ACTS

Smyth & Helwys Bible Commentary: Acts
Publication Staff

President & CEO
Cecil P. Staton

Publisher & Executive Vice President
Lex Horton

Vice President, Production
Keith Gammons

Senior Editor
Mark K. McElroy

Book Editor
Leslie Andres

Graphic Designer
Dave Jones

Assistant Editors
Betsy Butler
Kelley F. Land
Erin Schneider

Smyth & Helwys Publishing, Inc.
6316 Peake Road
Macon, Georgia 31210-3960
1-800-747-3016
© 2007 by Smyth & Helwys Publishing
All rights reserved.
Printed in the United States of America.

The paper used in this publication meets the minimum
requirements of American National Standard for Information
Sciences—Permanence of Paper for Printed Library Materials.
ANSI Z39.48–1984 (alk. paper)

Library of Congress Cataloging-in-Publication Data

Chance, J. Bradley.
The Acts of the Apostles / J. Bradley Chance.
p. cm. — (The Smyth & Helwys Bible Commentary ; v. 23)
Includes bibliographical references and indexes.
ISBN 978-1-57312-080-7 (alk. paper)
1. Bible. N.T. Acts—Commentaries. I. Title.

BS2625.53.C43 2007
226.6'07—dc22
2007037520

SMYTH & HELWYS BIBLE COMMENTARY

ACTS

J. BRADLEY CHANCE

SMYTH&HELWYS
PUBLISHING INCORPORATED • MACON, GEORGIA

PROJECT EDITOR
R. SCOTT NASH
Mercer University
Macon, Georgia

OLD TESTAMENT
GENERAL EDITOR
SAMUEL E. BALENTINE
Union Theological Seminary and
Presbyterian School of Christian
Education
Richmond, Virginia

NEW TESTAMENT
GENERAL EDITOR
R. ALAN CULPEPPER
McAfee School of Theology
Mercer University
Atlanta, Georgia

AREA
OLD TESTAMENT EDITORS
MARK E. BIDDLE
Baptist Theological Seminary
at Richmond, Virginia

AREA
NEW TESTAMENT EDITORS
R. SCOTT NASH
Mercer University
Macon, Georgia

KANDY QUEEN-SUTHERLAND
Stetson University
Deland, Florida

RICHARD B. VINSON
Baptist Theological Seminary
at Richmond, Virginia

PAUL REDDITT
Georgetown College
Georgetown, Kentucky

ADVANCE PRAISE

Prof. J. Bradley Chance has written an intelligent, informed, illuminating, and accessible commentary on the Acts of the Apostles. This work is a fine addition to the already impressive Smyth & Helwys Bible Commentary series. Professional scholars and students alike will find themselves in Chance's debt as they use this volume to further their study of Acts.

Marion L. Soards
Professor of New Testament Studies
Louisville Presbyterian Theological Seminary

Chance's solid scholarship provides insightful observations upon the historical and narrative world of the Acts of the Apostles. His interpretations, clear writing style, and ability to find analogies present a fresh reading of this often neglected New Testament work. Chance excels in uniting the biblical world of our ancestors in faith with the world of contemporary Christians. This commentary reflects an author who has thoroughly engaged Acts on both a critical and personal level. Chance is to be commended for an outstanding addition to the Smyth & Helwys Commentary series.

David M. May
Professor of New Testament
Central Baptist Theological Seminary

Followers of Jesus have, for two millennia, looked to the book of Acts for guidance and inspiration about how to live faithfully and missionally in the face of changing cultures and unexpected challenges. J. Bradley Chance helps us listen wisely and deeply to the text, inviting us to hear through it the contemporary voice of the Spirit. His commentary is grounded in thorough familiarity with the work of other scholars, but there is also a refreshing originality in his reading of Acts, especially in his connecting of "then" and "now"—of "there" and "here."

Guy Sayles
Pastor, First Baptist Church
Asheville, North Carolina

CONTENTS

DEDICATION

For Jay, my beloved son in whom I am well pleased—

Too soon the race is run
Too soon the wreath is won

Eternal Lord God, you hold all souls in life: Give to your
whole Church in paradise and on earth your light and your
peace; and grant that we, following the good examples of
those who have served you here and are now at rest, may at
the last enter with them into your unending joy; through
Jesus Christ our Lord, who lives and reigns with you, in the
unity of the Holy Spirit, one God, now and for ever. Amen.
(*The Book of Common Prayer*, 253)

ABBREVIATIONS USED IN THIS COMMENTARY

Books of the Old Testament, Apocrypha, and New Testament are generally abbreviated in the Sidebars, parenthetical references, and notes according to the following system.

The Old Testament

Genesis	Gen
Exodus	Exod
Leviticus	Lev
Numbers	Num
Deuteronomy	Deut
Joshua	Josh
Judges	Judg
Ruth	Ruth
1–2 Samuel	1–2 Sam
1–2 Kings	1–2 Kgs
1–2 Chronicles	1–2 Chr
Ezra	Ezra
Nehemiah	Neh
Esther	Esth
Job	Job
Psalm (Psalms)	Ps (Pss)
Proverbs	Prov
Ecclesiastes	Eccl
or Qoheleth	Qoh
Song of Solomon	Song
or Song of Songs	Song
or Canticles	Cant
Isaiah	Isa
Jeremiah	Jer
Lamentations	Lam
Ezekiel	Ezek
Daniel	Dan
Hosea	Hos
Joel	Joel
Amos	Amos
Obadiah	Obad
Jonah	Jonah
Micah	Mic

Nahum	Nah
Habakkuk	Hab
Zephaniah	Zeph
Haggai	Hag
Zechariah	Zech
Malachi	Mal

The Apocrypha

1–2 Esdras	1–2 Esdr
Tobit	Tob
Judith	Jdt
Additions to Esther	Add Esth
Wisdom of Solomon	Wis
Ecclesiasticus or the Wisdom of Jesus Son of Sirach	Sir
Baruch	Bar
Epistle (or Letter) of Jeremiah	Ep Jer
Prayer of Azariah and the Song of the Three	Pr Azar
Daniel and Susanna	Sus
Daniel, Bel, and the Dragon	Bel
Prayer of Manasseh	Pr Man
1–4 Maccabees	1–4 Macc

The New Testament

Matthew	Matt
Mark	Mark
Luke	Luke
John	John
Acts	Acts
Romans	Rom
1–2 Corinthians	1–2 Cor
Galatians	Gal
Ephesians	Eph
Philippians	Phil
Colossians	Col
1–2 Thessalonians	1–2 Thess
1–2 Timothy	1–2 Tim
Titus	Titus
Philemon	Phlm
Hebrews	Heb
James	Jas
1–2 Peter	1–2 Pet
1–2–3 John	1–2–3 John
Jude	Jude
Revelation	Rev

Other commonly used abbreviations include:

AD	*Anno Domini* ("in the year of the Lord")
(also commonly referred to as CE = the Common Era)	
BC	Before Christ
(also commonly referred to as BCE = Before the Common Era)	
C.	century
c.	*circa* (around "that time")
cf.	*confer* (compare)
ch.	chapter
chs.	chapters
d.	died
ed.	edition or edited by or editor
eds.	editors
e.g.	*exempli gratia* (for example)
et al.	*et alii* (and others)
f./ff.	and the following one(s)
gen. ed.	general editor
Gk.	Greek
ibid.	*ibidem* (in the same place)
i.e.	*id est* (that is)
LCL	Loeb Classical Library
lit.	literally
n.d.	no date
rev. and exp. ed.	revised and expanded edition
sg.	singular
trans.	translated by or translator(s)
v.	verse
vv.	verses
vol(s).	volume(s)

Selected additional written works cited by abbreviations include the following. A complete listing of abbreviations can be referenced in *The SBL Handbook of Style* (Peabody MA: Hendrickson, 1999):

AB	Anchor Bible
ABD	*Anchor Bible Dictionary.* 6 Vols. Ed. David Noel Freedman. New York: Doubleday, 1992.
ANTC	Abingdon New Testament Commentaries
EDB	*Eerdmans Dictionary of the Bible.* Ed. David Noel Freedman. Grand Rapids MI: Eerdmans, 2000.
ET	English Translation
ICC	International Critical Commentary
LXX	The Septuagint

MCB	*Mercer Commentary on the Bible.* Ed. Watson E. Mills and Richard F. Wilson. Macon GA: Mercer University Press, 1995.
MDB	*Mercer Dictionary of the Bible.* Ed. Watson E. Mills. Macon GA: Mercer University Press, 1990.
MT	Masoretic Text
NAC	New American Commentary
NIV	New International Version
NRSV	New Revised Standard Version
NT	New Testament
OT	Old Testament
RSV	Revised Standard Version
SacPag	Sacra Pagina
SBLDS	Society of Biblical Literature Dissertation Series
SBLSP	Society of Biblical Literature Seminar Papers
SNTSMS	Society for New Testament Studies Monograph Series
TDNT	*Theological Dictionary of the New Testament.* Ed. G. Kittel and G. Friedrich. Trans. G. W. Bromiley. 10 volumes. Grand Rapids MI: Eerdmans, 1964–1976.
TNTC	Tyndale New Testament Commentaries

TRANSLATIONS

Unless otherwise noted, translations are from the following sources.

Bible	New Revised Standard Version. Division of Christian Education of the National Council of Churches of Christ in the United States of America. 1989.
Classical Literature	Loeb Classical Library. Cambridge: Harvard University Press.
Josephus	*The Works of Josephus: Complete and Unabridged.* Trans. William Whiston. Peabody MA: Hendrickson, 1987.
Philo	*The Works of Philo. Complete and Unabridged.* Trans. C. D. Yonge. Peabody MA: Hendrickson, 1993.
Qumran Literature	*The Complete Dead Sea Scrolls in English.* Trans. Geza Vermes. New York: Penguin Press, 1997.

AUTHOR'S PREFACE

In our religion classes at William Jewell College we offer our students a model of biblical interpretation that is by no means distinctive or unique, but it is quite workable. We encourage students to recognize that interpretation emerges out of the *intersection* of the interpreter and the biblical text. That is, interpretation is not the result of the interpreter passively absorbing "*the* meaning" of the text and then simply offering a paraphrase of this internalized, objective meaning. Nor is ethically responsible interpretation a matter of the reader *imposing* her or his own meaning onto the text, making it say whatever one wants or needs the text to say. While ethically responsible interpretation requires "listening" to the text, we think it important to guide our students to understand that interpreters do wield some power—that interpretations are, in fact, the *readers'* interpretations and, as such, readers need to take accountability for their interpretations.

Such a model at least offers students an understanding of why there exist different interpretations of the same text. And it also allows students to understand why their own interpretations of a given text can mutate over time. As readers change, what they bring to the text changes, and the resulting interpretation that emerges out of the intersection of reader and text can change, as well.

As I explain in the Introduction, what follows in this commentary are my readings. I worked on this commentary far longer, I'm sure, than the editors at Smyth & Helwys would have preferred, and I feel obliged to thank them for their patience. But when one works on a reading of a text for as long I did, it was inevitable, as I look back on my own story during this interpretive journey, that my own life would go through quite a few changes, some incredibly joyous, some downright tragic. A handful of readers who read these words and who shared my journey will know what I'm talking about.

Suffice to say that I learned on the journey of writing this commentary what I have been telling my students for years: as I changed, what I brought to my reading of the text changed and, while I'm hopeful that a certain editorial consistency is present in the completed manuscript, I can certainly recognize places where this or that experience "informed" my reading of the text. I've noted, for example, as I have read back through the completed manuscript (a number of times!) that as I was struggling the most with just how God really works in the nooks and crannies of life, where, at least in my experience, transformative miracles were sorely lacking, my Connections more explicitly reflected on how God is present when life is marked primarily by seeming silence and absence. Such is the way of engaged, active reading.

As I read over and over the text of Acts through the years, I never read alone. I was accompanied by many other readers, all from whom I've learned and who are duly recognized in the footnotes. Footnotes are a bit sterile, so I express my appreciation to the many other readers of Acts who offered me invaluable help and guidance in my own reading. Readings are so varied these days that it's impossible to agree with everyone. So, at times, I've had to disagree with the readings of others. But I learned from all of them and know that I am a more informed reader of this biblical text because of their knowledge and, more importantly, wisdom.

Finally, I would like to thank Alan Culpepper, my immediate editor, and Scott Nash, the editor of the series, for their guidance and help. Alan was an editor who offered helpful counsel, while always giving me the freedom to present my own readings of Acts in my own way. Consequently, I have to take full responsibility for the reading of Acts that follows. My hope is that it will prove to be helpful to others as they engage in their own reading of this incredibly important story of the church's earliest ancestors.

J. Bradley Chance
September, 2007

SERIES PREFACE

The *Smyth & Helwys Bible Commentary* is a visually stimulating and user-friendly series that is as close to multimedia in print as possible. Written by accomplished scholars with all students of Scripture in mind, the primary goal of the *Smyth & Helwys Bible Commentary* is to make available serious, credible biblical scholarship in an accessible and less intimidating format.

Far too many Bible commentaries fall short of bridging the gap between the insights of biblical scholars and the needs of students of God's written word. In an unprecedented way, the *Smyth & Helwys Bible Commentary* brings insightful commentary to bear on the lives of contemporary Christians. Using a multimedia format, the volumes employ a stunning array of art, photographs, maps, and drawings to illustrate the truths of the Bible for a visual generation of believers.

The *Smyth & Helwys Bible Commentary* is built upon the idea that meaningful Bible study can occur when the insights of contemporary biblical scholars blend with sensitivity to the needs of lifelong students of Scripture. Some persons within local faith communities, however, struggle with potentially informative biblical scholarship for several reasons. Oftentimes, such scholarship is cast in technical language easily grasped by other scholars, but not by the general reader. For example, lengthy, technical discussions on every detail of a particular scriptural text can hinder the quest for a clear grasp of the whole. Also, the format for presenting scholarly insights has often been confusing to the general reader, rendering the work less than helpful. Unfortunately, responses to the hurdles of reading extensive commentaries have led some publishers to produce works for a general readership that merely skim the surface of the rich resources of biblical scholarship. This commentary series incorporates works of fine art in an accurate and scholarly manner, yet the format remains "user-friendly." An important facet is the presentation and explanation of images of art, which interpret the biblical material or illustrate how the biblical material has been understood and interpreted in the past. A visual generation of believers deserves a commentary series that contains not only the all-important textual commentary on Scripture, but images, photographs, maps, works of fine art, and drawings that bring the text to life.

The *Smyth & Helwys Bible Commentary* makes serious, credible biblical scholarship more accessible to a wider audience. Writers and editors alike present information in ways that encourage readers to gain a better understanding of the Bible. The editorial board has worked to develop a format that is useful and usable, informative and pleasing to the eye. Our writers are reputable scholars who participate in the community of faith and sense a calling to communicate the results of their scholarship to their faith community.

The *Smyth & Helwys Bible Commentary* addresses Christians and the larger church. While both respect for and sensitivity to the needs and contributions of other faith communities are reflected in the work of the series authors, the authors speak primarily to Christians. Thus the reader can note a confessional tone throughout the volumes. No particular "confession of faith" guides the authors, and diverse perspectives are observed in the various volumes. Each writer, though, brings to the biblical text the best scholarly tools available and expresses the results of their studies in commentary and visuals that assist readers seeking a word from the Lord for the church.

To accomplish this goal, writers in this series have drawn from numerous streams in the rich tradition of biblical interpretation. The basic focus is the biblical text itself, and considerable attention is given to the wording and structure of texts. Each particular text, however, is also considered in the light of the entire canon of Christian Scriptures. Beyond this, attention is given to the cultural context of the biblical writings. Information from archaeology, ancient history, geography, comparative literature, history of religions, politics, sociology, and even economics is used to illuminate the culture of the people who produced the Bible. In addition, the writers have drawn from the history of interpretation, not only as it is found in traditional commentary on the Bible but also in literature, theater, church history, and the visual arts. Finally, the *Commentary* on Scripture is joined with *Connections* to the world of the contemporary church. Here again, the writers draw on scholarship in many fields as well as relevant issues in the popular culture.

This wealth of information might easily overwhelm a reader if not presented in a "user-friendly" format. Thus the heavier discussions of detail and the treatments of other helpful topics are presented in special-interest boxes, or Sidebars, clearly connected to the passages under discussion so as not to interrupt the flow of the basic interpretation. The result is a commentary on Scripture that focuses on the theological significance of a text while also offering the reader a rich array of additional information related to the text and its interpretation.

An accompanying CD-ROM offers powerful searching and research tools. The commentary text, Sidebars, and visuals are all reproduced on a CD that is fully indexed and searchable. Pairing a text version with a digital resource is a distinctive feature of the *Smyth & Helwys Bible Commentary.*

Combining credible biblical scholarship, user-friendly study features, and sensitivity to the needs of a visually oriented generation of believers creates a unique and unprecedented type of commentary series. With insight from many of today's finest biblical scholars and a stunning visual format, it is our hope that the *Smyth & Helwys Bible Commentary* will be a welcome addition to the personal libraries of all students of Scripture.

The Editors

HOW TO USE
THIS COMMENTARY

The *Smyth & Helwys Bible Commentary* is written by accomplished biblical scholars with a wide array of readers in mind. Whether engaged in the study of Scripture in a church setting or in a college or seminary classroom, all students of the Bible will find a number of useful features throughout the commentary that are helpful for interpreting the Bible.

Basic Design of the Volumes

Each volume features an Introduction to a particular book of the Bible, providing a brief guide to information that is necessary for reading and interpreting the text: the historical setting, literary design, and theological significance. Each Introduction also includes a comprehensive outline of the particular book under study.

Each chapter of the commentary investigates the text according to logical divisions in a particular book of the Bible. Sometimes these divisions follow the traditional chapter segmentation, while at other times the textual units consist of sections of chapters or portions of more than one chapter. The divisions reflect the literary structure of a book and offer a guide for selecting passages that are useful in preaching and teaching.

An accompanying CD-ROM offers powerful searching and research tools. The commentary text, Sidebars, and visuals are all reproduced on a CD that is fully indexed and searchable. Pairing a text version with a digital resource also allows unprecedented flexibility and freedom for the reader. Carry the text version to locations you most enjoy doing research while knowing that the CD offers a portable alternative for travel from the office, church, classroom, and your home.

Commentary and Connections

As each chapter explores a textual unit, the discussion centers around two basic sections: *Commentary* and *Connections*. The analysis of a passage, including the details of its language, the history reflected in the text, and the literary forms found in the text, are the main focus of the *Commentary* section. The primary concern of the *Commentary* section is to explore the theological issues presented by the Scripture passage. *Connections* presents potential applications of the insights provided in the *Commentary* section. The *Connections* portion of each chapter considers what issues are relevant for teaching and suggests useful methods and resources. *Connections* also identifies themes suitable for sermon planning and suggests helpful approaches for preaching on the Scripture text.

Sidebars

The *Smyth & Helwys Bible Commentary* provides a unique hyperlink format that quickly guides the reader to additional insights. Since other more technical or supplementary information is vital for understanding a text and its implications, the volumes feature distinctive Sidebars, or special-interest boxes, that provide a wealth of information on such matters as:

- Historical information (such as chronological charts, lists of kings or rulers, maps, descriptions of monetary systems, descriptions of special groups, descriptions of archaeological sites or geographical settings).

- Graphic outlines of literary structure (including such items as poetry, chiasm, repetition, epistolary form).

- Definition or brief discussions of technical or theological terms and issues.

- Insightful quotations that are not integrated into the running text but are relevant to the passage under discussion.

- Notes on the history of interpretation (Augustine on the Good Samaritan, Luther on James, Stendahl on Romans, etc.).

- Line drawings, photographs, and other illustrations relevant for understanding the historical context or interpretive significance of the text.

- Presentation and discussion of works of fine art that have interpreted a Scripture passage.

Each Sidebar is printed in color and is referenced at the appropriate place in the *Commentary* or *Connections* section with a color-coded title that directs the reader to the relevant Sidebar. In addition, helpful icons appear in the Sidebars, which provide the reader with visual cues to the type of material that is explained in each Sidebar. Throughout the commentary, these four distinct hyperlinks provide useful links in an easily recognizable design.

AΩ

Alpha & Omega Language

This icon identifies the information as a language-based tool that offers further exploration of the Scripture selection. This could include syntactical information, word studies, popular or additional uses of the word(s) in question, additional contexts in which the term appears, and the history of the term's translation. All non-English terms are transliterated into the appropriate English characters.

Culture/Context

This icon introduces further comment on contextual or cultural details that shed light on the Scripture selection. Describing the place and time to which a Scripture passage refers is often vital to the task of biblical interpretation. Sidebar items introduced with this icon could include geographical, historical, political, social, topographical, or economic information. Here, the reader may find an excerpt of an ancient text or inscription that sheds light on the text. Or one may find a description of some element of ancient religion such as Baalism in Canaan or the Hero cult in the Mystery Religions of the Greco-Roman world.

Interpretation

Sidebars that appear under this icon serve a general interpretive function in terms of both historical and contemporary renderings. Under this heading, the reader might find a selection from classic or contemporary literature that illuminates the Scripture text or a significant quotation from a famous sermon that addresses the passage. Insights are drawn from various sources, including literature, worship, theater, church history, and sociology.

Additional Resources Study

Here, the reader finds a convenient list of useful resources for further investigation of the selected Scripture text, including books, journals, websites, special collections, organizations, and societies. Specialized discussions of works not often associated with biblical studies may also appear here.

Additional Features

Each volume also includes a basic Bibliography on the biblical book under study. Other bibliographies on selected issues are often included that point the reader to other helpful resources.

Notes at the end of each chapter provide full documentation of sources used and contain additional discussions of related matters.

Abbreviations used in each volume are explained in a list of abbreviations found after the Table of Contents.

Readers of the *Smyth & Helwys Bible Commentary* can regularly visit the Internet support site for news, information, updates, and enhancements to the series at **www.helwys.com/commentary**.

Several thorough indexes enable the reader to locate information quickly. These indexes include:

• An *Index of Sidebars* groups content from the special-interest boxes by category (maps, fine art, photographs, drawings, etc.).

• An *Index of Scriptures* lists citations to particular biblical texts.

• An *Index of Topics* lists alphabetically the major subjects, names, topics, and locations referenced or discussed in the volume.

• An *Index of Modern Authors* organizes contemporary authors whose works are cited in the volume.

INTRODUCTION

The genre "commentary" requires the discussion of certain matters of "introduction," among which are issues of authorship, date, possible sources, and the like. In addition, specific biblical books require exploration of issues distinctive to that book. With respect to the Acts of the Apostles, three issues warrant attention: the textual history of Acts, the speeches of Acts, and the value of Acts as a reliable source for the history of early Christianity. These issues are interrelated, as the discussion below will make apparent. It is also helpful to readers for the introduction to discuss some prominent theological themes and issues that the Commentary will explore.

Title, Authorship, Date, and Sources[1]

Title[2]

The title "Acts of Apostles" is represented among the best manuscripts of the New Testament, some of which date to the late second and early third centuries. One also finds among the manuscripts "The Acts of the Apostles," the title often employed today. The original manuscript of the narrative is not available for examination, so one cannot know what title the original work bore. The Greek word *praxsis* (acts) was employed in the larger culture to denote great deeds of either historical or mythological characters. The title attributed to the narrative at least shows that early Christian readers understood the narrative to describe the "acts" of the great ancestors of the church, specifically the apostles.

This is interesting for a number of reasons. First, Acts itself does not highlight Paul *as an apostle* (see [Paul and Barnabas as Apostles]), even though he is most certainly the main character of the second half of the book. Second, the narrative devotes attention to Stephen, Philip, and James, none of whom Acts considers to be apostles. Acts, with the exception of 14:4, 14, confines the title apostle to the Twelve (see [Twelve Apostles]), yet it does not focus attention exclusively on the Twelve and devotes considerable attention to those outside this circle. Such considerations allow the tentative conclusion that whatever "original" title the author might have placed on his narrative, it would not have been the Acts of the *Apostles*. Church tradition, however, did view Paul as an apostle (as did Paul, of course!), as well as James, and many confused Philip the Evangelist with Philip the apostle (see [Philip]). Hence, the title is appropriate, given how the church understood the word *apostle*.

Authorship[3]

Discussion of authorship begins with the recognition that the author of Acts is the same as the author of the Gospel of Luke. The respective prologues of the two books (Luke 1:1-4; Acts 1:1-5) certainly link the two narratives. It is safe to say that the consensus of both critical scholarship and church tradition is that Luke and Acts were written by the same person. The separation of Luke from Acts by the Gospel of John requires the (obvious) conclusion that the church did not think it imperative to join the books in the canon. For about the last century, following the work of Henry Cadbury, scholars have more deliberately viewed Luke and Acts as a unity (Luke–Acts). Despite recent protests from some readers,[4] the critical consensus is to see the two volumes as a narrative and theological unity, *at least nominally*. The fact that commentaries, as well as critical groups and seminars, still give focused attention to the separate volumes allows the conclusion that each is viewed as having its own literary integrity.

While there is consensus that Luke and Acts come from a single author, critical scholars are not unanimous regarding the identity of this author. The very title "The Gospel of Luke" speaks for itself with respect to the assessment of church tradition. The attribution of the Gospel—and, hence, Acts—to Luke, the companion of Paul, has an ancient history, going back to the last third of the second century. Some critical scholars are slow to accept this tradition. First, the theology of the narrative does not always comport with that of Paul.[5] One would suspect that a companion and admirer of Paul would have understood better the theology of his hero. Second, a comparison of historical data that can be gleaned from Paul's letters with historical claims made by Acts often do not easily—or, some think, even tortuously—harmonize.

On the other hand, in spite of these issues, one is left wondering why the church would have attributed these narratives to Luke, given that he was hardly a famous person in his own right in church tradition and history. The so-called We Passages certainly play a role in the debate (see [We Passages]). The passages imply that the person who penned the narrative accompanied Paul on occasion. It is quite possible that the church tradition of Lukan authorship emerged by the attempt to deduce who might have been the anonymous voice behind the We Passages who, apparently, was in Paul's company on some of his journeys. One seeking to associate a name with the anonymous narrator would likely rule out persons specifically named in Acts as Paul's companions, persons such as Silas and Timothy, especially since the character hiding behind the *we* tends to distinguish himself from these and other "named" characters (cf., e.g., 16:1, 10 and 16, 19). A known companion of Paul not named in Acts is Luke (Phlm 24; cf. Col 4:14). This is the person whom church tradition has identified as the author.

It is hardly necessary to assume that an occasional companion of Paul fully understood all the nuances of Pauline theology or even felt compelled to agree with such. The author, whoever he was, has chosen to employ narrative as a means of presenting *his own* distinctive theology. But Paul, though admired, need hardly have been the author's only source of theological thinking. There are, admittedly, historical differences between Acts and data that can be gathered from the Pauline corpus, but such differences need not exclude an occasional companion from being the author. History is not an exact science today, much less two millennia ago. Further, the more serious conflicts between the chronological presentations of Acts and history that is constructed based on Paul's letters are found in the sections of Acts *before* the We Passages begin (especially Acts 9, 12, and 15), that is, before the author participated in some events of Paul's life.

One can suspect that Paul's part-time companion, despite claims to careful investigation (see Luke 1:1-4), did not spend all his time pressing Paul for the precise chronological details of his exploits that occurred fifteen or so years before the author met him. If Luke were the author, Paul knew him as one of his fellow workers (Phlm 24), not his chronicler. Luke may very well have viewed himself in a similar light. That is, there is no reason to claim with any certainty that while Luke was journeying with Paul he knew that one day he would write a history. It is *possible* that Luke was careful to take notes that he safely tucked away and pulled out many years later to consult for his history.[6] But this is only *possible* and should not serve as an unquestioned foundation on which to build arguments about the author and his historical veracity.

Saint Luke Evangelist

El Greco (Domenikos Theotokopulos). *Saint Luke Evangelist.* Canvas, 98 x 72 cm. Cathedral, Toledo, Spain. (Credit: Erich Lessing / Art Resource, NY)

The simplest way to understand the We Passages is to conclude that the author of the narrative spent some time with Paul. The Commentary, following tradition, will call this occasional companion and author "Luke." And it is certainly possible, though by no means certain, that the Luke mentioned in the Pauline corpus was, in fact, this author. However, the authority and value of Acts does not lie in the identity of the author. It is the narrative that carries the theological freight, not the name of the person who penned it. To acknowledge this is to respect the deliberate anonymity of the author.

Date[7]

Dating the Acts of the Apostles is tenuous business, as such dating rests on other conclusions—or assumptions—that critics hold regarding significant dates of early Christian history, as well as dates assigned to other New Testament texts. Generally, historians date Paul's arrival in Rome (Acts 28) to c. AD 61. Acts speaks of Paul's preaching there for two years, bringing the last events narrated to c. AD 63. Such dates assume the general historical reliability of Acts, an assumption not taken for granted by many critical readers. But assuming the accuracy of such a rough chronology, the earliest date that one can propose for the composition of Acts would be c. AD 63. Justin Martyr, whose apologies date to around the mid-second century, appears to allude to the content of Luke–Acts (e.g., *1 Apol.* 50.12). If so, this would mean that the latest possible date of composition would be the mid-second century. Thus, a date range for the composition of Luke–Acts is rather wide: mid-60s to mid-second century.

The fact that Acts is connected with the Gospel of Luke must shape hypotheses about the date of composition. A commonsense reading of Acts 1:1 requires one to conclude that Acts was not composed until after the writing of the Gospel. Dating the Gospel has its own problems, however. Critical consensus—though it is hardly unanimous—affirms the Gospel of Mark to have been one of Luke's sources for his Gospel. But dating Mark is also tenuous. Mark's interest in the fall of Jerusalem, assuming this historical event to be the subject matter of Mark 13, leads many to date his Gospel to c. AD 70. If Luke used Mark as a source, the composition of the Gospel of Luke, as well as its companion volume of Acts, would have to date to after AD 70. This would seem to be confirmed by the Gospel's apparent awareness of the siege and fall of Jerusalem in 70 (see, e.g., 19:41-44; 21:20-24).

Some critics argue for a later date of composition, suggesting the late first or early second centuries, perhaps even as late as 130. Such proposals have not persuaded the majority of critics. The consensus seems to fall within a range between c. 70 to the early 90s.[8] Thus, some events of which Acts speaks pre-date its composition by as much as forty to sixty years, while the later events narrated in Acts would pre-date Acts' composition by around ten to thirty years. Such distance offers the author the hindsight necessary to construct a volume that narrates "the fulfillment of things accomplished among us" (cf. Luke 1:1). It also allows sufficient time for traditions to fade away or take on such embellishments that their historical value may be minimal.

Sources[9]

While generalizations are always risky, critical scholars believe that Luke did use sources for Acts. However, there is little agreement regarding the specific content of such sources. The comparison of Luke's Gospel with those of Matthew and Mark gave rise to the Two-Source hypothesis of the Synoptic Gospels, namely that Matthew and Luke used two common sources in the composition of their Gospels, Mark and Q (a hypothetical source consisting primarily of sayings of Jesus). The Two-Source hypothesis gave critics confidence that Luke employed sources in the composition of his narratives, both the Gospel and Acts. With such confidence, the quest for sources behind Acts was on. A generation ago Dupont surveyed these quests for sources and offered an assessment that still holds true today: "Despite the most careful and detailed research, it has not been possible to define any of the sources used by the author of Acts in a way which will meet with widespread agreement among the critics."[10] More recently, C. K. Barrett has offered sober counsel on this issue: "It is probably better at this stage to think of traditions, without specifying their form, that of written or even oral sources, if oral sources are understood as verbally fixed."[11]

Still, many interpreters attempt to isolate such sources. For example, Luke may have employed a source emerging from the Jerusalem church, called a *Jerusalem* or *Palestinian* source. In addition, he may have employed a source from the church at Antioch, an *Antiochene* source. Mention has already been made of the We Passages, and these passages may represent a source employed by the author, assuming that these passages do not, in fact, represent the author's own presence at the events narrated therein. Some have argued that Luke had access to an itinerary of Paul's various stops during his missionary journeys, which one could label the *Pauline* source. And then there will be the slippery "oral traditions," stories that Luke simply heard. A source that Luke likely did not use was the Letters of Paul. Luke likely did not know of their existence. If he knew of their existence, he ignored them—an odd thing for him to do if he investigated things as carefully as he claimed (Luke 1:3). Either way, there is no evidence that Luke used these letters.

Discussion of sources hinges on one's conclusions regarding other issues. For example, accepting that the We Passages denote the participation of the author in certain events allows for some tentative observations. Most obvious, of course, is that the author was an eyewitness to many events of which he speaks—he was his own "source." Further, because Paul was Luke's companion, Paul could have served as a "source" for events at which the author was not present. Recall, however, the caveat offered above: picturing Luke as pressing Paul for details and copiously taking notes is only a *possibility*.

Note also Acts 21:8: "We entered the house of Philip the evangelist, who was one of the seven, and stayed with him." Again, it would be a stretch to assert that Luke took advantage of his stay with Philip "to do research," milking Philip for all the historical information he possibly could. Yet it is not far-fetched to suppose that during the stay Philip told some stories about his days in Jerusalem and his efforts to preach the gospel in the surrounding regions. The passing comment of 21:8, in other words, would allow the tentative conclusion that, with respect to events of Acts 6–8, Luke may very well have had as one of his "sources" Philip the Evangelist. This would certainly have a bearing on the value of Acts as a *historical* document, but, again, that is a matter that will be given more attention below.

The Text of Acts[12]

Textual criticism does not usually excite readers outside the specific field. However, it is a crucial feature of critical scholarship, and its labors affect *every* reader of the Bible today. Readers who pick up any modern version of the New Testament are reading a translation of Greek manuscripts. However, it is not the case that translators can consult the "original" edition of any New Testament (or Old Testament, for that matter) text and translate it. The "original manuscripts," called *autographs*, are nonexistent. What scholars do possess are many copies and copies of copies.

Over the decades and centuries as these copies of copies evolved, there emerged certain characteristics among various "families" or textual traditions. Imagine a letter written by the matriarch of a family chronicling the family history. Both of her immediate heirs, say her two children, want a copy so that they can pass it on to their children. Of course, today one would simply go to a copy machine or scan the document and store it on a computer. But imagine attempts to preserve the letter at a time when handwritten copies were one's only option for duplicating the letter.

Imagine something like this: As the two children make their own copies of the letter, each introduces some changes. The matriarch who wrote

Codex Bezae Cantabrigiensis Excerpt from Luke

(Credit: James R. Adair, "Codex Bezae Cantabrigiensis," [cited 20 September 2007]. Online: http://alpha.reltech.org/cgi-bin/Ebind2html/BibleMSS/U5?seq=426.)

the letter, for example, might have made reference to "the farm." The son, for the sake of clarity should one day his children read the letter, expands this simple reference to say "the family farm in Ohio." This expanded version of the matriarch's letter is then passed along to this particular copyist's descendants. The daughter, as she makes a copy of the letter to pass along to her heirs, introduces some expansions of her own, again to offer clarity of the letter's content for her descendants. Perhaps the matriarch's original letter made reference to "my beloved husband." The daughter modifies her copy to read "my beloved husband, Frank, to whom I was married for more than fifty years." Now this emendation is part of the "textual tradition" that is passed along to the daughter's immediate descendants. And, of course, each might have introduced into her or his respective copy inadvertent changes, such as accidentally omitting or repeating words and using alternate spellings of words.

"Two recensions" of the "original letter" now exist. The son's copy would read "the family farm in Ohio" and "my beloved husband." A textual critic might call this *Tradition S*, with *S* standing for "son." There is another copy that reads simply "the farm" and "my beloved husband, Frank, to whom I was married for more than fifty years," which a textual critic might call *Tradition D*. Add to this the unfortunate fact that the matriarch's original letter was lost in a flood that swept away the lockbox where the original letter had been preserved for safekeeping.

All that now exist are copies. Imagine that a couple generations later someone gained access to *both* copies, on the basis of which she prepared her own handwritten copy. Confronted with two versions of the original letter, this later copyist might choose to conflate the two versions, creating a hybrid text that read "the family farm in Ohio" *and* "my beloved husband, Frank, to whom I was married for more than fifty years." Now there exists yet *another* textual tradition, which a textual critic might label *Tradition SD,* recognizing it to be conflation of *Tradition S* and *Tradition D.*

Though the above example is highly simplified, this is precisely the kind of thing that happened as New Testament texts were copied and passed along: "textual traditions" emerged. Textual critics identify four major textual traditions, or families, of copies of the Greek New Testament: the *Alexandrian* tradition, the *Western* tradition, the *Caesarean* tradition, and the *Byzantine* tradition. The Caesarean tradition is actually something of a hybrid of the Alexandrian and Western traditions.[13] The Byzantine tradition is the "latest" tradition and includes, overall, the most "additions" to the text. By far, most Greek manuscripts that exist today represent this tradition. Despite the large numbers, however, most textual critics consider this tradition to be the least reliable "witness" to the *autograph.* This was the textual tradition upon which the KJV of the New Testament was based, explaining why there are often many differences between the KJV and more modern translations. The Alexandrian and Western traditions are "earlier" and represent, overall, better witnesses to the oldest Greek copies of the New Testament. With respect to Acts, however, the Western tradition presents a most intriguing mystery for textual critics. The Western recension of Acts is actually about ten percent longer than the Alexandrian recension. Which recension or tradition best represents the original text of Acts?

Some have argued that Luke is responsible for *both* traditions. That is, Luke wrote two editions of Acts, a long version and a short version, with one giving rise to one "family" of texts and the other another family. But among such critics there is no agreement as to which version of Acts, the longer or the shorter, represents the version that Luke, finally, preferred as his "polished draft." Most textual critics today do *not* ascribe the longer Western version to Luke. Rather, most argue that the Western recension emerged out of the originally shorter version.

This volume follows the consensus of textual critics that the Western tradition does *not* represent the "best" tradition as one attempts to reconstruct the oldest, most original version of Acts. However, the Commentary will, on occasion, make reference to the Western tradition of Acts. Readers will note that one of the tendencies of this tradition was to clarify the shorter text of Acts by adding comments that filled gaps left by the shorter version or "updated" the shorter version to make it more "relevant" to later readers (see [Textual Criticism and the Apostolic Decree]). Further, the Western tradition also can show an "anti-Jewish" bias (see [The Western Addition of vv. 6b-8a]). In other words, the Western tradition actually represents something of a commentary on the Acts of the Apostles, with such commentary being embedded in the text itself, much like the son and daughter in the hypothetical example above embedded into their mother's letter their own interpretive comments.

The Speeches of Acts[14]

Examination of the speeches of Acts spills over into discussion of the value of Acts as a source of history. Hence, many items pertaining to this discussion will lay a foundation for the next section of the introduction.

The speeches of Acts deserve focused examination for the simple reason that there are so many of them. Approximately one-third of Acts consists of speech material. Though scholars may disagree as to the exact number of speeches (depending on how one defines what constitutes a speech), most would agree that there are at least twenty-four speeches in Acts. Peter delivers eight speeches,[15] and Paul delivers nine.[16] In addition, other characters present speeches: Gamaliel (5:35b-39), Stephen (7:2-53), James (15:13b-21), Demetrius of Ephesus (19:25b-27), the anonymous town clerk of Ephesus (19:35b-40), Tertullus (24:2b-8), and Festus (25:14c-21, 24-27). Some count the words of the risen Christ as a speech (1:4-5, 7-8), as well as the brief words of the Twelve (6:2b-4) and Gallio (18:14b-15). Some of these "speeches" consist literally of only a couple verses, too short for some critics to consider a "speech."

It is the critical consensus that the speeches in Acts *in their present* form are Lukan compositions. For example, even if one were to argue that the words attributed to Gallio in 18:14b-15 actually reflect the gist of what the proconsul said, it is hard to imagine that this is *all* he said. At best, the "speech" represents an incredibly brief précis that would relate to the reader the finding of the proconsul, as such was relevant to the story at hand. In fact, even the "longer" speeches of Acts are not all that long, as speeches go; Stephen's speech, the longest in Acts, would take only a few minutes to recite. If the speeches are précis, one must conclude that, *in their present form,* they are the compositions of the author. On that issue, there is no debate among critical readers.

Debate centers around whether the speeches are, in fact, précis of things actually said or artistic, rhetorical creations of the narrator. Here critics are divided. Much debate revolves around the statement of the historian Thucydides:

> With reference to the speeches in this history, some were delivered before the war began, others while it was going on; some I heard myself, others I got from various quarters; it was in all cases difficult to carry them word for word in one's memory, so my habit has been to make the speakers say what was in my opinion demanded of them by the various occasions, of course adhering as closely as possible to the general sense of what they really said (*Histories,* 1.22.1).[17]

How is one to assess what this statement says about the nature of speeches in ancient historical writing? The first sentence is easy enough to understand: it is hard to recall accurately what was said on any given occasion, whether Thucydides or someone else heard the speech. The second sentence contains internal tension. In the first part of the sentence Thucydides states that his practice was *to make the speakers say what was in my opinion demanded of them by the various occasions.* This statement gives Thucydides a lot of freedom. But the second half of the sentence qualifies the first part by saying *of course adhering as closely as possible to the general sense of what they really said.*

Critical scholars are not in agreement as to how to assess speeches in ancient historiography in general or Luke's speeches in particular. Martin Dibelius represents one approach. He sums up succinctly the tension of Thucydides' statement: "The ambiguity of this remark presents a real problem. As a result, no agreement has yet been reached among the interpreters of Thucydides concerning the relationship of the subjective judgment and objective reproduction of the speeches."[18] Dibelius, based on his survey of other speech material in ancient historiography, gives most weight to the first part of the ambiguous sentence, emphasizing the *freedom* of ancient historiographers in producing speeches. His statement is worth quoting in full.

> This survey was merely intended to show concerning historical writing in ancient times that, where it contains speeches, *it follows certain conventions.* What seems to the author his most important obligation is not what seems to us the most important one, that of establishing what speech was actually made; to him, it is rather that

of introducing speeches into the structure in a way which will be relevant to his purpose. *Even if he can remember, discover or read somewhere the text of the speech which was made, the author will not feel obliged to make use of it.*[19]

Dibelius goes on to say that speeches in ancient historiography served primarily either to "enliven the whole" narrative or to "serve as an artistic device to help achieve the author's aims."[20]

Dibelius studies some major speeches of Acts and concludes that such speeches serve primarily artistic aims and, in the context of the extended quotation above, are simply not interested in conveying actual words or even offering a précis of an actual speech; rather Luke fashions the speeches only to serve his own aims, and those aims are directed *at the reader*, not the "audience" of the speech in the story. In short, one is to assess the speeches not according to their word-for-word accuracy or even whether they represent generally what was actually spoken, to allude to Thucydides, but their literary and artistic function *within the narrative.* One simply misses the mark and is "looking for the wrong thing" to seek in the speeches a record, even a précis, of "what the speeches really said."

Ben Witherington represents a critical assessment of the Lukan speeches that leads to different conclusions.[21] To be sure, good Greek historiography was sensitive to rhetorical matters. Writing was to be artful.

> It was not, however, a matter of the nonrhetorical historians versus the rhetorical ones. The debate was over whether distortion or free invention was allowable in a historical work in the service of higher rhetorical aims. No one was seriously arguing that composers of written history should eschew all literary considerations.[22]

Witherington concedes there was "debate" in antiquity whether "distortion or free invention" was acceptable in historiography.

Witherington wants to put Luke in the camp of "good historians," those who, while alert to rhetorical concerns, did not succumb to distortion or free invention. Representing the best of historiography were historians like Thucydides (c. 455–400 BC) and Polybius (c. 203–120 BC), who were both concerned to offer an accurate presentation of "what happened." Polybius's understanding of good history writing can be seen in his critical assessment of the historical writing of Timeaus. Note especially his comments as they pertain to speech material:

When we find one or two false statements in a book and they prove to be deliberate ones, it is evident that not a word written by such an author is any longer certain and reliable. But to convince those also who are disposed to champion [Timeaus] I must speak of the principle on which he composes public speeches, harangues to soldiers, the discourses of ambassadors, and, in a word, all utterances of the kind, which, as it were, sum up events and hold the whole history together. Can anyone who reads these help noticing that Timaeus had untruthfully reported them in his work, and has done so of set purpose? For he has not set down the words spoken nor the sense of what was really said, but having made up his mind as to what ought to have been said, he recounts all these speeches and all else that follows upon events like a man in a school of rhetoric attempting to speak on a given subject, and shows off his oratorical power, but gives no report of which was actually spoken. (*The Histories of Polybius*, 12.25a).[23]

With respect to Thucydides, *immediately* following his statement quoted above concerning speeches, one finds the following:

And with reference to the narrative of events, far from permitting myself to derive it from the first source that came to hand, I did not even trust my own impressions, but it rests partly on what I saw myself, partly on what others saw for me, the accuracy of the report being always tried by the most severe and detailed tests possible. My conclusions have cost me some labour from the want of coincidence between accounts of the same occurrences by different eye-witnesses, arising sometimes from imperfect memory, sometimes from undue partiality for one side or the other. The absence of romance in my history will, I fear, detract somewhat from its interest; but if it be judged useful by those inquirers who desire an exact knowledge of the past as an aid to the interpretation of the future, which in the course of human things must resemble if it does not reflect it, I shall be content. In fine, I have written my work, not as an essay which is to win the applause of the moment, but as a possession for all time (Thucydides, *The History of the Peloponnesian War*, 1.22.3-4).[24]

With respect, specifically, to speeches, all this is not to say that speeches, even in "good" historiography, were verbatim reports. Witherington summarizes J. Wilson's assessment of the speeches of Thucydides: the speeches were offered in Thucydides' own words; they represent a selection of speeches; they contain a selection of ideas that represent the "general sense" of what was said; they may be either abbreviated or expanded if such editing does not detract from the general sense; expansion in order to make the general sense clearer is quite acceptable.[25] In short, the speeches are

"Thucydidian compositions," but one finds within them a fair presentation of "the general sense of what they really said."

Witherington quotes with approval the summarizing statement of C. W. Fornara:

> We are not entitled to proceed on the assumption that the historians considered themselves at liberty to write up speeches out of their own heads. That some or many or most actually did so is perhaps hypothetically conceivable. We must recognize, however, that such a procedure would have been contrary to convention and *not, as all too many seems to suppose, a convention in its own right.*[26]

Witherington's critical assessment yields different conclusions from that of Dibelius. Following Dibelius's understanding of the *conventions* of historiography, one simply looks in vain in the Lukan speeches to find a "general sense of what they really said." Despite Thucydides' assertion, this was not what ancient historians were interested in offering. Luke was a literary artist and therein one finds the value of the speeches. Witherington's assessment leads to the conclusion that while rhetorical, artistic concerns are not absent, and while the speeches in their present form are most certainly Lukan compositions, it was not a convention of ancient historiography for historians to compose speeches with little to no concern for what was actually said. Hence, one would find in Luke's speeches, assuming that he followed the proper conventions of good historiography, words that give the reader a sense of what was actually said. The question boils down to whether Luke followed the proper conventions of good historiography, as Witherington understands such conventions.

Readers are confronted with two opposing interpretations of exactly what the proper conventions were of ancient history writing. The statement of Fornara (cited above) that Witherington embraces provides something of a two-edged sword: "That some or many or most actually did [write up speeches out of their own heads] is perhaps hypothetically conceivable. We must recognize, however, that such a procedure would have been contrary to convention and not, as all too many seem to suppose, a convention in its own right." One the one hand, Fornara insists that liberty in the composition of speeches was not the convention, in spite of the fact that many wrongly believe that to be the case. On the other hand, Fornara concedes that, at least hypothetically, it is possible that most ancient historians did freely construct speeches. Witherington states,

It must be acknowledged that such standards [of good historiography] were not observed a good deal of the time in antiquity. Thucydides and Polybius *were* in various regards exceptional, but it is also true that it was not impossible for a well-educated and apparently well-traveled person like Luke, who claims to have taken time and pains to investigate matters closely, to follow in the footsteps of other exceptional historians.[27]

What constitutes *convention*? Is *convention* what a handful of "exceptional" historians of a bygone era (Thucydides and Polybius) claimed to practice or what "most" did?

Granting Witherington's understanding of convention, it is possible that Luke followed the exceptional standards of historians who preceded him by centuries. Indeed, if Luke were a historian of the caliber of Thucydides and Polybius, he would have been quite exceptional. The second-century AD satirist Lucian offers his own opinion of the historians of his time in his treatise to Philo, *How to Write History*. He laments: "You cannot find a man but is writing history; nay, every one you meet is a Thucydides, a Herodotus, a Xenophon. The old saying must be true, and war be the father of all things, seeing what a litter of historians it has now teemed forth at a birth" (§ 2).[28] Lucian also held up Thucydides as one of the standard bearers of good historiography, whose high standards Lucian describes succinctly: "For history, I say again, has this and this only for its own; if a man will start upon it, he must sacrifice to no God but Truth; he must neglect all else" (§ 39).

Interestingly, despite Lucian's praise for Thucydides' commitment to the God of Truth, he offers no unambiguous allusion to or comment on what Thucydides has to say about *speeches*, though it appears likely that Lucian would have been familiar with the passage in question.[29] Furthermore, in offering his counsel to Philo, Lucian seems to give the historian some latitude when it comes to speeches: "When it comes in your way to introduce a speech, the first requirement is that it should suit the character both of the speaker and of the occasion; the second is (once more) lucidity; but in these cases you have the counsel's right of showing your eloquence" (§ 58).[30] Speeches need to be appropriate to both the character offering the speech and to the occasion. They must be clear. But Philo is also given leave to show his "eloquence." Nothing is said of accuracy. This hardly sounds like Polybius's castigation of Timeaus: "He recounts all these speeches and all else that follows upon events like a man in a school of rhetoric attempting to speak on a given subject, and shows off his oratorical power, but gives no report of which was actually spoken" (*Histories,* 12.25a).

If one understands *convention* to mean "what people actually did," Dibelius seems to win the debate with Witherington. The Commentary will focus on the speeches as they help to convey to readers Lukan theology and purpose. Little attention will be given to offering a defense of their veracity to the "general sense of what they really said." Readers who side with Witherington and other scholars who agree with him can choose to "hear" these speeches as Lukan compositions that reflect "the general sense of what they really said." Such an assumption will not detract from the role the speeches play in communicating the aims of the narrative. Even if one grants Witherington's position, a careful writer like Luke would not have ignored the plot and aims of his narrative as he compressed, expanded, and composed the speeches as they now stand.

The Value of Acts as a Source for Early Christian History[31]

The assessment of the value of Acts as a good historical source hinges, as so many other issues of introduction, on one's assessment of other matters. For example, the We Passages clearly leave the impression that the author was an eyewitness to some events narrated in Acts. If one concludes that the insertion of a first-person narrator is, itself, simply a literary device—and something of a deceptive one, at that—one will not be reticent to assert that Acts would be of limited value, historically. An author willing to insert himself falsely into the story would be more inclined to insert other material as well. Readers assuming that the author was an eyewitness to some events (with access to others who witnessed other events) will be more inclined to view the narrative as having historical value.

One's assessment of the genre of the narrative will affect one's overall assessment of its historical value as well. Richard Pervo has argued that Acts is a historical novel; that is, it makes no pretense to offer history.[32] Pervo has alerted critics to many popular features of narrative that the author has incorporated into his work. He has not won consensus that Acts is a deliberate novel. Most interpreters view Acts as belonging to the genre of history, though Charles Talbert has made a valiant effort to view Luke–Acts as a special type of biography—a succession biography.[33] Following the consensus of critics that Acts at least purports to be history, the question then focuses on how trustworthy a historian Luke was.

To be sure, in the prologue to the Gospel, which can serve both volumes, Luke claims to have investigated things carefully and consulted numerous eyewitnesses. Because such claims were quite conventional within the genre, they cannot always be taken at face value.[34] One suspects that Lucian, whose work on writing history was consulted above, would not have taken well to the attention given in Acts to the workings of God, the risen Christ, and the Holy Spirit. As Witherington notes, Polybius was not reticent to write a history that lays out the workings of Fortune—hence, such a type of history was not foreign to the world of antiquity, most certainly when one considers biblical and Jewish histories.[35] Notably, however, Polybius did not make Lucian's list of commendable historians, for whatever reason.

Still, when one considers what Lucian notes as characteristics of good historical writing, Acts measures up rather well in many instances. Luke does not present a pretentious and wordy prologue (Lucian, *How to Write History*, § 23). Luke does not burden the reader with lengthy descriptions of geographical locations (§§ 19, 56–57). His narrative is not filled with major geographical errors (§ 24). Luke's language offers a good balance, avoiding artificially highbrow language, while not bereft of "impressive and exalted tones" (§ 45). In the We Passages the author makes an implicit claim to being an eyewitness, which would satisfy Lucian's exhortation to Philo not to make "exaggerated" claims to being such a witness (§§ 28–29). And while one suspects that Lucian would not have approved of the abundance of miracle stories in Acts, he does allow for such stories in histories: "It may occasionally happen that some extraordinary story has to be introduced; it should be simply narrated, without guarantee of its truth, thrown down for anyone to make what he can of it; the writer takes no risks and shows no preference" (§ 60). Certainly, the author of Acts believes the stories to be true, but he narrates them in a straightforward manner and offers no *apologia* for their content.

Candidly, critics differ widely on the historical value of Luke. Gerd Lüdemann represents one school of thought.[36] Essentially, Lüdemann believes the narrative of Acts to be a heavily redacted text. Buried within the Lukan compositions are snippets of inherited traditions. And buried within the snippets of traditions are snippets of *historical* tradition. Acts is valuable as a historical document *not as a whole* but in the fragments of historical tradition that the critic can excavate from the narrative.

While the Commentary will give focused attention to such issues where appropriate, one example will illustrate the fruits of

Lüdemann's method and labor.[37] Acts 18 tells of Paul's ministry in Corinth. Two pieces of accurate historical information are embedded in Luke's narrative: Claudius's expulsion of the Jews from Rome and Gallio's tenure as proconsul. Each of these historical events is linked with Paul's Corinthian ministry. However, Lüdemann dates the expulsion of the Jews from Rome to c. AD 41 and Gallio's tenure to about a decade later. Hence, there are in fact two visits of Paul that Acts has collapsed into one visit. As one can see, following this approach, Luke's value as a historical *writer* is minimal; it is not "good historiography" to collapse two visits to a city separated by ten years into one visit. But Luke does, even if unwittingly, preserve helpful historical information.

Martin Hengel represents another approach.[38] While he reads Acts critically, he believes that Acts does present an overall good and competent historical narrative: "Luke is no less trustworthy than other historians of antiquity. People have done him a great injustice in comparing him too closely with the edifying, largely fictitious, romance-like writings in the style of the later acts of apostles, which freely invent facts as they like and when they need them."[39]

This is not to say that Hengel is a naïve and credulous reader. He is a critical reader, but, as such, is not averse to a reasonable conflation of source material. For example, he cautions readers not to "play off II Cor. 11.32f. and Acts 9.23ff. in this connection."[40] If Hengel can find a credible way to synthesize the sources, in this instance, Acts and Paul's own writings, he will do so. He does not, however, strain credulity. For example, Hengel simply acknowledges that Paul could not have made the journey from Antioch with Barnabas to deliver famine relief to Jerusalem, as Acts 11:29-30 records.[41]

Readers should keep in mind that commentaries serve different purposes. This Commentary is not focused on the historical reconstruction of early Christianity. Rather, its focus is to offer Commentary and Connections on the theological significance of the narrative. Hence, while the Commentary will give attention to historical issues, that will not be the focus, with such attention generally confined to the sidebars. Joel Green gives voice to the approach of this Commentary:

> To learn theological interpretation from Luke, then, is to set aside the hyper-concern with historical validation that has occupied so much biblical scholarship, even biblical theology, in the modern era, in favor of renewed attention to signification. That is, rather than concerning ourselves primarily with whether things happened in this

way, we attend to what significance these have when construed within this narrative. That is because we recognize that *theological interpretation* takes as its starting point the theological claim that the church has received as canon these particular narrative representations of those events that appear in Scripture (rather than the church's having declared canonical a particular set of historical facts).[42]

In this volume, Luke's theological insights are not contingent on *first* offering an apology for the historical accuracy either of words attributed to characters or events depicted. Such lack of focus does not mean that the volume takes a hypercritical stance toward history as presented in the narrative, though historical problems will not be avoided or minimized. [A Chronology of Early Christianity]

Theological Themes of Acts

As stated above, the primary purpose of this Commentary is to explore theological features of the narrative, not to employ the narrative as a source for historical reconstruction. A number of themes come forth in the Commentary and Connections sections of the volume.[43]

Christianity's Connection with Judaism

Christianity is not a new religion; rather, it is the fulfillment of the hopes of Judaism as such hopes are given expression in Israel's Scriptures. Many of the speeches of Acts devote attention to the explication of Scripture in order to demonstrate the continuity between Judaism and the movement initiated by Jesus, which Acts designates not as "Christianity" but as "the Way" (see [The Way]).

Another way that Luke shows continuity is through his attention given to the city of Jerusalem and the temple, in both the Gospel and Acts. The Gospel begins in Jerusalem and the temple, and much of the birth narrative takes place within these environs. The central panel of the Gospel speaks of Jesus' journey to Jerusalem. Jerusalem and the temple are the locations of Jesus' passion *and* resurrection. The early chapters of Acts take place in Jerusalem, with much action happening at the temple. Even as the message of the gospel moves outward to "the ends of the earth" (cf. Acts 1:8), primarily through Paul, the reader (and Paul) is regularly brought back to Jerusalem to remind the reader of the Way's roots in this city. Like Jesus, Paul makes a final trip to Jerusalem where he faces a trial before numerous authorities (see [Jesus and Paul]).

The narrative's concern to show continuity with Judaism spills over to another area: continuity between the early Jerusalem church and the expansion of the Way beyond the boundaries of Jerusalem and Judea. The Jerusalem church, through its representatives (usually Peter, though not exclusively), offers its approval of the expanding mission of the Way. Peter and John, for example, visit the newly established Samaritan churches in Acts 8. Barnabas visits the church of Antioch in Acts 11. As noted above, as Acts focuses on Paul as the primary instrument of Christ to carry the gospel to the ends of the earth, Paul's connection with Jerusalem is highlighted (Acts 9, 11, 15, 18, and 21).

Another way that Acts demonstrates continuity between the Jerusalem church and the geographically expanding church is to narrate the story in a manner that highlights similarities between Peter, a chief representative of the Jerusalem church, and Paul, the chief representative of the geographically expanding church.

Both offer about the same number of speeches. The respective initial speeches of each highlight the fulfillment of Jewish Scripture in Christ (Acts 2 and 3 for Peter, Acts 13 for Paul). Both are arrested and interrogated by various Jerusalem authorities (Peter: Acts 4, 5, 12; Paul: Acts 21–24). Furthermore, the "trials" of each are regularly narrated in a way that highlights similarities with the trial of Jesus before various Jerusalem authorities (see Commentary, ch. 10 on Acts 12 and [Jesus and Paul]). Both heal a lame man (Peter: Acts 3; Paul: Acts 14). Both heal indirectly (Peter's shadow, Acts 5:15; Paul's cloths, Acts 19:12). Both confront magic (Peter: Acts 8:18-24; Paul: Acts 13:6-11; 19:11-20). Both raise someone from the dead (Peter: Acts 9:36-41; Paul: Acts 20:9-12). Both miraculously escape from prison (Peter: Acts 12:6-11; Paul: Acts 16:25-41). [Apostles Peter and Paul]

Such "parallels" serve to demonstrate the continuity between the missions of each major representative of "the Way" in the first and second halves of the book and in the geographical regions in and around Jerusalem (Peter) and beyond (Paul). Such narrative links offer the reader a sense that "the Way" emerges smoothly out of its Jewish roots. Jesus' deep connections with the historic faith of Israel, Peter's connections with Jesus and this same Jewish faith, and Paul's connections with both Jesus (demonstrated through *literary* parallels) and Peter (also demonstrated through *literary* parallels),[44] mixed with Paul's own credentials as one once steeped in a blindly zealous commitment to his Jewish heritage (cf. Acts 22:3-5), all combine to affirm that the narrative of the Gospel and Acts presents not the story of the establishment of a "new religion," but the fulfillment of a very old and true religion.

A Chronology of Early Christianity

The following table offers a rough chronological sketch of some key events of the first generation of church history. It assumes the *overall* historical reliability of Acts, supplemented *and corrected* by data from the Pauline corpus. Those who assume Acts to be essentially unreliable will not agree to such a constructed chronology. Those who assume Acts to be an infallible source of historical data will disagree with some features, as well.

Date Ranges (all dates are AD)	Event	Explanation
28/29	Jesus' public ministry begins	Luke 3:1 states that Jesus began his ministry in the fifteenth year of the reign of Emperor Tiberius (AD 14–37).
30	Death of Jesus	The Synoptic Gospels offer no specific indication of the length of Jesus' ministry. John's Gospel indicates a ministry of two, possibly three, years, if one can accept as historically reliable this Gospel's record of Jesus' frequent trips to Jerusalem during various Jewish festivals.
30–33	Acts 1–8. Early period of the Jerusalem church. Martyrdom of Stephen.	If one can follow Acts, which places the events of Acts 1–8 before the call of Paul, one would date these events prior to the time of Paul's call.
33	Acts 9. Call of Paul	To a great extent, dating Paul's call requires that one work backward from dates that one can ascertain with more assurance, such as Paul's work in Corinth (see below) and information provided by Paul's letters, especially Galatians 1–2.
36	Acts 9. Paul visits Jerusalem	Acts 9:23-26 is very imprecise regarding the time span between Paul's call and his first trip to Jerusalem. Paul says in Gal 1:18 that he did not visit Jerusalem until three years after his call, a trip to Arabia, and his return to Damascus (Acts makes no mention of these last two events; see [Acts and Galatians]).
33–46/47 or 49/50	Acts 10–14. Expansion of Christianity into Judea, northern Syria, and Asia Minor. The conversion of Cornelius fits into this period (prior to 44, Herod's death). Paul and Barnabas bring famine relief to Jerusalem (mid-40s). Martyrdom of James, brother of John (c. AD 44).	Events of Acts 10–14 would be placed between the call of Paul (33) and Paul's trip to Jerusalem for the so-called Jerusalem Council (see below). Luke is likely in error to state that Paul made the famine relief trip (see [Chronological Issues]). The execution of James is recorded in Acts 12:2. Acts 12:20-23 records the death of Herod Agrippa I (AD 44), shortly after the narration of the death of James, implying a date of c. 44 for James's death.
46/47 or 49/50	Acts 15. Paul visits Jerusalem a third time, according to Acts. The Jerusalem church issues the so-called apostolic decree, not requiring Gentiles to be circumcised.	Paul says in Gal 2:1 that he returned to Jerusalem "after fourteen years." But does he mean fourteen years after the first visit (36) or after his call experience (33)? Scholars are not sure. Assuming the latter would render a date of c. 49 or 50. The former would render a date of c. 46 or 47. Most scholars equate the visit of Gal 2:1 with the meeting described in Acts 15.

46/47 or 49/50–50/52	Acts 16–17. Paul's missionary travels, including Philippi, Thessalonica, and Athens.	If Paul arrived in Corinth no later than AD 51 (Acts 18; see next panel), all events spoken of in Acts 16–17 must occur in the narrow time frame between the meeting of Acts 15 and Paul's arrival in Corinth. Assuming an earlier date for the Jerusalem meeting of Acts 15 allows more time for events of Acts 16–17 to transpire.
50/51–51/52	Paul in Corinth	Acts 18:12 indicates that Paul was in Corinth when Gallio was proconsul. Inscriptional evidence allows historians to date the likely beginning of Gallio's tenure to the summer of 51, possibly the summer of 52. He began his tenure after Paul had spent as much as eighteen months in Corinth. This provides a touchstone date around which to date other events.
50/52–58	Paul's missionary travels of Acts 19–21	Paul spent two, possibly three, years in Ephesus (Acts 19), visited various churches he had established earlier (Acts 20), then went to Jerusalem, making a number of stops along the way (Acts 20–21).
Spring 58	Paul returns to Jerusalem where he is arrested and imprisoned (Acts 21–26)	If one can consider as reliable the reports in Acts regarding Paul's imprisonment under Felix (52–60) and Festus (60–62), one may conclude that Paul arrived in Jerusalem c. 58, in the spring (cf. Acts 20:16). Acts 24:27 indicates that Paul was imprisoned in Caesarea during the last two years of Felix's reign (58–60). Paul's letters confirm that he was planning a trip to Jerusalem (e.g., Rom 15:25) to deliver relief for the church there (see [The Collection]). Acts minimizes the significance of the collection.
Fall 60	Paul leaves for Rome	Acts 26 indicates that it was not long after Festus assumed leadership that Paul left for Rome. Acts 27:9, with the reference to the Fast (the Day of Atonement), indicates that the voyage began in the fall, approximately two-and-a-half years after Paul arrived in Jerusalem.
Early 61	Paul arrives in Rome	Again, one must rely on Acts. Acts 27:1–28:14 states that the voyage to Rome took place over the winter season. The voyage was interrupted by a shipwreck that required the crew and prisoners to holdover on Malta for the winter, after which Paul continued and finished his trip to Rome.
61–63	Paul's stay in Rome	Acts ends with reference to Paul's preaching in Rome for two years, offering no word on the outcome of Paul's hearing. Later church traditions asserted that Paul was released and continued his missionary work. He was then martyred during Emperor Nero's persecution of Christians.

The above table is a revision of the chronological table prepared by the author and found in J. Bradley Chance and Milton P. Horne, *Rereading the Bible: An Introduction to the Biblical Story* (Upper Saddle River NJ: Prentice-Hall, 2001), 272–73.

Apostles Peter and Paul

Peter and Paul are "the apostles" upon whom the Acts of the Apostles focuses. The painting by El Greco may show awareness that, historically (though certainly not in Acts), there was tension between the two (cf. Gal 2). Though not touching, the near touch of the hands shows reconciliation. However, it would appear that Peter is reaching out to Paul more than Paul to Peter. Note how Peter looks in Paul's direction, while Paul looks away from Peter's direction. Though barely discernable, one can see in the shadows that Peter holds "the keys to the kingdom" in his lowered left hand. While the keys, symbolic of the power of Peter and the church (based on Matt 16:18-19), are hidden in the shadows, the book to which Paul points, representing a Bible, is given prominence. Though both the church (Peter and the keys) and the Bible are present in the picture, it is the Word that shines more prominently. This interpretation shows my deep, free-church roots and makes no claims to represent El Greco's intention. Though the Acts of the Apostles focuses on Peter and Paul, in the narrative it is Paul, as perhaps in this painting, who is the more dominant figure.

El Greco. *Apostles Peter and Paul*. 1592. Oil on canvas. The Hermitage, St. Petersburg. Web Gallery of Art.

To be sure, Acts urges readers through its narrative to reread and to interpret in fresh ways just what lies at the heart and mission of this very old religion, that is, to paraphrase Paul, to come to grips with the "scandal of the gospel" as Luke interprets it. The gospel requires Israel to revisit and rethink its own story and heritage, recognizing the far-reaching and universal implications of its own story. Therein lies the rub and cause of much conflict in the narrative between the followers of the Way and those of Israel for whom the old wine tastes good (cf. Luke 5:39), who cannot let go of the "old" way of being Israel. This leads to the next theme.

The Universal Gospel

As stated above, while the Way is the fulfillment of Israel's own Scriptures and hopes, such fulfillment requires Israel *to be Israel* in a new "way." The God of Abraham, Isaac, and Jacob is not the God of only the physical descendants of these ancestors; God is the God of all. It is precisely this "way" of understanding Israel and Israel's mission to which the Lukan narrative gives emphasis. And it is precisely this way of being Israel that creates the greatest conflict within the narrative.

Luke has radically rewritten Mark's terse story of Jesus at Nazareth in Luke 4:16-30. When one notes the Lukan expansions to the skeleton of Mark 6:1-6 four themes emerge: Jesus as the fulfillment of Scripture (Luke 4:16-21), the initial openness of Israel to the message of fulfillment (Luke 4:22), the implications of Jesus' mission for those beyond the boundaries of Israel (Luke 4:23-27), and Israel's violent rejection of these implications (Luke 4:28-30). Within this programmatic pericope lies the Lukan pattern. The good news of Israel's God fulfills Israel's hopes, as expressed in Scripture. But it is not only for Israel's glory, but is also a light for revelation to non-Jews (cf. Luke 2:32). It is this second feature of Israel's mission that most of Israel resists, according to Luke (e.g., Acts 13:44-47; 14:1-6, 19; 17:4-5, 13; 18:4-6; 22:17-23).

Luke's universal gospel revolves around the God of Israel and God's Messiah, to be sure. Israel, who already worships the true and living God, is not called upon to repent in order to worship this God. But Israel is called upon to repent—to turn—and recognize Jesus as God's Messiah. Such recognition is not simply a matter of doctrinal consent, but recognition that, in Christ, God has visited God's people to show them the way to be Israel, including the universal implications of being God's people. Gentiles are also to repent, turning from the empty worship of idols to the true and living God of Israel—and of all.

The Connections section of the volume explores for the contemporary faith community the universal implications of being the people of God. The Connections are not interested merely in describing how "the Jews back then" resisted the universal gospel. As the portion of Scripture called Acts engages and challenges contemporary readers, such readers need to reflect on their "way" of being the people of God. The church has done its fair share of erecting barriers that close off the liberating word of God from those whom the church insists remain outside the gates. The inclusiveness of the gospel message finds resistance in the Lukan narrative quite often from those who were "the people of God," Israel. Those who claim to belong to the people of God today in the context of the church can still exclude people, though the criteria of exclusion may be very different from the criteria that faced the author of Acts through the protests of "the Jews." The topic of inclusion is potentially no less controversial today than it was "back then."

The Community of Faith

Acts offers numerous portraits of the church, the community of faith. The Commentary and Connections do not advocate a mere imitation of the patterns discerned in Acts. There are no calls for contemporary Christians to sell their possessions and lay the proceeds at the feet of the apostles, attempting to discern who the equivalent of "the apostles" would be today before whom contemporary Christians are to lay their goods and money. Yet Luke's descriptions of the faith community offer numerous opportunities for reflection and "connections."

Prayer was a crucial dimension of community life. In Acts, prayer makes things happen. Numerous Connections and sidebars will offer some reflections about this significant dimension of community life. *Fellowship*, the breaking of bread, is also an important dimension of community life. Breaking of bread requires presence, not only the presence of the living Lord, but also the presence of flesh-and-blood believers sharing the same space. Fellowship in Acts is not an abstract concept; it assumes and requires face-to-face interaction among the people of faith.

The *interpretation of Scripture* also plays a crucial role in the life of the community. As the Commentary and Connections will note, the interpretation of Scripture was very much rooted in the experiences of the community of faith. In fact, as much as it pinches the methods of critical scholarship, Acts does not portray the community as very interested in the "original meaning" of a text as it goes about the task of interpreting Scripture. While responsible interpretation today cannot ignore the fruits of critical scholarship, the *critical interpretation* of Acts makes clear that the "original meaning" of a text did *not* dictate what Luke–Acts understood the only or perhaps even primary "meaning" of Scripture to be. To interpret Scripture as the early community of faith interpreted Scripture requires that we not confine our interest to its "original meaning," but that we allow Scripture to address our own contexts, issues, and questions.

The community plays a crucial role in the interpretation and application of Scripture and, with that, the discernment of the will of God. Though Acts is not reticent to speak of visions offered directly to key individuals to guide these persons in discerning the divine will, the community consistently plays an important role in legitimating and sanctioning such visions and personal experiences. An obvious example would be the role played by the Jerusalem church in offering legitimacy and sanction to the mission to those who were not Jewish (cf. Acts 11, 15). It is not an exaggeration to say that the Spirit finds its voice in the voice of the community (cf. Acts 15:28).

The community also devotes itself to the teaching of the apostles (cf. Acts 2:42). The devotion to the apostles is also demonstrated symbolically through laying one's goods at the feet of these apostles (cf. Acts 4:34-37). Application to the contemporary community of faith is varied. Churches that embrace an episcopal structure (e.g.,

Catholic, Anglican, Methodist, Lutheran) carry such deference to the apostolic teaching over into the structure of church governance, giving heed to the counsel and guidance of bishops (*episkopoi*). For all Christians, including those who follow bishops, the apostolic voice of guidance is certainly found in the New Testament. Christians aware of the realities of the process of canonization, itself slow, methodical, and not without controversy, and the history of biblical interpretation within the church know, however, that the apostolic voice contained in the New Testament does not exist in a vacuum apart from the larger faith community, both past and present.

It was, after all, the larger community of faith that "canonized" certain texts as Scripture. And it was the community of faith, over the centuries, that wrestled with the meaning of such texts, offering itself guidelines as to how one should read these texts. Responsible interpretation of *Scripture as Scripture* does not exist apart from the community of faith, both past and present. While Acts, as noted above, gives due weight to the *experiences* of individual believers in discerning the will of God and the meaning of Scripture, it seeks to balance such experience with the counsel of the community. For Acts, that Christian community and its leadership reach across a couple of generations. For the contemporary church, the community and its leadership reach across a couple of millennia. Acknowledgment of *the community of saints*, both past and present, is part of responsible scriptural interpretation and discernment of the will of God. Finding the wisdom to delicately negotiate passage between Scylla and Charybdis, between personal experience and community tradition, is necessary for responsible discernment of Scripture and God's will. Readers will encounter numerous Connections and sidebars that provide humble attempts to offer such wisdom.

The Providence of God and Human Participation in the Divine Drama

These two theological themes go together. There is no question but that God is "behind" the action in Acts. Visions and miracles are numerous, denoting the direct action of God to guide the church in its mission. The volume does not minimize the importance of this kind of divine acting. The story of Acts is "going somewhere," and where it is going is in accordance with the "plan," "will," or "purpose of God" (see, e.g., [The Whole Purpose of God]).

Yet exclusive focus on "God's action" through vision and miracle can leave many modern Christian readers feeling a bit out of the loop. Most do not experience God like this. To be sure, some still do, but many do not, especially modern, Western Christians who are the implied readers—the envisioned audience—of this volume. The volume does not browbeat readers to pretend to have the worldview of first-century Jews and Christians. The fact is, much of the providential care of God manifests itself in Acts in the ebb and flow of human choices and action, including human beings who are not at all interested in discerning and acting on the will of God. God very much works in partnership with people, most especially God's people, to accomplish God's purposes, aims, and goals.

Readers will detect sympathy in the Commentary and Connections with ways of thinking and talking about God that highlight this *relational partnership*. As such, readers will find some exploration of ways of talking and thinking about God that one finds today in so-called "open theism" and "process theology." This is not to say that the Commentary or Connections will argue that Luke was an open or process theist. This would be as grossly anachronistic as arguing that Luke was Roman Catholic, Orthodox, Anglican, Lutheran, Calvinist, or whatever label one can put on various expressions of Christianity that have emerged over the centuries. All are later theological constructions. None, whatever advocates might claim, is a mere replication of Lukan, Pauline, or biblical theology. Still, readers especially bent on certain expressions of Calvinism had best be prepared to gird up their loins in order to engage in some fairly serious resistant reading.

A Personal Word

Readers will find numerous places where I talk about "gaps" in the Lukan narrative. In fact, it would not be far-fetched to say that the *commentary* genre is all about filling in gaps that one finds in the text. If the text had no gaps, commentary, frankly, would not be required. There are many ways that commentators fill the gaps. Those informed by historical criticism appeal to issues of historical or social background to "fill the gap." For example, Acts 2 talks about Pentecost, but leaves a gap as to exactly *what* Pentecost is. The commentator fills the gap by offering some background on the nature of the Jewish festival, including its biblical roots and the evolution of its meaning over Jewish religious history.

Or one may fill a gap by reconstructing the history behind the story that one finds in the narrative. For example, Acts 9:23 says that "after many days" Paul left Damascus and went to Jerusalem. That's a very indeterminate time frame, leaving quite a gap. Galatians 2:18 states that Paul made his first trip to Jerusalem *three years* after becoming a follower of Jesus, possibly filling in this

Lukan gap. The above examples offer readers a taste of how historical criticism can fill in narrative gaps. One must be cautious, however, as the Commentary will show from time to time, that interpretive comments not stray from offering comment on the *Lukan narrative* to offering comment on the *reconstructed history* that might lie behind the narrative.

Commentators also can fill gaps by alluding to other texts within the Lukan narrative. For example, Acts 1:3 says that the risen Lord spoke to the disciples about the kingdom of God, but the text itself offers no comment on what this "kingdom of God" is. One can appeal not only to "historical criticism" to fill this gap, but also to Luke's Gospel, which devoted much attention to talking about and illustrating the kingdom of God.

A very candid admission that every commentator should make to readers, and I offer this now, is that all interpretations, all expositions, all "gap filling" that one encounters in a commentary *are the readings and interpretations of the commentator*. That could go without saying, but I choose to come right out and say it. It would be annoying and rhetorically ineffective for every comment to begin with "I understand this to say," or "I think this text means," or "I read the text this way," or some such comment. Commentators do not tend to do that. In reality, commentators— and I have followed their example—tend to hide their voices behind other voices.

I might hide my voice behind the voice of the author or narrator of Acts, saying things like, "the author wants to make clear" or "the narrator implies such and such here." Readers will find that I tend to "hide my voice" more often behind "the narrator," who is "present" to the reader, than "the author," the person I'm calling Luke, who held the pen, lest readers think that, somehow, I can discern what this human author was thinking or intending as he wrote this or that text.

I might hide my voice behind the narrative itself, saying things like, "the narrative implies" or "the narrative demonstrates irony in this passage." Or I might hide my voice behind "readers." Sometimes I'll hide behind "real readers," quoting other readers of Acts, other commentators. Occasionally, I'll even endorse their "readings," saying something like, "as so-and-so rightly observes." What I'm really saying is that I think so-and-so is right. Or I might hide my voice behind hypothetical readers, urging such readers to understand the text in question a certain way. "Readers should recall that . . . " or "alert readers will detect the irony here." I am hopeful that my readings are informed and thoughtful. I am hopeful that my readings do not leave too many gaps for *my* readers to have to fill. But keep in mind that the readings are *my* readings of the Lukan text.

Given all of this, rhetorically, I will employ a third-person voice in the Commentary sections, using expressions such as those offered above. The Connections sections strive to "connect" the biblical passage to *our* own issues and questions. Hence, in this section I will regularly employ a first-person plural voice, attempting to pull the reader (you), author (me), and text (Acts) into a more explicit kind of interpretive *relationship*.

Also, the Connections will offer a more explicitly *canonical* approach to the reading and application of Acts, drawing on the whole of Christian Scripture to "connect" to our time and place various issues that *I* see expressed in Acts. In addition, the Connections will draw on other thinkers whose counsel, I believe, can help us make connections between the narrative of Acts and our own time (Justin, Augustine, Irenaeus, John Wesley, Walter Rauschenbusch, Paul Tillich, Karl Barth, Martin Luther King Jr., Henry Nouwen, Sallie McFague, John Sanders, Clark Pinnock, Molly Marshall, Marjorie Suchocki, and the list could go on). Canonical reading, combined with insights from the "communion of saints," past and present, allows us to bring out the richness of the text in question.

Finally, I need to make explicit what should certainly have been at least implicit in my above introductory comments. Ultimately, I interpret Acts *as Scripture*. I do not attach to the word Scripture what some do; most especially I do not attach to Scripture the heavy freight of inerrancy, *however one might choose to define that term*. By Scripture I mean a text recognized by the church, the body of our spiritual ancestors, to speak the word of God. But, as I hope comments just above have made clear, *interpretation* is a crucial dimension of *hearing* the word of God. Thoughtful interpretation is to give rise to serious *reflection* on the implications of God's word for the faith community. And, finally, such reflection is to lead to the *transformation* of readers, both as individuals and in community. These three dimensions of reading Scripture are discussed in the excellent volume of essays *Reading Luke: Interpretation, Reflection, and Transformation*, which I highly recommend.[45] These three interconnected steps together allow the *reading* of Scripture to serve the *purpose* of Scripture, as *stated by* Scripture: to be "useful for teaching, for reproof, for correction, and for training in righteousness, so that everyone who belongs to God may be proficient, equipped for every good work" (2 Tim 3:16-17).

NOTES

[1] For a good overview of introductory issues see Luke Timothy Johnson, "Luke–Acts, Book of," *ABD* 4.403–20, and Raymond B. Brown, An Introduction to the New Testament (New York: Doubleday, 1997), 279–332.

[2] Joseph A. Fitzmyer, *The Acts of the Apostles* (AB 31; New York: Doubleday, 1998), 47–49.

[3] Fitzmyer, *Acts*, 49–51; Ben Witherington III, *The Acts of the Apostles: A Socio-Rhetorical Commentary* (Grand Rapids MI: Eerdmans, 1998), 51–60.

[4] E.g., Mikeal C. Parsons and Richard Pervo, *Rethinking the Unity of Luke and Acts* (Minneapolis: Fortress, 1993).

[5] See, e.g., Philipp Vielhauer, "On the 'Paulinism' of Acts," in *Studies in Luke–Acts*, ed. Leander Keck and J. Louis Martyn (Philadelphia: Fortress, 1966), 33–51. See also J. Bradley Chance, "The Seed of Abraham and the People of God: A Study of Two Pauls," *1993 SBLSP*: 384–411.

[6] Some scholars claim as much. See Jacob Jervell, "The Future of the Past: Luke's Vision of Salvation History and Its Bearing on His Writing of History," in *History, Literature, and Society in the Book of Acts,* ed. Ben Witherington III (Cambridge: Cambridge University Press, 1996), 104–26, esp. 117.

[7] Fitzmyer, *Acts*, 51–55; Witherington, *Acts*, 60–63.

[8] John B. Polhill, *Acts* (NAC 26; Nashville: Broadman, 1992), 27–31, proposes the early 70s; C. K. Barrett, *Acts*, 2 vols. (ICC; Edinburgh: T&T Clark, 1994/1998), 2.xlii, proposes the late 80s to early 90s. Witherington, *Acts*, 62 proposes the late 70s to early 80s; Fitzmyer, *Acts*, 54, the 80s. All acknowledge that such suggestions are tentative.

[9] Jacques Dupont, *The Sources of Acts* (New York: Herder and Herder, 1964); Fitzmyer, *Acts*, 80–89; Barrett, *Acts*, ICC 2.xxiv–xxx.

[10] Dupont, *Sources*, 166.

[11] Barrett, *Acts*, ICC 1.53.

[12] F. J. Foakes Jackson and Kirsopp Lake, *The Beginnings of Christianity: The Acts of the Apostles*, 5 vols. (Grand Rapids MI: Baker, 1979), vol. 3: "The Text of Acts," esp. ccxxi–ccxlvi; Fitzmyer, *Acts*, 66–79.

[13] Eldon Jay Epp, "Textual Criticism: New Testament," *ABD* 6.412–35, though he employs different terminology (Alexandrian = B text group; Western = D text group; Caesarean = C text group; Byzantine = A text group). Bart D. Ehrman, "Text of the New Testament," *EDB* 1292–95, identifies three major traditions, Alexandrian, Western, and Byzantine. Recall that the Caesarean is a hybrid of Alexandrian and Western traditions.

[14] Henry J. Cadbury, "The Speeches of Acts," in *Beginnings of Christianity*, 5.402–427; Eduard Schweizer, "Concerning the Speeches of Acts," in *Studies in Luke–Acts*, 208–16; Marion L. Soards, *The Speeches in Acts: Their Content, Context, and Concerns* (Louisville KY: Westminster/John Knox, 1994); Fitzmyer, *Acts*, 103–108, 111–13.

[15] 1:16-22; 2:14-36, 38-39; 3:12-26; 4:8-12, 19, 20; 5:29-32; 10:34-23; 11:5-17; 15:7-11.

[16] 13:16-41; 14:15-17; 17:22-31; 20:18-35; 22:1-21; 24:10-21; 26:2-23, 25-27; 27:21-26; 28:17-20.

[17] *"The History of the Peloponnesian War," By Thucydides, Written 431 B.C.E.,* Translated by Richard Crawley, http://classics.mit.edu/Thucydides/pelopwar.1.first .html (14 July 2006).

[18] Martin Dibelius, "The Speeches in Acts and Ancient Historiography," in *Studies in the Acts of the Apostles*, ed. Heinrich Greeven (Mifflintown PA: Sigler Press, 1999), 138–85, quotation p. 141.

[19] Ibid., 144. Emphases added.

[20] Ibid.

[21] Witherington, *Acts*, 24–49.

[22] Ibid., 41.

[23] *The Histories of Polybius Published in the Loeb Classical Library, 1922–1927* [public domain], http://penelope.uchicago.edu/Thayer/E/Roman/Texts/Polybius/ 12*.html (14 July 2006).

[24] *"The History of the Peloponnesian War"*; see n. 17 for complete bibliographical information.

[25] Witherington, *Acts*, 47.

[26] Ibid., 48; emphasis added by Witherington.

[27] Ibid., 26.

[28] All translations of Lucian's *How to Write History* and references are from *Internet Sacred Text Archive, Lucian, How to Write History*, http://www.sacred-texts.com/cla/luc/wl2/wl210.htm (14 July 2006).

[29] Lucian offers a clear paraphrase of Thucydides, *History* 1.22.4. Thucydides states: "I have written my work, not as an essay which is to win the applause of the moment, but as a possession for all time." Lucian's paraphrase: "our work is to be a possession for ever, not a bid for present reputation" (42). The paraphrased statement from Thucydides occurs just a few lines after Thucydides' statement on speeches. It would seem that if Lucian knew the lines he paraphrases, he would have been familiar with the lines immediately preceding them.

[30] Lucian's advice that the speech suit the speaker and occasion *could* allude to Thucydides' comment that speeches "make the speakers say what was in my opinion demanded of them by the various occasions." If so, and this is by no means certain, it is significant that Lucian makes no allusion to Thucydides' comment that his speeches reflected the general sense of what was actually spoken.

[31] Witherington, *Acts*, 24–51; Barrett, *Acts*, ICC 2.xxxii–lxii; Fitzmyer, *Acts*, 124–28; Ernst Haenchen, "The Book of Acts as Source Material for the History of Early Christianity," in *Studies in Luke–Acts*, 258–78.

[32] Richard I. Pervo, *Profit with Delight: The Literary Genre of the Acts of the Apostles* (Philadelphia: Fortress, 1987).

[33] Charles Talbert, *What Is a Gospel? The Genre of the Canonical Gospels* (Philadelphia: Fortress, 1977); see also J. Bradley Chance, "Talbert's New Perspectives on Luke–Acts: The ABCs of Ancient Lives," in *Cadbury, Knox, and Talbert: American Contributions to the Study of Acts*, ed. Mikeal C. Parsons and Joseph Tyson (Atlanta: Scholars Press, 1992), 181–201.

[34] Charles Talbert, *Reading Luke: A Literary and Theological Commentary on the Third Gospel* (New York: Crossroad, 1986), 8–11.

[35] Witherington, *Acts*, 32–33.

[36] Gerd Lüdemann, *Early Christianity according to the Traditions in Acts: A Commentary* (Minneapolis: Fortress, 1989).

[37] Ibid., 195–204.

[38] Martin Hengel, *Acts and the History of Earliest Christianity* (Philadelphia: Fortress, 1979).

[39] Ibid., 60.

[40] Ibid., 85. See [Acts and Galatians].

[41] Ibid., 111. See [Chronological Issues].

[42] Joel B. Green, "Learning Theological Interpretation from Luke," in *Reading Luke: Interpretation, Reflection, Formation*, ed. Craig G. Bartholomew, Joel B. Green, Anthony Thiselton (Scripture and Hermeneutics Series 6; Carlisle UK: Paternoster/Zondervan, 2005), 55–78 (quotation, 57; emphasis original).

[43] One can offer an overview of theological themes by discussing a list of various "-ologies": Lukan *eschatology, pneumatology, Christology, ecclesiology, missionology*, etc. The themes discussed here emerged out of a review of the Commentary and Connections upon their completion. The kinds of issues here may not always fit traditional *theological* categories, but are theologically relevant and reflect the actual themes and issues that readers will encounter in the pages that follow. Further, since the issues discussed in this section emerged from a synthesis of numerous discussions throughout the Commentary, rather than a review of critical writers for the specific purpose of writing this section of the introduction, this section does not present bibliography that surveys the topic under discussion. Relevant bibliography is presented in appropriate places in the Commentary and Connections sections.

[44] Though Peter and Paul share the stage on occasion (cf. Acts 9:27; 15:4, 12), they *do not directly interact* in the narrative. "Connections" between Peter and Paul are constructed by the way the narrator tells stories about each.

[45] Green, *Reading Luke: Interpretation, Reflection, Formation*, n 42.

WAITING FOR THE PROMISE OF THE FATHER

Acts 1:1-26

COMMENTARY

This chapter has two scenes. Verses 1-11 present a second dedication and echo some themes found in the conclusion of the Gospel. Additionally, they offer supplementary information to prepare the reader for the Acts narrative. Verses 12-26 focus attention on Judas's replacement, completing the circle of the Twelve.

Reviewing What Jesus Began to Do and Teach, 1:1-11

Acts begins with a second dedication to Theophilus (Gk., "lover of God"). This dedication ties Acts to the Gospel of Luke, also dedicated to Theophilus (Luke 1:1-4). Many narrative details of the introduction hark back to the conclusion of the Gospel. [Comparison of Acts 1 and Luke 24] Still, comparisons between Luke 24 and Acts 1 do not yield precise agreement. Luke 24 leaves the impression that the resurrection, appearances, and the ascension all took place on the same day, while in Acts Jesus appeared regularly to his followers over a forty-day period (v. 3). In the Gospel, the ascension brings dramatic closure to the story about Jesus. In Acts, the ascension stands at the beginning of the narrative and points toward the future of apostolic witness. Jesus' periodic and ongoing fellowship with and instruction of the apostles prior to his ascension enhances the authority of these apostolic witnesses. [The Ascension]

Verse 3 states that Jesus spoke to his followers of the kingdom of God. How do readers relate this speaking of the kingdom of God with what Jesus focused on in Luke 24, especially Jesus' word that his death and resurrection and the preaching of forgiveness to the nations were all in fulfillment of Scripture? Jesus does not speak explicitly of the kingdom of God in Luke 24, but he speaks much about it in the Gospel. Is Luke inviting readers to pull in what they have learned from the Gospel about the kingdom and synthesize it

Comparison of Acts 1 and Luke 24

Comparison of the two narrative sections reveals that Acts does not offer an exact recounting of the Lukan narrative. Important themes, however, are found in each of the narrative accounts of post-Easter encounters between Jesus and his disciples.

Acts 1	Luke 24
Jesus gave instructions through the Holy Spirit (v. 2).	Can allude to the whole activity of Jesus' teaching of the disciples in Luke 24. Cf. vv. 25-27, 32, 44-48.
Jesus presented himself alive by many proofs (v. 3a).	See the story of the Emmaus travelers (vv. 13-32), the notation of Jesus' appearance to Simon (v. 34), and the narration of Jesus' appearance to the disciples (vv. 36-40).
Appeared for forty days (v. 3b).	Not in Luke 24.
Spoke of kingdom of God (v. 3b).	Not explicitly in Luke 24. May compare with Jesus' discussion of his fulfillment of the Scriptures (see vv. 27, 45-47).
Ate with the disciples (v. 4a).	Cf. vv. 41-43; Jesus requests something to eat, and he receives and eats some fish.
Commanded disciples not to leave Jerusalem (v. 4b).	Cf. v. 49b; "but stay in the city."
Instructed disciples to wait for the promise of the Father (v. 4b).	Cf. v. 49; "stay in the city, until you are clothed with power from on high."
Disciples asked about restoration of kingdom to Israel and Jesus' response (vv. 6-7).	Compares thematically with the Emmaus traveler's hope that Jesus was to redeem Israel (v. 21).
Jesus reiterates promise of Holy Spirit and the command to be witnesses.	Cf. vv. 48-49; "You are witnesses of these things. And behold, I send the promise of my Father upon you."
Ascension described (vv. 9-11).	Cf. v. 51; states that Jesus ascended.
Disciples returned to Jerusalem from Olivet (v. 12).	Cf. v. 50; ascension takes place at Bethany, which connects with Olivet. Verse 52, disciples return to Jerusalem.
Disciples went to "upper room" (v. 13).	Cf. v. 53; disciples go to the temple (they go to the temple in Acts 3).

with what Jesus says about his suffering and death and the proclamation of forgiveness?

Readers first encounter the kingdom of God in Luke 4:43: "I must preach the good news of the kingdom of God to other cities also; for I was sent for this purpose." The statement climaxes a chapter of purposeful activity, wherein Jesus had withstood the onslaught of the devil (Luke 4:1-13), visited Nazareth and announced the fulfillment of the Scriptures that heralded the coming of God's liberating activity (Luke 4:16-30), and performed

The Ascension

Only Luke–Acts and the extended ending of Mark offer a *narrative* of the ascension of Jesus. Many texts within the New Testament do speak of Jesus "going up to heaven," to use somewhat non-technical language (see Eph 4:10 [cf. Eph 1:20-22]; Col 3:1; 1 Tim 3:16; Heb 4:14; 9:24-26; 1 Pet 3:21-22). However, nothing in the texts cited *requires* one to understand that Jesus' "going up to heaven" was thought of as an "event" distinct from the resurrection itself. Earliest Christian tradition may not, therefore, have always distinguished resurrection from ascension. Both were ways of speaking of the glorification and exaltation of Jesus Christ. The Gospel of John seems to distinguish between resurrection and ascension, given the risen Jesus' statement to Mary that he has not yet *ascended* (John 20:17). Jesus' statement, however, implies that his ascension is quite imminent, perhaps immediate. Luke clearly distinguishes resurrection from ascension, explicitly stating in Acts 1:3 that Jesus had fellowship with and instructed the apostles periodically for a duration of forty days. Luke's Gospel itself (24:50-51) easily reads that the ascension was the same day as the resurrection (similar to John). Subsequent Christian traditions extended the duration of Jesus' continued fellowship with the apostles to eighteen months (Valentinians) or even twelve years (*Pistis Sophia*). Luke's view of things became normative in Christian tradition: Jesus was resurrected and forty days later ascended into heaven, to sit at the right hand of God on the throne of the Messiah.

a series of healings and exorcisms that demonstrated the liberating activity of God through Jesus. Jesus then declares that he has been proclaiming the kingdom of God (Luke 4:43). Readers should understand this kingdom about which Jesus speaks in Acts to allude to this work of liberation—"release"—from the bonds of Satan, sin, sickness, and possession. Recognizing the connection between the kingdom of God and the message of "release"/liberation, readers can hear an echo of what Jesus said explicitly in Luke 24:47: "repentance and forgiveness [lit., "release"] of sins should be preached in his name to all nations." The text also invites readers to make some connection between this kingdom of God and the death and resurrection of Jesus, which receives attention in Luke 24:26-27, 45. Whatever one understands this liberating "kingdom of God" to include, one now connects it with the significance of the death and resurrection of Jesus. The message of "the gospel," which focuses on Jesus, and especially his death and resurrection, becomes central and subsumes in itself the liberating message of God's dawning reign. The "good news of the kingdom of God" and "the good news" itself merge into one message.

"Now when they had come together" (v. 6) implies a change of physical location, though the subject matter discussed in v. 6 connects with the topic of the Holy Spirit found in v. 5. If one reads v. 4 as "while he [Jesus] was eating with them," that might imply a setting somewhere in Jerusalem, especially in light of Luke 24:33-43, which tells of Jesus'

Mount of Olives

Garden of Gethsemane. (Credit: Alex Slobodkin, istockphoto.com)

The Spirit and the Last Days

Scholarly consensus maintains that it was widely held in Judaism that the Holy Spirit, understood primarily as "the spirit of prophecy," was no longer active in Israel. Often cited is the rabbinic tradition, "When the last prophets, Haggai, Zechariah, and Malachi, died, the holy spirit ceased out of Israel; but nevertheless it was granted them to hear [communication from God] by means of a mysterious voice" (*Tos Sotah* 13, 2; see Moore, 1.421-22). It was, however, also widely held that with the coming of the new age of restoration, this spirit of prophecy would be renewed for *all* of God's people. "The Holy One, blessed be He, said, 'In this world only individuals are endowed with prophecy, but in the world to come all Israel will be prophets" (*Numbers Rabbah* on 15:25).

Interestingly, this text then quotes Joel 2:28 (3:1 in the Hebrew Bible) as a "proof text" to back up this claim, even as does Luke in Acts 2:17ff.

G. F. Moore, *Judaism in the First Centuries of the Christian Era*, 2 vols. (New York: Schocken Books, 1971, 1927).

The Ascension of Jesus

Pietro Perugino (1448–1523). *Ascension*. Duomo, Sansepolcro, Italy. (Credit: Scala / Art Resource, NY)

The text of Acts places angels ("two men in white robes" [1:10]) at the scene of Jesus' Ascension, but their attention is directed solely at the disciples. In Perugino's *Ascension* angels and cherubs surround and welcome Jesus to the messianic throne. The positioning of Jesus' hands can allude back to Luke, which says that Jesus, "lifting up his hands, ... blessed them" (Luke 24:50). Both the Lukan narrative and the artist's portrayal imply a priestly blessing, though a priestly Christological theme is not given much attention in Luke–Acts. Finally, Mary is given prominence in Perugino's *Ascension*, a status not given her in the narrative of Acts at the Ascension. The prominence of Mary is not without precedent, both in classical and contemporary depictions of the Ascension.

appearing to and eating with the disciples in the city. But v. 6 initiates a small narrative unit that continues right up to the ascension in vv. 9-11, which took place *outside* the city (see Luke 24:50; Acts 1:12). This concluding scene begins with the disciples asking a question that was not explicitly raised in Luke 24: "Lord, will you at this time restore the kingdom to Israel?" (but cf. Luke 24:21).

Perhaps the question is prompted by Jesus' discussion of the kingdom (v. 3) and his promise in v. 5 that the disciples would receive the Holy Spirit. The return of the Spirit was regularly associated with the restoration of God's people in "the last days," and talk of God's kingdom might naturally lead to talk of "restoring the kingdom to Israel." [The Spirit and the Last Days] If one understands this kingdom to be God's liberating work of releasing people from the grip of evil, especially "release from sins," then the restoration of the kingdom to Israel *will* begin with the coming of the Spirit. At this time, according to Luke 24:47, the worldwide proclamation of "forgiveness of sins, beginning from Jerusalem" will commence. For Israel, the restoration of the kingdom, at least in part, "means its reception of the Holy Spirit . . . and its enjoyment of the messianic blessings of spiritual fellowship and harmony."[1]

Jesus directs the disciples' attention away from times and seasons set by the Father (v. 7). This reference points beyond the story time of Luke's narrative to the final culmination of things (cf. Luke 21:8, 24; Acts 3:20). This "second coming," or *Parousia*, brings the ultimate closure to the story of the kingdom and the gospel. But that is not to be the focus of the disciples' attention. Thus, Jesus redirects their attention to the mission of being worldwide witnesses of Jesus (v. 8).[2] The fact that this verse offers something of a concise outline of the story to follow reinforces its significance. Disciples, both inside the story and outside the story (the readers), are encouraged to focus attention on the mission of being witnesses.

Luke concludes this opening scene with the ascension. The more detailed narration of the story enriches the telescoped narrative of Luke 24. What was simply *told* to readers in the Gospel is *shown* to readers in Acts. The use of "and behold" (v. 10) invites readers to visualize the scene. Readers witness, along with the disciples, the ascension of Jesus to the messianic throne. In Luke 22:69 Jesus had said, "From now on the Son of Man shall be *seated* at the right hand of the power of God." Acts provides fulfillment within the narrative of this declaration. The two men use direct discourse, allowing readers to "hear" what was said. Readers are there with the disciples. The words promising that Jesus "will come in the same way as you saw him go into heaven" (v. 11) recall Luke 21:27 when "they will see the Son of man coming in a cloud with power and great glory." Luke 21:28 states that Jesus' audience (the disciples and the Jewish people gathered to hear him speak at the temple) is to "look up and raise your heads, because your redemption is drawing near." This allusion in Acts 1:11 to Luke 21:27-28 helps readers to answer the question asked by Acts 1:6: "Will you at *this* time, restore the kingdom to Israel?" No. The story of Israel's restoration does not reach its conclusion a few days hence when the Spirit comes. The conclusive event of restoring the kingdom to Israel comes only when people see Jesus return on the clouds, even as the disciples (and readers) witnessed him depart on a cloud. But, for now, there is work to be done.

Taking the Place of Judas, 1:12-26

Verse 12 states that the disciples returned to Jerusalem from Mount Olivet, which Luke describes as being "near Jerusalem, a sabbath day's journey away." [Sabbath Day's Journey] This reminder keeps readers focused on Jerusalem, or

Sabbath Day's Journey

ΑΩ A Sabbath day's journey is the distance one can walk on the Sabbath and not be considered in violation of the legal prohibition from work (Exod 20:8-11). Legal scholars of Judaism calculated this distance to be 2,000 cubits, based on Num 35:5, or six *stadia* (about one-half mile). Josephus records the distance from Olivet to Jerusalem to be five or six *stadia*, in agreement, therefore, with Acts. However, John records that Bethany itself, which Luke locates at Olivet (Luke 19:29), is fifteen *stadia*, or about two miles, from Jerusalem (John 11:18).

its immediate environs, as the place where the key events following the resurrection took place. The Lukan narrative emphasizes this Jerusalem connection (compare the Galilean resurrection traditions of Matt 28:16-20). The center of God's saving activity is the holy city of Jerusalem, the city that Jews believed was the place where God would manifest to all God's saving power (see, e.g., Isa 2:2-4). Luke 24:50 associated Bethany with the ascension, but according to Luke 19:29 Bethany was located at this mount. There may also be symbolic significance in Mount Olivet as the place of the ascension of Jesus as the messianic king. According to Zechariah 14:4, this place was associated with the manifestation of the Lord's power on behalf of God's people.

According to Luke 24:52-53, the disciples returned to Jerusalem and went to the temple to praise God. In the opening chapters of Acts, the disciples will spend much time in the temple area. However, prior to this, they return to "the upper room" (*to hyper-oion*). The use of the definite article implies a specific place. Luke 22:12 spoke of an "upper room" (*anagaion*) as the place of Jesus' last meal. Identification of the two rooms would mean that this place had become for the disciples a semi-permanent place of residence in Jerusalem. This allows readers to understand how this itinerant group of men from Galilee could have a common gathering place where the resurrected Lord could appear to them in Luke 24:33, 36. Luke does not specifically speak of an "upper room" in Luke 24, nor does he specifically say that the room of Acts is the same as the room of the Last Supper. But authors can never tell readers everything; readers must always fill in gaps left by authors.

Though presented in a different order, the list of disciples that follows (v. 13) is identical to that found in the Gospel (Luke 6:14-16), less Judas Iscariot. In Acts, Peter and John are mentioned together (John is the fourth name listed in the Gospel). Their juxtaposition in v. 13 anticipates their being mentioned together in following narrative (there are ten references to "Peter and John" in Acts, in addition to this one).

Verse 14 states that others were in the room praying with the disciples. Present are Jesus' brothers and some women, including Jesus' mother and perhaps also the women who had witnessed Jesus' death (Luke 23:49) and burial (Luke 23:55) and had visited the tomb (Luke 24:10). According to Luke 24:10, one of the women who visited the tomb was "Mary the mother of James." This could be a veiled reference to Jesus' mother, who did have another son named James (cf. Gal 1:19). But it would be curious that Luke chose to introduce Jesus' mother at the empty tomb in such a cryptic manner. Luke 24:33 notes that others, in addition to the eleven, were gathered in one place when Jesus appeared. Those gathered with the eleven in the Gospel are not identified as they are here. Nothing compels or prevents readers from understanding that the others who saw the resurrected Lord in Luke 24:33 included those mentioned in Acts 1:14 (the women, Jesus' mother, and his brothers). If readers do assume those of Acts 1:14 to have been present in Luke 24, they might wonder why Luke offered no specific word in the Gospel of their presence. Does Luke assume that readers should include them, perhaps especially the women, in the group to whom Jesus appeared? Or does his silence indicate that he wished to remove women from the group of people to whom the resurrected Lord appeared? How any particular reader fills this gap will say more about the reader, perhaps, than the author of Luke–Acts.

Luke mentions only Jesus' brothers, not his sisters. Mark 6:3 and Matthew 13:56 state that Jesus also had sisters. Luke does not mention Jesus' sisters in either the Gospel or Acts. He does refer to Jesus' brothers in Luke 8:19-21, who appear with Jesus' mother as in Acts 1. The Gospel presents Jesus' family in a positive light, with Jesus describing them as "those who hear the word of God and do it" (Luke 8:21).

The reference in v. 15 to "in those days" implies a minor shift of time, though not necessarily a shift of location. The phrase introduces a section of narrative filled with language imitating the LXX. Similar to Luke 1–2, which also imitates Greek biblical style, Luke uses language to place the reader into a "biblical world." Readers feel as though they are in the world of the Jewish Scriptures as they read this story about the church's beginnings. One hundred twenty people are now gathered. This may have symbolic significance, in that some interpreters of Jewish law required a city to have at least 120 persons in order for a legitimate Jewish synagogue to exist (*m.Sanh.* 1:6).

After explicitly noting the presence of women in v. 14, the focus is now on men (see vv. 15 and 16). The women, if present, are silent and even ignored. The focus of this section on selecting a twelfth apostle may account for the masculine air. Whatever roles Luke assigns to women, they were not considered for apostleship. This fact has no direct bearing on the role of women in ministry today, since Luke portrays "apostleship" as a unique, unrepeatable office that neither women nor men today can fill.

Verses 16 and 17 present direct speech, introducing the first major speech in Acts. Peter, who in the Gospel had denied Jesus, has now been restored to a position of leadership, fulfilling what

Relief of the Death of Judas

The Crucifixion of Christ. Late Roman, c425 AD. Plaque from an ivory casket; the earliest known narrative portrayal of the Crucifixion. It is combined with the suicide of Judas, his payment for betraying Christ at his feet. British Museum, London, Great Britain (Credit: HIP / Art Resource, NY)

Christian tradition has latched on to Matthew's version of Judas's death, which is that he hanged himself. The relief depicts the irony of Judas's death, showing Judas hanging from a rope at the same time that Jesus hangs from a cross. Judas's hanging brought him shame and infamy. Jesus' hanging brings redemption. Around Jesus are Mary, John, and the Roman centurion. Their attention is focused on Jesus. Judas dies alone.

Jesus prophesied in Luke 22:31-32. Peter's first words point to the idea of the fulfillment of Scripture. Jesus had opened the minds of those to whom he had appeared to understand that the Scriptures found their fulfillment in the story of his death and resurrection, as well as the story of the church's proclamation to the nations (Luke 24:25-26, 45-46). Readers of Luke 24 were not told which Scriptures were fulfilled by Jesus' death and resurrection. The speeches of Acts will fill this gap.

The Scriptures are presented as "fore-speakings" (*pro* [fore] *eipen* [to speak]) of the Holy Spirit through the human author David, the traditional composer of many of the psalms. This view of the Scriptures, which portrays them as divine oracles concerned to address a time beyond that of the human author, was common to first-century Judaism. Both the author of Acts and his characters share this perspective.

Verses 18-19 offer a kind of flashback, providing new information to fill a gap left by the Gospel of Luke concerning the fate of Judas. Interpreters debate whether the verses represent a continuation of Peter's speech or an intrusion of the narrator's voice. Either way, readers learn that Judas bought a field with his "wicked wages" and killed himself, presumably by jumping headfirst off a precipice of some sort, bursting his body open upon impact. Luke leaves it to readers to picture precisely "the how" of the suicide, but leaves little to the imagination as he presents to readers the final picture. [Death of Judas]

Following vv. 18-19 the selection of a new apostle becomes the focus. Peter refers to Psalm 69:26 (LXX; 69:25 in ET) in v. 20a and Psalm 109:8 in 20b. The Scriptures anticipate even the destiny of Jesus' betrayer.

According to vv. 21-22, the replacement is to come from among "one of the men" (*andrōn*) who accompanied Jesus throughout his public ministry and shared fellowship with Jesus after the resurrec-

Death of Judas

The New Testament offers two versions of Judas's death. Matthew states that Judas repented and returned the money to the Jewish leaders and then hanged himself. The Jewish leaders then bought a field (Matt 27:3-10). This differs from Acts, which states that Judas bought the field himself (1:18). Luke states that Judas jumped headfirst to a violent, literally gut-busting fall. This is not another way of saying that Judas "hanged himself." Opinion regarding the historicity of the story ranges widely. Some argue that Matthew's and Luke's accounts can be reconciled, implying both to be historically accurate, but incomplete in and of themselves (Marshall,

65). Others contend that the whole account of Judas's suicide is legendary, built on the popular motif of the death of an enemy of God (Lüdemann, 33-36). Common elements between Matthew and Luke include a field called "Field of Blood" and association of its purchase with the money paid to Judas to betray Jesus. Both understand Judas to have committed suicide. If Matthew and Luke are working independently of one another, this at least implies a relatively early tradition about the death of Judas.

I. Howard Marshall, *The Acts of the Apostles: An Introduction and Commentary*, TNTC (Leicester: Inter-Varsity Press, 1984); Gerd Lüdemann, *Early Christianity according to the Traditions in Acts: A Commentary* (Minneapolis: Fortress, 1989).

---

tion. It is imperative that the replacement be able to bear witness to the resurrection. Two persons are put forward, Joseph, who is also called Barsabbas and surnamed Justus, and Matthias. The details regarding Joseph may lead one to suspect that he will be chosen, making the selection of Matthias something of a surprise. God, "who knows the heart" (v. 25), does not choose according to expected criteria—the one "known better" by human beings, including the narrator.

Prayer and casting lots are the means of selection (v. 26). [Casting Lots] What most moderns would call "luck of the draw," the early apostles called divine guidance. Once the Holy Spirit comes, casting lots is no longer mentioned, cautioning contemporary Christians from confusing the roll of the dice with the will of God.

Casting Lots

A traditional means within Judaism to determine God's will (see Lev 16:8; Num 26:55-56; 33:54; Josh 19:1-40; 1 Chr 26:12-16; Mic 2:5; Jonah 1:7-8), the practice of casting lots was also employed at Qumran. Stones were marked to designate certain persons and placed in a jar or a bag. The container was shaken until a stone fell out determining the one on whom "the lot fell." Chance was viewed as divinely determined: "Before Pentecost, before the presence of the Spirit to lead it, the church sought the direction of God and used the Old Testament procedure of securing divine decision" (Polhill, 95).

John B. Polhill, *Acts* (NAC 26; Nashville: Broadman, 1992).

The Twelve are now reconstituted. Why is this important? Are not eleven witnesses to the resurrection sufficient? The 120 persons in v. 15 may be relevant to this question. The number twelve and the related number, 120, may signify something important. Verse 6 spoke of the restoration of the kingdom to Israel. Luke–Acts is a story about God and God's dealings with Israel, the people whose Scriptures find fulfillment in the Jesus story and its aftermath. Hinted at in the reconstituted twelve apostles and the 120 who formed the nucleus of the early community is the restoration of Israel, the nation of twelve tribes. Jesus promised in Luke 22:28-30 that his followers who had been with him throughout his ministry had been assigned a kingdom—a rule. And what they are to rule

Twelve Apostles

For Luke, the twelve apostles serve as the leaders of the restored Israel (Luke 22:28-30) and the eyewitness link between Jesus and the early followers (Acts 1:8, 21-22). As the leadership of the restored "twelve tribes of Israel," Judas must be replaced; there must be "twelve" to lead the restored Israel. However, once the Spirit is bestowed and the faith community and gospel message that founded this community is firmly established, it is not necessary for the ongoing welfare of the church for "the twelve apostles" to continue. Thus, when James is killed (Acts 12:2) there is no move to fill his place (Johnson, 39). Luke uses the word "apostle" in a much more limited sense than Paul, virtually limiting the word to denote only "the Twelve"

(but cf. Acts 14:14). Scholars debate the question of the historical character of "the Twelve." Was it a post-Easter Christian tradition "read back" into the time of Jesus, or did Jesus intentionally pick twelve special followers, symbolic of his ministry of restoring Israel in the context of the dawning of God's kingdom? If Jesus did view his work as, in part, initiating the eschatological restoration of Israel, it could follow that he chose twelve special disciples to symbolize the restoration and renewal of God's people.

F. J. Foakes Jackson and Kirsopp Lake, *The Beginnings of Christianity: The Acts of the Apostles*, 5 vols. (Grand Rapids MI: Baker, 1979), 5.3–41; Luke Timothy Johnson, *The Acts of the Apostles* (SacPag 5; Collegeville MN: Liturgical Press, 1992).

and judge is "the twelve tribes of Israel." The "restoration of the kingdom to Israel" may not come to full fruition in the imminent future when the Spirit arrives. But a decisive thing will take place that has to do with the restoration of Israel and the offering of God's liberating reign to all people. With the twelve apostles restored, this larger story of restoration can now begin. [Twelve Apostles]

CONNECTIONS

One impressive feature of the text is its conviction that the Scriptures speak an immediate and relevant word to the community seeking guidance. We note Peter's assurance that the psalm, written by David centuries before, offered an explicit word "concerning Judas" and his treachery (v. 16).

We are told that the text from David explicitly "concerns Judas." Modern readers, who tend to focus attention on the meaning of a text in its *originating* context, must acknowledge that first-century Jews, including Bible writers, did not have our concern for originating context. Thus, while we might feel more comfortable speaking of how a Scripture might "apply" to a contemporary situation, ancient readers had no hesitancy to say that the Scripture *explicitly* concerned a contemporary issue. [Bibliography on New Testament Use of the Old] We should not abandon our conviction to pay attention to the originating context of the Scriptures' word. But attention to Peter's use of the psalms can renew our awareness that the Scriptures can address our own contexts, as well as those of the ancient author or audience.

Acts 1:20a loosely quotes Psalm 69:25; the LXX forms the basis of the quotation. The LXX reads, "Let *their* habitation be made desolated [participle] and in their tents let there not be the inhabitant." Acts reads, "Let *his* habitation be made desolate [adjective], and let there not be the inhabitant." The most obvious alteration is the change of the plural "their habitation" to the singular "his habitation." This change is comprehensible since Peter approaches the psalm with the *belief* that it "concerns Judas" (v. 16). Peter's assumption informs his way of reading the text. If the text is about Judas, an individual man, the text is reread to make this clear. While this might be

Bibliography on New Testament Use of the Old

Dodd, C. H. *The Old Testament in the New.* Revised ed. Philadelphia: Fortress, 1971. A modern classic on the subject.

Beale, G. K. *The Right Doctrine from the Wrong Texts? Essays on the Use of the Old Testament in the New.* Grand Rapids MI: Baker, 1994. A collection of essays on the subject, written from an evangelical perspective. Several essays respond to arguments of other essays presented in the collection, allowing readers to encounter differing points of view.

Evans, Craig and James A. Sanders. *Luke and Scripture: The Function of Sacred Tradition in Luke–Acts.* Minneapolis: Fortress, 1993. A collection of essays by the authors dealing specifically with the use of Jewish Scripture in Luke–Acts.

disturbing to readers who strive to read a text "on its own terms," it emphasizes Peter's conviction that the Scripture spoke a living word to the faith community of his own time as it looked for guidance from the Scriptures.

Early Christians often employed Psalm 69 to tell the story of Jesus. Psalm 69:4 is found in John 15:25; Psalm 69:9 in John 2:17; and Psalm 69:21 in Matthew 27:48, Mark 15:36, and John 19:28-29. Paul quotes Psalm 69:22-23 in Romans 11:9-10 to offer scriptural testimony concerning Jewish unbelief. A reading of the psalm in its entirety reveals why Luke would have been drawn to the text. A reader who assumed that the Jewish Scriptures anticipated and foretold the Jesus story would find ripe material here. The psalm is about a righteous person who suffers at the hands of his enemies and seeks vindication from God. One who identifies Jesus with the righteous sufferer would naturally identify the persecutors of the righteous man with those responsible for the suffering of Jesus. Judas would fall in that lot.

Psalm 109 is another psalm offering the lament of a righteous sufferer. Again one drawn to this psalm *looking* for connections with the Jesus story could find a collage of texts that could refer to Jesus' opponents (those in the psalm responsible for tormenting the righteous sufferer). If a Christian were reading with an eye to identify texts pertinent to Jesus' opponents, Judas being among them, many texts would easily apply (especially vv. 6-15). In Acts 1:20b one finds Psalm 109:8, quoted almost verbatim from the LXX.

Our first exposure to an example of how the Scripture finds its fulfillment in the Jesus story, including his suffering, refers to "fore-speakings" of what Judas had done. The persuasive success of such appeals requires that readers assume that Scripture is to be read a certain way, that Scripture indeed contains quite specific "fore-words" about quite specific events associated with the Jesus story. We can learn from our early Christian ancestors the power of reading the biblical text with our own concerns and issues in the forefronts of our minds. With a bit of empathy, we can see how texts about righteous sufferers and their enemies could easily have spoken volumes to Christians who read the texts from the context of their own experiences, looking to their Scriptures to tell them something about Jesus' life, mission, death, and resurrection, as well as their own mission.

Ascension Day

Christian tradition, going back to at least the fourth century, celebrated Ascension Day on the sixth Thursday, or fortieth day, after Easter. The appropriate Sunday on which to celebrate this event would be, therefore, the sixth Sunday after Easter. Celebrants used to observe Ascension Day with a processional, to remember Jesus' journey to the Mount of Olives with his disciples before he ascended. Psalms traditionally associated with Ascension Day are 8, 15, 21, 24, 47, and 108.

In that same spirit, we turn to the opening chapter of Acts, not concerned primarily with a reconstruction of history or the history of traditions, but to hear a word from God that speaks to our context. What do the ascension and the observance of Ascension Day say to us? [Ascension Day] Most obvious is our realization that the Lord, under whose direction we carry on our mission of witness, is the one who now sits at the right hand of God (Ps 110:1). God has highly exalted him and bestowed upon him the name that is above every name (Phil 2:9). Scholars may debate whether the resurrection and ascension were at one time not distinguishable, as is now the case in Luke–Acts. But in the drama of our own worship, we are grateful that Luke has presented the ascension as a distinct episode, for it allows us to reflect concretely and specifically on the significance of our faith that Jesus has ascended to "the heavenly places," positioned, even now, "far above all rule and authority and power and dominion, and above every name that is named, not only in this age but also in the age to come" (Eph 1:21). The church on mission today needs regularly to reflect on her conviction that in the ongoing struggles against the dark forces that continue to corrupt God's creation, we are led by the one who already sits on the throne, far above all other powers.

We should also reflect on the question of the angel, spoken as much to us as those who stood on Mount Olivet centuries ago, asking why we are looking into the sky when there is work to be done. But we should also be reminded that Jesus' ascension requires that we keep in mind that Jesus will return again in the manner in which we saw him leave. Such a thought might distract us from our immediate mission of being witnesses, encouraging some to keep their eyes ever-focused on the clouds, awaiting the triumphant return of the Lord.

But, actually, thoughtful reflection on the inevitable return of the Lord directs our attention not to the skies but to the task, especially if we heed the word of Jesus as he speaks of the Parousia. Luke 12:35-40, for example, offers a parable about the Parousia. The Parousia stands in this parable not as some pipe-dream after which one sighs. It serves as a reminder that the servants are blessed whom the master finds awake when he comes (Luke 12:37). Being "awake" is interpreted in the conclusion of the parable as being "ready." The parable does not specifically tell the reader what "readiness" means. Perhaps the parable of the ten pounds (Luke 19:11-27; cf. Matt 25:14-30) can help to fill the gap. Servants are to make responsible use of the resources that the "nobleman" gives to them before he leaves to "receive a kingdom" (19:12). Investing the resources given us so that they bear fruit results in reward. Squandering the resources offered by the Lord, playing it safe by doing nothing with our God-given resources, results in judgment. These parables of the Parousia leave the distinct impression that the one who will return expects to find his people readily engaged in the kind of work that bears results. We refocus our attention back on the ascension narrative of Acts and remember Jesus' final word before his departure that we were to be witnesses to him to all the ends of the earth. In the context of this final word, being "awake," "ready," and fruitful appears now as consisting of active involvement in the work of witness: telling the story of the liberating reign of God that is made real for us and others through the life, death, and resurrection of Jesus. In short, like Jesus, we are to "preach the good news of the kingdom of God" (Luke 4:43), which is subsumed in light of the work of Jesus in the preaching of good news of Jesus Christ.

NOTES

[1] Luke Timothy Johnson, *The Acts of the Apostles* (SacPag 5; Collegeville MN: Liturgical Press, 1992), 29.

[2] See I. Howard Marshall, "Political and Eschatological Language in Luke," in *Reading Luke: Interpretation, Reflection, Formation*, ed. Craig G. Bartholomew, Joel B. Green, Anthony Thiselton (Scripture and Hermeneutics Series 6; Carlisle UK: Paternoster/Zondervan, 2005), 157–77.

FILLED WITH THE HOLY SPIRIT

Acts 2:1-47

COMMENTARY

This chapter has three main sections: 2:1-13 describes the coming of the Spirit and the immediate reaction of the onlookers; 2:14-36 offers Peter's sermon that interprets the significance of the coming of the Spirit and its connection with the gospel of Jesus; 2:37-47 describes the response of Peter's audience.

When the Day of Pentecost Had Come, 2:1-13

Luke denotes the arrival of the day of Pentecost by saying, "And when the day of Pentecost was fulfilled." While "fulfill" can denote the arrival of a specific date, the word "fulfill" offers the impression that something significant is about to happen. The time is approaching for the fulfillment of the prophecy of the coming of the Spirit (cf. Luke 24:49; Acts 1:4-5, 8). That time would be Pentecost, known in the Old Testament as the Feast of Weeks. [Pentecost] The "all" in v. 1 can refer back either to the 120 of Acts 1:15 or only to the apostles. While the apostles are the focus of the ensuing narrative (see v. 14), the "gift of the Spirit" is for *all* believers. Luke is not specific with regard to "the same place" (*epi to auto*) at the end of v. 1.

Pentecost

The word comes from the Greek word for fifty, derived from the biblical injunction that the festival was to take place fifty days after Passover (Lev 23:16). The term was used occasionally within the Septuagint to denote the Jewish "Feast (or Festival) of Weeks" (cf. Tob 2:1; 2 Macc 12:32). The Feast of Weeks was the second of the three great feasts, held between Passover and Tabernacles (see Exod 23:16; 34:22; Lev 23:15-22;

Deut 16:9-12). The last two references explain that the festival takes place seven weeks after Passover, hence its name "Festival of Weeks." It was originally a festival to celebrate the first fruits of the harvest, though it later came to take on religious significance (see [Pentecost, Sinai, and Acts]). Some interpreters see a connection between Pentecost's original association with the "first fruits" and the giving of the "first fruits" of the Spirit on Pentecost.

Pentecost

El Greco (1541–1614). *The Pentecost.* Museo del Prado, Madrid, Spain (Credit: Scala / Art Resource, NY)

This depiction of Pentecost by El Greco employs the artist's well-known style of elongated figures. The dove at the top represents the Holy Spirit, and the tongues of fire falling on the apostles portray each of them receiving the power of the Spirit, which enabled them to speak in other tongues, or languages. Note the prominence given to Mary, the mother of Jesus, around whom the apostles gather. In ancient Christian art, including icons from the Eastern Church, prominent attention to Mary was common, reflecting the veneration given to the Virgin throughout Christian history.

The next verse identifies this place as "the house," and it may denote the "upper room" of 1:13. Few interpreters take it to mean the temple.

Luke describes the coming of the Spirit in something of an objective manner (cf. Luke 3:22). There is a sound like the rush of a mighty wind. "Wind" was a useful image for Luke, for the Greek word (*pnoē*) is formed from the same stem as the Greek word for spirit (*pneuma*). There appeared tongues as of fire. What is happening is something heard and seen, even if the narrator is compelled to use similes to offer a picture. What is happening has its origins in God, for it all came from "out of heaven" (v. 2). The heavenly origin and the precise similes place readers in the world of the biblical language of theophany ("appearance of the deity"). Wind or God's "breath" could be used in the Bible to represent the divine presence (e.g., 2 Sam 22:16; Job 37:10; Isa 66:15). Compare also the storm language of God's appearance at Sinai (Exod 19:16-19). Fire was a more common phenomenon to denote the divine presence (e.g., Exod 3:2 [the burning bush]; 13:21-22 [the pillar of fire in the wilderness]; 19:16-19 [Sinai]).

Luke's use of the word "tongues" to describe the fire foreshadows the "speaking in tongues" that comes in vv. 4-12. Philo, the first-century AD Jewish philosopher, combines in his discussion of Sinai the image of fire and the phenomenon of language. [Pentecost, Sinai, and Acts] Assuming such connections to be valid, Luke may be encouraging readers to compare Christian Pentecost with Israel's being given the law at Sinai. Just as the law was central to Jewish

Pentecost, Sinai, and Acts

By the second century AD, Judaism came to associate Pentecost with the giving of the Torah at Sinai. Some believe that the association of Pentecost and Sinai could reach back to the first century as well (Johnson, 46). The pre-Christian Jewish text known as *Jubilees* makes clear that before the birth of Christianity some Jews associated the festival with covenant renewal. The giving and the receiving of the Torah at Sinai signifies the moment in Israel's salvation history when Israel entered into a covenantal relationship with God (Exod 24:1-8). Hence, the association of Pentecost with the birth of a covenant people and covenant renewal allows readers to understand Luke's story of Pentecost as a story about the birth of God's new covenant people. This covenant is sealed not with the blood of oxen (Exod 24:5), but the blood of the Son of God (Luke 22:20; Acts 20:28). Central to this new covenant is not the law, carved in stone, but the Spirit, which indwells all believers (cf. 2 Cor 3:1-18).

Luke Timothy Johnson, *The Acts of the Apostles* (SacPag 5; Collegeville MN: Liturgical Press, 1992).

identity as God's people, the Spirit is central to Christians' identity as God's people of the new covenant (cf. Luke 22:20).

The narrator shifts attention away from a description of what was happening around those gathered in the room to what happened to the people themselves. First, "they were all filled with the Holy Spirit." Endowments with the Spirit empower God's people for the tasks to which they have been called (cf. Luke 24:49; Acts 1:8). Second, they spoke in other tongues. Only rarely are endowments by the Spirit accompanied by the phenomenon of "tongues" (10:46; 19:6). In this context, "tongues" likely means other human languages, representing the universal character of the gospel message. [Tongues]

The focus shifts in vv. 5-13 from the believers to the multitudes living in Jerusalem and attracted by the sound. In the story world, the multitude is obviously located near "the house," though Luke gives no indication precisely where in the city of Jerusalem the house is located. Given that subsequent public speeches by Peter take place in the temple courts, this encounter between the apostles and the multitude may be taking place in or near these courts. Readers can understand "this sound" that drew the crowd as the believers' speaking (see v. 4) or the sound of the wind (v. 2). Either way, an audience is now present.

> **Tongues**
>
> Acts states that after being filled with the Holy Spirit, the believers spoke in other tongues (2:4). Given the comments of the characters in the crowd, most understand "tongues" in 2:4 to mean other human languages. In other parts of the New Testament, including Acts, "tongues" appears to be used to denote a kind of ecstatic speech, which is generally called *glossolalia* (see Acts 10:46; 19:6; 1 Cor 14). This kind of speech was offered in the context of an ecstatic experience and was thought to be evidence of divine possession (see Johnson, 42, for discussion and ancient references). One might conclude that the tradition received by Luke originally had to do with *glossolalia*, which he changed to fit his story about preaching to Jews from around the world. Or one could argue that Luke understood the "tongues" as *glossolalia*, through which some heard words in their own language, while others heard only babbling. "Tongues" was understood in early Christianity to denote both human (ordinary) and divine (ecstatic) speech, both of which could be "inspired" (cf. 1 Cor 13:1).
>
> Luke Timothy Johnson, *The Acts of the Apostles* (SacPag 5; Collegeville MN: Liturgical Press, 1992).

The text identifies the crowd as "Jews, devout men from every nation under heaven" (v. 5). They are further identified as permanent dwellers in Jerusalem (*kataoikountes*), not merely visitors (*epidemountes*), like those identified from Rome in v. 10. One major ancient Greek manuscript (Sinaiticus) omits the word "Jews" from v. 5, but most manuscripts do contain the word, as do most text critics and translations. On several occasions, the amazement of the multitude is noted (vv. 6, 7, 12). They are amazed not so much at *what* is said ("the mighty works of God," v. 11), but that they can *understand* what is being said by these Galileans (v. 7). The last time one of these men was recognized as a Galilean (Luke 22:59), Peter was in the course of denying Jesus (Luke 22:60). Now those recognized as Galileans do not hesitate to communicate openly the mighty things of God. "What does it mean" that people

The List of Nations

Interpreters have tried to discern significance in the actual places listed and/or their order of presentation. The first four (Parthia, Media, Elam, and Mesopotamia) are situated to the east, beyond the boundaries of the Roman Empire. The list then moves toward the west, into the area of Asia Minor (Cappadocia, Pontus, Asia, Phrygia, and Pamphylia [vv. 9b-10a]).

The list inserts Judea just before Cappadocia in v. 9, which seems out of place since Luke appears to be moving readers directly westward. The inclusion of Judea directs readers temporarily toward the south. Two explanations are noteworthy here. One: Judea was added as a later insertion (Haenchen, 170). Perhaps "Armenia" originally stood here, given that both Tertullian and Augustine quote this text using "Armenia." If Armenia did originally stand here, a look at the map shows that it would be situated between Mesopotamia and Cappadocia. Two: Luke is using Judea in its "biblical" sense, to denote the full extent of Israel's territory "from the Euphrates to Egypt" (see Gen 15:18; 1 Kgs 4:21). If so, then "Judea" would reach up at its northern extreme between Mesopotamia and Cappadocia.

Luke then moves to northern Africa (Egypt and Libya, v. 10b) and westward to Rome (v. 10b). Some understand "Jews and proselytes" to refer to the *entire* list of nations. If so, it is curious that Luke follows this with "Cretans and Arabians" in v. 11 (why would Luke not wait and mention Jews and proselytes after he had finished his whole list?). Perhaps the Cretans and Arabians are later additions. Without Judea, Crete, and Arabia, there are exactly twelve places. This would appear to have some symbolic significance for Luke, who is talking about the restoration of Israel. However, "Jews and proselytes" may refer only to the inhabitants of Rome. One is still left asking why Luke, after having taken his readers as far west as Rome, then abruptly moves them back toward the southeast, with the mention of Crete and Arabia.

Generally, Luke covers much of the world east of the Roman Empire and the eastern Mediterranean. If Luke did employ some traditional list, he has apparently amended it so as to present the picture of a broad geographical sweep. This allows his audience to represent Diaspora Judaism and to foreshadow Christianity's reach "to the ends of the earth" (cf. Acts 1:8).

Ernst Haenchen, *The Acts of the Apostles: A Commentary* (Philadelphia: Westminster, 1971).

---

can hear words in their own native languages (v. 12)? The stage is set for the first public "sermon" ever preached.

Luke allows the characters, through a kind of choral speech, to identify the various "nations under heaven" represented (vv. 9-11). The multiple nations indicate that Jews from around the world see the sign of the coming of the Spirit and hear the first presentation of the gospel message. [The List of Nations] Luke–Acts, at least in part, is about the restoration of Israel (cf. 1:6). And in Luke's day "Israel" was a worldwide phenomenon, with significant numbers of Jews living all about the Roman Empire. The devout Jews in Jerusalem represent Jews of the Diaspora. Significantly, Luke portrays these Jews from around the world as seeing and hearing these events *in Jerusalem*, the city that was to be the gathering place of God's people when the time for the restoration of Israel was fulfilled.

But not all respond positively. Some mock, charging that the believers are drunk (v. 13). [New Wine] Apparently, the words spoken by the believers do not make sense to some. Perhaps the believers are speaking a kind of *glossolalia*, or

New Wine

"New wine" refers to wine from the most recent harvest, whereas "old" wine refers to wine from previous seasons' harvests. This is initially confusing, since the spring harvest would not yet have occurred as of Pentecost. "New wine" was only partially fermented, explaining why one does not place it into old, brittle wineskins that could burst as the fermentation process was completed (Mark 2:22). The ancients had developed a means to prevent further fermentation from taking place. Hence, "new wine" could refer to wine from earlier harvests that had been treated so as to prevent further fermentation.

ecstatic speech, which only the devout can understand. Perhaps the skeptics were hearing foreign human languages that they did not understand, so that it sounded to them like drunken gibberish. Readers may see here a review and foreshadowing of a motif that appeared in the Gospel and will appear again in Acts: Jesus and the word about him divides Israel into those who accept the word and those who do not (cf. Luke 7:29-30; 23:35, 39-43; Acts 3:22-23; 28:24-25). The restoration of Israel includes this kind of division between the faithful and dismissive.

Peter Stood and Addressed Them, 2:14-36

Peter's speech has three sections. First, he interprets the meaning of the tongues event (vv. 14-21). Second, he presents the basic kerygma, or proclamation of the gospel (vv. 22-32). Third, he connects the first two sections, speaking of the relationship between the coming of the Spirit and Jesus as the Christ (vv. 33-36). In the narrative world, Peter is speaking to his audience of Jewish inhabitants of Jerusalem. Readers are not merely "overhearing" something said long ago; readers are the primary audience of speeches.[1]

Peter serves as the spokesman for the twelve apostles, the rest of the eleven standing with Peter (v. 14). Peter's words are authoritative, apostolic proclamation and commentary, offered by one whose mind the risen Lord had opened to understand the Scriptures (Luke 24:45). The words are solemn and even inspired, as indicated by the Greek word *apephthegxato*, the same word found in 2:4 ("as the Spirit gave to them to utter" [*apophthengesthai*]). Inspired speech can take the form of miraculous "tongues" (be it ecstatic speech or foreign language) or of plain, sober speech (cf. 1 Corinthians 14). Many features demonstrate the solemnity of Peter's speech: the abundance of scriptural citations, the subject matter (interpreting the doings of God and the proclaiming the gospel), and the "scriptural style" that Peter employs.[2]

He begins by addressing quickly the detractors (v. 15). Their charge of drunkenness violates simple common sense, given that in Jewish custom one did not eat (or drink) until after morning prayers, which began at 9:00 A.M. One can note some dry humor in Peter's response: People don't get drunk until after morning prayers, and it's not even time to pray yet! In v. 16, he moves to the more serious interpretation of the meaning of the event. "This thing" that Peter needs to interpret refers to the whole of the phenomenon that the Jewish audience has witnessed, both the "mighty works of God" *and* hearing it in their own native languages (v. 11).

Peter's immediate explanation of "this thing" consists of an edited quotation of Joel 2:28-32a (3:1-5 in MT), based on the LXX. Peter offers no explicit interpretation of the Joel text; thus, readers must make sense of how the Joel passage interprets the meaning of "this thing." Peter edits the passage from Joel immediately. Acts 2:17 reads, "and it will be *in the last days, God says.*" The words in italics represent Peter's changes to Joel, which actually reads, "And it will be after these things" (Joel 3:28a, LXX). To what "things" is Joel referring? The setting of Joel is a locust plague that has devoured the land and signifies divine judgment. Joel calls upon the people to repent (2:12-17), which will result in God's removal of the plague and the beginnings of the restoration of the land (2:20-27). It is "after these things" that God will pour out God's Spirit, followed by the end of the captivity of his people and the judgment of the Gentiles (Joel 3). In short, the Joel text quoted by Peter is to *follow* the rebellious people's repentance and restoration.

But while the immediate context of Joel 2:28-32 does not match up with Peter's use of the text, use of Joel in the context of the Pentecost sermon is appropriate. First, the Joel text, even taking into consideration its "original context," has an eschatological ring to it. Second, the text is concerned about the restoration of God's people. Third, it is about the pouring out of God's spirit. The Lukan narrative is about "eschatological" things: the proclamation of the kingdom of God and the installation of Jesus to the messianic throne. It is about the "restoration of Israel" (Acts 1:6). And much has been made in the Lukan narrative about the coming of the Holy Spirit, which is now happening. Clearly, as early Christians read their Scriptures, they had a broader understanding of "context" than those modern readers who focus exclusively on "original" context.

Joel's words teach that "this thing" (v. 16) needing explanation is "prophecy." Prophecy is a fitting term to explain the believers' telling of "the mighty deeds of God." [Prophecy] But is it fitting to explain the phenomenon of "speaking in tongues"? Prophetic speech is not generally synonymous with "tongues," understood either as ecstatic speech or speaking in foreign languages. But prophetic speech is *inspired* speech, and Luke explicitly states that "speaking in tongues" is "inspired" speech (see v. 4). Thus, the notion of inspiration would connect prophecy and tongues. Though Luke does not always equate

Prophecy

The 1973 Society of Biblical Literature seminar on Early Christian Prophecy came to agree on the following definition of "prophecy" in the early church: "The early Christian prophet was an immediately-inspired spokesperson for God, the risen Jesus, or the Spirit who received intelligible oracles that he or she felt impelled to deliver to the Christian community or, representing the community, to the general public."

Eugene Boring, "Prophecy (Early Christian)," *ABD* 5.496.

the two, texts such as Acts 19:6 show a very close relationship between the phenomena.

The list provided by Joel of *who* will prophesy—sons and daughters, young men and old men, God's men and women servants—gives concrete definition to the phrase "all flesh" (vv. 17-18). Many prophets populate the world of Acts, including women (see 11:27-28; 13:1; 15:32; 21:9). The statement about visions and dreams serves to give further explanation as to what constitutes prophetic activity (see [Vision]). This allows readers to understand upcoming visionary experiences of Jesus' followers as inspired, prophetic, and, thus, authoritative experiences (see 9:3-9, 10-16; 10:3-4, 9-23; 11:5; 16:9-10; 18:9-10; 22:17-21; 27:23-26).

Understanding vv. 19-20, which quote Joel 2:30-32a with editorial additions, is more difficult. Acts alters the text from Joel. Acts 2:19 quotes Joel 2:30 as follows (Lukan additions are in italics): "And I will show wonders in heaven *above*, and *signs* upon the earth *below*, blood and fire and vapor of smoke." Acts 2:20's quotation of Joel 2:31 is almost exact.

The addition of the word "signs," coupling the word with "wonders," may be due to the fact that the phrase "signs and wonders" had become a very common expression in the first century (see [Signs and Wonders]). Note also that Peter's version of the Joel text draws attention specifically to signs and wonders both "above" and "below." Four observations are in order:

1. *The language of Acts 2:19-20 is eschatological, apocalyptic language.* This is seen especially in Acts 2:20 with its talk of cosmic, heavenly portents and the day of the Lord.

2. *Reference to heavenly portents preceding the coming of the day of the Lord (2:20) is very reminiscent of texts such as Luke 21:25-28, which speak of heavenly, cosmic signs preceding the Parousia of the Son of Man.*

3. *A few lines later, Peter talks of "signs and wonders" in reference to Jesus' ministry.* These "signs and wonders" that occur "upon the earth below" may be a referent of the words from Joel quoted in Acts 2:19b.

4. *The followers of Jesus also perform many "signs and wonders" in the forthcoming narrative of Acts* (see 2:43; 4:30; 5:12; 6:8; 14:3; 15:12). These too could serve as referents of "signs upon earth below."

The signs and wonders performed by Jesus and his followers are part of a cosmic, apocalyptic drama that culminates in the cosmic, heavenly signs immediately preceding the coming of the Son of Man. In short, signs and wonders indicate that the last days are

St. Peter Preaching to the Multitude

Masolino da Panicale (1383–1447). *St. Peter Preaching to the Multitude*. (Post-restoration). Brancacci Chapel, S. Maria del Carmine, Florence, Italy. (Credit: Scala / Art Resource, NY)

upon Israel. "In these last days" is precisely how Peter *changes* Joel as he begins his proclamation. With the coming of the last days come both the opportunity of restoration and the possibility of judgment. Thus the final appeal from Joel, "everyone who calls upon the name of the Lord will be saved," is most appropriate. Peter will provide opportunity to call upon "the Lord" and experience the beginnings of restoration before he is finished preaching.

Verses 22-32 turn attention directly to Jesus himself, giving further comment to "this thing" (v. 16) that the Jewish audience does not understand (v. 12). Peter's approach is to summarize the Jesus story (vv. 22-24) and then to quote and interpret Scripture in light of Christian experience (vv. 25-32).

Peter assumes that his audience knows about Jesus and the mighty works, wonders, and signs that God accomplished through him (v. 22). It is Philistine to ask how every Jew in Peter's audience could know this. The Lukan Gospel has offered many scenes where Jesus spoke the word and did the works of God before the people, with Jesus' ministry in Jerusalem being the culmination of his public ministry. Understanding the Jewish multitude as a "character" on the dramatic stage of the story allows readers to connect Peter's audience with "the people" who appeared on stage during the last week of Jesus' life.[3]

Peter claims that through the mighty deeds, God was "vouching for" or "legitimizing" (*apodedeigmenon*) Jesus to these Jerusalemites. Yet they rejected him: "you crucified and killed [him] by the hands of lawless men" (v. 23). Summarized here is Luke's Passion Narrative, free of the nuances of the more extended narrative. For example, Luke's tendency to place most of the blame on the Jewish leaders in the Gospel itself (see especially Luke 24:20) is appropriately omitted here, given that Peter's audience is the citizenry itself, not their leaders. The reference to "lawless" men likely refers to those who do not live under Jewish law, the Romans.

This death Peter declares was "according to the definite plan and foreknowledge of God." The juxtaposition, without comment, of human agency and divine plan, often leaves modern commentators looking for a logical reconciliation between two seemingly inconsistent ideas: human freedom and divine sovereignty.[4] The death of Jesus, however, was overcome by God's act of raising Jesus from the dead. According to Acts, this initial presentation of the gospel focused on the death and resurrection of Jesus. This is echoed by Paul's summary of the early kerygma that was delivered to him (see 1 Cor 15:3-4). This message lies at the heart of genuinely Christian proclamation from the earliest days of the church.

Peter describes God has having "loosed the pangs of death" (v. 24). This peculiar metaphor is explained in part by the fact that the Hebrew word for "bond," which would make perfect sense here ("God loosed the *bonds* of death"), was almost identical to the Hebrew word for "pangs," as in "birth pangs." On occasion, translators of the LXX would translate the Hebrew phrase "bonds of death" as "pangs of death" (see LXX of 2 Sam [LXX = 2 Kgs] 22:6; Ps 18 [LXX = 17]:5).[5]

The metaphor of "birth pangs" could denote the woes and tribulations that would precede the glorious manifestation of the "Age to Come" (Mark 13:8 ‖ Matt 24:8). It is possible that the use of this phrase to describe Jesus' death shows an early understanding of the death of Jesus as a piece of the trails, tribulations, and sufferings which must precede the end-time triumph of God.[6] For Jesus, this victory has been won through God's raising him from the dead. For Jesus' followers and the rest of creation the present is still a time to endure the "birth pangs" (cf. Rom 8:18-25, 28-30).

In vv. 25-28, Peter turns to Scripture, quoting exactly Ps 16:8-11 (LXX = Ps 15). Verses 29-32 interpret the text. The resurrection of the Messiah was not part of the standard stock of traditional Jewish belief. Peter wants not only to proclaim the resurrection of Jesus, but also to persuade his audience that the one whom God raised was the Messiah. Peter and his associates can claim that Jesus is resurrected and that they are witnesses to this (v. 32). But this claim will mean more to their Jewish audience if they also show that resurrection was the intended destiny of the Messiah. Peter appeals to the common Jewish tradition that David wrote the psalms (v. 25). Then he asserts in v. 25 ("For David says *concerning him*") and argues in vv. 29-31 that David was not speaking of himself in Psalm 16, despite the use of first-person singular language. Since David is dead and buried, with the site of his tomb well known to Peter's listeners, he could not have been referring to himself when

Jerusalem in the First Century

In this detailed model of ancient Jerusalem one can see in the far upper right-hand corner the temple area where Acts says early Christians gathered daily (2:46). The tall building in the upper center with pyramid-apex is the tomb of David to which Peter makes reference (2:29; see **Map of Jerusalem**). To the left of the tomb is the Palace of Caiaphas. Readers might imagine some scenes where priestly authorities question the apostles as taking place here, but one cannot be sure.

(Credit: Jim Pitts)

he said, "you will not abandon my soul to Hades, nor let your holy one see corruption" (2:27; Ps 16:10). If not speaking of himself, he must be speaking of his descendant. David knew that God had promised him that God would set one of David's descendants upon his throne (v. 30, which alludes to Ps 132:11 and 2 Sam 7:13-16, promises made to David concerning one of his descendants).

This "descendant" would be understood in the setting of early Christianity and first-century Judaism as "the Messiah," given that the Davidic throne had not been existence for centuries. Peter also puts Psalms 16 and 132 together. David's foresight that "he" would not experience corruption in the grave, combined with the promise that one day God would set one of David's descendants (the Messiah) on the throne, leads to the conclusion of v. 31: David "foresaw and spoke of the resurrection of the Messiah." Peter concludes his sermon with the declaration that God raised this Jesus up (v. 32). The basis for the claim that Jesus was raised up is the testimony of the apostles. Scripture does not prove that *Jesus* was raised; Scripture proves that *the Messiah* was to be raised. The personal testimony of the apostles concerning Jesus combined with the scriptural argument concerning the resurrection of the Messiah allows Peter to conclude that Jesus is the Messiah (v. 35).

But before moving directly to this conclusion, Peter says more about the resurrection/exaltation of Jesus and Jesus' connection to the spiritual phenomena that his audience has just witnessed (vv. 33-36). Peter makes two claims in v. 33: (1) Jesus was exalted to the right hand of God, and (2) Jesus received the Spirit that God has poured out. The first claim is rooted, as was the resurrection, in the experience and witness of the apostles and is a reference back to the ascension. Though the claim is grounded primarily in the experience of the apostles, it is not without scriptural support (see [Experience and the Believer]). Again, Peter appeals to Scripture (vv. 34-35) to argue that David himself foresaw the ascension of the Messiah to the right hand of God. He argues that in writing Psalm 110:1, David could not have been speaking of himself, since he did not ascend to the heavens. Thus, once again, David must be talking about his descendant, the Messiah. Jesus, through his ascension, fulfills this messianic prophecy of David, adding to Peter's argument that God has made Jesus the Messiah (v. 35). Peter does not appeal to Scripture to back up his claim that Jesus has poured out the Spirit, but the experience of his audience and what it is that they "see and hear" (v. 33c). *Their* experience—what *they* see and hear—serves to confirm that the one anticipated by Scripture to rise and to ascend to God's right hand is Jesus. Thus, Peter makes this inference specific in v. 35: "God has made him both Lord and Messiah." Calling Jesus "Lord" connects this conclusion with the scriptural claim of Joel 2:32a, which Peter quoted in 2:21: "Everyone who calls upon the name of the Lord will be saved."

"What Shall We Do?" 2:37-47

This section has two subunits: vv. 37-41 describe the immediate reaction of Peter's hearers, and vv. 42-47 present a summary portrait of early Christian life.

The people's immediate response is described by the biblical phrase "cut to the heart" (v. 37; cf. Ps 108:16 [LXX] = 109:16 [ET]). The phrase denoted sharp emotional pain due either to remorse or anxiety. Readers recalling Luke 23:48, which describes the crowds' "beating their breast" in response to Jesus' death, are prepared for the response here in Acts. The crowds offer their question to both Peter and the other apostles. Mention of "the other apostles" reminds readers that Peter's sermon represents authoritative, *apostolic* witness.

Peter instructs the audience to repent and be baptized in the name of Jesus (v. 38a). Repentance denotes a change of both mind and action. In this immediate context, such a turning involves a changing of one's mind regarding Jesus from one who was to be rejected and executed to one who is Lord and Messiah. Change of action requires committing oneself to this Jesus. Such commitment is realized in fulfillment of the instruction to be baptized in the name of Jesus (see [Baptism]). One is to claim total allegiance to Jesus Messiah, a claim outwardly demonstrated through baptism in his name.

The twofold result of such repentance and initiation into the restored people of God is forgiveness of sins and receipt of the Holy Spirit. The Greek word for forgiveness is *aphesis*, literally meaning "release." The word captures the liberating essence of Jesus' ministry of proclaiming the kingdom of God (see comments on 1:3, ch. 1). To be forgiven is to experience the liberating reality of God's reign, the reality of God's promised redemption for Israel (cf. Luke 1:68; 24:21) and the beginnings of his promised "restoration of the kingdom to Israel" (cf. 1:6). To receive the Holy Spirit involves being empowered by the personal presence of God so that one may join the ranks of the folk who will be God's prophets for new age of salvation, which is now dawning (see [The Spirit and the Last Days]). As such prophets, they, like Peter, have the capacity to testify to the gospel and be Jesus' witnesses.

Closely related to v. 38 is the exhortation of v. 40: "Be saved from this crooked generation." "Crooked generation" alludes to Deuteronomy 32:5, which uses the term to denote those who rebelled against God. Luke's Gospel regularly uses the term "this generation" to denote those opposed to God and God's way and will (Luke 7:31; 9:41; 11:29-30; 17:25). Hence, "this generation" is headed for judgment (Luke 11:31-32, 50-51; 21:32). It is from this rebellious, perverse, and crooked generation headed for judgment that Peter's audience must be saved. The word "saved" harks back to 2:21 wherein Peter quoted Joel 2:32a. Luke will later conclude this story with a summary statement, saying that many of those who heard Peter's sermon joined the number of "those were were being saved" (2:47): "*Hoi sōzomenoi* ['those who are being saved'] is the Remnant of Israel destined to survive the End."[7] To call upon persons "to be saved" is to call upon them to join the remnant of God's people, those who constitute restored Israel under allegiance to the one whom God made Lord and Messiah. It is an offer that God makes to all Jews, both in Jerusalem and the Diaspora, both in the present and in the future (v. 39). It is an offer, however, that people must choose to receive. On this day of Pentecost, a day associated with the birth of God's covenant people, Luke reports that 3,000 souls "received his word [and] were baptized" (v. 41). The large number communicates that the restoration of God's people for the new age of salvation is well underway.

Verses 42-47 present a Lukan summary of the newly restored faith community (see [Lukan Summaries]). This particular summary offers an ideal portrait of early Christian life. Verse 42 introduces features of such communal life upon which vv. 43-47 elaborate. First, the community was devoted to the apostles' teaching. Previous material in Acts allows readers to understand that this would have included scriptural (Old Testament) interpretation and gospel proclamation. Verse 43b adds that apostles also performed "signs and wonders." This recalls 2:19b, which speaks of "signs below." Apostolic teaching includes the mighty works that give demonstration to the reality of God's in-breaking rule.

Second, the community was devoted to "fellowship" (v. 42). At the root of the word *koinōnia* is the idea of sharing. While Christian fellowship can take on many characteristics, in this context such sharing manifests itself in the early community's practice of having all things in common (*koina*, v. 44). It was not uncommon for ancients to describe a community's origins in ideal terms, which include communal sharing.[8] [Communal Society] Given the formulaic character of such communal societies, some might be suspicious of the strict historical accuracy of Luke's description. Still, a community of sharing where people give to others "as any had need" is a goal, idealized or not, to which the covenant community of God's people should strive.

> **Communal Society**
>
> "The belongings of friends are held in common." Greek Proverb

Third, they broke bread together. [The Breaking of Bread] This would include both the celebration of "the Lord's Supper" and so-called "regular meals." The place where such meals took place was "at home" (v. 46), implying not one particular house, such as "the house" of 2:2, but various homes.

Fourth, they were devoted to "the prayers." The use of the definite article might imply specific prayers, such as those of daily Jewish prayer. This would complement the note in v. 46 that the early community daily attended the temple. It is possible that they went to the temple outer courts each day *only* to preach. But there may also be an allusion to Luke 24:53, which concluded the Gospel saying that the disciples "were continually in the temple blessing God." Acts 2:46 is the first reference to Jesus' followers being "in the temple." This text may represent the more detailed narrative realization of the

> **The Breaking of Bread**
>
> This was not a common phrase to denote eating, though the Jewish custom of breaking bread to begin a meal may lie behind the term. Perhaps due to Jesus' act of "breaking bread" in the context of the Passover meal, which was also the "Last Supper" shared between Jesus and his followers, the phrase came to represent for many early Christians meals that they shared with one another in the context of Christian fellowship. In this fellowship the presence of the risen Lord would be at the table. As time went on, the celebration of the Eucharist, or Lord's Supper, came to be separated from the context of "ordinary meals," and the phrase "breaking of bread" becomes synonymous with this ritual Communion meal.

initial reference found in Luke 24. Connection with temple worship related this early community to the Gospel's beginnings, which was also in the context of temple worship (see Luke 1). It also affirms that this remnant, restored Israel, is faithful to its heritage. Thus, other people in Jerusalem are favorably disposed to the new community, and many choose to join the ranks of the remnant, or "to be saved" (v. 47).

CONNECTIONS

This portion of Luke's narrative says much about the testimony, or witness, of God's people. Such testimony can only be accomplished when God's people are empowered by the Holy Spirit. We have witnessed this empowerment in the story of Pentecost and in the hearing of the first "Christian testimony" that follows this empowerment. Luke's narrative of the early community's experiences and testimony offers ongoing guidance to the contemporary faith community as it, too, engages in the offering of witness.

First, the experience of being touched by God's spirit is an essential element of one's witness. Those affected by the immediate presence of God in their lives will inevitably attract attention. [The Visible Church] We may not speak other human languages, or "the tongues of angels," or work "signs and wonders." More often than not, it will not be the more spectacular events that will attract people to those touched by the Spirit. Those marked by the Spirit may draw attention because there will always be the mockers in the crowd, those folk looking to find fault with those who have been touched by God. Paul's exhortation to the Philippian church is most fitting: "Do all things without murmuring and arguing, so that you may be blameless and innocent, children of God without blemish in the midst of a crooked and perverse generation, in which you shine as lights in the world" (Phil 2:14-15). Or the people of the Spirit may draw attention because some in the multitude see something in God's people that piques their curiosity, but which they cannot explain: a calm disposition, a forgiving spirit, a sense of conviction free of any stain of self-righteousness. But folk who experience God's spirit should be aware that others will be drawn for one reason or another. Once drawn, testimony is in order. [Pentecost Sunday]

The Visible Church

When historic Christianity speaks of the church, "it is not an invisible structure which is intended but quite a visible coming together, which originates with the twelve Apostles. The first congregation was a visible group, which caused a visible public uproar. If the Church has not this visibility, then it is not the Church" (Barth, 42).

Karl Barth, *Dogmatics in Outline* (New York: Harper Torchbooks, 1959).

Second, being "Jesus' witness" is to revolve around the interpretation of the Scriptures *in the context of the gospel*. In the commentary above, as well as in "Connections" of chapter one, we noted that for the early Christians the context for understanding Scripture was not limited to its ancient, originating context.

Pentecost Sunday
Also called "Whitsunday," it is the Feast of the Descent of the Holy Ghost. It is celebrated on the seventh Sunday after Easter. Celebration of Whitsunday can be traced back to the fourth-century Jerusalem church.

Finding "connections" between the ancient text and contemporary context is an ever-present priority. What are the implications that "sons *and daughters* will prophesy"? Do we rush as quickly as possible to other texts in the Bible to silence our wives, sisters, and daughters, breathing a sigh of relief to discover that within a few generations our own spiritual ancestors, for example, the author of 1 Timothy 2:8-15, offered us sanctions to quench the Spirit? Peter searched the Scripture to give explanation to the spiritual experience of his community, and he latched on to the text from Joel, which was as inclusive as possible. Ezekiel 39:29 could have worked quite nicely: "I will never again hide my face from them, when I pour out my Spirit upon the house of Israel, says the Lord God." It explicitly confines things to Israel and, without mention of women, doesn't even raise that potential problem.

But the gospel itself, Peter's recollection of the things that Jesus said and did, prevented him—and it prevents us!—from focusing on texts that are not inclusive. Could the Jesus we meet in the Gospel of Luke—the Jesus who speaks of the Good Samaritan, who teaches Mary at his feet, who visits the home of the tax collector Zacchaeus—really inspire us to find texts that allow us to exclude anyone from all the benefits and gifts of God's spirit? The gospel shapes our selection and reading of the Scriptures. And the gospel we preach is one of inclusion.

One theme with which the volume will regularly wrestle is that of divine will and our participation with God in God's work. The theme finds expression in the line from Peter's sermon: "This man, handed over to you according to the definite plan and foreknowledge of God, you crucified by the hands of those outside the law" (2:23). There is often an inherent tension between affirmations of divine sovereignty and experiences of human freedom. We may prefer consistency to tension and opt for affirmations of divine sovereignty that neglect human responsibility or endorse human freedom at the expense of God's lordship. But the tightrope of tension is where we must walk.

One thinks of the character in John Updike's novel *In the Beauty of the Lilies*, a Presbyterian pastor named Clarence Wilmot. Living during the early twentieth century, he is plagued by a sudden loss of faith, burdened by a constant refrain that rambles through his head: "There is no God." The realization came to him as he found himself unable to reconcile the claims of his Calvinistic piety with the claims of modern philosophy and science. Modern thought, which could not allow for a God who is active in the freedom of human affairs or the mechanisms of natural affairs, suffocated his faith in a God who is active in lives and history and with it "the chafflike riddle of predestination."[9] But with Wilmot's old worldview now lifeless, the pastor felt alone, living in a world where there was no direction, no "definite plan," to quote Peter. All that remained in his world were the brute facts of cruelty and death. A world void of divine direction and full only of human freedom turns empty.

And yet the steadfast assurance of his parishioners who were content to live according to divine fiat while giving little attention to human response is no more satisfying to Wilmot. The words of one parishioner, Mr. Orr, only confound Wilmot even more: "Well, if I'm not to be among the saved, it was laid down that way at the beginning of creation, and what can a body do? . . . But I can face the worst, if it was always ordained. God's as helpless in this as I am. If He's made His elections at the beginning of time, He is [helpless]. He can't keep changing His mind."[10] Mr. Orr's conclusions reveal that in a world where everything is fixed, God is just as absent as in a world where God simply doesn't exist. A God who fixes it all from the beginning and who can't "change his mind" can no more be a part of our lives than one who just isn't there. Both extreme views lead to the same dead end: a world where there is no experience of God. [Divine Will and Human Freedom]

The text can also offer insight as we reflect on what it means to be a community of faith. Living as a faith community is pictured ideally in the summary of 2:42-47. We are not less than "New Testament Christians" if we fail to meet in homes, worship at the ruins of the Jewish temple, or sell our goods and hold all things in common. We need not parrot our spiritual ancestors in order to learn from them.

Divine Will and Human Freedom

"A sovereignty of control would be impressive, but the sovereignty required to rule over a free and dynamic world is even more marvelous. What is needed to rule in this universe is infinite resourcefulness in the subtle use of power; what is required is a style of sovereignty that is open to the world and can respond to the unexpected" (Pinnock, 19).

Cynthia Rigby borrows an image from Elizabeth Johnson to illustrate how divine sovereignty and human/creaturely freedom work together. It is the image of a woman who carries a child.

The child is distinct from the woman as the world is distinct from God. And yet, because the world is encompassed by God and because God contains the world, God and the world exist in mutual relationship and mutually condition one another. As the baby is nurtured by the body of the woman, so the world is sustained by the sovereign God who contains it. As the woman is affected by the child who is both part of and distinct from her body, so God is affected by the world as it twists and cries and works to shape its distinctive identity. (Rigby, 58–59)

Clark H. Pinnock, "God's Sovereignty in Today's World, *Theology Today* 53/1 (1996): 15–21; Cynthia Rigby, "Free to Be Human: Limits, Possibilities, and the Sovereignty of God," Theology Today 53/1 (1996): 47–62.

First, the early believers likely participated in the worship life of their fellow Jews. The early Christians recognized that the old story of Israel was integral to their own story. They were not casting aside this old story, but bringing it to realization. After all, they were persuaded in part by Peter's arguments from their Scriptures that the Messiah was to rise from the dead. They heard this sermon on the day of one of their major festivals, the Feast of Weeks. The community of faith needs to rehearse and incorporate Israel's story into its own. The Old Testament is not a prologue to the real story, the New Testament. It is part of our Bibles, and its characters as much our spiritual ancestors as those of the New Testament. These first "Christians" consisted of "Jews from every nation under heaven," and that may explain the persuasiveness of the "Jewish Scriptures" and the ongoing participation in worship at the Jewish temple. But Peter was clear in the conclusion of his sermon: "The promise is for you, for your children, *and for all who are far away, everyone who calls upon the name of the Lord.*" Unless Gentile Christians somehow want to exclude ourselves from this promise, we had best get in touch with the literary and historical source of that promise, which is ours as well: the story and Scriptures of Israel.

Second, we claim our heritage when we, like our ancestors, devote ourselves "to the apostles' teaching." We hear their testimony today only indirectly, through the New Testament. But devotion to "the apostles' teaching," listening to their testimony in the New Testament, does not take place in isolation. The early community "devoted themselves to the apostles' teaching *and fellowship.*" We hear and study the apostolic testimony in fellowship with real people who have received the Holy Spirit and are prophets. And such fellowship reaches back through the centuries—what historic Christian faith calls the *communion of the saints*. The hearing of the apostolic word cannot be divorced from fellowship with real believers. We listen to the apostolic witness at the same time that we listen to the voices of God's people, past and present, their hopes and hurts, celebrations and concerns, praises and pains. Peter interpreted texts in a way that would speak genuinely to his real audience. We can do no less. When we study the apostolic testimony in a vacuum, we find empty propositions to drop on folks' heads. When we devote ourselves to the apostles' teaching *and fellowship*, we find living words that speak to the real lives of real people.

NOTES

[1] See the discussion on speeches in the Introduction to the Commentary.

[2] An example of such "Septuagintalisms" is the use of redundant introductory statements like "Men of Judea and all who dwell in Jerusalem" (v. 14), "Brothers, Israelites" (v. 22), and "Men, brothers" (v. 29).

[3] In biblical narrative, whole groups can function as a "character," with little regard for differences within the group. See Mark Allan Powell, *What Is Narrative Criticism?* (Minneapolis: Fortress, 1990), 51–67.

[4] The volume will regularly visit this issue in Commentary, Connections, and sidebars. See, e.g., [Divine Will and Human Freedom], [The Working of God], and [Human Freedom and Human Choice].

[5] F. J. Foakes Jackson and Kirsopp Lake, *The Beginnings of Christianity: The Acts of the Apostles*, 5 vols. (Grand Rapids MI: Baker, 1979), 4.23.

[6] Dale Allison, *The Ends of the Ages Has Come: An Early Interpretation of the Passion and Resurrection of Jesus* (Philadelphia: Fortress, 1985).

[7] Jackson and Lake, *Beginnings of Christianity*, 4.30.

[8] Hans Conzelmann, *Acts of the Apostles* (Hermeneia; Philadelphia: Fortress, 1987), 24; Luke Timothy Johnson, *The Acts of the Apostles* (SacPag 5; Collegeville MN: Liturgical Press, 1992), 62.

[9] John Updike, *In the Beauty of the Lilies* (New York: Alfred A. Knopf, 1996), 7.

[10] Ibid., 45, 48.

BY THE NAME OF JESUS, THIS MAN STANDS BEFORE YOU WELL

Acts 3:1–4:37

COMMENTARY

The people of God are being renewed through the Spirit (Acts 1) and repentance (Acts 2). The story of renewal in Jerusalem continues in Acts 3–4. This chapter has five sections: Peter heals a lame man (3:1-11); Peter preaches to the onlookers (3:12-26); the temple leadership arrests and interrogates the apostles (4:1-22); the community responds to persecution with prayer (4:23-31); and the narrator summarizes community life (4:32-37).

"In the Name of Jesus, Walk," 3:1-11

The summary of 2:43-47 leaves the impression that an indefinite duration of time has elapsed between the events of Acts 2 and Acts 3. Such lack of precision cautions readers from using the narrative as a source for the meticulous reconstruction of early Christian chronology.

Luke provides "local coloring" for the story he is telling: the setting of the temple, the time of prayer during the ninth hour (v. 1), and specific references to locations within the temple precincts—the Beautiful Gate (vv. 2, 9) and Solomon's Portico (v. 11). Such notices place the activity of Peter and John in the world of Jewish piety, for they are on their way to participate in the hour of prayer (v. 1). The setting elaborates on the notice of Luke 24:53 that the disciples returned to Jerusalem "and were continually in the temple praising God."

It is impossible to surmise how much Luke actually knew or expected readers to know about the layout of the Jerusalem temple or the rites that went on there. Still, it can help current readers to

Map of Jerusalem

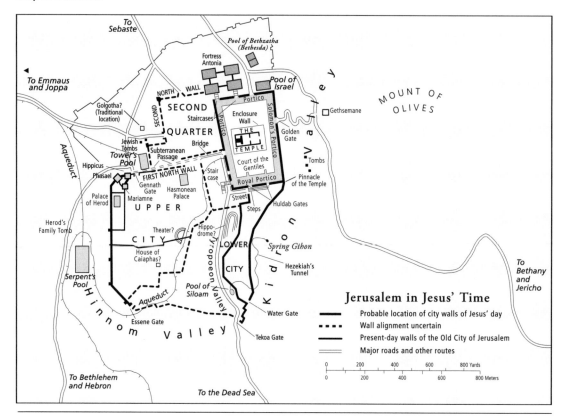

picture the scene with a greater sense of realism if they bring to the text a knowledge of the structure of the temple of Jerusalem.

First, Luke states that the time when Peter and John went to the temple was "the hour of prayer, the ninth hour" (v. 1), or about 3:00 P.M. It was customary to pray three times a day (see Dan 6:10); the prayer at the ninth hour was likely the second prayer of the day ("the afternoon prayer"), with the evening prayer offered toward the end of the day. Further, the afternoon prayer coincided with the afternoon whole offering, one of the main daily ceremonies of worship at the temple. The afternoon services would have been well attended. This high attendance explains both why a lame man begging for alms would want to be laid at the gate at this time and where the large crowd came from to hear Peter's preaching in 3:12-26.

Second, the lame man was laid at the gate called "Beautiful." [Beautiful Gate] Worshipers were perhaps more inclined to "show kindness" just before entering the temple for prayer and offering. [Pillars of Judaism] After Peter was asked for alms (v. 3), he gazed directly at the man and insisted that the lame man look at John and him

Beautiful Gate

Christian tradition has associated the Beautiful Gate with the Shushan Gate. This would be the gate closest to the viewer in the image of the temple labeled "The Inner Courts." But this gate accommodated the least traffic, and one can see from the map of Jerusalem that it would make no sense for Peter and John, if they were living in Jerusalem itself, to enter through this gate, as there were numerous other gates located to the south and north to allow entrance into the inner courts. Josephus describes a massive "Corinthian Gate" as that separating the Court of Women from the Court of Priests. In the image it is the gate located in the middle of the picture, with large steps leading up to it. Note the close-up in the second image below.

This may be a more a logical place for a lame man to be set and is the gate through which Peter and John would have *had* to pass to enter the courts for the afternoon prayer/offering service. It is reasonable, therefore, to imagine this "Corinthian Gate" as the equivalent for Acts' "Beautiful Gate," despite Christian tradition. One cannot be absolutely sure, for only Acts makes reference to a "Beautiful Gate." Further, Acts itself creates confusion, for if the Beautiful Gate is the gate within the inner court, v. 11 shifts immediately to Solomon's Portico. Note that Solomon's Portico is located *outside* the inner courts. The Western text, however, clears up this potential confusion. It reads: "He entered with them into the temple and all the people saw him . . . and when Peter and John went out he went with them, holding on to them, and (the people) stood in amazement in the Porch called Solomon's" (Lake, 484).

Kirsopp Lake, "Localities In and Near Jerusalem Mentioned in Acts: The Beautiful Gate," in F. J. Foakes Jackson and Kirsopp Lake, *The Beginnings of Christianity: The Acts of the Apostles*, 5 vols. (Grand Rapids MI: Baker, 1979), 5.479–86.

The Inner Courts

The Inner Courts. Model of Jerusalem. Holy Land Hotel, Jerusalem. (Credit: Jim Pitts)

Beautiful Gate Detail

Beautiful Gate. Model of Jerusalem. Holy Land Hotel, Jerusalem. (Credit: Jim Pitts)

(v. 4). Often, when we encounter a "street person," or anyone who approaches us for money, we either ignore the person or drop some loose change in the cup and quickly move on. This is not how Peter and John respond to the lame beggar.

The lame man's expectations were raised as he obeyed Peter's command and fixed his attention on them (v. 5). Peter confesses that he has no silver or gold, a possible allusion to the fact that the lame man now lay under the great Corinthian gate of brass, deco-

Pillars of Judaism

"Simeon the Just was one of the survivors of the Great Synagogue. He used to say: — 'Upon three things the world stands; upon Torah, upon Worship and upon the showing of kindness'" (*Aboth* 1:2). Herford understands the showing of kindness to include "unselfish beneficence" (22).

R. Travers Herford, ed. and trans., *Pirke Aboth. The Ethics of the Talmud: Sayings of the Fathers* (New York: Schocken, 1962).

In the Name of Jesus

AΩ The formula occurs frequently in Acts and can be divided into three categories: (1) "to be *baptized* in (or some similar preposition) the name" (2:38; 8:16; 10:48; 19:5), (2) to heal or exorcise in (or through) the name (3:6; 16:18; 4:30; 19:13), and (3) to preach or speak in the name of (4:18; 5:40; 9:27, 28). Each of these uses carries the connotation of power or authority. To be baptized in the name implies submission to the authority of Jesus; to heal or exorcise in the name appeals to the power of Jesus to perform the cure; to preach in the name of Jesus implies speaking on behalf of or under the authorized sanction of Jesus. However, "the name" is no magic formula, as readily evidenced by 19:13, where the sons of Sceva, who are non-believers, fail in their attempt to use the name of Jesus to cast out a demon.

rated with thick plates of silver and gold. Peter offers what silver and gold cannot: "In the name of Jesus Christ of Nazareth, walk" (v. 6b). Then Peter took him by the *hand* and *raised* him. This offers a faint echo of Luke 8:54, which states that Jesus took the *hand* of Jairus's daughter and commanded her to *arise*. Further, the scene of healing a lame man harks back to Jesus' miracle of healing a paralytic (Luke 5:17-26). [In the Name of Jesus]

The presentation of the story in Acts offers not only verbal echoes to the Gospel, but structural similarities also. In the Gospel, Jesus followed his "inaugural sermon," in which he spoke of the "release" that was to be offered to Israel (Luke 4:16-30), with a series of healings that manifested the "release" and liberation that Jesus has to offer. The healing stories culminate with the healing of a man who was paralyzed (4:31–5:25). The last healing, wherein Jesus made a claim about his authority ("the Son of Man has authority on earth to forgive sins" [Luke 5:24]), prompted confrontation with the Jewish leadership (5:21; 6:1-11).

Acts shows a similar pattern. Peter has concluded his inaugural Pentecost sermon (Acts 2). In the context of this sermon he spoke of "signs and wonders" to be seen "here on earth below" (2:19). He demonstrates these signs and wonders by healing a man who cannot walk. In the context of this miracle, a claim is made about the authority of Jesus ("in the name of Jesus the Messiah"). The claim concerning Jesus' authority made during the healing itself will be made explicit during Peter's sermon to follow in vv. 12-26. This prompts a confrontation with the Jewish leadership (Acts 4).

The verbal echoes and structural parallels between the Gospel and Acts show that Peter is doing what Jesus had done. Peter offers the liberating power of God's reign to those in need of such liberation. The liberation of the kingdom and gospel comes in many forms: "release from" or "forgiveness of" (it is the same word in Greek) sins, release from the demonic, and release from disease. The liberating power of God reaches into the darkness that hides in the nooks and crannies of life, corrupts people's lives, and renders them less than whole.

Whereas modern society is gradually changing attitudes and no longer views physically challenged people as less than whole, such was not the case in the first-century world. Though lame people were not expressly forbidden from entering the inner courts of the temple, language from the Old Testament that describes the qualifications of the priests would likely carry over to popular attitudes about the place of the lame in the religious life of Israel. Undoubtedly, this lame man had become used to sitting *outside* the Corinthian Gate, excluded from the worship of the court of the temple beyond this gate. Thus, v. 8 is a fitting climax to the story of this man's healing: he "entered the temple with them, walking and leaping and praising God." Restoring the kingdom to Israel includes restoring individual Israelites to full participation in the worship life of God's people.

The multitude at the temple confirms the success of the healing (vv. 9-11). "All the people" recognize this man to be the one who had once been lame. As the multitude marveled at the sign of the Spirit in Acts 2, it marvels at another of the "signs and wonders" performed here "upon the earth below" (cf. 2:19b): Peter, John, and the healed man exiting the inner court and moving out to Solomon's Portico with the crowd following (v. 11).

"Why Do You Wonder at This?" 3:12-26

The balance of Acts 3 falls into two subsections, representing different types of rhetoric. Verses 12-18 are judicial in style, while vv. 19-26 are deliberative. [Types of Rhetorical Persuasion]

In vv. 12-18 (judicial rhetoric), Peter focuses on four things that have happened that require consideration. First, Peter wants to persuade his audience that, though they acted in ignorance (v. 17; cf. Luke 23:34), they were wrong to have demanded the crucifixion of Jesus (vv. 14-15). [Titles for Jesus in Acts 3:14-15] Second, God vindicated Jesus by raising him from the dead, with Peter and John serving as the "two witnesses" (cf. Deut 17:6; 19:15). Third, Peter claims that what happened to Jesus was according to the plan of God, as evidenced by the claim that

Types of Rhetorical Persuasion

 Scholars of ancient rhetoric speak of three broad types of persuasive argument: Judicial rhetoric is concerned to persuade folk to understand in a certain way something that has happened *in the past*. Deliberative rhetoric is concerned to persuade folk to take certain action *in the future*. Epideictic rhetoric seeks to persuade folk have a certain point of view *in the present* about something or someone (Soards, 23n15). The courtroom can illustrate all three. A defense attorney attempts to persuade a jury that her client did not *in the past* do things of which he is accused (judicial). Thus the jury should now *in the present* hold to the view that her client is innocent (epideictic) and make *in the future* the decision to render a verdict of "not guilty" (deliberative [note that we speak in our legal system of a jury's "deliberations"]).

Marion L. Soards, *The Speeches in Acts: Their Content, Context, and Concerns* (Louisville: Westminster/John Knox, 1994).

Titles for Jesus in Acts 3:14-15

AΩ *Holy One.* The term "the Holy One" (*ho hagion*) was a designation for Jesus in the Synoptic tradition (Mark 1:24 and par.), the Johannine tradition (John 6:69; 1 John 2:20), and in the Apocalypse (Rev 3:7). Acts uses the phrase three times, twice when quoting the LXX (2:27; 13:35, which uses the Greek word *hosios*) and 3:14. Luke also uses *hagion* attributively in Acts 4:27 and 30 ("holy servant/child"). The term is not a "christological" or "messianic" title per se, but it does designate Jesus as one who belongs to and is set apart by God, making his murder particularly heinous.

Righteous One. Only in Acts is the adjective "righteous" used substantively with reference to Jesus: "the Righteous One" (3:14; 7:52; 22:14). The substantive use implies that the adjective is used as a title, not only as an indicator of Jesus' character. *The Similitudes of Enoch* use "the Righteous One" as a designation for the Messiah (38:2), but this does not allow the conclusion that it was a formal messianic title in Judaism. Not only do many question the pre-Christian dating of the *Similitudes*, but also one example hardly makes for a formal title. As "the Righteous One" Jesus was, therefore, totally undeserving of death (precisely the point of Luke 23:43, which uses the word *dikaios*); fittingly, it is through this One that people can, themselves, be made "righteous" (13:38-39; translated as "set free" in the NRSV).

Author of Life. There are four references to this term in the New Testament: Acts 3:15; 5:31; Heb 2:10; 12:2. The term can mean either "leader" or "originator." In ancient literature the latter sense (originator) could denote (quasi-) divine founders of communities or colonies; hence, Jesus may be portrayed as the "founder" of the Christian community. I. H. Marshall believes "originator" works well with Acts 3:15 and Heb 2:10, while "leader" works best with Acts 5:31 and Heb 12:2 (Marshall, 91–92).

I. Howard Marshall, *The Acts of the Apostles: An Introduction and Commentary* (TNTC; Leicester: Inter-Varsity Press, 1984).

God had foretold by the mouth of all the prophets that Jesus would suffer.

The primary thing that Peter wants his audience to understand is that the lame man was not healed by the power or piety of Peter and John, but by the power of the name of Jesus and faith in that name (see vv. 12, 13a, 16). Peter is careful to direct attention to Jesus and the God of Israel who stands behind him. By referring to God as "the God of Abraham, Isaac, and Jacob, the God of our ancestors" (cf. Exod 3:6, 15), Peter is explicitly connecting the healing of the lame man with the activity of the God who liberated Israel from the bondage of Egypt. Thus, God "glorified his servant Jesus" through the healing of the lame man (v. 13). In referring to Jesus as "the servant of God," Peter is using language to describe Jesus that intersects with the last of the Servant Songs of Isaiah (52:13–53:12, esp. 52:13; 53:11, 12). [Servant of God] Such explicit connections with the Jewish Scriptures again show the continuity between Israel's story and that of Jesus.

Peter insists that the healing was accomplished through the name of Jesus and faith in his name (v. 16). Here, "name of Jesus" refers to something done under the power and authority of the one named. Those acting "in the name of" are

Servant of God

AΩ Jesus is designated as "servant" four times in Acts (3:13, 26; 4:27, 30). In all instances, Jesus is understood to be "God's servant." The term "servant of God" is commonly used in the Old Testament, often for Moses (cf. Josh 1:7, 13; 9:24; 1 Chr 6:49). Minimally, the term denotes Jesus as one who served God. The term can have more specific meaning. The phrase "servant of God" could be applied to messianic figures (Ezek 34:23-24; 37:24-25; Zech 3:8) and the songs of 2 Isaiah refer often to Israel as God's Suffering Servant. All of these understandings of "servant" can apply to Jesus. The fact that the title faded from use may be due to the fact that the Greek word *pais* could also be translated as "child." Thus, referring to Jesus as "God's servant" was subsumed under the more widely used designation "God's Son."

H. J Cadbury, "The Titles of Jesus in Acts," in F. J. Foakes Jackson and Kirsopp Lake, *The Beginnings of Christianity: The Acts of the Apostles*, 5 vols. (Grand Rapids MI: Baker, 1979), 5.364–70; J. Jeremias, "*Pais Theou*," TDNT 5.677–717.

instruments; the one in whose name they act is the real source of power. But Peter also speaks of "faith in his name" and, further, "the faith that is through him [Jesus]." The objective source of power for healing is Jesus the Messiah. Yet it is a power only made effective in the context of human faith.

The second half of Peter's speech is deliberative, trying to persuade the audience to "repent" and "turn again" (v. 19). The two terms when used together imply a change of both mind and action.

Repentance results in three things. First, sins will be blotted out (v. 19; cf. Isa 43:25). This is identical to the result of repentance noted in 2:38, "the forgiveness of sins." The second result is that "times of refreshing may come." The word is used in 4 Ezra (2 Esd) 11:46 to refer to the earth's being "refreshed" and relieved by the Messiah from the violence suffered by oppression from Rome. Hence, the word can be used to denote "end-time," eschatological deliverance.

The third result of repentance is "that he may send the Messiah appointed for you" (v. 20). This likely "means that conversion properly prepares [one] for the Parousia, not that it brings it about."[1] The statement claims that God has "appointed" or "selected" Jesus to be the Messiah "for Israel." This reiterates that Israel's story finds its fulfillment and realization in Jesus. Israel, however, can enjoy the benefits of its Messiah only if it repents.

This Messiah now sits on the heavenly throne and must remain "in heaven . . . until the time for the restoration of all things" (v. 21a). Such restoration is not a fourth result of repentance, but provides further commentary on what is in store for Israel when the Messiah does come. The words "which God spoke by the mouth of his holy prophets from of old" (v. 21b) offer a clear echo of the words of Zechariah in Luke 1:68-75, especially v. 70. Zechariah praises God for keeping God's promises to Israel, promises that have to do with the liberation of Israel from its enemies. The blessings that accompany "the restoration of all things" can be Israel's as well, if only it will recognize that the one whom it rejected was the Messiah whom God appointed for the people.

But as is common in biblical narrative, the promise of blessing is coupled with the threat of judgment (see Deut 28:1-46). This pattern is evidenced at the end of this speech in vv. 22-23, where Peter quotes Moses (see Deut 18:15-20; Lev 23:29). Jesus is the "prophet like Moses," whom Moses warned Israel to heed. Furthermore, everyone who did not would be "cut off from the people." Continuing in the ranks of God's people is dependent upon "listening" to Jesus by recognizing him as the Messiah.

Peter claims that all the prophets anticipated the coming of the Messiah (v. 24). He concludes by reminding his audience that they are heirs of promises that God made through both the prophets and the covenant given to their ancestors (v. 25a; cf. Gen 12:3; 18:18; 22:18; 26:4). The promise was that through Abraham's "seed all the families of the earth would be blessed" (v. 25b).

In Galatians 3:16, Paul understood "seed" to denote Jesus, a specific descendant of Abraham. If one understands Acts this way, Peter is saying that through Jesus all the families of the earth, including Israel, would find blessing. Peter goes on to say in the next verse that God sent his servant *first* to Israel so that it might be the first among the families of the earth to be *blessed*. Such "blessing," however, comes only when Israel turns (or "repents") from its wickedness.

"We Must Speak of What We Have Seen and Heard," 4:1-22

This section divides structurally into four parallel units:
    A. The rulers' actions (vv. 1-7)
      B. The apostolic response (vv. 8-12)
    A'. The rulers' actions (vv. 13-18)
      B'. The apostolic response (vv. 19-22)

A. The Rulers' Actions, vv. 1-7

Unstated irony confronts the reader in the opening verses of chapter 4. It is just as the apostles present the word of salvation to "the people" (v. 1; cf. 3:9, 11) that representatives from the temple suddenly appear (*ephistemi*) on the scene. Three groups are identified: the priests (some manuscripts say "chief priests"), the captain of the temple, and the Sadducees. The irony lies in the fact that as "the people" hear word of how their own story is finding realization in the person of Jesus the Messiah, those who are responsible for the religious welfare of the people arrive not to listen, but to put a stop to things.

Given the time and setting, it is appropriate that "the captain of the temple" is among the intruders. [Captain of the Temple] "The priests" who accompany him may be those who assisted the captain in the maintenance of discipline. If so, then these would actually be Levites, persons who had assumed a role of *assisting* the priests after the exile.

Captain of the Temple

AΩ Rabbinic literature refers to this officer as the *sagan*. Josephus and the LXX use the same term as Acts to denote the *sagan, strategos*. This official, second in command only to the high priest, was responsible for both the daily offerings and the maintenance of discipline within the temple court areas.

The presence of the Sadducees is a bit confusing on the purely historical level, for Sadducees *per se* did not have official authority over the temple. [Sadducees] However, the priestly leadership, who did have authority over the temple, did come from the Sadducean ranks. On the literary level, their presence is more understandable, for this group consistently appears in Acts as the quintessential opposition group to the Christians, with their opposition being rooted in their insistence that there was no resurrection of the dead (see Luke 20:27; Acts 23:8).

It is precisely this "resurrection" that the apostles have been preaching (v. 2). This, combined with the fact that the apostles were teaching at all, motivates the intrusion. Officially, the responsibility of teaching the people, especially on the temple grounds, fell to the official priesthood. Thus, teaching of any kind from persons not sanctioned as priests would be viewed with suspicion. Affirming the idea of resurrection, and most especially that "in Jesus" the resurrection was a reality, would make temple officials who were sympathetic with Sadducean ideas even more suspicious of the apostles. The interruption of the apostles for "teaching the people" and talking of "resurrection" offers an echo of the Gospel narrative. Jesus also taught the people in the temple, confronted the authorities, and spoke of resurrection (cf. Luke 19:47-48; 20:27-40; 21:37-38). Such echoes offer subtle indications that Jesus' followers are doing what he did and, hence, are being faithful to their master.

Luke Johnson argues that a key issue for Luke concerns the question, "Who is the legitimate leadership of 'the people,' of Israel?"[2] Officially, the answer would be the temple leadership. But the Messiah, Jesus, had promised to confer upon his apostolic followers "a kingdom, that [they] may . . . sit on thrones judging [or ruling] the twelve tribes of Israel" (Luke 22:29-30). Acts presents a confrontation between "leaders."

The priestly leadership clearly has power, for they arrested the apostles and placed them in custody until the next day (v. 3). The apostles' arrest by this priestly leadership is reminiscent of Jesus' arrest by the "chief priests and officers of the temple" (Luke 22:52). It offers a reminder that those who follow Jesus can expect to be

Sadducees

They were not so much an "official party" as a circle of aristocrats, both lay and priestly, united by a common interest: the maintenance of order in Jewish life under the watchful eye of the Romans. Likely their name is derived from "Zadokites," the old ruling priestly family of the Jews. In New Testament times, however, the Sadducees are not Zadokites, though they may have hoped that their name, reminding folk of their Zadokite roots, would enhance their authority. Their "theology" tended to be conservative, rejecting increasingly accepted ideas within Jewish thought such as resurrection and divine providence. When one considers the central role both resurrection and providence play in Acts, it is easy to understand why Luke consistently presents this group in a bad light.

J. Bradley Chance, "Sadducees," *MDB* 784–85.

Sanhedrin

The Jewish ruling council in Judea existed under Roman authority to deal with legal matters involving Jewish people. Each town of any size had a local "sanhedrin." Acts speaks only of the "Supreme Sanhedrin" located in Jerusalem. Headed by the high priest, it consisted of seventy-one members, from three groups: the priestly aristocracy (referred to in the New Testament as "the priests" or "chief priests"), the lay aristocracy ("the elders" in the New Testament), and "the scribes," considered the legal (biblical) scholars of their day. The priests and elders would be aligned with the Sadducees while the scribes would tend to be aligned with the Pharisees (cf. Acts 23:6).

J. Bradley Chance, "Sanhedrin," *MDB* 795–96.

High Priest

Narrowly defined, the term refers to the person who held the appointment as the leading priest of the Jewish priestly system. Scripture and tradition had stated that this person was to be of the priestly family of Zadok, who emerged as the leading priest during the time of Solomon (see Ezek 40:46; 44:15; 48:11; Sir 51:12 [Hebrew version]). In fact, since the second century BC, the office was a political appointment and while the one who held it had to be a priest, the "Zadokite" requirement was forgotten. The high priest served as the "president" of the Sanhedrin. More broadly defined, the term "high priest" can be used to denote also former high priests and members of the family from which the high priest had been chosen (cf. Acts 4:6). The New Testament regularly uses the plural "chief priests" to denote the priestly aristocracy that served on the Sanhedrin (cf. Acts 4:23; 23:14 for two of many references).

treated like their Lord as they proclaim the message of God to those who hold power.

There is more irony in that even as the apostles are led away by the leadership, "many who heard the word believed" (v. 4). Despite the priestly leadership's efforts, the impact of the apostolic word is growing, with the ranks of the believing remnant of Israel now swelling "to about five thousand." The temple leadership may have *power*, but they cannot stop the response of the people to the *authoritative* word. Power and authority are not the same.

The next morning the "rulers and elders and scribes" gather together (v. 5). Luke likely is speaking of the supreme ruling council of the Sanhedrin; hence, the high priest is there as he was head of the council. [Sanhedrin] Annas is identified as the high priest, though Caiaphas was, in fact, the high priest at this time (see Matt 26:3, 57; John 18:13; Josephus). [High Priest] The high priest was the leader of the ruling council. Some have tried to explain this Lukan misstatement by arguing that Annas was the "real" power behind the throne. The fact remains that Luke explicitly states that Annas is the high priest, while saying nothing in this context about Caiaphas's association with the office. Nothing is known of John and Alexander, though one important manuscript (D) reads "Jonathan," which may be a reference to one of the sons of Annas who served as high priest in AD 36. [Jewish Rulers of Acts] Gathered also are "all who were of the high priestly family." Luke is setting the stage: the apostolic leadership is facing the whole of the official leadership of "the people."

The apostles are then placed "in the midst" of the semicircle around which members of the council sat (v. 7). The interrogation begins: "By what power or by what name did you do this?" The question harks back to the emphasis on "the name" of Jesus that Peter had preached in Acts 3 and the healing that was done in the power of that name. This does not square with v. 2, which indicates that those who arrested the apostles were bothered not by the miracle, but by the fact that the apostles were teaching and pro-

Jewish Rulers of Acts

The book of Acts refers to a number of Jewish rulers. (The rulers are listed in alphabetical order.)

Agrippa: See ch. 23, **[Agrippa]**.

Ananias: See Acts 22:12; 23:2; 24:1. High priest from AD 48–59. He was killed by Jewish rebels at the outbreak of the revolt (AD 66).

Annas: See Acts 4:6. High priest from AD 6–15. He likely continued to wield influence through successive high priests. Caiaphas was his son-in-law, and several of his sons held the office in later years. Despite what Acts 4:6 says, he was not the high priest at the time of the early church. Luke 3:2 leaves the impression that Luke may have thought that Annas and Caiaphas oversaw a kind of joint high priesthood, but this is unattested in the other ancient sources. Perhaps

Luke was aware of Annas's continuing influence in Jewish political affairs and assumed that such influence made it appropriate to call Annas "high priest."

Bernice: See ch. 23, **[Bernice]**.

Caiaphas: See Acts 4:6. The high priest from AD 18–37. He was, therefore, the leader of the Sanhedrin at the time of Jesus' arrest, trial, and execution.

Herod (Agrippa): See Acts 12. The grandson of Herod the Great, he ruled extensive territory in Judea from AD 37–44, with his domain eventually reaching the extent of his grandfather's.

Herod (Antipas): See Acts 4:27; also Luke 3:19-20; 23:6-12. The son of Herod the Great, he ruled the territories of Galilee and Perea from 4 BC–AD 39.

---

claiming in *Jesus* the resurrection of the dead. Now the interrogators want to know about the miracle and do not seem to know what "name" is involved (cf. 3:12). Luke has interests beyond historical transcription. The commentary stated above that v. 2 reminded readers of Jesus' encounters in the temple precincts with both the people and the religious authorities. The question of v. 7 is to set up Peter and to offer him yet another opportunity to preach. Luke is more concerned to construct a narrative that edifies than one that offers mundane, historical precision.

B. The Apostolic Response, vv. 8-12

Peter, again, plays the role of the apostolic spokesperson (cf. 3:11-12). He does not begin to speak until he is "filled with the Holy Spirit." Readers encounter here yet another echo of the Gospel. Jesus had said that when standing before rulers "the Holy Spirit will teach you . . . what you are to say" (Luke 12:11-12). Some argue that Luke, unlike Paul and the Johannine materials, did not view the Spirit as a permanent endowment of believers.[3] While the narrative can speak of special situations, such as this one, when God's help is needed, texts such as 2:38 and 9:18 indicate that believers receive the Holy Spirit through repentance and not only in moments of special spiritual need.[4]

Peter's response is judicial, addressing directly the question of his interrogators concerning what the apostles had done and in whose name. He refers in v. 9 to the "good deed done to one who was ill" and makes clear that the man was "made well," or "saved" (*sesotai*), by the "name of Jesus Christ of Nazareth" (v. 10a). Peter has employed the word *sōzō* in such a way so as to bring out the full range of its meaning. The word can be used to denote both restora-

Kerygma

A Ω From the Greek word for "proclamation," it is a shorthand way of referring to Christian proclamation of the gospel. C. H. Dodd has outlined the pattern of the kerygma found in Acts (21–24). He believed that the pattern found in Acts reflects the early kerygma of the Jerusalem congregation. Though this historical conclusion is frequently challenged, the outline of the kerygma, as presented in Acts, is still a helpful summary:

1. The age of fulfillment has dawned.
2. This fulfillment has come through the ministry, death, and resurrection of Jesus; a short account of which is given, backed up by scriptural proof.
3. Through his resurrection, Jesus is exalted to "the right hand of God" as Messiah of the new Israel.
4. The Holy Spirit is the sign of Christ's present power and glory.
5. The messianic age will shortly reach its consummation with the Parousia of Christ.
6. Folk need to respond through repentance.

C. H. Dodd, *The Apostolic Preaching and Its Developments* (1936; repr., Grand Rapids MI: Baker, 1980).

tion to physical health and "salvation" on a deeper level. The physical healing of a man in the name of Jesus points to this same Jesus as the one in whose name one can "be saved." For readers, this harks back to 2:21 where Peter quoted Joel 2:39: "All who call upon the name of the Lord shall be saved." Acts 2 defines such salvation in terms of "forgiveness of sins" (2:38), but, as in the Gospel, such salvation has more far-reaching effects. In "the name of Jesus" people can find the liberating power that delivers (saves) them from anything that binds them and makes them less than whole.

Peter presents a summary of the Christian proclamation, referring to Jesus' death and resurrection. [Kerygma] Jesus' death is said to be at the hands of those in Jerusalem who either masterminded or permitted his execution (v. 10b; cf. 2:23; 3:13, 14). But God raised this Jesus from the dead (v. 10b; cf. 2:24; 3:15). This "contrast formula" is common in Acts.[5] It contrasts what people have done with the reversal that God effects that brings honor to the rejected one.

Peter continues this pattern in v. 11, this time employing Scripture (Ps 118:22) to convey the same idea. Jesus is compared to a "stone which was rejected by you builders, but which has become the head of corner."

Acts echoes the Gospel again. In Luke 20:17 Jesus employed the same text in addressing the Jewish leadership, which had just asked Jesus "by what authority do you do these things?" (Luke 20:2). Jesus responded with the parable of the vineyard, using this psalm at the conclusion of the parable. In this parable, the tenants of the vineyard (the Jewish leadership) are judged for rejecting the owner's son. As punishment for the tenants' rejection, the owner will come "and destroy those tenants, and give the vineyard to others" (Luke 20:15). Note that the parable does not say that the vineyard (Israel) is destroyed, but only its tenants, or leaders.

Now in Acts 3, Luke employs the same psalm during the first direct encounter between two opposing groups of leaders of "the vineyard," the apostles and the Jewish hierarchy. Allusion to the parable of the vineyard reminds readers that Jesus had said that "the tenants" would be destroyed and the vineyard given to others. These "others" are the apostles who now stand in the middle of the

Sanhedrin. The Jewish leadership may not know it, but readers know who the real "leaders" of "the vineyard" are and what the destiny of the "official leadership" is: destruction.

Verse 12 reinforces this. Insisting that salvation is offered by no other name urges readers to conclude that if the leaders do not end their attempts to silence "the name," they will not be listening to the prophet like Moses and will be excluding themselves "from the people" (cf. 3:23).

A'. The Rulers' Actions, vv. 13-18

The reaction of the rulers to Peter's response does nothing to earn readers' sympathies. The rulers perceive these men to be "unlettered" and without professional credentials (*idiotai*) (v. 13). The observation is quite ironic given that the subtext of the whole encounter concerns the real leadership of Israel. The "official leadership" feels secure, for its opponents do not have the credentials to be leaders. The statement at the end of v. 13 can be read as almost calloused: now that they have been reminded of Jesus, they recall that these men had been with one whom, just a few weeks ago, they had condemned to death.

Further analysis of their reaction shows who the *real* leaders are. The official leaders have "nothing to say," as contrasted with the "boldness of Peter and John" (vv. 13-14). The whole scene reinforces the believing reader's confidence in the authority of the Jesus in whose name one is saved, for in the silence of the official leadership is fulfilled Jesus' prophecy that his followers' adversaries would be not able to respond to their testimony (Luke 21:15). The official leaders show their lack of integrity in that they do not question "the facts of the case." They acknowledge that the man was healed, and they cannot deny the reality of what has happened (vv. 15-16). But their only concern is to maintain their positions, and this requires that the message the apostles are preaching spread no further among "the people." Thus, they command the apostles neither to teach nor speak "in this name" (v. 17).

B'. The Apostolic Response, vv. 19-22

The Sanhedrin's commandment is one that the apostles cannot accept. Their response is not distinctively Christian, but quite proverbial in the ancient world (v. 19). [Divine and Human Authority] The apostles' loyalty is "to speak of what they have seen and heard" (v. 20). Faithfulness to the command to be witnesses overrides obedience to the command of the Sanhedrin to be silent.

Divine and Human Authority.

"I shall obey God rather than you, and while I have life and strength I shall never cease from the practice of teaching philosophy." Socrates (Plato, *Apol.* 29D)

Verse 21 offers yet another echo of the Gospel. In the Gospel the official leadership felt helpless in its confrontations with Jesus "because of the people" (cf. Luke 19:48; 20:19; 22:2, 6). But the people proved unreliable in the end, doing nothing to stop the schemes of their leadership to execute Jesus. Things appear to be different now, for "all persons praised God for what had happened" (v. 21), recognizing the special power that was unleashed with healing of the man born lame. Will the people remain loyal this time or prove fickle as they had before?

They Lifted Their Voices Together to God, 4:23-31

Upon their release, Peter and John return to "their own" (*idious*), denoting either the other apostles or the larger community. In their report of what happened, they do not mention "the scribes," even though the scribes were present (see v. 5). Such silence may subtly communicate that the core of opposition to Jesus' followers comes from the ranks of the priests and lay-aristocracy.

The response to the Sanhedrin's challenge is prayer and praise (vv. 24-30). The prayer falls into three parts: v. 24 offers words of praise to God; vv. 25-29a present a "narration" of what has happened, employing the use and interpretation of Scripture; vv. 29b-30 present the community's petition. [Structure of Prayer (Acts 4:24-30)]

The introduction of praise addresses God as *despota*, "master" (v. 24). Luke uses the term in only one other place (Luke 2:29) and there, as here, contrasts God as "master" with God's people as

---

Structure of Prayer (Acts 4:24-30)

The prayer of Acts 4 resembles the structure of King Hezekiah's prayer, recorded in Isa 37:16-20. Some commentators believe it significant that the Christian prayer differs from Hezekiah's in that it does not pray for deliverance from enemies, but boldness in preaching the gospel.

Outline	Hezekiah's Prayer (Isa 37:16-20)	Christian Community's Prayer (Acts 4:24-30)
Introduction of Praise	V. 16: God acknowledged as king and creator	V. 24: God acknowledged as "master" and creator
Narration of What Has Happened	Vv. 17-19: Speaks of the Assyrian threat	Vv. 25-29a: Speaks of plot against Jesus and threats against community
Concluding Petition	V. 20: Prays for deliverance that God may be vindicated	Vv. 29b-30: Prays for boldness of preaching and manifestations of God's power

"servants." God is also praised as the creator, a very common biblical theme (cf. Gen 14:19; Exod 20:11). As both "master" and creator of all, God is addressed in a manner appropriate for one whom the petitioner believes to be "the Lord of history," a conviction the petitioners make explicit by the end of their prayer.

At the heart of prayer is a "narration" of what has happened (vv. 25-29a). Verses 25-26 present an exact quotation of Psalm 2:1-2 (LXX). The introduction to the quotation, affirming that God spoke through the inspired David, is a feature of early Christian understandings of Scripture (see Commentary, ch. 1). Psalm 2 was a "royal psalm," which in its ancient context would have been sung by the people in honor of the Davidic king, the anointed one of God. Such psalms were easily open to messianic interpretation when the historical dynasty of David came to an end. It makes sense that followers of Jesus, who believed him to be the Messiah and king, would be drawn to the royal psalms. Verse 27 offers an interpretation of the psalm, applying it specifically to Jesus' passion. Herod (see Luke 23:6-12) is understood as "the kings" to whom the psalm refers, while Pontius Pilate represents "the rulers." The interpretation of v. 27 does not spell out whom "the Gentiles" or "the peoples" of the psalm denote, but they would likely refer to the Roman soldiers and those from among the people of Israel who participated in the execution of Jesus, especially the Jewish leadership.

The interpretation of v. 27 seems to put more blame on Herod and Pilate, than does Luke's Passion Narrative (see Luke 23). But in the speeches of Acts thus far, Luke has tended to flatten the more nuanced description of Jesus' passion found in the Gospel. For example, "the people" are accused of killing Jesus in the speeches, while in the Gospel, Luke goes to great lengths to place most of the blame on the *leadership* (see Luke 24:20). No matter how complex the interaction of various characters in the execution of Jesus may be, in the end, according to the speeches of Acts, no one who was in any way involved is without guilt.

Those offering the prayer take comfort that the complexities of history do not deter God from accomplishing God's purposes (v. 28). This declaration "shows with all possible clarity the conviction that the passion transpired by divine necessity and that God works in relation to human events with final authority."[6] Through praise that emerges out of crisis, the community expresses its deeply held faith in God's sovereignty. Declarations made in such a context make the pedantic utterances of cold propositions ring hollow. God's sovereignty is to be trusted in and celebrated, not figured out.

The community's conviction in the accomplishment of God's sovereign will allows it to call upon the Lord to "look upon their [the Sanhedrin's] threats" against God's people (v. 29a). God can use even threats to realize God's aims, the praying community believes. The community sees its own tribulations as closely related to those of Jesus, moving easily in their prayer from remembering Jesus' passion to recalling their own trials.

In the petition (vv. 29b-30), the people do not ask for deliverance from the trials, but that the master grant the servants to speak the word with "boldness." They pray that they may proclaim the gospel openly, frankly, confidently, and courageously (all representing good understandings of *parrēsia*). They do ask for God to manifest God's power ("stretch out your arm"), but they envision such power through demonstrations of God's liberation, such as healing, which comes with the proclamation of the gospel, not the destruction of the community's enemies.

The shaking of the room demonstrates that God answered their prayer (v. 31). [Divine Presence and Response] God responds through a renewed empowerment of the community with the Spirit so that it could speak the word in the manner it had requested.

Divine Presence and Response

The divine presence is regularly depicted through a shaking of the earth: Isa 6:4; Exod 19:18. "While he spoke to me, little by little the place where I was standing began to rock to and fro" (4 Ezra [2 Esd] 6:29). Roman literature speaks of a divine trembling in response to human prayer: "Grant, father, an omen, and inspire our hearts! Scarcely had I thus spoken, when suddenly it seemed all things trembled" (Virgil, *Aen.* 3.89–90).

There Was Not a Needy Person among Them, 4:32-37

The text offers a second Lukan summary, similar in content to the first (cf. 2:42-47). Both speak of the community holding things in common (v. 32; cf. 2:44) and the apostolic witness (v. 33a; cf. 2:43b). This summary also speaks explicitly of the believers being "of one heart and soul" (v. 32). It was not uncommon in literature of the Hellenistic period to find the expression "one soul," an idiomatic way of talking of friendship, joined with "holding all things in common." As with the previous summary, Luke is painting an ideal portrait, recognizable to Gentile readers of the early community: "What [Gentiles] esteemed as an ideal, had become a reality in the young Christian community."[7] The expression "there was not a needy person among them" (v. 34) is an echo of Deuteronomy 15:4. Deuteronomy 15:1-11 applies well to Luke's portrait of the early Christian community. The "people of God" dwelling in the land were to be a people who were generous so that there would be no needy persons among them. Recall that Luke is portraying the early Jerusalem community as the "restored" people. Thus, it is only fitting that in their life together they realize, through their generosity and sharing, God's intentions for God's people as spelled out in their Scriptures. Like the ideal portrait of God's people presented in Deuteronomy, the early community can best be described not so much as practicing communal *ownership*, as generous *sharing*. Verse 34, which employs imperfect tenses, can be read to say that people were *in the habit of selling* property and bringing the proceeds to the apostles. This implies a regular practice of disposing of property "as any had need" (v. 3b).

Laying the proceeds at the apostles' feet is fitting in this context. The larger issue is "Who is the true leadership of (restored) Israel?" Readers know it to be the apostles. Laying something at someone's feet symbolizes "a state of submission or obedience" (cf. Josh 10:23-24; 1 Sam 25:23-25; Ps 8:5-6; 110:1; Luke 7:38; 8:41; 10:39).[8] Thus, by entrusting their property to the apostles, these early followers show that they too understand wherein the real leadership resides. The scene concludes with a picture of Barnabas laying the proceeds from his property at the feet of the apostles. Herein exemplifies faithful obedience to those who rule over the twelve tribes of Israel. [Son of Encouragement]

> **Son of Encouragement**
>
> AΩ This is the etymology given by Luke for the name "Barnabas." "Bar-" does mean "son," but "-nabas" does not mean "encouragement." Literally, the name means "son of Nebo," a pagan god, a curious name for the apostles to give to the Levitical Jewish believer. Perhaps, though less likely, "-nabi" could be derived from the Hebrew word (*nabi*) "prophet," hence, "son of a prophet." This latter suggestion certainly makes more sense, but few commentators accept this etymology. Evidently, Luke was persuaded by the *type* of person Barnabas was as he attempted to explain his name. It is possible that Luke, for reasons of edification, added the detail that Barnabas's name was given to him by the apostles. In biblical parlance, to assign a name to someone can demonstrate authority over that person (cf. Gen 2:1; 17:5; John 1:42). Luke is portraying Barnabas as an ideal example of one who submits to the authority of the apostles.

CONNECTIONS

Luke again gives expression to the theme of God's sovereign design. The narrative of Acts offers constant reassurance that what happens on the field of history works, ultimately, in accordance with the divine purpose.

But Luke is careful not to ascribe "bad things" to God's initiative. People do bad things; God works through the bad we do to accomplish God's aims *on our behalf*: "whom you [human beings] crucified, whom God raised from the dead, by him this man is standing before you well" (4:10). This summary of early Christian preaching serves also as a summary of the mystery of the divine providence and mercy. Despite what the residents of Jerusalem had done, Peter says to them, "God raised up his servant and sent him to *you* first, to bless *you* in turning *every one of you* away from your wickedness" (3:26).

A word we encounter regularly in these chapters related to witness is the word "boldness" (4:13, 29, 31). In the midst of persecution the church prayed to offer bold testimony. The word *parrēsia* (boldness) has many connotations. It can mean to be "open" about something, as opposed to secretive or private (John 7:26; 18:20). To speak in a manner described by this word is to offer plain speaking (John 10:24; 11:14), the opposite of talking in rhymes or figures (John 16:25). The word also carries with it a sense of courage (Acts 18:26; Eph 6:19-20) and even confidence (2 Cor 3:12; 7:4; Heb 3:6; 10:35). Open, plain speaking exhibiting courage and confidence is what impressed the Sanhedrin about Peter and John and also stunned the council into silence (see 4:13-14). It is this kind of "boldness" for which the community prays.

The word should not be construed as "brashness," "arrogance," or "pushiness." Too often, "bold" preaching is confused with verbal brutality and red-faced, vein-popping sputtering. We can best keep in check our confusion of what "boldness" means by remembering that the word *parrēsia* is regularly used in the New Testament to describe the spirit in which we approach God (Eph 3:12; Heb 4:16; 10:19; 1 John 3:21; 5:14) and even face "judgment day" (1 John 2:28; 4:17). None would approach God or the judgment bar brashly or arrogantly. The "confidence" or "boldness" to approach God is grounded in an awesome sense of our own unworthiness and in the context of our total reliance on the mercy and grace of God. When we feel "confident" that we are approaching an opportunity to bear witness in the same spirit that we would approach the God who raised Jesus up for us, we can know that we have a sense of the kind of boldness for which our early spiritual ancestors prayed.

Witness does not always take place in a context of serenity. It can lead to a confrontation with the powers that be. Voices of a small, politically powerless group stood face to face with Judea's equivalent of the Supreme Court, White House, and Congress rolled into one. Recall that the subtext of the debate is "wherein lies the real leadership of the people?" When we focus attention on the powerful people who sat in the ruling chairs of the Sanhedrin we get an ugly picture of how "power," ironically frustrated by its own impotence, responds to the courageous, confident, and bold witness of a minority under conviction. Most striking is that these representatives of religious and political power have little interest in "the truth." The evidence literally *stands* before them: a formerly lame man. But they are unimpressed. Stopping and silencing the voices of the apostles are all that matter.

Martin Luther King Jr. preached a consistent theme to and about what he called "the forces of darkness." Much like the apostles who grounded their testimony in the Scriptures to which the Sanhedrin would have to give allegiance, King pressed his audience to recall the sacred texts, traditions, and heroes of the American story: the Declaration of Independence, our ideals of freedom and justice for *all*, and persons of character who made a difference because they stood for these ideals, persons like Thomas Jefferson and Abraham Lincoln. But "the truth" of these traditions, ideals, and even laws, made little difference to those who unleashed the police dogs, turned on the fire hoses, beat the freedom riders, and passed arbitrary laws designed only to harass those seeking liberty. In the context of struggle, people can generally know that truth is on their side, even if raw power is not, when the opposition has no interest in debate and can only respond to challenges with threats and commands of silence.

In the face of this kind of opposition, we can learn both from the apostles and those who confronted the segregated forces of darkness a generation ago. When pressed to voice allegiance, the apostles followed in the steps of those like Socrates and laid a path for the many people of conscience to follow, insisting that they must obey the just God rather than unjust people. Peaceful, nonviolent, determined action for that which is right, or just, is sometimes necessary. [Civil Disobedience]

But talk of the confrontation that can come with witness carries with it at least one caveat. Early Christians were a persecuted minority. In our culture, as "post-Christian" as it is, Christians are *not* a small sectarian group, pitting themselves against "the powers that be," like a modern-day David and Goliath.

Persons confessing allegiance to the Christian faith make up the vast majority of members of Congress. They consistently have sat in the White House. They sit on our local school boards and city councils. Christian denominations are multi-billion dollar incorporated entities, owning buildings, schools, and billions in assets in mutual funds. They can disseminate their message through massive publishing houses, radio, and television.

Civil Disobedience

"Nonviolent direct action seeks to create such a crisis and establish such creative tension that a community that has constantly refused to negotiate is forced to confront the issue. It seeks so to dramatize the issue that it can no longer be ignored" (King, 86).

Perhaps it is anachronistic to call the apostles' defiance of the Sanhedrin "civil disobedience." But they are portrayed as believing that they confronted Israel with an issue that could not be ignored. God was calling Israel to affirm its own heritage and to embrace the realization of its own hopes. From the perspective of Luke–Acts, Israel had threatened its own destiny in rejecting its Messiah at the instigation of the "powers that be" (the Sanhedrin). Israel had to make some choices, and the apostles of old, like many who have disturbed the civil order since, found ways to confront Israel with the choices it had to make: will you listen to the prophet like Moses or will you follow those who were intent on destroying him?

Martin Luther King Jr., "Letter from a Birmingham Jail," in *I Have a Dream: Writings and Speeches that Changed the World*, ed. James M. Washington (New York: HarperSanFrancisco, 1986).

In terms of power, we look far more like the temple and its personnel than the early followers of Jesus. In terms of power, Christians have become the Sanhedrin. We have taken our place in the councils of "the powers that be." Thus, we regularly need to spend as much time thinking about how to use power in legitimate ways, as on imagining ourselves, in every conflict, to be like the politically powerless apostles.

When there is little concern for the truth and much concern for gaining the upper hand, we act like the Sanhedrin. When we threaten harm rather than listen with reason, we act like the Sanhedrin. When we refuse to celebrate the healing of others simply because they are helped by those of whom we are skeptical or with whom we disagree, we act like the Sanhedrin. When we treat the sacred space of the church, pulpit, or classroom as "our turf" where folk can do and say only that of which we approve, we act like the Sanhedrin. And when we try to compel people to be silent, forbidding them to speak their heartfelt convictions, we act like the Sanhedrin. We act like those who knew they had the power and assumed that they also possessed divinely sanctioned authority. [Discerning Justice]

Luke depicts a community that found its power in prayer, not political maneuvering. Acts 3 begins with a notice of the hour of prayer in which the apostles participated and ends with the community praying for boldness in its proclamation. Sometimes we are too quick to scoff at ceremonies and rituals of prayer, thinking that structured times or modes of prayer are too formal and, somehow, "unreal." But our spiritual ancestors went to the temple at the ninth hour, along with thousands of others, to share in prayer. The fact is, there is a certain discipline required to pray regularly in communion with other saints.

Dietrich Bonhoeffer offers a call to such discipline in his small book *Life Together*. [Regular Christian Devotion] In continuing the traditions of our

Discerning Justice

What is a cause over which the creation of civil unrest is in order? Too often we claim that any cause with which we have the slightest disagreement emerged from the darkest shadows evil, which we must stop at any cost. Dr. King offered a simple, yet subtle and profound criterion:

One may well ask, "How can you advocate breaking some laws and obeying others?' The answer is found in the fact that there are two types of laws: there are just and there are unjust laws. . . . How does one determine when a law is *just* or *unjust*? A just law is a man-made code that squares with the moral law or the law of God. An unjust law is code that is out of harmony with the moral law. . . . Any law that uplifts the human personality is just. Any law that degrades human personality is unjust.

Martin Luther King Jr., "Letter from a Birmingham Jail," in *I Have a Dream: Writings and Speeches that Changed the World*, ed. James M. Washington (New York: HarperSanFrancisco, 1986), 89.

Regular Christian Devotion

"Every common devotion should include the *word of Scripture, the hymns of the Church, and the prayer of the fellowship*. . . . [Scripture]: Consecutive reading of Biblical books forces everyone who wants to hear to put himself [*sic*], or to allow himself to be found, where God has acted once and for all for the salvation of men. We become a part of what once took place for our salvation. . . . [Hymns]: It is the voice of the Church that is heard in singing together. . . . Thus all singing together that is right must serve to widen our spiritual horizon, make us see our little company as a member of the great Christian Church on earth. . . . [Prayer]: [W]e are to pray to God as a fellowship, and this prayer must really be *our* word, *our* prayer for this day, for our work, for our fellowship, for the particular needs and sins that oppress in common, for the persons who are committed to our care."

Dietrich Bonhoeffer, *Life Together* (San Francisco: Harper & Row, 1954), (selections from ch. 2).

ancestors, both of Israel and the church, he lays out the importance of morning, noontime, and evening *communal* devotions, consisting of Scripture, hymns, and prayer. Many who would read a discussion of this kind of devotion will be struck with the seeming impossibility of following such a regimen. We do not have time to gather with God's people, three times a day, to lift our praise and petitions toward God. And the truth is, we don't. We have created life-structures that make regular and disciplined devotion to God a virtual impossibility. Rather than pass judgment on such formalized, communal prayers while we don't pray at all in community, perhaps we should recognize that there may be much good to say about religious traditions, such as we meet in the temple services of Acts, contemporary Islam, the Roman Catholic tradition, or the Anglican Communion, which build formally into the day times of and prescriptions for prayer. For the most part, those in "free church" tradition have abandoned this kind of thing as "empty ritual." Consequently, many have abandoned the discipline of prayer altogether.

The prayer offered up by the community of Jerusalem saints in Acts 4:24-31 offers a helpful model for prayer of the Christian community of any generation. First, we observe that the community prays the psalms. Literally, it offers its prayer to God in the words of David. [Praying the Psalms] Second, as the community prays, it remembers the gospel story (vv. 27-28). Prayer is possible because of what God has done for us in Jesus Christ. Whenever we pray communally or privately, remembrance of the gospel story should be explicitly in our hearts and on our lips. Third, as our ancestors offered up their petitions, it was not so much for deliverance as for the grace to speak God's word with boldness. The request for boldness is a request for empowerment so that we can get on with the work we have been called to do. And that work is to testify that, in Christ, God is doing what God had always promised to do: offer salvation of liberation to all flesh.

Praying the Psalms

To "pray the psalms" is to read these ancient prayers as one's own; it is to follow the example of our Christian ancestors in Acts. It is to pray in "the communion of the saints."

When we Christians pray the Psalms, we pray from the formative spirituality of another people who wrote those Psalms so many generations ago. As we join them in this praying, they become a part of our own reality. In writing down their prayers to God, the Jews gave themselves not only to God, but also to all those who would follow them by lifting again the prayers they first voiced and sang. They gifted a people beyond themselves and even beyond their own tradition with some of their own spirit. . . . Praying the Psalms gently speaks to us of wider communities than our own Christian community, of other peoples who belong to God, of other languages breathed in the presence of God's own Spirit. The Psalms, even while speaking of and through and in our most personal of feelings, lift us to that wider community of God, joining us to it even as we are deeply ourselves.

Marjorie Heweitt Suchocki, *In God's Presence: Theological Reflections on Prayer* (St. Louis: Chalice, 1996), 41.

NOTES

[1] Hans Conzelmann, *Acts of the Apostles* (Hermeneia; Philadelphia: Fortress, 1987), 29.

[2] Luke Timothy Johnson, *The Acts of the Apostles* (SacPag 5; Collegeville MN: Liturgical Press, 1992), 79–82.

[3] Ernst Haenchen, *The Acts of the Apostles: A Commentary* (Philadelphia: Westminster, 1971), 216; F. J. Foakes Jackson and Kirsopp Lake, *The Beginnings of Christianity: The Acts of the Apostles*, 5 vols. (Grand Rapids MI: Baker, 1979), 4.43.

[4] See John B. Polhill, *Acts* (NAC 26; Nashville: Broadman, 1992), 143n45.

[5] Marion L. Soards, *The Speeches in Acts: Their Content, Context, and Concerns* (Louisville KY: Westminster/John Knox, 1994), 46.

[6] Ibid., 49.

[7] Polhill, *Acts*, 152.

[8] Johnson, *Acts*, 87.

THEY DID NOT CEASE TEACHING JESUS AS THE CHRIST

Acts 5:1-42

COMMENTARY

This chapter connects well with Acts 3–4. The story of the greed of Ananias and Sapphira offers a contrast to the preceding story of the generosity of Barnabas (4:36-37). The hearing before the Sanhedrin continues the conflict between the opposing leaders of Israel initiated in Acts 4. Acts 5 divides into three larger units: the story of Ananias and Sapphira (5:1-11), a third Lukan summary of the life of the early community (5:12-16), and the second hearing before the council (5:17-42). Cumulatively, the stories make clear to the readers who the true leaders of the restored Israel are.

Tempting the Spirit of the Lord, 5:1-11

The narrative of Acts introduces readers to Ananias ("Yahweh is gracious") and Sapphira ("beautiful"). Both names are quite ironic, given the plot of the story. Ananias sold some land (*ktēma* denotes real property) and, with Sapphira's knowledge, "kept back" (*enosphisato*, vv. 2-3) a portion of the proceeds. The verb translated as "kept back" implies embezzlement and is used in contexts to denote the keeping for oneself that which belongs to or has been entrusted to another. The verb is used in the LXX to describe Achan's action; he kept for himself some of the captured goods that were to be devoted to Yahweh (Josh 7:1).

Use of this verb, implying that Ananias *embezzled* the proceeds, creates some tension with v. 4, which clearly states that after the land was sold it remained "under Ananias' authority" or "at his disposal" (NRSV). If the proceeds remained at his disposal, how can one call it embezzlement that he retained some of the proceeds? Conzelmann explains the tension, stating that v. 4 is due to Lukan editing; the author wanted to emphasize the *voluntary* character of such disposal.[1] This does not really explain the gap on the *literary* level. Thus, Polhill has argued that one must assume either that it was *expected* that one was to devote all or none of the proceeds of a land sale or that Ananias had promised to devote the whole amount to the apostles' care.[2] Another possibility is that Luke employed the verb *enosphisato* because he wanted to draw readers' attentions to the relationship between the stories of Achan and Ananias and Sapphira.

To lay something at the apostles' feet served to represent one's recognition of their authority as the leaders of the restored Israel and one's commitment to this restored community (see commentary on 4:32-37). Thus, Ananias's act of laying only a part of the proceeds at Peter's feet (v. 2) shows his lack of total allegiance and commitment, both to the apostles and the community. This has dire consequences.

Peter's series of questions in vv. 3-4 levels some specific charges against Ananias. He asks "why Satan has filled his heart," which carries with it the harsh charge that Ananias is moved by the enemy. Perhaps readers will compare Ananias with Judas, into whom it was said that Satan entered (Luke 22:3). Both are said to have been moved by Satan *and money and property* (cf. Luke 22:5; Acts 1:18, 25). And yet the charge of satanic "filling" does not excuse Ananias, for Peter can also ask "How is it that *you* have contrived this deed in your heart?" (v. 4b). Twice, Ananias is accused of lying, once to the Spirit (v. 3) and once to God (v. 4). This lie consisted of his keeping back from the community and the apostolic leadership part of the proceeds (v. 3b).

Perhaps Ananias's mistake was to assume that in dealing with the apostles and the community, he was dealing with mere human beings and institutions. The congregation of faith is the renewed, eschatological, and prophetic community of the Spirit. The apostles are its God-appointed leaders. Peter demonstrates his authority by showing that, through the prophetic Spirit, he, like Jesus, *the* prophet, can see people's hearts (cf. Luke 5:22; 7:39; 9:47; 24:38). Behind human deception and confrontation lies the significant cosmic struggle between good and evil, God/Spirit and Satan. Ananias simply did not take the moral character of the world in which he lived seriously enough.

Ananias's punishment is swift and severe: death. Luke's terse comment on the community's reaction, "great fear," communicates the people's awareness that they had witnessed the judgment of God. Psychological or physiological explanations may be interesting for modern readers (e.g., "Ananias died of shock"), but the narrator appears uninterested in so-called secondary causes. Luke's description of Ananias's burial is as terse as his description of Ananias's demise: the young men wrapped him up, carried him out, and buried him. Ananias's story is through. As E. Haenchen notes, "all this is handled without pity, for we are in the presence of the divine punishment which should be witnessed in fear and trembling, but not with Aristotelian fear and pity."[3]

What happened for the next few hours, where Sapphira has been, why she has now come before Peter, and how the demise of her husband has been kept from her, are all gaps within the narrative that may prove interesting for speculation, but are not all that significant to make sense of the story. In v. 8, Luke allows Sapphira to hang herself and prove with her own words the charge the narrator leveled against her in v. 2: she was a co-conspirator with her husband in the deception. She and he "agreed together to tempt the Spirit of the Lord" (v. 9). In the Old Testament, the verb used for "tempt" (*peirasai*) consistently denotes the actions of the people of Israel in the wilderness (e.g., Exod 17:2; Deut 6:16; Pss 78:18, 41, 56; 95:8-9).

This verbal echo offers yet another invitation to readers to compare the story of the early eschatological community with their ancestors of ancient Israel. Israel of old often did not embrace the liberating salvation that God offered, but responded by pressing God's limits and seeing just how much they could get away with. So, too, elements within the community now experiencing the liberating salvation of this liberating God do the same. And the result is the same: judgment.

Sapphira now falls at Peter's feet. She has fully submitted to his power and authority, for now it is not her money that lays at his feet but her corpse (v. 10a). The description of her burial is just as terse as that of her husband's (v. 10b). And the community's reaction is just as appropriate as it was when word of Ananias's death spread: "great fear came upon the whole church" (v. 11).

This is Luke's first use of the word "church." Perhaps he has used it here to provide yet one more echo with the stories of Israel's first story of salvation. The term *ekklēsia* is used consistently throughout Deuteronomy to denote the community of Yahweh, God's people (cf. Deut 4:10; 9:10; 18:16; 23:2, 3, 8, 9; 31:12, 29, 30). Like its ancestors, this restored community is to fear God (cf. Deut 4:10; 31:12). The "restored Israel" has no less an obligation to be holy than the Israel of old. As this story makes clear, such holiness is manifested in truthfulness and integrity both toward God and

God's people. Further, apostolic leadership, like that of Moses and Joshua of old, involves not only the announcement of God's salvation and blessing, but also the declaration of God's judgment when it is called for. In Luke's story world, however, the actual dispensing of the judgment is left to God (see "Connections").

Believers Were Added to the Lord, 5:12-16

These verses offer the third and final of the so-called summaries found in the Jerusalem section of the narrative. [Lukan Summaries] Generally, this summary differs from the others in two respects: (1) it summarizes the life of the community from the perspective of its impact on outsiders, and (2) it emphasizes the miraculous dimension of the community's witness.

Commentators regularly note that v. 12a connects easily with vv. 15-16, thereby making vv. 12b-14 read like a redactional intrusion.[4] However, people's reaction in vv. 13-16—be it "keeping their distance," holding the apostles and community in high honor, becoming believers, or bringing their sick—is a response to the "signs and wonders" that the apostles were performing "among the people" (v. 12a; see [Signs and Wonders]). In this way the whole summary hangs together.

The apostles' performance of "signs and wonders" offers explicit word that the prayer of 4:30 has been answered. Such signs and wonders point to the apostles as inspired prophetic persons who fulfill the prophetic word of Joel (cf. Acts 2:19). Miracles demonstrate the liberating power of God, through which God releases people from the forces that corrupt their lives, be it sin (cf. 2:38; 3:19), sickness (cf. 3:1-10), or the satanic (demonic; cf. 5:16). This summary highlights a major theme of the narrative of 3:1–4:22: the people find in the apostolic leadership of Israel the power to offer the liberation that comes from God's reign and is made effective in the gospel.

The people recognize this, for they bring those who are bound by disease and demons to these apostolic leaders (vv. 15-16), not to the "official" temple leadership of Israel. Verse 12b ironically

---

Lukan Summaries

There are three major summaries in Acts (2:42-47; 4:32-35; 5:12-16) and a number of minor ones (5:42; 6:7; 9:31; 12:24; 19:20). They function in at least two ways. First, they "provide a sense of fullness to a narrative otherwise low in specific factual content" (Johnson, 9). Acts 1–5 offers only a handful of stories and accompanying speeches: the selection of Mattathias, Pentecost (with speech), the healing of the man at the temple (with speech), the arrest (and re-arrest) of the apostles and the hearings before the Sanhedrin (with speeches), and the stories of the generosity of Barnabas and duplicity of Ananias and Sapphira. Yet the reader senses a much fuller picture of early community life and history. The summaries give readers that sense of fullness. Second, summaries provide idealized portraits of early community life, which offer a context for assessing specific incidents within the narrative. For example, the duplicity of Ananias and Sapphira is even more reproachable against a background of the ideal of community sharing. Or the healing of the man at the temple, in light of the summary of 5:12-16, is seen not as an isolated incident, but an *example* of regular apostolic activity.

Luke Timothy Johnson, *The Acts of the Apostles* (SacPag 5; Collegeville MN: Liturgical Press, 1992).

reminds readers that a favorite place for the apostles to gather was on the priests' turf, Solomon's Portico, which was part of the temple complex. Modern readers may be confused or offended at the notion of people being healed by Peter's shadow (v. 15). Ancients believed the shadow was an extension of the personality and power of the person,[5] a view that the narrator assumes. It is appropriate to understand that biblical writers, inspired as they may have been, made sense and wrote of things in the contexts of their lives and accompanying worldviews. [Inspiration]

Verses 12b-14 create some confusion, or at least ambiguity, for interpreters. Who is denoted by the "all" of v. 12, all the apostles or all the Christian community?[6] Who are "the rest" of v. 13a? Does it denote everyone other than the apostles, be they Christian or non-Christian, who in reverent fear of the apostles' power "keep their distance" (one reading of the verb *kollasthai*)? Or do "the rest" refer only to the non-Christians, who think it best to keep their distance from the whole Christian community? These issues cannot be resolved definitively.

Clearly, the apostles, and perhaps the whole Christian community, are making an impact on the people of Jerusalem and the surrounding areas (see v. 16a). Such an impact is closely related to their power. Such power both repels and attracts, like anything beyond the ordinary. [The Awesome Power of the Holy] The same power that urges people to "keep their distance" also leads them to hold the apostolic leadership, and perhaps community, in high honor. It leads some to believe in the Messiah who stands behind this power. It leads still others to bring their sick, in hopes that they too can be liberated. One looking for the awesome and liberating power of God can find it in the leadership and community of Jesus the Messiah. Given this, what value has the "official" temple leadership? Not much,

---

Inspiration

One can understand inspiration in a manner that lifts human authors out of their social and cultural context, including the assumptions and presuppositions of that context. John Goldingay observes that the incarnation makes clear that God is quite content to speak God's word in a specific cultural and historical context:

> When God speaks, by a prophet or by a Son, inevitably this speaking takes place in a context, and any generalizations of absolute validity have to allow for that historicality. In becoming a member of a certain race at a certain time, the Word undertook a self-emptying that involved speaking as someone of a particular day and culture (239).

Surely, if this is true of the incarnate Word, it is true of the written Word and its authors.

John Goldingay, *Models of Scripture* (Grand Rapids MI: Eerdmans, 1994).

The Awesome Power of the Holy

The Holy, the most basic meaning of which is "Other," has the distinctive power both to repel and attract. This is true across time and culture. Extraordinary phenomena, things outside the ordinary and everyday, are "holy," set apart things. Think of how people are both repulsed by and drawn to such things: a burning home, a crime scene, video footage of scenes from 9/11, and the list could go on. The apostles radiate a kind of "holy," awe-full power that has the same paradoxical effect on those who witness their power. Rudolf Otto describes this paradoxical quality of the Holy as follows:

> The daemonic-divine object may appear to the mind an object of horror and dread, but at the same time it is no less something that allures with a potent charm, and the creature, who trembles before it, utterly cowed and cast down, has always at the same time the impulse to turn to it, nay even to make it somehow his own.

Rudolf Otto, *The Idea of the Holy: An Inquiry in the Non-Rational Factor in the Idea of the Divine and Its Relation to the Rational* (Oxford: Oxford University Press, 1923), 31.

and those of the Sanhedrin seem well aware of how insignificant they appear when compared to this rival circle of leadership.

Worthy to Suffer Dishonor for the Name, 5:17-42

This long section can be further divided into four smaller units: the arrest, escape, and recapture of the apostles (vv. 17-26); the hearing before the Sanhedrin (vv. 27-32); Gamaliel's speech (vv. 33-39); and the release of the apostles (vv. 40-42).

Elusive Apostles, vv. 17-26

The section begins by reminding readers that the high priest and his allies, the Sadducees, strongly oppose the followers of Jesus. [School] They are filled with "jealousy" (v. 17b), indicating that their motives for rounding up the apostles are petty. They appear to recognize that though they make up much of the "official leadership" of Israel, they are, in fact, ineffective when compared with the apostles. These officials might also have feared the political implications of the messianic message taught to the rabble on temple grounds. The political implications of the Christian movement may form a subtle subtext of this confrontation, given that Gamaliel will compare Jesus and his followers to two political rebels (vv. 36-37).

God, however, is on the side of the apostolic leadership. God sends an angel to open the doors and release the apostles. This miraculous escape is the first of three escape narratives of a similar type (cf. 12:6-11; 16:26-31). Release with the help of angels is perhaps ironic, given that the apostles' primary opponents (the Sadducees, v. 17) may not believe in angels (cf. 23:8). The apostles are told to go to the temple and proclaim the specific message that can bring "life" to the people ("speak to the all the words of *this* life," v. 20b).

A primary issue involves the identity of the real leadership of Israel. Appropriately, the apostles are sent to the temple. This space was the center of the high priest's power. Possession of the temple gave legitimacy to one's claims to authority. By speaking in the area of the temple, the apostles show themselves to be the *legitimate* authority figures over the people of Israel. [The Temple and Legitimacy]

School

AΩ Acts 5:17 refers to "the *hairesis* of the Sadducees." The Greek word literally denotes "choice," from the verb "to choose" (*hairetizō*). The NRSV translates the term "sect," while the RSV uses "party." While "sect" is technically appropriate, it could imply something pejorative in contemporary culture. "Party" might imply something more formal and institutional, like a political party. Ancient philosophers used the term to denote the various "choices" of philosophical *schools* one could join. Josephus used the term to denote the various movements within first-century Judaism (e.g., Pharisees, Sadducees, Essenes, etc.). Luke used the term to denote Sadducees (5:17), Pharisees (15:5; 26:5), and Christians (24:5, 14; 28:22). The word "school" seems appropriate, comparable to the phrase "school of thought." In New Testament epistles and especially later church history the term comes to take on a thoroughly pejorative meaning: "heretic" denoted one who chose the *wrong* things to believe.

Hans Dieter Betz, "Heresy and Orthodoxy in the NT," *ABD* 3.144–47; Jeffrey S. Lamp, "Heresy," *EDB* 577.

The Temple and Legitimacy

Jewish culture assumed a close association between legitimate authority and control of the temple. After the exile, Zerubbabel's legitimacy as the ruler of the Jewish people was associated with his rebuilding of the temple (Zech 4:6-10; cf. 6:9-13). The Hasmonean family, while fighting the Syrians, secured the legitimacy of their rule by rededicating the temple back to God and, later, holding the office of high priest, the ruler of the temple (1 Macc 4:36-61; 14:41-49). Herod the Great refurbished the Jerusalem temple, attempting to emulate other "kings of the Jews" who had preceded him and built temples (Solomon and Zerubbabel). Jesus' first public act upon entering Jerusalem was to seize control of the temple grounds, even if only symbolically (Mark 11:15-17). Awareness of this association allows modern readers to grasp the significance of Acts' portraying the apostles as free to carry on their work on the temple grounds.

This picture of legitimate authority is enhanced by their arrival at "daybreak," just when the people would be let in to observe the morning whole offering service. This service commenced at first light and was to be presided over by the *sagan* (see [Captain of the Temple]). As the worshipers of Israel gather for morning worship, entering with them are their true leaders who are teaching Israel what it must hear to find real life (v. 21a).

The scene switches to the chamber of the "council and the whole body of elders of Israel" (v. 21b, NRSV). The NRSV translation may be misleading. NRSV renders the Greek phrase "all the *gerousia*" as "the whole body of elders," implying *two* groups of rulers, "the council" and "the elders." The term *gerousia* was actually the older word used to denote the ruling council before the word "sanhedrin" became the common nomenclature. A more accurate translation would be "the Sanhedrin, that is, all the ruling council of the children of Israel," but "Luke uses [the two terms] in combination for sake of solemnity."[7] Who represents the true leadership of Israel? The apostles or the "Sanhedrin, that is, all the ruling council of the children of Israel"?

This contest of leaders must be delayed, for the "temple police" (v. 22) cannot find the prisoners. The term translated as "temple police" (*hyperetai*) is used in Acts only here and in v. 26, both times to denote the assistants of the "captain of the temple" (cf. vv. 24, 26). These "temple police" may be the "priests" who accompanied the captain of the temple and arrested the apostles in Acts 4:1. These forces from the staff of the captain of the temple confirm with their befuddled words of v. 23 the reality of the miracle narrated in v. 19. Ironically, "hostile witnesses" confirm that the prisoners are not there, though the prison is secure and well guarded.

The captain of the temple is present at the hearing (v. 24). Apparently, he has not been where he was supposed to be, overseeing the morning whole offering, for he knows nothing of what is going on at the temple precincts, until he, along with the rest of the council, is informed by a messenger (v. 25). Historically, this creates some problems, for the captain of the temple should have been at the morning service and, hence, should not have been unaware of the preaching being done by the apostles at the break of day! On the literary and dramatic level, however, the absence of the captain of the temple is wrought with irony. For while he is shirking his responsibilities of overseeing the morning whole offering, shirking these tasks because of his determination to silence the apostles, the apostles stand on *his* space teaching the people of Israel. Who are the real leaders of Israel? Who currently staffs the temple? Who is teaching the people at the temple? The "official leadership"? No. These roles are filled by the apostles.

Gingerly, therefore, the captain of the temple must go with his police staff to bring back the apostles for the hearing to continue (v. 26). The scene is almost humorous. The captain of the temple, until recently unaware of what was even going on in the precincts for which he was responsible, must go and carefully bring the apostles back to trial. Though Luke does not say it, the captain succeeds only because the apostles let him. If he could not use violence for fear of being stoned by his own people, just what was his plan for recapturing the apostles had they not been willing? It is clear that he did not have one. It is equally clear that the apostles are in charge here.

Defying the Council, vv. 27-32

The scene moves back to the council, where the apostles now stand in the middle of the semicircle, surrounded by their accusers. The high priest carries out the interrogation (vv. 27-28). In Luke's narrative world, readers need to imagine the speaker to be Annas (cf. 4:6). Verse 28a reminds readers of the Sanhedrin's prohibition of teaching in Jesus' name (cf. 4:18). Peter and John had said then that this was a command they could not obey (4:19). The fact that the apostles have filled Jerusalem with their teaching (v. 28b) provides for the high priest the evidence he needs that the prohibition was ignored. Ironically, readers hear from the high priest's own mouth that the city over which the Sanhedrin is to rule is, in fact, out of their control. The very thing they forbade from happening has happened. The word cannot be stopped.

The high priest also accuses the apostles of bringing "this man's blood upon us" (v. 28b). The phrase is idiomatic for "accusing us of Jesus' death" (cf. Gen 4:10-11; 2 Sam 1:16; Hos 12:14). It is true that on one public occasion, the apostolic preaching accused the Jewish leadership of having a hand in Jesus' death (see 3:17). And, privately, before the council, Peter made the accusation very explicitly (4:10-11). But the apostolic preaching also included the invitation to repentance (cf. 3:19-21). In short, the indictment of the rulers is not presented in the narrative of Acts as an attempt to bring God's wrathful judgment down upon them (though this appears to be how the high priest hears it), but to point out their error that they might turn back to God.

Peter responds not by offering any specific defense to the actual charges, but by preaching the gospel. The gospel is his and the other apostles' only defense (vv. 29-32). He reiterates what he said in 4:19: the apostles' loyalty must be to God. The kerygmatic summary is quite terse, for the reader by now knows well the essential outline of the story (see [Kerygma]).

One new feature is the description of Jesus' death with the phrase "whom you killed by hanging him on a tree" (v. 30), an echo of Deuteronomy 21:22-23. With this echo comes more irony. The Deuteronomic text makes clear that only one guilty of a sin worthy of death is to receive this punishment. Through this biblical allusion Peter offers his assessment of the rulers' estimation of Jesus: a sinner worthy of death. The irony is that through this Jesus, God offers repentance and forgiveness of sins—he offers "salvation." It is appropriate that Jesus is given the title "Savior" in this context (cf. Luke 2:11; Acts 13:23). Through Jesus, whom the leadership condemned as a sinner, God offers to all of Israel, even the leadership, forgiveness of its sins, including that of killing God's anointed one.

Verse 32 reiterates the apostolic witness to the truth of these things (cf. 1:8, 22; 2:32; 3:15) and adds the witness of the Holy Spirit. To those who respond in obedience to the kerygma, God grants the prophetic Spirit, and this Spirit also serves to authenticate for the believer the truth of the gospel's message of life and salvation (cf. Rom 8:14-17).

Gamaliel Speaks, vv. 33-39

Gamaliel attempts to calm the potentially volatile situation. [Gamaliel] The larger council wants to execute the apostles, but the revered teacher urges caution. [Death Penalty] Gamaliel presents a deliberative speech (see [Types of Rhetorical Persuasion]), urging the council to take a certain course of action: "consider carefully what you propose to do with these men" (v. 35). Gamaliel compares the movement of Jesus and his followers to other revolutionary groups,

Gamaliel

His name means "recompense of God." He was the grandson of the great teacher Hillel, the founder of one of two leading scribal schools of thought (Shammai was the founder of the other influential school). His son Simon was a leader of the revolt against Rome (Josephus, *J. W.* 4.159). Toward the end of the first century, his grandson, Gamaliel II, was the "prince" (*Nasi*) of the reorganized, post-revolt, Sanhedrin. This information allows modern readers to appreciate the stature of this man and to understand why Luke could portray him as having such influence over the Sanhedrin.

Death Penalty

The Sanhedrin's determination to carry out the death penalty is historically problematic, for there is debate whether this body had such power. John 18:31 indicates that this body had no such power, as does rabbinic literature. Texts such as Acts 5:33 and 7:58 (the killing of Stephen), and the execution of James, the brother of Jesus, under the priesthood of Ananus, the son of the high priest Annas of Acts 4:6 (Josephus, *Ant.* 20.200–201), make firm conclusions difficult to render.

J. Bradley Chance, "Sanhedrin," *MDB* 795–96.

Theudas and Judas

Josephus writes much about Judas: "But of the fourth sect of Jewish philosophy, Judas the Galilean was the author. . . . They have an inviolable attachment to liberty; and say that God is to be their only Ruler and Lord" (*Ant.* 18.23). "Under his [Coponious's] administration it was that a certain Galilean, whose name was Judas, prevailed with his countrymen to revolt; and said they were cowards if they would endure to pay a tax to the Romans" (*J. W.* 2.118). This matches well with Acts 5:37. The census to which Gamaliel refers is directly linked with the taxes that Judas exhorted Jews not to pay.

The problem is with Theudas. Josephus (*Ant.* 20.97–99) refers to a certain Theudas who was a rebel against Rome during the procuratorship of Fadus (AD 44–46), *after* the activity of Judas the Galilean and, more importantly, several years *after* Gamaliel supposedly gave this speech. (Fadus came to power after the death of Herod Agrippa and Herod does not die in Luke's narrative until Acts 12.)

Solutions to this riddle are very much shaped by ideological/theological assumptions about the nature of Scripture and its historical veracity. Interpreters assuming that Luke could or would not have "made up a speech" are compelled to say that the Theudas of Gamaliel's speech is a figure unknown in other historical annals, a statement that can neither be proved nor disproved. Those who find this line of argument untenable and are willing to allow for Lukan authorship of the speeches argue that he was simply confused regarding the order of Theudas and Judas, a confusion betrayed by the presence of a historical blunder that it would have been impossible for Gamaliel to have made.

those of Theudas and Judas (vv. 36-37). This comparison shows that Gamaliel does not adequately understand the kind of liberation and salvation that Jesus offers. For Gamaliel the comparisons with the two revolutionaries are obvious. [Theudas and Judas] All three would-be leaders gathered followers about themselves. All three were killed. In the case of Theudas and Judas, their followers "disappeared," being "dispersed" and "scattered."

Gamaliel then applies the comparison to the present situation. If "this plan" being spoken of by the apostles is of human origin, it will come to nothing, just like those schemes of Theudas, Judas, and their followers. And if it is of divine origin, the Sanhedrin will not be able to stop it anyway. In fact, opposing a movement that is of God may render the council guilty of opposing God (v. 39).

The speech could have a significant impact on first-century Christian readers. A revered Jewish leader has laid forth a clear criterion by which to judge whether a movement is of God or of human origin: if it is of God, it endures; if it is of human origin, it perishes and is scattered. As Luke's original readers read this narrative sometime in the last third of the first century, two facts confronted them: (1) the Christian movement was still enduring; (2) Jerusalem and the temple had been destroyed and the city's inhabitants killed or scattered among the nations (cf. Luke 19:43-44; 21:24). The very Sanhedrin that Gamaliel addresses had been disbanded and was in the process of having to reorganize itself in the city of Yavneh. By the very criterion Gamaliel presented, it was clear which movement was of God and which one was not. The movement of the apostles still lived on. The priestly aristocracy, the Jerusalem Sanhedrin, and the temple were no more. The implications of Gamaliel's words are quite clear: it was the Sanhedrin, and especially its priestly Sadducean leadership, that stood in opposition to God. It was the apostles who were doing the things of God. It is clear wherein resides the true leadership of "the vineyard" of Israel (cf. Luke 20:9-19). [A Rabbinic Parallel to Acts 5:38-39]

A Rabbinic Parallel to Acts 5:38-39

"Rabbi Johanan the sandal maker said: Every assembly which is for the sake of Heaven will in the end be established, and every assembly which is not for the sake of Heaven will in the end not be established" (*Aboth* 4:13). This rabbi lived during the first half of the second century, so he post-dates Gamaliel by a several generations. Still, the saying shows a sentiment similar to the counsel of Gamaliel.

The Release of the Apostles, vv. 40-42

The council follows the advice of Gamaliel, not so much, one suspects, because they have given serious consideration to the possibility that the apostles might be of God, but because they were so confident that the apostles were not. The Sanhedrin did, however, have the apostles flogged, which is no light punishment, assuming this to be the infamous thirty-nine lashes. Readers are naïve to imagine the apostles charging out of the council chamber and proceeding directly to temple, jumping for joy that they could suffer for Jesus. More realistically, the apostles were carried out and returned to the temple when their wounds had healed.

Two key points remain as this chapter concludes. First, suffering dishonor for the name is often necessary when one is truly on the side of God. Regularly, in the short term, those opposed to God's purposes have the power to make those doing God's work suffer. The vindication of God's people, like the vindication of Jesus, does not always come immediately or in ways that are apparent to those abusing God's people. Second, it is significant that, as the chapter ends, the apostles are *still* doing the very thing that got them into trouble in the first place, and they had twice been forbidden to do by "the powers that be": they are teaching and preaching *in the temple* that Jesus is the Messiah. The ruling priests' turf is still held by the new leadership of Israel.

CONNECTIONS

Reflections on this text for the life of the community cannot avoid the troubling story of Ananias and Sapphira. While we cannot ignore the harsh judgment against the couple, we should focus attention first on the *cause* of the judgment.

Permeating the story is the importance of being a person of truth and integrity. Being truthful means more than being honest about this or that particular thing. "Truth" and "integrity" go together,

Integrity

Stephen L. Carter says that integrity "requires three steps: (1) *discerning* what is right and what is wrong; (2) *acting* on what you have discerned, even at personal cost; and (3) *saying openly* that you are acting on your understanding of right from wrong" (7).

Ananias and Sapphira offer a clear contrast with the apostles on the issue of integrity. These two people failed to discern what was right, acted instead on what was wrong, and then failed to say openly (and honestly) what they had done. In contrast, the apostles discerned that it was "right" to obey God and speak in the name of Jesus, acted on this belief at great personal risk, and openly declared their intentions and motives to their interrogators.

Stephen L. Carter, *Integrity* (New York: Basic Books, 1996).

for the latter implies a wholeness and consistency of character that complements the virtue of truthfulness, understood in its broadest sense. [Integrity] Ananias and Sapphira were people without truth; they acted with neither honesty nor wholeness and consistency of character. They wanted to belong to the renewed people of God, yet they wanted to live like the people of darkness. The charges leveled against Ananias and Sapphira (vv. 3, 5, 9) make this clear.

Truth, understood in its fullest sense, is *the* hallmark of the community of God's people. This derives from the fact that truth is a key hallmark of the very God to whom God's people claim allegiance. God is true (John 3:33; 8:26). Jesus is "full of grace and truth" (John 1:14). The Holy Spirit who fills and inspires the renewed community of faith is "the Spirit of truth" (John 14:17; 15:26; 16:13; 1 John 5:6). Conversely, the Adversary of God and God's people stands on the opposite side of the truth (John 8:44). Consequently, the people of God are to be people of truth. The very message that defines our identity, the gospel, is "the word of truth" (Col 1:5). As a people, we are made holy and pure, marked off as God's people, by the truth (John 17:17, 19; 1 Pet 1:22). The truth is part of the armor of God that protects God's people from evil (Eph 6:15). Thus, we are to put away all falsehood and speak the truth to our neighbors (Eph 4:25), though we are to speak such truth with love (Eph 4:15).

Our devotion to truth is such that Jesus exhorts disciples not to fall into the snare of believing that "swearing" to tell the truth somehow binds us to a higher standard of integrity than simply letting our "yes" be yes and our "no" be no (Matt 5:33-37). People of integrity are truthful all the time. When Jesus exhorts his followers to be perfect, even as God is perfect (Matt 5:48), he is calling upon them to be imitators of God and to live in ways that are holistic and consistent: to be people of truth and integrity.

When we encounter a shocking story like this one, the very experience of the shock should allow us to feel just how crucial words such as "consistency," "wholeness," and "truthfulness" are to the Christian community's character. Initially, rather than side-step the shocking judgment, we should allow it to make its full impact on us and move us to feel just how abhorrent the lack of integrity is to the God we claim to follow.

But, then, what are we to do with such stories of harsh judgment? Dare we use such stories to sanction harsh treatment toward those who violate the standards of integrity and truth that are to shape the faith community? Do we read the story against its grain, challenging its message of wrath and judgment? [Resisting Reading] To a great extent, the way one answers such a question will say much about the interpreter. Those whose experiences of life and faith lead to a relishing of stories such as this one will not be persuaded to think differently by appeals to mercy and grace. And those who feel repelled by such a story will likely not feel better to be reminded that the New Testament speaks of judgment as well as mercy.

Resisting Reading

"Resisting reading is adversarial reading. It is reading against the grain of the text. It is reading in conflict with other possible readings of the text. . . . Persons professing biblical faith need not be fearful that resisting reading of the Bible is somehow unfaithful reading. To the contrary, one could argue that the most faithful reading of all is resisting reading. Some of the noblest moments in Jewish and Christian history are moments of resistance to officially approved oppression, injustice, or traditions gone sterile." (75)

Robert M. Fowler, "Reader-Response Criticism: Figuring Mark's Reader," in *Mark and Method: New Approaches in Biblical Studies*, ed. J. C. Anderson and S. D. Moore (Minneapolis: Fortress, 1992).

Perhaps an appropriate response is embodied in those characters within the story who, like readers, witnessed the judgment of the couple. "Great fear" descended upon the church (5:11). In the aftermath, many were both drawn to and wary of the apostles (5:13-14). Stories of terror, such as that of Ananias and Sapphira, create within us, the church today, the same kind of ambivalence that struck our spiritual ancestors. We are repelled by images reminding us that, indeed, "the wrath of God is revealed from heaven against all ungodliness and wickedness of people who . . . suppress the *truth*" (Rom 1:18). And yet the awe-full portrait of God's wrath in the opening chapters of Romans provides the meaningful context for hearing the words of grace that come with the gospel. Similarly, terrible texts such as this one of Ananias and Sapphira remind us that God's forgiving grace stems not from a deity who has simply grown weary of demanding consistency and wholeness from God's people. Occasionally, we need reminding that the God of grace is the God of judgment. Occasionally the church needs reminding that God expects that those who say that they live in Christ should walk even as he walked (1 John 2:6); and the way of our God and God's Christ is truth. And thus we are drawn to God, seeking salvation, grounded in God's mercy, while, at the same time, working out our own salvation in fear and trembling (Phil 2:12).

It is imperative to note the judgment of Ananias and Sapphira is a judgment *from God.* Peter makes the charge. God exacts the judgment. The text does not invite us to help God out as all-too-willing instruments of divine wrath. When we take this task upon ourselves, we begin to resemble more the religious leaders of the Sanhedrin.

Divine sovereignty guides the action and plot of the story of God's people. Through Gamaliel the narrative lays down a rather simple criterion to know whether things are of God or of human design: that which is of God endures, and that which is not of God does not endure. Implied here is a rather simple faith in God's providential participation in the long haul of history. It is our task, so says even Gamaliel, to "leave alone" those whom we think are on the wrong side of God's ways (5:38). Jesus offered similar advice in Matthew's parable of the wheat and the weeds when the householder counsels his zealous servants not to attempt to separate the wheat from the weeds, but leave them both until the harvest (Matt 13:28-29). Even the Pastoral Epistles, hardly known for their irenic spirit, offer similar advice: to avoid controversies, dissensions, quarrels and to admonish factious persons once or twice then have nothing more to do with them—in other words, to leave them alone (Titus 3:9-10).

When we apply this criterion, we are compelled to come to at least one conclusion: *Many* religious traditions *other than our own* must be of God or at the very least—should we trust God's providence—serve some meaningful purpose as they continue to exist and even thrive. Look around. We do not see *only* our own tradition alive and well. We see many that we oppose and that we know oppose us. It is tempting to follow the instincts of the Sanhedrin and ignore the counsel of Gamaliel.

The Crusades, the Inquisition, the Salem witch hunts, Fundamentalist/Modernists wars, and the emergence of strange parasitic creatures that blend their racism or homophobia with godly conviction all bear witness that the world is filled with those who love God too much to follow the guidance of God's word on this matter. Like the Sanhedrin, the best many can do is to listen to sober counsel, only to feel the need to lay a few licks on the heretics just to be sure that they get the message.

But in the story of Acts, which is permeated with a calm confidence in the divine sovereignty of the Author of both life and history, it is consistently those who take the matter of God's judgment into their own hands who come off as the villains. There is simply no way to avoid this reading. The true people of God are the victims of the abuse of the so-called righteous. The faithful "suffer dishonor for the name." The self-assured righteous "inflict pain for the name."

NOTES

[1] Hans Conzelmann, *Acts of the Apostles* (Hermeneia; Philadelphia: Fortress, 1987), 38.

[2] John B. Polhill, *Acts* (NAC 26; Nashville: Broadman, 1992), 156.

[3] Ernst Haenchen, *The Acts of the Apostles: A Commentary* (Philadelphia: Westminster, 1971), 239.

[4] Ibid., 243.

[5] Polhill, *Acts*, 164.

[6] Luke Timothy Johnson, *The Acts of the Apostles* (SacPag 5; Collegeville MN: Liturgical Press, 1992), 95 understands the text to refer to the apostles. Most other commentators surveyed understand it to refer to the whole of the community.

[7] Ibid., 97.

STEPHEN: FULL OF GRACE
AND POWER

Acts 6:1–8:3

COMMENTARY

This story brings to completion the first section of Acts, that period focusing on the "witness to Jerusalem" (cf. 1:8). This period of witness ends on a tragic note, with the lynching (or execution?) of Stephen. And yet, as readers have grown accustomed to seeing, out of such tragedy, the gospel moves onward. This section has four parts of unequal length: the selection of the seven (6:1-7), the seizing of Stephen (6:8–7:1), Stephen's speech (7:2-53), and the killing of Stephen (7:54–8:3).

Seven Men of Good Repute, 6:1-7

The narrative begins with a general time reference ("in those days," v. 1), allowing readers to date these events to the early 30s. The number of disciples was increasing. The neglect of the widows in the daily distribution may have been caused by this numerical influx. [Widows] [Daily Distribution] The story introduces two groups within the early Jerusalem community, the Hellenists and the Hebrews. The narrative leaves the impression that the two groups were primarily

---

Widows

Granting that the Hellenist women of Acts 6 were of the Diaspora and had migrated to Judea, the means provided by Jewish law or tradition to care for them might have proved difficult to practice. For example, biblical law prescribed levirate marriage (Deut 25:5-10), whereby the brother of the widow's late husband was to marry the widow. The widow could also return to her original home or join the household of her in-laws. Or she could remarry someone outside her late husband's family. But if these widows were immigrants from the Diaspora, the brothers or larger household of her deceased husband or her original

family might still have lived far beyond the borders of Judea, making it virtually impossible for these to care for her. While the widows could have remarried, in some circles of Judaism and early Christianity, remaining a widow was considered an act of piety (see Judg 8:1-8; Luke 2:36-38; 1 Cor 7:39-40; 1 Tim 5:9). At any rate, care for the widow on the part of the community was not contingent upon whether all other means of support had been exhausted.

S. Safrai, "Home and Family," in *Jewish People in the First Century: Historical Geography, Political History, Social, Cultural and Religious Life and Institutions*, ed. S. Safrai and M. Stern, 2 vols. (Philadelphia: Fortress, 1976), 2.728–92; esp. 2.787–91.

Daily Distribution

Jewish practice provided a means to distribute food to the poor. One means was to distribute weekly funds to poor *residents* in order for them to *purchase* food. This was called *quppah*, so named after "the box" that was used to collect the funds. A daily distribution of food was provided for non-residents and was called *tamhuy*, named after the "tray" on which foodstuffs were placed for distribution (Jeremias, 130–32). It appears that the Christian community was imitating the *tamhuy* with its "daily distribution." But does this mean that the widows were not considered "residents"? And one may ask, "Why did Christian Jews have to set up *their own means* of caring for the poor?" One can only speculate whether the neglect of "the widows" by the *larger* Jerusalem community might indicate that the Hellenistic Christian community was viewed by the residents of Jerusalem as a distinct enough group that it did not "qualify" for either the *quppah* or *tamhuy*.

Some interpreters believe that "the conflict is a creation of Luke himself" (Lüdemann, 76). If this is the case, attempts to integrate scenes from Luke's story world with the historical world of Jerusalem that existed "behind the text" are futile, except to defend Luke's verisimilitude.

Joachim Jeremias, *Jerusalem in the Time of Jesus* (Philadelphia: Fortress, 1969); Gerd Lüdemann, *Early Christianity according to the Traditions in Acts: A Commentary* (Minneapolis: Fortress, 1989).

---

divided along linguistic lines and that the "neglect" was inadvertent. [The Hellenists and the Hebrews] Still, the Old Testament made clear that "widows" are a special group that God's people are not to neglect (see Deut 24:19-21; 26:12-13); intentional or not, this oversight requires correction.

The Hellenists and the Hebrews

There is consensus regarding the identification of the two groups. "'Hellenists' means 'Hellenistic diaspora Jews' whose mother-tongue was Greek and Luke uses 'Hebrews' . . . to refer to Aramaic-speaking Jews born in Palestine" (Haenchen, 267). But were their distinctions only linguistic? Some have proposed that the Jerusalem Christian Jewish community consisted of two relatively distinct groups: Diaspora Jews who had migrated to Jerusalem and Palestinian Jews, Jews born and reared in the land. Due to cultural differences arising from being reared in different worlds, there existed some tension between the two groups, the evidence of which is minimized by Luke, but still present.

For example, the "neglect" in the distribution of food may point to tension. Further, Acts *implies* that, *historically*, when the persecution arose because of Stephen, only Hellenist Christians were actually affected by it (see the Commentary on 7:54–8:3). If this is so, this provides other evidence that more than language divided "the Hellenists and Hebrews."

Ernst Haenchen, *The Acts of the Apostles: A Commentary* (Philadelphia: Westminster, 1971); see also Hans Conzelmann, *History of Primitive Christianity* (Nashville: Abingdon, 1973), 56–59; Martin Hengel, *Acts and the History of Earliest Christianity* (Philadelphia: Fortress, 1979), 71–80.

The apostles quickly move to address the oversight (vv. 2-3). As leaders, the apostles take the initiative and present a plan of action, lay forth the criteria of those who will help in the distribution, and make the final appointment of the chosen men to carry out this service. Yet, as *servant leaders* (cf. Luke 22:24-27), they do not leave the "multitude of the disciples" (v. 2) out of the process. It is the *body* that will "pick out" (*episkepsasthe*, a verb that implies careful examination and inspection [v. 3]) and "elect" (*exelaxanto*, v. 5) the seven men.

The apostles present three criteria (v. 3). The ones selected are to be men of "good repute" (*martyroumenous*). The stem *martyr* in this descriptive participle is the same as the word for "witness." The good reputation is grounded in what others have witnessed. Those selected are to be "full of the Spirit." While all believers have the Spirit, Luke also speaks of being endowed with the Spirit for a specific task (e.g., offering witness [Luke 12:11-12]). The community is to be sure that those whom they select are spiritually equipped for leadership roles they are to play. Finally, they are to be "full of wisdom," which could be understood in ancient times, as well as now, as having the kind of practical knowledge and skills required for a task.

The specific task is described as "serving tables" (v. 2, *diakonein*). This verb is appropriate, given that "food distribution" will be the responsibility of these men. However, the verb could have broader connotations, namely "to cover the general financial administration of the community."[1] This is also appropriate in the flow of the Lukan narrative; recall that authority over possessions represents in Acts spiritual authority.[2] The seven who are chosen, therefore, are chosen to serve as leaders in a broader sense, not simply to distribute food, which none ever actually does in Luke's narrative!

[The Seven]

The apostles will also continue to "serve" (*diakonia*, v. 4), but their primary task will be "the service of the word" (v. 4), which is understood as "preaching" (v. 2). The apostolic focus on preaching does not stem from the apostles' belief that the kind of service the seven are to perform was beneath them. First, as the narrative unfolds, both the seven's and apostles' primary means of "service" is through witness and preaching. Herein lies the basis of the authority of both groups. Second, apostolic "service to the word" results in physical danger (recall Acts 5). There is nothing "elitist" about "serving the word" as opposed to "serving tables."

The congregation selects the seven who will serve the community. All the names are Greek, implying that the seven come from the ranks of the Hellenists. Stephen is singled out as "a man full of faith and the Holy Spirit" (v. 5). Such special notice prepares readers for the subsequent narrative where Stephen is the central character.

The apostles pray and lay hands on these seven (v. 6), the means whereby they appoint (cf. v. 3) these men to their tasks. Laying on of hands denotes a sharing of authoritative power. This leadership

---

The Seven

The seven are the men chosen to "serve tables." Yet there is no record that they do any such thing. Only two of the seven are treated in any detail, Stephen (chs. 6–7) and Philip (ch. 8; 21:8-9). It is difficult to distinguish sharply between the activities of these two representatives of "the seven" and the actions of "the Twelve": both groups work wonders and preach. *Historically*, "the seven" were perhaps not merely a group appointed by the Twelve to "serve tables"; rather, they served as the *leaders* of the Hellenist Christians, with "the Twelve" serving as the leaders of the "Hebrew" Christians. The Hellenists looked to *seven* leaders since "local officials of the Jewish community and also ancient councils consisted of seven members" (Conzelmann, 45).

Luke, attempting to offer a simplified and unified portrayal of the early church, relegated "the seven" to a less significant role. Still, the traditions he inherited reveal perhaps that this group of seven played a more significant role in the early Jerusalem church. Regarding other members of the seven, later church tradition said that Prochorus became an associate of the Apostle John and Nicanor founded the heretical Nicolaitans of Rev 2:6.

Hans Conzelmann, *Acts of the Apostles,* Hermeneia (Philadelphia: Fortress, 1987).

group coming out of the Hellenists, thereby, received apostolic sanction. Hence, in subsequent narratives, such as Acts 8, as the witness of the gospel spreads beyond Jerusalem to Judea and Samaria through Philip, another of these Hellenistic seven, readers can rest assured that such extended proclamation goes forth under the authority of the twelve apostles.

Verse 7 offers a mini-summary, affirming that what has just transpired has the blessing of God. The word of God, that is, the message of the gospel, is increasing, and even more disciples are being added to the ranks. Given that increased numbers (v. 1) likely created the problems that led to the appointment of the seven in the first place, the resulting increase of disciples assures readers that things are now under control. Curiously, the narrator adds that many priests also joined the movement and were "obedient to the faith," that is, the gospel message (cf. 1 Tim 1:19; 4:6; 6:10). Quite a social chasm existed between the chief priests and the other priests, who were generally poor and only served "part time." Perhaps Luke is implying that among the ranks of the non-aristocratic priests, many were recognizing wherein the real community of Israel lay: among those who follow "the faith" and the apostles. [Priests]

Priests

Luke's notice that some priests joined the Jesus movement implies a distinction between "ruling priests" and "regular priests." The Jewish historian Josephus sees a distinction, and even speaks of tension between the two groups of priests: "The high priests . . . had the hardness to send their servants into the threshing floors, to take away those tithes that were due to the priests, insomuch that it so fell out that the poorer sort of the priests died for want" (*Ant.* 20.181).

They Seized Stephen, 6:8–7:1

Stephen is reintroduced as being "full of grace and power" (v. 8a). "Grace" communicates divine favor (cf. Luke 2:40), and "power" is another way of saying that Stephen was a man of the Spirit, the Spirit being the source of the disciples' power (cf. 1:8). Doing great wonders and signs not only allows for the public demonstration of the divine favor upon this man of the Spirit, but also shows this Hellenist leader to be comparable to the apostles, who also did signs and wonders (see [Signs and Wonders]). Also, like the apostles, some Jews confront Stephen when he displays such wondrous signs.

There is some confusion over exactly how to understand v. 9. Does the opposition come from one synagogue called "the Synagogue of the Freedmen" whose membership came from all the areas mentioned in the verse? Or are readers to imagine a number of synagogues in the city, one "of the Freedmen" and another "of the Cyrenians" and yet another "of the Alexandrians" to which

Synagogues in Jerusalem

Later rabbinic tradition, as recorded in the Jerusalem Talmud (*Meg* 73d), claims there were 480 synagogues in Jerusalem. Even assuming this to be an exaggeration, such a tradition indicates that numerous synagogues existed in the city. Rabbinic literature also speaks of the purchase of a "synagogue of the Alexandrians" in Jerusalem, indicating that synagogues were known by their primary constituencies, such as "Alexandrians" or "Freedmen" (cf. Acts 6:9).

An inscription discovered in Jerusalem, dating to c. AD 70, and possibly earlier, describes how a certain Theodotos, son of Vettenus (a Latin name), restored a synagogue that had originally been built by his ancestors. There is speculation that since Theodotos's father had a Latin name, the father was a former slave who took Vettenus as his name. Hence, Theodotos may have been the son of a freedman; thus, the Theodotos synagogue may have been the synagogue (or, at least, *a* synagogue) of "the Freedmen." (See below for a picture of the inscription and translation.) Scholars generally identify these "freedmen" as the "liberated descendants of the Jews who had been taken to Rome by Pompey" (Conzelmann, 47).

The Theodotos Inscription. (Credit: Image courtesy of Israel Antiquities Authority)

Translation:
Theodotos, son of Vettenus, priest and head of the synagogue, son of a head of the synagogue, grandson of the head of a synagogue, built the synagogue for the reading of the law and for the teaching of the commandments, and the guest-house and the rooms and the supplies of water as an inn for those who have need when coming from abroad, which synagogue his fathers and the elders and Simonides founded (Jackson and Lake, 4.68–69).

Hans Conzelmann, *Acts of the Apostles*, Hermeneia (Philadelphia: Fortress, 1987); F. J. Foakes Jackson and Kirsopp Lake, *The Beginnings of Christianity: The Acts of the Apostles*, 5 vols. (Grand Rapids MI: Baker, 1979).

"those from Cilicia and Asia" belonged? [Synagogues in Jerusalem] Despite this lack of clarity, it is apparent that Stephen's opposition comes from fellow Hellenists. There was division among the Hellenists, for while some are obviously open to rather radical reinterpretations of the Jewish tradition (e.g., Stephen), others are zealous defenders of the traditional institutions of Judaism, such as the law and the temple (Stephen's opponents). [Hellenists and Internal Disputes]

While Stephen's opponents come initially from the ranks of the Hellenists, as the story progresses, the Sanhedrin, as well as "the people" (v. 12), participate in bringing charges against Stephen. This leaves the impression that those from all quarters of Judaism, "the people," the "leadership," and the "Diaspora," are united in opposition against Stephen and the Christian community for which he speaks. The so-called "Jerusalem springtime" is drawing to a close. Literarily, the transition is rough, for readers are left without explanation as to why "the people" are now siding with their leaders. Readers should not be totally surprised, for, equally inexplicably, "the people," whose presence had regularly protected Jesus against the leadership in the Gospel, failed to raise any voice

Hellenists and Internal Disputes

The Jews Luke describes as "Hellenists" were not a unified group. Some of these Jews from the Diaspora were attracted to the Christian message and, if Stephen's speech in any way reflects their views, did not hesitate to offer a critical reading of the Jewish tradition. On the other hand, some "Hellenists" appear as arch defenders of Jewish institutions and traditions (see Acts 6:9-11; 9:29; as well as the many Jews of the Diaspora who confronted Paul during his travels). The "Hellenists" were no more a unified body of Jews than the natives of Palestine, some of whom were attracted to the message of Jesus' followers and most of whom were not.

Some Jews of the Diaspora, absent frequent contact with the temple, its priestly leadership, or distinctive interpretations of the Torah that grew up in and around Jerusalem, would not have felt the close ties to the traditional institutions of the temple and the Torah, at least as the latter would have been understood and applied in Palestine. It is also easy to imagine other Diaspora Jews being doubly zealous for the distinctive characteristics of their Jewish heritage as a way of maintaining a sense of identity while living in a foreign land and culture. Luke's portrait of both "Hebrew" (Palestinian) and Hellenist (Diaspora) Jews shows both groups to be diverse and discourages simplistic stereotypes.

of protest when Jesus actually fell into the hands of the Sanhedrin (cf. Luke 23). Perhaps readers are to recognize that being one of God's faithful followers does not ensure support from the masses. "Popular support" is shallow and fickle.

Stephen's detractors, like the apostles' opponents in the Sanhedrin, cannot successfully argue against Stephen (v. 10). Again, a prophecy of Jesus is finding fulfillment before the readers' eyes (cf. Luke 12:11-12; 21:13-15). They charge Stephen with blasphemy (v. 11), saying things against Moses and God. Verses 13-14 offer more specific charges: Stephen speaks against the temple by saying that Jesus would destroy it; he speaks against Moses by changing the customs delivered by Moses. [Blasphemy]

The charges are very intriguing. Readers familiar with the other two Synoptic Gospels will detect some similarities between the charges against Stephen and those brought against Jesus before Sanhedrin. First, the charge against both is said to be "blasphemy" (v. 11; cf. Matt 26:65; Mark 14:64). Second, both involve charges brought by false witnesses (v. 13; cf. Matt 26:60; Mark 14:56). Third, both involve a charge that Jesus would destroy the temple (v. 14; cf. Matt 26:61; Mark 14:58). This parallelism offers a rich comparison between Jesus and his loyal follower, but, curiously, is a comparison that Luke's original readers could not have made had they not known Matthew and Mark, for Luke does not have these three details in his account of Jesus' trial before the Sanhedrin. Readers who have a possible advantage over Luke's original readers and who can read Acts in its *canonical* context can recognize the way that Stephen's

Blasphemy

AΩ "For wisdom is a kindly spirit, but will not free blasphemers from the guilt of their words" (Wis 1:6). This proverb conveys the seriousness of blasphemy in the Jewish tradition. In the narrower, more technical sense, blasphemy denoted use of the divine name in an improper manner (cf. 2 Kgs 19:4 [LXX has *blaspheme*, trans. as "mock" in NRSV]). It could also be used, as in the charge against Stephen, in the broader sense of acting or speaking against Israel (cf. Ezek 35:12; 2 Macc 10:4, 35-36; 15:24) or its revered and sacred practices and institutions (Isa 66:3 [LXX uses the word as a synonym for "idolatry"]; 1 Macc 2:6; 2 Macc 9:28).

persecution/prosecution follows the example of Jesus' persecution/prosecution.

As Stephen stands before the council (v. 15), his face is said to be like that of an angel. God affirms this witness and what he will say as he responds to charges against him (7:1).

"Brethren and Fathers, Hear Me," 7:2-53

Stephen's response, the longest of any of the speeches in Acts, has proven very difficult for readers to interpret, leading Ernst Haenchen to speak of problems "about which the experts have cudgeled their brains."[3] For example, at least two issues present themselves as regular stumbling blocks. First, numerous details in Stephen's version of Israel's history do not match up with the biblical testimony. [The Biblical History according to Stephen: A Comparison with the Jewish Scriptures]

Second, Stephen does not directly address the charges against him (review 6:13-14). Rather, Stephen recites the history of Israel, which is not the most effective way to defend oneself against specific charges. One would expect Stephen to tell his own story, which would be relevant to his defense (cf. how Paul regularly tells his own story when he wishes to defend himself [22:3-21; 24:10-21; 26:2-23]). It is difficult for Stephen to defend himself when he refuses to talk about himself. Hence, after reading the speech, we will have no idea, based at least on Stephen's words, whether Stephen did or did not claim that Jesus claimed he would destroy the temple. And while Stephen accuses his listeners of not obeying the law (v. 53), readers have no idea, based on his "defense," whether Stephen did or did not claim that Jesus, or anyone else, would change the customs that Moses delivered to the people. [Historical Recitation]

On the *narrative* level this problem is relatively easy to comprehend: the narrator has already told the reader that the charges were leveled by "false witnesses" (6:13). Thus, the *reader* does not really need to hear Stephen's denials of the charges or the evidence he might present to prove the charges false. But, at least indirectly, Stephen's lack of self-defense requires readers to recognize that *they* are the real audience of this speech. In the narrative world Stephen addresses his words to his accusers in the story. But the speech will make more sense to readers if they keep in mind that *they* are the audience the narrator is most interested in addressing. Even if one wishes to claim that what is recorded in Acts 7 is an abbreviation of some things Stephen actually said, that does not change the fact

The Biblical History according to Stephen: A Comparison with the Jewish Scriptures

The following table summarizes some of the more notable differences between Stephen's telling of the biblical story and biblical record. The table shows that Stephen (and/or Luke) "reads" the Jewish Scriptures within the context legend and variant scriptural traditions.

Stephen's Speech	Biblical Text	Possible Explanations
V. 2-3: Cites Gen 12:1, stating that God said this to Abraham "before he lived in Haran."	According to Gen 11:27–12:5 (see esp. 12:1, 4-5), God made the call of Gen 12:1 while Abraham was in Haran.	Gen 12:1, if read without attention to its narrative context, could be understood has having been said while Abraham still lived in his "own country." Gen 15:7, another version of "the call," also leaves this impression.
V. 4: States that Abraham left Haran and moved to Canaan after his father (Terah) died.	Terah was seventy years old when Abraham was born (Gen 11:26). When Abraham was seventy-five years old (making Terah 145), Abraham moved from Haran to Canaan (Gen 12:5). Terah lived until he was 205 (Gen 11:32), meaning that he had to be alive when Abraham left Haran.	Since Gen 11:32 reports the death of Terah, followed a few verses later by notification that Abraham left Haran (Gen 12:5), it would seem natural to conclude that Terah died before Abraham left Haran. Philo read Genesis the same way as Stephen (*Migration* 177).
V. 14. Seventy-five persons migrated to Egypt.	Gen 46:27; Exod 1:5; Deut 10:22 report seventy persons.	LXX of Gen 46:27 and Exod 1:5 report seventy-five persons. The MT and LXX editors counted persons differently. Gen 46:26 speaks of sixty-six persons, to which one adds Joseph, his two sons, and Jacob himself, totaling seventy (46:27). LXX also started with the sixty-six of 46:26, but says that Joseph had nine sons, equaling seventy-five. Philo is aware of the numerical discrepancy, which he interprets allegorically (*Migration* 200–202).
V. 16. Joseph and Jacob buried in Shechem.	Jacob was buried at Hebron (Gen 49:29-32), and Joseph was buried at Shechem (Josh 24:32).	May be due to Luke's agenda to de-emphasize "the land." Having both patriarchs buried in Shechem (not an active city in Stephen's time, but located near Mount Gerizim in Samaritan country) would serve Luke's theological agenda.
V. 22. Moses was instructed in the wisdom of Egypt.	Not in the Bible.	Widely attested in Jewish traditions and legends about Moses (e.g., Philo, *Moses*, 1.20–24).
V. 23. Moses was forty years old when he visited his kinsmen and fled Egypt. Cf. v. 30: Moses spent forty years in Midian.	Exod 2:11 says only that Moses had grown up. Exodus gives no time reference. The closest is Exod 2:23, "after a long time."	Based on the biblical tradition of the forty-year wilderness period and the 120 total years of Moses' life, rabbis divided Moses' life into three equal periods of forty years each: years until Moses fled Egypt, years Moses spent in Midian, and years of exodus and wilderness wandering.
Vv. 38, 53. The law was mediated by angels.	Not in Hebrew Bible.	Seems to have been a common Jewish tradition. LXX of Deut 33:2 translates a confusing Hebrew text to include angels. Josephus (*Ant.* 15.136) seems to know of such a tradition. Gal 3:19 and Heb 2:2 speak of such a tradition.

that the speech, in the form now presented, functions to speak to Christian readers in the form of a response to the Sanhedrin and Stephen's other accusers. It is designed to assure Christian readers that charges that Christians are blaspheming renegades are groundless.

What concerns the reader of Acts is "the truth of the things about which you have been informed" (cf. Luke 1:4). Central to Luke's theological agenda is the claim that Jesus

and, by extension, his followers fulfill the story of Israel as contained in its Scriptures (cf. esp. Luke 24:25-27, 45-47). The various speeches of Peter presented to this point have regularly emphasized this issue. A corollary of this issue concerns the identity of the legitimate leadership of the restored Israel. Is it the Sanhedrin or the apostles? The flip side of this question is, "Where does one find the legitimate remnant of God's people, those who follow the apostles or those who follow the Sanhedrin?" Stephen's speech, when read with *these* questions in mind, assures the reader that the story of Israel was pointing ahead to the coming of Christ and that Israel's story finds its realization in Christ and those who follow him. [Implied Reader]

In a broad sense, therefore, Stephen's speech informs (implied Christian) readers that they are the legitimate heirs of Israel's story; therefore, they (and Stephen) are not "blasphemers" against the heritage of Israel, a heritage closely connected with two great institutions of that tradition, the law and the temple (cf. 6:11). In fact, Israel's story was one of continual rebellion against God, a point that this speech will make abundantly clear.

Four themes will guide the reading of Stephen's words: (1) God's presence is not tied to a particular place or land; (2) the calling of God's people is to worship him; (3) Israel's history was of one continual rebellion, manifested most clearly in a rejection of the ones whom God chose and sent to Israel to deliver it and resulting in false worship; (4) Israel's story anticipated and pre-pared the way for the coming of Jesus, in whom this story finds its realization. The overall impact of these themes is that the legitimate remnant of God's people is found in the followers of Jesus and the apostles, not in the Sanhedrin and its followers.

The speech has four sections: Abraham and the patriarchs (vv. 2-16), Moses (vv. 17-43), the tabernacle and the temple (vv. 44-50), and Stephen's concluding accusation (vv. 51-53).

The Patriarchs, vv. 2-16

Stephen begins the story of the patriarchs with Abraham (vv. 2-8) followed by a summary of the story of Joseph (vv. 9-16). Immediately, the theme that God is not bound to a certain place or land is evident, for God called Abraham "when he was in Mesopotamia, before he lived in Haran" (v. 2). Even though Abraham did eventually find his way to "this land in which you [Stephen's narrative audience] are now living" (v. 4), God gave Abraham no inheritance in the land. Abraham, the great patriarch, was a man without "the land." And so were his descendants for a long while, for a key element of Israel's early story was that they would be a people living as "aliens in a land belonging to others" (v. 6). The theme that God is not bound to the land continues as Stephen recites the story about Joseph, for though Joseph was "sold . . . into Egypt . . . God was with him" (v. 9), delivering him from all his afflictions (v. 10). Even Joseph's family was saved from star-vation outside the land of Canaan and in the land of Egypt.

The theme that Israel's calling was to worship God finds laconic but clear expression in Stephen's retelling of the patriarchal story: "But I will judge the nation that they [Israel] serve . . . and after that they shall come out and worship me in this place" (v. 7). Interpreters debate whether "this place" refers specifically to the temple (cf. 6:13) or the land. Regardless, the essential message is clear: Israel's reason for living in the land or for having a temple is to worship God. Worship is Israel's reason of being.

Stephen refers to the rebelliousness of Israel when he speaks of how the patriarchs were "jealous of Joseph" (v. 9). It was *they* who sold him into Egypt. By means of the rebellious "jealousy" of the patriarchs, God rescued Joseph from his own "afflictions" (or "tribulations," v. 10) and exalted him to a ruling position so that he might deliver Israel from the "great affliction" (or "tribulation," v. 11) of famine. Christian readers can see a comparison between Joseph and Jesus, both of whom were rejected by their own people, but whose rejection God had used to make deliverance possible.

Subtle comparisons between Jesus and a character from the Jewish Scriptures are a way for the narrator to address the fourth theme: Israel's story anticipated and prepared the way for Jesus. [Typology] Joseph's rejection by his own brothers is but one example. Other features of the Joseph story lend themselves to typological reading. For example, it is said that God gave Joseph "grace" (*charis*, [translated as "favor" in NRSV]) and "wisdom" (v. 10). It was said of Jesus also that God's "grace" was upon him and that he was filled with "wisdom" (Luke 2:40; cf. 2:52). Only *readers* of the narrative could make such a connection.

It may also be significant that Stephen speaks of a first and second visit (vv. 12-13) of Joseph's brothers to Egypt, and only during the second visit did "Joseph make himself known" (v. 12). Polhill sees another typological connection to the Jesus story:

> What Stephen did emphasize, however, was the seemingly insignificant detail that the brothers made two visits and only recognized Joseph on the second. Why this emphasis? . . . One is strongly tempted to see here a reference to the two "visits" of Christ. The Jews had rejected him on his first coming. Would they now accept him when confronted by Christ through Stephen's preaching?[4]

Typology

Typology assumes that persons or events of the Old Testament prefigured persons or events in the story of Jesus and his followers. Paul, for example, speaks of Adam as a "type" (Gk. *typos*) of Christ (Rom 5:14). He interprets events that occurred during the exodus, the passing through the Red Sea and manna and water provided by God for the people, as "types" of Christian baptism and the bread and wine of the Lord's Supper (1 Cor 10:6 [NRSV translates *typoi* as "examples"]). Moses clearly serves as a "type" of Jesus in Stephen's speech, even though Luke does not use the word *typos* explicitly in this sense in the speech.

Typology was developed as a more systematic means of reading the Bible by the Antiochene school, which intentionally contrasted typology with "allegory." Allegory, like typology, sought a "deeper meaning" from the Old Testament, but, unlike typology, emphasized the symbolic character of the Old Testament to such an extent that the "historical" character was virtually ignored.

R. M. Grant and D. Tracy, *A Short History of the Interpretation of the Bible*, 2d ed. (Philadelphia: Fortress, 1984), chs. 6–7. For selections from the writings of representatives of the Antiochene school on biblical interpretation, see K. Froehlich, *Biblical Interpretation in the Early Church* (Philadelphia: Fortress, 1984), chs. 7–9.

Others may find this kind of typological interpretation strained.[5] The point remains, however, that *any* interpreter who suggests this as a possible meaning of Stephen's words can do so only if such an interpreter is assuming that Stephen is assuming a "Christian" audience. And, of course, Stephen can speak to the Christian readership only as he speaks as a character within a narrative that is the creation of the narrator. One cannot plausibly argue that the *historical* character Stephen had hoped that his *Jewish* audience would have seen the *christological* significance of this detail about Joseph or that, one day, later Christian readers would be reading his speech.

Moses, Ruler and Judge over Israel, vv. 17-43

This is the longest section of the speech, and it too offers many connections with the four primary themes that drive this speech. First, the reader sees that God continues not to be bound to any

The Martyrdom of St. Stephen

Peter Paul Rubens (1577–1640). *The Martyrdom of St. Stephen*
(triptych). Oil on wood; oil on canvas. (Credit: Réunion des
Musées Nationaux / Art Resource, NY)

particular place. Though Israel is being oppressed in Egypt, God is there, taking steps to deliver God's people. While Moses was living in "exile in the land of Midian" (v. 29), God was revealed to Moses at Mount Sinai (vv. 30-34). "Holy ground" (v. 33) can be found outside the land. Moses can perform signs and wonders that bring deliverance to God's people "in Egypt and at the Red Sea, and in the wilderness" (v. 36). The power of God is not limited to "the land."

The theme of Moses' rejection leads to Israel's failure to fulfill its *raison d'être* of proper worship. But as Stephen speaks of Moses' rejection by Israel, he makes it quite clear just *who* this Moses is whom Israel rejects: God's chosen deliverer of Israel. Verse 17, which speaks of the time drawing near for God to fulfill God's promise to Israel (cf. vv. 5, 7 for reference to God's promise to give Israel a land—a place—that it might worship God), allows readers to anticipate that God is about to do something significant. It was "at this time [that] Moses was born" (v. 20). Stephen's detailing of Moses' accomplishments in v. 22 also allows the reader to realize that Moses possessed the requisite gifts and skills to be the deliverer that Israel needed.

Moses' role as a savior/deliverer is manifested in numerous ways in the story. First, he kills an Egyptian because an Israelite was being "wronged" and "oppressed" (v. 24). The voice of God confirms Moses' role as God speaks to him at Mount Sinai in v. 34: "I have come down to deliver them. And . . . I will send you to Egypt." Moses serves as God's instrument of deliverance. Stephen's narration continues to make explicit Moses' liberating role as he speaks of Moses as a "ruler and deliverer" whom "God sent" and who "led out" Israel while performing "signs and wonders" (vv. 35b-36). Finally, it was through this Moses that Israel received "living oracles," indicating that the words that Moses gave the people offered them life.

After making clear just who this Moses was, Stephen makes equally clear that Israel's consistent response was one of rejection. In fact, each explicit act of deliverance or liberation on the part of Moses is met with a response of rejection on the part of Israel. Just after Moses defended the oppressed man in v. 24, Stephen comments that Moses' fellow Israelites did not understand "that God was giving them deliverance by [Moses'] hand" (v. 25). Then, on "the following day" an Israelite cast Moses aside, asking, "Who made you a ruler and a judge over us?" (v. 27). The Israelite implicitly threatens Moses by communicating that he knows that Moses had killed an Egyptian. This causes Moses to flee (vv. 28-29).

As Stephen continues his narration, it is immediately after God commanded Moses to return to Egypt as God's instrument of deliverance (v. 34) that Israel refused "*this* Moses" (v. 35). Commentators often note that Stephen regularly uses the near demonstrative pronoun ("this") to draw attention to Moses (see vv. 35, 36, 37, 38, 40) as though Stephen wants to say, "It was *this* Moses, the Moses whom God had chosen to be Israel's deliverer, whom Israel rejected." Similarly, just after Stephen describes the deliverance of Israel through Moses (vv. 36-38), he explicitly states, "Our ancestors refused to obey him, but thrust him aside, and in their hearts they returned to Egypt" (v. 39), saying "'as for this Moses who led us out from the land of Egypt, we do not know what has become of him'" (v. 40b). Clearly, the Moses whom Israel so emphatically rejected was the one whom God had appointed and sent to be Israel's deliverer.

Such rejection manifests itself in Israel's failure to fulfill its own God-appointed calling of worshiping him. Verse 39, which speaks of Israel's refusal to obey Moses, is immediately followed by the incident of the calf: they "offered a sacrifice to the idol and rejoiced in the works of their hands" (v. 41). This act of false worship results in God "giving them over" (cf. Rom 1:24-25) to even more thoroughgoing idolatry and false worship (v. 42a).

In vv. 42c-43 Stephen employs the LXX version of Amos 5:25-27, one of the "book[s] of the [twelve] prophets" (v. 42b), to say that Israel did *not* offer its sacrifices to God during the wilderness period (v. 42c) but to false gods such as Moloch (a Canaanite-Phoenician sun god) and Rephan, perhaps a variation of the name Repa, by which Egyptians referred to Saturn (v. 43a).[6] Israel's call to worship God (v. 7) was a total failure as it chose to worship the figures (*typoi*) that it created (v. 43b). As a consequence, Israel suffered the deportation "beyond Babylon" (v. 43c). [Exile]

Moses had offered liberation and deliverance. Israel rejected him, resulting in false worship

Exile

📖 Stephen, like his Jewish contemporaries, argues that the Babylonian exile (587–539 BC) was due to Israel's failure to show obedience and loyalty to God. For Stephen true worship demonstrated such loyalty and obedience. True worship was Israel's "reason to be." It had failed. Therefore, it experienced God's judgment in the form of exile, a punishment that, even in Stephen's day, Israel was still experiencing to some degree. Surely, the Israel of Stephen's time could still have uttered without qualification the same prayer uttered by the refugees who had returned to Jerusalem centuries before: "Here we are, slaves to this day—slaves in the land that you gave to our ancestors to enjoy its fruit and its good gifts" (Neh 9:36).

N. T. Wright, *The New Testament and the People of God*, vol. 1 of *Christian Origins and the Question of God* (Minneapolis: Fortress, 1992), 268–72.

and bondage in the form of exile. For Stephen, the rejection of the deliverer Moses offered a clear foreshadowing of the way in which Israel would respond to the final deliverer whom God would send. The Moses story, like that of Joseph, anticipated and prepared the way for the coming of the final deliverer, Jesus. Stephen employs the Moses story to anticipate the Jesus story in a number of ways.

First, he uses language to describe Moses that is similar to language used to describe Jesus, creating verbal allusions, many of which could only be "caught" by the reader. Verse 22 describes Moses as "mighty [*dynatos*] in his words [*logois*] and deeds [*ergois*]." This compares easily with Luke 24:19, where Jesus is described as "a prophet mighty [*dynatos*] in deed [*ergō*] and word [*logō*]." Verse 25 describes Moses as an instrument of deliverance or salvation (*sōtērian*). Luke–Acts is full of references or allusions to Jesus as the one who offers "salvation" (e.g., Luke 2:11, 30; 19:9; Acts 4:12; 5:31; 13:23). Moses is described as a "ruler" (*archōn*, vv. 27, 35, 36), which is similar to the title "leader" used of Jesus earlier in Acts (3:15; 5:31 apply *archēgon* to Jesus). It is also said that Moses was Israel's "redeemer" (*lytrōtēn*), which compares with Luke 24:21, where the two travelers to Emmaus say about Jesus, "We had hoped that he was the one to redeem [*lytrousthai*] Israel." Finally, Moses anticipates the coming of Jesus in that Moses' rejection by his own people prefigures Jesus' rejection by Israel. In his person, Moses typologically prefigures the role and function of Jesus as the rejected leader and liberator.

An extremely crucial way in which Moses anticipates the role of Jesus in relation to Israel is as the prophet. Verse 37, referring to Deuteronomy 18:15, explicitly compares Jesus to a prophet who will be like Moses. This text appears earlier in Acts 3:22, where Peter referred to the same passage. Jesus as "the prophet" is one of Luke's regular descriptions of Jesus (cf. Luke 4:24; 7:16; 13:33; 24:19). Moses as "the prophet" anticipates Jesus not only typologically, but in *predicting* the coming and "raising up" of Jesus: "God will raise up for you a prophet" (v. 37). Of all the things Moses is recorded as having said in the Jewish Scriptures, Stephen picks out this one line: Moses prophesying the "raising up" of Jesus.

Related to Moses as a prophet who predicts the coming of Jesus the prophet is the phrase Stephen uses to describe the law that Moses gave to Israel. Verse 38 states that Moses received "living oracles" to give to the people. The word "oracles" could be employed in the Septuagint to denote "the law" (Deut 33:9, Isa 4:24, and numerous texts from Ps 118 [= 119 in ET]). But the term could also be used to denote "prophetic pronouncements"

(Num 24:4, 16; Isa 28:12; 30:27) or "promises" from God (Pss 11:7; 17:31; cf. Rom 3:2). In using the word "oracles" to denote what Moses gave to Israel, Stephen is implying that these sayings from God are more than "law." That which Moses gave to Israel includes prophetic pronouncements and promises; that is, they point to something (or someone) coming in the future. For Stephen that someone is Jesus. Hence, Moses anticipates the coming of Jesus not only in the way he prefigures Jesus' functioning as deliverer and redeemer, but also through his predicting the coming of Jesus and giving Israel "oracles" that prophesy and promise his coming.

The Tent and the Temple, vv. 44-50

This penultimate section of the speech will display prominently the theme of worship, Israel's *raison d'être*. The themes of divine presence, proper worship, and rebellion are tightly intertwined. The theme of prefiguring Jesus is implicit at best in this section, reading the references to Joshua (Hebrew form of "Jesus") and David (the messianic forerunner) in an anticipatory manner.

This section makes clear that there is no guarantee that God is present simply because the people are in the land (or have a temple, for that matter). Exploring the themes of worship and rebellion bring out the full implications of this theme.

The text presents a contrast between "the tent of witness" and the "house" or temple. God provides Moses what is necessary for God's people to have a proper place for worship. God shows Moses the "pattern" (*typon*) in order to build the tent (v. 44; cf. Exod 25:40). This contrasts with the calf and other idols, which are described as *typoi*, or figures, stemming from human hands (cf. v. 41). Israel can worship according to a true pattern (*typos*) offered by God, as given in the tent provided by Moses, or according to false patterns (*typoi*) that come from human hands.

Though vv. 45-46 are terse, they leave the impression that during the period extending from Joshua through David, worship in the land was according to God's will. The lack of any comments about the people rejecting Joshua or David implies that Israel followed the God-sent leaders during this period. Regardless of how one responds to this reading, it remains true that as the people were employing the tent provided by Moses, God was throwing out the nations before them (v. 45). These nations were primarily a threat because they tempted Israel to worship God falsely (cf. Deut 7:1-6). Things were going well. Even David, who is described as finding favor (*charis*), wants to continue the tradition of this "tent" (*skēnē*) by planning to build, not a "house" (*oikos*) for God, but a tent-like habitation (*skēnōma*).

Stephen is offering a certain "spin" on the story of David's inquiry in 2 Samuel 7:1-9 to build a place to hold the ark. Review of the Old Testament story clearly implies that David, who seemed to feel it inappropriate that he lived in a "house" while God lived in a "tent," wanted to build God something *other than* a "tent." Nonetheless, the story of 2 Samuel 7:5-6 says quite clearly that David was *not* to build a "house" for God and goes on to predict that David's descendant would be the one to build this house (2 Sam 7:13). Stephen picks up on this fact, noting in v. 47 that Solomon did build a "house" for God. But while Jewish tradition, and, indeed, the narrative of 1 Kings, interprets this act of Solomon quite positively, Stephen's statement of v. 48, backed up with words from Isaiah 66:1-2 in vv. 49-50, is difficult to read positively.

Stephen claims point blank that God "does not dwell in houses made with hands" (v. 48). Is Stephen offering a *reminder* to his story audience that Jewish tradition did not claim that God was confined to the temple (cf. 1 Kgs 8:27)? Or is he implying that his audience believed that God lived in the temple and he was *challenging* this idea? The fact that Stephen speaks of the temple as "made with hands" is significant. Earlier in the speech, Stephen used the phrase as a synonym for making idols (v. 41). Later, Paul will use the phrase to debunk pagan idolatry and shrines (17:24-25). Attaching the phrase "made with hands" to the temple gives Stephen's critique a decidedly polemical tone: this temple is idolatrous.

Is Stephen condemning the temple *per se*, claiming that the very act of building and worshiping in the temple was, and always has been, an act of idolatry? Stephen's way of contrasting the "tent" and "house" could lead one to read this way. Or is he saying that the Jerusalem temple, given what it has actually come to be, has *become* a place of idolatry? Because the Lukan narrative tends to portray the temple in a positive light, one could justifiably read the speech to say that the temple *has become* an instrument of idolatry. [Luke's Picture of the Temple]

Luke's Picture of the Temple

On the whole, Luke offers a positive portrait of the temple. The Gospel begins in the temple (Luke 1:5-23), and important other scenes take place at the temple setting in the birth narrative (Luke 2:22-40, 41-51). Luke confines his narrative of the resurrection to Jerusalem (the city of the temple) and its environs (Luke 24) and concludes his narrative by having the apostles "in the temple blessing God" (Luke 24:53).

Acts' opening chapters take place in Jerusalem, and the temple is an important location of the action, with Luke portraying the early Christians participating in the prayer services there (Acts 2:42, 46; 3:1). Paul undergoes the appropriate purification and plans to present offerings there (Acts 21:24-26). When employed properly (as Jesus, his parents, and his followers do), the temple can be a legitimate place of worship. But it becomes an instrument of idolatry when employed in the wrong spirit: a spirit that attempts to confine God's presence or leads one to reject God's appointed leaders for Israel (see Commentary).

J. Bradley Chance, *Jerusalem, the Temple, and the New Age in Luke–Acts* (Macon GA: Mercer University Press, 1989).

What both of these ways of reading have in common is their agreement that *the temple as it now exists at this juncture within the narrative is an instrument of idolatry*. Therefore, it fails in its God-assigned role as the "place" where Israel is to worship God (cf. v. 7). The question is "why?" Recalling the other themes that have carried through this speech will help answer this question.

God's presence is not limited to any particular place. A point the speech consistently makes is that any view of God that limits and confines God misunderstands the character of this God. The God of Israel is one who moves with God's people. The "tent," therefore, was a most appropriate place for this God to be manifest. A "house," on the other hand, is a stationary dwelling place, a place where one is immobile, or a place where one "rests" (cf. v. 49b). One implication of the speech is that one who approaches God as one who dwells and rests in "this place" fashioned by "human hands" so misunderstands God's essential being that she or he approaches the Deity no differently than one would approach an idol. The polemical tone of the speech implies that Stephen's story audience *does* approach God in such a restrictive manner.

True worship hinges on obediently following the God-sent liberators and leaders, most aptly represented by Moses. Failure to follow Moses led *directly* to false worship, wherein the people "rejoiced in the works of their hands" (cf. vv. 39-41). Applying this pattern to the acceptance or rejection of Jesus as the liberating leader sent by God, the implication is clear: refusal to accept this liberating leader can only lead to false, idolatrous worship whereby the temple itself becomes a "house made with hands" (v. 48).

In summary, the temple is not idolatrous just because it is a temple. It is idolatrous as it functions in a context that attempts to confine God and denies the mobile (omnipresent) understanding of God *and* attempts to practice worship while simultaneously rejecting the God-sent liberating leaders. Worship that is true and non-idolatrous must be accompanied by a proper understanding of God's universal presence *and* obedient following of God's appointed leaders of Israel.

It is crucial to understand that it is precisely at the intersection of these two issues that Luke's view of God and God's chosen Messiah collides with Luke's presentation of the opposing Jews' views of God and the chosen Messiah. From Luke's perspective, those who align themselves with the Sanhedrin have rejected God's chosen liberating leader, Jesus the Messiah. Also, from Luke's perspective (and as the narrative will show more clearly as the story of Acts progresses), those from Israel who align themselves *against* Jesus and his followers and *with* the Sanhedrin and other official structures of Jewish leadership have a view of God in which God is limited and confined to a particular place and *especially* to a particular people: ethnic Israel. Both actions can only result in false worship and a failure to live up to the essence of Israel's calling, which is to worship God.

The Final Accusation, vv. 51-53

Stephen employs traditional accusations from the Scriptures to offer his final charge against his accusers. "Stiff-necked" (v. 51) is found a number of times in the LXX to describe stubborn and rebellious Israel (e.g., Exod 33:3, 5; 34:9, Deut 9:6, 13; Neh 9:29). The LXX used the figure of an uncircumcised heart to denote Israel gone astray (e.g., Lev 26:41; Jer 9:25 [ET = 9:26]). Stephen is charging his accusers, as well as their ancestors, with being a stubborn, rebellious, and wayward people. These are people who "resist the Holy Spirit" (cf. Isa 63:10, LXX). For Luke's readers, receipt of the Holy Spirit is the mark that one is of the remnant of the covenant people. To be charged with resisting the Spirit, combined with other, more traditional accusations from the Jewish Scriptures, is tantamount to accusing the accusers and their ancestors of not being God's people. Recall that Peter had earlier said that those who rejected the prophet of whom Moses spoke would be destroyed from the people (3:23).

The charge is vindicated, according to Stephen, by the further indictment that the Israelite ancestors persecuted and killed the prophets, again rejecting those whom God sent to lead Israel. Stephen's charge of persecuting and killing the prophets had been commonly believed among Jews for quite some time (cf. Neh 9:26 and various Jewish legends).[7] Israel's pattern of rebellion and rejection, action that was directly linked to Israel's failure to worship God properly, reached its zenith in the rejection of Jesus, whom the prophets had foretold (v. 52). If the rejection of Moses led to false, idolatrous worship in the wilderness, the rejection of the one whom Moses and the other prophets foretold must also lead to false, idolatrous worship at the temple. To be sure, Israel received the law, but it was Israel that did not keep it, for through rejection of God's chosen leaders Israel failed to live up to its calling to worship God.

The speech is complex and much easier to understand if readers do not restrict themselves to hearing it as it would have made sense to the Sanhedrin and Stephen's other accusers. Heard against the background of the whole of the Lukan narrative, Stephen's words assure Luke's readers, most of whom were not Jewish and lived beyond the land, that they are the remnant of God's people. God's people exist to worship God. This God is not bound to a particular place and, hence, can be worshiped anywhere. God has provided God's people with chosen liberators and leaders. To follow these liberating leaders is to show faithfulness to God; to reject them leads to false and idolatrous worship. Luke's readers follow the ultimate liberating leader sent by God, Jesus the Messiah. This can offer assurance that they are not guilty of false worship or "blasphemy against Moses and the temple" (6:11), for it is not *they* who are guilty of rejecting God's appointed leaders.

They Ground Their Teeth against Him, 7:54–8:3

The accusations that Stephen makes enrage his audience. The narrator employs colorful language to depict their anger. He says in v. 54 that they were "ripped through their hearts," denoting anger that goes to the very seat of their volition and will. "Grinding teeth" was a common biblical expression denoting "hostility and rage, especially of the wicked against the righteous" (see LXX Pss 34:16 [ET = 35:16]; 36:12 [ET = 37:12]; 111:10 [ET = 112:10]).[8] But as angered as they are by Stephen's accusatory retelling of Israel's story, it is his description of his heavenly vision that drives them to kill him (vv. 57-58).

In v. 55 the narrator speaks directly, saying that Stephen was a man of the Spirit. Thus, when his audience members oppose him, they are only showing Stephen's charge of v. 51 ("you always resist the Holy Spirit") to be true. Observing Stephen as he gazes into heaven itself and sees the glory of God and Jesus standing at God's right hand further vindicates Stephen and his testimony in the eyes of the reader. When Stephen reports in v. 55 that he sees the heavens opened and the Son of Man standing at the right hand of God, readers know that he speaks the truth. This magnifies the guilt of his story audience who rush and kill him precisely because he speaks truthfully of what he sees. [The Son of Man Standing at the Right Hand of God]

However, Stephen's audience does not want to hear it. They cry out and plug up their ears in order to block out his voice of testimony. And killing him will silence him for good. The reader

---

The Son of Man Standing at the Right Hand of God

Acts 7:56 is the only place in the New Testament where someone other than Jesus uses the term "Son of Man" as a designation for Jesus. Acts 7:56 echoes Luke 22:69, where Jesus had said to *his* accusers, "But from now on the Son of Man shall be seated at the right hand of the power of God." Note that in Stephen's vision Jesus is standing, while in Jesus' own prediction the Son of Man sits. The image of standing may be interpreted in one of two ways: (1) Jesus is rising to receive his witness, affirming Stephen as a faithful man of the Spirit; (2) Jesus is rising in judgment against those who are killing his servant. Given Stephen's prayer, it would be odd for Jesus to rise to judge the people whom Stephen had requested that God forgive. Either we should lean toward the interpretation that Jesus is rising to receive his servant, or see some bitter irony in Stephen's prayer.

Is Stephen's Death a Lynching or Formal Execution?

On the whole, the evidence leans in the direction of Stephen's death being a lynching. What is known of "formal executions" by stoning comes from later Jewish materials, specifically the Mishnah (*Sanh* 6). The procedure was not for a large group of people to throw hand-sized stones, but for the guilty party to be stripped and thrown off a precipice. If that did not kill him (or her), a boulder would be rolled on the person to crush the chest. If the person still lived, another boulder was rolled to crush him.

Given this description, the picture painted by Acts 7:59-60 is curious. Stephen prays with a large boulder on his chest, and then presumably, after he pushed the boulder off his chest, he stood up so that he could then kneel down (v. 60). The procedure spelled out in the Mishnah may not have been in force in the first century or Luke may not have known the procedure, forcing him to construct the scene as best he could. Adding the fact that Roman law likely did not allow the Sanhedrin the authority to carry out executions (see [Sanhedrin]), the scene makes most sense if understood as a lynching, with the Sanhedrin being portrayed by Luke as a no better than a mob that does not keep the law (cf. 7:53).

is led to conclude that, ultimately, what drives the opposition to persecute, silence, and even kill the followers of Jesus is their claim that this Jesus, whom the inhabitants of Jerusalem under the leadership of the Sanhedrin are responsible for killing, is the one vindicated by God. It is Jesus to whom Israel must look for its salvation (cf. 4:12; 5:31), forgiveness (cf. 2:38; 5:31), and even continued status as God's people (3:23). It is precisely this testimony that those Sanhedrin-aligned Jerusalem residents will not accept.

Though the Sanhedrin is present, the text portrays the actions of a mob. This depicts the Sanhedrin as out of control and willing to join the mob to achieve its ends. One of Luke's narrative agendas is to present the apostles as the *true* leaders of the remnant of Israel; this negative depiction of the Sanhedrin can only help Luke's cause. [Is Stephen's Death a Lynching or Formal Execution?]

Readers are now introduced to "a young man named Saul" (v. 58). As the narrative progresses, Saul will personally assume the role as the persecutor of the church, not only consenting to the death of Stephen (8:1), but dragging both men and women off to prison (8:3). While Saul emulates the character and action of the Hellenists and Sanhedrin who oppose the followers of Jesus, Stephen emulates the way of his Lord. Like Jesus, he dies with a prayer on his lips, asking Jesus to "receive his spirit" (v. 59). This is a clear echo of Jesus' dying prayer to God: "Father, into your hands I commit my spirit" (Luke 23:45). And, like Jesus, Stephen prays so that his killers may hear him: "Lord, do not hold this sin against them" (v. 60; cf. Luke 23:34, though the Lukan text is disputed in the ancient manuscripts).

Persecution does not end with Stephen. The whole church of Jerusalem is the object of persecution, so that "they were all scattered throughout the region of Judea and Samaria, except the apostles" (8:1). Two comments are in order. First, it is the attempt to silence the testimony of God's people that actually serves the divine plan. The narrator's reference to "Judea and Samaria" reminds readers that the next phase in the mission of Christ's witnesses after Jerusalem was "Judea and Samaria" (1:8). Second,

The Martyrdom of Saint Stephen

Both Annibale Carracci and his less famous nephew and student Antonio Carracci produced artistic interpretations of the martyrdom of Stephen. The painting depicts Stephen being stoned outside the city (Acts 7:58). Being cast outside the city may serve to make Stephen's death more like that of Christ, who was executed outside the city as well. Stephen is depicted praying that the Lord receive his spirit and for his persecutors (Acts 7:59-60). The viewer of the painting, like Stephen, is allowed to see "heavens opened and the Son of Man standing at the right hand of God" (Acts 7:56). The angel descending to receive Stephen is not a specific feature of the text of

Annibale Carracci (1560–1609). *The Stoning of Saint Stephen*. Louvre, Paris, France. (Credit: Erich Lessing / Art Resource, NY)

Acts. The man sitting on the right, guarding the clothes of Stephen's attackers, is clearly Paul (Saul). Is he reaching out imploring Stephen's killers to stop, foreshadowing his eventual repentance? Or does he want to participate?

Luke's notification that the apostles were left in Jerusalem makes initial sense, but can also create some confusion.

Initially, if Luke wants to emphasize that the apostles are the true leaders of the restored, remnant Israel, then to portray the Twelve as remaining in Jerusalem indicates that they cannot be removed from the city over which they are to rule "the twelve tribes of Israel" (cf. Luke 22:28-30). There is some confusion, however, for as the narrative progresses it's clear that the apostles are not the only followers of Jesus who remain in Jerusalem (cf. 9:26-28; 11:1-2, 22, 27, 29; 12:1, 12). Many interpreters explain this inconsistency *historically*, arguing that what Luke intends to say is that it was only the Hellenist Christians, or, even more narrowly, only the *leaders* of Hellenist Christians, who were run out of the city. Indeed, *historically* speaking, this is likely true. But why doesn't Luke simply say this?

One can only speculate. If *historically* only the Hellenists or their leadership were scattered (and Luke knew it), perhaps he wanted to offer simultaneously a picture of a unified church and of an apostolic leadership holding its ground in God's city of Jerusalem. Had Luke explicitly said that *only* Hellenists had been run out of the city, that could have implied to the reader a church more internally divided (as, indeed, historians claim it was; see [The Hellenists and the Hebrews]) than Luke wanted to portray. Thus, the portrait of a unified church requires the claim that "they were *all* scattered." On the other hand, had Luke not added the statement, "except the apostles," his whole narrative attempt to portray the Twelve as the true leaders of the restored remnant of Israel may very well have collapsed. Had they been scattered at this crucial juncture in the story, it would have appeared that the Sanhedrin and its cohorts really controlled the situation in Jerusalem.

Previous narratives in Acts have portrayed historic Israel as divided between those who follow Jesus and those who do not. To remain a part of God's people, one must follow Jesus the Messiah. As Luke ends the Jerusalem section, he ends with a final reminder that Jerusalem is still divided (8:2-3). Some "devout men" bury Stephen and offer proper public mourning for his death. Taking seriously Luke's comment that the apostles were the *only* followers of Jesus left in the city implies that these "devout men" are non-Christian Jews. There are still some among the residents of Jerusalem who recognize that men like Stephen are not the blasphemers others accuse them of being. And then there are men like Saul (v. 3) who ravage the church. But as the subsequent narrative will show, even he is not beyond forgiveness and salvation. Stephen's prayer that the Lord not hold the sin of his murderers against them will be answered as it concerns at least this one who consented to Stephen's death.

CONNECTIONS

We learn from this narrative much about the witness and life of the community. With respect to being a witness, we learn at least that there are two kinds of people in this story: those willing to die for their convictions and those willing to kill for their convictions. A persistent theme that permeates the Lukan narrative is that the *true* people of God do not kill others for what they believe, but are willing to die for what they believe. Too often, religious zealots confuse the two results of holding firmly to convictions.

Willingness to die for one's convictions is a strange thing to talk about in days like these when people who "die for their convictions" come from Jonestown, Waco, or Heaven's Gate. It seems that the only people willing to die for their convictions are people who are convicted about the wrong things. It is important to note that Stephen does not seek martyrdom, yet he does not avoid it by attempting to placate his accusers. Most of us are fortunate in that we don't have to give serious consideration to dying for what we believe. Hence, an issue for us to consider is not so much whether martyrdom is a good thing that we, like Ignatius of Antioch, should seek, but whether the "story we tell" is one that so shapes and molds our beings that we will stand up to the powers that be, be they secular or religious, and speak the truth as best we can. [Consequences]

Consequences

📖 "A person of integrity is willing to bear the consequences of her convictions, even when this is difficult, that is, when the consequences are unpleasant."

Lynne McFall, "Integrity," *Ethics* 98 (1987): 5.

As we speak further of "witness," it is *not* a good thing to use Stephen's speech as a model for how to picture "Judaism" and its relation to Christianity. Stephen's witness, when read as the words of a "Christian" to "the Jews," becomes anti-Semitic invective. Stephen is addressing not "the Jews," but speaks as one Jew to other Jews who are zealous defenders of their own convictions (the Hellenists) or desperately holding on to their own power (the Sanhedrin). A better application for us is how Christians who find themselves in the minority are to stand up to Christians who find themselves holding both the minds of the majority and the reins of institutional power. We speak boldly, yet we seek ultimately not the punishment of our accusers, but their reconciliation to God, pleading that God not hold their sin against them. In short, perhaps on a moral level, we have the "right" to employ the sharp rhetoric of a Stephen against our accusers only when we sincerely seek their reconciliation with God, not their judgment.

The text also speaks to the theme of community life. Stephen's claim that the *raison d'être* of God's people is proper worship deserves careful attention, especially in light of Stephen's warnings that God's called people can slip too easily into idolatry. We should recall the two things that can tempt God's people to fall into idolatrous worship: (1) attempts to confine God and (2) failure to follow faithfully God's appointed leaders. For the Christian community, these two features are intertwined, for the faithful following of Jesus Christ will prevent his people from grasping a theology or ideology that confines God and forces God into our own molds.

Jesus is continually portrayed in the New Testament as attempting to break through the barriers that limited the reach of God. Marcus Borg offers the thoughtful insight that Jesus encouraged people to understand God primarily within the framework of a paradigm of *compassion*, as contrasted to the dominant paradigm of his own Jewish society, which was one of *holiness*. [Compassion] A paradigm of holiness, while certainly not inappropriate for God's people, risks, if it serves as the community's *dominant* paradigm, legiti-

Compassion

📖 "Compassion, not holiness, is the dominant quality of God, and is therefore to be the ethos of the community that mirrors God."

Marcus Borg, *Meeting Jesus Again for the First Time* (New York: HarperSanFrancisco, 1994), 54.

mating a pattern of life that emphasizes separation and distinction from others.

Jesus associated with the sinner, the leper, the woman, and even the occasional Gentile not because he was moved primarily by a vision of God that emphasized the *otherness*, separateness, and distinctiveness, that is, the *holiness* of God and God's people. Moved by a vision of compassion, Jesus associated with the untouchables of his culture. To follow faithfully our Lord's vision of God is to dare to think of God primarily as a God of compassion who is anxious to embrace those in need of reconciliation, rather than a God of holiness who primarily desires us to separate ourselves from such folk. It was only because many of his followers dared to believe such a vision of compassion that they would dare, eventually, to extend to the most untouchable of all the groups—the Gentiles—the love of God.

A vision of God that emphasizes God's holiness moved the opponents of Stephen to place inappropriate value on the temple, viewing it as a stationary house situated in a certain place and designed to serve a certain people. Christians, who are predominantly Gentile, should reflect on where we would be if our spiritual ancestors had embraced as their primary vision of God the stationary "Lord who is in his holy temple," as opposed to the ever-moving God of the tabernacle.

We can also recognize in Stephen's retelling of Israel's story what some call a hermeneutics of suspicion. Such a hermeneutic can, to be sure, degenerate into a hermeneutics of radical skepticism or even paranoia, wherein we assume that *whatever* values and assumptions the larger culture holds to be true *must* be false and, therefore, *must* be challenged. We need not use the term in this way. Rather, such a hermeneutic encourages us always to be on guard that the prevailing assumptions and values of the groups that inform our way of thinking, be they groups as large as a culture or as small as intimate community of faith, *might* not, on a given issue, always have the proper vision. [Hermeneutics of Suspicion]

Stephen's speech warns us that one of the greatest temptations facing God's people is that of assuming that God is our own tribal totem whom we worship primarily as one who serves *us*. We cannot hold God forth as the one true God who is the creator of all and, at the same time, treat God as a mascot deity whose only concern is us and others like us with whom we are willing to share fellowship.

How often did our immediate ancestors assume that our racially segregated society was divinely ordained and that to challenge the

Hermeneutics of Suspicion

This phrase is often employed in the context of "Liberation Theology." Hermeneutics, which has to do with *how* one goes about the task of interpretation, occurs in a circular pattern (the "hermeneutical circle"). According to Juan Luis Segundo, this circle involves a "suspicion" of the various ideological elements that influence the religious community's interpretation of the Bible. First, some new experience of reality leads one to suspect on a general level that the prevailing ideology (one could add "theology") that undergirds the larger society's way of reading the Bible is amiss. Second, this initial suspicion leads one to suspect the *entirety* of the ideological and theological structures that underpin a whole society. Third, this suspicion leads one to suspect that the Bible has been read primarily to support the prevailing social ideology and, therefore, needs a fresh reading. Fourth, suspicion that the Bible has been read to sanction the prevailing social ideology leads to a new reading of the text (Segundo, 7–9).

Each of these steps can be applied to the Stephen speech: (1) Something in Stephen's experience (the gospel) has led him to suspect that something is amiss in the way his Jewish contemporaries have understood their calling as God's people. (2) This initial suspicion leads Stephen to suspect that his society's whole way of understanding God (God is bound to a particular place and a particular people) is in need of critique. (3) Knowing that his society employs the biblical story of Israel to justify its view of God and its exclusive relationship with God, Stephen suspects that the story of Israel needs to be read in a new light. (4) Stephen retells the story of Israel, trying to show that the Bible that his Jewish contemporaries used to justify their view of God and their favored relationship with God actually shows that (a) God is not confined to any land or place and (b) Israel has been a rebellious people who have failed to fulfill their calling of worshiping God.

John Luis Segundo, *The Liberation of Theology* (New York: Maryknoll, 1976).

social structures of racism and segregation was tantamount to "speaking blasphemous words against God" (cf. Acts 6:11)? How often do we assume that our "American way of life," which consumes inordinate proportions of the limited resources of *God's* earth, is evidence of God's blessings upon *us*? How often do we assume that it is an affront to God to believe that God can call to ministerial service creatures whose genetic code is embedded in two X chromosomes? How often do we assume that our own intellectual constructs through which we give expression to our understandings of God, the atonement, the incarnation, the Trinity, or the Bible are to be equated with what God really is, what God has done for us, or how God has revealed and continues to reveal the divine character and will to us? Do we recognize that our ways of talking about God can become golden calves to which we bow down in idolatrous worship? A healthy hermeneutic of suspicion does not call us to stop our talking about God ("theologizing"), but invites us to do so with humility and an openness to new vision.

Stephen dared to offer such a new vision. He dared to say that false, idolatrous worship can lie at the core of his fellow Jews' most revered and holy institutions. For us to use this speech to talk about "the Jews" and how "they" got it wrong misses the point. The word of Stephen's speech becomes the word of God for us when we ask how it warns us about how close we always stand to worshiping that which we have made with *our* hands—or our minds.

NOTES

[1] F. J. Foakes Jackson and Kirsopp Lake, *The Beginnings of Christianity: The Acts of the Apostles*, 5 vols. (Grand Rapids MI: Baker, 1979), 4.64.

[2] Luke Timothy Johnson, *The Acts of the Apostles* (SacPag 5; Collegeville MN: Liturgical Press, 1992), 110–11.

[3] Ernst Haenchen, *The Acts of the Apostles: A Commentary* (Philadelphia: Westminster, 1971), 286.

[4] John B. Polhill, *Acts* (NAC 26; Nashville: Broadman, 1992), 192.

[5] E.g., Haenchen, *Acts*, 279–80.

[6] Polhill, *Acts*, 201n71.

[7] Jackson and Lake, *Beginnings of Christianity*, 4.82.

[8] Johnson, *Acts*, 139.

THEY WENT ABOUT
PREACHING THE WORD

Acts 8:4-40

COMMENTARY

These narratives about the exploits of Philip take readers into the second major phase of Acts, as outlined by Jesus' command of 1:8. This phase involves Judea and Samaria, the geographical regions that provide the focus of the stories of 8:4–12:25. Readers are regularly returned to Jerusalem (e.g., Acts 9; 12), the historic city of God's people, to remind them of the gospel's deep roots in the story of Israel and its Scriptures.

One may divide the chapter into two subsections, focusing on the *geographical* locations of the story. Verses 4-25 tell the story of what happened in a Samaritan urban center while vv. 26-40 tell of events on a deserted road to Gaza. One can also divide the narrative focusing on the characters, resulting in a three-fold division:

A. Philip in Samaria (vv. 4-13)
B. Peter (and John) in Samaria (vv. 14-25)
A'. Philip on the road to Gaza (vv. 26-40)

This structure allows readers to see how Luke tells the story to show the central role of apostolic representatives in the narrative. Though one other than an apostle takes the gospel to its next phase of "Judea and Samaria," the story offers assurance that it moves forward with apostolic involvement, blessing, and sanction.

Philip Went Down to Samaria, 8:4-13

The narrator links this section of the narrative with the conclusion of the previous episode by making reference to the "scattering" (*diasparentes*, v. 4; cf. 8:1) of Jesus' followers. But this scattering moves forward the divine plan of reaching the "ends of the earth": "Scattered Christians transform their flight into a missionary tour."[1]

Philip

In addition to Acts 8, readers of Acts meet Philip in 6:5, as one of "the seven," and 21:8. As early as the second century, church tradition blended the Philip of Acts with the apostle Philip, an apostle mentioned in all New Testament lists of apostles, including Luke–Acts (see Luke 6:14-16; Acts 1:13). The two men are similar in that the Philip of Acts takes the gospel to non-Jews while, according to John 12:20-22, the Apostle Philip is responsible for bringing the Greeks to Jesus. Critical scholars are divided. Some argue that Philip the Apostle and Philip the Deacon are identical, in which case Luke is responsible for leaving the impression that there were two important men by this name (e.g., Matthews). Others argue that it was church tradition that erroneously blended two persons into one (e.g., Watson).

Later Christian apocryphal literature was attracted to Philip. He had one gnostic gospel named after him and he played a significant role in the gnostic text, *Pistis Sophia*. According to the *Acts of Philip*, a late apocryphal acts, he was martyred. Given that much of church tradition identified Philip the Apostle and Philip the Deacon, much of this apocryphal literature reflects this identification.

Christopher R. Matthews, "Philip," *EDB* 1047; JoAnn Ford Watson, "Philip," *ABD* 5.311–12.

The narrative reintroduces readers to Philip, one of the seven Hellenists of Acts 6. [Philip] The text states that he "went down" to "a city of Samaria," understanding "Samaria" to denote the region north of Judea (in biblical idiom one always goes "down from" and "up to" Jerusalem). Some manuscripts read "to *the* city of Samaria." In Luke's time this city was known as "Sebaste"; hence, most interpreters understand Samaria to denote the region. Proclamation to Samaria has now begun.

Philip preaches the word (v. 4), proclaims Christ (v. 5), and speaks "the good news of the kingdom of God" (v. 12). All Christian proclamation, whatever its precise terminology, has to do with offering people the liberating power of God, which frees people from that which binds and corrupts their lives (see ch. 1, Commentary on 1:3). Philip performed signs that offered the liberating power of God over demons and disease. Such "signs" of liberating power provide a concrete link between the work of the Hellenist Philip and that of the twelve apostles (cf. 2:19, 22; 4:16, 22, 30; 5:12) and Jesus, whose characteristic demonstration of liberating power was healing and exorcism (cf. Luke 4:38-44). The gospel message proclaimed by those other than the Twelve is the authentic liberating word.

The people of this Samaritan city gave, "with one accord," careful attention (*proseichon*) to Philip's proclamation (v. 6). Readers see a distinct contrast between the way the Samaritans and the inhabitants of Jerusalem received the word. The latter were divided in their response and, toward the end of the Jerusalem period of witness, almost united in opposition against the Christians. The united receptivity of the Samaritans foreshadows the gospel's more positive reception among those who live beyond Jerusalem.

Receipt of the word brings "much joy" to the city. "Joy" is an appropriate response to the gospel, and even serves to frame the narrative of Luke's Gospel (cf. Luke 1:14; 2:10; 24:52). One of Jesus' parables speaks of people who receive "the word with joy," only to fall away with the coming of temptation because they have no root (Luke 8:13). The Samaritans, too, will face temptation.

Map of Palestine in New Testament Times

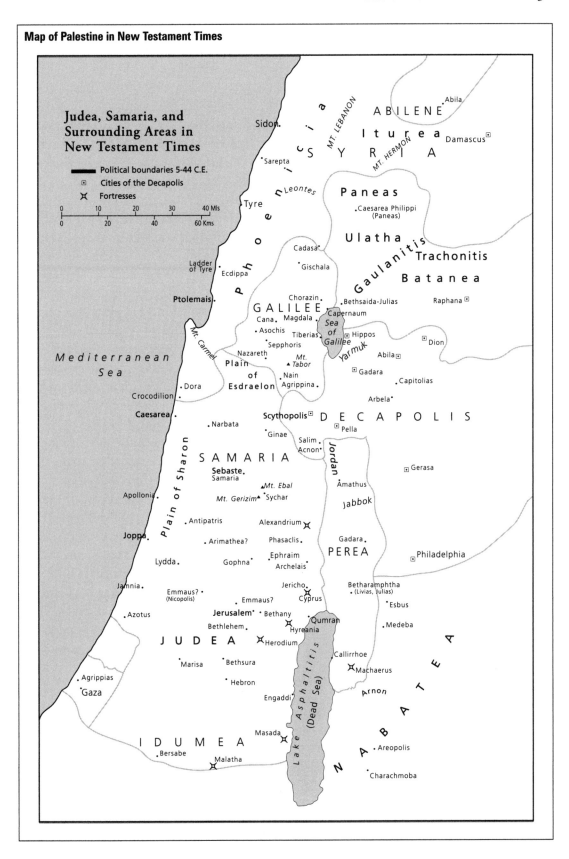

Judea, Samaria, and
Surrounding Areas in
New Testament Times

▬▬▬ Political boundaries 5-44 C.E.
⊡ Cities of the Decapolis
✕ Fortresses

0   10   20   30   40 Mls
0   20   40   60 Kms

Temptation comes in the person of Simon Magus. Verses 9-11 likely present a narrative flashback, filling readers in on what had been happening in this city *before* Philip arrived. The story of Simon is linguistically linked to the story of Philip by the word *prosechō*, "to give heed" (see vv. 6, 10, 11). Just as the Samaritan crowd, "with one accord gave heed" to the gospel (v. 6), they had "all . . . from the least to the greatest" once "given heed" to Simon (v. 10). [Simon Magus]

Simon Magus

He became an infamous character in later church lore, being credited as the first heretic. Justin Martyr speaks of Simon's eventual travels to Rome with his consort, Helen. Their followers revered both of them as divine (*1 Apol.*, 56). Irenaeus (*Haer.*, I. 23), and Hippolytus (*Ref.* VI.4–15) portray Simon's theology as gnostic. The fictional Clementine *Homilies* (esp. XVIII–XIX) greatly dramatize the encounter *between* Peter and Simon, transforming the simple story of Acts into a series of public debates between the orthodox Peter and gnostic Simon. The specifics of these later Christian traditions cannot be verified. It is likely that Simon did have a following at least into the second century and as far away as Rome.

Simon did two things that contrast with and can provide tempting alternatives to the gospel. First, he claimed divine power, perhaps even actual divinity, for himself (v. 10). Second, he worked magic (v. 11). What is meant by the epithet for Simon, "that power of God that is called Great" (v. 10)? The people perceived Simon to be an embodiment of divine power, even a god. The word "power" can serve as a reference to God (cf. Mark 14:62). Following this reading, readers would understand the genitival phrase "of God" as explanatory ("the Power, which is God"), rather than as a genitive of origin ("the power that comes from God").[2]

Magic has also tempted the Samaritans. It is difficult to define the term precisely, but it was generally used as a pejorative term. It denotes counterfeit demonstrations of supernatural power. Some might consider such demonstrations counterfeit because hucksters perform them. Or one might consider "magic" counterfeit because it finds its source in the dark side of the spiritual world. Acts likely leans toward the latter (cf. 19:18-19). [Magic]

Magic

On the theoretical level, magic is regularly distinguished from religion in that magic "attempts to rationally control transcendent powers through precise rituals and recipes with automatic and predictable results" (Johnson, 147). One feature of magic, apparently, was the attempt to manipulate supernatural forces to help one control his or her life. Johnson and other scholars are aware that such neat definitions are theoretically helpful, but practically very difficult to maintain. In ancient literature, "magic" is regularly used to denote activities that the observer wishes to disparage. "Our group" is religious; "your group" practices magic. One can easily imagine that stories such as those found in Acts 5:14-15 and 19:11-12 could be open to the charge of magic from unsympathetic readers. In a world where the immediate intervention of the supernatural was assumed, "magic" was a helpful way to attribute the supernatural workings of an opposing group or person to the dark side of the spiritual universe.

Luke Timothy Johnson, *The Acts of the Apostles* (SacPag 5; Collegeville MN: Liturgical Press, 1992); Susan R. Garrett, *The Demise of the Devil: Magic and the Demonic in Luke's Writings* (Minneapolis: Fortress, 1989); Howard Clark Kee, *Medicine, Miracle, and Magic in New Testament Times* (New York: Cambridge University Press, 1986).

But the power of the gospel is greater than that of a false god or power from the dark side that a false god can manipulate. The Samaritans did not continue to yield to the temptation of Simon, but believed the gospel of the reign of (the true) God and were baptized (v. 12). Even Simon potentially experiences liberation from the dark forces that had moved him before; he also believed and was baptized (v. 13). Readers recall from the story of Ananias and Sapphira (5:1-11) that being a member of the community of faith does not make one immune to temptation. Wealth can be such a temptation (cf. Luke 8:14). Temptation finds Simon an easy target.

Samaria has received the gospel of the *true* God, accompanied by the *true* liberating and *miraculous* power and signs (v. 13) of this God. This first story of Christian success beyond the boundaries of Jerusalem is quite telling. If readers bring to this story what is known *historically* about the Samaritans, they could view them as "marginalized Jews." [The Samaritans] For Luke, Samaritans represent an interesting category of people. Luke classifies them neither as "Gentiles" nor as "marginalized Jews." But they behave very much like some of the Gentiles that readers will encounter later. There is no hint in Luke–Acts that the Samaritans know a version of the Pentateuch, that their ancestor is Abraham, or that they are descendants of the tribes of Israel. They are people who *all* had "given heed" to the claims of a false god who demonstrated demonic power through the working of magic. Readers will not encounter anything more "pagan" even as the gospel reaches to the farthest extremes of "the ends of the earth." The gospel, as Luke tells the story, has not so much moved into "marginalized Jewish territory," as into the world of deepest spiritual darkness: a territory that stands between Jerusalem/Judea and "the ends of the earth." And yet the gospel was successful, even here. Readers can read on with confidence that the gospel can move forward victoriously.

The Apostles Send Peter and John, 8:14-25

Two incidents require attention: (1) the significance of the laying on of hands and the coming of the Spirit (vv. 14-17) and (2) the encounter between Peter and Simon (vv. 18-24).

Hans Conzelmann's overall assessment of vv. 14-17 is helpful: "The point here is not the idea of baptism, but an understanding of the church: the Samaritan church is legitimate if it has been sanctioned by Jerusalem."[3] Attempts to extract from this story of the laying on of hands "data" for the construction of a systematic

The Samaritans

 Luke pays special attention to these people (Luke 9:51-55; 10:25-37; 17:11-19). The region of Samaria was located between Judea and Galilee (see the map located in this chapter). Samaritans were viewed as descendants of the northern kingdom of Israel, whose capital was Samaria (called Sebaste in the New Testament times). Many Israelites intermarried with their Assyrian conquerors who had settled in the land. The Samaritans continued their tradition of Yahweh worship. They had their own version of the Pentateuch, built a temple on Mount Gerizim (which was destroyed by the Hasmoneans in the second century BC), and even looked forward to a messianic-type deliverer, called the *taheb*. Relations between the Samaritans and Jews were hostile (cf. 2 Kgs 17:24-41; Ezra 4:1-4). Awareness of this hostility adds richness and irony to Luke's stories involving Samaritans. However, the Lukan narrative shows no explicit awareness of the history and beliefs of the Samaritans.

Baptism, the Laying on of Hands, and the Holy Spirit

Only the most determined reader can construct from Acts a systematic pattern of the way God bestows the Spirit.

- Receipt of the Spirit without mention of laying on of hands or baptism (2:4).
- Baptism joined with receipt of the Spirit (2:38).
- Baptism, followed by laying on of hands, followed by receipt of the Spirit (8:16, 17).
- Baptism, with no mention of laying on of hands or the Spirit (8:38; 16:15).
- Laying on of hands, followed by receipt of the Spirit, followed by baptism (9:17-18).
- Receipt of the Spirit, without laying on of hands, followed by baptism (10:47-48; cf. 11:15-16).

"There is no doctrine of the Spirit which would shield us against ever-new surprises by the living God, of whose love we know, but not how he will act on us" (91–92).

Eduard Schweizer, *Luke: A Challenge to Present Theology* (Atlanta: John Knox, 1982).

Simony

Simon's attempt to purchase the power to bestow the Holy Spirit gave rise to the term "Simony" to denote the purchase or sale of spiritual things. It was consistently condemned in various church councils (such as Chalcedon [5th c.] and Trent [16th c.]) and the writings of influential church thinkers, such as Aquinas [13th c.]). Such regular official denunciations actually serve as evidence that the practice was widespread, for one generally does not exert energy condemning something that does not exist.

"doctrine" of the Holy Spirit are futile. Luke's narrative descriptions of the ways in which the Holy Spirit comes to believers defy the construction of a coherent "doctrine." [Baptism, the Laying on of Hands, and the Holy Spirit]

The story shows that in those who follow the apostles, as opposed to the Sanhedrin, one finds the true remnant of God's people. Philip's Samaritan mission is the first step beyond the initial Jerusalem phase of witness. The story makes clear that both God and the apostolic leadership sanction this phase of witness. Readers have grown accustomed to seeing Peter and John play the role of "apostolic representatives" (3:1, 3, 4, 11; 4:1, 13, 19). Where they act and speak, the apostles act and speak. In this crucial opening scene as the witness about Christ moves into its next phase, the duo will make their last appearance together as apostolic representatives. As they lay their hands on the Samaritans, they communicate all the apostles' support for and approval of Philip's work. The Samaritans' reception of the Holy Spirit communicates God's blessing both upon the *witness* presented beyond Jerusalem's boundaries and the *people* who stand outside the fold of "the Jewish people."

The story of Peter and Simon (vv. 18-24) continues a theme readers have encountered before: the misuse of wealth. Simon does not misuse money in that he wants to hoard it (recall Ananias and Sapphira, 5:1-11). Rather, he wants to acquire "power" (v. 19) through offering money to Peter. [Simony] In earlier stories, people laid material possessions at the apostles' feet to symbolize their loyalty to these leaders of the renewed Israel. Simon's offer is a parody of this gesture, for he offers money not to signify loyalty, but to aggrandize himself. He wants to treat a gift of God as something he can buy and add to his bag of magical tricks (v. 20).

Peter's response is unequivocal. He reveals his prophetic powers once again, as he discloses the intentions of Simon's heart (v. 22). His words are harsh, declaring that Simon has "no part or lot in this word" (v. 21, RSV). The word "lot" echoes the last time Peter spoke of Judas's "lot" (cf. 1:17). Use of this word on Peter's lips places Simon in company with Judas, another man who experienced judgment. To lose one's lot in "the word," probably denoting here the message of the gospel, is to lose one's hope of experiencing the liberating power offered by God's reign. Peter's call to repentance, therefore, is justified (v. 22). One who so grossly misunderstands the nature of God's gift can only be moved by a heart whose intentions are warped. Peter employs biblical language to describe the root of Simon's intentions: "the gall of bitterness" and "the chains of wickedness."

"Gall of bitterness" echoes Deuteronomy 29:18. This Old Testament text uses the phrase in connection with the worship of false gods. This is quite appropriate, given that Simon had presented himself as a god for the Samaritans to worship. Isaiah 58:6 uses the phrase "chains of wickedness" in the context of speaking of the lack economic justice within Israel. Misuse of money lies at the root of Simon's wickedness.

Simon's response (v. 24) shows appropriate deference and even fear. Readers are left wondering whether he repented; later Christian tradition was sure he did not. However, the Lukan text leaves open Simon's personal destiny. The story leaves at least two impressions on the reader. First, through the words of Peter, Luke impresses upon the reader that the forces of darkness, represented by Simon, can exist *within* the church (cf. 20:28-30). Second, the story assures readers that the legitimate power of God, represented by Peter, is more powerful than the dark forces that move Simon. Simon's plea of v. 24 shows that even he recognizes the superiority of Peter and the power that Peter represents.

Verse 25 renders a quick conclusion, indicating that the witness to the regions of Samaria continues. Perhaps Philip returns with the apostles as they go back to Jerusalem. The Greek text says only that "they" returned (NRSV's "Peter and John" is a gloss). As they return, the word continues to spread throughout Samaria. Perhaps Philip returned with them, as the directions he receives from God in v. 26 use Jerusalem as a point of reference.

An Ethiopian Eunuch, 8:26-40

This story has puzzled interpreters because it appears to offer an account of the conversion of a Gentile. Yet the attention Luke gives to the conversion of Cornelius (Acts 10–11) would seem to indicate that Luke's narrative portrays *the Cornelius episode* as the *initiation* of the "Gentile mission" (see 11:18 and 15:7, 14). If Peter

Ethiopia

Ancient Ethiopia is not identical to the modern country by this name. Ancient Ethiopia is the same as the nation of Cush in the Old Testament (Gen 10:6-8) and was located in area of modern Sudan. The civilization of Cush lasted until c. AD 350. The culture was a source of fascination to the ancients. Pliny the Elder (*Nat.* VI.186–92) speaks of reports that certain regions of Ethiopia produced human monstrosities: people without noses, upper lips, or tongues. Some tribes were said to follow a dog as their king, while others followed a one-eyed king. Awareness of these popular stereotypes of Ethiopians makes God's directing of Philip to invite an Ethiopian into the fold of God's people especially provocative. This gospel really is for all types of people! Other relevant biblical texts are Isa 11:11 and Zeph 3:10.

Eunuchs

Castrated men regularly served in positions of governmental responsibility, particularly in overseeing financial matters and the royal harem. Philostratus tells an amusing story of a eunuch who was attracted to one of the royal concubines. The king wanted to execute the offender, but Apollonius of Tyana recommended that a more fitting punishment would be to let him live, given that he would never be able to satisfy his sexual longings (*Apollonius of Tyana*, I.36).

The Candace

"Candace" was a title (like Pharaoh) for the queen of ancient Ethiopia. The queen was the official head of this government (see Pliny the Elder, *Nat.* VI.186). A novelistic biography of Alexander seems to understand "Candace" as the queen's name, for a certain Queen "Kandake" appears in one portion of this novel (Psuedo-Callisthenes, *Alexander Romance*, III.18–23).

is the instrument through whom God "first visited the Gentiles" (15:14), how does one make sense of Philip's encounter with this non-Jewish (Gentile) man from Ethiopia? [Ethiopia]

The story echoes texts such as Deuteronomy 23:1 and Isaiah 56:3-7. The Deuteronomic text explicitly states that castrated men cannot enter the assembly of the Lord. Yet the Isaianic text states that in the new age of salvation, even the eunuchs and foreigners would be admitted into God's house (see Isa 56:3-7). [Eunuchs] It is significant that this man was a *eunuch* from a *foreign* land, for he embodies those of whom Isaiah 56:3-7 speaks.

In Isaiah, the eunuch and the foreigner were to find full acceptance in God's house, the temple. It is significant that in the Lukan narrative the promise of Isaiah, the promise of full inclusion among God's people of *foreigners* and *eunuchs*, finds its fulfillment *not* in Jerusalem and the temple, from which the eunuch is returning, but in his hearing and receiving of the gospel. Readers miss much of the punch of this story if they fail to observe that this man, as a foreigner and eunuch, is *excluded* from the fold of Israel. Thus, whatever sense readers make of this story, it is best not to downplay the Gentile (foreign) status of this character.[4]

This eunuch is certainly sympathetic with the Jewish faith. He is, after all, returning to his homeland after having made a pilgrimage to Jerusalem to worship (v. 27). [The Candace] While the text leaves a gap, not saying one way or the other whether the eunuch would have been welcomed into the inner courts, it is legitimate for readers to fill the gap with the assumption that he would not have been welcomed into the inner courts of the temple. Nothing Luke has said to this point would imply the welcoming of the eunuch, and readers later will learn of staunch, even violent resistance to the idea of allowing non-Jews into the temple (21:29). This eunuch represents a Gentile who is sympathetic with the Jewish faith, but who is not "qualified" to be a full participant within this faith.

Readers would profit to pause and reflect further on the notice that the eunuch has been to Jerusalem to worship (*proskyneō*, v. 27). Recall that Israel's *raison d'être* was to worship (*latreuō*) God (7:7). Luke does not employ the same Greek word in 8:27, but he does not sharply distinguish between the two words (see, e.g., Luke 4:7, 8; Acts 7:42, 43; 24:11, 14). This non-Jewish person, one excluded from the temple by those who have run Philip out of Jerusalem, satisfies better in his life Israel's reason to be than does Israel itself.

One can appeal to Luke's use of sources to address the problem of the tension between this story about the conversion of a Gentile and the more detailed story of Cornelius. For example, Hans Conzelmann argues that the Ethiopian story served as the Hellenist Christians' account of the conversion of the first Gentile.[5] It existed as a rival narrative to the Hebrew Christians' account of the first Gentile conversion, the Cornelius story. Luke wanted to employ the Philip story, despite the tension it would create with the Cornelius story, for it offered a concrete tradition about the activities of the Hellenist Christians. He apparently did not have an abundance of traditions from these circles on which to draw. Luke then tried, without much success, to downplay the tension it would create with the Cornelius story by avoiding the term "Gentile" to describe this eunuch.

Robert Tannehill offers a literary solution to the problem. He argues that within the flow of the narrative the story of the eunuch serves to foreshadow *for the reader* the Gentile mission "to the ends of the earth."[6] He thinks it significant that only the two characters in the story and the reader of the story know of this incident. It is a private foreshadowing offered to readers, so that by the time they come to Acts 10–11, they can watch the Jerusalem Christians come to realize what they already know: God has granted repentance and life to the Gentiles.

Another intriguing point of comparison with the Cornelius/Peter story of Acts 10–11 is the emphasis that the narrative gives to divine guidance and direction. The guidance of God is unmistakable in this story. An angelic command begins the action (v. 26). Though the angel sends Philip down a deserted road, he comes across a eunuch who is quite positively predisposed to hearing the gospel. He worships the God of Israel (even if he is forced to stand outside the main temple), and he is reading from the Jewish Scriptures. [Desert Road]

The Spirit explicitly directs Philip to approach this man (v. 29). As Philip approaches, he hears (ancients tended to read aloud, even

Desert Road

The Greek text literally reads, "this is a desert"
or "this is a deserted place" (the word "road" is
not present, but is usually the understood antecedent of
"this"). Interpreters have understood the phrase in one of
three ways: (1) A road going through a desert region. But
the region becomes desert only to the south of Gaza. (2)
A road not frequently traveled, "a deserted road." (3) A
road leading to the "old Gaza," which was located
between Ascalon and "new Gaza." Old Gaza was
destroyed and deserted in the late fourth century BC.
Hence, the meaning would be "the road from Jerusalem
to Gaza, this is the deserted city." Most commentators
will opt for the first or second reading.

when reading to themselves) the eunuch as he reads from Isaiah (v. 30). More importantly, he is reading a text he cannot understand (vv. 31, 34). The text is about the Suffering Servant (vv. 32-33; Isa 53:7-8). Further, the two verses the narrator identifies give clear expression to what lies at the heart of the gospel: the suffering/death and vindication/resurrection of God's servant. Isaiah speaks about the humiliation and denial of justice (v. 33a), as well as the servant's life being taken up from the earth (v. 33b). All of this provides Philip the opportunity to open the eunuch's mind to understand the Scriptures (cf. Luke 24:45).

[Augustine and Biblical Interpretation]

Another indication of the divine direction is the coming upon water for baptism (vv. 36-39a). The narrative offers one final reminder of the Spirit's direct involvement in the action as it tells readers that the Spirit moved Philip on to yet other opportunities to preach the gospel "to all the towns till he came to Caesarea" (v. 40). Perhaps notification of Philip's preaching to other towns serves to provide readers what they need to know to fill some gaps that come *later* in the narrative. Acts speaks later of saints in the cities of Lydda (9:32) and Joppa (9:36), as well as Caesarea (10:1). Perhaps the man who brought the gospel to Caesarea brought it to Lydda and Joppa as well.

Tannehill's reading of this story as a foreshadowing of the witness to the ends of the earth is on target. The story prepares readers for what is coming in Acts 10–11 and beyond. In the many stories to follow, the gospel will confront essentially three types of people:

Augustine and Biblical Interpretation

Augustine thought biblical interpretation to be so crucial to the Christian life that he devoted a whole treatise on the subject (*On Christian Doctrine* [*CD*]). Augustine conceded that God could offer *direct* illumination to a reader of Scripture, "but the condition of our race would have been much more degraded if God had not chosen to make use of men as the ministers of His word to their fellow-men" (*CD* Preface 6). Augustine employs the story of Philip and the eunuch to illustrate the importance of human teachers in the interpretation of Scripture:

And we know that the eunuch who was reading Isaiah the prophet, and did not understand what he read, was not sent by the apostle to an angel, nor was it an angel who explained to him what he did not understand, nor was he inwardly illuminated by the grace of God without the interposition of man; on the contrary, at the suggestion of God, Philip, who did understand the prophet, came to him, and sat with him, and in human words, and with a human tongue, opened to him the Scriptures (*CD* Preface 7).

Augustine, *On Christian Doctrine*, NewAdvent.org, http://www.newadvent.org/fathers/12020.htm (21 June 2006).

Jews, Gentiles who sympathize with Judaism, and Gentiles who live in darkness of idolatry and demonic deception. The Jerusalem section (Acts 1–7) has prepared readers for what they will see when the Jews around the world hear the gospel. This gospel will create division and, regrettably, meet mostly with rejection. The word of the gospel will also divide the Gentiles. Yet the overall movement of the narrative will impress upon the reader that the Gentile world is more receptive to the gospel. And this is precisely what Acts 8 prepares readers to see. The Samaritans and the Ethiopian eunuch, respectively, represent the kinds of non-Jewish folk readers will meet in the ensuing chapters: those who live in the total darkness of demonic deception and those who live sympathetically on fringes of Judaism. And these two representatives also foreshadow in their *response* to the gospel the response of the Gentiles that readers will meet in later chapters: joyfully (see vv. 8, 39) they receive the good news.

CONNECTIONS

This narrative connects directly with a number of key theological issues of Acts. We will focus first on the theme of witness. Through Philip's witness of the gospel, "outsiders" are invited to participate fully in the worship of God. Whether people live under the oppression of darkness or exclusivism, the gospel offers liberation from the forces that enslave and alienate.

Application to our own contexts requires thoughtful translation. We appear trite and irrelevant if our application of Luke's message of liberation from the forces of magic is nothing more than a diatribe against reading over the horoscopes or attending a David Copperfield "night of magic." Philip is not offering the gospel to liberate people from mundane forms of amusement.

Perhaps we should recall what "magic" was: the desire to control one's fate and circumstances through the manipulation of forces that made the world go round. But the narrative assumes, ironically, that submission to the magic of Simon, manipulative tricks that promised liberation, itself became a force of bondage from which the Samaritans needed to be liberated. What do persons of our world identify as the forces that promise freedom, but which, when followed blindly, deliver only another kind of bondage? Are we slaves to that better-paying job that promised greater financial independence? Do we acquire power to liberate ourselves from those who would lord over us, only to discover that the fear of

Philip Baptizing Ethiopian Eunuch

Alexandre-Denis Abel de Pujol (1787–1861). *St. Philip baptising the Queen of Ethiopia's eunuch on the road from Jerusalem to Gaza.* 1848. Oil on canvas. (Credit: Réunion des Musées Nationaux / Art Resource, NY)

losing power now enslaves us? False liberators, like Simon and his magic, become the oppressors.

The gospel to which we bear witness promises liberation from the seductive forces that offer only counterfeit freedom. The gospel does not liberate by providing some better means to find so much money that we don't need to worry about the bills anymore or so much power over other people that we don't have to worry about being pushed around anymore. A "gospel" that offers these is only another form of magic, preached in the name of Jesus rather than Simon. The gospel to which we bear witness has the potential to liberate from the very need of false liberation.

Simon offers his money to Peter in order to expand his bag of manipulative tricks. Simon shows he's still not liberated from his need to try to manipulate life and seduce people with his charisma. Barnabas (4:36-37) offered his money to demonstrate his submission to the gospel and, by this very act of submission, showed himself liberated from the need to hoard for himself resources he did not need (contrast Barnabas with the rich fool of Luke 12:13-21). We end our reading of this story with the sense that Simon is still not truly free. We likely have many in the pews every Sunday who, like Simon, have believed and been baptized, but are still not free. What does the gospel to which we bear witness say to them? Perhaps one thing that still enslaves many of our people is an attitude of exclusiveness, which brings us to the story of the Ethiopian eunuch.

The gospel to which we bear witness is an inclusive gospel. It delivers to the Ethiopian eunuch what texts such as Isaiah 56:3-7 could only promise: full participation in the worship of God. As with our connections with the narrative's talk about magic, we must connect this story in a way that is meaningful and on-target. Not too many churches these days wrestle with the dilemma of admitting castrated Ethiopians into the congregation.

The narrative assumes that we are dealing with a person who *wants* to worship God. This Ethiopian traveled hundreds of miles to Jerusalem to stand in the outer courts and pray to God. His disqualification from full participation was rooted not in some kind of blind Jewish prejudice, but in the written word of God (Deut 23:1). The tough task for us is to decide how we respond to those who *want* to worship with God's people, but whom our traditions, *even scriptural traditions*, seem to disqualify.

What do we say to the woman who has given birth to an illegitimate child who wants to come to our place to worship and raise her child among God's people? Do we follow the counsel of Deuteronomy 23:2, banning from our congregations "those born of an illicit union . . . even to the tenth generation"? What should be our word to that unmarried, cohabiting couple who want to come and worship among us? There is no question but that these "fornicators" do not qualify; Scripture offers testimony no less ambiguous than Deuteronomy 23:1 (for example, 1 Cor 5:11). And despite attempts at revisionist re-readings, it is very difficult to make scriptural testimony regarding homosexual behavior read positively, or even neutrally. Texts such as Romans 1:26-27 seem to be just as clear regarding homosexual behavior as Deuteronomy 23:1 is regarding castrated men. But what do we say when the gay or lesbian couple comes and stands outside the gates leading to our sanctuary because they want to worship with God's people?

Are *we* the ones who send the bastards, fornicators, and homosexuals off to read their Bibles alone on a deserted road? Or are we the ones who track them down, join them in the chariot, and talk about how Scripture finds its meaning in the gospel of Jesus Christ? Perhaps it is not accidental that the witness who speaks to the Samaritans and the eunuch had, himself, been run out of God's holy city by God's holy people. That often happens to those who preach God's liberating word to *all* people.

The themes of the providential design and human participation in the divine drama also deserve brief connecting commentary. As we showed in the Commentary section, the text describes the divine guidance of Philip's opportunity to preach to the eunuch. To what extent do contemporary Christians really believe that they live in a world where God is so active? How would most who sing praises and offer prayers to God each Sunday really respond if someone claimed that an angel or the Spirit had instructed them in some very specific task (cf. 8:26, 29)? The statement attributed to comedienne Lily Tomlin seems true: "When we talk to God it's called prayer; when he talks to us it's called schizophrenia."

Many contemporary Christians have internalized the Enlightened, Newtonian, mechanistic model of the universe as a self-contained system of cause and effect. How does divine action fit into this kind of world? We may need to begin with blunt

Lenses of Life

With regard to the issue of the involvement of God in the affairs of life, Robert John Russell, director of The Center for Theology and the Natural Sciences at Berkeley, offers the following statement:

Metaphorically, one could say that what we normally take as "nature" is in reality the activity of "God + nature." . . . It is as much a leap of secular faith to view "God + nature" as just "nature" as it is a leap of theistic faith to view "nature" as "God + nature," although the former is the working assumption of modernity (and with it, science). One could say that we are presented with a choice between naturalism and theism: The same evidence from science is available to both, and the choice of presuppositions is crucial.

Robert John Russell, "Does the 'God Who Acts' Really Act?: New Approaches to Divine Action in Light of Science," *Theology Today* 54/1 (1997): 58.

honesty, admitting that much of how we make sense of the world in which we live is shaped by the various presuppositions and assumptions about life that we bring to those experiences. Do we dare to believe that God is so much a part of the fabric of the world and events that surround us that God's words and deeds are not intrusions upon "nature"? We "act" in our worlds every day, and we hardly see our workings as intrusive on some "natural" order, as though we live "outside" nature, rather than integrated within it. [Lenses of Life]

Aside from the explicit references to the angel (v. 26) and the Spirit (vv. 29, 39), most of what "moves the story along" one could credit to happenstance. We are not *told* that Philip's decision to talk to the eunuch, the eunuch's reading from Isaiah or his inquisitive and open spirit, or the sudden appearance of water for baptism were "divinely planned." It's a fair reading to think that they were, because we know our narrator presents readers with a narrative world that operates under divine guidance. But readers could *choose* to view these events in the story as happenstance. It may not be too different with life. We can choose to view history as a series of events, related only by mechanical causality, but signifying nothing. Or we can choose to view the world as something in which God participates, even as we do, not as some outside intruder, but as an integral member. [Providence, Prayer, and Presuppositions]

Providence, Prayer, and Presuppositions

The March 31, 1997, edition of *Newsweek* ran a cover story on prayer. A couple of responses from readers to the story (found in the April 21, 1997, issue) illustrate just how "presuppositions" shape the way that people understand God's participation, or lack thereof, in the affairs of life.

One reader responded:

God always answers prayers. . . . Sometimes it is his perfect timing to answer "yes" to a person's prayer, and sometimes it is for the person's benefit for him to answer "no" or "wait." God is not a genie: he is a loving Father who gives his children things they ask for *in his will* and when it is best for them.

Another said:

Life is a crap shoot—some people luck out and some people don't. . . . When [people] pray and get they wished for, they are sure that their prayers were "answered." When they pray and don't get what they wanted, it was "God's will." Actually, it is always just random chance.

Neither statement can be tested in some so-called objective fashion. Each reveals the presuppositions that one brings to the experience of life. Each reveals its own kind of "leap of faith."

When we understand life this way, we do not become passive observers. One cannot read the Acts of the Apostles and offer any legitimate interpretation that claims that this narrative advocates passive non-involvement. Philip was on the lookout for opportunities to work in partnership with God as a witness for the gospel. And when he lived with eyes open, opportunities presented themselves. Belief in divine providence and human beings' partnership in such divine activity spurs the characters of Acts to action.

NOTES

[1] Ernst Haenchen, *The Acts of the Apostles: A Commentary* (Philadelphia: Westminster, 1971), 301.

[2] "'[T]he great power' was a Samaritan designation for the supreme deity" (ibid., 302.)

[3] Hans Conzelmann, *Acts of the Apostles* (Hermeneia; Philadelphia: Fortress, 1987), 65.

[4] Contra Luke Timothy Johnson, *The Acts of the Apostles* (SacPag 5; Collegeville MN: Liturgical Press, 1992), 159–60.

[5] Conzelmann, *Acts*, 67–68.

[6] Robert W. Tannehill, *The Narrative Unity of Luke–Acts: A Literary Interpretation*, 2 vols. (Minneapolis: Fortress, 1990), 2.107–110.

SAUL: A CHOSEN INSTRUMENT OF CHRIST

Acts 9:1-31

COMMENTARY

Acts 8 has set the stage for the expansion of the gospel beyond the boundaries of Jerusalem. The narrator will now introduce in detail the man who will be the Messiah's primary instrument for carrying the gospel to "the ends of the earth," Saul of Tarsus. The story divides into three smaller sections: the story of Saul's conversion (vv. 1-19a), Saul's preaching in Damascus (vv. 19b-25), and Saul's brief exploits in Jerusalem (vv. 26-31). [Saul of Tarsus]

He Regained His Sight, 9:1-19a

The words used to describe Saul in v. 1 call the reader back to 8:1b-3. In Semitic idiom, anger was associated with breath. The "threats" and "murder" that Saul breathes indicate the depth of his anger toward the disciples. While Saul is the focus of the narrative, the narrator will not allow readers to forget that the Sanhedrin plays a central role in the persecution of the renewed Israel. Saul goes to the high priest (Annas in Luke's narrative world, see 4:6 and [Jewish Rulers of Acts]) "for letters to the synagogues at Damascus." These letters would somehow assist Paul to bring to Jerusalem followers of the Way who resided in this northern city. [The Way]

Saul of Tarsus

Only Acts uses the name Saul or speaks specifically of Tarsus as his hometown. Paul, in his letters, says nothing explicit either to confirm or contradict this. He claims descent from the tribe of Benjamin (Phil 3:5), the tribe of Israel's first king, Saul (1 Sam 9:21). It is quite possible that one who claimed to be a Benjaminite would bear the name of the first king of Israel. In another passage, Paul says that after he visited Jerusalem for the first time he "went into the regions of Syria and Cilicia" (Gal 1:22). Tarsus is located in Cilicia. Candidly, one would never read this statement to mean that Paul hailed from Tarsus. However, one can read Gal 1:22 as "matching up" with Acts 9:30, at least allowing one to say that there is no contradiction between Paul and Acts on this matter.

The Way

AΩ The word literally means road or path, but can take on the metaphorical meaning of the "path" one follows in life (cf. Pss 1:1, 6; 2:11; Rom 3:17; 1 Cor 12:31b). Luke occasionally uses the term metaphorically with some type of descriptive genitive ("way of salvation" [16:17]; "way of the Lord" [18:25]; "way of God" [18:26]). Luke extends this metaphorical meaning and uses "the Way" in an absolute sense to denote the movement whose message led one to "the way" of salvation, the Lord, or

God (9:2; 19:9, 23; 22:4; 24:14, 22). Scholars debate whether the term originated among non-believers to designate this movement (Jackson and Lake, 4.100) or as a self-designation, created by believers (Haenchen, 320; Polhill, 234).

F. J. Foakes Jackson and Kirsopp Lake, *The Beginnings of Christianity: The Acts of the Apostles*, 5 vols. (Grand Rapids MI: Baker, 1979); Ernst Haenchen, *The Acts of the Apostles: A Commentary* (Philadelphia: Westminster, 1971); John B. Polhill, *Acts* (NAC 26; Nashville: Broadman, 1992).

The narrative creates numerous gaps for the reader. What are these letters, precisely? Perhaps they are official letters of extradition or formal letters outlining Saul's assignment and requesting the assistance of the synagogue leaders to identify disciples. [The Jurisdiction of the Sanhedrin] And why is Saul going to Damascus? How did these Christians get there? Is Saul going to round up Jews who have escaped from Jerusalem or any Christian Jews who reside there? Does he bypass the Samaritans because neither the narrator nor the character Saul understood these people to be Jews? Such questions illustrate how much Luke's narrative is driven by concerns other than composition of a complete *historical* narrative. The narrative makes the main literary point: Saul is the personified persecutor of the church, the arm of the Sanhedrin who will go to any length to find and destroy the people of the Messiah. The tone of vv. 1-2 makes the upcoming reversal of Saul's loyalties even more impressive.

Verses 3-9 describe Saul's encounter with the risen Lord. As Saul approaches Damascus, a flash of light from heaven interrupts the action (v. 3). [Damascus] Readers familiar with biblical imagery would suspect that Saul is about to experience a divine manifestation, or theophany. Biblical narrative regularly employed light (Isa 2:5; 60:19) and flashes of light (Exod 19:16; Ezek 1:4, 13) to denote the presence of the divine. Saul falls to the ground, either out of reverence or fear, and readers and he

The Jurisdiction of the Sanhedrin

The issue of Saul's delegated authority to bring Jews back to Jerusalem creates quite a conundrum. Many argue that there is no good evidence that the Sanhedrin of Jerusalem, or its leader, the high priest, had the power to reach beyond Judea and round up Jews from other jurisdictions and bring them forcibly to Jerusalem. 1 Macc 15:15-21 offers perhaps the strongest evidence, aside from Acts itself, that the high priest and Sanhedrin did have such powers of extradition. It records a letter from Lucius Calpurnius Piso, consul of the Romans (140–139 BC) to Ptolemy VII Physcon that says, among other things: "Therefore if any scoundrels have fled to you from their [the Jews'] country, hand them over to the high priest Simon, so that he may punish them according to their law" (v. 21). Verses 22-24 report that the same letter was sent to numerous rulers throughout the empire. But some scholars question the authenticity of this letter, arguing not that a fraudulent letter was circulated, but that it exists only in the narrative world of 1 Maccabees (e.g., Conzelmann, 71).

Others argue that even if we grant its authenticity *and* assume that this policy was still in force some 200 years later, the letters from the high priest should *not* have been addressed to the synagogue leaders, but the non-Jewish authorities (Lüdemann, 106–107). As with so much in Acts, those who read skeptically will question Acts' veracity, while those who read with a less skeptical eye will give Luke the benefit of the doubt.

Hans Conzelmann, *Acts of the Apostles* (Hermeneia; Philadelphia: Fortress, 1987); Gerd Lüdemann, *Early Christianity according to the Traditions in Acts: A Commentary* (Minneapolis: Fortress, 1989).

Damascus

Located in southern Syria, this old city (dating back to the second millennium BC) was literally an oasis that stood along a major trade route connecting Mesopotamia and Egypt. Like other cities of the Decapolis, Greek culture dominated, though a substantial Jewish population lived there (according to Josephus, *J. W.* 2.561, 7.368, *thousands* of Jews living there died in the revolt of AD 66). Given that this was a major urban center heavily populated by Jews along a major trade route, it is reasonable that the gospel message would find its way there relatively quickly. Luke, however, offers no word on how the gospel came to Damascus.

together hear a voice (v. 4). Readers know that either God or Jesus speaks. Saul, however, is baffled—in the dark, so to speak, as his question makes clear: "Who are you, Lord?" (v. 5a). Readers hear the question ironically, for Saul is addressing "the Lord" whose own disciples he is threatening to kill (cf. v. 1). Saul's confusion is quickly clarified as the Lord Jesus identifies himself as the one whom Saul persecutes (v. 5b). Readers learn something also about how close the relationship is between Jesus and his followers: "Whoever persecutes Christians persecutes Christ" (cf. John 13:20).[1]

The risen Jesus continues to speak to Saul in v. 6, informing him that he will receive further instructions after he has entered the city. Both the reader and Saul must wait to see what the Lord has in store for this persecutor of Christ's people. Will it be judgment or grace?

While Saul's encounter with the Lord is a personal experience, having heard his name spoken by the voice, the narrator also wants readers to understand it as an objective event. This is the function of v. 7. Saul's companions stand speechless. They are as shocked as he. They have heard the sound (*phōnēs*). The Greek word could be translated as "voice," but readers are given no clues that, even if the companions did hear a "voice," they understood the words addressed to Saul. Further, the text says most explicitly that they did not see anyone. Employing the vehicle of descriptive narrative, Luke leaves the impression that while something "objective" happened, something also intensely personal with regard to Saul happened within this event.

In obedience to the command "to arise" (v. 6), Saul gets up. He now discovers on a literal level what readers already knew to be true about him on a spiritual/metaphorical level: he is blind (v. 8). Ironically, through this physical blindness he will come to see spiritually what he had not to this point been able see: that Jesus is the Messiah in whom God's promises to Israel find fulfillment. His companions lead him to Damascus. He waits in darkness for three days, neither eating nor drinking. The text offers no reason for this fast, but later clues (e.g., "praying" [v. 11b], visionary experiences

The Conversion on the Road to Damascus

Though inspired by the Carracci family (see [The Martyrdom of Saint Stephen]), Michelangelo is generally credited with the creation of the Baroque style. To be noted is his realism and use of light. The light almost beats down on Saul as he lies on the Damascus road, offering a sense of the overwhelming power of the light that has blinded him. The outstretched arms communicate a desperate reaching out for help. The man with him, cowering behind the horse, is in no position to help Saul. Saul's help must come from the Lord.

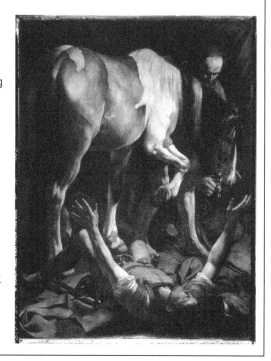

Michelangelo Merisi da Caravaggio (1573–1610). *The Conversion of Saint Paul.* S. Maria del Popolo, Rome, Italy. (Credit: Scala / Art Resource, NY)

Ananias

The name means "Yahweh is gracious." Whereas the name is ironic when applied to the Ananias of 5:1-11, it is fitting for this Ananias. Even more skeptical readers (e.g., Lüdemann, 113) acknowledge that Luke inherited this basic story from tradition, for he would not have "made up" a character with the same name as two other infamous characters in Acts (5:1-11; 23:2-5). How he came to be a follower of Jesus is left unsaid. Readers might assume that he is either a refugee from Jerusalem (though v. 13 implies that he is not) or that he learned of Jesus from refugees who had fled Jerusalem. Some scholars suggest on a *historical* level that followers of Jesus from the time of his ministry, quite independently of the apostles, carried his message to various places within the region, such as Damascus (Jackson and Lake, 4.102). This may true, historically, but Luke is so concerned to establish "Jerusalem ties" that it is not prudent to understand the Lukan narrative to be saying this.

Gerd Lüdemann, *Early Christianity according to the Traditions in Acts: A Commentary* (Minneapolis: Fortress, 1989); F. J. Foakes Jackson and Kirsopp Lake, *The Beginnings of Christianity: The Acts of the Apostles*, 5 vols. (Grand Rapids MI: Baker, 1979).

[v. 12], and eventual baptism [v. 18]) imply penance.

The scene switches to an unspecified locale in Damascus and a new character, Ananias (v. 10). The narrative does not distract the reader from the main action by offering any information about him. Ananias's vision contrasts with that of Saul. Key, of course, is that Saul must respond to the voice he hears with a question (see v. 5), while Ananias, as a disciple, responds in a manner reminiscent of great persons of faith from the biblical story: "Here I am, Lord" (cf. Gen 22:1, 11; 1 Sam 3:4-14; Isa 6:8). [Ananias]

The vision (vv. 11-12) indicates divine direction, something with which readers are growing quite accustomed. Note the specificity: the name of the street (Straight), the specific home (Judas's), the name of the one Ananias is to help, and even some details about Saul. By listening in on Ananias's vision, readers learn that Saul is in prayer, pointing to his sincerity. Further, readers learn that, even as Ananias is having a vision about Saul, Saul is having a vision about Ananias. This informs readers that God is very much involved in the action. Further, Saul's vision that he will regain his sight through Ananias assures readers that the Lord will show mercy to Saul. God is answering Stephen's prayer (7:60), as well as Saul's.

It is not uncommon in biblical visionary narratives for the one who receives a visionary call to offer a question, mild protest, or incredulous comment (see, e.g., Gen 15:1-3; 17:17; Exod 3:13; 4:1, 10; Luke 1:18, 34). Similarly, Ananias reminds the Lord (and the reader) who this Saul is (vv. 13-14). Imitation of biblical narrative patterns gives a sacrosanct feel to the story, allowing readers to sense that the unfolding of the drama of Acts stands on a continuum with the whole of the biblical story. But Ananias's words also remind *readers* that this Saul has been a tool of the Sanhedrin to oppose those who call upon Jesus' name. This reminder sets the stage for what the Lord has in store for Saul.

Whereas Saul had been a tool of the Sanhedrin, he will now be an instrument (lit., "vessel," cf. 2 Cor 4:7) of Jesus. Whereas Saul had caused those who called upon Jesus' name to suffer, he will now suffer on behalf of the name (vv. 15-16). Saul's loyalties are radically transformed. Foreshadowed in this response is Saul's task of spreading the gospel to Gentiles and standing before various rulers (see esp. 24:10; 25:9-10, 13-14; 26:2-23). Readers also learn that Saul's mission continues to include "the children of Israel." This gospel is rooted in God's enduring promises to Israel.

Ananias and the readers learn of Saul's mission before he does. Perhaps readers are to conclude that Ananias was the one who communicated this calling to Saul (a tentative conclusion confirmed by Paul's retelling of this story in 22:15). God has brought Ananias and the reader into God's confidence regarding Saul. This serves to form a bond between "the Christian community" (represented by Ananias and the reader) and this new follower of the Way. As great as Saul's mission may be, he can only learn of and act upon his calling in the context of the community of faith—an impression confirmed by the rest of this narrative about Saul.

The narrator wastes little time getting Ananias to Judas's home (v. 17a). He lays hands on Saul, confirming him to be a Christian "brother," while sharing that the Lord had told Ananias that Jesus was the one "who appeared" (*ophtheis*) to Saul. The narrator's description of Saul's experience, coupled with Ananias's report of the vision he received concerning Jesus' appearance to Saul, informs readers that this "instrument" of the Lord has received a commission from Jesus himself. This call is further confirmed by Saul's receipt of the Spirit, that Spirit of prophecy that he will need to proclaim the gospel to all people.

Saul's eyes then are opened (v. 18). The end of physical blindness, pictured by the scale-like substance falling from his eyes, brings with it the end of spiritual blindness. Saul has regained his sight on both levels of understanding. Because he now sees spiritually, he is initiated through baptism into the faith community (see [Baptism]). With this initiation, his fast ends as he strengthens himself for the mission that lies ahead (v. 19).

He Proclaimed Jesus, 9:19b-25

Luke introduces this section with his customary general indication of time ("several days," v. 19b; see also v. 23 [and cf. 2:47b; 6:1; 8:1). This narrative device gives the story a sense of chronological movement. It also informs readers that the larger faith community in Damascus has accepted Saul. Historically, one might surmise that Saul was learning some more about the teachings of Jesus or the "kerygma," but such instruction is not part of Luke's narrative world (see [Kerygma]). Hence, one should offer such "commentary" cautiously, in full awareness that suggestions such as these are not "commentary" on the Lukan text, but speculations on events taking place outside the text.

In the narrative world, Luke clearly states that Saul's preaching in the synagogues began "immediately" (v. 20). This preaching in the synagogues, readers will later learn, foreshadows the pattern Saul will employ as he moves toward "the ends of the earth." By preaching in the synagogues, Saul can fulfill his calling to carry the name of Jesus to the "children of Israel" (cf. 9:15). The narrative does not allow readers to hear one of Saul's sermons, but only quick summaries of their essential thrust: Jesus is "the Son of God" (v. 20) and the Christ (v. 22b). Verse 20 offers the only explicit use of "Son of God" in Acts. It could be significant that it is found on the lips of Saul, given that Paul often employed the term in his letters.[2] However, one should not think it striking to find use of this phrase in Acts; it was not foreign to the narrator (cf. Luke 1:32, 35; 4:3, 9, 41; 8:28; 22:70).

More significant to the flow of the story is the response of Saul's audience to his conversion and preaching. [Conversion] To this point, Luke has employed the word "Jews" quite sparingly (2:5, 10). Even the Gospel used the term infrequently

Conversion

"By conversion we mean the reorientation of the soul of an individual, his deliberate turning from indifference or from an earlier form of piety to another, a turning which implies a consciousness that a great change is involved, that the old way was wrong and the new is right" (Nock, 7).

Since the publication of Krister Stendahl's classic essay, "Paul Among Jews and Gentiles," scholars have debated whether one should think of Paul's experience as a "call," like that of an Old Testament prophet, or as a conversion. Stendahl notes, "Here is not a change of 'religion,' that we commonly associate with the word *conversion*. Serving the one and the same God, Paul receives a new and special calling in God's service" (7).

The issue hinges on how one defines "conversion." If one means "to change from one religion to another," Stendahl is quite right. Neither Paul nor Acts thinks of Paul ceasing to be a Jew and joining a "new" religion, Christianity. If one focuses on Nock's definition, one can call Paul's experience a "conversion," for it did result in a "turning . . . from one form of piety to another" including a "consciousness . . . that the old way was wrong and the new is right."

A. D. Nock, *Conversion* (London: Oxford University Press, 1933); *Krister Stendahl Paul among Jews and Gentiles* (Philadelphia: Fortress, 1976).

and always within the title "king of the Jews" (see Luke 23:3, 37, 38). Yet now that the Messiah has appointed the instrument to carry the gospel to all people, "the Jews" emerge as a voice of opposition. Luke was aware that Jesus, Peter, Stephen, Saul, and the many thousands of Jerusalem disciples (cf. 2:5, 10; 21:20) were "Jews." And Luke can use the term "Jews" to denote folk out of whom believers, or at least sympathetic listeners, emerge (13:43; 14:1; 17:11). However, perhaps reflecting the actual context out of which Luke penned his narrative, he depicts "the Jews" primarily as the group that opposes the gospel (see [The Jews]). The response of "the Jews" to Saul ("amazement" [v. 21], "agitation/consternation" [v. 22], violence [v. 23]) foreshadows what is to come.

Contemporary readers must use caution and not transfer today to Jewish people the generally negative portrayal of "the Jews" one finds in Luke's narrative world. Further, in Luke's narrative world the Christian characters do not abandon the Jews; persons like Saul/Paul continue to offer the word of the gospel to them, even as he offers the word to all, until the end of the narrative. Even more importantly, Christian characters *never* respond with violence or "hate speech" toward "the Jews."

Due to threats of violence from the Jews of Damascus, Saul is forced to leave the city, being lowered in a basket. The suffering promised in 9:16 is already beginning to find fulfillment. [Escaping from Damascus]

Escaping from Damascus

Acts 9:25 forms an intriguing intertext with 2 Cor 11:32-33, including the colorful detail of escaping in a basket. Acts states that Saul was fleeing Jewish persecution. Paul states that he was fleeing King Aretas IV (9 BC–AD 38/40). Paul said he went to Arabia (the Nabataean Kingdom, ruled by Aretas, see **Map of Palestine in New Testament Times**) shortly after he became a follower of Jesus, then returned to Damascus (Gal 1:17). One can surmise from this that he did something while in Arabia to lead Aretas to try and seize him. Luke has none of this. Since Luke has spoken only of Saul's preaching in Damascus to Jews, only one group can be responsible for Saul's troubles: the Jews.

Scholars who attempt to reconcile Acts and Paul can argue that "Acts pictures a coalition against the common enemy, the Jews watching the gates from within and the Nabataeans from without" (Polhill, 242). Such readings *may* offer a plausible reconstruction of "what really happened," though such ways of reconciling Acts and Paul are regularly criticized (see Lüdemann, 119). Such harmonized reconstructions of history do not really comment on the Lukan narrative world, but a world that exists *behind* or *outside* the Lukan text. In fact, Acts does *not* "picture a coalition against a common enemy," even *if* that is what "really happened." Acts "pictures" the Jews of Damascus, and only the Jews of Damascus, trying to kill Saul.

John B. Polhill, *Acts* (NAC 26; Nashville: Broadman, 1992); Gerd Lüdemann, *Early Christianity according to the Traditions in Acts: A Commentary* (Minneapolis: Fortress, 1989).

He Went in and out among Them in Jerusalem, 9:26-31

Saul now returns to Jerusalem. The narrative offers no clues about how much time has passed since Saul left for Damascus with the intention of harming disciples, save for the reference to "many days" in v. 23. The fact that the disciples of Jerusalem are still afraid of him and suspect his motives (v. 26) would likely not encourage readers to conclude that years had gone by (cf. Gal 1:17-18). [Acts and Galatians]

Acts and Galatians

Acts 9 offers one of the few texts dealing explicitly with information that other, independent, New Testament texts address. The way one compares and contrasts the text of Acts 9 with Galatians 1 will offer more insight into the assumptions of the interpreter than firm conclusions as to "what really happened." The following table lays out the relevant intertexts between Acts and Galatians, along with comments that illustrate how one can read the two texts emphasizing what they have in common, or how they differ.

Acts 9	Galatians (and other relevant Pauline texts)	Comparisons and Contrasts
Saul journeys to Damascus under the authority of the high priest to bring disciples back to Jerusalem (vv. 1-2).	Paul was a violent persecutor of the church, motivated by zeal and wanting to destroy it (1:13-14).	*Comparison*: The "zeal" that motivated Paul is consistent with the portrait of Acts. Words like "destroy" and "violently" match with Acts. *Contrast*: Paul makes no mention of the Sanhedrin connection, nor does he ever specifically say that he was going to Damascus when he met the Lord. One can read Gal 1 to say that he was already in Damascus.
On the way to Damascus, Saul has a vision of the Lord and is struck blind (vv. 3-9).	Paul speaks of God revealing his Son to him (1:15-16a; cf. 1 Cor 9:1; 15:8). He does not speak of being struck blind.	*Comparison*: Both agree that Paul encountered the risen Lord. Since Paul speaks of "returning" to Damascus after his Arabian tour (Gal 1:17b), one can infer that this experience took place somewhere in or around Damascus. *Contrast*: The *specific* story of Acts, so important to Luke, finds no parallel in Paul's Letters. If Paul already lived in Damascus, the whole story of what happened on the road to Damascus must be called into question.
Ananias heals and, presumably, baptizes Saul (vv. 10-19). Verses 6 and 15-16 imply that Saul learned the specifics of his calling from Ananias. This calling was to preach to Gentiles and Jews.	Paul makes no mention of this character or this incident. He summarizes the essence of his calling as "preaching [Jesus] among the Gentiles" (1:16). In other texts, Paul emphasizes his mission to the Gentiles (cf. e.g., 2:2, 7-9). Further, he never leaves the impression that his call was mediated to him by another human being; rather, it was a direct revelation from God.	*Comparison*: One might argue that Paul's silence regarding Acts 9:10-19 proves nothing (being an argument from silence). While Paul might emphasize in letters to predominately Gentile readers his calling to preach to Gentiles, he was not unconcerned about Jews (cf. Rom 9:3), and he obviously had run-ins with Jewish authorities, implying frequent contact with Jews (2 Cor 11:24, 26). *Contrast*: Paul's insistence that his call was to Gentiles and came directly from God is simply not what Acts says. Acts has an "agenda" (or Tendenz): to show Paul's dependence upon the Jerusalem church and to show the connections between Paul and Jerusalem by having him preach both to Jews and Gentiles, even as Peter did.
Saul leaves Damascus due to Jewish persecution (vv. 23-24).	Paul implies that he left Damascus, noting that he later returned after he went to Arabia (1:17). Paul's account of the basket escape makes no mention of Jews, but only the ethnarch under King Aretas (2 Cor 11:32-33).	Regarding the basket escape, see [**Escaping from Damascus**]. *Comparison*: There is no reason not to believe that Paul encountered persecution from Jews. *Contrast*: Since Paul explicitly says he left because the governor was seeking him, one could conclude that Luke has spun the tradition to emphasize Jewish persecution of Jesus' followers.

There is no mention of this in Acts.	Paul goes to Arabia (v. 17b) and then returns to Damascus. Presumably, Paul would have preached to Gentiles in Arabia, in obedience to his call (1:16).	*Comparison*: Luke writes an abbreviated history. He is not obliged to note all events. Contrast: Paul immediately began to fulfill his call of preaching to Gentiles. Luke cannot say this, for Peter must officially open the doorway; thus, the Lukan Paul must confine his work, for now, to Jews.
Paul goes to Jerusalem and is presented by Barnabas to the apostles (vv. 26-27).	Paul "after three years," goes up to Jerusalem and sees only Peter and James, the brother of Jesus (1:18-20).	*Comparison*: Both agree that Paul met with "apostles." Given the rhetorical situation of Galatians, it makes sense that Paul would not mention Barnabas's role. He does not lie to keep silent about this. *Contrast*: Acts does not leave the impression that Paul visited Jerusalem only after a couple of years. One would not construe the "many days" of Acts 9:23 to denote years without the intertext from Galatians. Luke's tendency to show Paul's close association with Jerusalem has motivated him to leave the impression that Paul visited with the apostles before he preached anywhere, except the "many days" he spent in Damascus. This leaves the wrong impression, historically.
Saul moved among the disciples, preaching to the Jews in Jerusalem (vv. 28-29).	Paul stayed for two weeks (1:18). Verse 23 notes that people of Judea did not know Paul by sight even after he had left Judea. He does not mention that he preached or that he was persecuted.	*Comparison*: Given the rhetorical point of Galatians, there is no reason for Paul to mention his meeting with other Christians or his preaching among the Jews. Verse 23 says, however, that the Judean Christians heard that Paul was "preaching the faith." Could this not imply that he was preaching in Jerusalem? *Contrast* : It is difficult to reconcile how Paul could say that he was still not known by sight to the Judean churches with Acts' statement that he moved about among the disciples. More significantly, the fact that Paul says he was not known by sight indicates that he was not from Jerusalem/Judea, as Acts clearly says. On this major point, Acts is simply wrong, calling into question all the stories involving Paul's persecution of Stephen, association with the Sanhedrin, trip to Damascus, and the Damascus road experience.
Paul went to Tarsus, setting sail from Caesarea (v. 30).	After going to Jerusalem, Paul went into the regions of Syria and Cilicia (1:21).	*Comparison*: Tarsus is in Cilicia, so this matches. *Contrast*: Galatians implies a land journey through the regions of both Syria and Cilicia. Acts implies a sea voyage.

Interpreters who tend to emphasize the contrasts between Paul and Acts include Haenchen (318–36), Conzelmann (70–75) and Lüdemann (106–20). Interpreters emphasizing the similarities and the possibility of harmonizing Acts and Paul include Polhill (230–45), Marshall (166–77), Witherington (324–25), and Hengel (81–91). Johnson offers a helpful summary of essential agreements between Acts and Paul: Paul was called around Damascus, ministered for some period of time before visiting Jerusalem, had to escape from Damascus, visited Jerusalem relatively early during missionary career, met with some apostles there, and went to the region of Cilicia afterward (173).

Ernst Haenchen, *The Acts of the Apostles: A Commentary* (Philadelphia: Westminster, 1971); Hans Conzelmann, *Acts of the Apostles*, Hermeneia (Philadelphia: Fortress, 1987); Gerd Lüdemann, *Early Christianity according to the Traditions in Acts: A Commentary* (Minneapolis: Fortress, 1989); John B. Polhill, *Acts* (NAC 26; Nashville: Broadman, 1992); I. Howard Marshall, *The Acts of the Apostles: An Introduction and Commentary* (TNTC; Leicester: Inter-Varsity Press, 1984); Ben Witherington III, *The Acts of the Apostles: A Socio-Rhetorical Commentary* (Grand Rapids MI: Eerdmans, 1998); Martin Hengel, *Acts and the History of Earliest Christianity* (Philadelphia: Fortress, 1979); Luke Timothy Johnson, *The Acts of the Apostles* (SacPag 5; Collegeville MN: Liturgical Press, 1992).

It is fitting, however, that the Lukan narrative should portray the Jerusalem community as accepting Saul relatively quickly after he became a disciple. While the Jerusalem leaders will not be the primary instruments to carry the gospel "to the ends of the earth," it is they who have the responsibility of verifying and sanctioning this mission.[3] Quickly establishing a bond between the Jerusalem leadership and Saul helps to sanction and legitimate Saul and his mission.

Barnabas plays the role of intermediary (v. 27). His appearance recalls his introduction in 4:36, where the narrator portrayed him as a loyal disciple and interpreted his name to mean "son of encouragement." He clearly plays such an encouraging role here, vouching for Saul. In describing Barnabas's role as Saul's advocate before the apostles, the narrative establishes a bond between Barnabas and Saul, providing a foundation for the close association between them that readers will see in Acts 11–15. The narrative leaves the reader wondering why Barnabas trusted Saul or how he (seemingly) was the only Jerusalem disciple who knew of Saul's experiences in and around Damascus. Readers simply do not need to know these things to understand Barnabas's narrative role as "the son of encouragement," indicating, once again, how narrative concerns drive the author.

The community accepts Saul, as evidenced by his easy movement among the disciples (v. 28a). Saul does in Jerusalem what he did in Damascus: he preaches "in the *name* of the Lord" (v. 29a), again fulfilling partially the call of 9:15 to carry Jesus' *name* to the children of Israel (see [In the Name of Jesus]). Saul's loyalty to the gospel leads the disciples of Jerusalem to accept him. It leads the nonbelieving Jews, however, to the opposite response (v. 29b). Luke could have referred to these opponents of Saul as "Jews." But he calls them "Hellenists." Recalling that "Hellenists" denotes Greek-speaking Jews of the Diaspora who have now settled in Palestine, the narrator may be offering both an ironic flashback and ominous foreshadowing. Flashing back, the last time Saul was associated with some Diaspora Jews in Jerusalem, Stephen was being executed (6:9; 7:54–8:3). Now Saul is their target. Looking ahead, the Hellenists' violent opposition to Saul foreshadows the way many Diaspora Jews will respond to the gospel as Saul carries the word to the ends of the earth.

As in Damascus, the disciples of Jerusalem help Saul to escape trouble, taking him to Caesarea, which Luke knows to be a port city (18:22), from which he embarks a ship for Tarsus, his native city (9:11). In the story world of Acts, Saul will leave the stage while the narrator lays the final foundation stone for the gospel to move to the ends of the earth: the conversion of the Gentile Cornelius. When this is done, Saul will re-enter the narrative and begin to fulfill the other part of his call: to carry Jesus' name "before Gentiles" (9:15).

Just after Saul exits, the text presents a brief pause. Readers are not told why this respite occurs, why the "Hellenists," "Jews," or "Sanhedrin" leave the church at peace, allowing it to be "built up" throughout Judea and Galilee and Samaria. Perhaps one should find God's providential care behind this scene. Regardless, the entire region in which Jesus ministered has heard and is responding to the gospel. Expectations are raised that the next phase, "to the ends of the earth," is about to begin. Narratively, the short summary leaves the impression of the passage of time, providing a pause in the action before the next, very dramatic, story is told (see [Lukan Summaries]). Also, within the flow of the story, a pause is appropriate, given that the one individual most responsible for "making havoc" (9:21) now is a follower of Jesus Christ. The church, for a moment, is at peace.

CONNECTIONS

This text illustrates well the theological theme of human participation in the divine drama. The essential feature of Paul's (to employ Saul's more popular name) call from the risen Lord acknowledges the fact that God chooses human beings to be "instruments" to carry forth God's work. We can learn something of the character of being vessels as we reflect on Paul's call story.

The Commentary noted that the story of Paul's physical blindness served to represent in narrative form something of his inner, spiritual blindness. Hence, when the scales fell from his eyes, Paul had regained more than physical sight. On spiritual matters he saw more clearly than he had to this point. The irony, of course, is that Paul, while breathing threats and murder against the church, likely believed that at *this* time he saw with extreme clarity. Generally, people do not harm other people in the name of God unless they are quite confident of God's will. [Blind Zeal]

Blind Zeal

Charles Kimball's book on the dangers of religion becoming an instrument of evil offers the following apropos statements:

In every religion, truth claims constitute the foundation on which the entire structure rests. However, when particular interpretations of these claims become propositions requiring uniform assent and are treated as rigid doctrines, the likelihood of corruption in that tradition rises exponentially. . . . Authentic religious truth claims are never as inflexible and exclusive as zealous adherents insist. . . . With potentially destructive consequences, people presume to know God, abuse sacred texts, and propagate their particular versions of absolute truth.

Charles Kimball, *When Religion Becomes Evil* (New York: HarperSanFrancisco, 2002), 41, 46.

In his own letters, Paul offers a terse, yet explicit, rationale for his violent and destructive persecution of the church: "As to zeal a persecutor of the church" (Phil 3:6). Paul offers his own definition of "zeal" in another comment he makes regarding his days of wreaking havoc: "I advanced in Judaism beyond many of my own age among my people, so extremely zealous was I for the traditions of my ancestors" (Gal 1:14). It was not some generic kind of zeal that drove Paul into a murderous rage; it was zeal for his religious tradition and heritage. Undoubtedly, he saw himself as a vessel of God, an instrument of righteous judgment, wielding the sword of the Lord. There was no doubt in his mind; he saw clearly the will and way of God.

And yet Paul was blind. He did not see at all. He was not a vessel of the Lord, but an instrument of evil. He was not beyond redemption, for no one is beyond the reach of God; but he lived in a kind of spiritual darkness no less real than the physical darkness that overwhelmed him on the way to Damascus. The Acts narrative, which plays on the image of Paul's sight, provides an intriguing intertext with what Paul himself has to say about seeing: "When I was a child, I spoke like a child, I thought like a child, I reasoned like a child; when I became an adult, I put an end to childish ways. For now we see in a mirror, dimly, but then we will see face to face. Now I know only in part; then I will know fully, even as I have been fully known" (1 Cor 13:11-12).

It is fascinating that immediately after Paul asserts that he has "grown up," no longer speaking, thinking, or reasoning like a child, he acknowledges that "we see in a mirror, dimly," gazing only at indistinct, puzzling, and even enigmatic images (the word that NRSV translates "dimly" is *ainigma*). [We See in a Mirror, Dimly] It is the *mature* Paul, the one who claims to have given up childish ways, who acknowledges that the vision is fuzzy and that making sense of life is like figuring out a riddle (the literal meaning of *ainigma*). The Paul who moved defiantly toward Damascus, armed with the authority bestowed upon him by the religious powers and motivated by righteous rage, suffered no such blurred vision. Or so he thought. He learned, however, that while he thought he saw perfectly, he actually saw things as "through a *glass* eye darkly." He didn't see at all.

Effective vessels, or instruments of the Lord, are *not* driven by righteous rage. They are not driven by zeal for the traditions of the elders (or deacons or even trustees, for that matter!). They are not

We See in a Mirror, Dimly

We know so little. Who is to say what truth is? When the door has been closed and the light turned off for the night, who is to say what goes on in that room we call God?

Excerpt from Anthony S. Abbott, "Point of Light," *Theology Today* 54/1 (1997): 84.

driven by a cocksure confidence that they see all things clearly. Paul was no vessel of the Lord when his life was driven by such forces from the shadows. He became an effective vessel only after he learned that he couldn't see at all. And as he matured, he acquired the quiet confidence to acknowledge that he did not see as an adult nearly as clearly as he thought he saw as a child. We needn't feel sorry for Paul. The light that revealed to him just how dark his life was also healed him. The ones we must feel sorry for (and, perhaps, fear) are the ones who think they've seen the light, but live, think, and act like this religious zealot *before* he met the Lord.

This story also offers some insights into the theme of community. Because of accusations that Paul's apostolic authority was something less than genuine, Paul, in his Letter to the Galatians, felt it necessary to portray his relationship with the Jerusalem church as distant. Acts wishes to emphasize Paul's close association with a larger community of faith. At times, the situation demands that we emphasize our distinctiveness, as Paul did in Galatians. Equally, there are times when it is appropriate "to make every effort [*peirazō*] to join the disciples" (9:26).

In the stories of Paul's association with the churches of Damascus and Jerusalem, the larger community plays primarily the role of deliverer or protector. Paul's disciples in Damascus helped him escape death (v. 25). The disciples of Jerusalem help Paul to escape the Hellenists when they threaten his life (v. 30). Most of us can be grateful today that we don't need the church literally to escape death. But these brief narratives imply that the church is *essential* for the life of the believer. The New Testament does not portray the believer as the rugged, self-contained individualist, dependent on nothing or no one, save for his or her own wit and resources. Disciples are interdependent persons who do not hesitate, simultaneously, to support and depend upon one another. For the modern, enlightened individualist who would call this weak, Paul would totally agree: "If I must boast, I will boast of the things that show my weakness. . . . At Damascus, the governor under King Aretas guarded the city of Damascus in order to seize me, but I was let down in basket through a window in the wall, and escaped his hands" (2 Cor 11:30, 32-33). Which fundamental understanding of life do we embrace?

NOTES

[1] Ernst Haenchen, *The Acts of the Apostles: A Commentary* (Philadelphia: Westminster, 1971), 322.

[2] John B. Polhill, *Acts* (NAC 26; Nashville: Broadman, 1992), 239.

[3] Robert W. Tannehill, *The Narrative Unity of Luke–Acts: A Literary Interpretation*, 2 vols. (Minneapolis: Fortress, 1990), 2.113.

THE GENTILES RECEIVE
REPENTANCE UNTO LIFE

Acts 9:32–11:18

COMMENTARY

Readers have witnessed the startling conversion of Saul, from one who persecuted the Lord to the one who would be the Lord's primary instrument to bring Christ's name before Gentiles and the people of Israel (9:15). The mission to the "ends of the earth" seems ready to swing into full motion. But the mission to "Judea and Samaria" is not yet complete. And Luke's interest in demonstrating the apostolic sanctioning of the progress of the church's mission will require that Peter play a central role in leading the Jerusalem church to take the incredibly important step of openly welcoming Gentiles into the fellowship of God's people. Though the narrative will continue to focus much attention on Judea and Jerusalem, the story of Cornelius and the story of the church at Antioch (11:19-30) allow the reader to infer that the stage is being made ready for the full mission "to the ends of the earth."

   This chapter divides into two larger sections: Peter's mission in the region of Judea (9:32-43) and the Cornelius episode (10:1–11:18). The Cornelius episode is further divided into seven scenes, which will be presented in the context of the discussion of Acts 10–11.

Many Believed in the Lord, 9:32-43

Philip's missionary work in Samaria, then south toward Gaza, and then back north to Caesarea in Samaria offered readers a glimpse of the mission to Judea and Samaria. Peter and John offered Jerusalem's sanction to Philip's work in Samaria. Peter now continues the Judean mission, represented by Peter's work in the Judean cities of Lydda and Joppa. The narrator does not explicitly state that these are cities of Judea, but a glance at the map shows them to be located in the northern extremities of the Judean region. Absent a definitive word from the narrator that Peter is outside Judea, readers are wise to view these stories as descriptions of Peter's witness to Judea. Though the narrative is terse, it serves to illustrate the claim of 9:31 that the church was growing in the regions of Judea, Galilee, and Samaria (though the narrator has not spoken of specific churches in Galilee).

Two miracle stories will provide a transition to the decisive stories of the encounter between Cornelius and Peter and its aftermath (10:1–11:18). Luke will tell these stories in a manner that offers verbal echoes of other narratives of healing, either from the ministry of Jesus or the Old Testament prophets. [Miracle Stories] In so doing, readers can see the connection between Peter and his spiritual predecessors. Thereby, "Peter is validated once more as an authentic representative of the line of prophets who 'work signs and wonders among the people.'"[1]

Verses 32-35 recount the first miracle. Peter is traveling "among them all," denoting either among all the saints (so NRSV, "believers") or all the villages and towns in which the saints lived. The narrative last left Peter in Jerusalem, to which he had returned after visiting the Samaritans who had recently become followers of Jesus (8:25). Likely, readers should imagine Peter in the narrative of Acts 9 to be on a similar tour, vis-

Miracle Stories

In the New Testament, miracle stories follow a form or pattern common to miracle stories across cultures and time. The miracle story describes a condition of need that ordinary means cannot address. The sick (or even dead!) person and the miracle worker encounter each other. The miracle worker does or says something that results in a (usually instantaneous) cure, accompanied by some confirmation, including the amazement of any onlookers. As with other features of biblical narrative, worldviews and assumptions of readers will shape their judgments regarding the historicity of miracles. Throughout church history, even before the Age of Reason and the Enlightenment, the allegorical and/or typological interpretation of miracle stories—as well as the rest of the Bible—was not uncommon. The Reformers tended to favor a literal approach, both with respect to miracle stories and other biblical texts.

Harold E. Remus, "Miracle: New Testament," *ABD* 4.856–69.

City of Caesarea

Ancient City of Caesarea, Israel. (Credit: Stella Levi, istockphoto.com)

iting recently established churches in order to bring them into the fold of the Jerusalem church. Peter's travels bring him to Lydda, a city located about twenty-five miles northwest of Jerusalem. "Saints" likely denotes those led to the Lord either by Philip or other Christians who were scattered due to persecution in Jerusalem (see 8:1b, 4).

While in Lydda, Peter found Aeneas, who had long been paralyzed (v. 33). Given that the text has just informed readers that Peter was visiting the saints, it would be reasonable to conclude that Aeneas is a follower of Jesus. Yet Luke's silence on this issue may imply that Aeneas's status is not the important feature of the story. What is important is that Peter serves as an instrument of Jesus Christ. At Peter's declarative word, "Get up and make your bed," Aeneas immediately rises. The story echoes that of Luke 5:17-26, which further indicates Peter's role as an instrument of Jesus; Peter imitates his Lord. The Gospel story also involved a paralytic whom Jesus healed with words similar to those that Peter used: "Rise, take up your bed and go home" (Luke 5:24). Candidly, the verbal echoes are closer in English than in Greek, but the echoes exist, nonetheless. The precise meaning of the phrase translated in the NRSV as "make your bed" (*strōson seautō*) is open to dispute—one could also translate it into idiomatic English as "set the table," since one spread out a mat to prepare for dining. However one translates the phrase, the message conveyed is that the man is now able to walk; the miracle is a success. Peter does what Jesus does; Peter speaks for Jesus. Peter is an authoritative figure.

As a consequence of this demonstration of Jesus' power, "all" those who lived in Lydda and the Plain of Sharon to the north "turned to the Lord." Readers can confidently consider Luke's "all" as a generalization, denoting a significant number of people. Luke's statement that people "turned to the Lord" would imply that he is thinking of Jews. Jews already believed in God; they needed only to "turn to the Lord [Jesus]." Luke will regularly speak of Gentiles as "turning to *God*" (see 14:14; 15:19; 26:20).

The next story offers an even more dramatic demonstration of power, as Peter raises a disciple from the dead (vv. 36-43). Luke further illustrates Peter's association with mighty prophets who preceded him by telling the story in a manner reminiscent of similar stories from the Jewish Scriptures and the Jesus tradition. [Scriptural Patterns of Resuscitation Narratives] The narrative further confirms Peter's authoritative status as it approaches the story of Cornelius.

Scriptural Patterns of Resuscitation Narratives

The patterns employed in the story of Peter's resuscitation of Tabitha offer numerous echoes of images found in similar stories elsewhere in the Bible. Such echoes implicitly invite readers to make comparisons between Peter and Old Testament prophets and even Jesus, thereby enhancing Peter's authority as a man of God. Compare Acts 9:36-42 with 1 Kgs 17:17-24, 2 Kgs 4:32-37, Mark 5:35-43, and Luke 7:11-17.

Acts 9:36-42	Biblical Parallels
Tabitha's friends place her in an upper room (*hyproio*), v. 37.	Elijah places the dead child in an upper room (*hyproon*), 1 Kgs 17:19, 23.
Peter removes the mourners from the room, v. 40a.	Jesus commands the mourners to leave him alone with Jarius's daughter, her family, and his closest disciples (Mark 5:40). Both Elijah and Elisha perform their miracles of resuscitation in private (1 Kgs 17:18; 2 Kgs 4:32).
Peter prays, v. 40b.	Elijah "cried out" to God (1 Kgs 17:20-21); Elisha "prayed to the LORD" (2 Kgs 4:33).
Peter commands the woman to rise with the words "Tabitha, rise" (Tabitha *anastethi*), v. 40.	Jesus commands Jarius's daughter to rise with the expression *talitha koum* (Mark 5:41), offering a verbal echo with "Tabitha" of the Acts story.
Tabitha "opened her eyes," v. 40c.	The child raised by Elisha "opened his eyes" (2 Kgs 4:35).
Tabitha "sat up," v. 40c.	The young man resuscitated by Jesus "sat up" (Luke 7:15).
Peter "gave her his hand," v. 41a.	Jesus took Jarius's daughter by the hand as he resuscitated her (Mark 5:41).
Peter presented Tabitha to the former mourners alive, v. 41b.	Elijah gave the resuscitated child to his mother (1 Kgs 17:23); Elisha presents the Shunammite woman's son to her (2 Kgs 4:36); Jesus gave the resuscitated son to his mother (Luke 7:15).
The miracle results in a response of faith, v. 42.	The woman recognizes Elijah to be a man of God (1 Kgs 17:24); the people recognize that in Jesus a prophet has arisen among them and God has visited them (Luke 7:16).

The text introduces a certain woman disciple who lived and died in the nearby coastal city of Joppa. She went by the Aramaic name of Tabitha, or "Dorcas" in Greek. Both words meant "gazelle" and were common names in both languages. Dorcas had lived a life of sincere piety, being both good and generous (v. 36b). After she died, she was washed, a custom practiced by both Jews and Gentiles, and placed in an upper room. [Washing the Dead] On the practical level the upper room offered better ventilation; the detail also allows this miracle story to echo similar Old Testament stories. One can only wonder pre-

Washing the Dead

This was considered standard preparation for burial, important enough that "they may make ready [on the Sabbath] all that is needful for the dead, and anoint and wash it, provided that they do not move any member of it" (*m. Shab.* 23:5).

cisely what the disciples who sent for Peter at Lydda expected Peter to do. Did they expect Peter to bring Dorcas back to life? Why was it necessary that Peter hurry? Does this imply a hope of resuscitation, given the popular Jewish belief that on the third day the soul shall have passed permanently into Sheol, the realm of the dead? [Sheol]

Peter goes with the disciples from Joppa, and they take him directly to the upper room where Dorcas lay. The widows (see [Widows]) who had been the beneficiaries of Dorcas's generosity mourn her death. In imitation of scriptural patterns of resuscitation, Peter requires everyone to leave; he prays and then offers his only words in this story, "Tabitha, rise" (v. 40), using the same word for "rise" that he had used in v. 34. Both physical healing and bodily resuscitation serve to point beyond themselves to the promise of "rising" to the new life that believers eventually will share with Christ.

Luke permits the reader, who is alone with Peter and Dorcas in the narrative world, to witness the resuscitation as Dorcas opens her eyes, sits up, is taken by the hand, and lifted up (vv. 40b-41a). The narrative confirms the reality of the miracle, as Peter presents Dorcas alive to "the saints and the widows" (v. 41b). Luke distinguishes the saints and widows not to imply that the widows are not saints, but to bring attention to the fact that these women who had relied on Dorcas now have her back. As with the cure of Aeneas in Lydda, the resuscitation of Dorcas leads many Jews to "believe in the Lord" (v. 42). Peter's stay in Joppa, at the home of Simon the tanner, sets the stage for Peter's encounter with Cornelius. [Tanner]

With the narration of these stories, both of which climax with the notice that many people turned to the Lord, "the task in Palestine proper has been accomplished."[2] The climactic speech of Stephen (Acts 7) fulfilled the "Jerusalem" phase of the mission (1:8). Now the Judea/Samaria phase draws to a conclusion. Philip has been to Samaria (v. 4); the apostles have preached "the gospel to many villages of the Samaritans" (8:25); Philip has preached in the more southern regions, toward Gaza, before he moved toward Caesarea, preaching "the gospel to all the towns" (8:40). Readers

Sheol

In the Old Testament, Sheol denoted the place of the dead where departed "shadows" existed in a kind of numbed forgetfulness (Pss 6:5; 115:17). The fate of all people was the same, and it was not a pleasant prospect (cf. Eccl 3:18-21). Later, many Jews embraced the concept of a resurrected life beyond the dust of the grave that distinguished between righteous and unrighteous human beings (Dan 12:1-3). Texts such as Luke 16:22-23 show evidence that Jews could also conceive of reward or punishment *immediately* after death, where souls would experience either bliss or torment until they were resurrected for the final judgment.

Tanner

Because tanners, by necessity, worked with dead animals, they were chronically unclean. The Mishnah compares the tanner's uncleanness to that of persons afflicted with boils or polyps or who collected dogs' excrement. Some rabbis even required tanners and others who lived in such uncleanness to "put away their wives"; that is, they did not require women to remain married to such men (see *m. Ket.* 7.10). For readers who know this, Peter's residing with "Simon the Tanner" ironically sets up the following scene where Peter appears so scrupulous about matters of ritual cleanness. Peter's residence may also foreshadow his eventual association with another group of "unclean people," the Gentiles.

know that there are Christians in Damascus, even if Luke leaves them wondering how these believers got there (Acts 9). And now Peter's work has led many on the western plains of Palestine to turn to the Lord. Hence, "it is time for the Christian mission to seek goals farther afield."[3]

Who Was I That I Could Withstand God? 10:1–11:18

Peter's statement of 11:17 conveys the central point of the story: God wants to include the Gentiles in the sphere of God's blessing. Acts 10:1–11:18 is a complex tale, discussing two separate, but closely interrelated issues: the admission of the Gentiles into the ranks of God's people and social interaction between Jews and Gentiles, symbolized most appropriately by food taboos.[4]

One can find other places within the New Testament that associate the issues of Gentile inclusion and food laws. For example, Mark 7 offers a controversy story that deals with the issue of clean and unclean food (Mark 7:1-23), central to which is Mark's explicit declaration that Jesus declared all foods clean (Mark 7:19b). Immediately following this story about food, Mark narrates two stories of Jesus' encounters with non-Jews, extending to these people the healing and liberating powers of the kingdom (Mark 7:24-30, 31-37). Mark connects the issues of food and Gentile inclusion.

Similarly, Galatians 2 offers such a connection. In Galatians 2:1-10 Paul narrates how the Jerusalem church offered its blessing to Paul's work among the Gentiles—the Gentiles were to be included among the people of God through the gospel that Paul preached. *Immediately* following this passage, Paul narrates the story of his conflict with Peter regarding association with Gentiles in the context of table fellowship—fellowship that, of course, would involve issues of food purity laws (Gal 2:11-14).

The two issues would go together. Inclusion of the Gentiles into the ranks of God's people would require that people give thought to how Jews would associate with these who, because of their failure to observe Jewish kosher laws, would be considered "unclean." Acts 10:1–11:18, as well as Acts 15, which the commentary considers later, offers Luke's contribution to this important and complex conversation.

Given the importance and complexity of the issue and this Lukan narrative, there is debate over the historicity of the Cornelius episode. The commentary will focus attention on the theological message of the story in the flow of Luke's narrative. [The Historicity of the Cornelius Story]

The Historicity of the Cornelius Story

Interpreters rarely assess the historicity of biblical narratives with cold objectivity. Assumptions that one holds about the Bible invariably shape methods scholars employ to analyze texts, the types of arguments interpreters offer, and the conclusions they reach. Readers' responses to these scholars are also informed by readers' assumptions and overall approaches to the biblical text.

For example, I. H. Marshall surveys the views of some of the more skeptical exegetes on the matter of historicity, only to conclude that such "thorough-going scepticism is unjustified" (182); he adds, "it is unlikely that Luke would have invented it [the essence of the story], or the place of Peter in it" (183). Further, "the way in which the Spirit fell on the Gentiles before their baptism is so unprecedented that it is hardly possible for it to be invented" (183). Note Marshall's appeals to common sense and his sympathetic approach to the text, which would affirm that "thorough-going scepticism" is simply not a justifiable stance.

Gerd Lüdemann represents another approach, subjecting the Cornelius episode, and every text in Acts, to a thorough analysis typical of German critical methods. His analysis consists of identifying Lukan redactional elements, based on a close study of vocabulary, style, and tendencies. These elements denote material that Luke added to traditions he received.

This allows Lüdemann to identify and then analyze the traditional material inherited by Luke. In this particular story, Lüdemann isolates three core pre-Lukan traditions: the conversion of Cornelius, Peter's vision, and the controversy that followed. While these are traditional, they may very well have been discrete traditions and Lukan redaction is responsible for bringing them together; in other words, the tradition of Cornelius's conversion was *originally* unrelated to the tradition of Peter's vision about eating non-kosher foods.

Finally, Lüdemann offers some historical judgments. Likely a Gentile named Cornelius became a Christian under the influence of Peter's preaching, though, *historically* speaking, this conversion only later came to be viewed as having the ground-breaking, history-setting significance that one now sees in Acts. It is also possible, Lüdemann argues, that the story of Peter's vision may be loosely rooted in some type of historical event that served to legitimate Jewish-Christian emancipation from Jewish food laws, but "we know nothing about who received the vision or where" (133).

Note Lüdemann's appeal to rigorous analytical methods, especially his division of the narrative into redactional and traditional layers, from which he then moves to historical judgments. Readers who approach the text with a more sympathetic bent will likely not be persuaded by such dissections and analyses of the text.

I. Howard Marshall, *The Acts of the Apostles: An Introduction and Commentary* (TNTC; Leicester: Inter-Varsity Press, 1984); Gerd Lüdemann, *Early Christianity according to the Traditions in Acts: A Commentary* (Minneapolis: Fortress, 1989).

Commentators divide the story in different ways. Some modern interpreters, representing a diverse range of perspectives, opt for a seven-fold division of the story.[5] This division has an ancient history in the reading of Acts.[6]

Scene One: Cornelius's vision at Caesarea (10:1-8)
Scene Two: Peter's vision at Joppa (10:9-16)
Scene Three: The meeting of Peter and Cornelius's servants at Joppa (10:17-23a)
Scene Four: Peter's visit to Cornelius (10:23b-33)
Scene Five: Peter preaches the gospel (10:34-43)
Scene Six: The Gentile Pentecost (10:44-48)
Scene Seven: Peter's defense at Jerusalem (11:1-18)

Scene One: Cornelius's Vision at Caesarea, 10:1-8

The first scene is set in the seaport city of Caesarea. [Caesarea] Readers recall that Philip had settled in this city (Acts 8:40). The

Caesarea

Caesarea Maritima was originally a small anchorage called Strato's Tower. Herod the Great transformed Strato's Tower into a major port city and renamed it for Caesar Augustus, who had given it to him.

It was a predominantly Gentile city and the official seat of government for the Roman procurators. It was home to a theater, as any decent Gentile city would need, which seated about 3,500 people. Herod also built an aqueduct to bring fresh water to the city. Caesarea plays a significant role in Acts' story of early Christianity. Philip settled there (8:40; 21:8); Paul was imprisoned there (23:23–26:32), and Cornelius's Gentile household experienced the Spirit there (10:44-48).

Caesarea Theater.
(Credit: Tim Frodsham, Portland, OR)

The ruins of a Roman aqueduct leading to Caesarea in Northern Israel. (Credit: Jeffery Borchert, istockphoto.com)

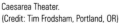

Cornelius

The name may indicate that Cornelius was a descendant of a former slave. In 82 BC Cornelius Sulla freed some 10,000 slaves, many of whom joined the military ranks and took on Cornelius's name, passing it along to their descendants.

Centurion

The centurion was the commander of a unit of 100 men (cf. the English word "century"). Six such units combined to form a cohort of 600 men. Ten cohorts formed a Roman legion. A centurion plays a central role in two well-known Gospel stories, the healing of the centurion's slave (Luke 7:1-10, par.) and the scene of Jesus' death (Luke 23:47, par.).

The Italian Cohort

An ancient inscription makes reference to "the Second Italian Cohort of Roman Citizens," which was based in Syria from around AD 69 onward. There is no specific evidence outside the Acts narrative to confirm the presence of this military unit or a detachment of it in Caesarea during the period of this story (early 40s).

T. R. S. Broughton, "The Roman Army," in F. J. Foakes Jackson and Kirsopp Lake, *The Beginnings of Christianity: The Acts of the Apostles*, 5 vols. (Grand Rapids MI: Baker, 1979), 5.427–45, esp. 5.441–42.

narrative offers no clues, however, that Cornelius had heard Philip's preaching. [Cornelius] Yet the narrative offers abundant clues that this centurion of the Italian cohort was an extremely pious man. [Centurion] [The Italian Cohort] Pious also were his whole household (v. 2) and military aide (v. 7).

The text describes Cornelius as a God-fearer (v. 2a), a term that most commentators understand to denote a Gentile who was quite sympathetic to Judaism, but not a full convert (or proselyte). [God-fearer] Cornelius's behavior, in addition to his overall sympathy with Judaism, portrays his piety. Cornelius regularly practiced two significant modes of traditional Jewish piety, prayer and almsgiving (v. 2b; see [Pillars of Judaism]). Fasting was also a traditional practice of piety, but the narrative does not note this of Cornelius. [Prayer and Almsgiving]

The narrative specifically states that Cornelius received a vision from an angel "about the ninth hour of the day." Given that this was the time of prayer (3:1), the text implies that it was during the act of prayer itself that the vision came to Cornelius. This is appropriate since prayer is an

God-fearer

AΩ One can find a number of references in the New Testament to "fearing God" (e.g., Luke 18:2; 23:40; Acts 10:2, 22; 13:16, 26 [cf. v. 35]; Rom 3:18; 2 Cor 7:1; 1 Pet 2:17; Rev 14:7). One also finds references to those who are "reverent" or "reverence God" (e.g., Acts 13:50; 16:14; 17:4, 17; 18:7). The two terms appear synonymous. The references in Acts 13:16 and 26 are quite intriguing, for here the phrase "those who fear God" is apparently used to denote an identifiable group *other than* Jewish people found within the synagogue community. This has led to the hypothesis that the term "those [or 'one'] who fear[s] God" served in Acts and the ancient world as a semi-technical term to denote Gentiles sympathetic with the Jewish faith, but who were not formal converts to Judaism, or proselytes (cf. Acts 13:43). That such Gentiles did exist is beyond question, and it is quite likely that Luke uses the term, often translated as "God-fearer," to denote these Gentiles attracted to Judaism. It is doubtful, however, that "God-fearer" was a *formal* title used to denote some officially recognized class of religious person. Scholars generally conclude that such God-fearers would have been fertile soil for early Christian missionaries. Joseph Tyson has argued that this group was Luke–Acts' primary audience (Tyson, ch. 1).

Joseph B. Tyson, *Images of Judaism in Luke–Acts* (Columbia: University of South Carolina Press, 1992); see also L. Lake, "Proselytes and God-Fearers," in F. J. Foakes Jackson and Kirsopp Lake, *The Beginnings of Christianity: The Acts of the Apostles*, 5 vols. (Grand Rapids MI: Baker, 1979), 5.74–96, esp. 5.84–88.

act of communication with the Deity. In this instance, God responds unambiguously to the pious Gentile's prayer. Obviously, this Gentile does *not* pray as even the Jesus tradition had stereotypically portrayed Gentiles' prayers: empty words that did not receive God's attention (Matt 6:7). God has heard this pious man's prayers, noted his pious behavior, and now speaks to him. Cornelius responds with fear, but such a response is typical of Lukan characters who encounter the awesomeness of God's messengers (e.g., Luke 1:12, 29; 2:10).

The angel explains, both to Cornelius and the readers, that God has received Cornelius's prayers and alms as he would receive a pleasing sacrifice that "ascends as a memorial" (v. 4). The Septuagint of Leviticus 2:2, 9, 16 connects memorial and sacrifice (NRSV translates the term for "memorial" as "token portion"). One regularly can find instances in both the New Testament and Jewish literature that allude, as Acts 10:4 does, to spiritual sacrifice. This text reinforces the notion that God is far more interested in

Prayer and Almsgiving

 Jesus speaks of prayer and almsgiving in the same context in Matt 6:2-6. The Apocryphal/Deuterocanonical book of Tobit clearly gives highest praise to almsgiving: "Prayer with fasting is good, but better than both is almsgiving with righteousness. . . . For almsgiving saves from death and purges away every sin. Those who give alms will enjoy a full life" (Tob 12:8-9). The Christian tractate *The Didache* (late first or early second century AD) offers praise for prayer and almsgiving, so long as they are done in accordance with the teachings of Jesus (presumably as found in Matt 6): "As for your prayers and acts of charity and all your actions, do them all just as you find it in the Gospel of our Lord" (Did 15:4). An early Christian sermon, *2 Clement*, dating from the early to mid-second century AD, clearly privileges the act of almsgiving: "Charitable giving, therefore, is good, as is repentance from sin. Fasting is better than prayer, while charitable giving is better than both, and love covers a multitude of sins. . . . Blessed is everyone who is found full of these, for charitable giving relieves the burden of sin" (*2 Clem* 16:4).

Spiritual Sacrifice

📖 While the Old Testament assumes the world of literal sacrifice, it regularly speaks of the futility of such a practice apart from a proper moral and spiritual disposition (see, e.g., Isa 1:11-17; Jer 7:21-22; Hos 6:6; Amos 5:21-24; Mic 6:6-8). Awareness that the proper spiritual disposition was truly pleasing to God allowed some Jewish groups, including early Christians, to employ the language of sacrifice to refer to *spiritual* or *moral* attitudes and behavior. The community at Qumran, which produced the Dead Sea Scrolls, interpreted sacrifice non-literally and spiritually: "They [the members of the community] shall atone for guilty rebellion and for sins of unfaithfulness that they may obtain loving-kindness for the Land without the flesh of holocausts and the fat of sacrifice. And prayer rightly offered shall be as an acceptable fragrance of righteousness, and perfection of way as a delectable free-will offering" (1 QS 9:4-5). Texts such as Rom 12:1, Phil 4:18, and 1 Pet 2:6 reveal a similar perspective within the Christian community.

sincere devotion than sacrificial ritual. The fact that God accepts as the equivalent of priestly sacrifice the sincere devotion of even a Gentile implies that something significant is about to happen. [Spiritual Sacrifice]

God responds to Cornelius's prayer by asking him to do something else: send for Peter (v. 5). Pious behavior is not always immediately rewarded. Sometimes, God's response of blessing is not apparent, for rather than rewarding Cornelius, God gives him something else to do. Because Cornelius is faithful, he obeys the divine charge (vv. 7-8). The result will be blessing, going beyond what even the devout Cornelius might have imagined.

Scene Two: Peter's Vision at Joppa, 10:9-16

Scene two switches to "the next day" as the envoy from Cornelius approaches Joppa (v. 9a). If Luke means "the next day" to refer to the day after Cornelius received his vision (which, recall, was in the middle of the afternoon), he must want readers to conclude that the envoy had traveled throughout the night. Thirty-five miles, hence about sixteen hours, separate the two cities. If the envoy left Caesarea the day after Cornelius had his vision, they could easily have made Joppa by noon the following day, even allowing for a night's rest. Hence, Luke may mean by "the next day" the day after the envoy set out from Caesarea, or two days after Cornelius's experience.

The narrator's perspective shifts from the travelers to Peter, whom readers find on the housetop, preparing to pray (v. 9b). The time is about noon, which is not one of the prescribed times for daily Jewish prayer. However, one need not assume that people can pray only at "prescribed" times. Luke notes that Peter was hungry (v. 10). Again, noon is not the normal time for Jews of Palestine to eat, given that their custom was to eat a late morning and mid-afternoon meal. Apparently, Luke thinks it important to note Peter's hunger, perhaps to provide a transition to, or even a primitive psychological explanation for, the upcoming vision of food. Perhaps Luke, in setting the stage for the vision, is simply assuming the more customary noontime "lunch" of Roman society.

Regardless of these details, Peter, like Cornelius, has an intense communicative experience with the Deity while being in a state of prayer. The narrative reports that he saw something descending from heaven like a great sheet (v. 11). I. Howard Marshall suggests that Peter would have been under a large awning that served to provide shade on the rooftop; seeing this awning might have prompted this vision.[7] One, of course, cannot prove or disprove such interpretations.

Central to the visionary experience is Peter's seeing the animals within the sheet, described as "all kinds of four-footed creatures and reptiles and birds of the air" (v. 12). The phraseology is reminiscent of biblical categorizations of animals (cf. Gen 1:30; 6:20). In response to the command to "kill and eat" (v. 13), Peter offers a very strong protest and objection (*mēdamōs*, rendered "by no means" in the NRSV). The intensity of the objection may imply that the vision portrayed *only* unclean animals. If both types of animals appeared, one wonders why Peter could not have understood that he was to "kill and eat" from among the clean animals, simply avoiding the unclean. [Unclean Animals] Contemporary readers who cannot empathize with the Jewish repugnance to eating unclean food would benefit from reading the stories of the Maccabean martyrs. [Eleazar and the Seven Brothers and Their Mother]

Despite the depth of Peter's commitment to traditional *and legal* dietary regulations, the divine voice is quite clear that it wants Peter to consume these animals he considers unclean. First, the heavenly voice declares that Peter should not call "common" what God has cleansed. The food that repulses Peter is now clean (v. 15). Presumably, he is free to eat of it. Second, lest there be any ambiguity for either the reader or Peter, the vision and its accompanying divine command happens two additional times (v. 16).

Readers attempting to find an immediate connection between the preceding story of Cornelius's vision and this story of Peter's vision regarding unclean food may feel frustrated.

Unclean Animals

The Old Testament lays out in summary fashion the categories of clean and unclean animals in Lev 11 and Deut 14. Curious to modern readers is the whole notion of dividing the world into things clean and unclean. Anthropologists have noted that across human cultures all people are inclined to organize and categorize their worlds into spheres of clean and unclean. Hence, "the clean/unclean distinction is Israel's symbolic means of structuring the world. Clean animals stay in their own sphere (land, water, air) and move in a way appropriate to that sphere (walking, swimming, flying). Unclean animals cross between the spheres and use inappropriate locomotion" (Watts, 167; see [Purity]). Though moderns tend not to "divide up" the world as did Jews in the first century, even modern people have a sense of "clean" and "unclean." For example, there are foods that modern Westerners tend not to eat: road kill and domesticated, in-home animals (pets). They would consider this "gross," or "unclean." And moderns certainly know what "dirty words" are and even have appropriate rites to "cleanse" the mouth: washing it out with soap.

J. W. Watts, "Leviticus," *MCB* 157–74.

Eleazar and the Seven Brothers and Their Mother

Their stories are found in the Apocryphal/Deuterocanonical books of 2 and 4 Maccabees (2 Macc 6:12–7:42; 4 Macc 5–12). The former likely was written in the first half of the first century BC and the latter likely between 63 BC and AD 70. The stories speak in graphic detail of the tortures endured by Eleazar, an old and revered priestly leader, and seven brothers for refusing to eat food forbidden by biblical law. The mother of the seven bravely watches her sons die, encouraging them to remain faithful to God even in the face of tortuous death. Such stories can provide modern readers with a sense of the depth of Jewish conviction about demonstrating faith in God through strict observance of God's commands forbidding the eating of unclean foods.

What, after all, does God's acceptance of a Gentile's piety have to do with eating pork or some other (formerly) unclean food? The connection, to be sure, is indirect, but present. Recall the discussion above of the two other places in the New Testament where other writers connected the issue of Gentiles with the issue of dietary regulations. The Old Testament provides a clear connection between the two: "I am the LORD your God; I have separated you from the peoples. You shall therefore make a distinction between the clean animal and the unclean. . . . And I have separated you from the other peoples to be mine" (Lev 20:24b, 25a, 26b). Note how the text *explicitly* associates the Israelites' distinction from non-Israelites and the distinction between clean and unclean foods. In this vein, one should also review 1 Maccabees 1:11, 63. Separation from the Gentiles and separation from unclean food went together.

Thus, the association between the two stories is subtle, but understandable. If God has accepted the piety of a Gentile and, on the basis of that acceptance, called that Gentile to bring Peter to Caesarea, Peter is going to have to associate with a non-Jew. The same disposition that encouraged pious Jews to separate themselves from Gentiles encouraged separation from unclean foods. Peter's vision, informing him that God has cleansed what Peter had thought common, is beginning to break down the categories of purity and cleanness by which Peter had ordered his world. This system of categorization would have discouraged Peter from associating with the "other peoples."

Scene Three: The Meeting of Peter and Cornelius's Servants at Joppa, 10:17-23a

This brief scene describes Peter's encounter with Cornelius's servants. Verse 17a connects this scene of Peter's encounter with Gentiles with the preceding vision about God's declaring formerly common things "clean." Peter's perplexity regarding the meaning of the vision invites readers to attempt to make a connection between the vision and this scene.

The narrative offers readers many additional reminders of God's direct involvement in this story. The servants knew to ask for Simon's house (v. 17b) only because Cornelius had been given Simon's name in his vision (v. 6). Verse 22 employs the servants' words to remind readers of the specific content of Cornelius's vision, even adding some new information at the very end of the verse (Cornelius wants to hear what Peter has to say). Verse 19 is the most explicit indicator of continued divine involvement, for the Spirit expressly commands Peter to accompany these men, informing him that the Spirit had sent them to Peter.

The Spirit commands Peter to accompany the men "without hesitation." This properly translates the Greek expression *mēden diakrinomenos*. Yet it is significant that the term *diakrinomenos* means more basically "to differentiate," "to make distinction," and "to separate." Peter's habit of discriminating between clean and unclean food naturally carried over to a habit of discriminating between people with whom he could associate. His vision has told him that he must not call common what God has cleansed (v. 15). While contemplating this vision, he is now told by the Spirit not to hesitate to accompany these men who are seeking him. By not differentiating or distinguishing between himself and these men, he will obey this command. He takes the first steps toward such obedience when he invites these men to be his guests.

The servants' brief narration of Cornelius's experience that led to their coming to Joppa (v. 22) testifies to God's direction. It also reminds readers of Cornelius's piety, describing him as "upright and God-fearing." Perhaps it is significant that the verb translated as "receive a guest" (v. 23) has as its base meaning "foreigner." Though these men are foreigners—Gentiles—Peter welcomes them.

Scene Four: Peter's Visit to Cornelius, 10:23b-33
On the following day, Peter, the envoy of Cornelius, and "some of the believers from Joppa" depart for Caesarea (v. 23b). Why would Peter take along fellow believers from Joppa? The text does not say. Later, however, when Peter tells his story before the Jerusalem congregation (11:1-18), these believers serve as witnesses to Peter's report (11:12b), helping implicitly to give credence to his narrative. Their accompanying Peter and the servants might further indicate divine guidance: God has provided the witnesses Peter would need to help to persuade the Jerusalem congregation.

The group reaches Caesarea the following day, and Cornelius is waiting for them, along with "his relatives and close friends" (v. 24). How would Cornelius have known when Peter was arriving so that he could have this crowd assembled? The Western textual tradition addressed this question by amending the text accordingly: "And as Peter was approaching Caesarea one of the slaves ran ahead and announced his arrival. And Cornelius leapt up and met him."[8] Such emendations are understandable, but hardly necessary. With all of the divine guidance that readers have witnessed thus far, no one should be surprised that Peter has an audience waiting to hear what God has sent him to say.

Cornelius's response to Peter's entrance, falling at his feet and worshiping him, is not appropriate. Recognition of apostolic authority, represented by placing one's goods at the apostles' feet, is fitting (cf. Acts 4:35). Idolizing the apostles, or any human authority, is wrong. Luke will remind readers again of this fact in Acts 14:15.

Verses 28-29 exhibit judicial rhetoric (see [Types of Rhetorical Persuasion]). In this instance, Peter is attempting to persuade his audience (including the reader) that what has happened is due to *God's* initiative.[9] Verse 28 is especially crucial. Here, Peter makes explicit what the crucial problem is that this story addresses: relations between Jews and Gentiles. Through Peter's voice, readers learn that it is "unlawful for a Jew to associate with or to visit a Gentile." Interaction between Jews and Gentiles was a bit more complex than this. Yet, as Paul's testimony shows, Christian Jews from Jerusalem did not always associate freely with Gentiles (Gal 2:11-14). [Jewish and Gentile Relations] Peter's words also interpret explicitly his understanding of the visionary experience on the rooftop: it is *people* whom God had commanded Peter not to call common or unclean. Peter has learned that laws requiring one to distinguish between clean and unclean animals had encouraged him to distinguish between clean and unclean people. The vision on the rooftop, combined with his experiences of meeting Cornelius's servants, has shown Peter that being a Gentile does not disqualify one from fellowship (v. 29).

Cornelius tells Peter his story (vv. 30-33). This offers the reader yet another reminder of God's involvement in this encounter between the centurion and the apostle. Yet this reiteration also points again to Cornelius's piety, speaking of his visionary experience during prayer. God has brought Peter to the household of this pious man. His audience, "here in the presence of God," is anxious to hear what Peter has to say. It is God who has set the stage for the next most important scenes: the proclamation and of the gospel the results of such proclamation.

Scene Five: Peter Preaches the Gospel, 10:34-43

Marion Soards classifies this speech as epideictic, a persuasive speech that attempts to convince the audience to hold to a certain point of view.[10] Specifically, this speech affirms the good news of salvation in Jesus Christ and its efficacy for all people.

Jewish and Gentile Relations

In first-century Judaism, different Jewish groups had relationships with Gentiles according to varying degrees of strictness. In the regions of Palestine, "the degrees of 'avoidance' compatible with loyalty to Torah were debated by the various parties within Judaism, and distinguished the more extreme separatists like the Essenes from the more moderate like the Pharisees, and from the least observant 'people of the land' ('*am-ha-ares*)" (Johnson, 190). "In the Diaspora, relationships with non-Jews were apparently not avoided in principle" (Conzelmann, 82).

Luko Timothy Johnson, *The Acts of the Apostles* (SacPag 5; Collegeville MN: Liturgical Press, 1992); Hans Conzelmann, *Acts of the Apostles* (Hermeneia; Philadelphia: Fortress, 1987).

Verses 34-35 make explicit the gospel's universal implications. The God behind the gospel is the God of all, "a central theological axiom," according to Luke Johnson.[11] This God shows no partiality with regard to race, ethnicity, or national origin. Yet v. 35 makes clear that God's lack of partiality is directed "in any nation [toward] anyone who fears him and does what is right." It is precisely these people who are "acceptable to him." The *piety* of Cornelius, of which readers were reminded in v. 31, *does* have a bearing on his standing before God. [Human Piety and God's Partiality]

To make his case that the blessings of the gospel are for all people who fear God and do what is right, Peter presents the essential kerygma (vv. 36-42; see [Kerygma]). Close reading of this presentation of the kerygma, curiously, does *not* explicitly make Peter's case that God shows no partiality. God sent the message of the gospel (*logos*) to *Israel* (v. 36a). "That message spread throughout Judea" (v. 37a), the "country of the Jews" (RSV), culminating in "Jerusalem" (v. 39). Even v. 42 states that Jesus commanded his disciples "to preach to the people," *not* noting for Cornelius that Jesus explicitly commanded his disciples *twice* to preach to non-Jews (Luke 24:47; Acts 1:8). Peter does conclude with an emphatic statement that "all the prophets testify . . . that everyone who believes in him receives forgiveness" (v. 43). Still, if one listens to this kerygmatic summary as *Cornelius* would have heard it, one wonders what exactly would have convinced him that this gospel is for all people.

Readers should recall that the speeches of Acts, as much as they may bear some connection with history, are directed primarily to the *readers*. Perhaps the opening words of Peter's speech, "You know" (v. 36, NRSV; v. 37, Greek NT), give away to readers the real audience of these words, for Peter had no reason to assume that Cornelius "knew" the gospel story. But readers do! The primary actors within the kerygmatic summary, God and Jesus, are not unknown figures to the reader. The God who acts in this summary is the God with whom the reader has become quite familiar in the whole narrative of Luke–Acts to this point. It is this God whose Spirit inspired Simeon to proclaim at the beginning of the story that Jesus would be a light to Gentiles (Luke 2:31-32). This same God has just now brought Peter and the Gentile Cornelius together.

Human Piety and God's Partiality

"God does discriminate between those whose behavior is acceptable and those whose attitude is not acceptable. Those who reverence God and practice what is right are acceptable to him. . . . One should note that even Paul was capable of describing the impartial justice of God as being based on one's good or evil works (Rom 2:9-11). . . . The stress on both Cornelius' devoutness *and* his works is perhaps, then, a good corrective to an abused doctrine of grace with no implications for behavior and a reminder of James' dictum that at base, faith and works are inseparable." (260–61)

John B. Polhill, *Acts* (NAC 26; Nashville: Broadman, 1992).

Parenthetically, Peter notes that Jesus is "Lord of all" (v. 36). This *could* speak directly to Cornelius, if he understood *pantōn* ("all") to include "all people," a possible, though not necessary, rendering of the Greek word. Readers, however, recalling that Jesus did command his disciples to proclaim forgiveness of sins to *all* nations in his name (Luke 24:47), would easily recognize the universal implications of the expression "Lord of all."

Finally, while Cornelius must simply trust Peter's declaration that the prophets testify to the universal efficacy of the gospel (v. 43), readers can recall the climactic line of the prophetic quotation that introduced the first sermon preached in Acts: "Then everyone who calls on the name of the Lord shall be saved" (Acts 2:21, quoting Joel 2:32a). Recollection of this prophetic declaration, especially when combined with the readers' knowledge of Jesus' command to preach forgiveness to all nations "*in his name,*" should convince the reader that the gospel is for all people. The next scene will confirm this, both for the reader and for the characters within the narrative.

Scene Six: The Gentile Pentecost, 10:44-48

Though brief, the point of this portion of the narrative is clear: God publicly accepts these Gentiles. Even as Peter is speaking, God acts by pouring out the Spirit on all who heard (v. 44). God apparently is anxious to include this Gentile household among God's people. The narrator makes clear that the Jewish believers witnessed the evidence of God's blessing upon Cornelius and his household (v. 45). The explicit notice that these Jewish believers were amazed confirms the reality of divine action: the Jewish witnesses are not projecting their own wishful thinking onto events.

The evidence offered was "speaking in tongues and extolling God" (v. 46). The reference to tongues calls readers back to the first outpouring of the Spirit, Pentecost (2:1-4). There, the "tongues" represented the gifted ability to proclaim the gospel in various human languages (cf. 2:5-12; see [Tongues]). Yet there is no linguistic barrier to be overcome at Cornelius's house (quite a bit of conversation has already taken place!). Likely, one should conclude that tongues in this context represents something more akin to what one finds in 1 Corinthians 14, perhaps even standing as a virtual synonym for "extolling God."

The language of the narrative may be urging the reader to make connections between this event and initial outpouring of the Spirit in Acts 2. The reference to "tongues," regardless how one might interpret the precise meaning of the term in this context, accomplishes this. Peter's words make the connection between the two scenes explicit, as he compares what he is witnessing to his and other earliest believers' experiences. He notes that these Gentiles before him "have received the Holy Spirit *just as we have*" (v. 47). Readers must supply the implications of what it means that Gentiles have received the Spirit. Again, remembrance of the first Pentecost story helps, for there Peter declared that the coming of the Spirit accompanied "the forgiveness of sin" (2:38). God has cleansed these Gentiles (cf. 10:28) and forgiven them.

It is now necessary for the church to be as inclusive as God has been. Peter recognizes this necessity and calls for the Gentiles' baptism (vv. 47-48; see [Baptism]). These Gentiles are baptized into Jesus' name, just as other believers who had preceded them (cf. 2:38; 8:12). Like the repentant Jews of Jerusalem in Acts 2, these pious Gentiles who have been led by God to hear the proclamation of the gospel now stand on an equal footing among God's people: they too have received the Spirit, forgiveness, and baptism. It is now time to let the larger church know what God has done.

Scene Seven: Peter's Defense at Jerusalem, 11:1-18

This final scene brings the Cornelius narrative to closure. Upon returning to Jerusalem Peter must offer a speech that summarizes for the audience in the story the gist of the narrative of Acts 10 (11:4). At the same time, the speech functions to review the key features of the preceding narrative for the reading audience. Peter's audience within the story is described as "the apostles and the believers [lit., 'brothers'] who were in Judea" (v. 1). Verse 2 then makes reference to "the circumcised believers." Some commentators argue that "the circumcised believers" are synonymous with the apostles and other Judean believers.[12] Others contend that "the circumcised believers" denote a subgroup among the apostles and Judean believers.[13] Given that Luke is able to distinguish between various Christian Jewish groups within Jerusalem (recall Acts 6; cf. Acts 15), one cannot dismiss the possibility that Luke portrays the objections coming from a small element within the Judean congregation. Yet the text is ambiguous. [Circumcised Believers]

Peter Baptizing the Centurion Cornelius

It is not uncommon in ancient art for the same person to be depicted in the representation at different stages within a story. Hence, the figure kneeling at the feet of Peter and the figure standing to Peter's right could both represent Cornelius at different points in the story. Cornelius kneeling at Peter's feet might represent Acts 10:25, which notes that Cornelius fell at Peter's feet and worshiped him. Or it might denote the moment of his baptism; though Acts does not say that Cornelius knelt for the baptism, other Christian art regularly portrays him in this position. Cornelius standing beside Peter might depict Acts 10:30-33, when Cornelius related to Peter his own vision from God.

Baptism of the legionnaire Cornelius by Saint Peter. Detail from the sarcophagus of the "Miraculous Source." Late 4th century. Musee de l'Arles antique, Arles, France. (Credit: Erich Lessing / Art Resource, NY)

Circumcised Believers

AΩ This phrase, found in the NRSV and other modern translations, would more literally be translated as "those out of circumcision." The Greek phrase found in 11:2 is exactly the same as that found in 10:45 to denote those who accompanied Peter to Cornelius's house and were so shocked to see the Spirit come upon the Gentiles. Acts likely means to say something other than "the men who made this criticism were circumcised men." The narrator would likely expect his readers to assume that *all* the men at this meeting in Jerusalem were circumcised. Thus, Acts is likely employing the phrase to denote a religious/theological stance rather than a physical condition. Commentators tend to view "those out of circumcision" as "especially conservative Jewish Christians" (Polhill, 266) or, more pejoratively, "extremists among the Jewish Christians" (Neil, 142). Perhaps they can be linked or even identified with those whom Acts describes as "zealous for the law" (21:20). Though they believe that Jesus is the Messiah, they firmly believe that one is to follow this Messiah while at the same time maintaining strict faithfulness to the law that God had revealed to Moses. Thus, gospel or no gospel, they would have expected neither to see God treat Gentiles just as God treated Jews (10:45) nor to condone a Jew sharing table fellowship with non-Jews.

John B. Polhill, *Acts* (NAC 26; Nashville: Broadman, 1992); William Neil, *Acts: Based on the Revised Standard Version* (Grand Rapids MI: Eerdmans, 1987).

Once news came to Jerusalem that "the Gentiles had also accepted the word of God" (v. 1), Peter's detractors (however one precisely understands "those of the circumcision") accused him of eating with uncircumcised men (v. 3). This appears a curious response to news that Gentiles accepted the word of God. However, if Gentiles have embraced the same God as these Jews, this will have implications on how open Jewish followers of the Messiah will have to be toward these non-Jewish people. It is not difficult to imagine people who have lived separated from other races or ethnic groups being willing to acknowledge that people of other races can love and be loved by God, while at the same time having no intention themselves of associating with these racially different people.

In his response, Peter chooses to focus *explicit* attention on *God's* acceptance of the Gentiles, *not* his social association with them. According to Soards, Peter's deliberative speech functions primarily to convince audiences that God is responsible for what has happened.[14] The fact that "God gave them the same gift that he gave us when we believed" (v. 17) requires one to conclude that "there is nothing that might suggest a status as 'second-class citizens' for the Gentiles."[15] Verse 18 would indicate that Peter was successful in convincing his audience that God had offered life-giving repentance to non-Jews. But Peter's speech at least offered a tacit response to the accusation that he had table fellowship with the Gentiles: "Peter's argument implicitly claimed that Gentiles were full members of the church, and therefore that circumcision and keeping of the law were unnecessary for salvation; it also contained the wider implication that the Jewish distinction between clean and unclean foods and people was abolished."[16] In short, if God has accepted Gentiles, so too must the body of believers.

Acts states that "when they heard this, they were silenced. And they praised God saying, 'Then God has given even to the Gentiles the repentance that leads to life'" (v. 18). Acts notes that before these men offered this praise "they were silenced," implying that the text refers to those who had criticized Peter. That would seem to indicate that they had been persuaded that God had fully accepted the Gentiles. With this conclusion, the story can now move on more deliberately toward "the ends of the earth." Readers will later learn, however, that traditional attitudes die hard, for the church will, again, have to address the controversy over the full acceptance of Gentile believers (Acts 15).

CONNECTIONS

When offered the opportunity to do so, Peter preached the gospel message to Cornelius and his household (10:36-43). The proclamation of the gospel message is the means whereby the church fulfills its calling as "witnesses" (cf. 10:41). That gospel, even in its abbreviated form as presented here by Peter, culminates in the proclamation that Jesus has been ordained by God to be judge of the living and the dead (10:42). This clear affirmation of the cosmic lordship of Christ is *the* essence of the gospel message. The miraculous deeds, the agonizing death, the triumph of resurrection, and the glory of ascension all bear witness to the central confession that "Jesus is Lord." Appropriately, therefore, Peter *begins* his witness with the central confession (10:36) and ends with an affirmation of that same confession as he acknowledges Jesus as the judge of both the living and the dead (10:42), which encompasses that which was, is, and will be.

Peter and the other apostles were privileged to be witnesses to this in a distinctive and unique way, having witnessed the historical ministry of Jesus and his resurrection (10:39, 41). Our experiences are not identical to the historically distinctive experiences of this first—and *only*—generation of apostles. Yet our experiences of God and the living Christ are no less real. And on the basis of our experience of God and Christ, we too share an authoritative witness to the lordship of Christ. If we did not believe this, the important Christian tradition of one's "personal testimony" would be meaningless. To be sure, personal experience cannot legitimate all things, without any accountability to Scripture and even the communities of faith (religious institutions) of which we are a part. "Soul competency" is not the same as "individual arbitrariness." But through the power of our own experiences of the Lord in our own lives, we too can fulfill the calling of being witnesses, wherever we may find that God has led us to be.

A major theme of this story is the role that God plays in directing Cornelius and Peter to their historic encounter. The direction of God manifests itself in this narrative primarily through visionary experiences and the action of the Holy Spirit. It was a vision that prompted Cornelius to send for Peter (10:5-6). It was Peter's vision of the animals that prepared him eventually to understand that God shows no partiality (10:34). It was a vision from God that led Peter to receive into the home where he was lodging the three envoys of Cornelius, though they were not Jewish (10:19-20).

The action of the Holy Spirit in the lives of the Gentile members of Cornelius's household also offers evidence that "this thing is of God." The text says that those with Peter were utterly surprised—"beside themselves" might be one way to translate the verb *exestēsan*—to see that "the gift of the Holy Spirit had been poured out even on the Gentiles" (10:45). This is significant, for it tells readers that God was offering direct evidence to the witnesses that God had accepted these Gentiles. Peter appeals to this action of the Spirit when he defends himself before his critics in Jerusalem: "The Holy Spirit fell on them just as on us at the beginning. . . . Who was I that I could withstand God?" (11: 15, 17). Peter's testimony to his own observation of the action of the Spirit silenced his critics and transformed their criticism into the glorification of God (11:18).

The climate of our age is not readily receptive to claims of new and direct actions of God. When thrown into the pile along with Scripture and community, it often is given the least weight. Candidly, most of us simply do not know what to do when someone justifies an action based on a vision from God. Susan Howatch's novel *Glamorous Powers* tells the story of Jonathan Darrow, a mystic and member of the Fordite Order of St. Benedict and St. Bernard. What drives the plot is a visionary experience he has, which, he is convinced, is calling him to *leave* the Order. [Jonathan Darrow's Vision]

The incredulity of Jonathan's Abbot General, Father Francis, captures well how many in our time respond to such claims of visions. After listening to Jonathan share the content of his

Jonathan Darrow's Vision

"The vision began at a quarter to six; around me the room was suffused with light. . . . I was sitting on the edge of my bed when without warning the gold lettering on the cover of the Bible began to glow. . . . After the initial fear comes the equally instinctive acceptance. I had closed my eyes to lessen the terror of disorientation but now I forced myself to open them. . . . I was . . . walking along a path through a wood of beech trees. . . . I glanced to my left at the chapel in the dell below. . . . I faced the chapel . . . [and] noticed the suitcase, . . . sprinkled with labels. . . . [Darrow then enters the chapel.] Sinking to my knees I covered my face with my hands, and as the vision at last dissolved, the knowledge was branded upon my mind that I had to abandon the work which suited me so well and begin my life anew in the world I had no wish to rejoin."

Susan Howatch, *Glamorous Powers* (New York: Ballantine Books, 1988), 1–2.

vision, Father Francis responds, "Is that all? . . . There weren't for example six naked women dancing merrily in the glade? . . . It's a dull sort of vision, isn't it? No naked ladies, no heavenly choirs, no disembodied voices exhorting you to great spiritual feats."[17] Father Francis continues to embody the modern spirit as he hands Jonathan a note to carry to the cloister's infirmary with the words, "Take this to the infirmary. . . . The first thing to do with any monk who has visions is to give him a thorough medical examination."[18]

We are especially uncomfortable when one claims, based on spiritual experience, to have been offered insight that *challenges* some longstanding view that we have held. In short, we tend to recognize as legitimate those "actions" of the Holy Spirit that confirm theological positions we already hold to be valid. For example, those who believe, for whatever reason, that God does not call women to the pastoral ministry simply will not accept as valid the testimony of a woman who claims to have experienced the call of God through the activity of the Spirit in her life. She may have experienced *something*, her critics charge, but surely not the call of God! It is fair to conclude, however, that attitudes about Gentiles and associating with Gentiles were as deeply entrenched in the consciences of many Jews as are attitudes of some Christians today regarding the appropriate roles of women in ministry. And yet even those "circumcised believers" were willing to give serious attention to Peter's testimony regarding a spiritual experience. Are the bastions of tradition willing today to do the same?

The implications of this story can be both humbling and frightening. The idea that God really can offer fresh insights and directions that are so contrary to both tradition and the assumptions of the communities of which we are a part humbles our arrogant assurance that we always know the will of God. Yet it is frightening, for to move away from the comfort zones offered by tradition and community is perilous. We risk not only confusion ("But, Lord, I have never eaten anything common or unclean. How can you be asking me to do this?"), but also censure ("Those of the circumcision criticized him").

One's conviction of the truth of such novel experiences rarely can survive unless one does two things. First, it helps us to affirm our own convictions if we can convince the faith communities of which we are part to rethink their own assumptions, inviting them to reexamine the bases of their criticisms. This is what Peter did as he shared his story. His faith community, the Jerusalem church, though initially skeptical, was willing to hear Peter and to acknowledge that God had granted repentance to Gentiles. Yet one wonders whether the Jerusalem community was *really* ready to accept this newly revealed truth. A few chapters later, in Acts 15, the issue of the Gentiles will have to be addressed again.

And Galatians 2 offers an intriguing story about Jews and Gentiles eating together in Antioch, one of the crucial issues supposedly addressed in Acts 10–11. According to Paul, representatives from James, the leader of the Jerusalem congregation, convinced the Christian Jews at Antioch—including Peter!—not to eat with Gentile Christians. Peter, it seems, did not have the will to stand up to his community. Paul, perhaps a rare personality type, clearly did, literally standing *alone* against the Jerusalem envoy and all the Jewish Christians in Antioch. In hindsight, we can admire Paul's courage. We suspect that at the time he simply appeared arrogant and stubborn. Still, the story illustrates that only rarely can people hold to their "own truths" without the support of a larger community of faith to support them.

Our goal, then, should be to lead the community to embrace understandings of spiritual and ethical matters that we are fully convinced are right. But we must be prepared to conclude that communities can be wrong and be willing to stand on the strength of our own convictions.

Second, "new insights" into the truth can best be maintained if we can revisit our traditions, including our scriptural traditions, and see if our new insights can be reconciled with our inherited traditions. To many, such "revisitations" appear to be doing nothing more than accommodating Scripture or tradition to match up with our own, newly held ideas. But do we really imagine that our "old" readings of Scripture were not, to a great extent, simply accommodating the old ideas that we held before? Honest readers of Scripture admit that they do bring to the interpretive task the best insight that they happen to have at the moment. Given that, fresh insights will bring fresh readings of Scripture (see [Hermeneutics of Suspicion]). We will see in Acts 15 how James is portrayed as revisiting his scriptural tradition to justify the conclusion that Gentiles have been called of God to be his people, apart from circumcision. [Religious Certainty]

The action of God requires human participation. Ernst Haenchen argued that the Cornelius narrative so thoroughly emphasized the action of God that "by the end of the story the reader will no longer forget that it was *God* who brought about the whole of these events: and thereby instituted the mission to the Gentiles."[19] Yet Haenchen actually takes issue with the seeming

---

Religious Certainty

Peter offers an authoritative word, confirmed by the *experience* of the power of the Holy Spirit, which was poured out on the Gentiles. This offered to Peter and even his critics in Jerusalem a kind of "certainty" that God had acted in a decisive way.

But how can one be "certain" of one's religious convictions? Peter Berger speaks of three ways that contemporary Christians seek certainty:

There are those who offer certainty through the Bible, understood as literally inspired by God and therefore without errors ("inerrant"). . . . Since the literal and "inerrant" understanding of the Bible is very implausible as a result of modern historical scholarship, this offer of certainty tends to be taken up by people relatively distanced from contact with the results of this scholarship. . . . There is the offer of certainty by way of an inner "spiritual" experience . . . of conversion, of being "born again," of having been "filled with the Spirit." . . . But it is undermined . . . by modern psychology and sociology of religion. We now have a pretty good understanding of how these experiences of certainty are induced. . . .

The third type of certainty . . . [comes] by embracing the institution [the Church]. . . . The formula here is to give oneself up to the institution and thereby attain a conviction of certainty. . . . Christian faith, like any other religious or moral commitment, requires institutional anchorage. It

seems to me that the preferred choice for Christians should be to gather around a box from which the gospel is preached and around which one tries, feebly, to reach out to the cosmic liturgy. But one should not absolutize the choice of any particular box (Berger, 141–43).

Religious "certainty" emerges from a synergistic synthesis of sources: Scripture, experience, and community (institution, under which one can also speak of tradition). It is a distinctive sort of certainty; it is not like the certainty one has that she sits in a chair or holds a book or embraces a child. Acts 10–11 focuses on two of these elements: experience, to be sure, but also the community, the believers in Jerusalem who hear Peter's experiential testimony and offer their own assessment. This is a crucial dimension of the story. And while Scripture is not explicit in these chapters, Scripture plays a crucial role in the whole of Acts. Viewed with a certain eye, one can easily see in Acts the synthesis of Scripture, experience, and community (institution and tradition) to be the means through which the narrator guides his readers "to know the truth concerning the things about which you have been instructed" (Luke 1:4).

Peter L. Berger. *Questions of Faith: A Skeptical Affirmation of Christianity* (Malden MA: Blackwell, 2004).

---

heavy-handiness of God, concluding that "in all of us there exists a longing to have the weight of personal decisions lifted from our shoulders by abandonment to the will of God."[20]

Other commentators have rightly taken issue with Haenchen. Robert Tannehill says it well: "The narrative presents a more sophisticated and complex account of humans discerning the will of God than Haenchen thought."[21] Tannehill notes that, in fact, what we find are (1) divine promptings, (2) obedient responses, (3) openness to other persons, and (4) mutual sharing of visions, culminating (5) in public conversation and even debate (Acts 11 and, eventually, Acts 15). Discerning and carrying out the will of God in this narrative is hardly free of "the weight of personal decisions."

Imagine how this narrative would have stalled had Cornelius not responded obediently to the vision to send for Peter; if Peter had simply dismissed the vision of the sheet of animals, rather than allowing himself to be grabbed by his own perplexity over what the vision might mean (10:17); if Peter had resisted the visionary command to accompany unclean Gentiles (10:20); if Peter and those Jewish Christians who had accompanied him simply refused to acknowledge the evidence of God's spirit in the lives of Cornelius's household (10:47-48). Obedient response to divine promptings is crucial.

Within this narrative, coming to an understanding of God's will involves hearing other people and the mutual sharing of visions. Acts 10:34 is most illustrative of this: "Truly I perceive that God shows no partiality." Note that nowhere in this narrative did God ever say directly to Peter, "I show no partiality." It was Peter who came to "perceive" this. The verb translated as "perceive" (*katalambanō*) means to "seize," "take," or "make one's own." In the middle voice, as in this verse, the verb takes on a metaphorical meaning of coming to understand something, as though one were grasping an idea and laying hold of it as one's own. Such grasping comes to Peter as a result of *his* joining together and reflecting upon his own visionary experiences and the experience of Cornelius. Refusal to listen to others can regularly shut people off from grasping new insights from God.

The preceding discussion has already broached the theme of fellowship, as we reflected on Peter's willingness to listen to the personal testimony of Cornelius. The theme of fellowship addresses the fifth element of Tannehill's rubric above: public conversation and even debate.

The discernment and accomplishment of God's will require *public* conversation, and perhaps even healthy debate. To be sure, we do not want to ignore Paul's counsel, wherein he reminds us that we do not admit folk into the fellowship merely "for the purpose of quarreling over opinions" (Rom 14:1). The faith community's primary reason for being is not debate. That does not imply that genuine conversation, and even debate, is not part of the process of discernment, however.

Recall again the counsel of Paul to guide the gathering of the faith community: "Let two or three prophets speak, and let the others weigh what is said" (1 Cor 14:29). A narrow reading would lead to the conclusion that as these "others weigh what is said," they sit silently in a pensive mode, keeping their musings entirely to themselves. But it is just as likely that Paul here is exhorting the Corinthians to think out loud with one another as they weigh the Spirit-prompted utterances offered by the prophets. The Greek verb *diakrinō*, translated in the NRSV as "weigh," literally means to "judge through." It carries various meanings: "to pass judgment," "to judge correctly," "to deliberate," and "to render a decision."

Discerning the will of God involves *both* the inspired utterances of the prophet *and* the careful deliberations of the community. In

Acts, Peter conveyed to the church his vision and his witness of the action of the Spirit. The church weighed what he said and rendered a judgment: God has granted repentance to the Gentiles (11:18). With this judgment made, the story can now move forward, both in the world of Acts and in the world of the contemporary church.

NOTES

[1] Luke Timothy Johnson, *The Acts of the Apostles* (SacPag 5; Collegeville MN: Liturgical Press, 1992), 180.

[2] Ernst Haenchen, *The Acts of the Apostles: A Commentary* (Philadelphia: Westminster, 1971), 341.

[3] Ibid.

[4] See on this interrelationship F. J. Foakes Jackson and Kirsopp Lake, *The Beginnings of Christianity: The Acts of the Apostles*, 5 vols. (Grand Rapids MI: Baker, 1979), 4.112, and John B. Polhill, *Acts* (NAC 26; Nashville: Broadman, 1992), 249.

[5] See, e.g., Haenchen, *Acts*, 357–69, and Polhill, *Acts*, 250.

[6] Polhill, *Acts*, 250n64.

[7] I. Howard Marshall, *The Acts of the Apostles: An Introduction and Commentary* (TNTC; Leicester: Inter-Varsity Press, 1984), 185.

[8] Jackson and Lake, *The Beginnings of Christianity*, 4.117.

[9] Marion L. Soards, *The Speeches in Acts: Their Content, Context, and Concerns* (Louisville KY: Westminster/John Knox, 1994), 71.

[10] Ibid., 70–71.

[11] Johnson, *Acts*, 191.

[12] Hans Conzelmann, *Acts of the Apostles* (Hermeneia; Philadelphia: Fortress, 1987), 86; Haenchen, *Acts*, 355; Marshall, *Acts*, 195–96.

[13] Johnson, *Acts*, 197; Polhill, *Acts*, 266.

[14] Soards, *Speeches*, 77.

[15] Marshall, *Acts*, 197.

[16] Ibid., 198.

[17] Susan Howatch, *Glamorous Powers* (New York: Ballantine Books, 1988), 29.

[18] Ibid., 34.

[19] Haenchen, *Acts*, 358.

[20] Ibid., 363.

[21] Robert W. Tannehill, *The Narrative Unity of Luke–Acts: A Literary Interpretation*, 2 vols. (Minneapolis: Fortress, 1990), 2.131.

FROM JERUSALEM TO ANTIOCH

Acts 11:19-30

COMMENTARY

This brief narrative, which describes succinctly the movement of the gospel from regions of Judea and Samaria to the first, transitional phases of "the ends of the earth" (cf. Acts 1:18), consists of two short scenes: preaching to non-Jews at Antioch (vv. 19-26) and the prophecy of the great famine (vv. 27-30).

They Spoke to Greeks Also, 11:19-26

The rather abrupt reference to "those who were scattered" (v. 19) harks back to 8:1b, leading some scholars to conclude that in 11:19-26 Luke employs a source that perhaps originated in Antioch. [Antioch] These scholars argue that Luke follows this source throughout Acts

---

Antioch

This city was the capital of the Roman province of Syria (see **Map of Paul's First Missionary Journey**). It was founded by Seleucus Nicator c. 300 BC, who named the city after his father. The city may represent an ancient example of "urban sprawl," for it was actually a combination of four cities that eventually grew into one another during the first 125 years of Antioch's existence. Estimates of the population of the city in the first century AD range from 500,000 to 800,000 (Jerusalem, by comparison, is estimated to have had a population of between 25,000 and 50,000). The Jewish historian Josephus stated that Antioch was third among cities of the Roman world, ranking only behind Rome and Alexandria. Antioch was made a free city by Pompey in 64 BC.

F. J. Foakes Jackson and Kirsopp Lake, *The Beginnings of Christianity: The Acts of the Apostles*, 5 vols. (Grand Rapids MI: Baker, 1979), 4.127–28; T. C. Smith, "Antioch," *MDB* 34–35.

Antioch on the Orontes.
(Credit: Library of Congress, LC-matpc-02183/LifeintheHolyLand.com)

Greeks/Hellenists

AΩ The manuscripts of Acts 11:20 offer a variant reading that creates some confusion. Some manuscripts indicate that the preachers from Cyprus and Cyrene "spoke also to the Greeks" (*Hellēnas*), while others indicate that they "spoke also to the Hellenists" (*Hellēnistas*). The text is easier to understand if it reads "Greeks," given that Luke consistently defines "Hellenists" to mean "Greek-speaking Jews" (see [The Hellenists and the Hebrews]). It would make little sense for Luke to say in Acts 11 that some spoke *only* to Jews (v. 19), while some spoke also to "Greek-speaking Jews." Did Luke imagine that a significant number of Jews in Phoenicia, Cyprus, and Antioch spoke something other than Greek?

A principle of textual criticism is that later copyists would alter the text to make it clearer, not to make it more obscure. Thus, if the oldest reading of v. 20 was "Greeks," it is difficult to imagine what would have inclined later copyists to have changed it to "Hellenists," thereby inserting confusion into an already clear text. For this reason, some scholars are inclined to argue that the text originally read "Hellenists" and, due to the confusion created by such a reading, was later changed to read "Greeks."

Regardless, the *context* clearly communicates that v. 20 refers to non-Jews, regardless of the specific Greek word employed.

11:19-26, lays it aside, and begins to follow the source once again in 13:1.[1]

Within the flow of the narrative, however, Luke's notice that these scattered disciples preached the gospel shows how even persecution and tribulation can serve the advancement of the gospel; the gospel spreads *because of*, not in spite of, tribulation. Historically, it seems highly unlikely that those who preached in Antioch (v. 20) waited for the conclusion of the Cornelius episode to begin preaching—how would they have even known that the Jerusalem church had approved of such preaching? [Greeks/Hellenists] Luke may delay informing readers of this proclamation to non-Jews until after he has narrated the Cornelius episode in order to allow the latter to legitimize such preaching.[2] The characters *in* the story may not know that Jerusalem has recognized the legitimacy of preaching to Gentiles, but the reader *in front of* the story does. Conzelmann observes that the preaching to Jews in v. 19, *followed* by preaching to non-Jews in v. 20, also foreshadows a pattern for the missionary preaching to follow, where the proclaimers regularly preach to Jews first, then to non-Jews.[3] The narrative identifies those who preached to non-Jews as coming from Cyprus and Cyrene, denoting Jews who were of the Diaspora. Hence, they might "have been more accustomed to speak and to deal with Gentiles."[4] The subject of their preaching was "the Lord Jesus" (v. 20).

The narrative makes clear that God sanctioned the proclamation of "the Lord Jesus" directly to non-Jews, for it says that "the hand of the Lord was with them" (v. 21). This phrase is common to the Old Testament (cf. 1 Sam 5:3, 6, 9; 2 Sam 3:12) and, therefore, may denote the hand of *God*, not the Lord Jesus, despite the immediate antecedent. Luke's use of "Lord" interchangeably for God and Jesus may indicate an implicitly higher Christology on Luke's part than scholars regularly assume.[5] It might also indicate that Luke is not terribly precise or systematic with his titles. The explicit notification that many believed and turned to the Lord offers concrete evidence that God was with these preachers. Indications of impressive numerical growth recall texts such as Acts 2:41, 47, 4:4, 5:14, 6:7, and 9:31, which speak of the numerical success of the Jerusalem mission. The witness to Jesus has successfully moved into the regions of "the ends of the earth."

When Philip, another follower of Jesus who was scattered because of the persecution, preached the gospel to the Samaritans (see 8:4-24), the Jerusalem church, upon hearing of the Samaritans' receiving the word, "sent [*apesteilan*] to them Peter and John" (8:14). So, too, when news of the success at Antioch reached Jerusalem "they sent [*exapesteilan*] Barnabas to Antioch" (v. 22). Perhaps Barnabas was selected to visit the church because he, like some of those who preached to non-Jews at Antioch, was from Cyprus (cf. 4:35). Barnabas might have been sent "to investigate . . . and allay the concerns of the more conservative 'circumcision' group in Jerusalem (cf. 11:2)."[6] Perhaps this is true historically. But in the narrative world this group has supposedly been "won over" to the Gentile cause. More likely, Barnabas represents the continuity between Jerusalem and churches beyond its immediate environs. In Acts 9, Barnabas provided a connection between Paul and the apostles. Here he provides a link between the apostles of Jerusalem and Antioch: "We see Luke's concern to secure continuity between the restored people of God in Jerusalem, and the ever extending messianic people, now including great new areas and entire new races."[7]

Upon his arrival, Barnabas, being "full of the Holy Spirit and faith," can easily infer that the grace, or favor, of God was with these new believers. Barnabas, true to his name (recall 4:36), "exhorts" or "encourages" the new believers "to remain in the Lord with steadfastness of heart" (v. 24, which the NRSV translates as "faithful . . . with steadfast devotion"). The appropriate response of those who have experienced the grace or favor of God is loyalty to this graceful God. God's favor is further displayed as yet more people were added to the ranks of God's people (v. 25b).

The narrative had left Saul in Tarsus (9:30). Luke does not tell readers why Barnabas decided to go to Tarsus to look for Saul and bring him back to Antioch (v. 25). Yet, as the narrative will later make clear, Saul's connection with Antioch will prove decisive as the mission to the ends of earth progresses (cf. 13:1-3). However, the indication that Saul and Barnabas spent a year meeting with

Christians

AΩ Acts 11:26 states that "it was in Antioch that the disciples were first called 'Christians'" (*Christianoi*). The term represents the combination of "Christ" with the Latinized suffix "*-ianos*," which indicated "partisan of" or "belonging to" (cf. Mark 3:6, which refers to *Herodianoi*, or "Herodians"). According to Joseph Fitzmyer, the Greek term translated "were called" could be understood to say either that the followers of Jesus designated themselves by the term "Christian" or were so designated by others (478). Ben Witherington observes that the two other instances of the word "Christian" in the New Testament (Acts 26:28; 1 Pet 4:16) indicate that it was *outsiders* who used the term to refer to followers of Jesus (371). Non-Christians did employ the term to refer to followers of Jesus (e.g., Josephus, *Ant.* 18.64; Tacitus, *Ann.* 15.44). Most likely, "Christians" was an appellation given *by outsiders* to followers of Jesus (Polhill cites opposing views [273n127]).

Joseph A. Fitzmyer, *The Acts of the Apostles* (AB 31; New York: Doubleday, 1998); Ben Witherington III, *The Acts of the Apostles: A Socio-Rhetorical Commentary* (Grand Rapids MI: Eerdmans, 1998); John B. Polhill, *Acts* (NAC 26; Nashville: Broadman, 1992).

and teaching the church (v. 26) allows readers yet another comparison of this congregation with that of Jerusalem: just as the apostles taught the church of Jerusalem, these two, who have each in some way received the blessing of Jerusalem (cf. 9:26-30), teach this new company of believers.

The narrative establishes clear connections between the community in Antioch and the Jerusalem church. And yet there is something distinctive about these people, for they are, for the first time, called Christians. Even non-followers can see that "Christianity is no mere variant of Judaism."[8] It is religious loyalty, not ethnic identification, that offers the church at Antioch its distinctiveness. [Christians]

Prophets Came Down from Jerusalem, 11:27-30

The second short scene concerns the prophetic announcement of the famine and the church's response to the announcement. Luke does not offer any reason why the prophets came to Antioch. Their presence may further solidify the connection between the two cities. While there, the prophet Agabus "predicted by the Spirit that there would be a severe famine over all the world" (v. 28). [Famine over All the World] As far back as 2:17, Luke has connected prophecy with "the Spirit." This text indicates that Luke understands inspired prophecy to include "foretelling" (though the Greek word *esēmanen* can, in other contexts, simply denote "to declare" or "to signify"). [Prophets]

The response of the Antioch church is to send relief. The word employed here is

Prophets

📖 Acts 2:17 indicates that the Holy Spirit was identified with the spirit of prophecy. The balance of Acts 2 would imply that prophecy could denote the proclamation of the gospel and accompanying exhortations to repentance. Acts 15:32 includes within prophetic speech exhortations that give encouragement to God's people (cf. 1 Cor 14:3). Yet Acts 2:17 implies that prophecy also includes ecstatic experiences, such as visions. Acts 11:27-28 places "foretelling" within the sphere of prophecy, perhaps understood as a certain type of visionary experience. A number of persons in Acts are designated as prophets: Agabus (11:28; 21:10 [assuming this to be the same Agabus]), Saul, Barnabas, and other persons at Antioch (13:1), Silas and Judas (15:32), and the daughters of Philip (21:8-9).

Famine over All the World

Interpreters who insist on strict historical accuracy within the Lukan narrative stumble over this line from Acts 11:28, for evidence of a worldwide famine is lacking, just as evidence of a worldwide census is lacking (cf. Luke 2:1). However, readers who are willing to allow the narrator some hyperbolic license, or not insist on strict accuracy, can note that during the reign of Claudius the Roman Empire was hard hit in various places by famines. Accordingly, Johnson (202, 205–206) suggests the following rendering for Acts 11:28: "He predicted a great famine would come on the whole of the empire."

Various historians of antiquity refer to the famines that affected the empire during Claudius's reign:

Many prodigies occurred during the year [c. AD 44]. . . . A shortage of corn, again, and the famine which resulted, were construed as a supernatural warning. . . . It was established that the capital had provisions for fifteen days. (Tacitus, Ann. 12.43)

When there was a scarcity of grain because of the long-continued droughts, he [Claudius] was once stopped in the middle of the Forum by a mob and so pelted with abuse and at the same time with pieces of bread, that he was barely able to make his escape to the Palace by a back door. (Suetonius, *Claudius* 18.2)

Under these procurators that great famine happened in Judea, in which queen Helena bought corn in Egypt at great expense, and distributed it to those that were in want. (Josephus, *Ant.* 20.101)

Especially hard hit was Egypt, c. AD 45/46, due to the flooding of the Nile. If readers are to assume that Acts does, indeed, refer to an actual, identifiable famine, this Egyptian famine is likely the best candidate. This would imply that Judea was hit by the effects of this famine no earlier than c. AD 46, though Witherington dates the visit to c. 47/48 (368).

Luke Timothy Johnson, *The Acts of the Apostles* (SacPag 5; Collegeville MN: Liturgical Press, 1992); Ben Witherington III, *The Acts of the Apostles: A Socio-Rhetorical Commentary* (Grand Rapids MI: Eerdmans, 1998).

diakonian, which is commonly used in the New Testament to denote financial help (cf. Rom 15:31; 1 Cor 16:15; 2 Cor 8:4; 9:1, 13; Acts 6:1, 4; 12:25). Earlier in Acts, money seemed to have a symbolic function, with laying one's goods at the feet of the apostles signifying acknowledgment of the apostles' authority (4:32-37). Given this, there may be implied here Antioch's acknowledgment of the authority of Jerusalem or, more likely, the apostolic gospel, which goes forth from the holy city. Given that Saul is one of the persons who presents the relief, the story may also be subtly implying that this one who will later be so instrumental in preaching the gospel "to the ends of the earth" recognizes the authority of the apostolic witness, which finds its home in Jerusalem. [Chronological Issues] But even granting this, one should not overlook the more obvious meaning that the gift may also represent, simply, the generosity of the community of faith. The church of Antioch emulates the generosity of the Jerusalem community, but even exceeds it, sending of its resources beyond its immediate community.[9]

Luke concludes with a terse notice that Barnabas and Saul delivered the relief "to the elders" (v. 30). Luke offers no clue as to how this leadership group arose or its precise connection with the apostles. However, by introducing the group at this juncture, readers are

Chronological Issues

Acts 11:30 indicates that Paul visited Jerusalem to deliver famine relief to the church. If one can conclude that the famine being referred to is the famine created by Egyptian food shortages, this would indicate that Paul visited Jerusalem c. AD 46 or even 47/48 (see [Famine Over All the World]). This immediately creates a problem for the historian, for according to Paul's own testimony, he visited Jerusalem for the second time some fourteen years either after his apostolic call or his first visit to Jerusalem (see Gal 1:18; 2:1).

While it is difficult to date Paul's call with precision, most offer a date between AD 32–34 (e.g., Lüdemann, 262 [though possibly as early as 30]; Hengel, 91; Jewett, 99), thereby placing the date for his "second trip to Jerusalem" as early as 46 (fourteen years after the early date range for Paul's call) or as late as 51 (fourteen years after Paul's first visit, which Paul indicates was three years after his call [Gal 1:18]). Thus, one can see that it is quite possible, but by no means certain, that Paul could have visited Jerusalem between AD 46–48. It certainly appears that AD 46 is the *earliest* that one can reasonably reckon this "second visit" to have taken place.

Yet other weightier matters concern historians. Acts 12 *implies* that Herod (Agrippa) died either while Paul and Barnabas were in Jerusalem delivering the famine relief *or* after they had delivered the relief, left Jerusalem, and returned yet again (see Acts 12:20-23, followed by the notice of 12:25 [the textual problem of 12:25 will be explored in the next chapter]). Yet historians are quite certain that Herod Agrippa died in AD 44, before the likely date of the famine visit and before the earliest time that Paul likely could have visited Jerusalem for the second time (AD 46).

Also, according to Paul's own testimony, the primary reason for his second visit to Jerusalem was to deal with the issue of Gentile circumcision (see Gal 2:1-10). Yet, according to Acts, Paul did not visit Jerusalem to deal with the circumcision issue until Acts 15, which by Acts' reckoning would either be Paul's third or possibly even fourth visit to Jerusalem (depending on how one understands Acts 12:25).

Commentators can read Acts in such a way so as to minimize or obliterate these historical complexities (see, e.g., Witherington, 368–69). But even scholars such as Witherington concede that Luke's historical veracity does not mean chronological precision. Perhaps the most one can expect from Luke is that he correctly clusters key events (the famine and death of Herod) around the same general time frame (mid-40s), but without a precise ordering of events.

Gerd Lüdemann, *Early Christianity according to the Traditions in Acts: A Commentary* (Minneapolis: Fortress, 1989); Martin Hengel, *Acts and the History of Earliest Christianity* (Philadelphia: Fortress, 1979); Robert Jewett, *A Chronology of Paul's Life* (Philadelphia: Fortress, 1979); Ben Witherington III, *The Acts of the Apostles: A Socio-Rhetorical Commentary* (Grand Rapids MI: Eerdmans, 1998).

not so surprised to find them in leadership roles later in the story (cf. 15:2, 4, 6; 16:4; 21:18). [Elders]

CONNECTIONS

Two recurring theological themes that are especially relevant to this passage are human participation in the divine drama and the life of the community of faith.

Readers know that the divine drama includes the offering of the gospel to all peoples (1:8). The preceding story about Cornelius has revealed that God led the Jerusalem church to recognize that God "has given even to the Gentiles the repentance that leads to life" (11:18). What is impressive about these who were scattered by persecution is that they acted on values implied by the gospel itself, without waiting for direct, divine promptings. Luke reports that these scattered followers spoke also to non-Jews only *after* he has told the story of Cornelius. But the text offers no clue that these missionaries themselves were aware of what had happened to Peter, Cornelius, and the Jerusalem church. They are not preaching to non-Jews because Peter did and because the Jerusalem church told them that it was all right to do so.

When one compares the clarity of vision of these scattered missionaries with that of Peter, one wonders why it should have even taken a triple vision from God to get Peter to see that the day had now come for all people to see the revelation of the glory of God (cf. Isa 40:5). The Scripture text Peter employed to preach his first sermon concluded with the declaration, "*Everyone* who calls on the name of the Lord shall be saved" (Acts 2:21, quoting Joel 2:32a). Peter had heard the resurrected Jesus say that "repentance and forgiveness of sins is to be proclaimed in [my] name to all nations" (Luke 24:47) and "you will be my witnesses . . . to the ends of the earth" (Acts 1:8).

> **Elders**
>
> ΑΩ The early chapters of Acts employ "elder" to denote persons within the Jewish leadership of Jerusalem (4:5, 8, 23; 5:21; 6:12). Acts also uses the term to refer to Jewish leaders at the end of the narrative (22:5; 23:14; 24:11; 25:15).
>
> Beginning in Acts 11:30, Acts employs the term to denote leaders *within the church*, both in Jerusalem (15:2, 4, 6, 22, 23; 16:4; 21:18) and around the empire (14:23; 20:17). Other texts within the New Testament refer to elders within the church (1 Tim 5:1, 2, 17, 19: Titus 1:5; Jas 5:14; 1 Pet 5:1, 5; 2 John 1; 3 John 1), as do several early fathers (e.g., Clement, Ignatius, and Polycarp). Acts 20, which refers to elders (v. 17), later uses the term *episkopoi* ("bishop" or "overseer") as a synonym for "elder," implying a very close, if not identical, relationship between the offices. Note also that Titus 1:5-9 appears to use "elder" (v. 5) and "bishop" (v. 7) interchangeably, thereby granting to the elder the responsibility of preaching, teaching, and even discipline within the church. By the time of Ignatius, however, the offices and bishop and elder were distinct, with the bishop ranking higher than the elder.
>
> The Jewish roots of Christianity may account for the emergence of this leadership position within the church. The fact that Acts first mentions elders as part of the Jerusalem church may lend substance to this hypothesis.
>
> W. McWilliams, "Elder," *MDB* 241–42; M. H. Shepherd Jr, "Elder in the NT," *IDB* 2:73–75.

In some "objective" sense, Peter knew what God's intentions were. But Peter was slow to allow this "objective" value to become, for him, an internalized "subjective" value, until God twisted his arm. Yet these scattered missionaries, without angelic fanfare or profound visions, had already internalized and made subjective what readers had known all along to be the objective value of God: the good news is to be preached to all nations.

To *make disciples* of all nations (cf. Matt 28:19) God's people have to make personally and subjectively real the transcendent values that they would readily affirm to be objectively real. Then they can be effective human instruments in the divine drama. [The Internalization of Proper Values] This is what the scattered missionaries had done, and, due to their insight and courage, the church began its movement "to the ends of the earth."

The passage also says something about life within the community of faith. While the community of faith at Antioch came into being

The Internalization of Proper Values

Timothy. O'Connel argues that the internalization of proper values is imperative in order to fulfill the command of the Great Commission to "make disciples of all nations." While people are quick to *affirm* many good values, they tend to internalize subjectively the values that they *prefer*. In a world of conflicting values, any number of which can have legitimacy, the task is not so much to convince people that Value A is wrong and Value B is right, but that Value B is to be preferred over Value A.

As applied to the preaching of the gospel also to Gentiles, one might apply this insight in this manner: There is certainly value in preaching to Jews only (Value A): they understand the Old Testament promises, there is a ready cohesion and community, and there is risk in inviting

"outsiders" into the community of faith for such is surely to bring changes to the community that none could foresee. Those who would want to preach to outsiders (Value B) should not insist that everything pertaining to Value A is wrong. Rather, this approach to value clarification would strive to show why Value B is to be *preferred*, even in the face of Value A's legitimate concerns.

For example, while acknowledging the risks of bringing outsiders into the community, Value B is preferable in order to live consistently by the gospel, for if God is one, then God must be the God of all, even outsiders (cf. Rom 3:29-30). Further, such openness is clearly consistent with Jesus' pattern of ministry.

Timothy E. O'Connel, *Making Disciples: A Handbook of Christian Moral Formation* (New York: Crossroad, 1998), 57–64.

initially without the sanction of Jerusalem, both the churches of Antioch and Jerusalem recognize their mutual interdependence. Just as the Jerusalem church sent Peter and John to Samaria, following its evangelization by Philip (8:14-25), so here the Jerusalem church sends Barnabas to Antioch. Perhaps Luke is trying to assert that the Jerusalem church must *sanction* the church at Antioch before one can consider it a valid congregation. Readers can just as easily understand the text as demonstrating *continuity* between Jerusalem and Antioch. Readers can also understand the symbolism conveyed by sending money to Jerusalem to denote recognition of apostolic authority and the apostolic gospel.

But readers should not overlook the "more obvious meaning." We find enacted in Acts the principle that Paul laid out in his Letter to the Romans as he spoke to this congregation about a financial gift that he was taking to Jerusalem toward the end of his career. Paul explained the meaning of this gift, in part, by saying: "Indeed they [the Gentiles] owe it to them [the Jerusalem Christians]; for if the Gentiles have come to share in their spiritual blessings, they ought also to be of service to them in material things" (Rom 15:27).

Both Acts 11 and Romans 15 affirm that we offer assistance to others, insofar as we are able (11:29; cf. 2 Cor 8:10-15), in order to address their genuine needs. The Gentiles *needed* the good news. Followers of Jesus, coming forth from Jerusalem shared what they had to share: the gospel. The community of Jerusalem *needed* food. Followers of Jesus, springing forth in Antioch, met the needs of the Jewish believers, sharing what they had to share: relief from the famine. That is the way of Christian *koinōnia*.

NOTES

[1] Hans Conzelmann, *Acts of the Apostles* (Hermeneia; Philadelphia: Fortress, 1987), 87; Joseph A. Fitzmyer, *The Acts of the Apostles* (AB 31; New York: Doubleday, 1998), 474; F. J. Foakes Jackson and Kirsopp Lake, *The Beginnings of Christianity: The Acts of the Apostles*, 5 vols. (Grand Rapids MI: Baker, 1979), 4.127.

[2] Robert W. Tannehill, *The Narrative Unity of Luke–Acts: A Literary Interpretation*, 2 vols. (Minneapolis: Fortress, 1990), 2.146.

[3] Conzelmann, *Acts*, 87.

[4] Fitzmyer, *Acts*, 476.

[5] See, e.g,. H. D. Buckwalter, "The Divine Savior," in *Witness to the Gospel: The Theology of Acts*, ed. I. H. Marshall and D. Peterson (Grand Rapids MI: Eerdmans), 107–23 for a rigorous case in defense of a "high Christology" in Luke–Acts. See Buckwalter's fuller treatment of Luke's higher Christology in *The Character and Purpose of Luke's Christology* (SNTSMS 89; Cambridge: Cambridge University Press, 1996). While provocative, Buckwalter has overreached in his thesis. See my review of his book in *Review of Biblical Literature* 1 (1999): 276–79.

[6] John B. Polhill, *Acts* (NAC 26; Nashville: Broadman, 1992), 272.

[7] Luke Timothy Johnson, *The Acts of the Apostles* (SacPag 5; Collegeville MN: Liturgical Press, 1992), 207.

[8] Ernst Haenchen, *The Acts of the Apostles: A Commentary* (Philadelphia: Westminster, 1971), 371.

[9] Tannehill, *Narrative Unity*, 2.148.

VIOLENT HANDS AND THE RESPONSE OF GOD'S PEOPLE

Acts 12:1-25

COMMENTARY

This chapter offers both a disturbing and inspiring story: disturbing in that it reminds readers of the opposition that God's people can encounter, inspiring in that it illustrates the power that God's people have in the face of such violent opposition.

Broadly, the story moves from notification of King Herod's persecution of certain leaders of the Christian community (vv. 1-5), to the story of Peter's deliverance from Herod (vv. 6-19), to the account of Herod's death (vv. 20-23, 24-25).

Luke brackets the whole story with a reminder of the relief that the church of Antioch sent to Jerusalem (see [Chronological Issues] for the chronological problems this raises). The transitional phrase of v. 1, "about that time," connects the narrative that follows with the Antioch relief mission. The conclusion of the narrative (v. 25) implies that Saul and Barnabas, emissaries from Antioch, had been in Jerusalem during this trying and tumultuous period. Through the structure of the narrative, Luke communicates that the Christians of Jerusalem do not face trial and persecution alone: "The continued presence of the Antiochian delegation in Jerusalem throughout the persecution served Luke as a demonstration of the heartfelt communion between the mother church and the daughter congregation."[1]

Violence against the Church, 12:1-5

At about the same time that the church of Antioch extended a helping hand to Jerusalem (11:29-30), King Herod (Agrippa I) lays violent hands on the church there (v. 1). [King Herod] The narrative gives no immediate rationale for Herod's motivation for executing James (v. 2), the brother of John. [James, the Brother of John] The phrase "killed with the sword" might conjure up decapitation for ancient

King Herod

The Herod of Acts 12 was more commonly referred to as Agrippa I. He was a grandson of Herod the Great. Agrippa was friends with Emperor Caligula, who became the Roman emperor in AD 37 and appointed Agrippa I ruler of the territory located northeast of Galilee and formerly ruled by one of Herod the Great's sons. When Agrippa's uncle, Herod Antipas (the Herod of Luke's Passion Narrative), was deposed in AD 39, Agrippa was given the regions that he had ruled, Galilee and Perea. In AD 41 Agrippa became the ruler of Samaria, Judea, and Idumea as well. He now ruled territory as extensive as that of Herod the Great. He died in Caesarea in AD 44.

R. O. Byrd, "Agrippa I and II," *MDB* 16.

James, the Brother of John

James and John, the sons of Zebedee, were among the first disciples whom Jesus called to follow him (Luke 5:10). According to Mark 10:35-37, the two brothers asked Jesus for a special position in his kingdom. According to Mark 10:39, Jesus predicted that the two brothers would "drink the cup" of and be "baptized" with Jesus, implying that they too would suffer a violent death. Acts 12 narrates James's death. Based on Jesus' implied prophecy of a violent death for John, as well as traditions attributed to Papias (early 2d century AD), some scholars have argued that John was also martyred early in the history of the church. More widely accepted church tradition says that John lived to a ripe old age.

F. J. Foakes Jackson and Kirsopp Lake, *The Beginnings of Christianity: The Acts of the Apostles*, 5 vols. (Grand Rapids MI: Baker, 1979), 4.133–34.

readers. This could indicate a type of formal Roman execution (crucifixion was not the only mode of Roman capital punishment), implying that Herod perceived James to be some type of political threat. But this is not explicitly stated. Readers familiar with Jewish law would know that the rabbis limited decapitation to murderers and "the people of an apostate city."[2] In this case, the narrative is implying that Herod is siding with the Jerusalem opposition to the Christians and viewing these followers of Jesus as apostates— persons who had turned their backs on their Jewish faith and heritage. Again, this is not explicitly stated.

When Judas killed himself at the beginning of Acts (Acts 1), the apostolic leadership considered it imperative to replace him. Luke's passing over the loss of James with no hint that the Jerusalem church gave any consideration to replacing the vacancy now left among the Twelve implies that "in terms of salvation history the phase of the earliest community is over."[3] The Twelve served an important function to lay a foundation of leadership and proclamation upon which others, such as Saul and Barnabas, could build. In his silence, Luke communicates that such a foundation is complete and can continue to endure without the individual apostolic office holders that laid that foundation.

Verse 3 states that Herod arrested Peter "when he saw that it [the execution of James] pleased the Jews." This does not say that Herod's motive for executing James was to curry the favor of the Jews; it only states that *after* the execution he observed that it was pleasing to some Jews. John Polhill offers documentation from Josephus that Herod Agrippa sought the favor of his Jewish subjects.[4] Significantly, Luke does not single out the Jewish *leaders* in v. 3 as the ones whom Herod is trying to please, but "the Jews" (see [The Jews]). The climate has clearly changed from the so-called

"Jerusalem springtime" of the early chapters of Acts when the people, as opposed to their leaders, were open to hearing the apostolic word. That the line between "the people" and their leaders has blurred is confirmed by the conclusion of v. 4, which states that Herod intended after Passover to bring Peter out before "the people," presumably to pronounce the same death sentence that James had received. [Passover]

Readers recall that Peter had escaped from prison before (5:18-19, 23). Herod has taken precautions, perhaps more elaborate than those taken by the Sanhedrin in Acts 5, to prevent another escape. He has set up four squads of soldiers to guard Peter for the duration of his incarceration. Each squad would have consisted of four soldiers, with each squad serving a three-hour watch before being relieved. Escape may prove more difficult this time (see [Prison Conditions])

Passover

Acts 12:3-4 states that Agrippa I arrested Peter during the "Days of Unleavened Bread" but that Agrippa was not going to bring Peter out until "after the Passover," implying that Passover followed the Days of Unleavened Bread. Passover was celebrated on 14/15 Nisan to commemorate the exodus from Egypt. The celebration of the "Days of Unleavened Bread" began on 14 Nisan and continued until 21 Nisan. Technically, therefore, Passover would have been completed when Herod arrested Peter. The two celebrations, however, were very closely associated (see Exod 12:1-20; Deut 16:1-4). The Jewish historian Josephus could use either Passover or Feast of Unleavened Bread to refer to the whole of the weeklong festival (*Ant.* 6.423; 17.213). Luke also thought of Passover and the Days of Unleavened Bread as synonymous (Luke 22:1).

F. J. Foakes Jackson and Kirsopp Lake, *The Beginnings of Christianity*, 4.134; Joseph A. Fitzmyer, *The Acts of the Apostles* (AB 31; New York: Doubleday, 1998), 487.

The church responds to this crisis with the only means at its disposal—prayer. Legal maneuvering, peaceful public protest, a daring commando rescue attempt, and other such responses that modern readers might think of are not within the realm of possibility for the first-century church. In the current social climate, where Christians no longer feel totally powerless against the state, prayer might be a last resort or, at best, a tandem strategy that accompanies other, more practical responses to hardships. First-century Christians had no option but prayer.

The Deliverance of Peter, 12:6-19

The story of Peter's deliverance unfolds in three scenes: vv. 6-11 take place in prison and its immediate environs; vv. 12-17 move the reader to the house of Mary, mother of John Mark; and vv. 18-19 move back to the prison.

Scene One, vv. 6-11
The scene opens with the dramatic notification that it was the eve before Herod planned to take Peter out before the people (v. 6a). Peter has been in prison now for a number of days, given that the period of his imprisonment was during the "*Days* of Unleavened

Bread" (see v. 3). To this point, the earnest prayers of the community have seemingly gone unanswered. Time is running out on Peter. The hope for an escape seems diminished by the fact that Peter is chained to two of the soldiers responsible for guarding him, a practice documented by ancient historians (see, e.g., Josephus, *Ant.* 18.196, who reports that Herod the Great [Herod Agrippa's grandfather] was so guarded while imprisoned in Rome). As Haenchen writes, "All possibility of escape seems precluded."[5]

Perhaps in contrast to readers' anxiety over Peter's dilemma, the narrative portrays Peter as sleeping calmly, with the angel having to "tap" (v. 7, NRSV; the Greek word *patassō*, the same word employed later in 12:23, implies something more than a gentle nudge) the apostle to rouse him from sleep. The angel clearly controls the action, commanding Peter to "get up" (v. 7), get dressed (v. 8), and follow him out of the prison (v. 8). The angel is also responsible for loosing the chains from Peter's hands without disturbing the guards (v. 7).

Angelic control of the action continues as he leads Peter past the guards to the final gate that opens of its own accord (v. 10). The narrator impresses upon readers the passivity of Peter, who suspects that what is happening is not real, but a vision (v. 9). It is only after Peter finds himself in the street outside the prison that he realizes the Lord has delivered him (v. 11).

Peter's musing to himself in v. 11 is primarily for the benefit of readers, who are told explicitly through his voice that the Lord had rescued Peter both from Herod and the expectations of "the Jewish people." The reference to "the Jewish people" is telling, for to this point Luke has used the word "people" (*laos*) in a more positive sense, regularly portraying the people as receptive to the apostolic word, in contrast with their leaders (see, e.g., 2:47; 3:9-10, 11-12; 4:1-2, 8, 10; 5:13, 25, 26; but cf. 6:12). In 12:2 Luke employed the term "the Jews" as a sweeping term to denote a group siding with Herod and opposed to the Christians. Luke has used "the Jews" before to denote those opposed to Jesus (10:39) or his followers (9:22, 23). But this is the first time that he has used "people" and "Jews" together, as if to say that "the people" who have failed to join the disciples are now aligned with "the Jews" who are opposed to the Messiah and his people. All this represents a tragic point in the progression of the narrative, for "the Jewish people," as a whole, have now elected to join the ranks of the leadership, a leadership consistently opposed to the gospel and its messengers.

Scene Two, vv. 12-17

The scene shifts to the home of Mary, the mother of John Mark. [John Mark] Peter goes directly to this home, indicating that it was a regular meeting place of the Jerusalem community. The text implies a large house with its reference to an outer gate that likely entered into a courtyard separating the street from the dwelling where people were gathered. The fact that Mary retained ownership of her home indicates that members of the Jerusalem community did not literally sell *all* their possessions (cf. 2:44-45). Yet the fact that her home is open for prayer, even during the night, indicates that she willingly shared what she had with the larger community, as this community had need (cf. 2:46).

The irony of the story is apparent. The community of believers had enough faith to gather for prayer, apparently for several days, even holding their prayer vigils well into the night and early hours of the morning. Yet when their prayer is answered, they respond with incredulity. First, they conclude that Rhoda, the maid who heard Peter's voice outside the gate, is "out of her mind" (v. 15). Following her insistence, the community is willing to grant that maybe she did hear *something*, but at best it was Peter's angel. [Angel] It is only Peter's persistent knocking, which would have to be rather loud to reach across the courtyard and be heard by the buzzing crowd inside the house, that moves people out to the courtyard to open the gate. Peter had less trouble exiting the gates of prison than entering the gates of the church!

The narrator does not say whether Peter entered the courtyard, much less the house. Peter briefly tells the people gathered there of

John Mark

The character introduced in Acts 12:12, 25 assisted Paul and Barnabas on the missionary journey described in Acts 13. He did not remain with them, returning to his Jerusalem home (13:13) for reasons that Luke does not disclose. Following the council meeting of Acts 15, Barnabas wanted John Mark to rejoin Paul and him. Paul objected, however, so Barnabas and Mark went their own way (15:36-41). Colossians 4:10 refers to "Mark the cousin of Barnabas," referring undoubtedly to the John Mark of Acts (see also 2 Tim 4:11; Phlm 24). These references in Pauline letters, with Philemon being most assuredly authentic, indicate a reconciliation between Paul and John Mark.

First Peter 5:13 refers to a Mark, described as the son of Peter, indicating a very close relationship between Mark and Peter. Again, one cannot be certain if this Mark is the John Mark of Acts, though tradition asserts the two to be the same person. Even if the many critical scholars who question the authenticity of 1 Peter are correct, the reference to Mark in 1 Peter at least assumes a tradition among Christians that a certain Mark was a co-worker of Peter. Bishop Papias (early second century AD) ascribed the second Gospel to this Mark. Later church tradition says that Mark evangelized Egypt and became the first bishop of Alexandria.

F. J. Foakes Jackson and Kirsopp Lake, *The Beginnings of Christianity*, 4.137; Luke Timothy Johnson, *The Acts of the Apostles* (SacPag 5; Collegeville MN: Liturgical Press, 1992), 212–13; J. A. Reynolds, "Mark," *MDB* 549.

Angel

Behind the speculation that Peter's angel was knocking at the gate lies the Jewish and Christian belief in "guardian angels" (cf. Tob 5:22; Matt 18:10). The mid-second-century treatise *Shepherd of Hermes* expresses belief that each person is attended by two angels, "one of righteousness and one of wickedness" (*Mandate* 6.2.1–2).

Saying that Peter's angel was nearby might also imply that those in Mary's house thought that Peter had died, for "it was believed that one's angel often appeared immediately after a person's death" (Polhill, 282; cf. Luke 24:37).

John B. Polhill, *Acts* (NAC 26; Nashville: Broadman, 1992).

his miraculous deliverance and instructs them to report this "to James and the believers" [lit., "brethren"]. Luke regularly will introduce, almost in passing, characters who will play a more important role later in the narrative (cf. 4:36, 6:5; 8:1; 12:12). This establishes a kind of intimacy with the readers, since the narrator is giving readers the benefit of the doubt that they know as much as the narrator. Those who do know appreciate the compliment. Those who do not know are perhaps more inclined to pay careful attention to the narrative to follow, having been tersely introduced to a new character. James is so introduced here. He will play a more significant role in Acts 15. At this juncture in the story, readers who *do not* know about James can only infer that this new character has assumed some leadership position, since Peter thinks it important that the community inform him of what has happened.

This scene concludes tersely, stating that Peter went away to another place. Such a laconic and enigmatic statement sparks speculation as to the location of this "other place." Some circles of church tradition speculated that Peter went to Rome and established the Roman church. Such suggestions cannot be proven or disproven.[6] In this immediate context, the narrative may only want to say that Peter left the city for his own well-being. Answered prayer is no excuse to put oneself in the position of needing yet another miracle. However, the introduction of James, as blunt as it was, leaves readers assured that the Jerusalem church is not without leadership. Peter himself, with his instructions to inform James of what had happened, has implicitly endorsed the one who will emerge as the new leader of the Jerusalem congregations.

Scene Three, vv. 18-19

The third scene shifts quickly and briefly back to the prison. Day has come, the day that Peter was to be led out before the people (vv. 4, 6). But Peter is gone. Though Luke does not say so, readers familiar with the practice of a rotating guard (see v. 4) would infer that Peter must have been delivered after the final changing of the guard, for one can only surmise that had he left earlier, his absence would have been noted when the new guard detail came on watch. This retrospect heightens the drama of the miracle, for readers now see that Peter was not delivered until, literally, the final hours before he was to be presented to the people and, likely, handed over for execution.

The picture painted by v. 19 is almost comical, as readers imagine the king himself running through the damp corners of the prison, looking for Peter. Only when he has satisfied himself that

Peter is gone does he "examine" the guards. Torture would not be out of the question, and here readers may feel pity for the guards. Their interrogators would be seeking information that the guards could not deliver, for they truly had no idea how Peter escaped. The guards were then led away for execution. Roman custom required that guards receive the penalty due their escaped prisoners.[7] This last word confirms what readers likely suspected: Peter *was* headed for execution. The scene ends with a brief announcement that Herod went to Caesarea.[8]

The Striking Down of Herod, 12:20-25

When chapter 12 began, Herod appeared to have the upper hand, executing James and arresting Peter. But as the story progresses, the text reverberates with echoes of Mary's Magnificat: "He has brought down the powerful from their thrones, and lifted up the lowly" (Luke 1:52). Peter is lifted up and out of prison; Herod is brought down to death.

Modern commentators know nothing substantive about the dispute between Herod and the people of Tyre and Sidon (v. 20). The important feature may be the conclusion of v. 20, which states that the people of Tyre and Sidon were *dependent* upon Herod's country for food. This notice serves to say something significant about the power of Herod, at least as far as the narrative world was concerned. On his throne, wearing his regal robes and offering kingly oration to his subjects (v. 21), Herod is back in the position to which he was accustomed. Here is a man whose plans for evil have been foiled by God and who has ordered the torture and execution of innocent guards. But that is all behind him now. Good times have returned.

Verses 22-23 further inform readers of Herod's view of himself, for when the people offer him divine accolades, Herod refuses to reject such honors and to give glory to God. In the larger narrative context, Herod's failure to give glory to God extends beyond his acceptance of divine honors. He also failed to give God glory when he executed and imprisoned some of the apostles. Perhaps failure to give glory to God extends to Herod's arrogant and callused torture and execution of prison guards. It never occurred to Herod that the inexplicable escape of Peter might just have been evidence of divine deliverance. Ironically, whereas an angel "strikes" (v. 7, *protassō*) Peter to awaken and deliver him, an angel of God now "strikes" (v. 23, *protassō*) Herod to render God's ultimate judgment. Employing a common motif found in ancient literature,[9] Luke's

The Death of Herod in Josephus

Josephus offers an explanation similar to Luke's to explain Herod's (Agrippa's) death. Josephus says nothing of the dispute between Agrippa and the citizens of Tyre and Sidon, but does describe in *great* detail the splendor of Agrippa's royal apparel. Indeed, it was the grandeur of the king's clothing that inspired the people to hail him as a god. Josephus specifically says what Luke only implies, namely that Agrippa's failure to rebuke such divine accolades led to Agrippa's illness, which began with a severe stomach pain and eventuated in his death five days later. According to Josephus, Agrippa saw an owl, which he took as an omen, and immediately recognized that he had done wrong. He told his friends that he willingly accepted the punishment of divine Providence that he knew was he to endure (*Ant.* 19.343–352). Luke offers Herod no such redeeming moment.

narrative describes how another tyrant who persecutes the lowly bites the dust. There *is* justice in the world, especially a world under the reign of God. [The Death of Herod in Josephus]

Verse 24 represents clear understatement. Despite the attempts of the mighty Herod to stamp out a religious menace, it is God's word, which is dependent upon God, that moves forward triumphantly. The concluding notice states that Barnabas and Saul returned *from* Jerusalem to Antioch. [Returned from Jerusalem] When the story shifts back to this city in Acts 13, readers will see just how much the "word of God was to grow and multiply."

CONNECTIONS

This text opens our eyes to a number of life-connecting theological reflections: (1) being witnesses of Christ, (2) the workings of God in history, and (3) the life of the community of faith.

Luke skillfully narrates the story of Herod's persecution of Jesus' followers to highlight the similarities between the sufferings (passion) of Jesus and those of his disciples.[10] In such similarities lies the disciples' capacity to be witnesses of Christ. The two most obvious connections between the narratives of Jesus' passion and the apostles' suffering are the Passover setting (Luke 22:1; Acts 12:2) and the involvement of "King Herod" (Luke 23:6-12; Acts 12:1). The latter is especially telling, for it is only Luke's Gospel that involves King Herod (Antipas) in Jesus' passion. Further, ancients tended to refer to the Herod of Acts 12 as Agrippa (I). Some readers might assume that the Herod of Jesus' passion and

Returned from Jerusalem

AΩ The NRSV translates 12:25 as "Barnabas and Saul returned to Jerusalem." This translation should confuse the reader, for Acts 11:30 has Saul and Barnabas going *to* Jerusalem, and Acts 12 never spoke of their return to Antioch. Further, immediately after 12:25, the scene is Antioch, and Saul and Barnabas are there. The textual evidence of the ancient manuscripts is rather evenly divided with some saying "returned from [using either the preposition *ek* or *apo*] Jerusalem" and others saying "returned to [*eis*] Jerusalem." Since the preposition "to" is the more

difficult reading, many textual critics believe this to be the more authentic reading.

However, even if one retains the preposition "to," one can read the phrase "to Jerusalem" to go with the phrase "having completed their mission," rather than with the verb "returned." This would render the translation: "Then having completed their mission to Jerusalem Barnabas and Saul returned and brought with them John." This allows the retention of the more difficult *eis* while still allowing the narrative to make sense.

the apostles' persecution is the same. The Lukan narrative does not discourage such confusion.

Close, intertextual reading of Acts 12 and Luke's Passion Narrative reveals other similarities. Jesus and Peter are *seized* (Luke 22:54; Acts 12:3), *handed over* (Luke 23:25; 24:7; Acts 12:4), and *brought before* potential accusers (Luke 23:1; Acts 12:4). Luke's stories of the resurrection of Jesus and the deliverance of Peter employ similar vocabulary. Readers find the appearance of *angels* in both (Luke 24:23; Acts 12:7). News of Jesus' and Peter's deliverance by God is met by disbelief (Luke 24:11; Acts 12:15), with the disciples imagining Jesus to be a ghost (Luke 24:37) and Peter an angel (Acts 12:15). Jesus and Peter meet and speak with the disciples (Luke 24:36-49; Acts 12:17) and then depart (Luke 24:50-53; Acts 12:17).

Luke constructs a narrative world that encourages readers to recognize that Peter's role as a witness requires him also to imitate the pattern of Jesus' passion, all in the hope of eventual deliverance by God. For many, this way of imitating Christ is the scandal—the stone of stumbling—of Christian discipleship. Yet the pattern permeates the New Testament (e.g., Rom 8:15-17; Phil 3:10; cf. 1 Pet 2:20-25; 3:17-18).

The pattern does not encourage reveling in suffering for suffering's sake. Jesus suffered for bearing witness to the kingdom of God; his followers suffered for bearing witness to this messenger of God's reign. When one confronts the world with the message of God's reign, most especially those corners of the world controlled by those like Herod who exploit power and position for their own self-aggrandizement, one can expect to encounter stiff resistance. Darkness does not yield to light without a struggle. Suffering in the context of the struggle is the kind of suffering that the New Testament expects and consoles.

During a guided tour of the Mammoth Caves of Kentucky, we were led into a cavern into which absolutely no natural light could penetrate. The ranger turned off the electric lights that had illuminated our paths, and, for about a minute, all in the cave experienced *total* darkness. The guide lighted one small match. All were amazed at how much light one small match could produce when lit in the context of total darkness. It takes only a little light to bring illumination to a darkened world.

While contemporary Christians need not seek out prison cells to inhabit, God's people today might begin to suspect that something is wrong if they never feel the pinch of living in the nooks and crannies of life. The experience of Mammoth Cave reminds us that even a flicker of light *cannot* go unnoticed in darkness. What does it imply if no one is noticing—and pinching—God's people? Perhaps those who never feel the pinch are either avoiding the dark caverns altogether or snuffing their matches before they enter the darkness that they might blend unnoticed into the blackness. The experiences of James and Peter remind us that the world notices those whom Jesus called the light of the world. Truly a city on a hill cannot be hid—it will draw attention to itself.

Peter's deliverance is God's doing: "Now I am sure the Lord has sent his angel and rescued me from the hands of Herod," Peter declares to the reader (Acts 12:11). Once again, Luke employs his literary skill to tell the story in such a way so as to invite readers to compare Peter's deliverance with other acts of salvation that demonstrate God's working in history.

Robert Tannehill offers some insightful comparisons between Luke's narration of Peter's deliverance and God's rescuing of Israel from its bondage in Egypt.[11] The association of Peter's imprisonment with the Passover season connects Peter's story not only to Jesus' passion, but also to ancient Israel's experience of the exodus, which Passover served to commemorate. Just as Luke employed intertextual echoes to relate Peter to Jesus' passion, he also offers such echoes to connect Peter's experience of deliverance with Israel's exodus.

One finds three key phrases in the narration of both the church's and ancient Israel's persecution and deliverance:

- "Herod the king laid hands *to afflict* [*kakōsai*] some of the church" (Acts 12:1; literal translation). The language echoes the Septuagint's rendering of the words of God spoken to Moses at the burning bush: "I have surely seen the *affliction* (*kakōsin*) of my people that is in Egypt." This particular Greek word translated *affliction* occurs frequently in the Bible's telling of the exodus story (Gen 15:3; Exod 1:11; 5:23; Acts 7:6, 19, 34).
- After Peter discovered himself a free man standing in the streets of Jerusalem, he said, "I know truly that the Lord sent his angel and *rescued me out of the hand of* Herod" (Acts 12:11; literal translation). Again, readers find similar language at the burning bush: "I have come down to *rescue them out of the hand of* the Egyptians" (Exod 3:8; literal translation of LXX). The biblical tradition commonly employed the phrase "to rescue out of the hand" to speak of the exodus (see Exod 18:4, 8-10; Acts 7:4).
- Acts employs the following phrase to describe what Peter told those gathered at Mary's home: Peter "described how the Lord *led*

him out of [*exēgagen ek*] the prison" (Acts 12:17). Again at the scene of the burning bush one reads God saying "to lead them out of [*exagagein ek*] that land [Egypt]" (Exod 3:8; literal translation of LXX). The Bible regularly employs the verb *exagō* to refer to God's leading of Israel out of the bondage of Egypt (Exod 18:1; 32:1, 23 Acts 7:36, 40; 13:17).

Such intertextual echoes drive home the idea that the liberating works of God provide continuity and connection between the people of God across history. Luke narrates the story of Peter's deliverance in the language of Scripture. Ironically, many readers today do not know the language of Scripture well enough to recognize what Luke is doing.

As we address contemporary audiences we should make it a priority to do what Luke has done: connect our stories and experiences with those of our biblical ancestors, learning to employ the language and imagery of Scripture to create for ourselves a meaningful symbolic world with which we can find connection and roots. [Biblical Imagery and Language] We used to be able to rely on the larger Western culture to educate people in the language, imagery, and symbolism of the Bible. We cannot any longer. The faith community needs with renewed earnestness to inculcate the language and symbolism of faith into the members of the community. In so doing we imitate the way our biblical ancestors communicated their faith—a way that proved effective for millennia.

The devotion of the Jerusalem church in offering prayers for Peter's rescue offers us meaningful, connecting insights regarding the life of the community of faith. There is sad irony in this story of answered prayer. The characters pray earnestly (12:5) and continually, praying for days even into the dark hours of the early morning. The irony is that they, apparently, were not really expecting their prayers to change things. One thinks of the humorous story of the drought-blighted community that called a special prayer meeting to plead with

Biblical Imagery and Language

Human beings are linguistic and symbolic creatures. Imagine trying to communicate without language. Imagine how narrow communication would be without symbols and imagery. Through language and symbols, humans construct the worlds in which they live as social beings. The awareness of humans' capacity for constructing worlds from language and symbol should increase awareness of the significance of employing regularly and consistently Christian language and imagery. Such language and imagery can be internalized individually through Bible reading and study. Corporately, such internalization can occur in the context of worship that intentionally employs biblical language and imagery in the context of prayer, sermons, and music.

Attempts to make the Christian message "relevant" are commendable, but if such relevance sacrifices specific biblical imagery and language, the message itself can be changed. Rather than allow the larger secular culture to shape the church's language, the church would do better to retain its own language and socialize the members of the community into biblical imagery and language.

J. Callahan, "The Bible Says: Evangelical and Postliberal Biblicism," *Theology Today* 53/4 (1997): 449–63; B. K. Smith, "Christianity as a Second Language: Rethinking Mission in the West," *Theology Today* 53/4 (1997): 439–48. Both articles are influenced by the works of George Linbeck, *The Nature of Doctrine: Religion and Theology in a Postliberal Age* (Philadelphia: Westminster, 1984) and "Scripture, Consensus, and Community," in *Biblical Interpretation in Crisis*, ed. R. J. Neuhaus (Grand Rapids MI: Eerdmans, 1989).

Answered Prayer

"God is not deaf, but listens; more than that, he acts. God does not act in the same way whether we pray or not. Prayer exerts an influence upon God's action, even upon his existence. That is what the word 'answer' means." (386)

Karl Barth, *Prayer* (Philadelphia: Westminster/John Knox, 1985). Cited from J. R. Tyson, *Invitation to Christian Spirituality: An Ecumenical Study* (Oxford: Oxford University Press, 1999).

God to send rain. Only one person brought an umbrella. [Answered Prayer]

Yet there is great comfort in this story. God *heard* the prayers of the people. God did not choose to answer them only after having done a kind of "faith inventory" to measure the depth of their confidence that God would, in fact, listen and respond. The act of prayer itself is the act of faith sufficient to move mountains—*even when we may not really believe that the mountain will move.* That can bring assurance to God's people who may think that what they ask of God is, actually, too much to ask.

NOTES

[1] Ernst Haenchen, *The Acts of the Apostles: A Commentary* (Philadelphia: Westminster, 1971), 387.

[2] Luke Timothy Johnson, *The Acts of the Apostles* (SacPag 5; Collegeville MN: Liturgical Press, 1992), 211.

[3] Gerd Lüdemann, *Early Christianity according to the Traditions in Acts: A Commentary* (Minneapolis: Fortress, 1989), 140.

[4] John B. Polhill, *Acts* (NAC 26; Nashville TN: Broadman, 1992), 278.

[5] Haenchen, *Acts*, 383.

[6] Joseph A. Fitzmyer, *The Acts of the Apostles* (AB 31; New York: Doubleday, 1998), 498–90.

[7] Polhill, *Acts*, 283.

[8] Earlier editions of the NRSV stated that *Peter* went to Caesarea. This nonsensical reading was corrected in later editions of the NRSV.

[9] A most thorough treatment of the motif of the tyrant who comes to a just end, with the application of this motif to Acts 12, is found in the dissertation of O. Wesley Allen, Jr., *The Death of Herod: The Narrative and Theological Function of Retribution in Luke–Acts* (SBLDS 158; Atlanta: Scholars Press, 1997).

[10] Johnson, *Acts*, 218–19.

[11] Robert W. Tannehill, T*he Narrative Unity of Luke–Acts: A Literary Interpretation*, 2 vols. (Minneapolis: Fortress, 1990), 2.153–55.

SENT OUT BY THE
HOLY SPIRIT

Acts 13:1-52

COMMENTARY

Acts 13 begins in earnest the third phase of the church's mission, taking the gospel to the "ends of the earth" (Acts 1:8). The narrative has foreshadowed this significant phase of the mission, not only in Acts 1:8, but in the call of Saul, in the context of which Jesus declared that he would be his instrument to preach both to Jews and Gentiles (9:15). Further, the exploits of Philip in Acts 8, Peter's preaching to Cornelius in Acts 10, and the notification that the church in Antioch consisted of both Jews and Gentiles (11:19-26), collectively, have prepared readers for this phase of the story.

Acts 13 introduces the first of three missionary journeys that will help to structure the narrative from 13:1–20:38. [Paul's Missionary Journeys] Acts 13 falls easily into two main sections. Verses 1-12 speak of the commissioning of Barnabas and Saul and their first missionary adventure on the island of Cyprus. Verses 13-42 tell of the preaching of Paul in Pisidian Antioch and the response there.

Paul's Missionary Journeys

The book of Acts divides Paul's missionary exploits into three journeys, weaving these journeys around Paul's connections with Syrian Antioch and Jerusalem. Interpreters recognize the Lukan artistry, but differ among themselves whether a solid historical chronology lies behind such artistry.

> **The First Missionary Journey** (Acts 13:1–14:26). Saul and Barnabas depart from Antioch. Paul and Barnabas return to Antioch (14:27-28), go to Jerusalem (15:1-29), and then return to Antioch again (15:30-35).
>
> **The Second Missionary Journey** (Acts 15:36–18:21). Beginning from Antioch. Paul visits the church in Jerusalem, then goes to Antioch (18:22).
>
> **The Third Missionary Journey** (Acts 18:23–20:38). Departs from Antioch. Sets sail for Jerusalem at end of third journey (21:1).

They Sailed to Cyprus, 13:1-12

The scene begins in Antioch, the city to which Barnabas and Saul have just returned, having completed their mission of delivering famine relief to Jerusalem (12:25). The text introduces readers to various prophets and teachers (see [Prophets]). Acts understands prophets both as foretellers (cf. 11:27-28) and speakers of encouragement (15:32; cf. 1 Cor 14:3). When combined here with "teacher," the prophetic role appears to be that of helping the larger community to discern the will of God.

Included among these prophets and teachers, in addition to Barnabas and Saul, are "Simeon who was called Niger [Simeon the Black One], Lucius of Cyrene, [and] Manaen" of the court of Herod the Tetrarch (v. 1). Commentators have speculated about the identity of these persons, equating, for example, Simeon with Simon of Cyrene or Lucius of Cyrene with Luke, the author of Luke–Acts.[1] Ben Witherington speculates that Manaen was Luke's special source for the goings on at the court of Herod Antipas.[2] The list of the prophets and teachers displays the diversity of the Antiochene church, from African Gentiles to a member of the Jewish, Herodian royal court.

Luke is not clear in v. 2 whether the "they" who are worshiping denotes only those listed in v. 1 or the whole church. Accordingly, it is unclear who the "they" are of v. 3 who lay hands on Barnabas and Saul. Is the leadership of the Spirit offered to the whole church[3] or the leadership group?[4] Readers must decide and will likely decide based on their own views of church polity. The text is clear, however, that such leadership of the Spirit came in the context of worship and fasting. The fact that "they" are fasting may indicate a sense of expectation that God was to move in a decisive way. [Fasting]

Through the Spirit, likely speaking through one of the prophets, God moves, commanding the church or its leadership to "set apart . . . Barnabas and Saul for the work to which I have called them" (v. 2). This "work" harks back to Acts 9:15 where Jesus had said that Saul was to be his instrument to bring Jesus' "name before Gentiles and . . . the people of Israel."

After continued fasting and prayer, "they" lay their hands on Barnabas and Saul. The laying on of hands may represent "a sign of transmitting power and authority"[5] or "a commissioning service for the two missionaries."[6] While Johnson's language may strike one as

Fasting

Fasting is well rooted in the Old Testament. The practice was often associated, either individually or corporately, with mourning and contrition. There are also instances of fasting in preparation for or in anticipation of divine revelation (Exod 34:28; 1 Kgs 19:8; Dan 9:3; 10:3). This last context for fasting most closely resembles the Antiochene church of Acts 13:1-3. Mourning, contrition, and the expectation of revelation from God are all settings that are appropriate for prayer. Hence, fasting and prayer regularly accompanied one another.

M. G. Reddish, "Fasting," *MDB* 296–97.

being more formal, even the language of "commissioning" implies some kind of "authorization." The key issue is not so much what the text may or may not say about ecclesiastical authority, as the text's recognition that the expansion of the gospel was not the work of individualistic mavericks, but the response of the *church* to the guidance of the Spirit. Authorization by the faith community does not magically transfer some mystical quality to the individuals. Rather, it offers testimony that the work they do is recognized as valid by a larger community, guarding against the danger of individuals being led by their own whims or idiosyncrasies.

Though it is the church that "sends off" Barnabas and Saul (v. 3), the narrator reiterates his belief that the church functions as an instrument of God's spirit, for v. 4 immediately says that they were "sent out by the Holy Spirit." The two, accompanied also by John Mark (v. 5; see [John Mark]), head for the port city of Seleucia, about fifteen miles west of Antioch, and sail to Cyprus. The narrative has established that the church at Antioch had a number of connections with Cyprus: Barnabas was from there (4:36), as were some of the Hellenist Jewish missionaries who initially preached the gospel in Antioch (11:19-20). That may have influenced the stop at this island.

When they arrive at the port city of Salamis on the eastern shore, they go to the synagogues to preach. This pattern of going to the synagogues will become paradigmatic in Acts. Verse 6 compresses

Map of Paul's First Missionary Journey

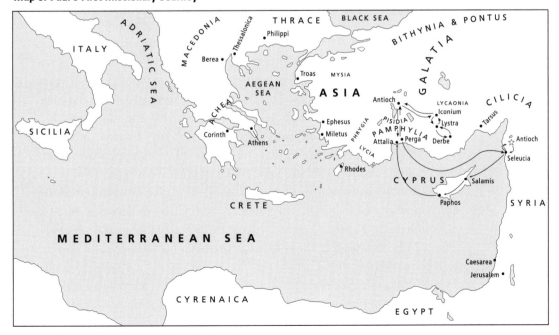

Sergius Paulus

Acts identifies him as the proconsul, which is the correct technical term for the governor of a senatorial province. Cyprus had been a province of the Roman senate since 22 BC. Some scholars have connected a number of inscriptions, located throughout the Roman Empire, including Cyprus, with this Sergius Paulus, or at least his family. For example, inscriptions near Pisidian Antioch refer to a family bearing the name Sergius Paulus (see below). An inscription located on Cyprus refers to a proconsul named Paulus. Yet the inscription itself is difficult to date, with possibilities ranging from the late first century BC to the early second century AD. The relevance of such inscriptional evidence for assessing the historical reliability of Acts varies from interpreter to interpreter.

F. J. Foakes Jackson and Kirsopp Lake, *The Beginnings of Christianity: The Acts of the Apostles*, 5 vols (Grand Rapids MI: Baker, 1979), 5.455–459; Ben Witherington III, *The Acts of the Apostles: A Socio-Rhetorical Commentary* (Grand Rapids MI: Eerdmans, 1998), 399–400.

Sergius Paulus Inscription from Antioch of Pisidia.
(Credit: Image courtesy of www.holylandphotos.org)

the trek across the island of Cyprus into a few words, with their journey ending in Paphos, the official capital of the island. The narrator focuses only on cities. This is typical of the way Acts presents Paul's missionary travels, a presentation surely grounded in history. Paul was the founder of the "first urban Christians."[7]

The short story about the witness to Sergius Paulus represents the anecdotal character of Acts. [Sergius Paulus] As Fitzmyer observes, this one story represents Paul's evangelization of the whole of Cyprus.[8] Readers should not infer that Paul's encounter with Sergius Paulus was the only such encounter on the whole island. Furthermore, 11:19 indicates that Christians had already preached on Cyprus. Luke is telling a memorable story that crystallizes and summarizes the advancement of the gospel.

Sergius Paulus apparently seeks the counsel of a certain magician, named Bar-Jesus (see [Magic]). It might surprise readers that one described as "intelligent" (v. 7) would have a magician as one of his advisors. The Roman culture, including its informed leaders, put high stock in practices that modern culture would call superstition. Divination (augury) was a respectable business in the Roman world.

Magic, while not the same as divination, moved in that orbit of fascination with the mysterious aspects of the supernatural. The Jewish philosopher Philo speaks very positively of what he calls "the true magical art," noting that initiation "into the mysteries of the magi" was almost a prerequisite for one who wanted to be a successful ruler (*Spec. Laws* 3.100). A *Jewish* magician would be even more appealing, as the Jewish religion had its own mystique. Josephus records the story of how Felix (see [Felix]), the Roman appointed procurator of Judea (AD 52–60), solicited the services of a Jewish magician from Cyprus to attempt to lure Drusilla, a married woman, away from her husband (*Ant.* 20.141-143). It worked, though Josephus does not tell the story in an approving manner.

Sergius's interest in supernatural things offers a credible rationale for his summons to Barnabas and Saul (v. 7). But Bar-Jesus, now referred to as "Elymas the magician (for that is the translation of his name), opposed them" (v. 8). Commentators are confused over the name change from Bar-Jesus to Elymas and the translation of his name. Regarding the latter, some have suggested that Elymas may be the Greek rendering of the Arabic name *'Alim*, which does mean "wise man," or *magos* (cf. the "magi/wise men" of Matthew's Gospel). Luke's addition of this information about Elymas does not, however, add much to the story. The name "Bar-Jesus," meaning "son of Jesus/Joshua [son of God-saves]," is loaded with rich irony, which Luke seems ready to exploit, with Paul referring to him as "son of the devil" (v. 10). Bar-Jesus earns this rebuke, for he attempted to turn Sergius "away from the faith" (v. 8) and "the word of God" (v. 7). It is ironic that one whose name proclaims his loyalty to the God who saves tries to inhibit one from hearing the saving message.

Saul, "who is also called Paul" (v. 9), is filled with the Holy Spirit in his confrontation with Bar-Jesus. ["Who Is Also Called Paul"] Such spiritual filling is Luke's typical way of describing one's empowerment by God for some specific task that God has given one to do (Luke 1:15; 4:1, 14; Acts 2:4; 4:8, 31; 6:3, 5; 7:55; 11:24). While Paul is filled with the power of God, Bar-Jesus is "full of all deceit and villainy" (v. 10). The charge offers a faint echo of Jeremiah's charge in Jeremiah 5:27, claiming that Judah consisted of houses "full of deceit" (NRSV = "treachery"), a condition sure to bring judgment (Jer 5:29).

Paul asks rhetorically whether Bar-Jesus will "not stop making crooked the straight paths of the Lord" (v. 10b). Here again, Luke employs scriptural echoes. The phrase translated "making crooked the straight paths" echoes the LXX version of Proverbs 10:9 and

---

"Who Is Also Called Paul"

AΩ Romans generally had three names, the *praenomen, nomen,* and *cognomen.* The *cognomen,* like modern culture's "last name," was the surname, or family name, like Gaius Julius Caesar. This example is informative, for most know this Roman ruler either as Julius Caesar or simply Caesar. The point is that one did not need, in ancient, as in modern times, to use one's "full name" for identification. It is possible that "Paul" (*Paulos*) was the apostle's *cognomen* and his first two Roman names are not known. If Paul was the apostle's *cognomen,* there is no evidence that he was related to Sergius Paulus (common "last names" do not necessitate a familial relationship).

It was not uncommon in Roman Judaism for Jews also to have a Semitic name, called a signum. Since Paul was from the tribe of Benjamin (Phil 3:5), whence the first king of Israel came, it is not at all implausible that his Semitic name would have been that of this first king. It is obvious from Paul's letters that he used the name Paul in the Greco-Roman world. Perhaps the shifting of the Lukan narrative focus from the regions of "Judea and Samaria" to the "ends of the earth" explains the change of name at this point in the narrative. The reference to Sergius Paulus may have provided an appropriate setting to segue to this new name.

F. J. Foakes Jackson and Kirsopp Lake, *The Beginnings of Christianity: The Acts of the Apostles,* 5 vols. (Grand Rapids MI: Baker, 1979), 4.145–46; Gerd Lüdemann. *Early Christianity according to the Traditions in Acts: A Commentary* (Minneapolis: Fortress, 1989), 151; John B. Polhill, *Acts* (NAC 26; Nashville: Broadman, 1992), 295.

Hosea 14:10, with the former referring to "crooked paths" and the latter referring to "straight paths." Both Old Testament texts make clear that judgment awaits those who pervert or stray from God's paths. There is also a clear echo of Luke 3:4, itself a quotation of Isaiah 40:3. John the Baptist's mission was to make the path of the Lord straight to prepare for the coming of Jesus. Bar-Jesus's demonic mission is to make the straightened paths crooked to inhibit the coming of the Lord Jesus into the life of Sergius.

The Old Testament texts that Paul's words echoed promised judgment for those who deceived and perverted God's ways or paths. Paul pronounces such judgment on Bar-Jesus, cursing him with a punitive miracle. The miracle calls to mind Paul's experience of temporary blindness, including the small detail that Bar-Jesus had to be led around "by the hand" (v. 11; cf. 9:8). The text does not suggest that Bar-Jesus came to see the error of his ways, but the connection with Paul's experience does imply that God's judgment has the potential of being redemptive.

There is certainly a redemptive dimension to the punitive miracle as far as Sergius is concerned, for the text states that when he "saw what had happened, he believed" (v. 12). Yet, while the display of divine power might open one to belief, this *alone* is not sufficient. The final clause of the verse grounds the proconsul's faith in his being "astonished at the teaching of the Lord" (v. 12b). Luke offers no summary of what this "teaching" was. One could read it to say that teaching was conveyed in the miracle itself: God punishes the rebellious. But vv. 7 and 8, which make reference to "the word of God" and "the faith," imply that Sergius did hear about the Lord Jesus. The message of power, backed by the demonstration of power, combined to produce faith.

They Came to Antioch in Pisidia, 13:13-52

This extended story falls into three parts: (1) an introduction (vv. 13-16a), (2) Paul's sermon to the synagogue (vv. 16b-41), and (3) the response of the audience (vv. 42-52). This represents one of three major speeches that Paul offers in the course of his journeys, with one speech during each of the three journeys. In this speech Paul preaches in the synagogue to Jews and Jewish sympathizers. During the second journey Paul delivers his speech to Gentiles informed by the Greek philosophical tradition (17:22-31). In the course of the third journey, he delivers a farewell address to the Ephesian bishops at Miletus (20:18-35). Hence, the narrative offers three representative types of address: to the Jews and others informed by the Jewish scriptural tradition, to the Gentiles

Pisidian Antioch

The city, which rested some 3600 feet above sea-level, was located on the border between the ancient districts of Phrygia and Pisidia. To distinguish this Antioch from several other cities that bore the same name, it was known as *Antioch facing Pisidia*, *Pisidian Antioch*, or *Antioch of Pisidia*. The Greek manuscripts of Acts reflect the last two options listed, with *Pisidian Antioch* the preferred name. (Antioch was not actually assigned formally to the Pisidian administrative jurisdiction, hence was not literally "*of* Pisidia," until AD 295. The reading *Antioch of Pisidia* may reflect this later, jurisdictional situation.)

In 25 BC the city came under the governance of the Roman province of Galatia and became a Roman colony in 11 BC. Antioch was an important governmental city for this region of the Galatian province. A sizable Jewish community lived in Antioch when Paul was there. They were descendants, most likely, of Jews who had migrated there in the late third century BC.

Pisidian Antioch cardo. (Credit: Todd Bolen, "Pisidian Antioch cardo," [cited 20 September 2007]. Online: http://www.bibleplaces.com.)

Joseph A. Fitzmyer, *The Acts of the Apostles* (AB 31; New York: Doubleday, 1998), 509; T. C. Smith, "Antioch," *MDB* 35; Ben Witherington III, *The Acts of the Apostles: A Socio-Rhetorical Commentary* (Grand Rapids MI: Eerdmans, 1998), 404–406.

informed by the Greek philosophical tradition, and to the church informed by the Christian tradition. Paul, the effective orator of Acts, can address all audiences and settings.

Introduction, vv. 13-16a

The introduction begins with the notification that Paul is now taking the lead; no longer will the reader encounter "Barnabas and Saul." It is now "Paul and his companions" (v. 13). The group leaves Pamphos and sails north to the province of Pamphylia, which had only recently become a Roman province (AD 45). Likely, the company did not go directly to Perga, which is actually a few miles inland. Though sitting along a river, it is inaccessible today by a sizable sailing vessel and was likely impassable in ancient times, as well. Thus, readers can infer that the ship harbored at Attalia, situated a few miles south of Perga. The narrator tersely reports that John (Mark) departed. No reason is given for John's departure, but it did create tension later on between Paul and Barnabas (15:37-40).

The trip to Pisidian Antioch (v. 14) would have taken time, with more than 100 miles of mountainous terrain lying between Perga and this city. [Pisidian Antioch] Once there, however, Paul and Barnabas attend synagogue worship. As part of the worship experience, there are readings from the law and prophets (v. 15). [Synagogue Worship] It seems curious that the narrative speaks of mul-

Synagogue Worship

Though not mentioned in the Old Testament, the synagogue emerged in the Greco-Roman era throughout the world as the important center of Jewish worship, education, and community life. Whereas the priestly class provided the leadership of the temple services in Jerusalem, the community was central to the life and services of the synagogue, with "lay" persons leading in prayer, Scripture readings, and even exposition. Women and children, as well as Gentile sympathizers with Judaism ("God-fearers"), attended synagogue worship, but Jewish men took the active leadership roles.

The order of worship in the synagogue had apparently achieved some structure by the first century AD, though interpreters need to keep in mind that more detailed descriptions of synagogue worship date later than the first century.

• Worship began with the recitation of the *Shema*, consisting of Deut 6:4-9, 11:13-21, Num 15:37-41, and, some scholars say, the Decalogue.
• The *Shema* was followed by prayer. Synagogue prayers may have resembled some version of what came to be known as the *Shemoneh'esreh* (see [Eighteen Benedictions]). These benedictions are a series of specific affirmations of the blessings God has bestowed and will bestow on Israel. Some scholars argue that prayer preceded the *Shema*.
• Scripture reading (cf. Luke 4:17-19; Acts 13:15a). Likely there existed some ordered sequence of reading from the Law in the first century (similar to a Christian lectionary), though such sequenced readings were not identical to what eventually developed in Judaism. Readings from the prophets were also a regular part of worship. Pronouncements of blessings introduced and concluded the reading of Scripture. Readings from the Scripture in Hebrew were followed by translations into the common language of the synagogue worshipers.
• Sermonic exposition (cf. Luke 4:21-27; Acts 13:15b-41). Exposition was actually an extension of the scriptural reading, being viewed as part of the study of Scripture, and would not have been a part of every Sabbath service.
• Concluding blessing.

S. Safrai, "The Synagogue," in *The Jewish People in the First Century, Historical Geography, Political History, Social, Cultural and Religious Life and Institutions*, 2 vols., ed. S. Safrai and M. Stern (Van Gorcum/Philadelphia: Fortress, 1976), 2.908–944.

tiple synagogue rulers, for it was the norm for each synagogue to have one ruler. Some commentators argue that the title could be used as an honorary title or that anyone who had ever held the position could retain the title.[9] Modern readers should not view this as typical, similar to the modern church of multiple, professional ministers.

The narrative offers no hint as to why those in charge of the synagogue service gave the visiting worshipers the opportunity to speak (v. 15b). Attempts to find psychological or historical explanations are speculative. In the Lukan narrative world, the subtle but ever-present guidance of Providence is likely behind this. Paul, regularly portrayed as the able orator by Luke,

St. Paul's Church

The church actually belongs to a much later period (c. 4th century). Tradition has it that the church was built over the site of the synagogue where Paul preached. The official archaeological report of the University of Michigan was open to the possibility: "Who shall say that this building may not stand upon the site of the synagogue where Paul and Barnabas preached (Acts XIII)?"

Church of St. Paul, Pisidian Antioch
(Credit: Todd Bolen, "Church of St. Paul," [cited 17 September 2007]. Online: http://www.bibleplaces.com.)

George W. Swain, "Archaeological Results of First Importance Attained by the Near East Research of the University of Michigan During Its First Campaign," 19 August 1924, Francis W. Kelsey papers, box 73, p. 4, Kelsey Museum Collection, Bentley Historical Library, University of Michigan, Ann Arbor MI. Report can also be found online: http://ella.slis.indiana.edu/~zestrada/Antioch/Articles%20and%20Reports.html (5 July 2006).

offers the typical orator's wave of the hand to begin his address (v. 16a).

Paul's Sermon at the Synagogue, vv. 16b-41

In Paul's sermon he narrates the story of Israel. It is a narrative driven by a theology of promise and fulfillment. As Tannehill notes, "This speech is basically the announcement, with supporting argument, that the promised heir has come and has been installed as Messiah through resurrection."[10]

The study of rhetoric as a guide to interpretation is not an exact science, as evidenced by the division among commentators whether this speech represents deliberative[11] or epideictic[12] rhetoric (see [Types of Rhetorical Persuasion]). The implicit calls to the audience for repentance (v. 24) and belief (v. 39), along with the warning not to scoff at the message (vv. 40-41), imply that Paul wants the audience to *do* something. That would indicate deliberative rhetoric.

Interpreters have outlined the speech itself a number of ways.[13] The tendency of modern oral and written presentations to have three main points might commend Polhill's organizational outline: (1) the promise to Israel (vv. 16b-25), (2) the promise fulfilled in Christ (vv. 26-37), and (3) the appeal to accept the promise (vv. 38-41).[14]

The Promise to Israel, vv. 16b-25

This survey of the history of Israel is told with an eye to the promises that God had made. Paul begins by identifying his audience as consisting of Jews and "God-fearers" (see [God-fearer]). Verses 17-20 cover quickly the eras of ancient Israelite history from the ancestors through the period of Samuel, just before the rise of the monarchy. In this narration, "all stress is on God's mercy—his election of Israel, his exaltation of his people, his gift of an inheritance in the promises land, his gift of rulers and kings."[15] Paul can be brief in telling this part of the story, for the reader can fill in the details concerning the patriarchs and Moses from Stephen's speech of Acts 7.

Textual evidence is divided over whether v. 18 should read that God "cared for" (*etrophophrēsen*) or "put up with" (*etropophorēsen*) Israel in the wilderness. The Old Testament interprets the wilderness period both ways (see Deut 1:31; Num 14:33). Perhaps the emphasis on God's promises to Israel should favor the reading "cared for," but scholars are divided. One may find the seven nations of v. 19 in any number of places in the Old Testament (e.g., Deut 7:1). There is also some confusion on what precisely the

450 Years

AΩ Greek manuscripts of Acts 13:19 offer two significant variant readings. One connects the reference of 450 years to v. 20, indicating that the duration of the period of the judges was 450 years. This very extensive period for the judges is similar to other ancient Jewish reckonings of the duration of this period. Josephus reckoned the period to be more than 500 years, while the rabbis reckoned some 383 years. Biblical scholars who take seriously the biblical traditions of the exodus, the conquest/settlement, the period of judges, *and* archaeological evidence regularly calculate the duration for the period of the conquest/settlement and judges to be less than 200 years (c. 1200–1020 BC).

Other Greek manuscripts of Acts 13:19 construct the Greek to indicate that the 450 years represents the total number of years for the events of 13:17b-19. The captivity of Egypt lasted for 400 years (cf. Gen 15:13; Acts 7:6; but see Exod 12:40); the wilderness wandering continued for forty years (the reference to forty years in 13:18 is included in the total of 450, according to this way of reckoning), and the conquest is estimated to have taken about ten years.

period of 450 years refers to (v. 19). [450 Years] It makes most sense to apply this period of time to the period from the captivity in Egypt up to the *beginning* of the period of judges. *After that period*, the judges ruled, until Samuel arose, which led to the rise of the monarchy (v. 20).

Verses 21-23 focus on the monarchy. Saul is a transitional figure. His reign of forty years serves to round out to 490 years the period from Egyptian bondage to the rise of David. [Forty Years] David is Paul's real concern, for it was to David that God made the promise of a savior (v. 23). Paul introduces David by saying that God "raised him up" (v. 22). The Greek word *ēgeiren*, like the English verb *raised up*, can conjure up, at least for the reader, an allusion to the *raising up* of Jesus at the resurrection.

Paul weaves together various Scripture texts to describe David (v. 22b): "I have found David" echoes Psalm 89:20; "a man after my heart" echoes 1 Samuel 13:14; "who will carry out my wishes" resonates with Isaiah 44:48. This last intertext is quite intriguing, for Isaiah 44:48 actually refers to Cyrus, the Persian king who ruled from 539–530 BC. Apparently, Paul can apply the text to David, for, like David, Cyrus is God's anointed (Isa 45:1) and is even described as a shepherd (Isa 44:48). At the very least, Paul's weaving of texts reveals that early Christians did not read their Bibles with wooden literalism; applying a text about Cyrus to David requires openness to an artful and poetic reading of the Scriptures.

Forty Years

AΩ The duration of Saul's reign is difficult to calculate with precision. The Hebrew text of 1 Sam 13:1 is corrupt (see the NRSV translation, with the numbers necessary for calculation missing.) The LXX offers no help, for it omits this verse altogether. Subsequent Jewish tradition is also confusing. Josephus, for example, reckons Saul's reign to be twenty years in one place (*Ant.* 10.143) and forty years in another (*Ant.* 6.378). Paul agrees with this latter tradition in Acts 13:21. Critical reconstructions of ancient Israelite history tend to date Saul's reign from c. 1020–1000 BC.

Verse 23 is crucial for Paul. Here he alludes specifically to a promise that God made to David, a promise that involved David's posterity (literally, *seed*). Paul declares that the promise finds its fulfillment in Jesus, a Savior. Paul will revisit this declaration in the next section of the speech. Paul does not quote any scriptural texts, but his words echo 2 Samuel 7:12 and 22:51. Second Samuel 7:12 speaks of God *raising up* David's *seed* and establishing his kingdom. The LXX version of 2 Samuel 22:51, which concludes a psalm attributed to David (cf. Ps 18), makes reference to "the salvation of [God's] king," God's anointed (*christos*), and David's *seed*. Paul affirms Jesus to be David's seed and a Savior.

Luke must assume his readers to be immersed in scriptural language and imagery (see [Biblical Imagery and Language]). The appeal of Paul's speech only works for the audience that can hear the subtle allusions. Early Christian readers of Scripture were often quite nuanced and subtle, suggestive and allusive in their ways of reading the Bible.

Verses 24-25 summarize the work of John the Baptist, including his preaching of repentance (cf. Luke 3:3, 8) and the fact that John was not the one who fulfilled the promise (cf. Luke 3:15-16). As Paul presents the story, John belongs to the period of "promise." Readers who know the story of John can fill in the blanks. What could Paul's audience in Antioch have been expected to know about John the Baptist? Understanding the speech to be composed primarily for the *reader* makes the question moot, for the narrator can assume the reader's knowledge of John from the Gospel narrative. Those who read the speech as a précis of an actual speech offered by Paul can appeal to Acts 19:3-4 for evidence that John was known among the Jews of the Diaspora or can argue that this Lukan presentation is very much a précis, and Paul would have given more detail in the actual speech.

The Promise Fulfilled in Christ, vv. 26-37

Verse 23 made reference to a promise that God made to David regarding the coming of a Savior. Verse 26 declares that "the message of this salvation" has been sent to these who are now proclaiming the word to the Jews and God-fearers. According to the canons of ancient rhetoric, v. 26 is the *proposition*, or main thesis, of the speech.[16] The verses following will offer the justification for this main thesis: vv. 27-31 present the supporting kerygmatic testimony (see [Kerygma]); vv. 32-37 offer supporting scriptural testimony.

The kerygmatic testimony offers a concise summary of what is central to the proclamation of the gospel, the death and resurrection of Jesus. Verses 27-29 briefly summarize the Passion Narrative of Luke 23. The laconic summary removes the more nuanced presentation of Jesus' passion that one reads in Luke's Gospel. For example, Luke 23 tends to lay more blame on the rulers than the people; there is no such distinction in this summary. Luke 23:50-53 states that a righteous man, Joseph of Arimathea, took Jesus down from the cross and buried him. Paul's summary leaves the impression that the same inhabitants of Jerusalem who were guilty of executing Jesus buried him (v. 29). Focusing on the rhetorical effect of the speech on the reader, recall that Acts 12 has dissolved the distinction between the Jewish leaders and the rest of the Jewish people. This presentation of the kerygma may reflect this lack of distinction that now controls the narrative.

The kerygmatic synopsis adds an interpretive element not explicitly found in the Passion Narrative, namely, that the Jews fulfilled Scripture unwittingly as they carried out the execution of Jesus (v. 27b). Paul makes the charge that the Jews do not understand their own Scriptures. Recalling the resurrection narrative of Luke 24 helps to explain this charge. There, it is made clear that even Jesus' followers *did not* understand that the Scriptures found their fulfillment in the death and resurrection of Jesus (Luke 24:25-27). Only the resurrected Jesus could "open their minds to understand the scriptures" (Luke 24:45). Fellowship with the resurrected Lord is the prerequisite to understand that the Scriptures find their fulfillment in Christ. Scriptural proof *alone*, apart from a receptive hearing that is at least open to faith in the Resurrected One, will not prove persuasive.

This kerygmatic summary of the death and resurrection of Jesus is grounded in the claim that Jesus appeared alive for many days to those who had known him prior to his death (v. 31). That Jesus died was beyond dispute—it was a public event. His resurrection appearances were limited to his followers. Like scriptural testimony, such eyewitness testimony of Jesus' resurrection can prove persuasive only to those faithfully receptive to such testimony.

Paul moves explicitly to scriptural testimony in vv. 32-37. Verse 32 reiterates that God had made promises to the ancestors of Israel, promises recorded in the Scriptures (cf. esp. v. 23). He declares that the resurrection of Jesus is *the* act of God that fulfills these promises (v. 33a), moving directly to a quotation of Psalm 2:7 to make his case.

The use of Psalm 2:7 illustrates the point made above that the persuasive power of scriptural testimony is limited, apart from a receptive and faithful hearing. The words of Psalm 2:7 do not explicitly offer testimony about the resurrection of a crucified Messiah. This is evidenced not only by a reading of the whole psalm, but by the fact that other places in the New Testament, including Luke, employ the same psalm in reference to Jesus' baptism (cf. Matt 3:17; Mark 1:11; Luke 3:22). Hebrews 1:5 also applies Psalm 2:7 to Jesus, but not in reference to any specific event, such as the baptism or resurrection. The varied application of Psalm 2:7 would indicate that Christians were likely drawn to Psalm 2 because of its reference to the anointed one (cf. Ps 2:2) and the son (Ps 2:7), both of which Christians could easily apply to Jesus, *given their faith that Jesus is Messiah, the Son of God.* Application of Psalm 2:7 to the resurrection is only *one* possible reading and can take place only *after* one comes to believe that Jesus is the Messiah whom God raised from the dead.

Verses 34-37 continue the scriptural witness, making use of two biblical texts to show that Jesus' resurrection is the fulfillment of Scripture. Key to the argument that Israel's Messiah was to be resurrected is the biblical promise that he was not to experience corruption (v. 34). This line of argument was apparently crucial to Luke, for Peter employed a similar argument in Acts 2:25-31. Perhaps Luke expects readers to bring to their reading of Paul's speech Peter's employment of a similar argument.

The first text to help Paul offer scriptural testimony to the resurrection is Isaiah 55:3, quoting verbatim a few words from the LXX—the words translated in NRSV as "to you the holy promises made to David" (v. 34b ["I will give" is added to the LXX text]). The Greek is very difficult to translate, but one must consider a literal translation in order to understand the logic of Paul's argument: "I will give you [plural] the holy things of David which are faithful."[17] Verse 35 begins with "therefore," claiming thereby that the reference to Psalm 16:10 that follows connects with the text from Isaiah 55:3. Verse 35 reads, literally, "Therefore he says also in another [psalm], 'You will not give your holy one to see corruption.'" What connects the two texts are the words "give" and "holy things"/"holy one" and the association with David (the stated author of Ps 16). The intertextual interpretation of the two texts renders the following scriptural support.

God promised that he would give *the holy things of David* to "you," the audience of Isaiah 55:3. The plural "you" and the larger context of Isaiah 55 indicate Israel to be the audience of this oracle. Paul can connect this with Psalm 16:10 by virtue of the words "give" (though it is Luke/Paul who adds the word "give" to the quotation of Isa 55:3) and "holy things"/"holy one." Interpreting the two texts in conversation with one another allows the "holy one" of Psalm 16:10 to define the "holy things" of Isaiah 55:3. Understanding the "holy one" to be the Messiah renders the interpretation that the "holy things of David" that God promises to give to Israel denote the Messiah. God fulfills his promise "to *give* the holy things of David" (Isa 55:3) to Israel by *not giving* the Holy One to see corruption (Ps 16:10). The context of Psalm 16 makes clear that the "corruption" that the Holy One does not experience is continuing death. Thus, in the resurrection of God's Holy One, the promises made to Israel's ancestors concerning what God would give to Israel find fulfillment. That David is not understood to be the subject of Psalm 16:10, despite the literal meaning of the words, is proven by the fact that David has died and has experienced corruption (vv. 36-37). Only Jesus, whom eyewitnesses affirm as resurrected, fulfills the scriptural promises.

The intricacy of the above interpretation reveals the complexity and subtlety of the New Testament's use of Jewish Scriptures. Such finely tuned intertextual interpretations imply that early Christians read their Bibles very carefully, interpreting the Scriptures through the lens of faith that Jesus is Messiah. However, the very complexity and subtlety of the arguments also might imply that such arguments were actually more for use *within* the church, to affirm an already existing faith, than to persuade those outside the church. Luke Johnson's statement may be apropos: "The argument [of vv. 34-37] would obviously not be convincing for anyone who was not already committed to its governing premise, namely that Jesus was the resurrected one 'begotten this day' (13:33), but then the speech is not really a report of what Paul said to the Jews at Antioch, but a reflection on the first mission by the apologetic historian Luke."[18]

The Appeal to Accept the Promise, vv. 38-41

Paul begins his appeal by making explicit that the Messiah offers forgiveness of sins (v. 38). For Luke, forgiveness of sins manifests God's liberating reign. Luke's version of the "Great Commission" is to proclaim "repentance and forgiveness of sins" (Luke 24:47). *This* is the disciples' mission. Hence, the proclamation of such forgiveness receives ample attention throughout Acts (2:38; 5:31; 10:43; 13:38; 26:18).

In v. 39, Luke couches his central message of forgiveness in the language for which Paul had become famous: "justification by faith." Translated more literally, the verse would read, "And from all things from which you could not be justified by the law of Moses, by this one (Jesus) everyone who believes (has faith) is justified."[19] Though Paul did not speak much of "forgiveness of sins" (see Rom 4:7; cf. Col 1:14), in one place where he does speak of such "forgiveness of sins" he juxtaposes forgiveness with "justification by faith" (see Rom 4:1-8, esp. vv. 6-8).

Paul concludes his appeal by quoting Habakkuk 1:5. He warns his audience not to behave in a manner that would make the words of Habakkuk apply to them. Paul warns his audience not to scoff and respond only with amazement, failing to believe the deed done by God and proclaimed to them (v. 41). The "deed" done by God refers to the whole of what Paul has just preached: the death and resurrection of Jesus and the offering of forgiveness, all in fulfillment of the promise that God made to Israel's ancestors.

The Response of the Audience, vv. 42-52

The audience initially responds positively; at least they appear open to hearing more on the next Sabbath (v. 42). The impression of v. 43 is that numerous "Jews and devout converts" (i.e., Gentiles) continued to carry on conversation with Paul and Barnabas. [Devout Converts]

Luke is silent regarding the events of the week before the arrival of the next Sabbath. The large crowd that shows up to hear the word of God (v. 44) indicates that Paul's message created a stir throughout the predominately Gentile city. Large numbers of Gentiles would be in "the crowds" that the Jews observed at their synagogue (v. 45a). But whereas the Gentiles hunger for the word of God, the Jews "were filled with jealousy." Do these jealous Jews include the "many

---

Devout Converts

ΑΩ Paul refers to those who "fear God" in 13:16 and 26, setting these people in both instances alongside Jews. These who fear God are generally understood to be "God-fearers" (see [God-fearer]), that is, Gentile sympathizers with Judaism, but not full converts. In 13:43 the narrator sets alongside "the Jews" not God-fearers, but *sebomenōn prosēlytōn*, which NRSV renders as "devout converts." This denotes Gentiles who were full converts to Judaism, not merely God-fearers. If one takes the language seriously, then the Gentiles of 13:16 and 26 are not the same group as the Gentiles of 13:43, but it seems curious that Luke would forget about the God-fearers whom he mentioned earlier and abruptly introduce full converts. Johnson is probably correct to say that, regardless of specific terminology employed, "Luke obviously wants the reader to perceive, in the environs of the synagogue, a fringe element of interested Gentiles among whom the messianic message will find its most eager listeners" (240).

Luke Timothy Johnson, *The Acts of the Apostles* (SacPag 5; Collegeville MN: Liturgical Press, 1992).

The Temple of Augustus

Acts 13:44 reports that almost the entire city of Antioch came to hear Paul preach. The temple of Augustus, the ruins of which are pictured here, serves as an enduring reminder of the thoroughly Gentile character of the city.

The Temple of Augustus, Pisidian Antioch (Credit: Todd Bolen, "The Temple of Augustus," [cited 17 September 2007]. Online: http://www.bibleplaces.com.)

Jews" of v. 43 who, the week before, were receptive to hearing more of Paul's message? The narrator presents the Jews of v. 45 as one group, implying a change of heart among those who were initially receptive to Paul's appeal. In contrast to the Jews, the Gentiles of v. 43, as well as the newcomers, will respond quite positively to the word that Paul declares (v. 48).

The word "jealousy" deserves focused attention. The Greek word *zēlos* can be translated either as "jealous" or "zealous." To be "zealous" was to be a faithful Jew (cf. Acts 21:20; 22:3; Gal 1:14; 1 Macc 2:24, 26, 27, 50, 54, 58; 4 Macc 16:16, 20). Contemporary readers should not understand Jewish resistance as grounded in what moderns would think of as "petty jealousy." Centuries before, Ezra had concluded that faithfulness to God required the Jewish community to separate itself from Gentiles (see Ezra 10:6-44; cf. Neh 13:1-3). The Jews of Antioch, unlike the reader, do not know that God has cleansed the Gentiles (Acts 10:28). They do not know that God intended God's word to be proclaimed "to all nations" (Luke 24:47) and "to the ends of earth" (1:8). Their zeal is commendable, but uninformed (cf. Rom 10:2). The Antiochene Jews were open to worshiping with *some* Gentiles who had shown their sympathy to Jewish ways and traditions. Having one's synagogue overrun with masses of Gentiles was another matter, however. These hoards of Gentiles could represent a threat to distinctive religious traditions.

When faced with what they perceive to be a threat to their tradition they attack both the message and the messenger that created this threat. "Blaspheming, they contradicted what was spoken by Paul" (v. 45), which can only mean the message that God had fulfilled his promises to Israel through the death and resurrection of Jesus. From the perspective of the narrator, to speak against this message of salvation, what Luke has several times called "the word of God," is to "blaspheme" (see [Blasphemy]).

Paul's response to such blasphemy is direct. First, Paul reiterates what Peter had said (3:25-26; cf. Rom 1:16; 2:9) and what the literary structure of Acts demonstrated with its focus on Jerusalem in Acts 1–7: that the word is preached first to the Jews. Such an affirmation offers readers assurance that God is not forsaking or "bypassing" Israel; the saving word of God has been offered to Israel in Jerusalem and also in the Diaspora.

Second, Paul asserts that rejection of this gospel message results in self-condemnation. Essentially, Paul is declaring that his audience is bringing to fulfillment the prophetic warning of v. 41.

Through their blasphemy, they scoff and refuse to believe the deed declared to them. Thus, as the prophetic warning of v. 41 threatened, they will perish, judging themselves unworthy of eternal life.

Third, Paul will now turn to the Gentiles. This important declaration deserves extensive comment.

1. *Paul does not mean that the Gentile mission is the mechanical result of Jewish rejection in Antioch, as though God offers the Gentiles the gospel only because the Jews of Antioch rejected it.* Texts such as Luke 2:29-32, 24:47, Acts 1:8, and 9:15 make clear that the salvation of the Gentiles was part of God's plan from the beginning.

2. *God does not turn to Gentiles because Jews reject the gospel; Jewish rejection is the secondary cause for the gospel's movement toward the Gentiles.* Rejection of the invitation by those on the original guest list prompted the householder of Jesus' parable to invite "the poor, maimed, blind, and lame" (Luke 14:21). Similarly, Jewish rejection of the gospel's invitation spurs the outward movement of the word. But just as one would not conclude that Jesus cared for the infirmed only because the healthy rejected his invitation, one cannot conclude that God cares for Gentiles only because Jews rejected the gospel. One must distinguish between the primary cause of the preaching to Gentiles (God's merciful will) and the secondary causes through which, in the context of history, God's will finds its realization (e.g., Jewish rejection).

3. *There is no hint that Jewish rejection of the gospel is due to some predetermined plan of God that eliminates the free will of the Jews who have heard the gospel.* Paul uses active verbs in v. 46: "you thrust the word of God from you" and "you judge yourselves unworthy of eternal life." God does not dictate that the Jews of Antioch will reject God's word so that the gospel can now move on to the Gentiles.

Paul concludes his harsh statements against his Jewish audience by quoting Isaiah 49:6. The quotation comes from one of the Servant Songs of Second Isaiah. In its original context the words are addressed to God's servant who was to restore the survivors of Israel and be "a light to the nations [Gentiles]." Paul quotes only the part of Isaiah pertaining to "the Gentiles," which is appropriate given that he has *just* announced this direction to his mission. Yet, by preaching to both Jews and Gentiles, Paul actually fulfills the inclusive role of the servant, to be an agent for the restoration of Israel and the salvation of the Gentiles.

The Gentiles' reaction is opposite that of the Antiochene Jews; while the Jews scoff, the Gentiles rejoice; while the Jews blaspheme against the word of God, the Gentiles glorify the word of God

(v. 48). If this incident serves a programmatic function in the narrative, it foreshadows that Gentiles will generally be more receptive to the gospel than the Jews. Verse 48 concludes with the affirmation that the Gentiles who "had been destined to eternal life became believers."

The language of the NRSV could imply a kind of determinism that the text does not demand. The Connections section will address this further. At this point, note that the text smoothly, yet unsystematically, blends the mystery of God's initiative, by using a passive form of *tassō* ("destined"), and human volition, using the active form of the verb *pisteuō* (believe). The structure of the Greek text actually puts the emphasis on the importance of human response to the divine initiative by bringing the verb "believe" to the front of the clause: "and they believed—as many as had been appointed to eternal life."

Verses 49-52 offer assurance that the word of God did not fail in Antioch or the entire region (v. 49), despite continued resistance and even persecution, tragically instigated by the Jews (v. 50). Luke acknowledges that persons of means and power can come to embrace the gospel (recall Manaen of Herod's court [13:1]). He also knows that persons of influence are often threatened by the challenge of the gospel (cf. Luke 18:14). Both women and men of high social standing are incited. The feminine participle *sebomenas* (devout) denotes the women (v. 50). Hence, Luke would mean by "devout women of high standing" *Gentile* women high on the social ladder who worshiped at the synagogue. The "leading men of the city" would also be Gentiles. This shatters any simple notion that "all Jews" reject the gospel while "all Gentiles" accept it. The world of Luke is not divided between ethnic groups, but between those who hear the gospel with faith and those who do not. Jews and Gentiles can make up both groups.

Persecution again spurs the gospel onward (cf. 11:19-21). Run out of town, Paul and Barnabas shake the dust from their feet and move on to Iconium. ["Shake the Dust from Their Feet"] Luke does not say what becomes of the believers who remain in Antioch, except that they are filled with joy and the Holy Spirit. The readers do not know whether they too faced hardship, but clearly the gospel is well established in Antioch.

"Shake the Dust from Their Feet"

The symbolic act of Paul and Barnabas in 13:51 is open to interpretation. Some have attempted to interpret the gesture in the context of Jewish culture. Jewish concerns over purity led to the practice of shaking the dust of a pagan city or some other unclean area off one's feet when one left so as not to become a bearer of ritual impurity. Such interpretations are interesting, but make little sense in the context of the Lukan narrative. Lukan readers can recall Luke 10:10-12 to find the significance of the act in Luke's narrative world. The gesture served as a warning to a city that rejected the gospel message that the kingdom of God had come near and it could expect severe judgment due to its rejection of the gospel. The gesture complements the verbal warnings of texts such as 13:41 and 46.

CONNECTIONS

This narrative, formally inaugurating the final phase of the book of Acts ("to the ends of the earth"), is rich in theological connections. First and foremost is the larger theme of the providential design of the story. Within this larger theme, three related sub-themes find expression in Acts 13: the activity of the Holy Spirit, salvation history, and the fulfillment of Scripture. The story also connects theologically with the theme of human participation in the divine drama. In the flow of the narrative of Acts 13 these themes and sub-themes move in and out of each other, supplementing and complementing each other like the patterns in a rich tapestry.

The opening scene of Acts 13, where Barnabas and Saul are commissioned by the church of Antioch, illustrates the providential design of the story as well as human participation in the divine drama. The activity of the Spirit, a significant aspect of God's providential design, explicitly finds expression in vv. 2 and 4. In v. 2 the Spirit speaks; in v. 4 the Spirit sends. Yet we can only imagine that the Spirit speaks through human prophets, who have gathered together in the context of worship. The inspired prophet need not speak, for, as Paul reminds us in 1 Corinthians 14:32, the spirits of the prophets are subject to the prophets. And we can only imagine that the Spirit sends disciples who are willing to go. None was compelled to go, as evidenced by John Mark's free decision to return to Jerusalem. Part of the mystery of divine leadership in the biblical story is how God relies on the free obedience of God's people for the accomplishment of the divine will through the intricacies of history.

God and Jesus are regularly portrayed as shepherds and their people as sheep. They are not portrayed as cowboys and their people as cattle. Cowboys *drive* cattle; shepherds *lead* sheep. In Acts 13 one can detect the leadership of God as the church in Antioch resolves to commission and send out Saul and Barnabas. Further, these two respond obediently to their commission. But the text clearly does not portray God as a taskmaster, compelling mechanical obedience from God's church, its missionaries, or even from those who share in the divine drama through repentance and faith upon hearing the gospel.

Salvation history and the fulfillment of Scripture are two very significant features of the theme of the providential design of the story. Acts 13 addressed these two features of providential guidance through Paul's sermon at Antioch. More subtly, through the manner in which Luke narrates the story of Paul's experience at

Antioch, Luke gives further expression to this important theme of salvation history.

Paul's sermon solidly grounds the gospel story in the larger biblical story, as it speaks of the eras of the patriarchs, exodus, wilderness, conquest, judges, and monarchy. In this particular telling of Israel's story, Paul stops with the rise of David. Missing are any words about Solomon, the temple, the other kings, the exile, and the return from exile. Such an abbreviated telling allows Paul to make clear the connection between David and Jesus within the context of God's saving history.

Direct linkage of Jesus with David helps Paul to emphasize that Jesus is *the* fulfillment of the hopes centering on David. The hopes for the restoration of the Davidic throne were not universal in first-century Judaism, but they certainly were widespread. And it was not uncommon for such hopes to include the idea that the grand descendant of David would conquer the enemies of God's people. The royal psalms, often interpreted in the Greco-Roman era as referring to the ideal king to come, the Messiah, speak regularly of the conquering of God's and the nation's enemies (Pss 2:8-9; 110:1, 5-6). The postexilic prophet Haggai hoped that David's royal descendant, Zerubbabel, would be God's instrument to overthrow the nations (Hag 2:21-23). A pseudepigraphic text written in the name of Solomon during the first century BC echoes similar themes: "Undergird him with strength to destroy the unrighteous rulers, to purge Jerusalem from Gentiles who trample her to destruction; in wisdom and righteousness to drive out the sinners from the inheritance; to smash the arrogance of sinners like a potter's jar" (*Pss Sol* 17:21-23).[20] Paul insists that Jesus fulfills the messianic hopes. Yet the primary victory of the Messiah for God's people is the offering of forgiveness of sins (13:38).

As mentioned in the Commentary, Paul spoke rarely of "forgiveness of sins," yet he spoke often of the "enemies of God." However, he consistently spiritualized these enemies, identifying the enemies of God with various spiritual forces from the dark side that waged war against God's people: death (1 Cor 15:26; Rom 5:14, 17); Satan (Rom 16:20; 1 Cor 5:5; 2 Cor 2:11); rule (1 Cor 15:24; Rom 8:38); rulers (1 Cor 2:6, 8) authority (1 Cor 15:24; Rom 13:1); power (1 Cor 15:24; Rom 8:38); sin (Rom 5:21; 6:12; 7:11-23).[21] Paul emphatically affirmed that God's Messiah, Jesus, would conquer these enemies of God and his people, the last one being death (1 Cor 15).

Paul's spiritualization of the enemies of God in his letters and the Lukan Paul's focusing on "forgiveness of sins" as the primary benefit of the Davidic Messiah's mission move in a similar orbit. Luke also speaks of the deliverance of God's people from their "enemies" in connection with the coming of the Messiah (Luke 1:68-73). Yet, as the Gospel narrative unfolds, the reader senses that the ultimate enemy of God's people is the malevolent forces that hold creation in bondage, for Jesus levels his attacks on disease, demons, and sin, offering healing, exorcism, and forgiveness (see, e.g., Luke 4:31-44; 5:17-26). As Jesus' followers assessed what this one whom they believed to be Messiah actually did for them, they concluded that liberation from spiritual enemies and the restoration of fellowship with God were his primary blessings. The gospel, as it was actually experienced by Jesus' earliest followers, became the primary lens through which Christians interpreted the Jewish Scripture and tradition. But this regularly necessitated a spiritualized reinterpretation of the Scriptures.

Thus, the theme of the fulfillment of Scripture cannot be separated from the Christians' tendency to reread their scriptural traditions spiritually. The Christian commentator Origen (c. AD 200) claimed that the primary reason that Jews of his time did not accept that Jesus was the fulfillment of scriptural hopes was because they insisted on a *literal* reading of the Scriptures. [Origen] Refusal to read the Old Testament as the earliest Christians read these Scriptures, as a repository of images, symbols, and metaphors that gave expression to deeply spiritual experiences of salvation, can result in missing significant connections between our worlds and the world of Scripture. Contemporary preachers will find it much easier and *relevant* to connect the Old Testament with the New Testament if they do not insist on a literal reading of the Jewish Scriptures at every turn, and, following the cue of the New Testament preachers, allow the Scriptures to "interpret spiritual things to those who are spiritual" (1 Cor 2:13).

Origen

"Those advocates of circumcision whose hearts were hardened and who had no understanding refused to believe in our Savior. It was their intention to follow the letter of the prophecies which spoke of him . . . . Failing to see any of [these prophecies] happening in a physical sense at the advent of the one whom we believe to be the Christ, they did not accept our Lord Jesus but crucified him as one who had claimed to be the Messiah against the law." (*On First Principles*: Book Four, II, 1)

K. Froehlich, *Biblical Interpretation in the Early Church* (Philadelphia: Fortress, 1984), 54–55.

Salvation history and the fulfillment of Scripture play a role not only in Paul's sermon, but in the manner that Luke narrates the story of Paul's experiences at Antioch. Luke has carefully crafted this narrative in a manner that reflects a pattern similar to another carefully crafted Lukan narrative, the rejection of Jesus at Nazareth (Luke 4:16-30). [Jesus at Nazareth and Paul at Antioch] By telling the story to show the similarities between Jesus' inaugural public proclamation and Paul's, Luke gives testimony to the *continuity* between

Jesus at Nazareth and Paul at Antioch

A close reading of the two inaugural sermons of Jesus and Paul reveals Luke's artistry in constructing the two narratives.

Event	Luke 4	Acts 13
The setting of synagogue worship	16	14
An invitation to Jesus/Paul to read or speak	17	15
An appeal to Scripture (Acts tells the story contained in Scripture and quotes frequently from Scripture)	18-19	16b-41
Announcement of the fulfillment of Scripture	21	23, 27, 32-33
The audience initially responds positively, or at least with openness, to the preaching	22	42-43
Inclusion of the Gentiles	23-27	44, 48
Violent reaction, including physical removal from city/district	28-29	45, 50
Escape/departure from Nazareth/Antioch	30	51-52

Jesus and Paul. Demonstration of continuity allowed, and allows, Christian interpreters to recognize and affirm the providential hand of God in the movement of history to achieve God's ends for salvation.

Observe in both stories a pattern of scriptural reading, interpretation, declaration of fulfillment, initial positive response, word of Gentile inclusion, and violent reaction. The fact that Acts 13 follows the pattern of Luke 4 so closely can hardly be coincidence. Conscious, literary artistry is part of the process of biblical composition, whatever one may believe about the inspiration of Scripture (see [Inspiration]).

The paradigmatic pattern constructed by Luke provides for him, and his readers, a key by which to make sense of one of the more profound mysteries of the gospel: the fact that most Jews did not recognize or understand Jesus to be the fulfillment of their Scriptures and its promises (13:27). In both Luke 4 and Acts 13 the people respond with a sense of openness and expectation to the announcements that Jesus fulfills the Scriptures. Yet, by the end of each story, both audiences have responded violently to the messenger of God's good news. In both, what moved the audience from initial acceptance, or at least openness, to the declaration that Jesus fulfilled the Scriptures was the indication that *Gentiles were included in God's good news of salvation*. The implication is that recognition of Jesus as the one who fulfills the Scripture requires one to understand these Scriptures in the context of a faithful hearing of Jesus and his messengers. More importantly, *such faithful hearing requires that we be willing to allow our well-worn assumptions about God and God's will to be challenged.*

The eventual inclusion of the Gentiles among the worshipers of God was well established in Jewish eschatological thought. [Inclusion of the Gentiles] And certainly the Jews of Antioch were not totally opposed to allowing Gentiles to worship with them, as evidenced by the presence of "God-fearers" in the synagogue. It is one thing to embrace an idea in the abstract or to allow in some exceptional cases for the abstract idea to find limited, concrete realization. It is quite another, however, to embrace the radical openness of the gospel fully and completely.

With the exception of hate groups that intentionally read the Bible through their lens of bitterness and paranoia, readers of the Bible acknowledge God's love of people of different races and classes. Christians acknowledge that all are one in Christ, male and female, slave and free, Jew and Greek (Gal 3:16). And we may even, from time to time, allow this ideal to be practiced

> **Inclusion of the Gentiles**
>
> The expectation for the eventual inclusion of the Gentiles within the people of God was widespread in much Jewish thought, both within biblical and extra-biblical traditions. Within the Bible, see such texts as Isa 2:2-4, 56:6-7, 66:23, and Zeph 3:8-10. The deuterocanonical book of Tobit (14:6-7) envisions the pilgrimage of the nations to Jerusalem, where they will worship God. Various rabbinic traditions, though later than the New Testament period, echo a similar expectation. One example comes from a text titled *Pesiqta de-Rab Kahana*: "Jerusalem is destined to become a beacon for the nations of the earth, and they will walk in its light" (21:4).

in some exceptional circumstances. Baptists have made two women, Lottie Moon and Annie Armstrong, their primary symbols of missions. We have an occasional joint worship service with a congregation of a different racial group. But if one dares to declare that *today* the time has come for the full and complete realization of scriptural ideals, for the full inclusion of women into the life of the church, for the full integration of God's people to shatter the caste system of "Jew and Greek" (read "white and everybody else," in our culture), there is resistance. Faithful or open hearing ceases. And reaction against those who proclaim the word of God may be violent, if not in action, then in word. Ironically, the violence is rooted in religious *zeal*, not in lukewarm apathy (see the Commentary on the issue of zeal).

The irony of grace is that God's providential care can work through the resistance of even misguided religious zeal. Jesus was forced to move beyond Nazareth. And so he went to other cities to proclaim the kingdom of God to them also (Luke 4:43). Paul and Barnabas move on to Iconium, and, as Acts 14 will show, the word spread. The history of God's saving work regularly unfolds in the face of resistance and even persecution, but it moves onward. In the narrative of Acts, Paul will reach "the ends of the earth."

The theme of human participation in the divine drama of salvation requires a closer look at Acts 13:48b: "and as many had been destined for eternal life became believers." The New Testament is clear that God's initiating grace is the reason that people can experience the restoration of fellowship and the forgiveness of sins. The Reformed tradition of Christianity, especially, has placed emphasis

Providence and Fatalism

📖 "Providence . . . is to be distinguished from what is usually called "fate." A belief in fate accepts that whatever happens has been determined in advance by some sovereign power, perhaps God, or even some agency more ultimate than God. A true fatalism therefore excludes free will, and thus human responsibility. . . . Calvin rightly maintains that providence is not a mere foreknowledge or prevision; the doctrine of providence is important only if God actively has a part in bringing events about. . . . But Calvin goes on to make it clear that he does not think of this as only a general control or direction over events. It is a direct act of governing which regulates every single happening. . . . He asserts that even human actions (including bad actions) merely carry out what God has previously determined. . . . If this were the case, it would make utter nonsense of any belief in human responsibility. . . . Calvin's view must be rejected as unworthy not only of man but of God as Christians understand him, for God is not exalted but debased by being turned into the author of fate."

J. Macquarrie, *Principles of Christian Theology*, 2d ed. (New York: Charles Scribner's Sons, 1966/1977), 244–45.

on the sovereignty and initiating grace of God. The initiating grace of God, through the Spirit, convicts one of sin, extends the call to repentance and faith, illuminates the minds of hearers of the gospel to recognize its divine truth, and enables the individual to respond to the call of the gospel.[22]

It is imperative, however, that we not equate graceful providence with blind fatalism, as though God, whimsically and arbitrarily, selects those to whom God will offer such conviction, call, illumination, and enablement. [Providence and Fatalism] The text often cited about the *convicting* power of the Spirit is John 16:8, yet this text does not say that the Spirit convicts "the elect," but "the world." Further, Paul speaks of the human conscience as having a convicting power in Romans 2:15-16. Second, it is God who stands behind the *call*, and yet the call comes through the preaching of the gospel itself (Rom 10:13-15; cf. 2 Thess 2:13-14). That is precisely the point Paul makes at the conclusion of his sermon in 13:41, when he warns his audience not to scoff at the word he has just proclaimed. Paul is an instrument of the call to reconciliation; hence, he can, with integrity, urge people who hear him to accept the reconciliation that God offers (2 Cor 5:18-21). The Great Commission, both in the Matthean (Matt 28:19) and Lukan (Luke 24:47) versions, makes "the nations" the object of proclamation, not some faceless elect hidden in the masses.

Paul addresses the *illuminating* work of God in 2 Corinthians 3:12-4:6. Two points are quite important. First, Paul acknowledges that a veil lies over the minds of nonbelieving Jews, so that they cannot understand that the old covenant points beyond itself to "the end of the glory that was being set aside" in Christ (v. 13). Paul insists that it is only in Christ that such illumination comes, but he further states that "when one turns to the Lord, the veil is removed." Paul employs the passive voice to speak of the removing of the veil, implying that this work of illumination is accomplished by God. But he employs the active voice of the subjunctive mood in v. 16a, stating, "if one should turn [*epistrepsē*, one of the New Testament words for *repent*] to the Lord." It strains credulity and empties the meaning from the biblical notion of repentance to argue that such turning has nothing to do with human volition. Second, Paul states in 2 Corinthians 4:3-4 that the truth of the gospel "is veiled to those who are perishing" (v. 3), stating that "the god of this world has blinded the minds of the *unbelievers.*" It is those who do not believe who are denied illumination. Again, it empties faith, which at its core means *trust*, of any meaning to insist that such faith is not directly associated with human volition. It is those who are unbelievers, not those who are predetermined to be unbelievers, who are blinded by the god of this world.

Finally, God is said to *enable* one to respond to the gospel; it is the divine initiative and power that makes repentance and faith possible. But are we to understand such enabling to be offered only to some elect and to hell with—literally—those who do not repent and believe because God simply chooses not to *enable* them to do so? Such a conclusion does not go well with affirmations such as 2 Peter 3:9: "The Lord is not slow about his promise, as some think of slowness, but is patient with you, not wanting any to perish, but all to come to repentance." The word translated "wanting" is *boulomai*, which, when used with reference to God's "wants," denotes the will of God. It is God's will that none should perish, but that *all* should repent. This cannot be easily reconciled with any theology that insists that God enables only *some* to repent and believe. One can say, reasonably, that God's will that *all* repent can be thwarted by the freedom to reject what God offers to God's creation. One cannot say, reasonably, that God's will that *all* repent is thwarted by God's own action of only enabling *some* to do so. So, indeed, these Gentiles who believed have been destined by God to eternal life—as has everyone who believes.

NOTES

[1] For details, see Joseph A. Fitzmyer, *The Acts of the Apostles* (AB 31; New York: Doubleday, 1998), 496; Luke Timothy Johnson, *The Acts of the Apostles* (SacPag 5; Collegeville MN: Liturgical Press, 1992), 220.

[2] Ben Witherington III, *The Acts of the Apostles: A Socio-Rhetorical Commentary* (Grand Rapids MI: Eerdmans, 1998), 392.

[3] John B. Polhill, *Acts* (NAC 26; Nashville: Broadman, 1992), 290.

[4] Witherington, *Acts*, 393.

[5] Johnson, *Acts*, 221.

[6] Polhill, *Acts*, 290.

[7] See Wayne A. Meeks, *The First Urban Christians: The Social World of the Apostle Paul* (New Haven: Yale University Press, 1983), esp. ch. 1.

[8] Fitzmyer, *Acts*, 499.

[9] Polhill, *Acts*, 297; Witherington, *Acts*, 406.

[10] Robert W. Tannehill, *The Narrative Unity of Luke–Acts: A Literary Interpretation*, 2 vols. (Minneapolis: Fortress, 1990), 2.166–67.

[11] Witherington, *Acts*, 407.

[12] Marion L. Soards, *The Speeches in Acts: Their Content, Context, and Concerns* (Louisville KY: Westminster/John Knox, 1994), 79.

[13] See, e.g., Witherington, *Acts*, 407 and Soards, *Speeches*, 80.

[14] Polhill, Acts, 287.

[15] Ibid., 300.

[16] Witherington, *Acts*, 407; Soards, *Speeches*, 79.

[17] Following the translation of F. J. Foakes Jackson and Kirsopp Lake, *The Beginnings of Christianity: The Acts of the Apostles*, 5 vols. (Grand Rapids MI: Baker, 1979), 4.155.

[18] Johnson, *Acts*, 238–39.

[19] Following, with modification, the translation of Jackson and Lake, *The Beginnings of Christianity*, 4.157.

[20] R. B. Wright, "Psalms of Solomon: A New Translation and Introduction," *The Old Testament Pseudepigrapha*, 2 vols., ed. J. H. Charlesworth (Garden City NY: Doubleday, 1985), 2.639–734.

[21] See the short but helpful discussion on Paul's views of "the enemies of God" in J. Neyrey, *Paul, In Other Words: A Cultural Reading of His Letters* (Louisville KY: Westminster/John Knox, 1990), 162–63.

[22] Stanley J. Grenz, *Theology for the Community of God* (Nashville: Broadman and Holman, 1994), 536–41.

PROCLAIMING THE GOSPEL TO THE SURROUNDING COUNTRY

Acts 14:1-28

COMMENTARY

Acts 14 divides into three sections: Paul and Barnabas at Iconium (vv. 1-7), their preaching and healing at Lystra (vv. 8-20a), and the return of Paul and Barnabas to Antioch of Syria (vv. 20b-28). (See the map of Paul's first missionary journey in the previous chapter to track Paul's movements in Acts 14.)

Preaching in Iconium, 14:1-7

Persecution at Antioch of Pisidia in the preceding chapter required Paul and Barnabas to move on to Iconium (13:51). [Iconium] Acts 14:1 states that "the same thing occurred in Iconium" (NRSV). The phrase "the same thing" renders the Greek phrase *kata to auto*, which can also be rendered "together" (RSV). The translation offered by NRSV makes the point that the pattern of the preceding chapter will repeat itself in Iconium: Paul and Barnabas will preach in the synagogue, some will believe, and some will not. Those who do not believe will oppose the proclamation of Paul and Barnabas.

Paul's preaching to Jews in the synagogue clarifies his declaration of 13:46 that he will turn to the Gentiles. It does not mean that he would never preach to Jews again. It reflects the providential pattern that Jewish rejection, rather than impeding the gospel, urges such proclamation forward to whomever will receive it.

Iconium

Located about 90 miles southeast of Antioch along the *Via Sebaste* (the Royal Road that accommodated trade and troop movements), Iconium was founded around 1200 BC by the Phrygians. It was an important and wealthy commercial and trade center, known especially for its orchards and wool industry.

John Laughlin, "Iconium," *MDB* 399; John B. Polhill, *Acts* (NAC 26; Nashville: Broadman, 1992), 309n53.

It is not unlike what one sees in Luke 4:24-27. Jesus stated that a prophet is not accepted in the prophet's hometown, yet the prophetic ministry continues. Elijah and Elisha were hardly silenced by Israel's rejection of their prophetic word. Rather, they shared the beneficence of God with Gentiles, the widow of Sidon, and Naaman of Syria. One who knows, however, the stories of these prophets knows that their preaching to Israel did not cease with such "turning to the Gentiles."

In Iconium, as in Antioch, many believed the gospel (14:1b). Also, as in Antioch, there were those who did not believe. The participle employed to describe the "unbelieving Jews" (v. 2) is *apeithēsantes*, which literally means "disobedient." The term is also used in the New Testament to denote the opposite of "faith" or "belief" (John 3:36; Heb 3:18-19). The LXX regularly used this word to denote egregious disobedience toward and rebellion against God (Lev 26:15; Num 11:30; Deut 1:26; 9:7; 32:51) and even failure to believe or trust in God (Deut 9:23-24). The narrative portrays these particular Jews of Iconium, therefore, as sharing company with the unfaithful and rebellious lot of their own ancestry.

The text says that these disobedient/unbelieving Jews "poisoned the minds" of the Gentiles "against the brothers" (v. 2). The phrase "poisoned the minds" renders a Greek phrase that literally means "made evil [*ekakōsan*] the souls." Acts has earlier employed this verb or its cognates to describe the oppression of Egypt against Israel (7:6, 19) and Herod against the church of Jerusalem (12:1). These particular Jews of Iconium not only share company with the rebellious Israelites of old, but also with those who have oppressed the people of God, in both the past and the present. It is not clear whether "the brothers" denotes only Paul and Barnabas or these two, plus those who believed. At this stage persecution is apparently limited to verbal attacks.

Curiously, the response of Paul and Barnabas is to remain in Iconium for a long time. Verse 3 includes the particle *oun*, which can be rendered "therefore," implying that the verbal persecution provided the *reason* for the two remaining in the city. The curious logic has urged some interpreters to suggest that vv. 2 and 3 should be transposed.[1] This would allow the narrative to say that because many believed (v. 1), Paul and Barnabas remained a long time (v. 3). Only later did persecution arise (v. 2). The Western text of Acts also discerned a problem with the logical flow of the narrative, inserting at the end of v. 2, "but the Lord soon gave peace."[2] Such textual variations at least testify to the careful reading that subsequent copyists gave to Luke's laconic narrative. The Western copyist was not merely a copier, but a *reader* and *interpreter.*

If one follows the generally accepted text (represented by NRSV) one can understand v. 3 to say that persecution only brings resolve—a resolve manifested in bold preaching, undergirded by concrete demonstrations of God's presence through signs and wonders. Such signs and wonders, however, are not in themselves unambiguous indicators of the presence of God (cf. Luke 11:14-22). Signs and wonders, like the proclamation of the gospel itself, can bring division, not only between believing and unbelieving Jews (cf. Acts 3:22; 13:42), but believing and unbelieving Gentiles. [Signs and Wonders]

Luke's passing reference to Paul and Barnabas as apostles in v. 4 creates some confusion, given Luke's tendency to employ the term only to designate the Twelve (see [Twelve Apostles]). Ben Witherington suggests that Luke may be employing the term in a manner similar to what one finds in 2 Corinthians 8:23, namely, "to refer to those commissioned or sent out by a particular local church to perform some sort of Christian service."[3] [Paul and Barnabas as Apostles]

The division created by the preaching of the gospel deepens and the hostility increases so that now both Jews and Gentiles, along with their rulers, plan to physically accost Paul and Barnabas (v. 5). Those sympathetic with the gospel do not seem to be the object of the intended violence. Learning of the planned violence, Paul and Barnabas move on to Lystra and Derbe where they continue to preach the gospel message. Once again, opposition to the good news does not silence it, but only spurs its advancement.

Signs and Wonders

When used in the Gospel of Luke to denote miraculous deeds, "signs and wonders" tend to take on a negative or pejorative connotation (see Luke 11:16, 29-30; 23:8). However, in Acts "signs" or "signs and wonders" denote evidence of the presence of the power of God (2:19). In Acts the doing of signs or signs and wonders is characteristic of God's people, instruments through whom God displays salvific power: Moses (7:36), Jesus (2:22; 4:30), the apostles (2:43; 4:16, 22; 5:12), Stephen (6:8), Philip (8:6, 13), and Paul and Barnabas (14:3; 15:12).

Paul and Barnabas as Apostles

It is curious that Luke would, almost in passing (14:4, 14), refer to Paul and Barnabas as apostles, given his tendency to limit the term to the Twelve. Interpreters offer several explanations:

• Luke has copied uncritically from a source at this juncture. However, in more recent years scholars are reluctant to assume that the author of Luke–Acts employed sources "uncritically."

• Luke viewed Paul and Barnabas as apostles; that is, Luke had a broader understanding of apostles similar to that of the historical Paul (Marshall, 233–34).

• Luke acknowledged that Paul and Barnabas played a role *similar to that* of the Twelve. Paul and Barnabas are fulfilling in their ministry that feature of the Lukan Great Commission to be witnesses "to the ends of the earth" (1:8). The phrase echoes the language of Isa 49:6, which Paul applied to himself and Barnabas in 13:47. In short, Paul and Barnabas are fulfilling the apostolic commission as it pertains to offering witness to the ends of the earth. In that sense, they are "apostles," persons commissioned and "sent out" by Christ (Clark).

I. H. Marshall, *The Acts of the Apostles: An Introduction and Commentary* (Grand Rapids MI: Eerdmans, 1980); Andrew C. Clark, "The Role of the Apostles," in *Witness to the Gospel: The Theology of Acts,* I. Howard Marshall and David Peterson, eds. (Grand Rapids MI: Eerdmans, 1998), 169–90.

Lystra

This small town, which had been made a Roman colony in 6 BC, was located about 20 miles southeast of Iconium. It served as a military outpost and was inhabited primarily by Greeks and Romans. The fact that Timothy, whose mother was Jewish, came from Lystra (16:1) indicates that the town was not bereft of Jews.

Clayton K. Harper, "Lystra," *MDB* 532.

Healing and Preaching in Lystra, 14:8-20a

The story of Paul and Barnabas at Lystra divides into four sections: vv. 8-10 describe a healing; vv. 11-14 portray the response of the crowds at Lystra to that healing; vv. 15-18 present Paul's brief speech to these crowds; vv. 19-20a speak of the persecution of Paul. [Lystra]

The Healing, vv. 8-10

Verse 7 concluded the previous episode with word that Paul and Barnabas went to Lystra and Derbe and preached the gospel. Verses 20b-21 will offer a brief statement about the preaching at Derbe. The introduction to the narrative about Lystra (v. 8) offers no hint as to how much time has elapsed between the arrival of Paul and Barnabas and the healing episode.

The story of the healing (vv. 8-10) echoes the story of 3:2-8, where Peter also healed a man lame from birth. The story in Acts 14 portrays Paul engaging in the same kind of ministry as Peter, which itself imitates the healing work of Jesus (cf. Luke 5:17-26). This further establishes Paul's credentials as an authoritative and prophetic proclaimer of the word of God, for Paul does what both Peter and Jesus do. Readers can only infer from the transitional statement of v. 7 and the response of faith of the lame man that what Paul spoke in v. 9 was the gospel message.

The lame man is said to have the faith necessary to be healed. The Greek word translated "healed" is *sōzein*, which also can mean "to save" or "to deliver"; that is, the text could also be translated "he had faith to be saved." The Gospel of Luke commonly employed the verb *sōzein* in stories of healing (Luke 7:50; 8:48, 50; 17:19; 18:42), thereby providing the verb with something of a double meaning. Though the healing stories clearly indicate that those suffering from infirmities were physically healed, the implication is that such healing is deeper, going beyond physical healing and including a more holistic deliverance.

The Response of the Crowd, vv. 11-14

Paul's healing miracle attracts much attention from the Lystrian crowds. They talk among themselves in their own Lycaonian language about what has happened (v. 11). One can interpret this added bit of detail about the crowd's language as an actual historical reminiscence or a bit of Lukan coloring to add verisimilitude to the story. Either way, the crowd's slipping into their local dialect explains why Paul and Barnabas were so slow to offer their horrified response to the crowd's inference that these men were Greek gods: they did not understand what the crowd was saying.

Commentators who believe that the reference to the use of the Lycaonian language reflects historical reminiscence speculate that the people would probably not have actually referred to Zeus and Hermes, who were Greek gods. Rather, the crowd would have referred to local, Lystrian gods, who, given the syncretism of the age, came to be identified with Greek counterparts within the pantheon.[4]

The confusion of human beings with gods is a popular motif in ancient Greek novels. A novelistic biography of Alexander the Great portrays him, like Paul and Barnabas, as refusing such divine accolades.[5] Further, Paul and Barnabas, in refusing such accolades, offer a sharp contrast with Herod, who accepted divine honors and was immediately punished for it (12:22-23). The identification of humans with gods in Greek novels does not necessitate the conclusion that the story told in Acts is fictional. The prevalence of the motif in novels is presumably rooted in the fact that such identifications actually happened from time to time. [Greek Novels]

Awareness of a local legend also adds some insight as to *why* the crowds identified Paul and Barnabas with Greek gods. According to the legend, Zeus and Hermes had appeared in human form in this region, only to be rejected by the populace, with the exception of one elderly couple. The couple was rewarded, while the inhospitable populace was punished.[6] The legend offers at least partial explanation as to why these people would jump to the seemingly illogical conclusion that these two strangers were these particular gods—a somewhat exaggerated response, even if they had witnessed a miracle.

While Paul and Barnabas cannot understand what the people are saying, they can infer from what they see that something untoward is happening. A priest of Zeus is preparing to offer a sacrifice of oxen (v. 13), animals reserved for grand occasions. The location for the sacrifice is said to be at the gates, though it is not clear whether Luke means the gates of the city or the temple of Zeus. If the latter, then the story offers yet another echo of the healing story involving

Greek Novels

The narrative of Acts reflects many features of Greek novels. The feature noted in the Commentary, the confusion of human characters with gods, is one among many. Others include the pervasiveness of religious themes, the setting of the story on a worldwide stage, adventure-filled sea voyages, mob violence, miracles and magic, and confrontations with powers that regularly result in imprisonment. Richard Pervo has argued that Acts is actually an ancient novel, albeit of a particular sort—the historical novel. One need not accept Pervo's conclusion that Luke intended to write a *novel* to recognize that Luke employed narrative devices similar to known ancient novels.

Richard I. Pervo, *Profit with Delight: The Literary Genre of the Acts of the Apostles* (Philadelphia: Fortress, 1987). For a translation of ancient Greek novels, see B. P. Reardon, ed., *Collected Ancient Greek Novels* (Berkeley: University of California Press, 1989).

The Sacrifice of Oxen
Though this relief is found on the northern frieze of the Parthenon of Athens, it illustrates that bulls were among the animals sacrificed in Greek religion. According to Acts 14:23, the priest of Zeus attempted to sacrifice oxen to Paul and Barnabas, whom the people of Lystra considered to be gods.

Phidias (c.490–430 BC). Youths leading an ox to sacrifice. Frieze from the Parthenon Temple. Acropolis Museum, Athens, Greece. (Credit: Scala / Art Resource, NY)

Peter in Acts 3, where the temple gate was the setting of the miracle (3:2). Whichever gate it might be, it is a logical location for the whole incident. The lame man would likely have positioned himself at a place where many people would pass, in hopes of receiving alms.

Once Paul and Barnabas recognize what is happening, they protest with the tearing of their clothes (v. 14). The tearing of one's clothing is a stock response in the biblical and Jewish tradition to convey anguish in the face of either blasphemous words and deeds (Mark 14:63; *m. Sanh* 7:5) or other traumatic events (Gen 37:29; Esth 4:1; Jdt 14:16-18). [Rending Garments] The pagan sacrifice prompts Paul to speak to the crowds, in hopes of dissuading the people from empty and meaningless worship.

Rending Garments

M. Sanh 7:5 describes how "the judges stand up and rend their garments" when they hear from witnesses that one blasphemed by uttering the holy Name of God.

Herbert Danby, *The Mishnah: Translated from the Hebrew with Introduction and Brief Explanatory Notes* (Oxford: Oxford University Press, 1933).

Paul's Response, vv. 15-18

The text actually says that both made the speech. "Group speech" is common in the Bible (cf. 6:2-3). But Paul has been identified as the primary speaker (v. 12). Paul's speech is brief and to the point. Soards classifies the speech as epideictic "since it seeks to convince the hearers to hold to a particular point of view in the present, but there are clear *judicial* tones in the speech" (see [Types of Rhetorical Persuasion]).[7]

This speech offers the first example of how Luke presents the proclamation of the gospel to non-Jews; Acts 17:22-31 will offer a more detailed example. One feature to note is that, whereas Paul's speech in Antioch of Pisidia began with reference to the patriarchs of the Jews (13:17), this speech avoids such explicit appeal to the Jewish tradition. Rather, it attempts to persuade the Gentile audience by appealing to God as the creator, a more universal premise.

In v. 15 Paul announces that he is offering "good news" to the crowds. Such good news calls them to turn from useless worship to the living God, who is the creator. The language Paul employs echoes certain scriptural texts (Exod 20:11; Ps 146:6), though there is no hint that his audience picks up on this. This call to turn to the true God echoes also 1 Thessalonians 1:9b-10, allowing the inference that behind Luke's composition is at least a partial reflection of the way Paul actually called Gentiles to repentance.

Verse 16 states that in the past God had permitted the Gentiles to walk in their own ways. This might imply a kind of permissiveness on God's part in the past, as though, up until now at least, God did not hold Gentiles accountable for such ways. The text does not say that explicitly, but it is a valid reading, especially when one compares this statement with 17:30, found in the context of Paul's more elaborate speech to a Gentile audience.

Verse 17 is connected logically with v. 16 by *kaitoi*, meaning "yet" or "although." Despite the fact that God had permitted Gentiles to walk in their worthless ways (cf. v. 15), the providential care that God had offered the creation and its human inhabitants actually provided a witness to God. Joseph Fitzmyer notes, "Such gifts from heaven should make humans aware of the source of them, or at least should make them inquire into whence such blessings of nature come."[8] Such a witness from creation could imply that the Gentiles are, in fact, "without excuse" (cf. Rom 1:20). If so, God's permissiveness in the past can only be grounded in God's mercy. Yet now, with Paul's explicit proclamation, these Gentiles have the opportunity to worship the one true God. Being offered the opportunity to come to have genuine fellowship with God is what makes Paul's speech "good news." While v. 18 indicates that the pagan sacrifice was not completed, it also leaves the impression that Paul was not overwhelmingly persuasive.

The Persecution of Paul and Barnabas, vv. 19-20a

The transition to vv. 19-20a is a bit rough, explaining why the Western text added "and when they had stayed there and taught" to introduce v. 19. This textual variation makes explicit what the gap in the most commonly accepted text implies, namely, that some time has passed. Verse 20, which makes reference to disciples who assisted Paul after he had been stoned, indicates that enough time had elapsed for the formation of a core community of believers.

The theme of continued Jewish opposition is quite obvious here. Antioch is some 100 miles from Lystra, indicating that Paul's opponents are persistent. The reference to Jews from Iconium implies that the Antiochene Jews have pursued Paul to Iconium and, not finding him there, gathered some of the Jews from that city to join in pursuit. How these Jews would have known where Paul was is not said.

Acts portrays these Jews as thoroughly determined to silence the proclamation of the gospel, even going so far as attempted murder. Increasingly, Acts is portraying the Jewish opponents as flat characters, whose primary purpose is to impede the proclamation of the *universal* gospel. This is especially evident in this story, for Acts portrays Lystra as a *Gentile* city.[9] There were Jews in the city (cf. 16:1), but that is not the point. At this juncture in the story, the narrative fails to offer any hint that Paul encountered Jews who were natives of Lystra. The pursuit of Paul to this Gentile city leaves the impression that the Jews pursuing Paul are not concerned for the welfare of any *Jewish* community, as though their motives were to preserve their own tradition from corruption from this wandering preacher. Their motive, rather, is to stop the proclamation of the good news *to Gentiles*—to stop Gentiles from turning to the true and living God. With such an implied accusation, Luke's own view of Jews who resist the gospel is becoming increasingly strident.

The Return of Paul and Barnabas to Antioch of Syria, 14:20b-28

Luke triumphantly reports that Paul and Barnabas left the next day and moved on to Derbe (v. 20b), a town about which little is actually known. Candidly, Luke's claim that Paul and Barnabas left the next day strains credulity. It takes more than a good night's rest to recover from a stoning that leaves one so battered that his attackers would take him for dead. Luke may be implying a miraculous recovery for Paul.

Luke offers a terse summary of what happened in Derbe: Paul preached and won many disciples (v. 21a). Paul and Barnabas backtrack, returning to the cities of Lystra, Iconium, and Antioch of Pisidia. Paul's return indicates that he wants not only to establish communities of faith, but to maintain them as well.

Such maintenance, according to vv. 22-23, involves at least three features. First, encouragement and strengthening (cf. 1 Thess 3:2 to see where Paul writes in his own hand of this concern). Paul offers *specific* encouragement, not just a general motivational speech. He exhorts the communities "to continue in the faith" (v. 22). The use of the term "the faith" could indicate maintaining loyalty to a body of teaching, not as mere intellectual consent, but as existential commitment. Jewish disciples must hold the conviction that, in Jesus, God fulfills the promises God made to their ancestors (see 13:12). Gentile disciples must continue to reject their polytheism and idolatry and remain true to the living God (see 14:15). Staying in the faith for both requires swimming against the streams of their respective cultures.

Second, Paul offers these young communities of faith explanation. These disciples had witnessed, and in some instances experienced, persecution (13:50; 14:2, 5, 19). *Understanding* such trials and tribulations, which were quite likely to continue if these disciples maintained their course against their cultures, is necessary if these communities are to endure.

Paul says that it is necessary that entrance into God's reign be accompanied by persecutions (*thlipseōn*, v. 22). The kingdom of God in Luke–Acts has both a present and future dimension. Presently, the reign of God includes salvation and forgiveness, in a word, *liberation* from sin and its corrupting consequences (see, e.g., Luke 4:43; 9:2, 11; 10:9; 11:24). Luke also uses "reign of God" to refer to the future consummation, often called in Jewish antiquity "the age to come" and regularly portrayed as a glorious banquet (see, e.g., Luke 13:28; 14:15; 17:20-21; 19:4; 22:16, 18).

Judaism of the Greco-Roman era, as well Christians who inherited many Jewish traditions, believed that, prior to the manifestation of the "age to come," God's people would experience severe persecution. Some Jews and Christians interpreted such tribulation as the last, desperate attempts of Satan and his allies to inflict as much damage on God's people as possible, for the hosts of evil knew that their days were numbered (see, e.g., Rev 12:10-12). Paul seems sure that persecution is the inevitable destiny of God's people who are about to enter into the blessings of God's eternal reign.[10]

The third feature of this return journey is the establishment of local leaders, called elders (see [Elders]). Elders first appeared within the leadership structure of the early church in Jerusalem (11:30). The appointment of such leaders in "each church" that Paul and Barnabas had established shows continuity with the mother church of Jerusalem. That the elders were appointed "with prayer and fasting" points not only to the fact that Paul and Barnabas sought divine guidance, but also echoes 13:2-3. There, the church of

Antioch had commissioned Paul and Barnabas with prayer and fasting. This echo demonstrates further continuity and connection among the emerging churches.

The balance of the chapter describes the return of Paul and Barnabas to Syrian Antioch, traveling back through the regions of Pisidia and Pamphylia. Luke mentions specifically their preaching in Perga (cf. 13:13-14). Attalia (v. 25) was the main port city of the region of Pamphylia, from which Paul and Barnabas departed for Antioch of Syria. Though not mentioned before in the narrative, Attalia would have been the likely port of entry when Paul and Barnabas came to Asia Minor from Cyprus (13:13).

Back in Antioch, Paul and Barnabas summarize the results of their journey, saying that God had opened a door of faith to the Gentiles. This summary statement allows readers to infer confidently what Luke thinks is important about the last two chapters of his narrative: Gentiles are entering the fold of the people of God.

CONNECTIONS

In the previous chapter, Paul had applied to himself and Barnabas words from Isaiah: "'I have set you to be a light for the Gentiles, so that you may bring salvation to the ends of the earth'" (Acts 13:47, quoting Isa 49:6). In the larger context of Isaiah 49, the words that Luke applies to Paul envisioned God's servant, Israel (Isa 49:3), or perhaps some special person or group within Israel, to be *both* the light to the nations *and* the one to raise up and restore Jacob (Isa 49:6a).

This says something about the witness of the gospel. Bound up with Israel's hopes of salvation was the eventual worship of God by the Gentiles (see [Inclusion of the Gentiles]). When God returned to Zion to visit and redeem God's people, the nations would witness the power of the true God and acknowledge this God (it is profitable to read Isa 49 in its entirety).[11] Luke believes God's redeeming visitation has arrived in Jesus (Luke 1:68). Tragically most of Israel did not recognize the time of its visitation (Luke 19:44). And yet, with the offering of repentance a second time to Israel, both in Jerusalem and beyond the borders of Judea, the restoration of the kingdom (1:6) comes to Israel through the offering of the forgiveness of sins (see, e.g., 2:38).

Paul, as a representative of the restored Israel, embodies in his own person the mission of the servant of Isaiah 49:6, whose mission was both to raise up and restore Israel *and* be a light to the nations. This is precisely Paul's call, according to 9:15. Hence, Paul's journey to Lystra, which Luke portrays as a thoroughly Gentile city barely touched by Jewish influence, is most appropriate in the flow of the Lukan narrative. The restoration of Israel is underway. Fittingly, the time has come for the invitation to and drawing of the nations to worship the God of Israel.

Central to Paul's message to the Gentiles of Lystra is the call to turn from false worship to the worship of the living God (v. 15). Based on Paul's own testimony in 1 Thessalonians 1:9, it is reasonable to conclude that such a call was, in fact, at the core of his proclamation to Gentiles. There is, therefore, something non-negotiable about the good news that Paul preaches in Lystra. Those who accept and embrace *his* gospel (cf. Rom 2:16; 16:25) will have to abandon "worthless things," which in this immediate context refers to false worship, in order to turn "to the living God, who made the heaven and the earth and the sea and all that is in them" (v. 15). The *inclusive* gospel offers the invitation to participate in the worship of the one true God; it offers the invitation to recite the opening line of the Apostles' Creed: "I believe in God, the Father almighty, the creator of heaven and earth."

Such a demand by Paul sounds so *exclusive* by the contemporary standards of inclusion and diversity. Our liberal, democratic tradition, informed as it is by the Enlightenment, emphasizes individual choice in matters of religion, unhindered by governing and ecclesiastical authorities. This valuing of religious liberty is a very important feature of our American Christian heritage, and certainly of Baptists and other Christian traditions of dissent.[12] And yet, in the context of an increasingly secular culture, the result has been to make religion increasingly a "private matter." The larger culture tends to view it, in the description of Stephen L. Carter as "just another hobby: something quiet, something private, something trivial—and not really a fit activity for intelligent, public-spirited adults."[13]

This is not at all to imply that our society does not consider itself religious. A Gallup poll, released on Christmas Eve of 1999, showed that ninety percent of Americans consider religion either to be "important" (30 percent) or "very important" (60 percent).[14] Eighty-six percent of Americans explicitly believe in God. However, when making important decisions affecting one's life, only forty-eight percent give primary attention to their religious teachings. About the same number give heed to their own views and those of friends (45 percent). So while the vast majority believe in God, or are religious, almost half do not take their religious convictions too seriously when it comes to making decisions that affect "real life."

Perhaps is it not surprising, then, that many religious people would affirm the statement, "I determine what God is."[15] Such an attitude can be illustrated by a young person who was interviewed about religion: "I have pieced together my own religion . . . because, if you pick out a bit of truth everywhere, then you have the absolute truth, namely your own truth."[16] The advent of postmodern thought has seen the folly of such individualism run wild.[17] But the postmodern solution seems to replace the individual with the community, so that the creed remains the same—only the subject has changed: "*We* determine what God is!"[18]

According to Howard Batson, one can find evidences of the reshaping of God to fit our fancy in the church, even in the pockets of the church that would be the first to insist that they would never compromise the integrity of the gospel: "Many of us would have concluded that evangelical Christianity, especially in its fundamentalist form, would never fail to issue a clear call to commitment to would-be disciples. What we find, ironically, is an emphasis—especially in fundamentalist churches—on doing whatever is necessary to attract new worshippers, even if the message must be diluted."[19] Batson illustrates his point by quoting the advertising brochures from various churches. All appeal to people's self-interest, promising such things as the "Compact Mini 22-Minute Worship Service," early completion of worship "so you can get on with your day," and "the hassle-free church."[20]

Paul's word to the religious people in Lystra speaks clearly today as well: "turn from these worthless things to the living God." The invitation is extended to all, yet all are invited to turn to someone real, to give up that which inhibits them from a genuine encounter with this living God.

The story of Paul and Barnabas at Lystra invites us to engage in thoughtful reflection on the importance of religious experience (see [Experience and the Believer]). Even if we have a "religious experience," an experience of something out of the mundane, we still are compelled to interpret or make sense of that experience. And in so doing, we must rely on the tools of interpretation that we happen to carry about inside us: language, concepts, symbols, traditions, and the like.[21]

When the people of Lystra saw the lame man walk, they knew they were experiencing awesome power. These people did what all people do: they proceeded to try to make sense of what they had experienced and to interpret it. Hence, they relied on the interpretive tools that they carried about inside them and concluded that Zeus and Hermes were in their midst!

Christians, too, are compelled to interpret religious experiences by employing the hermeneutical tools that we happen to carry about with us. Paul begins to offer his audience those tools as he speaks to them of "the living God, who made the heaven and the earth" (v. 15). The tendency of our age, which seems to *encourage* the picking and choosing of traditions off the "cafeteria religion" line, is actually an encouragement to people to construct their own bag of hermeneutical tools. The church is to offer thoughtful instruction to provide the people the concepts, traditions, and symbols to make sense of sacred experiences from within the framework of the Bible and the Christian heritage. This is imperative if we really believe that such frameworks provide the most meaningful and, dare one say, even *true* contexts in which to make sense of religious experiences.

Christians must be cautious, even as we instruct one another in "the faith." We can run the risk of exalting our understandings of God and the particular traditions, symbols, and concepts that we employ to speak of God, to a kind of protected status that lies beyond question or critical examination. Precisely because we do believe that behind and beneath our religious experiences is the *true* and *living God*, we must always be willing to concede the contingency of our own understandings of this God. [Reality of the Living God] Failure to recognize the contingencies of our own imperfect understandings risks the possibility, even probability, that we will make idols of our ideas. This type of idolatry is certainly more sophisticated than carving a god from a piece of wood to set upon the family hearth, but it is no less lethal.

Reality of the Living God

Ingolf Dalferth, professor of systematic theology at the University of Zürich, offers the following suggestions to Christians who desire to take seriously their commitment to interpreting responsibly their encounters with God:

• Preserve the distinction between your understanding of God and God.
• Deepen your understanding of God by keeping company with God.
• Understand yourself, your life, and your world entirely . . . in light of the effective presence of God.
• Expose your understanding of God to criticism without reservations and be prepared to justify it to others.

Ingolf Dalferth, "'I Determine What God Is!': Theology in the Age of 'Cafeteria Religion,'" *Theology Today* 51/1 (April 2000): 5–23 (esp. 22).

NOTES

[1] John B. Polhill, *Acts* (NAC 26; Nashville TN: Broadman), 310–11, offers a good discussion of such interpreters, though he does not opt for this position.

[2] J. Foakes Jackson and Kirsopp Lake, *The Beginnings of Christianity: The Acts of the Apostles*, 5 vols. (Grand Rapids MI: Baker, 1979), 4.161, offer a full translation of the Western text of this passage.

[3] Ben Witherington III, *The Acts of the Apostles: A Socio-Rhetorical Commentary* (Grand Rapids MI: Eerdmans, 1998), 419.

[4] See Jackson and Lake, *The Beginnings of Christianity*, 4.164; Joseph A. Fitzmyer, *The Acts of the Apostles* (AB 31; New York: Doubleday, 1998), 531.

[5] Luke Timothy Johnson, *The Acts of the Apostles* (SacPag 5; Collegeville MN: Liturgical Press, 1992), 249, cites a reference from Pseudo-Callisthenes, *Life of Alexander of Macedon* 12:22: "I beg off from honors equal to the gods."

[6] The story may be found in Ovid's *Metamorphoses* 8.611–724.

[7] Marion L. Soards, *The Speeches of Acts: Their Content, Context, and Concerns* (Louisville KY: Westminster/John Knox, 1994), 88.

[8] Fitzmyer, *Acts*, 532.

[9] Polhill, *Acts*, 313. But Acts 16:1 indicates that Timothy, who had a Jewish mother, was from Lystra, indicating Luke's perception that there was at least a Jewish presence in the city.

[10] See Dale C. Allison, Jr., *The End of the Ages Has Come: An Early Interpretation of the Passion and Resurrection of Jesus* (Philadelphia: Fortress, 1985), esp. 62–65.

[11] N. T. Wright, *The New Testament and the People of God* (Minneapolis MN: Fortress, 1992), 267–68.

[12] See Walter B. Shurden, *The Baptist Identity: Four Fragile Freedoms* (Macon GA: Smyth and Helwys, 1993), esp. ch. 4, "Religious Freedom."

[13] Stephen L. Carter, *The Culture of Disbelief: How American Law and Politics Trivialize Religious Devotion* (New York: Doubleday/Anchor Books, 1993), 22.

[14] "Americans Remain Very Religious, but Not Necessarily in Conventional Ways," http://www.gallup.com/poll/releases/pr991224.asp (20 April 2000). All Gallup statistics cited are from this source.

[15] Taken from the title of Ingold R. Dalferth's essay, "'I Determine What God Is!': Theology in the Age of 'Cafeteria Religion,'" *Theology Today* 57/1 (April 2000): 5–23.

[16] Ibid., 8, quoting from *Psychologie Heute*, July 1995, 25.

[17] A good introductory discussion of postmodernism and the theological implications of this philosophy and/or movement is Stanley J. Grenz, *A Primer on Postmodernism* (Grand Rapids MI: Eerdmans, 1995).

[18] Dalferth, "I Determine What God Is!," 13.

[19] Howard K. Batson, *Common-Sense Church Growth* (Macon GA: Smyth & Helwys, 1999), 116.

[20] Ibid., 115–17.

[21] See Luke Timothy Johnson, *Religious Experience in Earliest Christianity: A Missing Dimension in New Testament Studies* (Minneapolis: Fortress, 1998), esp. ch. 2, "Getting At Christian Experience."

GENTILES: A PEOPLE FOR GOD'S NAME

Acts 15:1-35

COMMENTARY

This chapter divides into three sections. Verses 1-5 provide an introduction, explaining the need for the meeting to take place in Jerusalem. Verses 6-29 focus attention on the Jerusalem Council. Verses 30-35 narrate the aftermath of the council, leaving the impression that a satisfying resolution was attained and that relations were good between Jerusalem and Antioch. [Jerusalem Council]

The Controversy: "They Must Keep the Law of Moses," 15:1-5

An indeterminate length of time has passed (see 14:28). Men from Judea visit the church at Antioch and are less than pleased that God "had opened a door of faith for the Gentiles" (14:27). The text does not identify these Judeans precisely, but readers may recall certain "circumcised believers" who criticized Peter after the Cornelius episode (11:2). Peter's response seemed to assuage the critics and resolve the issue (11:18). The controversy of Acts 15 over Gentile inclusion indicates either that the issue was not fully resolved or enough time has lapsed that the important issue needs revisitation.

The precise demand of the Judeans is that Gentiles be circumcised. [Circumcision] Given that this demand echoes the demand of certain

---

Jerusalem Council

This term is a shorthand way to refer to the gathering of the church described in Acts 15. One may also refer to the gathering as the "Apostolic Council." Calling the meeting a council is somewhat anachronistic, since the term generally refers to "a solemn assembly of authorities from all over the church" (Fitzmyer, 543). However, when one considers that later councils served the purpose of helping the church to negotiate its way through controversial disputes (e.g., Nicea [325], Constantinople [381], and Chalcedon [451], which dealt primarily with christological issues), this gathering did function as a council of sorts.

Joseph A. Fitzmyer, *The Acts of the Apostles* (AB 31; New York: Doubleday, 1998); James L. Blevins, "Jerusalem Council," *MDB* 443–44.

Circumcision

The history of this ceremony among the ancient Israelites is shrouded in mystery. Scholarly consensus connects the pivotal story of Gen 17 with the priestly source of the exilic period, which may indicate that by this time the ceremony had emerged as a most significant feature of Jewish religion. This story portrays circumcision as the mark of being a member of the covenant people. Jewish texts composed during the Maccabean period (c. 160s BC), such as Jubilees and 1 Maccabees, communicate the depth of commitment among pious Jews to be faithful to the law and tradition that required males belonging to God's people to be circumcised (see in the Apocrypha 1 Macc 1:54-64 for a good illustrative text of the importance of being circumcised and keeping the law of Moses within the Jewish community).

John B. Polhill, "Circumcision," *MDB* 156–57.

Pharisees

Luke consistently portrays Pharisees negatively in both of his narratives (e.g., Luke 11:37-4; Acts 5:34-39). Here, Luke portrays even believing Pharisees in a less than positive light (see Johnson, 260, for an exhaustive list of references and more discussion). The term likely means "separated ones," which communicates something of the importance that the school placed on being a holy people. Pharisees were primarily laypersons, devoted to the study and application of the law. They may have found their origins during the crucial period of the Maccabean revolt, initially supporting the Maccabees' attempts to throw off their Gentile oppressors. Dedication to their understanding of the law led them not only to oppose non-Jewish leaders, but some Jewish rulers as well. For example, Pharisees were regular agitators of numerous Hasmonean rulers, who ruled the Jews after the successful Maccabean revolt. Knowing something of their roots helps contemporary readers to understand why they insisted that Gentiles keep the law of Moses.

Luke Timothy Johnson, *The Acts of the Apostles* (SacPag 5; Collegeville MN: Liturgical Press, 1992).

Proselytes

Luke has introduced readers to a group whom scholars have come to identify by the term "God-fearers" (see [God-fearer]). God-fearers were non-Jews sympathetic with Judaism. Proselytes denoted people who converted to the Jewish faith. Generally, this required accepting essential instruction in Judaism, circumcision (males), undergoing a baptism of ritual cleansing, and offering a sacrifice at the temple (while it still stood). Acts makes explicit reference to proselytes in Acts 2:10; 6:5; 13:43 (see [Devout Converts]).

Pharisaic believers back in Jerusalem, who say that the Gentiles must be circumcised *and* keep the law of Moses (v. 5), it is reasonable to conclude that there is an explicit connection between the Judeans of v. 1 and the Pharisees of v. 5. Further, one may infer that the voices of dissent come not from the Jerusalem church *as a whole*, but only a segment from within the church. [Pharisees]

The matter needs clear resolution. The Pharisaic believers' demand does not seem unreasonable. Genesis 17:9-14 is emphatic that Abraham's descendants are the blessed people and circumcision is the mark of such descent. Texts such as Deuteronomy 5:28-33 demand that God's people "follow exactly the path that the LORD your God has commanded you" (v. 33). If Gentiles, *as Gentiles* and not as proselytes, were to be incorporated into the sphere of God's salvation, important theological implications will ensue; therefore, the issue needs clear discussion and resolution.[1] [Proselytes]

Paul encountered similar objections from Christian Jews who tried to persuade Gentiles within the orbit of Paul's Galatian ministry that they needed to be circumcised (see Gal 1:6-9; 5:3-6). If one follows the standard reconstructions of the history behind Acts 15 then the controversy over circumcision in Galatia arose *after* the meeting of Acts 15. This would indicate that, in fact, the issue was still *not* resolved to everyone's satisfaction, even after James and the church made their decision. Gerd Lüdemann writes, "Luke gives the impression that the dispute ended with the Jerusalem conference. But the Letters of Paul tell another tale."[2] [The History behind Acts 15]

Acts, however, portrays a much more definitive resolution to the controversy than historical reconstruction may warrant. The church of Antioch is concerned enough about the issue to "appoint" (*etaxan*) Paul, Barnabas, and "some others" to journey to Jerusalem to discuss the matter with the apostles and elders there (see [Elders]).[3] Attention focuses on this appointed band, with the narrator being silent as to what became of the Judean visitors (did they journey with Paul and his fellow travelers, return to Jerusalem in their own group, remain in Antioch, or move on to other places?). The narrator reports that as Paul and his companions made the 250-mile trek to Jerusalem they shared with churches in Phoenicia and Samaria reports of success among the Gentiles (v. 3).[4] These reports were well received, giving readers the sense that the Judeans who insist on Gentile circumcision have little support. The narrative reinforces this impression as it reports that Paul's entourage was "welcomed by the church and the apostles and the elders" (v. 4). The Pharisees of v. 5, who repeat the demand for circumcision, appear as believers on the fringe.

The Council, 15:6-29

The central panel of this narrative unfolds in three sections. Verses 6-12 offer the testimony of Peter. Verses 13-21 offer the testimony of James, including scriptural testimony. Verses 22-29 present the letter that the church produced to share the decision with the churches beyond Jerusalem.

The Testimony of Peter, vv. 6-12
Verse 6 reports that "the apostles and elders met together." Apparently, this smaller group, accompanied by Paul and Barnabas (v. 12), separated from the larger church to debate the matter. Such a reading would understand "the whole assembly" of v. 12 to mean the assembly of elders and apostles, which did not rejoin the larger church until v. 22. However, it is apparent from v. 10 that Peter is addressing the Pharisaic believers ("you are putting God to the test"), indicating that the meeting includes the Pharisaic believers. That would indicate that v. 6 does not assume a closed meeting, involving only the leadership, consisting of the presbytery and apostles (see [Twelve Apostles]).

In the midst of the debate (v. 7a), which readers can assume essentially pits the Pharisaic believers against the larger congrega-

The History behind Acts 15

This thorny issue has given rise to multiple reconstructions. There are interpreters, such as Ernst Haenchen, who give little historical credence to Luke's account of the meeting or the decree, while allowing that some kind of events lie behind the narrative. For example, the prohibitions found in the decree of James reflect some actual practices of the early church, but "for this, Jerusalem does not come into consideration, and James cannot be thought of as the author. . . . These prohibitions must have come into force in a strongly mixed community of the diaspora" (Haenchen, 471). Fitzmyer argues that the prohibitions *do* come from James, though from a time *other than* the meeting dealing with the matter of circumcision. Luke has collapsed two meetings and issues into one (Fitzmyer, 52–53).

Among scholars who believe that interpreters can employ Acts as a useful historical source, there are generally two schools of thought, both of which center on the issue of Pauline chronology as portrayed in Acts (see [Chronological Issues]).

Many interpreters, representing a range of theological perspectives, argue that the meeting described in Acts 15 equates with the meeting Paul describes in Gal 2:1-10 as his second trip to Jerusalem (see, e.g., Polhill, 321–22, Fitzmyer, 539–41, Johnson, 269–70, and Lüdemann, 166–73, esp. 171). Though the details of Acts 15 and Gal 2 are not identical, the respective descriptions are similar enough to warrant this conclusion. The following list broadly illustrates the common features (Lüdemann, 171).

1. *Barnabas and Paul go to Jerusalem* (Acts 15:2; Gal 2:1).
2. *The matter under consideration is the mission to the Gentiles* (Acts 15:12; Gal 2:1, 9).
3. *Meetings are held at both the community level* (Acts 15:12; Gal 2:2a) *and in the context of a smaller group* (Acts 15:6; Gal 2:2b).
4. *Paul states that persons of note, specifically James, Peter (Cephas), and John, were present* (Gal 2:9). Acts speaks of elders and apostles and mentions Peter and James by name (Acts 15 passim).
5. *At the meeting are those who want Gentiles to undergo circumcision.* Paul calls them "false brethren" (RSV; Gal 2:4), while Acts speaks of believing Pharisees (15:5).
6. *The church affirms the Gentile mission* (Gal 2:9; Acts 15:10-11, 19).

Those who insist that Gal 2 does not describe the events of Acts 15 note that according to Acts 11, Paul made his second trip to Jerusalem sometime before the meeting of Acts 15. Given that Gal 2:1 states that the meeting of Gal 2 was Paul's *second* visit to Jerusalem, Gal 2 must equate Acts 11. Scholars who accept this conclusion then empha-

size the *differences* between Acts 15 and Gal 2. Ben Witherington (441) offers a good example of this line of argument.

1. *Acts states that Paul went to Jerusalem at the direction of the church of Antioch* (15:2-3). Paul states in Galatians that he went up by revelation (Gal 2:2a).
2. *Paul says he met privately with the apostles* (Gal 2:2), *while in Acts the meeting is public* (15:12).
3. *Galatians refers to those with an opposing viewpoint as "false brothers," while they are identified as Pharisees in Acts.*
4. *Paul does not mention the decree.*
5. *Paul plays a major role in Galatians, but hardly any role in Acts.*
6. *The issue in Acts is circumcision and food, while in Galatians the issue is Paul's gospel.*

Readers must decide for themselves whether the differences between Acts 15 and Gal 2 justify concluding that the two are speaking of different meetings. But readers must also decide whether what Paul describes in Gal 2, with his speaking of false brothers and the defense of his gospel, should most reasonably be construed as Paul's version of what is described in Acts 11: a trip to Jerusalem to deliver famine relief. It is problematic that Witherington, who is so bothered by the minor discrepancies between Acts 15 and Gal 2, is not bothered by the *major* discrepancies between the reports of Acts 11 and Gal 2.

The matter of Paul's silence regarding the "apostolic decree" is curious. This leads some, such as Haenchen (471), to doubt the veracity of Luke's report that such a decree ever emanated from Jerusalem. Lüdemann argues that Paul may offer an indirect reference to the decree in Gal 2:6. Paul's statement that the Jerusalem leaders added nothing to *him* may mean that the prohibitions were relevant to the mixed congregation at Antioch, but not Paul's predominately Gentile churches (171). In short, Paul concluded that the decree simply did not apply to him. Fitzmyer argues that Luke has collapsed two events into one: the decision not to require circumcision occurred at one meeting (the meeting described in Gal 2), while the decree actually came later and may have been a decision with which Paul was not even familiar (544–45). Either Fitzmyer's or Lüdemann's interpretations could explain why Paul makes no *explicit* reference to the decree in any of his letters.

Ernst Haenchen, *The Acts of the Apostles: A Commentary* (Philadelphia: Westminster, 1971); John B. Polhill, *Acts* (NAC 26; Nashville: Broadman, 1992); Joseph A. Fitzmyer, *The Acts of the Apostles* (AB 31; New York: Doubleday, 1998); Luke Timothy Johnson, *The Acts of the Apostles* (SacPag 5; Collegeville MN: Liturgical Press, 1992); Gerd Lüdemann, *Early Christianity according to the Traditions in Acts: A Commentary* (Minneapolis: Fortress 1989); Ben Witherington III, *The Acts of the Apostles: A Socio-Rhetorical Commentary* (Grand Rapids MI: Eerdmans, 1998).

tion, Peter rises to offer his insight. This is Peter's final appearance on the Lukan stage, giving special significance to his words. Peter's final words will be a ringing endorsement of the full inclusion of Gentiles into the people of God.

Most commentators view the speech as deliberative,[5] though Fitzmyer says it is judicial,[6] all of which cautions modern readers that strict categorization is difficult (see [Types of Rhetorical Persuasion]). It appears that Peter's primary motivation is to urge the hearers to take in the future a certain course action with respect to Gentiles, the function of deliberative rhetoric.

Peter's speech falls into two parts. Verses 7-9 recount Peter's experience with Cornelius and his household, complete with reflections on the implications of the experience. Verses 10-11 apply Peter's reflections to the current situation and draw precise conclusions and recommendations for future action. Crucial to understanding the flow of Luke's narrative is to realize that Peter—as well as Paul and Barnabas in v. 12—is offering an argument from his own *experience* of the workings of God in his life (see [Experience and the Believer]). Tannehill comments, "Specific signs of God's work among the Gentiles in an effective mission constitute part of the evidence on which a decision must be based."[7]

Verses 7-9 refer back to the Cornelius episode of Acts 10–11. Peter refers to this incident as having occurred "in the early days"; some considerable time has lapsed between Acts 11 and Acts 15. The lapse of time may account for the need to revisit the issue of Gentile inclusion. Ernst Haenchen insists that the whole scene of Acts 15 lacks veracity, for he finds it inconceivable that such a (seemingly) public and significant event as recorded in Acts 10–11 could have been ignored or forgotten by the Pharisaic believers. Luke's desire to have the full Jerusalem congregation legitimate the Gentile mission necessitates that the issue be revisited, thus requiring Luke to set the stage by positing that the Pharisees have forgotten what happened in Acts 11.[8] While there are certainly historical problems with Acts 15, Haenchen is naïve to assume that because a religious body reached some consensus on a very controversial issue years before, dissent could not possibly reoccur years down the road.

In reflecting on past experience, Peter says that God had chosen (*exelexato*) him to be the instrument through whom Gentiles would first hear "the message of the good news" (v. 7). The narrative of Acts 10–11 does not speak explicitly of God's "electing" Peter. Peter's speech reflects an interpretation of the significance of the series of events that led Peter to journey to Cornelius's home and preach the good news to him and his household. His words require his audience, especially his reading audience, to recall the events of Acts 10. The providential guidance of God constitutes the apostle's "election" to preach to the Gentile Cornelius.

The result was that the Gentiles, represented by Cornelius and his household, came to "believe." Again, the narrative of Acts 10–11 does not explicitly say that these Gentiles "believed," but Peter offers a very legitimate interpretation of what happened, given what one reads in 10:43 and 11:17. The evidence that the Gentiles did, indeed, come to believe the gospel was God's bestowal of his Spirit upon them (v. 8; cf. 10:44-45; 11:15-17).

Peter further interprets the meaning of the Cornelius episode to mean that God "knows the heart," an interpretive allusion to the premise of Acts 10. The narrative there states that Cornelius is acceptable to God because he is a devout man (10:2, 4, 35). Johnson writes, "God is able to make judgment in terms of internal dispositions rather than on external criteria."[9] This God, who knows and views the heart, makes "no distinction" (*diekrinen*) between Jews and Gentiles (v. 9). This interpretive claim explicitly harks back to Acts 11:12, where Peter shared with his Jerusalem critics "the Spirit told me to go with them and not to make a distinction [*diakrinanta*] between them and us."

Closely associated with God's refusal to distinguish between Jews and Gentiles is the affirmation that God has cleansed the hearts of the Gentiles by faith. Acts 10:15 and 11:9 made direct reference to God's "cleansing" of the Gentiles. However, it is Peter who understands such cleansing to be explicitly associated with faith.

Through this brief rehearsal of Peter's experience, combined with Peter's interpretive reflections and inferences, Luke shapes the reader's understanding of the significance of that event: God makes no distinction between Jews and Gentiles and offers to both groups the Holy Spirit on the basis of their response to faith in the word of the gospel.

With this in mind, the narrator has Peter move to his concluding application. First, Peter accuses some of his listeners of "putting God to the test" (v. 10, *peirazete*). These are strongly accusatory words, given that such an action violates Jesus' own word of Luke 4:12 (using *ekpeiraseis*), as well the word of Scripture that Jesus is quoting in Luke 4 (Deut 6:16; cf. Exod 17:2, 7; Num 14:22; Ps 78:18, 41, 56 [Ps 77 in LXX]). Fitzmyer captures the seriousness of the charge, saying that to test God is "to approach God in a spirit of unbelief and mistrust."[10]

Second, Peter charges the Pharisaic believers with placing on the Gentiles a "yoke" or "burden" (*zygon*) that neither the Christian Jews nor their ancestors could carry. Commentators are divided on whether the term "yoke" is used negatively or positively as a reference to the law of Moses. Haenchen assumes a negative, pejorative usage, and concludes that (the historical) Peter could not have said such a thing.[11] Polhill, who assumes historical veracity of the Acts material, insists that Peter is not being disparaging to refer to the law as a "yoke." He rightly points out that the term "yoke" could be used positively in the gospel tradition (Matt 11:29-30).[12] This is true, but when Jesus uses the term he does not describe his yoke as something that no one is able to bear, nor does the larger Jewish tradition add a gloss to the term "yoke," speaking of it as an unbearable burden. Hence, it is probably better to view Peter's representation of the law as "yoke" *that none can bear* as a negative characterization.[13] Regardless of whether one reads the words of Peter as an accurate summary of an actual speech or strictly as a Lukan composition, the meaning in this context is clear: It is wrong for Pharisaic believers to attempt to impose on Gentiles a burden that even Jews, past or present, found impossible to carry. Luke may view the Jewish law as a venerable and even honorable institution of Jewish heritage and religion. But it is for Jews only, apparently, and is certainly not something necessary for the salvation of the Gentiles.

The law is not necessary for the salvation of any person, Jewish or Gentile. This third point of application provides Peter's powerful conclusion to his speech. Jews and Gentiles, alike, will be saved through the grace of Jesus Christ. [Will Be Saved] And though Peter does not add in this concluding formula "by faith," it is certainly implied by v. 9 ("cleansing their hearts by faith"). If the grace of Christ, received by faith, is what saves both Jews and Gentiles, the law is certainly not necessary that Gentiles might *be saved*, which was what the Judean believers were insisting (v. 1). Further, if Jews are saved on the same bases as Gentiles, as Peter insists, it follows that the law is not necessary for the salvation of Jews either. Jews are certainly free to keep the

Will Be Saved

"For Luke salvation at its very core has to do with God's gracious act of forgiving sins through Jesus which causes the moral, mental, emotional, spiritual, and sometimes even the physical transformation of an individual" (Witherington, 160). Luke 19:1-10 can illustrate many facets of this understanding of salvation. Such a description of salvation in Luke–Acts focuses on the *present* dimension of salvation: "For Luke, salvation, in the present, means the forgiveness of sins, the cleansing of the heart by the Holy Spirit and through faith" (ibid., 161). But there is also a future, more explicitly eschatological dimension to salvation. Witherington explains, "In the future, salvation means entering God's Dominion and being a participant in the messianic banquet when the Lord returns" (ibid., 161). Luke 18:26-30 illustrates this.

In Acts 15 the crucial issue being decided is whether Gentiles can experience God's salvation, both now and in the future, apart from circumcision and following the Law of Moses. Pharisaic believers said "no." Peter came to the important conclusion, affirmed by the larger church, that salvation for both Jews and Gentiles comes "through the grace of the Lord Jesus Christ" (15:11).

Ben Witherington III, "Salvation and Health in Christian Antiquity: The Soteriology of Luke–Acts in Its First Century Setting," in *Witness to the Gospel: The Theology of Acts*; I. Howard Marshall and David Peterson, eds. (Grand Rapids MI: Eerdmans, 1998), 145–66.

law as an important part of their ethnic customs, but such practices have no effect on the Jews' or Gentiles' salvation before God.

The personal testimony of Paul and Barnabas (v. 12) is almost anticlimactic after Peter's speech. Luke can be terse, for readers have just read of their exploits. Reference to "signs and wonders" (see [Signs and Wonders]) serves to remind readers of Paul's and Barnabas's legitimacy as prophetic spokesmen for God. Such personal legitimacy grants legitimacy to their work of Acts 13–14, through which God "had opened a door of faith for the Gentiles" (14:27).

The Testimony of James, vv. 13-21

Luke does not identify the James of Acts 15, who was first introduced as an offstage character in 12:17. (Acts 1:14 makes reference to Jesus' brothers being among the post-Easter believers, but does not give any names.) Readers can only infer from what he does that he has assumed some important leadership role within in church. Were it not for sources external to Acts, one would never surmise that that James was Jesus' brother. [James, the Brother of Jesus] Though James's familial status is important historically, it is not important, seemingly, in the Lukan narrative, given the narrator's silence.

James's speech is also deliberative, for he wants to urge the community of faith to a certain course of action in the future.[14] The speech falls into two main parts. Verses 14-18 present James's summary of the importance of Peter's speech and offer scriptural witness to confirm Peter's experience. Verses 19-21 offer James's judgment concerning what the church should do with respect to Gentile believers.

James, the Brother of Jesus

Acts does not explicitly identify James as the brother of Jesus. Interpreters infer this relationship from other sources, such as Paul (Gal 1:19; 2:9) and Josephus (*Ant.* 20.200). Josephus recounts the story of the execution of James by the order of the high priest Ananus, shortly after the end of Festus's governorship (AD 62). Josephus reports that "those who seemed the most equitable of the citizens, and such as were the most uneasy at the breach of the laws," disagreed with this action. Josephus implies that Ananus's accusations against James, namely that he was a breaker of the law, were not just.

Church tradition assigns authorship of the canonical Epistle of James to this person. Later Christian sources, such as Clement of Alexandria and Eusebius, also pass along traditions about James. An apocryphal Gospel about Jesus' infancy is attributed to him.

James refers to Peter as "Simeon," the Aramaic rendition of Simon, likely reflecting the narrator's desire for verisimilitude.[15] James summarizes the significance of Simeon's experience, confirming that Peter's encounter with Cornelius describes "how God first looked favorably on the Gentiles" (v. 14). In the Lukan narrative, the NRSV does not translate the Greek verb "to visit" (*episkeptomai*) consistently, sometimes using "looks favorably" (Luke 1:68; 7:16), "break upon" (Luke 1:78), or "visit" (Acts 7:23; Luke 19:44 [substantive "visitation"]). To speak of God's visitation is "shorthand for God's intervention in history,"[16] usually with such intervention pertaining to *Israel.*[17] Now God has *visited,* intervened in history, on behalf of Gentiles. And such intervention has resulted in God's taking from among these Gentiles "a people for his name" (v. 14).

Two terms are very important. First, James employs the word "people" (*laos*) to refer to Gentiles. Luke consistently employs the word *laos* to denote ethnic Israel as the people of God,[18] so to apply this word to Gentiles is most significant. Second, lest there be any ambiguity, James modifies the appellation "people" with the phrase "called by his name." The phrase "his name" is a circumlocution for God. James is saying simply that Peter's recounting of the Cornelius episode was nothing less than a narration of how God called Gentiles to be included within God's people "in the full sense that Israel is."[19]

James now turns to Scripture to confirm this conclusion. While James appeals to Scripture to confirm Peter's experience, one must not minimize that James explicitly states that "with this [experience and conclusion] the words of the prophets agree" (RSV).[20] It is Peter's *experience* and James's *interpretation* of it that guide James's interpretation of Scripture. *Scripture agrees with what James has experienced to be true!* The reason this is so important is that it offers candid admission, from the Bible itself, that Scripture is not interpreted in a vacuum, free of the context—and experience—of the interpreter.

The scriptural text that James quotes is essentially the Septuagintal version of Amos 9:11-12, though one can also hear echoes of other prophetic texts. [Amos 9:11-12] The presence of numerous prophetic voices explains James's affirmation that "the words of the *prophets*" (v. 15) agree with Peter's experience. Verse 16 focuses on the rebuilding and restoration of the fallen "dwelling of David." Most commentators see this as referring to the restoration of the Davidic house, the royal dynasty of David.[21]

From the perspective of Jewish history, the house of David had been in a state of disrepair ("fallenness") for centuries, effectively coming to an end with the destruction of Jerusalem, the temple, and the Babylonian exile (587/86 BC). Hope for the restoration of the Davidic house seems to have blossomed for a while shortly after the end of the exile, with such hopes focusing on Zerubbabel, a descendant of the royal line (see Hag 2:20-23). Such hopes failed to materialize, however, and messianic expectation was increasingly moved to the more remote future.

Luke and the believing characters within his narrative world believed that the fallen house of David had been restored with the coming of Jesus. The angel Gabriel declared as much in his words

---

Amos 9:11-12

Acts portrays James as quoting Amos 9:11-12 to show that Scripture agrees with the testimony of Peter regarding Gentile inclusion. The table below offers in translation a comparison of the text from Acts, the Hebrew Bible, and the Septuagint. As one can see, Acts follows closely the Greek version of Amos, though, as noted in the Acts column, Acts also alludes to texts from other prophets. Most interesting is the fact that the point James wants to make using Amos, namely, "that all other peoples may seek the Lord," *requires* his dependence on the Greek version of Amos.

Would James have used the Greek version of Amos? Haenchen says simply, "[T]he Jewish Christian James would not in Jerusalem have used a Septuagint text, differing from the Hebrew original, as scriptural proof" (448). Polhill represents interpreters generally willing to grant historical veracity to Acts. He says, "It is not impossible that James knew Greek and quoted the Septuagint text in a conference that had a number of Greek speaking delegates" (329n93).

It might do well to remember that the "Hebrew text" was hardly a fixed entity at this time. What became the "received text" of the Jewish faith community, the Masoretic Text, existed in its nascent form at this time, but had not yet attained the status of the officially accepted recension of the Jewish Scriptures. The Jews of Palestine employed more than one *Hebrew* recension. The discovery among the Dead Sea Scrolls of numerous Hebrew mss. that follow the Septuagint text verifies this. Thus, it is possible that James was quoting from a "Hebrew" version of the Jewish Scriptures—just not the Hebrew version that later would be officially sanctioned by the Jewish community (Barrera, 284–97; 318–23).

Acts 15:16-18 (NRSV)	Amos 9:11-12 Masoretic Text*	Amos 9:11-12 Septuagint**
[16] After this I will return, (cf. Jer 12:15)	[11] On that day	[11] In that day
and I will build the dwelling of David, which has fallen; from its ruins I will rebuild it, and I will set it up,	I will raise up the booth of David that is fallen, and repair their breaches, and raise up his ruins and rebuild it as in the days of old;	I will raise up the dwelling of David, which has fallen; from its ruins I will rebuild it, and I will raise up the parts of it that have been broken down, and I will rebuild it just as in the ancient days;
[17] so that all other peoples may seek the Lord—even all the Gentiles over whom my name has been called.	[12] in order that they may possess the remnant of Edom and all the nations who are called by my name,	[12] so that all other peoples may seek [no explicit object] even all the Gentiles over whom my name has been called.
[18] Thus says the Lord, who has been making these things known from long ago (cf. Isa 45:12).	says the LORD who does this.	Thus says the Lord, the one doing all these things.

*To represent the Masoretic Text, I have followed the NRSV translation, following from the critical notes a more literal translation of the Hebrew.

**To represent the LXX, I have prepared my own translation, but employed the translation of the NRSV of Acts 15:16-18 when the Greek of Acts and Amos were identical or very close.

Ernst Haenchen, *The Acts of the Apostles: A Commentary* (Philadelphia: Westminster, 1971); John B. Polhill, *Acts* (NAC 26; Nashville: Broadman, 1992); Julio Trebolle Barrera, *The Jewish Bible and the Christian Bible: An Introduction to the History of the Bible* (Grand Rapids MI: Eerdmans, 1998).

---

to Mary: "The Lord God will give to him the throne of his ancestor David. He will reign over the house of Jacob forever, and of his kingdom there will be no end" (Luke 1:32b-33). Jesus' ascension provided for readers and characters alike a visual representation of Jesus' installation to the messianic throne (1:9), where he waits, as Messiah, to return in order to accomplish the restoration of all things (3:20-21).

The Lukan narrative has offered numerous indications that Jesus' installation to the messianic throne carried with it implications for Israel *and the nations*. The first such hint reaches as far back as Simeon's Nunc Dimittis (Luke 2:29-32), which culminates with the emphatic declaration that Jesus was "a light for revelation to the Gentiles and for glory to your people Israel" (2:32). The resurrected Jesus opened the minds of his disciples to understand the Scriptures. Such understanding involved two features: (1) that the Messiah must suffer and rise, that is, enter into glory (Luke 24:46, cf. v. 26) and (2) the message of repentance and forgiveness would be preached "to all nations" (Luke 24:47).

Hence, the text of Amos not only agrees with the experience of Peter and James's interpretation of it, but with the thrust of the Lukan narrative. A crucial feature of Jesus' restoration of the house of David is the offering of forgiveness to the Gentiles. With *this* the text of Amos agrees, saying that the Lord would rebuild the dwelling of David "so that all other peoples may seek the Lord— even all the Gentiles over whom my name has been called" (v. 17a).

The restoration of the Davidic throne was regularly seen as including the restoration of God's people, Israel. Texts such as Jeremiah 23:5-6 make this clear: "The days are surely coming, says the Lord, when I will raise up for David a righteous Branch, and he shall reign as king and deal wisely, and shall execute justice and righteousness in the land. In his days Judah will be saved and Israel will live in safety. And this is the name by which he will be called: 'The Lord is our righteousness'" (cf. Jer 33:15-16; Isa 11:1, 10-11).

The restoration ("raising up") of the Branch (v. 5) precedes the restoration of God's people, as Judah will be saved and Israel will live in safety (Jer 23:6). James's application of Amos moves in a similar orbit, but now the restoration of the people of God includes "all other peoples . . . even all the Gentiles" into the protective enclave of God's salvation.

Verse 18 emphatically states that the inclusion of the nations in God's plan of salvation is not new. Rather, it finds its origins in the word of God "who has been making these

Saint James the Lesser

Georges de La Tour (1593–1652). *St. James the Lesser*. Oil on canvas. (Credit: Réunion des Musées Nationaux / Art Resource, NY)

things known from long ago" (cf. Eph 3:4-6). According to James's reading of the Scriptures, God had always intended that the restoration of David's dwelling would involve the inclusion of Gentiles into the fold of God's people. James, Peter, and the rest are witnessing the actualization and fulfillment of the divine aim.

Peter had concluded that the Pharisaic believers should not place a yoke on the Gentile believers. James concurs, judging, or determining (*krinō*), that "we [the Jewish believers] should not trouble those Gentiles who are turning to God" (v. 19). Gentile believers will not have to be circumcised and keep the law of Moses in order to be saved (cf. vv. 1, 5). James, however, does add some requirements in v. 20. One should not understand the requirements as necessary for the Gentiles' salvation, for presumably James agrees with Peter's conclusion that all are saved through the grace of Jesus Christ (v. 11). The narrative offers no explicit rationale as to what motivated James to add certain requirements to the Gentiles. In fact, such restrictions might appear intrusive, giving rise to various historical reconstructions of Acts 15.

It is possible that the laws of Leviticus 17–18 inspire the rationale for the requirements that James lays upon the Gentiles. These laws, in part, served to guide the behavior of "aliens" who lived among Israelites in the land. Just as the Scriptures made certain requirements of aliens who lived among Israelites, even though the aliens were not required to adhere to all aspects of Israelite law, James can make certain requirements of Gentile believers who wish to have fellowship with Jewish believers, even though these Gentiles believers are not to be troubled with following all the laws of Moses as circumcised proselytes. Gentiles are required, according to this rationale, to observe basic requirements of purity so that they might share fellowship with Christian Jews. [Purity]

James's "decree," as it is often called, places four restrictions on Gentiles, with the last two being very closely related. First, he requires that Gentiles abstain "from things polluted by idols" (v. 20; *eidōlōn*). Later, as James composes a letter to Gentiles, he rewords this phrase, saying that Gentiles are "to abstain from what has been sacrificed to idols" (v. 29; *eidōlothytōn*). Obviously, this element of the decree forbids the Gentile believers' involvement in idolatry, and most especially from the sacrifices associated with idol worship. This restriction finds an echo in Leviticus 17:8-9, which forbids both the Israelite and the alien from offering sacrifice to any but the Lord.

The second requirement is that Gentiles abstain from "fornication" (*porneia*). *Porneia* designated improper sexual activity.

Leviticus 18:6-23 spells out, in great detail, types of sexual relations that were forbidden, including sexual unions with "anyone near of kin" (Lev 18:6), with women during menstruation (Lev 18:19), between men (Lev 18:22), and with beasts (Lev 18:23). Leviticus 18:26 makes explicit that such restrictions of sexual practice apply both to "the citizen *or the alien who resides among you.*" James, therefore, is requiring Gentile believers to stay away from sexual practices that are forbidden *both for Jews and non-Jews* in the Scriptures.

The last two requirements are closely related; they require abstinence "from whatever has been strangled and from blood" (v. 20b). Leviticus 17:10-13 specifically forbids both Israelites and aliens from eating blood. Before eating any animal, all the blood is to be poured out (Lev 17:13). Given this, the requirement to abstain from what has been strangled is consistent, for a strangled animal, as opposed to one that had been sacrificed, would still have its blood within it.

Thus, according to this line of interpretation, James is requiring that Gentile believers who wish to associate with Jewish believers must adhere to restrictions that are similar to laws that have always guided "aliens" who associated with Israelites. They must avoid food offered to idols—and presumably other things "polluted" by idols—forbidden sexual practices, and food that contains blood, due to improper methods of slaughter.

Verse 21 provides the basis for these requirements, noting that such requirements are not anything new. All James is requiring is what the Mosaic law had always required of aliens. Most Gentile believers were recruited from among the "God-fearers," Gentiles who had regularly frequented the synagogues (see [God-fearer]). Hence, they would have been familiar with Mosaic law, "for he has been read every sabbath in the synagogues" (v. 21b).

Purity

It is difficult for modern people, removed from the culture of ancient Judaism, to appreciate the importance of purity (see [Unclean Animals]). Purity and purity laws are grounded in the belief that things are to be ordered: there is a place for everything and everything is to be in its place. To be out of place is to be unclean. Bruce Malina uses the illustration that "dirt" in a garden does not render the garden "unclean," for dirt is "in place" in a garden. Yet even a little dirt on the carpet makes the carpet "unclean," for dirt on a carpet is "out of place" (Malina, 122–52).

Though Gentiles had their own views on matters of ritual purity (Ferguson, 186–87), they did not follow Jewish laws of purity. Hence, they ate food that was "unclean" (out of place) and engaged in types of worship that were "out of place," according to Jewish law. To do unclean things made one unclean. Uncleanness was "contagious." Imagine someone with dirty hands shaking hands with someone with clean hands; the dirty hand makes the clean hand unclean, not vice-versa. Jews wanting to remain clean, therefore, would need to avoid Gentiles who were not ritually clean.

Hence, according to one line of interpretation, James is requiring Gentiles to maintain at least basic purity requirements so that they would not make Jewish believers unclean.

Bruce J. Malina, *The New Testament World: Insights from Cultural Anthropology* (Atlanta: John Knox Press, 1981); Everett Ferguson, *Backgrounds of Early Christianity*, 3rd ed. (Grand Rapids MI: Eerdmans, 2003).

As prevalent as this approach to the judgment of James is, it is not a totally satisfying reading. Both Peter and James appear insistent that Jews and Gentiles stand on an equal footing before God. Peter spoke of how God "made no distinction between them and us" (v. 9) and that both Jews and Gentiles "will be saved through the grace of the Lord Jesus" (v. 11). James concluded that God has "visited" the Gentiles and taken out from among them "a people for his name" (v. 14). Yet Leviticus 17–18 assumes a clear distinction between Israelites and "aliens." If proper behavior of "aliens" who wish to associate with "Israelites" is what is driving James's judgment, it would appear that James is undermining the very point that both he and Peter have been trying to make: both Jewish and Gentile believers constitute the people of God, between whom God makes no distinction.[22]

Ben Witherington provides a possibly helpful alternative approach to James's decree.[23] James, Witherington argues, is not offering advice to Gentiles who wish to have fellowship with Jews; rather, he is urging Gentiles who have turned to the true and living God (cf. 14:15) to shun those practices that are indicative of pagan worship. The exhortation to avoid the pollutions of idols or food offered to idols amounts to requiring Gentile believers to shun pagan, idolatrous practices, most especially feasts at pagan temples. Even the reference to abstaining from blood and things strangled alludes to non-Jewish methods of cultic sacrifice. [Philo on Pagan Sacrifice] Finally, the exhortations to avoid *porneia* refer to the avoidance of cultic prostitution, though other sexually immoral practices are also forbidden by such a requirement.

James, therefore, is not *explicitly* motivated by a rereading of Leviticus 17–18 to place restrictions on Gentiles that they might have fellowship with believing Jews. He is making clear that there are patterns of worship and sexual activity found among pagans from which Gentile believers, by virtue of the fact that they are included among the people of God, must abstain. This is consistent with what Paul also required in his letters to Gentiles who had turned to God (1 Thess 1:9). Paul exhorts his readers to shun idolatry (1 Cor 8–10) and sexual immorality (1 Thess 4:1-9; 1 Cor 5:1-8; 6:15-20). Fortuitously, and even providentially, if Gentile believers were to follow James's counsel, Jewish believers sensitive to the legal requirements of Leviticus 17–18 regarding association with "aliens" should also be satisfied.

Philo on Pagan Sacrifice

The following statement illustrates the connection in Acts between avoiding eating blood and strangled animals:

Some men, . . . being wholly absorbed in the invention of senseless pleasures, . . . prepare sacrifices which ought never be offered, strangling their victims, and stifling the essence of life, which they ought to let depart free and unrestrained, burying the blood, as it were, in the body. For it ought to have been sufficient for them to enjoy the flesh by itself, without touching any of those parts which have an [sic] connection with the soul of life. (Philo, *The Special Laws*, 4.122)

This would be true, for in Jewish tradition idolatry and sexual immorality epitomized Gentile sin. It is informative to read the Wisdom of Solomon in this regard. Wisdom proposes that human beings had failed to discern the true God behind the created order (13:1-9), actually confusing the things God had made with gods (13:2-3). The confusion of that which God had made with gods led to the human folly of confusing that which humans made with God, or idolatry (13:10–14:11). Idolatry, Wisdom contends, then led to sexual immorality: "For the idea of making idols was the beginning of fornication" (*porneia*, Wis 14:12).[24] The close connection in Jewish tradition between false worship, including idolatry, and sexual immorality helps contemporary readers understand better the linkage James makes between false worship practices and fornication and explains James's explicit insistence that Gentiles refrain *both* from the false worship practices and the corresponding sexual practices that Jews believed accompanied such false worship.

In essence, the Lukan narrative portrays James as forbidding Gentiles from engaging in practices that good, pious Jews associated with typical Gentile, pagan behavior: idolatry and sexual immorality. In his own way, James is saying to Gentiles something similar to what the writer of Ephesians urged to his readers: "Now this I affirm and insist on in the Lord: you must no longer live as the Gentiles live, in the futility of their minds" (Eph 4:17).

The Testimony of the Church, vv. 22-29

The primary actors in the preceding discussion have been the leaders of the Jerusalem congregation, "the apostles and the elders" (cf. v. 6). Perhaps Peter speaks for the apostles, while James represents the voice of the elders. The Lukan narrative, unlike Galatians 1:19, does not, after all, include James among the apostles. This same leadership group remains on center stage as composers of a letter that will give expression to the decision of the church. [Letter] Yet Luke is quite clear that the whole church joins with the leadership in this decision (v. 22; the Greek text literally reads, "Then it seemed [good] to the apostles and the elders, together with the whole church"). A community needs

Letter

Letters were a common form of communication in the ancient world, "a substitute for oral communication" (Aune, 158). They provided a way for parties to remain in contact with one another in a world that did not allow for instantaneous communication or speedy travel. Since the genre was so widespread, there existed many types of letters. One type David Aune called the embedded letter: "Authors of historical, biographical, and fictional narratives of the Hellenistic period often inserted letters for documentary or dramatic reasons" (169). Aune says that embedded letters were often fictional, even when found in historical documents. Hence, one cannot, based on genre alone, make a determination as to the authenticity of the apostolic letter embedded in Acts 15. Ancient letters followed rather typical forms, which the letter embedded in Acts follows:

• Opening, consisting of the sender(s), the recipient(s), and a greeting (15:23)
• Body (15:24-29a)
• Exhortation, if relevant (15:29b)
• Closing, consisting of a closing greeting ("Farewell" of 15:29)

David E. Aune, *The New Testament in Its Literary Environment* (Philadelphia: Westminster, 1987); William G. Doty, *Letters in Primitive Christianity* (Philadelphia: Fortress, 1973).

leadership to come to resolution on difficult issues, but that does not deter from the real possibility that a community can reach consensus on such issues.

What the leadership and larger church resolved to do was to send back to Antioch with Paul and Barnabas two men from the Jerusalem congregation, Judas and Silas. They would carry a letter spelling out the church's decision. All the reader knows from the Lukan narrative to this point about Judas and Silas is that they were "leaders" (Gk. = "leading men") among the Jerusalem congregation; the text does not specifically say that they were "elders." [Judas Called Barsabbas] [Silas] The narrative does not say why it was necessary for representatives of the Jerusalem church to accompany Paul and Barnabas. But readers should recall the pattern of the Jerusalem church sending personal envoys to geographical locations when important breakthroughs in the advancement of the gospel occurred (see 8:14, 25; 9:31-32; 10:23-24; 11:22-23).[25]

The leadership of the apostles and elders is evident in the salutation of the letter: "The brothers, both apostles and elders."[26] Though this heading makes the leadership the technical authors of the letter, the larger congregation is not excluded from offering its voice, as the letter explicitly states that "we have decided unanimously to choose representatives" (v. 25). Reference back to vv. 22-23a makes clear that the "whole church" was involved in this decision to select representatives to accompany this letter.

The recipients of the letter are said to be the "brothers," or fellow-believers, among the Gentiles of Antioch and the region of Syria and Cilicia, of which Antioch was the capital (see [Antioch]). In addressing the letter directly to the Gentiles, their status as the people of God is enhanced. Had the letter been addressed to Jewish believers in Antioch, the missive would have left the impression that the Christian *Jews* were the primary object of Jerusalem's concern, not the Gentiles.

The letter makes explicit Jerusalem's commitment to the inclusion of the Gentiles by distancing itself from those who started the disturbance among the Gentiles in the first place. Verse 24 concedes that those who instigated the current controversy are from among the ranks of the Jerusalem church. However, the letter is

Judas Called Barsabbas

Barsabbas means "son of Sabbath." This is the surname of one of the apostolic candidates, Joseph Barsabbas (Acts 1:23). Luke does not identify any relationship between the two.

Silas

Unlike Judas Barsabbas, Silas becomes an important figure in the New Testament. Acts mentions Silas several other times in connection with Paul (15:41; 16:19, 25, 29; 17:4, 10, 14-15; 18:5). There is no good reason not to equate this Silas with the Silvanus mentioned in Paul's letters (2 Cor 1:19; 1 Thess 1:1; 2 Thess 1:1). 1 Pet 5:12 claims Silvanus as Peter's amanuensis. Later church tradition distinguished Silas and Silvanus, stating that the former became the bishop of Corinth and the latter the bishop of Thessalonica (*The Beginnings of Christianity*, 4.179).

F. J. Foakes Jackson and Kirsopp Lake, *The Beginnings of Christianity: The Acts of the Apostles*, 5 vols. (Grand Rapids MI: Baker, 1979).

equally emphatic that these persons were unauthorized to say what they did, having received "no instructions from us." The verse further distances the Jerusalem leadership and church as a whole from the unauthorized Christian Jews by using harsh language to describe the results of the latter's work, acknowledging that these believers disturbed and unsettled the Gentiles. The word that the NRSV translates as "unsettled" (*anaskeuzontes*) is quite harsh, denoting the reversal of "what has been done, tearing down what has been built, or canceling what has been agreed upon."[27] The actions of this faction of believers are clearly viewed as destructive.

This harsh language raises the question of how "unanimous" (NRSV, v. 25) the Jerusalem church was in rendering this judgment. The text does not help the reader, leaving the question unresolved. Did the circumcision and Pharisaic faction come to embrace the views of the larger church? That is, does Luke use "the whole church" (v. 22) and "unanimous" (v. 25) with strict literalism? Or did the Pharisaic believers continue to cling to their views and effectively experience further alienation from the Jerusalem church? Attempts at *historical* reconstruction of the story behind the narrative of Acts can render some tentative conclusions, but Acts itself offers no explicit word as to what became of these Pharisaic believers, choosing rather to focus on the harmony and unity of the Jerusalem church on this matter of Gentile inclusion.

The letter offers an explicit word of commendation regarding Paul and Barnabas, of whom it says that they had either "risked their lives for" or "dedicated their lives to" Jesus (v. 26; one may read the Greek either way). Such commendation is curious, for these men were already known in Antioch, while Judas and Silas, about whom the letter offers no word of commendation, were unknown to the letter's recipients. Judas and Silas have the important task, however, of confirming by their personal testimony the content of the ruling of the letter. Such personal confirmation and/or supplementation of a letter appears in some letters of antiquity.[28] Though the Antiochene audience and the readers were already acquainted with Paul and Barnabas, who forged the path into Gentile territory, the letter's commendation offers the narrator one more opportunity to show *Jerusalem's* unswerving affirmation of the inclusion of non-Jews.

Verse 28 explicitly claims the sanction of the Holy Spirit in the decision to include Gentiles. One rereads the story of Acts 15 in vain, trying to find some explicit reference to the working of the Holy Spirit in this gathering of the church.[29] One can only conclude that the gathered church assumed the presence and the guidance of the Spirit in the community's debates and deliberations. Significantly, the Holy Spirit finds its voice in *human* action—speeches, scriptural interpretations, and James's emphatic statement that "*I* have reached the decision" (v. 19).

Finally, after an extensive introduction, the letter arrives at its point (vv. 28b-29). No burden will be imposed on the Gentiles except the four things that James noted earlier (v. 20). It is curious, given that the specific question over circumcision is what sparked the debate, that the letter does not explicitly speak of this ceremony. But readers of the letter, both the readers in the text (the Antiochenes) and readers in front of the text, should infer this conclusion. The letter indicates only that Gentiles must abstain from food offered to idols, from blood, from that which is strangled, and from fornication. Whether it is necessary that Gentiles refrain in order to maintain fellowship with Jewish believers or in order to live a life worthy of their calling as people who have turned to the living God, the letter does not say (see comment above on v. 20).

Delivering the Letter, 15:30-35

Acts 15 began in Antioch (15:1; cf. 14:26). Fittingly, the narrator brings closure to the narrative with a final panel that reports the return of the Paul and Barnabas, accompanied by the Jerusalem emissaries, to Antioch (v. 30).

The church at Antioch "rejoiced at the exhortation" (v. 31). The word that the NRSV translates as "exhortation" (*paraklēsei*) has many nuances, approximated by the English words "exhortation," "comfort," or "encouragement." The letter from Jerusalem offered all of these to the Gentile believers. Comfort came in hearing that the Gentiles would not have to be circumcised and follow the Mosaic law to be fully included in the ranks of God's people. Exhortation came in hearing that Gentiles, as God's people, would be required to live lives consistent with their status. Encouragement came with the word of assurance that Gentile believers would "do well" (v. 29) if they followed the requirements of the Jerusalem missive.

Judas and Silas further "encourage [*parekalesan*] and strengthen" the believers of Antioch, though the narrative is silent as to what they said. Readers might reasonably imagine that "gaps" in the relatively brief letter would raise questions in the minds of the Antiochene believers. By offering such encouragement and strengthening, however, Judas and Silas are fulfilling their role as prophets (see [Prophets]). As prophets, Judas and Silas are empowered to enrich the written word through oral proclamation, presumably offering extended commentary and clarifying interpretation. Such living, human application is necessary for a written text, be it a word from the prophets of old (cf. vv. 15-18) or a word from contemporaries, to be vital and engaging to the gathered community.

Typically, Luke gives only a general time frame to indicate how long Judas and Silas remained in Antioch (v. 33; cf. 14:28). The fact that the Jerusalem prophets stayed "for some time," however, indicates that they were welcomed by the Gentile believers. Jewish and Gentile believers live and worship harmoniously. The narrative reinforces this picture of harmony by stating that eventually the church at Antioch sent Judas and Silas[30] back to Jerusalem "in peace" (v. 34). Paul and Barnabas, however, remain in Antioch, continuing, along with others, to lead that church in teaching and proclamation.

CONNECTIONS

Several theological themes connect this story with contemporary faith. Human participation in the divine drama of salvation and experience are quite prominent in this narrative. And both are closely connected with the life of the community of faith and the community's witness.

God's will, or the "plan of God," a favorite phrase in Luke–Acts (Luke 7:30; 2:23; 4:28; 5:38-39), is that which the church of Jerusalem attempts to discern at this critical juncture in the story. The group involved in the debate over discerning the will of God on the matter of Gentile inclusion consists of Jewish believers. That is, this is a dispute involving Christians of the same ethnic and cultural heritage. One cannot blame the internal division on differences in religion, cultural background, or history. That is worth noting if only to remind ourselves that disputes within churches today regularly involve people who have much in common. Despite such common features of faith and heritage, sincere disagreements over the will and plan of God can irrupt.

The Pharisaic believers appeal to the Scriptures and tradition— hardly a bad combination—to conclude that the divine will required that the inclusion of Gentiles was dependent on circumcision.[31] Rabbinic tradition, much of which found its roots in Pharisaism, stated that "it is the Israelites who have a share in the world to come" (*m.Sanh.* 10:1). And being a part of the people of Israel included circumcision. Genesis 17:1-9 established the

Ananias and Eleazer

Josephus tells of a Jew named Ananias who converted to Judaism Izates, the Gentile king of Adiabene (*Ant.* 20.17–48). When Izates' mother, Helena, discovered that her son was interested in converting, she tried to persuade him not to accept circumcision, fearing that his subjects would reject the legitimacy of his rule if they knew he were Jewish. Ananias agreed with her and told Izates that what was really important was the worship of God and, given the special circumstances, God would forgive Izates for not being circumcised. Later, however, another Jewish teacher, Eleazer, insisted to Izates that he could not ignore "the principal of those laws [of Moses]," and that circumcision was necessary to be faithful to God. Izates then agreed to circumcision.

The story illustrates that some Jews were willing, under special circumstances, to grant Gentiles an exemption from circumcision. Yet, in the end, the story affirms the necessity of circumcision, even in cases where an exemption might be prudent. The situation facing the Jerusalem church was not a special exemption for an individual, but the setting aside of circumcision for all Gentiles. If circumcision were necessary for a king, despite the fact that it might hinder his governing effectiveness, surely Jewish law and custom could not be set aside for whole masses of people who wanted to join the ranks of God's people.

covenant that Abraham's descendants will be those whom God blesses in a special way. This is followed by Genesis 17:9-14, which requires that Abraham and his descendants practice circumcision in order to keep this covenant that God had made. Exodus 12:43-49 makes clear that only Israelites and *circumcised* alien residents may celebrate the Passover (see [Passover]). Josephus tells of an incident that bears on our story: two Jewish teachers had differing views over the necessity of circumcising a Gentile convert to Judaism; the issue was settled *in favor of requiring circumcision.* [Ananias and Eleazer]

The Pharisaic believers clearly had Scripture and tradition on their side. To what did those Jewish believers on the other side of the debate appeal? The answer shakes every conservative religious tradition, regardless of that tradition's particular confession. What many first-century believers appealed to was their *experience* of God.

Among the churches of Galatia, Paul confronted an issue similar to that being discussed in Jerusalem. As in Antioch and Jerusalem, Jewish believers were insisting that Galatian Gentile believers be circumcised (Gal 5:2-4). Though we cannot be sure exactly how the Jewish believers argued their case to the Galatians, perhaps they appealed to the story of Abraham and the covenant of circumcision found in Genesis 17.[32] In his argument against such demands, Paul employs appeals to the immediate and personal experience of God.

In Galatians 1:14, Paul acknowledges his own expertise in and prior zealous commitment to Jewish law and tradition. According to Paul's own testimony, what changed him was an encounter with God (Gal 1:12, 15-17). Further, Paul appeals to the personal experience of his readers: "The only thing I want to learn from you is this: Did you receive the Spirit by doing works of the law or by believing what you heard?" (Gal 3:2). The receipt of the Spirit is an *experience* of the presence of the God. This immediate experience of God's presence served for the early Christians as the sure sign and seal of their incorporation into the people of God, being spoken of as God's "guarantee" of the believers' eventual and total redemption (cf. 2 Cor 5:5).

The appeal to experience is echoed in Acts. As Peter makes his argument for God's calling the Gentiles to cleansing and belief, he refers back to the receipt of the Holy Spirit by Cornelius and his household (v. 8). James summarizes Peter's account by declaring that this apostle had just recounted how God had visited the Gentiles and called out from among them people who would belong to him (v. 14).

But the early Christian Jews who advocated Gentile inclusion did not appeal only to experience. *Scripture* continued to play an important role in arguments offered by supporters of Gentile inclusion. Paul appeals often to Scripture in Galatians 3 and 4, as he attempts to persuade his readers that they are not to accept circumcision. James also appeals to Scripture in vv. 16-17, quoting Amos 9:11-12. Further, the whole of Acts is replete with appeals to Scripture that legitimate the essential gospel message. But what allows Paul's interpretations of the Abraham story or James's appeal to Amos to carry more weight in the argument than the traditionalists' appeal *to the same scriptural heritage*? Can anyone claim, on the basis of a personal experience, to offer an authoritative rereading of Scripture that overturns tradition?

One might argue that persons such as Peter, James, and Paul hold a special status. As apostles and elders of the first generation of the church, they were granted special insight and authority to interpret properly the scriptural tradition. Appeal to texts such as Luke 24:45 offers some support for this line of argument. The experiences of God that *these* persons had count for much while *our* experiences do not. These first-century leaders, in effect, have created a new tradition that provides the proper frame of reference for interpreting the Scriptures.

Such an explicit line of argument has a long tradition. The second-century church thinker Irenaeus, when faced with gnostic interpretations of Scripture that appealed to special revelation or personal experience, challenged the validity of such interpretations by appeal to the larger tradition of the church. Through the Spirit, the apostles had been given perfect knowledge; guarded by such perfect knowledge they preached the gospel and, later, recorded in the Scriptures this true gospel (*Haer.* 3.1.1). Further, that the true tradition might continue to be guarded, the church established bishops, directly appointed by apostles to preserve the true teaching of the gospel (*Haer.* 3.3.1-2). Consequently, it is only in the church—the *true* church with its established connection through apostolic succession—that valid and legitimate interpretation of Scripture can take place (*Haer.* 4.26.2). One can see how such a line of argument would preserve the church from being too easily persuaded by variant interpretations of the Scriptures. In our own time one can find repeated the appeal to the tradition created by the church. [Tradition and Contemporary Interpretation] Has "Christian tradition" replaced "Jewish tradition" as the proper framework for the interpretation of Scripture?

Is there any way out of this passage between Scylla and Charybdis? Do we lose all freedom in meaningful scriptural interpretation, crashing against the immoveable rocks of fixed tradition? Or does our ship get sucked down the whirlpool of Charybdis, as interpretation gets lost in a funnel of rampant subjectivity? Our course must be negotiated with care.

Responsible reading of Scripture requires the honest admission that just as "No one can be a Christian alone" (John Wesley), none reads the Scriptures alone. We may read privately, but as we read we carry a lot of "stuff": cultural assumptions, pre-understandings, even biases. We cannot navigate the narrow channel between Scylla and Charybdis simply by denying the reality and power of tradition. Christians read *as Christians*, as obvious as that may sound. And even free-thinking Christians who emphasize liberty of conscience or soul freedom (maybe even soul competency!), cannot pretend that "Christianity" is some ill-formed putty that we can mold into any shape. If bringing a tradition is unavoidable as we read, it is not a bad thing for Christians to bring a *Christian* tradition.

Tradition is *not* a bad thing. The author of Luke–Acts speaks of his own dependence on tradition as he wrote our narrative (see Luke 1:1-4). Paul alludes a number of times to his receiving and passing along of tradition (1 Cor 11:2, 23; 15:3; cf. 2 Tim 1:13-14; 2:1-2). Tradition can serve as a helpful framework or guideline in our talk of God and even our interpretation of Scripture. Or, to employ a metaphor offered by Eduard Schweizer, Christian tradition and teaching can provide the pilgrim with signposts to guide one's journey or even guardrails to deter the Christian from falling off the path altogether.[33] To allude again to the image of Charybdis, tradition can help prevent us from being sucked into idiosyncratic and eccentric oblivion.

Tradition and Contemporary Interpretation

In the "Faith" section of the *Kansas City Star* (21 July 2000), a reader asked how one is to understand seemingly conflicting statements in the Bible. The Reverend Patrick Rush, vicar-general of the Diocese of Kansas City-St. Joseph, wrote:

[H]ow do we know which teachings must be held as true? The measure for sorting through the biblical teachings is neither society's values today nor my personal feelings about a particular teaching. Rather, the measure is church tradition. Tradition is the developing life and teaching of the church through which God's saving truth, given in the Scriptures, is passed on to succeeding generations.

But tradition is no substitute for the Scriptures. And Scripture, as *script*, requires *readers*. While Scripture often embodies tradition and while readers regularly employ tradition to help them read, the Scriptures—most especially within the Protestant *tradition!*—have primacy over tradition. James appealed to Scripture to affirm Peter's insight that God was calling out from the Gentiles a people to be God's own. In so doing, he appealed to Scripture to challenge the long-held Jewish tradition that being Jewish, that is, accepting circumcision and following Moses, was necessary for salvation.

But we still stand at something of an impasse, for while James appealed to Scripture, so could the Pharisaic believers who insisted on circumcision. This is where it is necessary to bring back into play the mystery of religious experience, but with an important provision. Religious experience happens regularly in the witness of the Scriptures *in the context of community*—not "community" in some abstract sense like, "the financial community" or "the law-enforcement community" or "the scientific community." Such terminology regularly refers on the evening news to a faceless mass of some subgroup of humanity. The community that provides the context for the immediate experience of God consists of a concrete group of people, gathering in a real place at a particular point in time. This is where tradition, experience, and Scripture come together to be tested and tried.

Such is what we find in the early church. In Acts 15, the church (v. 22) is gathered to hear Peter tell his story and to hear Paul and Barnabas speak of signs and wonders God had accomplished among the Gentiles (v. 12). James shares his reading of Amos before the church. The Pharisaic believers stated their position before the whole body in v. 5, as did their allies in Antioch (v. 1). *All* have a voice and can share with the community their understanding of the purposes and will of God. Then, it is with the *consent* of the community that a letter is drafted regarding the issue of Gentile inclusion (v. 22, 25). Even when writing to the Corinthians, where private religion and self-edification seemed the order the day (1 Cor 14:4), Paul insisted that revelatory words uttered by the prophets were to be assessed and weighed by other members of the community (1 Cor 14:29).

The concrete community of faith provides the living context where the voices of tradition, Scripture, and experience are negotiated. [Community of Faith] The church of Acts dared to believe that out of such negotiation the will of God could be discerned: "For it seemed good to the Holy Spirit and to us" (v. 28). Such a view of the church, namely, that in *her* decisions the Spirit finds its voice,

---

Community of Faith

📖 "Free church" traditions, such as Baptists, which regularly emphasize personal, even private religion, might diminish the importance of the concrete faith community in guiding one's understanding of spiritual matters, including biblical interpretation. The following statements represent voices from the free-church tradition that call readers to give serious attention to the community.

Joel Green:

Given that no interpreter comes to Scripture "clean," that all of us bring with us our own commitments and interests, what is to keep the interpretative enterprise from degenerating into self-legitimating pragmatism? [Green lists several "communities of discourse" in which the interpreter must participate. Two are particularly important in this context.]

Communal—taking seriously that the biblical witness is itself concerned with the formation of faithful communities of God's people, and that biblical interpretation, in order to *be biblical*, must take place in the context of faith(ful) communities.

Global—taking seriously that our communities, which keep us from developing private and idiosyncratic interpretations, are themselves subject to tunnel vision and self-legitimation, and thus need the witness of believers who are "not like us" as conversation partners. (Green, 166–67)

Molly Marshall:

When the Anabaptists' stress on the covenant community is neglected, Baptists can and have taken "liberty of conscience," "soul competency," and the "priesthood of the believer" (accent on *the believer*) to mean that one can believe what one chooses and has the "right of personal judgment" in matters of faith and doctrine. [Quoting from and building on the ideas of Baptist ethicist Michael Westmoreland-White, Marshall states,] "Genuine Baptist liberty is twisted into normlessness" when the freedom of private interpretation is devoid of ecclesial context. (Marshall, 144)

David M. Scholer:

The history of Baptists and other groups within the Church suggest that however deeply held the commitment to the individual freedom of interpretation might be, there are, in actual practice, invariably community boundaries. These boundaries, although sometimes quite elastic, establish some beliefs that are drawn from the perceived implications of biblical authority and stand against the absolute exercise of private interpretation. (Scholer, 189)

Joel B. Green, "Biblical Authority and Communities of Discourse," 151–73; Molly T. Marshall, "Exercising Liberty of Conscience: Freedom in Private Interpretation," 141–50; and David M. Scholer, "The Authority of the Bible and Private Interpretation: A Dilemma of Baptist Freedom," 174–93, all of which may be found in *Baptists in the Balance: The Tension between Freedom and Responsibility*, ed. Everett C. Goodwin (Valley Forge: Judson Press, 1997).

---

invites both confidence and caution. It offers the confidence that the gathered people of God can rely on the direction of God to be mediated through God's spirit, the Scripture, and even tradition, even as the church experiences within its own ranks disagreements on important issues. This view of the church also urges caution and humility, for it can lead a gathered community to assume arrogantly that whatever it decides about any given issue is the decision of God. This can lead a gathered community down the dangerous path of confusing its words with God's word.[34]

Contemporary readers may be left wondering what the so-called apostolic decree has to do with the issue of witness. This decree was certainly important to Acts (see also 16:4; 21:25). But how does one apply its word to our time? [Textual Criticism and the Apostolic Decree]

We presented in the Commentary two interpretations of the decree, stating our preference for the second interpretation offered. Our preferred reading states that the decree is not so much concerned with the issue of maintaining fellowship *within* the church as maintaining a consistent witness to those *outside* the church. We will focus our connections on this line of interpretation.

We would need to recall that, according to this way of reading, James is starting with common, almost stereotypical Jewish notions of "the pagan lifestyle." This "lifestyle" was summed up in two words: idolatry and *porneia*. Both of these were very much rooted in culture. The task for us is to challenge Christians today to identify patterns of living, and perhaps even worship, that, despite cultural acceptance, are inconsistent with those who have been called out to be God's people.

Does worship that focuses more on the congregation as an audience that needs entertainment than on God as the audience who deserves meaningful praise succumb to contemporary paganism? Does preaching that offers practical pragmatism rather than proclamation, whose primary text is Stephen Covey's *Seven Habits of Highly Effective People* rather than the Bible, surrender to the culture of modern paganism?

Would we dare to hold up for critique under the light of Scripture those words from a text of "American Scripture," which say that "life, liberty, and the pursuit of happiness" form the core of each individual's "inalienable rights"? What if Jesus had been

Textual Criticism and the Apostolic Decree

The textual history of the apostolic decree anticipates the struggles of contemporary Christians to make sense of the decree. The textual tradition offers two major versions of this decree, with multiple variations springing from the two major traditions. The NRSV follows the textual tradition accepted as original by the majority of scholars. This version focuses on *cultic* restrictions (see the Commentary).

The Western textual tradition attempts to offer an ethical reinterpretation of the decree. The Western Text of Acts 15:20, 29, and 21:25 strikes the reference to "and from whatever has been strangled," perhaps because the tradition understood abstaining from blood as forbidding murder, in which case abstaining from strangulation (of a human being) would be redundant. It then replaced the prohibition against things strangled with a version of the Golden Rule: ". . . and not to do to others whatever they do not wish to be done to themselves." This rendered an ethical interpretation of the decree: Gentiles were to abstain from idolatry, murder, and sexual immorality and were to practice the Golden Rule. Transformation of the textual tradition from a cultic to ethical interpretation reveals the concern of later copyists to make the texts they were copying relevant to their contemporary readers.

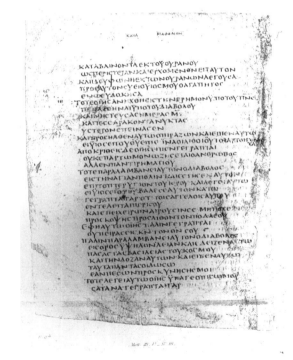

(Credit: James R. Adair, "Codex Bezae Cantabrigiensis," [cited 17 September 2007]. Online: http://alpha.reltech.org/cgi-bin/Ebind2html/BibleMSS/U5?seq=25.)

The commentary regularly makes reference to the Western Tradition of Acts. Codex Bezae, pictured above showing Matt 3:17–4:10, is the major Greek manuscript of the New Testament representing this tradition.

Hans Conzelmann, *Acts of the Apostles* (Hermeneia; Philadelphia: Fortress, 1987), 118.

driven by his desire to hold onto *his* inalienable rights, as defined by the "American experiment," as noble as it is? Would he then have given his life that others might live? Would Jesus, dedicated to his own liberty, have surrendered this liberty by devoting his life day after day to serving both the physical and spiritual needs of others? Do we really think that "the pursuit of happiness" as understood in the context of the American story (it was actually quite closely associated with the acquisition of property)[35] is what Jesus meant by "happiness" when he uttered the Beatitudes? These sayings define blessedness or *happiness* in terms spiritual poverty, meekness, sorrow, and the experience of persecution. Hardly the American Dream.

The decree of James, applied to our contemporary situation, dares to call upon the people to define themselves by patterns of worship and living that challenge fundamental assumptions and values of our own version of pagan culture. We would likely enjoy our Christianity much more if, when applying this decree, we focused on a few sexual sins—especially cultic prostitution—and relegated the rest of the decree to antiquated irrelevance. Surely, being a part of God's people does not really ask us to rethink the fundamental values of *our* culture, does it? If we pressed this too much upon the contemporary people of God our churches would not grow and we would be failures—at least as measured by the culture that we have made our standard.

NOTES

[1] This despite the fact that much Jewish eschatological expectation looked forward to the inclusion of the Gentiles in the "age to come." See [Inclusion of the Gentiles].

[2] Gerd Lüdemann, *Early Christianity according to the Traditions in Acts: A Commentary* (Minneapolis: Fortress, 1989), 172.

[3] Note that the Greek verb is active, not passive, as in the NRSV. Luke supplies no specific subject as to who appointed Paul and Barnabas, but v. 3 implies that it was the church ("they were sent on their way by the church").

[4] Luke has already reported the expansion of the gospel to these regions (see 11:19 for a passing reference to the region of Phonecia; 8:4-25 for a more detailed account of the spread of the gospel to Samaria).

[5] Marion L. Soards, *The Speeches in Acts: Their Content, Context, and Concerns* (Louisville KY: Westminster/John Knox, 1994), 90; Ben Witherington III, *The Acts of the Apostles: A Socio-Rhetorical Commentary* (Grand Rapids MI: Eerdmans, 1998), 453.

[6] Joseph A. Fitzmyer, *The Acts of the Apostles* (AB 31; New York: Doubleday, 1998), 543–44.

[7] Robert W. Tannehill, *The Narrative Unity of Luke–Acts: A Literary Interpretation*, 2 vols. (Minneapolis: Fortress, 1990), 2.184.

[8] Ernst Haenchen, *The Acts of the Apostles: A Commentary* (Philadelphia: Westminster, 1971), 462–64.

[9] Luke Timothy Johnson, *The Acts of the Apostles* (SacPag 5; Collegeville MN: Liturgical Press, 1992), 262.

[10] Fitzmyer, *Acts*, 547.

[11] Haenchen, *Acts*, 459. Witherington, who does assume that Peter offered such a speech, offers an equally plausible psychological explanation as to why Peter, a simple Galilean fisherman, would have found his experience of trying to keep the law very unsatisfying (*Acts*, 454). Speculations about what Peter could or could not have said will depend, of course, on prior assumptions that one holds about the historical veracity of the sources.

[12] John B. Polhill, *Acts* (NAC 26; Nashville: Broadman, 1992), 327. One could also note that the larger Jewish tradition employed "yoke" in a positive way, speaking of such "yokes" as the law or God's kingdom. The yoke, then, was a sign of Israel's election, which Israel should enjoy the privilege of carrying. See Fitzmyer, *Acts*, 548, and F. J. Foakes Jackson and Kirsopp Lake, *The Beginnings of Christianity: The Acts of the Apostles*, 5 vols. (Grand Rapids MI: Baker, 1979), 4.174.

[13] So Jackson and Lake, *The Beginnings of Christianity*, 4.174; Johnson, *Acts*, 263; Witherington, *Acts*, 454.

[14] Soards, *Speeches*, 92.

[15] Haenchen, *Acts*, 447.

[16] Johnson, *Acts*, 264.

[17] Tannehill, *Narrative Unity*, 2.187.

[18] J. Bradley Chance, *Jerusalem, the Temple, and the New Age in Luke–Acts* (Macon GA: Mercer University Press, 1988), 61.

[19] Tannehill, *Narrative Unity*, 2.187.

[20] NRSV translates v. 15 as "This agrees with the words of the prophets." It may seem like a small change, but the Greek text is very clear. It is not Peter's experience and James's interpretation of it that agree with the prophets; it is the prophets that agree with the experience and its interpretation.

[21] The restoration of the house of David: Johnson, *Acts*, 268, and Polhill, *Acts*, 329; the restoration of Israel: Fitzmyer, *Acts*, 555, and Witherington, *Acts*, 459.

[22] Historically, James might have made such a distinction, which may be reflected in the conflict between Paul and other Christian Jews in Antioch (Gal 2:11-14). Such possible distinction is minimized in Acts.

[23] Witherington, *Acts*, 462–67. His is a *historical* reading, though it also works well *literarily*.

[24] See James Barr, *Biblical Faith and Natural Theology* (Oxford: Clarendon Press, 1993), esp. ch. 4. Barr notes that the pattern discerned in *Wisdom* is very similar to the pattern of logic offered by Paul in Romans 1.

[25] See also Charles H. Talbert, *Reading Acts: A Literary and Theological Commentary of the Acts of the Apostles* (New York: Crossroad, 1997), 136.

[26] Some ancient Greek mss. included the larger church more explicitly in the salutation, reading "The apostles, the elders, and the brothers." A few of the ancient *translations* omit from the salutation any reference to "brothers."

[27] Jackson and Lake, *The Beginnings of Christianity*, 4.180. Cf. Polhill, *Acts*, 334, who says that the word was a military metaphor that could denote the looting and plundering of a town.

[28] See, e.g., 1 Macc 12:23; Eph 6:21-22; Col 4:7-8.

[29] Peter refers to the Holy Spirit in v. 8, but that is in reference to the Cornelius episode.

[30] Note that 15:40 states that when Paul left Antioch to visit churches he had earlier helped to establish, he took Silas with him. When did Silas return to Antioch? The text is silent. This gap prompted some ancient copyists to modify the text by adding v. 34: "But it seemed good to Silas to remain there."

[31] See Talbert, *Reading Acts*, 137–38.

[32] See E. P. Sanders, *Paul* (Oxford: Oxford University Press, 1991), 54–55.

[33] Eduard Schweizer, *Luke: A Challenge to Present Theology* (Atlanta: John Knox, 1982), 94.

[34] See, e.g., Stephen E. Fowl and L. Gregory Jones, *Reading in Communion: Scripture and Ethics in Christian Life* (Grand Rapids: Eerdmans, 1991), 110. Fowl and Jones argue that this is most especially prone to happen when the church fails to listen to all voices, even—and especially—the voices of the outsiders.

[35] Jefferson's "Declaration of Rights," in the context of which we find these profound words of secular, political philosophy, was actually based on a document penned a few weeks earlier by George Mason and included in the "Committee Draft of the Virginia Declaration of Rights." Jefferson's succinct phrase "life, liberty and pursuit of happiness" summarizes Mason's wordier phrase: "the enjoyment of life and liberty, with the means of acquiring and possessing property, and pursuing happiness and safety." See Pauline Maier, *American Scripture: Making the Declaration of Independence* (New York: Alfred A. Knopf, 1997), 126–27.

RETURNING TO EVERY CITY . . . AND BEYOND

Acts 15:36–16:40

COMMENTARY

The decision of the Jerusalem church spurs the "witness to the ends of the earth" onward. Acts 15:36 begins the second of Paul's so-called "missionary journeys" (Acts 15:36–18:21; see [Paul's Missionary Journeys]). The chapter divides into four episodes: 15:36-41 describes the separation of Paul and Barnabas; 16:1-5 introduces readers to Timothy; 16:6-10 narrates the Macedonian call; 16:11-40 tells of Paul's Philippian ministry.

Parting Company, 15:36-41

The phrase "after some days" (v. 36) signals a major transition.[1] Paul takes the initiative, indicating that he will continue as the main character, even as he played the leading role in much of Acts 13–14. Paul's plan offers no new bold initiatives: he wants to revisit churches already established in order to "see how they are doing" (v. 36). Actually, the ensuing narrative will give little attention to such visitation of established churches, for something major is about to happen.

The trip of Paul and Barnabas is delayed, however, for Barnabas wants to bring John Mark with them on this journey (v. 37; see [John Mark]). The narrator reminds readers that Mark had left Paul and Barnabas on their earlier journey while they were in Pamphylia (v. 38; cf. Acts 13:13). The narrator still leaves a number of gaps. First, Acts 13:13 states that Mark had returned to Jerusalem, leaving one wondering at what time and for what reason Mark had now returned to Antioch, the current narrative setting (cf. 15:35). Second, the narrator offers no clue as to why Barnabas wanted to include John on this journey. Colossians 4:10, which notes that Barnabas and "Mark" were cousins, might imply that Barnabas was driven by personal considerations and family ties. However, the narrative of Acts offers no such hints. Appeal to Colossians, as well as Philemon 24 and 2 Timothy 4:10, the latter two of which mention both Mark and Luke, also can give rise to historical speculation, particularly that Paul and Mark were reconciled.[2] Such historical speculation is warranted if one is interested in reconstructing early Christian history, yet its value for understanding the narrative of Acts is limited.

Apparently, it was because Mark had left Barnabas and Paul during the previous journey that Paul is quite reluctant to allow Mark to rejoin them (v. 39). The narrator is sympathetic with Paul. The word Luke uses to denote John's departure is *apostanta* ("deserted," NRSV). The English word "apostasy" is derived from this word.

The narrator sees Mark's early departure as a serious breach of commitment to missionary zeal. Luke Johnson suggests that Luke 9:52-62, which deals with the matter of faithful discipleship, offers a helpful commentary. The Lukan passage presents Jesus declaring that those who set their hands to the plow and then turn back are not fit for the kingdom of God.[3] This story in Acts may provide an application of Jesus' principle.

Some commentators observe that the dispute between Paul and Barnabas over Mark (v. 39) actually served to advance the gospel.[4] The departure of Barnabas and Mark to Cyprus, Barnabas's home (4:36), means that the gospel planted there (11:19; 13:4) can be further nurtured, even while Paul and his new companion, Silas, can further nurture the churches in Asia Minor. Such edifying readings are insightful, but speculative since the narrative offers no further comment on the work of Barnabas and John. One could also read v. 39b to mean that Barnabas went back home to Cyprus, even as John Mark had gone "back home" to Jerusalem in 13:13. However, the fact the Mark is leaving his hometown and accompanying Barnabas invites the more charitable reading.

The focus of the narrative shifts to Paul and Silas (vv. 40-41). It is only Paul to whom the church "commends . . . the grace of the Lord" (v. 40).[5] Further, the ensuing narrative will, henceforth, follow Paul's exploits and work, beginning with Paul's revisitation of the churches of Syria and Cilicia. Curiously, Acts 13–14 did not offer any great detail on the establishment of churches in these regions, though 15:23 clearly assumes missionary activity there. As for Barnabas and Mark, they fall off the stage of Acts, even if they do not fall off the stage of church history.

There Was a Disciple Named Timothy, 16:1-5

Paul visits Derbe and Lystra, cities explicitly noted in Luke's narration of Paul's so-called "first missionary journey" (cf. 14:6-22). Luke introduces readers to Timothy, a disciple of Lystra who was the son of a Jewish woman who was also a believer (v. 2; cf. 2 Tim 1:5). First Corinthians 4:17 implies that Paul converted Timothy, leading some commentators to conclude that such a conversion must have occurred during Paul's first visit to Lystra in Acts 14.[6] Such historical reconstructions are certainly possible, but the Lukan text offers no clues that any prior relationship existed between Paul and Timothy. [Timothy]

Paul's circumcision of Timothy (v. 3) has created much conversation among interpreters. It's likely that Timothy's circumcision indicates that he was Jewish. To be sure, some ancient, medieval, and modern interpreters argue that Timothy was not Jewish.[7] But in the flow of the Lukan narrative, it would make no sense for Paul to circumcise a Gentile. This is precisely what certain believing Jews insisted on in Acts 15:1, 5 and precisely what the Jerusalem leadership decided was not to occur (15:19, 28-29).[8]

The narrator appears, therefore, to want readers to conclude that Timothy is Jewish, despite the fact that his father was Greek. One cannot offer explicit documentation prior to the second century AD that the maternal lineage determined whether a child was Jewish.[9] But Luke apparently assumes the practice that was formally documented only later. But if Timothy was Jewish, why was he not already circumcised? The notification that Timothy's father was Greek might bear on the question.

Perhaps as a child of a "mixed union," Jewish and Gentile, Timothy would not have been considered a legitimate child of Abraham and, hence, not eligible for circumcision.[10] But if this were the case, then why would Timothy be eligible now? If it were "the Jews" who thought Timothy to be an illegitimate child because his father was Greek, it makes no sense to say that Paul circumcised Timothy "because of the Jews." Readers might infer that Timothy's Greek father, now dead presumably, forbade Timothy's circumcision as an infant.[11] His passing, combined with Paul's concern for the Jews, led to Timothy's circumcision. Admittedly, there is no sure way to fill this narrative gap.

Timothy

The Pastoral Epistles offer supplementary tradition regarding Timothy's upbringing, speaking of the influence of both his mother and grandmother (2 Tim 1:5). The indisputably authentic Pauline letters confirm the traditions of Acts that Timothy became an authoritative representative of Paul (1 Cor 4:17; 16:10-11; Phil 2:19-22; 1 Thess 3:1-6). Timothy's important role in Paul's mission is also highlighted by the fact that he is the co-author of a number of indisputably Pauline letters (Philippians, 2 Corinthians, 1 Thessalonians, and Philemon; cf. Colossians and 2 Thessalonians). The fact that two of the Pastorals are addressed to Timothy testifies that he was widely known in the late first or early second century (the likely date of these epistles) as a close associate of Paul—one worthy to be the recipient of these pastoral manuals.

Paul Ciholas, "Timothy," *MDB* 920; Jane S. Lancaster, "Timothy," *EDB* 1313.

The Jews

Numerous studies have attempted to interpret Luke's view of the Jews in his two-volume narrative. A survey of Luke's use of the term "the Jews" reveals that he uses the term rarely in the Gospel, and then only in the Passion Narrative and with greater frequency as the narrative of Acts develops. While Luke can use the term in a rather neutral manner, simply to describe the descendants of Abraham, he regularly employs the term to denote specifically those descendants of Abraham who oppose the Christian message and its messengers. He employs the term in this manner in the following texts: Acts 9:22, 23; 12:3; 13:45-50; 14:2, 4, 19; 17:13; 18:12, 14; 20:3, 19; 21:11; 23:27; 24:9, 27, 25:2, 7, 8, 9, 10, 15; 26:7, 21; 28:19. The one major exception is 21:20, which refers to thousands of Jews who are believers.

Robert L. Brawley, *Luke–Acts and the Jews: Conflict, Apology, and Conciliation* (Atlanta: Scholars Press, 1987); Jack T. Sanders, *The Jews in Luke–Acts* (Philadelphia: Fortress, 1987); Joseph B. Tyson, ed., *Luke–Acts and the Jewish People: Eight Critical Perspectives* (Minneapolis: Augsburg, 1988); Joseph B. Tyson, *Images of Judaism in Luke–Acts* (Columbia: University of South Carolina Press, 1992).

Luke does not say how this circumcision relates to "the Jews." Most likely, Luke means by "the Jews" non-believing descendants of Abraham. [The Jews] The gospel is not disloyal to Judaism or insensitive to the customs of the Jews, though such customs do not have explicit salvific value in Luke's estimation. This story challenges the claim made by Paul's opponents in Acts 21:21, to the effect that Paul ordered Jews *not* to practice circumcision.

Verses 4-5 summarize the activities of Paul, Silas, and, presumably, Timothy (cf. v. 3), as they "went from town to town" (v. 4). Timothy will fall out of the story, though he may be hidden in the anonymous "they" or "we" of Luke's narrative, until he reappears in 17:14. Luke notes that they "delivered . . . the decisions" reached by the apostles and elders concerning association between Jewish and Gentile Christians (Acts 15).

Luke employs two significant words here. *Paredidosan* ("delivered") is a semi-technical term that is a cognate of the Greek word for "tradition." This verb and its cognates are employed in such important texts as 1 Corinthians 11:2, which speaks of the Lord's Supper, and 15:3, which speaks of the resurrection. The use of this word implies that Luke sees this declaration as carrying some significant weight. The use of *dogmata* (cf. dogma), rendered as "decisions" in the NRSV, also implies that the word Paul and Silas pass along carries weight: "The term *dogma* derives from the verb *dokeō* (see 15:22, 28), and is widely used for official declarations and laws (see Plato, *Laws* 929D)."[12]

What is perhaps most significant is that Paul extends this "dogma" beyond the original recipients. James's letter was addressed to "the believers of Gentile origin in Antioch and Syria and Cilicia" (15:23). Luke is well aware that Derbe and Lystra—and presumably the cities to which Paul traveled when he left Lystra—were beyond the boundaries of Syria and Cilicia (see 14:6). By passing the tradition along to other churches that Paul had earlier established, Paul shows his respect for the Jerusalem decision that encouraged Gentiles to live lives that distinguished them from other Gentiles. Perhaps it is that very concern for such a spirit of unity that accounts for the strengthening of faith and the increase in numbers within the churches (v. 5).

"Come Help Us," 16:6-10

Verse 4 had made reference to "the cities" through which Paul and his companions passed and delivered word of the decision of the Jerusalem Council. The last cities specifically mentioned were Derbe and Lystra (v. 1). A look at the map implies that Paul is moving in a northwesterly direction. Verse 6 indicates that Paul and his companions then moved through the region of Phrygia and Galatia. If Luke means by this Galatian Phrygia,[13] it would imply that Paul is continuing to move in a northwesterly direction, perhaps toward Antioch, which is on the extreme northwestern border of Galatian Phrygia.

The narrator states that Paul is moving in this direction because they had "been forbidden by the Holy Spirit to speak the word in Asia" (v. 6). What is curious about this is that the large Roman province of Asia actually lies *beyond* Galatian Phrygia; that is, Paul would actually have to go through Galatian Phrygia to get to Asia. Some speculate that perhaps Paul was actually intending to move directly westward from Lystra, wanting to enter into the *southern* portion of the Asian province.[14] But if that were the case, then it

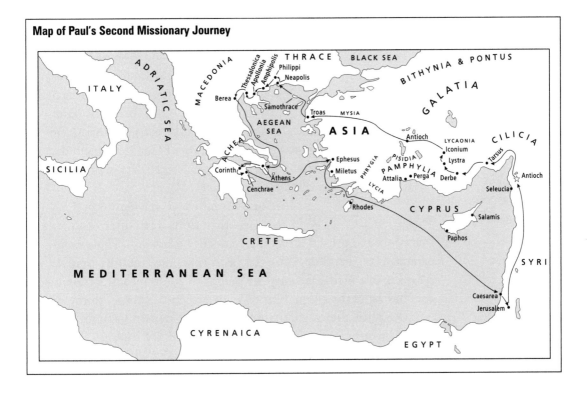

Map of Paul's Second Missionary Journey

appears that Paul would have been abandoning his original mission of visiting churches he had already established, since a direct westward movement from Lystra would have required that he bypass Iconium and Antioch. Verse 7 does not help to solve the geographical riddle, for it states that the missionaries proceeded to a point "opposite Mysia." One *must* pass through Asia to get near Mysia. Perhaps readers should conclude that while Paul actually did go through Asia, the Spirit, nonetheless, prevented him from preaching in this region.

The "Spirit of Jesus" also frustrates Paul's hopes of going north through Mysia to the region of Bithynia. So Paul bypasses Mysia and heads west toward the city of Troas (v. 8), a port city on the extreme western shore of Asia Minor. Even if one is befuddled by the seeming geographical confusion of the narrative,[15] the point seems clear. The providential care of God, offered through the Holy Spirit and the spirit of Jesus, is not allowing Paul and his companions to be distracted—even by preaching the gospel!—from reaching the edge of the subcontinent of Asia Minor.[16] The significance of this march toward Troas is about to become clear both to Paul and the readers.

While in Troas Paul receives the so-called Macedonian vision, as a man from Macedonia appears to Paul urging him to cross the Aegean Sea, enter into Macedonia, and help the people there (v. 9). [Macedonia] The narrator offers no clues as to the identity of the man, but commentators have offered a range of speculations, extending from Alexander the Great, who came from Macedonia, to Luke, the author the narrative.[17] Such speculations do not enrich the point that Paul is being guided by a vision, that is, by the providential direction of God, to expand the preaching of the gospel even farther toward "the ends of the earth" (1:8). [Vision]

Paul and his fellow travelers interpret his vision to mean that they were to go over to Macedonia to preach the gospel. Added, however, to Paul's companions is the narrator himself, as he intrudes now on the narrative, speaking in the first person: "*we* sought to go on into Macedonia, concluding that God had called *us* to preach the gospel to them" (v. 10). With the introduction of the first-person narrator, the reader encounters the first of several so-called We Passages or "we sections" within the narrative of Acts. [We Passages]

Macedonia

Prior to the rise of Rome, Macedonia reached its zenith of power under Alexander the Great (330s BC), who, as the leader of Macedonia, extended his reach as far east as the Persian Empire. Macedonia was unstable for many decades after Alexander's death, coming under Roman rule in 168 BC. The Romans divided Macedonia into four districts, but c. 146 BC reorganized it back into a single province, using this newly reunified province to launch invasions into Greece, which the Romans conquered. Augustus (27 BC–AD 14) made Macedonia a senatorial province, which his successor Tiberius combined in AD 15 with surrounding provinces to make one large province. In AD 44 Claudius again reorganized Macedonia, taking it back to the smaller province of Augustus's time.

Richard S. Ascough, "Macedonia," *EDB* 841–42; Joe R. Baskin, "Macedonia," *MDB* 537–38.

Vision

Employing Joel 2:28, Peter in Acts 2:17 listed seeing visions as one manifestation of the return of the Spirit of prophecy. Visions were an important medium of divine communication with Old Testament prophets (see, e.g., Isa 6; Jer 1:11-12, 13-19; 4:23-26; Ezek 1:4-14, 40-48; Amos 7:1-3, 4-9; 8:1-3; Zech 1:7–2:5; 2:1-5; 3:1-10), a trait that ancient Israelite religion shared with its larger environment. The fact that this vision is said to have appeared to Paul in the night implies that it came in the context of a dream—another common phenomenon in the Jewish tradition (see Dan 4:5, 9-10; 8:18, 27; *1 Enoch* 14; *T. Levi* 2:5-5:7; *2 Baruch* 52:7-53:12; *2 Enoch* 69:5-6). Appropriately, with the return of the Spirit of prophecy, visions play an important role in the narrative of Acts (9:10, 12; 10:3, 17, 19; 11:5; 18:9; 26:19).

Jenny Manasco Lowery, "Vision," *EDB* 1360.

Paul in Philippi, 16:11-40

Paul's Philippian ministry and adventures unfold in three scenes: Lydia and the slave girl (16.11-18), the imprisonment and release of Paul and Silas, in the context of which is the story of the Philippian jailor (16:19-34), and the departure of Paul from Philippi (16:35-40).

Lydia and the Slave Girl, vv. 11-18

Paul and his companions set a straight course to Samothrace (v. 11). Recollection of v. 10, which states that "we immediately tried to cross over to Macedonia," leaves the impression that the departure to Samothrace took place very soon after Paul received the vision.

Samothrace is an island in the Aegean Sea about halfway between Troas, the port of departure, and Neapolis, the port city of Macedonia, Paul's destination. The primary landmark of Samothrace is Mount Fengari, which towers 5,577 feet above sea level. With a good wind, the time required to reach Samothrace from Troas would be one day.[18] Hence, the group could easily reach Neapolis the following day.

The group of missionaries would then have to move inland about ten miles along the *Via Egnatia* to reach Philippi. [Philippi] The narrative's description of Philippi as "a leading city of the district of Macedonia" has confused both commentators and ancient copyists alike. Less confusing is the narrator's notation that Philippi was a Roman colony. ["A Leading City of the District of Macedonia"]

After spending a few days in the city, Paul and his companions journey on the Sabbath outside the city to a river, supposing that

We Passages

One finds within Acts a number of passages written in the first person plural, the so-called We Passages (see Acts 16:10-17; 20:5-15; 21:1-18; 27:1–28:16). The most obvious way to read these passages is to conclude that the author of Luke–Acts was actually present and an eyewitness to the events narrated in the first person, whether that author be identified with Luke or not. Many scholars read these passages this way (e.g., Witherington, 480–86). S. E. Porter surveys other ways that scholars understand these passages. (1) Some argue that the We Passages serve as a literary device to give the narrative a feel of historical veracity or literary vividness (e.g., Haenchen); (2) Robbins contends that first person narration was a stock literary convention employed by ancient authors to narrate sea voyages; (3) Some, including Porter, argue that the author employed a source penned by an eyewitness, though the author of this source was not the author of Luke–Acts.

Ben Witherington III, *The Acts of the Apostles: A Socio-Rhetorical Commentary* (Grand Rapids MI: Eerdmans, 1998); S. E. Porter, "The 'We' Passages," *The Book of Acts in Its First Century Setting*, ed. B. W. Winter, 6 vols. (Grand Rapids MI: Eerdmans, 1993–97), 2.545–74.

Philippi

Originally named Krenides, the city was renamed Philippi by Philip II, father of Alexander the Great, c. 358 BC. The city was brought under Roman rule in 168 BC. Inscriptions reveal a very religiously pluralistic city. In 42 BC, Philippi was the location of a key battle in which the forces of Antony and Octavian (Augustus) defeated the Republican forces. At that time, Octavian made the city a Roman colony. In 31 BC, when Octavian defeated Antony,

Octavian renamed the colony *Colonia Julia Augusta Victrix Philippensis*, adding *Augusta* to its name. The city became a popular place for Roman veterans to retire. As a Roman colony, Philippi had the right of autonomous government, did not have to pay tribute to Rome, and its citizens had the right of private ownership of property.

Richard A. Spencer, "Philippi," *EDB* 1048–49; T. C. Smith, "Philippi," *MDB* 683–84.

"A Leading City of the District of Macedonia"

AΩ The NRSV marginal note offers an alternative translation, based on the testimony of other Greek manuscripts: "a city of the first district of Macedonia." Macedonia was divided into four smaller districts and Philippi was located in the eastern district, which one might construe as "the first district." The Greek word *prōtē* can also have a titular sense, as in "chief" or "head" city, leading the Western textual tradition to understand the text to say "the capital city." However, Thessalonica was the capital of this Roman province.

Joseph A. Fitzmyer, *The Acts of the Apostles* (AB 31; New York: Doubleday, 1998), 584; F. J. Foakes Jackson and Kirsopp Lake, *The Beginnings of Christianity: The Acts of the Apostles*, 5 vols. (Grand Rapids MI: Baker, 1979), 4.187–89.

they would find there a place of prayer. Luke does not identify the river, but the most prevalent nearby river was known either as Gangites or Angites, located about one-and-a-half miles from the city. However, this distance violates the legal limitations for a Sabbath day's journey, which was 2,000 cubits, or a little more than one-half mile. Fitzmyer suggests, therefore, that "the river" may actually have been a smaller creek, Crenides, located closer to the city.[19]

Paul was looking for "a place of prayer." Interpreters debate whether this was an actual synagogue or an informal gathering place for Jews and Jewish sympathizers to pray.[20] It is true that Jewish synagogues could also be called "places of prayer."[21] It seems curious, however, that had Paul and his companions spent several days in the city they would not have been able to discern whether an actual synagogue was in or near the city. Luke clearly leaves the impression that on the Sabbath, Paul and his fellow travelers went *searching* for a place of prayer, *supposing* (*nomizō* means "think," "believe," or "consider")[22] that they would find such a place along the banks. The narrative, at least following the reading of the NRSV (see n 22), offers no clue as to why Paul supposed he would find a place of prayer alongside the river or creek. Possibly, water would be necessary to provide lustrations for ritual cleansing that would accompany prayer and study. If so, that

Philippi

Philippi. (Credit: Todd Bolen, "Philippi excavations from north," [cited 20 September 2007]. Online: http://www.bibleplaces.com.)

might explain why it was necessary for this place of prayer to be located *outside* the city—the Jews and devout Gentiles needed to be near a ready supply of water. Synagogues, to be sure, did have baths (*mikveh*) for ritual cleansing, but whether such would have been necessary for an informal gathering place is not known. The narrator simply leaves many gaps that readers are compelled to "fill in."

Despite these gaps, it is clear that Paul and his companions are seeking a group of people similar to the kind to whom Paul had customarily preached, Jews or those sympathetic with the Jewish tradition. Having found such a group, Paul and his fellow evangelists sit down, in customary Jewish fashion, and speak to the women who had gathered by the river (v. 13b). The focus on women need not imply that only women were present, but it does set the stage for role Lydia will play.

The narrative concerning the conversion of Lydia and her household (vv. 14-15) is quite laconic. What did Paul say to her? Readers likely will fill the gap by recalling earlier sermons that Paul had preached. Who is included among "her household" who were baptized? Slaves? Children? Readers concerned over the issue of infant baptism will insert or not insert small children into the household, depending on their own views concerning the practice. [Baptism of Households] The narrative implies that Paul and his friends accepted Lydia's invitation to stay at her house ("she prevailed upon us"), but does not report what took place there.

The presence of such gaps actually allows the *stated* features of the narrative to stand out more boldly. The narrator specifically

---

Baptism of Households

Acts 16:31-33 (cf. 16:14–15) speaks of whole households being baptized. Christians who view baptism as a personal and individual response of faith to the gospel might be troubled by statements that seem to indicate that the whole household can be saved based solely on the response of the head of that household (cf. 16:14b–15a, 31). To be sure, v. 32 makes clear that Paul and Silas spoke the word of the Lord to all who were in the jailer's house, allowing for the conclusion that baptism only followed personal confession.

While one likely can assume that confession of some sort preceded baptism, modern readers still must not assume that individualistic notions of personality and identity prevailed in the ancient world. Ancients had a more collectivist understanding of personality and identity. That is, persons in antiquity tended to find their identity and personality in the context of the larger significant groups in which persons were embedded. The most significant such group would be the kinship group, and especially the immediate household of which one was a part. Members of the household would likely take their "cues" even of *voluntary* religious identification from the head of the household, which was usually male (cf. 16:31–33), but could also be female (cf. 16:14–15). Texts within the gospel tradition do indicate, however, that the gospel message could divide families (see Matt 10:34-39 || Luke 12:51-53; 14:26; Matt 19:29 || Mark 10:29; cf. Matt 12:46-50 || Mark 3:31-35 || Luke 8:19-21).

Bruce J. Malina, *The New Testament World: Insights from Cultural Anthropology*, 3rd ed. (Louisville KY: Westminster/John Knox Press, 2001), chs. 2 and 5.

notes that Lydia is a dealer in purple cloth, a worshiper of God, and one who offers her home to Paul and his companions.

The city of Lydia's origin, Thyatira, was located in the region that shared Lydia's name. It was known for the production of wool and purple dyes.[23] Revelation addresses a letter to the church there (cf. Rev 2:18-29), though it makes no mention of the city's trade in textiles or dyes. Purple was associated with wealth and prestige, most likely because the production of this dark, colorfast dye required massive amounts of marine snails, from which the dye was produced.[24] The narrator's notation of Lydia's profession, along with her having a house large enough to accommodate Paul and those traveling with him, implies that she moved in circles of influence.

The note that Lydia was "a worshiper of God" likely indicates that she is non-Jewish (see [God-fearer]). Paul and Peter have encountered non-Jews before. Typically, when "God-fearers" hear the gospel their response is positive (e.g., Cornelius [Acts 10–11] and Paul's preaching at Antioch of Pisidia [Acts 13]). Gentiles who have no grounding in the Jewish tradition are often prone to misunderstanding, even if Luke presents some sympathetically (recall Lystra [Acts 14:8-20]). Thus, the narrative raises the expectation that Lydia, a worshiper of God, will respond positively to Paul's preaching, which she does. Yet the story of the Philippian jailer will make clear that *any* Gentile, regardless of prior understanding, can receive the benefits of the gospel.

Luke takes care to note that Lydia, following her baptism, was insistent that Paul and the others stay with her in her home. Such an invitation serves to legitimate her faithful response to Paul's words: "If you have judged me to be faithful to the Lord, come and stay at my home" (v. 15). Her insistent invitation indicates that faithful response to the gospel includes the sharing of responsibility to care for fellow believers.

Verse 16 probably represents a new scene, perhaps a week later on the following Sabbath as Paul and his companions are making their way again to the place of prayer. Luke Johnson has argued that v. 16 actually refers to the same trek spoken of in v. 13, with vv. 14-15 serving as a forward-looking narrative interlude.[25] This is certainly possible, but may offer a needlessly complex element to the more natural flow of the narrative. Regardless of how a reader imagines the sequence, vv. 16-18 serve to introduce vv. 19-24 and need to be placed here to allow the narrative to flow smoothly into the story of Paul's conflict with the soothsayer's owners.

The phrase that the NRSV translates as "a spirit of divination" (v. 16) is literally *a python spirit* (*pneuma pythōna*). In Greek mythology a python, or serpent, guarded the Delphi oracle and, hence, was associated with divination.[26] The narrator describes her activity with the Greek participle *manteuomenē*, which the NRSV renders as "fortune telling." *Manteuomenē* was a technical term in the Hellenistic world to denote ecstatic utterance[27] (compare the English word *mantic*). The woman's speech and behavior would have impressed one as curiously extraordinary.

In a narrative influenced by the Jewish and biblical tradition, *python spirit* could also imply the demonic/satanic character of the spirit. The serpent was a common symbol for Satan in the biblical and Jewish traditions (see esp. Rev 12:9, 14, 15; 20:2).[28] Luke clearly has a negative view of the practice. His observation that the slave-girl brought profit to her owners links the practice with the common charge in antiquity that divination and similar practices were the work of those who preyed on the naïvely credulous. [Charlatans] A charge of exploitation is certainly implied in the narrator's words.

The slave-girl's (or spirit's) constant mantra acknowledging that Paul and the men with him were servants of the Most High God and proclaimers of salvation (v. 17) is ambiguous and, perhaps, ironic. Readers know that the girl's words are true—Paul is a servant of God and does proclaim the way of salvation. Paul's silencing of the spirit "in the name of Jesus Christ" (v. 18) is quite reminiscent of Jesus' own silencing and casting out of demons in Luke's Gospel. [Exorcism] There, as here, the, voices of the possessed acknowledge the God whom the exorcist serves (cf. Luke 4:31-37). On the most obvious level, the story shows Paul to be, in fact, a servant of God who acts in a manner that emulates the ultimate servant of God, Jesus.

Witherington argues that Paul silences the girl because her words, without an appropriate Jewish/Christian context of interpretation, would actually be misleading, proffering a general message of salvation emanating from some generic god: "[Paul] was troubled about the content of her proclamation."[29]

Charlatans

"Certainly it is foolish and childish in the extreme to imagine that the god himself after the manner of ventriloquists enters into the bodies of his prophets and prompts their utterances, employing their mouths and voices as instruments" (Plutarch *Defect. Orac.* 414e; cited from Conzelmann, 131).

Hans Conzelmann, *Acts of the Apostles* (Philadelphia: Fortress, 1987).

Exorcism

Exorcism was widely practiced in the ancient world, in which it was commonly believed that a malevolent spirit could possess persons, either permanently or temporarily. The exorcist would generally call upon a benevolent supernatural power, perceived to be of greater strength than the evil spirit, to subdue or "cast out" the oppressive spirit (Jesus, for example, claimed to cast out demons by the power of the "spirit of God" or "finger of God" [see Matt 12:28 and Luke 11:20, respectively]). Jesus' followers would call on the power of the name of Jesus (cf. Acts 16:18) to cast out the malevolent spirits.

Charles Yeboah, "Exorcism," *EBD* 444.

The issue is not so much, however, that of challenging an ambiguous proclamation, as though Luke were concerned like some modern systematic theologian, to make sure that each phrase was appropriately nuanced. The woman's proclamation, to be sure, finds its source in the dark recesses of the cosmos—she speaks for the demonic underworld. Hence, Paul has every reason to be annoyed or troubled. But the *truth* of her proclamation, even if known only by the reader (the narrator's main concern!), affirms that the dark underside of the cosmos recognizes the power that confronts it. And Paul's silencing of the spirit, once it has duly recognized the power before it, *demonstrates* for readers and story characters alike the awesome power of this "Most High God." The power of Jesus Christ not only liberates a slave-girl from exploitative owners, but also, and more importantly, shows itself able to liberate, or *save*, people from the very forces of the cosmos that are forced to tremble before the name of the author of genuine liberation—Jesus the Messiah. The silencing of the spirit demonstrates that Paul, indeed, does offer *salvation*—liberation—from the chains that bind creation.[30]

"What Must I Do to Be Saved?" vv. 19-34

The story of Paul's exorcism of the "python spirit" immediately transits to the owners' reaction. The slave-girl was, to them, only an economic object of gain. They have lost their means to exploit the credulous masses. Their source of income now gone, they react with vengeance, seizing Paul and Silas and dragging them into the *agora*, the main public square of the city, which served as the center of public life. Appropriately, city officials are there. Excavations have uncovered this area, complete with a raised podium that would have served as the place where cases were heard.[31] The "rulers" of v. 19 are very probably the same as the "magistrates" of v. 20, local officials responsible to the larger power structures of the Roman Empire for maintaining order within their spheres of responsibility.

The angry slave owners do not offer charges as trivial as: "These men have taken away our means of exploitative gain." Rather, they appeal to the baser instincts of the officials: xenophobia, and particularly to the fact that Paul and Silas are Jews (v. 19). [Anti-Jewish Sentiment] The slave owners also appeal to loyalty to the state ("they advocate customs that it is not lawful for us Romans to practice," v. 20). Luke now pulls the crowd onto the stage. Mob scenes were typical in popular narratives that told of the travels and adventures of the story's heroes (see [Greek Novels]).[32]

The Agora of Philippi
According to Acts 16:19, Paul and Silas were brought before Philippian rulers at the "marketplace" (NRSV). The "agora" served as something of the town square where business such as this would be conducted.

(Credit: Linda Kane, image courtesy of www.holylandphotos.org)

As a result of charges and the emergent mob mentality, Paul and Silas are handed over for a beating (v. 22). The verb used for "beating" (*rhabdizein*) is a cognate of the noun employed later in the story in vv. 35 and 38 (*rhabdouchoi*). *Rhabdouchoi* were also city officials whose job it was to enforce the law, even with physical beatings (cf. 1 Thess 2:2; 2 Cor 11:25). This kind of swift justice was quite legal when applied against aliens, that is, non-Roman citizens. The city officials clearly assume these Jewish preachers to be such.

For ancient Christian readers of Acts, the charge of anti-Roman activity, leveled against Paul and Silas within the context of a Roman colony, would be quite relevant. Do Christians teach against Roman law? When one is finished with the story, it will be apparent that Romans, particularly at the local level, are often confused about Christians. And, as the physical torture and imprisonment of Paul and Silas show, such confusion offers a real threat to the followers of Jesus. But, in the end, Romans recognize that the gospel's message is not illegal, which is not to say that it's not subversive!

The charge against Paul and Silas, combined with a scene of mob reaction, is reminiscent of Jesus' trial. Like Jesus (Luke 23:2-5), political charges were made against Paul. And, like Jesus (Luke 23:18-24), the crowds are there, as well. Such allusions within the narrative serve at least two purposes. First, they show how the actions of the followers of Jesus emulate and imitate Jesus. The

Anti-Jewish Sentiment

While one finds "Jewish sympathizers" in the Hellenistic world, persons to whom Acts refers as "God-fearers" (see [God-fearer]), there was also much anti-Jewish sentiment in this world. Charges included attacks on Jewish xenophobia and ethnic exclusivism, Jewish denigration of that which most people held to be sacred, and a general spirit of sedition and rebellion against the state and society.

Charles Talbert, *Reading Acts: A Literary and Theological Commentary of the Acts of the Apostles* (New York: Crossroad, 1997), 152. Talbert offers illustrative quotations from ancient commentators on Judaism.

Master and the Master's followers walk the same path along "the Way." Second, the echoes of Jesus' passion can serve to inform readers that, even while Roman officials may recognize that Christianity is no real legal threat (this is the conclusion that, eventually, the officials of Philippi reach), this does not ensure adequate protection; Roman officials are easily swayed by mobs and other power brokers.

The legal troubles of Paul and Silas are like those of Jesus, but not identical. They are not executed after being beaten; they are imprisoned, apparently awaiting a continuation of the investigation concerning the charges leveled against them. Readers can only surmise this, as the narrator does not report what the plans of the officials were. The jailer responsible for their incarceration places them into the "inner prison," shackled in wooden stocks. Philippi had a complex prison structure, complete with a number of cells or chambers that allowed for maximum security, if such was deemed necessary.[33] Conditions of these prisons were merciless and horrendous. [Prison Conditions]

Time passes to the middle of the night when Paul and Silas are "praying and singing hymns to God" (v. 25). Luke offers just enough information to set a scene that depicts God's people, though wrongly imprisoned, offering a prayer to God, again, not unlike Jesus, who prayed from the cross (Luke 23:34, 46). Whether or not Paul and Silas were explicitly praying for deliverance is not said, but deliverance is what God offers. God delivers Paul and Silas and, ultimately, the jailer and his household. The story of deliverance begins with an earthquake.

Prison Conditions

Based on descriptions of ancient prisons found in the literature of antiquity, Charles Talbert offers a vivid description that allows one to imagine the setting:

Prison was the most severe form of custody. Jailers were notorious for their cruelty. . . . The inner prison was the worst possible site. . . . Many would be confined in a small area; the air would be bad; the darkness would be profound; the stench would be almost unbearable.

Charles Talbert, *Reading Acts: A Literary and Theological Commentary of the Acts of the Apostles* (New York: Crossroad, 1997), 154.

Acts has already offered other stories of miraculous escapes from prison (5:19-20; 12:6-11). The motif of the earthquake in this scene is appropriate, for the region of Philippi was known for such seismic activity. Furthermore, ancient literature commonly employed earthquakes to denote the presence of divine power. Though readers are not likely to view this earthquake as a mere coincidence, the story offers descriptions of the effects of the earthquake that render a somewhat "naturalistic" explanation: the earthquake shook things up so badly that the doors flung open and the prisoners' fetters shook loose.

Not surprisingly, an earthquake violent enough to shake open cell doors and loosen shackles awakened the hapless guard (v. 27). His response appears a bit melodramatic. It is curious that he is so quick to fall on his sword without taking a look to see if the prisoners had escaped.[34] Yet, within the logic of the Lukan narrative, the action makes sense, for alert readers would recall that when Peter escaped from a Jerusalem prison, the fate of the guards was execution (12:19). This echo allows readers to discern a similarity between Peter and Paul that offers subtle testimony to the unity of the witness of these two great characters in the narrative of Acts.

Yet this story takes a different turn from that of Peter, for Paul somehow knows what the guard is contemplating, and his immediate response is to try to dissuade him from such self-destruction (v. 28). Only now does the guard investigate, getting torches and moving into the bowels of the prison, directly to the cell of Paul and Silas (v. 29). The narrative does not say how he knew that it was Paul who called to him, but the narrative requires the jailer to find his way to Paul so that this story of the *guard's* deliverance can unfold.

There is perhaps some irony in the guard's question of v. 30: "Men, what must I do to be saved?" Salvation in the ancient world was not always a religiously loaded term;[35] the guard may have meant nothing more than, "What can I do to get out of this mess I think I'm in?" Readers inclined to offer psychological explanations can say that the jailer may have assumed a connection between the earthquake and the hymns and prayers, which, as a pagan, he might have heard as magical incantations. [Earthquakes and Theophanies] Filled with awe and fear, he is drawn to those whom he knew had been offering these "incantations" and seeks their help to deliver him from the situation that perhaps fate had handed him.[36] But Paul hears the *full* implication of the jailer's plea. Readers should also hear such a fuller meaning, for the guard's question echoes the question asked by Peter's hearers after his Pentecost sermon: "What shall we do?" (2:37).

Paul offers a succinct response: believe in Jesus for salvation (v. 31). The response is too succinct, candidly, to have made much sense to a pagan jailer, but readers can easily fill in the gaps, having heard many fuller explanations of the good news throughout the narrative. Perhaps readers should assume that v. 31 offers a very concise summary of a fuller explication of the

Earthquakes and Theophanies

In the biblical and larger Hellenistic tradition, the shaking of the earth commonly denoted the divine presence (see Isa 29:6; Matt 27:59; 28:2). In apocalyptic material, such quaking regularly denoted divine judgment (see Rev 6:12; 8:5; 11:3, 19; 16:18; 2 Esd 3:19). An interesting, though satiric example from Hellenistic literature comes from Lucian's *Lover of Lies*:

After a short time there came an earthquake and with it a noise as of thunder, and then I saw a terrible woman coming toward me, quite half a furlong in height. She had a torch in her left hand and a sword in her right, ten yards long; below, she had snake-feet, and above she resembled the Gorgon; . . . moreover, instead of hair she had the snakes falling down in ringlets, twining about her neck, and some of them coiled upon her shoulders. (ch. 22) gospel message (though a crumbling prison would not allow too much time for sermonizing!).

Though the narrative logic is a bit convoluted, the point of vv. 32-34 is clear enough. The scene quickly moves to the guard's home, and readers can easily infer that once the guard led Paul and Silas to his home they offered a fuller explication of the good news. As a result, the guard and his entire household were baptized. The jailer also took care to wash the wounds that had been the result of their beating earlier that day. A bit later, he fed Paul and Silas in his home, while he and his family rejoiced in their newly found salvation in God.

Yet the narrative leaves readers having to fill in some gaps. There is no narration of how Paul, Silas, and the jailer made their way to the guard's house. One would imagine that an earthquake of such magnitude would draw attention from other officials and that the absence of some prisoners and their guard would draw some response. No mention is made in the accepted text of Acts as to what the jailer did to ensure that other prisoners would not escape. However, the so-called Western text of Acts adds to v. 30 that before the guard brought Paul and Silas out of the prison, he secured the other prisoners. Haenchen exploits such narrative gaps to argue that the story is implausible historically.[37] Others will fill in the gaps in a manner that can preserve the historical basis of the story.[38] Still others will bypass historical questions and focus attention on the point of the *narrative*, making clear that its edifying style is intended to inspire readers with the realization that the gospel had been proclaimed and accepted by a representative of the Roman world, in a Roman colony, no less.[39]

"Do They Now Cast Us Out Secretly?" vv. 35-40

Verse 35 begins with a major gap, for there is no narration of the obvious return of Paul and Silas to the prison sometime during the night. As the scene opens, the narrative simply assumes that they are back in place. Further, v. 35 offers no explanation as to why the magistrates now have sent the police (*rhabdouchoi*—the "rod people)" to release these prisoners. Again, the Western text attempts to fill this gap by amending and adding to the more accepted text of Acts: "And when it was day the magistrates assembled together in the agora, and when they remembered the earthquake that had taken place they were afraid, and sent the police to say, 'Let those men go whom you received yesterday.'"[40] This modification of the text not only offers a rationale for the decision to let Paul and Silas go, but also gives more coherence to the narrative by allowing other characters in the story to notice a major event like an earthquake! The accepted text, however, offers no such explanation. Still, the story does make the point that, in the end, local Roman officials recognize that Christians and their message pose no legal threat to Rome.

The story line shifts the focus to Paul and Silas, who refuse the magistrates' offer simply to slip away peacefully and quietly. For the first time, both readers and characters in the story learn that Paul and Silas are Roman citizens (v. 37). As such, they had been publicly shamed in a manner that was illegal; the beating of Roman citizens without prior "due process" was forbidden. [Roman Citizens] That explains the magistrates' fear in v. 38. The magistrates do the only thing they can do when they have so violated the honor of Roman citizen. They "apologize" (*parakaleō*) or, more literally, attempt to *entreat, implore,* or *conciliate* Paul and Silas. In other words, they *groveled.* Their honor duly restored, the two leave the prison, apparently healed enough from the previous day's beating to make an exit. However, before leaving town, they visit Lydia and the newly established community of faith, offering them a final exhortation (v. 40; cf. 14:22; 15:41; 16:4).

CONNECTIONS

Two themes come forth in this chapter's text. The first has to do with the combination, found so often in Acts, of the guidance of God and human participation in the divine drama.

As we find ourselves in our present moment of life, it is sometimes useful to reflect on how we got where we are; to imagine how different things might be had a certain event not happened just as it did a long time ago; had we not taken a certain class in college or met a certain person at a social gathering, sports event, or some other place. Where would our lives be had we not been at *that* place, at *that* time? And, equally important, where would our lives be had we not made certain decisions at such crucial moments? Had we

Roman Citizens

Ancient authorities document that the beating of Roman citizens without due cause was forbidden (see Livy, *Historia* 10.9.4; Appian, *Bellum Civile* 2.26 sec. 98; Cicero, *Against Verres* 2.5.66, which reads: "To bind a Roman citizen is a crime, to flog him an abomination, to slay him almost an act of parricide" [Fitzmyer, 589, and Johnson, 301–302]).

Paul writes that he suffered the penalty of being beaten with rods three times (2 Cor 11:25). One wonders why he would have suffered such abuse, forbidden as it was by Roman law, if he had been a Roman citizen. Perhaps Paul was not, in fact, such a citizen, despite the testimony of Acts. Yet even very critical readers of Acts, such as Gerd Lüdemann, affirm that, "in all probability Paul was a Roman citizen" (241).

If so, one is left to account for Paul's being beaten at least three times. Several responses are possible: (1) Violations of official Roman policy did regularly occur (Lüdemann, 240); (2) Paul did not want "the claims of the gospel to rest on his claims to Roman citizenship" (Witherington, 501), for such might have implied to Roman authorities that loyalty to Rome superceded loyalty to the gospel, both for Paul and for his new converts; (3) "Paul could have chosen to use his Roman citizenship in an opportunistic way when it furthered his Christian purposes and not merely when it was personally advantageous" (Witherington, 501).

Joseph A. Fitzmyer, *The Acts of the Apostles* (AB 31; New York: Doubleday, 1998); Luke Timothy Johnson, *The Acts of the Apostles* (SacPag 5; Collegeville MN: Liturgical Press, 1992); Gerd Lüdemann, *Early Christianity according to the Traditions in Acts: A Commentary* (Minneapolis: Fortress, 1989); Ben Witherington III, *The Acts of the Apostles: A Socio-Rhetorical Commentary* (Grand Rapids MI: Eerdmans, 1998).

not taken a chance and changed our major course of study that fourth semester of college. Or had we not followed this particular professional opportunity, as opposed to some other option.

It is sometimes enlightening, and perhaps humbling, to contrast our current position in life with what we had planned for our lives. As the joke goes, "Want to make God laugh? Tell him your plans." How different reality, as opposed to best-laid plans and certain dreams, so often turns out to be.

It is also true that we often find ourselves on what appears to be a meaningless treadmill, plodding along and seemingly going nowhere. Life seems to be handing us one disappointment after the other. Where is God in all of this? Is life really a stringing together of one meaningless event after the other, without direction or purpose?

Acts 16:6-11 addresses with brevity, as well as clarity, these interesting and curious features of life. Paul and Silas operated according to the best-laid plans and with the best of intentions. It was their intention to visit churches that Paul had previously founded to check their progress as budding congregations of faith. Such work was successful in that the narrator declares that "the churches were strengthened in the faith and increased in numbers daily" (16:5).

It then appears that Paul and Silas attempted to move in directions that proved less fruitful. While the geographical movement of the two covers only two verses (16:6-7), a look at the map reveals that these men covered hundreds of very frustrating miles. The Spirit forbade them the opportunity to preach the word in Asia. They attempted to enter into Bithynia, but the spirit of Jesus did not allow that either. Then, when they had to bypass Mysia only to find themselves in Troas, things become a bit clearer. For here, in Troas, they were now in the *right* place to receive the call to move further westward.

The narrative makes clear that the seemingly hapless and frustrated movements of Paul and Silas were not without purpose. What appeared as meaningless misdirection was purposeful direction, after all. The Spirit was prodding Paul and party to an appropriate place so that the gospel could actually expand its boundaries even more.

Yet, while the Spirit is a main actor in moving the characters from place to place, the responses of Paul and Silas to such prodding play an equally important, even if understated, role. Earlier in the story, we were reminded that on the so-called first missionary journey, John Mark had chosen to return to Jerusalem (15:38). Abandonment of the hard work of discipleship is always an option—it was an option for John Mark and, presumably, could have been an option for Paul and Silas. Weeks of seemingly pointless movement across Asia Minor could easily have prompted either of these men to desert the cause and return to the safety of Antioch. Was not their original intention to strengthen already established churches successful? And yet they pressed on. Such willful human participation in the divine drama played an equally important role in the advancement of the gospel.

As we reflect on the complex tapestry that makes up our own lives, we can likely see an intricate intertwining of personal choices and things "bigger than we are," things that are beyond our control. Whether we understand such "things bigger than we are" as a random collection of circumstances or the subtle prodding of a benevolent God is also regularly our decision.

The second theme that finds clear expression has to do with the fellowship of the believers. Both characters whom Paul introduces to the way of discipleship offered Paul and Silas their homes. Lydia prevailed upon Paul and Silas to come to her home and stay with her. One can assume that such hospitality in her home would include the sharing of meals (16:15). The text explicitly states that the jailer offered food to Paul and Silas.

Christian fellowship, in the form of hospitality that includes opening up one's home and sharing one's table, comes to the fore. To be sure, such "Christian hospitality" was crucially needed, given that lodging while on the road promised only merciless conditions. [Inns] Friends and family, including the kind of fictive-kin that is formed by fellowship in Christ, would recognize the obligation of providing hospitality for travelers who were fellow pilgrims on the way.

But there is more happening than the meeting of the pragmatic needs of hospitality. The early Christian practice of hospitality, including "the breaking of bread" (cf. Acts 2:42, 46; 20:7, 11; 27:35; cf. Acts 11:3), offers a continuation of the pattern of table fellowship initiated by Jesus. Luke is aware of Jesus' pattern of eating with all sorts of folk, good and bad (see Luke 5:30; 7:34, 36, 37; 14:1; 15:2).

John Dominic Crossan offers a thoughtful understanding of Jesus' pattern of eating and his teaching on the subject. Crossan, borrowing from cultural anthropology, refers to this pattern as "open commensality." Crossan summarizes anthropological studies that argue that patterns

Inns

 Everett Ferguson offers a vivid description of the condition of ancient inns:

The wine was often adulterated, . . . sleeping quarters were filthy and insect and rodent infested, innkeepers were extortionate, thieves were in wait, government spies were listening, and many were nothing more than brothels. The literary complaints are supplemented by the graffiti from taverns in Pompeii (kissing, gambling, and fighting).

Everett Ferguson, *Backgrounds of Early Christianity*, 3rd ed. (Grand Rapids MI: Eerdmans, 2003), 89.

of table fellowship mirror larger social patterns of association.[41] For example, a CEO might have a large cocktail party, including heavy hors d'oeuvres, at the office for all employees, a lunch in a restaurant for middle managers, and a private dinner party in his home for his board of vice presidents. Each kind of food fellowship reflects appropriate etiquette and social boundaries within our culture: the closer various workers are to the status of the CEO, the more intimate the meal setting.

Crossan argues that Jesus practiced and encouraged open table fellowship (open commensality) in a deliberate attempt to demonstrate that within the sphere of the reign of God, the boundaries and barriers that humans establish to distinguish and separate people are broken down: "Then people will come from east and west, from north and south, and will eat in the kingdom of God" (Luke 13:29). Table fellowship, then as now, offered a very specific way to testify to how genuinely open one was to all different types of people. [Open Commensality]

The narrative of Acts offers concrete illustrations of the attempts of Jesus' followers to put into practice Jesus' call to open table fellowship. Peter went to the home of Cornelius and there led the centurion and his household to faith. We are told at the end of the narrative that Peter and his Christian Jewish companions remained in Cornelius's household for some days (10:48). Upon his return to Jerusalem, fellow Christian Jews chastised Peter for eating with uncircumcised men (11:3). The violation of the clear boundaries between Jew and Gentile were well established in biblical and postbiblical Jewish tradition. The issue was not simply eating, but what such sharing of table fellowship represented: the erasure of clear lines that demarcated "insiders" from "outsiders" in the sphere of God's people. Such boundaries are shattered again in Philippi, as Paul and Silas stayed in the home of Lydia and sat at the table of the Philippian jailer.

We have all noticed within our congregations, where all are "officially" welcome, as well as in our own patterns of social behavior, that we continue to erect barriers to divide people. Those with whom we will share "the Lord's table" during Communion or with whom we will associate at a church social, we do not include in our

Open Commensality

Peter Farb and George Armelagos describe the importance of commensality in their study on the anthropology of eating:

In all societies, both simple and complex, eating is the primary way of initiating and maintaining human relationships. . . . Once the anthropologist finds out where and with whom food is eaten, just about everything else can be inferred about the relations among the society's members. . . . To know what, where, how, when, and with whom people eat is to know the character of their society.

Quoted in John Dominic Crossan, *Jesus: A Revolutionary Biography* (New York: HarperSanFrancisco, 1994), 68.

after-church lunch bunch or invite to be our guests in our homes (unless we are sponsoring the Sunday school social!). Jesus' call to open commensality and the practice of early congregations to live obediently to such a call serves to remind the church that we still fall short of the demands of the kingdom—often in ways that we might not even conceive.

NOTES

[1] So, e.g., Ernst Haenchen, *The Acts of the Apostles: A Commentary* (Philadelphia: Westminster, 1971), 473, and Ben Witherington III, *The Acts of the Apostles: A Socio-Rhetorical Commentary* (Grand Rapids MI: Eerdmans, 1998), 471.

[2] See, e.g., John B. Polhill, *Acts* (NAC 26; Nashville: Broadman, 1992), 341.

[3] Luke Timothy Johnson, *The Acts of the Apostles* (SacPag 5; Collegeville MN: Liturgical Press, 1992), 288.

[4] E.g., Joseph A. Fitzmyer, *The Acts of the Apostles* (AB 31; New York: Doubleday, 1998), 570 and Polhill, *Acts*, 341.

[5] The Greek participle, which the NRSV translates as "commending," can apply only to Paul. It cannot apply to Paul and Barnabas.

[6] E.g., Polhill, *Acts*, 342; Witherington, *Acts*, 474n14.

[7] See Fitzmyer, Acts, 574–75 for a survey. For a modern interpreter see Gerd Lüdemann, *Early Christianity according to the Traditions in Acts: A Commentary* (Minneapolis: Fortress, 1989), 173.

[8] Lüdemann, ibid., 173, claims that the circumcision of Timothy does not contradict Acts 15, but only shows the limit of the scope of Acts 15, which is concerned with relations between Jewish and Gentile Christians, whereas the circumcision of Timothy is concerned with a mission to Jews. But it seems odd that Luke would remind readers in v. 4 of the Acts 15 decree if he assumed it had such a limited scope in v. 3.

[9] Johnson, *Acts*, 284.

[10] F. J. Foakes Jackson and Kirsopp Lake, *The Beginnings of Christianity: The Acts of the Apostles*, 5 vols. (Grand Rapids MI: Baker, 1979) 4.184; Hans Conzelmann, *Acts of the Apostles* (Hermeneia; Philadelphia: Fortress, 1987), 125; See Johnson, *Acts*, 283–84; Fitzmyer, *Acts*, 575.

[11] Johnson, *Acts*, 284.

[12] Ibid., 284.

[13] Witherington, *Acts*, 477; Conzelmann, *Acts*, 126.

[14] Polhill, *Acts*, 344.

[15] "Luke fashioned the route from a minimum of hard data. Nothing about Paul's real plans or work during this period can be concluded from these notes" (Conzelmann, *Acts*, 126).

[16] "Paul's evangelization of Asia is temporarily suspended in the interest of the evangelization of another field" (Fitzmyer, *Acts*, 580).

[17] See Witherington, *Acts*, 480.

[18] Jackson and Lake, *The Beginnings of Christianity*, 4.186.

[19] Fitzmyer, *Acts*, 585.

[20] Arguing that the place is not a synagogue are Fitzmyer (*Acts*, 585) and Polhill (*Acts*, 348); arguing that it is a synagogue is Johnson (*Acts*, 292).

[21] Eric M. Meyers, "Synagogue," *ABD* 6.252–53.

[22] Several mss. of Acts put *nomizō* in the passive voice, rendering the translation "where, according to custom, there was a place of prayer." Lake and Jackson, *The Beginnings of Christianity*, 2.155, prefer this variant, though Metzger prefers the text followed by NRSV (Bruce M. Metzger, *A Textual Commentary on the Greek New Testament* [United Bible Societies, 1971], 447). Either variant leaves the impression that Paul and companions were not *certain* they would find such a place, though the variant rejected by the NRSV does, at least, offer some rationale as to why Paul went looking for a place of prayer along the river—it was a customary place.

[23] John E. Stambaugh, "Thyatira," *ABD* 6.546.

[24] Frederick W. Danker, "Purple," *ABD* 5.557–60.

[25] Johnson, *Acts*, 293. Polhill, *Acts*, 350, and Witherington, *Acts*, 493, read v. 16 to refer to a subsequent visit.

[26] Fitzmyer, *Acts*, 586.

[27] See Johnson, *Acts*, 293–94.

[28] The serpent was and is a common symbol in world religions, and not always associated with negative imagery. In the ancient Near East, however, the serpent, especially the sea serpent, was commonly associated with chaos and the potential threat of the power of the dark "underworld." See Lowell K. Handy, "Serpent (Religious Symbol)," *ABD* 5.1113–16.

[29] Witherington, *Acts*, 495.

[30] See Haenchen, *Acts*, 502 for helpful discussion along this line.

[31] Polhill, *Acts*, 352.

[32] Richard I. Pervo, *Profit with Delight: The Literary Genre of the Acts of the Apostles* (Philadelphia: Fortress, 1987), 34–39.

[33] Karel van der Toorn, "Prison," *ABD* 5.468–69.

[34] Pervo, *Profit with Delight*, 23, views this as a stock literary motif. Johnson also leans in that direction (*Acts*, 300). Readers such as Polhill, *Acts*, 355 and 283n159, and Witherington, *Acts*, 497, wish to lend historical credence to the scene by referring to the Code of Justinian, 9.4.4, which stated that a guard who allowed prisoners to escape would be subject to receive the punishment the escapee was to receive.

[35] "In the common Greek of the first century, 'salvation' meant rescue from a difficult situation; it was not a specifically God-oriented word, just as our word 'redemption' when used of trading stamps is not a God-oriented word" (Bruce J. Malina, *The New Testament World: Insights from Cultural Anthropology*, 3rd ed. [Louisville KY: Westminster/John Knox, 2001], 94).

[36] Jackson and Lake, *The Beginnings of Christianity*, 4.196–97, offer a good discussion of various possibilities, including a psychological explanation, similar to the one offered here.

[37] Haenchen, *Acts*, 500–501. Pervo, *Profit with Delight*, 23–24, also questions the historicity, but more on formal grounds: the story is full of stereotypical features of ancient fiction.

[38] Witherington, *Acts*, 498, e.g., suggests that the jailer's house was immediately adjacent to the prison. This would partially explain the apparent ease of movement from the prison to the jailer's home.

[39] E.g., Tannehill, *The Narrative Unity of Luke–Acts: A Literary Interpretation*, 2 vols. (Minneapolis: Fortress, 1990), 2.204.

[41] Jackson and Lake, *The Beginnings of Christianity*, 4.200.

[42] John Dominic Crossan, *Jesus: A Revolutionary Biography* (New York: HarperSanFrancisco, 1994), 66–70.

THEY CAME TO THESSALONICA, BEROEA, AND ATHENS

Acts 17:1-34

COMMENTARY

Acts 17 follows Paul upon his departure from Philippi to the cities of Thessalonica (vv. 1-9), Beroea (vv. 10-15), and, finally, Athens (vv. 16-34). In Athens, Paul presents the gospel, offering a glimpse of how the gospel could be proclaimed to a thoroughly Hellenistic audience. Bertil Gärtner writes, "Whether Pauline or not, the Areopagus speech can legitimately be considered a typical expression of the first Christian sermons to the Gentiles."[1]

Acceptance and Resistance in Thessalonica and Beroea, 17:1-15

Departing from Philippi, Paul continues along the Roman highway that brought him there, the *Via Egnatia*. Paul and his party, consisting of Silas and, presumably, Timothy, passed through two cities along this route, Amphipolis and Apollonia (v. 1). The former was approximately thirty-one miles west of Philippi and was the capital of the first, or southern, district of Macedonia (see [Macedonia]). Apollonia was approximately twenty-five miles southwest of Amphipolis. There is no word on missionary activity. The cities may have served as stopping points. If on horseback, the party could make each city in a day's time.[2]

The group arrives at Thessalonica where they found a synagogue of the Jews. [Tessalonica] Fitzmyer speculates that the presence of a synagogue implies that *this* was the reason Paul stopped here.[3] That is, this was the first city that Paul came to that had a synagogue.

Luke's narration of events in Thessalonica follows a familiar pattern. As was Paul's custom, he goes to the synagogue (vv. 2-3; cf. 13:5, 14; 14:1; 16:13), where his preaching meets with some success

Thessalonica. (Credit: Todd Bolen, "Thessalonica from north," [cited 20 September 2007]. Online: http://www.bibleplaces.com.)

among Jews and Gentiles (v. 4; cf. 13:43, 48; 14:1). As in other places, however, Paul also meets opposition from some Jews who pull others of the city into the fray (vv. 5-9; cf. 13:45, 50; 14:2, 4, 19).

Verse 2 states that Paul preached in the Thessalonian synagogue for three weeks (lit., "three sabbaths"). With respect to historical matters, 1 Thessalonians implies a relatively long stay in Thessalonica (see 1 Thess 2:9, which indicates that Paul earned his own keep). Hence, Luke may be presenting an unreasonably short duration for Paul's stay.[4] However, one need not read Acts to say that Paul was in Thessalonica for only three weeks. Perhaps Paul preached for three consecutive weeks in the synagogue of that city, regardless of how many weeks he was there prior to initiating such preaching. Paul's evangelistic activity could have preceded his visiting the synagogue. If, in order to support himself (see 1 Thess 2:9), Paul "set up shop," he could have used his place of business and emerging business contacts as contexts for preaching.[5]

Luke employs formal rhetorical language to describe Paul's preaching. For example, the word *dielexato*, translated in the NRSV as "argued" (v. 2), "does not mean preach but refers rather to the presenting of arguments using Scripture as a basis or the engaging in dialogue and debate over the meaning of scriptural texts."[6] Further, the participles *dianaoigōn* and *paratithemenos*, translated by the NRSV, respectively, as "explaining" and "proving" (v. 3), "indicate the process of opening the mind and understanding of the hearers followed by the putting forward of proper proofs in good rhetorical form."[7] Luke presents Paul as employing the Jewish Scriptures to "prove" that it was necessary for the Messiah to suffer and rise from the dead (v. 3). [Paul and Rhetoric]

Clearly, *the narrator* wants to leave the impression that the gospel can have a certain intellectual appeal. Ironically, however, the narrator fails to present to the reader the substance of this intellectual and logical appeal. Readers are told neither *which* Scriptures Paul employed nor *how* he employed them.[8] Rather, the narrator calls upon readers to trust him that Paul could offer a rhetorically and logically powerful presentation of the gospel. The characters in Thessalonica are not required simply to "trust" Paul; readers are, however, required simply to "trust" the narrator.

As a result of Paul's appeal, many people "were persuaded" and joined Paul and Silas. Luke is not clear in v. 4a who "they" are, of whom "some" were persuaded. Yet, given that he states explicitly in v. 4b that "a great many of the devout Greeks" were *also* persuaded, it is likely that the "they" of v. 4a denotes Jews of the Thessalonian synagogue.[9] In other words, Luke perhaps wants to contrast that while only *some* Jews responded affirmatively to Paul's message, *many* Gentiles accepted the gospel, among whom were many leading women, that is, women of relatively high social status.

If *some* Jews accepted the gospel, they were exceptional, for, generally, "the Jews" responded with "jealousy" (*zēlōsantes*) and violence (v. 5; see [The Jews]). The narrative does not state what made these Jews jealous. Perhaps these Jews enjoyed the legitimacy and financial support that Gentiles brought to their synagogue and were afraid of losing such.[10] Or perhaps they viewed these devout Gentiles as potential proselytes (see [Proselytes]).

Literarily, Thessalonian Jews are playing "the role" that Jews increasingly play in Acts. They are opposed to Paul. The word translated "jealousy" can also be translated as "zeal" (see Commentary, ch. 11, on Acts 13:45). These Thessalonian Jews, zealous to protect their religious traditions, view Paul's message as subverting their understanding of what faithful Judaism represents. Paul would be leading astray *any* who would follow him, Jews or Gentile God-fearers (see [God-fearer]). The narrator would view such "zeal" as uninformed and misguided. In fact, it is this kind of "zeal," faithful to a certain *and misguided* understanding of the Jewish tradition, that actually undermines God's intentions: to bring both Jews and Gentiles into the saving power of the kingdom.

Luke makes no attempt to provide an objective portrayal of these opponents of Paul. They employ violence to achieve their goals. Whereas "devout Greeks" and "leading women" are persuaded by Paul's gospel, the jealous Jews march down to the city square and round up the "low-lifes" in order to set the city in an uproar. The word that the NRSV translates as "ruffians" (*agoraiōn*) is a cognate of the word for "market place." Loafers and malcontents who had nothing better to do than hang about the city market came to be called "market people." The term was pejorative and not merely descriptive in Luke's world. Jealous Jews and urban hoods (Luke is not above ethnic and social class stereotyping) join together to "create a crowd" (*ochlopoiēsantes*) and incite a riot. These are the kinds of people who oppose the gospel.

The mob makes its way to Jason's house in an attempt to find "them" (Paul and his party) and drag them out before the "assembly" (*dēmos*) (v. 5b). Calling the rabble created by the Jews and ruffians "the assembly" drips with sardonic irony. This term was normally used to denote the gathering of the city's citizens to conduct business.

The narrator leaves some gaps, particularly with his brief intro-duction of Jason. He may have been a Diaspora Jew, since Jason was the common Roman equivalent for the Hebrew name Jesus or Joshua. The mob assumes that he was offering hospitality to Paul and his companions (v. 7). This might imply that Jason was a recent convert who, like Lydia in Philippi, opened his home to those who brought him to Christian faith. This makes most sense given that v. 6 indicates that the crowd dragged both Jason and fellow believers (lit., "brothers") before city authorities. Presumably these fellow believers were found at Jason's home, which was perhaps being used as a house church. Church tradition clearly viewed him as a convert, for it claimed that he eventually became the bishop of Thessalonica.[11]

When the mob cannot find Paul and his companions, they are content to drag Jason and other believers before the city authorities to file charges (vv. 6-7). First, Jason has harbored subversive charac-ters—Paul and company, "who have been turning the world upside down"—and have now made their way to Thessalonica (vv. 6b, 7a). Second, and closely related to the first charge, these subversives have vio-lated the decrees of Caesar by claiming loyalty to a rival king (v. 7b). [Caesar]

Caesar

AΩ Originally, this was the family name of Julius Caesar, but in time "Caesar" became a title for the emperor of Rome, independent of any familial connec-tion with Julius Caesar.

The word that the NRSV translates as "world" is *oikoumenēn*, a word commonly used to denote the *inhabited* world, as opposed to "the whole earth." Hence, it can also mean "the Empire," a most fitting translation in this context. It is ironic that an "assembly" put together by local rabble-rousers who have put the city in turmoil charges others with being a threat to Roman order. Yet the local authorities appear obliged to take the charge seriously (v. 9). Luke uses the term *politarchas* to denote these local rulers of a free city, of which there would have been five or six.[12] This is the technically correct term for a free city like Thessalonica. Though a free city, "local officials would be expected to enforce loyalty to Caesar in order to maintain the peace and help the city stay in the good graces of the emperor."[13]

The second charge of subversion claims that Paul and his party have violated the decrees of Caesar, claiming there to be another king, Jesus. Witherington believes that he has identified the specific decree that the "assembly" would have had in mind. In AD 16 Tiberius issued a decree that prohibited predicting the demise of any current ruler. Paul's proclamation of the kingship of Jesus, particularly if combined with language of Jesus' victorious Parousia, could have been interpreted as such a violation.[14] Though an interesting reconstruction of history, one wonders whether this mob, or Luke's readers for that matter, would have known specific Roman law as well as Witherington does. Within the Lukan narrative, regardless of what one assumes about the author's, characters', or readers' knowledge of specific law, the messianic claims of Jesus are commonly portrayed as *misunderstood* if interpreted as *political* claims (cf. Luke 23:1-5).[15]

The Thessalonian authorities respond more sensibly than did those of Philippi, where the government officials exacerbated the tense situation by beating Paul and Silas and throwing them into prison (16:22-24). The Thessalonian authorities "take bail" from Jason and the other believers and then let them go. The narrative leaves a rather large gap, offering no explanation of what exactly this "bail" represents. Perhaps the authorities were holding Jason and the others charged with harboring potential subversives accountable to make sure that such activity came to an end. Perhaps the authorities ordered the expulsion of Paul and his companions from the city and were leaving it to Jason to make sure that their orders were carried out—or else they would forfeit their bond. That would explain why the believers *immediately* sent Paul and Silas away that very night (v. 10).

In moving toward Beroea, Paul and his party depart from the main Roman highway and head south toward Beroea, located some sixty miles from Thessalonica. The city was located on the eastern slopes of Mount Vermian in the Olympian mountain range and had, at one time, served as the capital city of one of the four Macedonian districts.[16] Consistent with Paul's pattern, he visits the synagogue (v. 10).

Though one can discern patterns in the way Luke presents stories of Paul's encounters with Jews and Gentiles in the synagogues, his account of Paul's experiences in Beroea shows that Luke can be nuanced in his presentations. Specifically, the narrator praises the Jews of this city, describing them as "more noble." The word *eugenesteroi* literally means "well born" or "well bred," but came to take on the more general meaning of "open," "tolerant" or "generous."[17] Luke also describes them as "eager" to receive the good news and to examine for themselves the Scriptures to confirm the truth of Paul's proclamation. Again, Luke does not allow readers to know precisely what Scriptures Paul appeals to, leaving readers unable to follow the characters' example. As a consequence of their eagerness and willingness to search the Scriptures, *many* came to believe, in direct contrast to only *some* (or *none!*) of the Thessalonian Jews. As in other cities, Gentiles also come to believe. Again, Luke takes care to note that women were among such believers and that they, as well as the men, were of high standing (v. 12).

The Thessalonian Jews remain consistent with the character they displayed in their own city. They make the sixty-mile journey all the way to Beroea to challenge Paul's work and, as in their hometown, stir up the crowds against Paul (v. 13). Given such dedication to their own cause, readers might conclude that, in fact, *zeal*, rather than simple jealousy, does motivate their behavior (cf. comments above on v. 5). The narrator offers no explicit statement regarding the believers' motives for sending Paul away (v. 14). Did the authorities take notice of him? Did they fear for Paul's life? Did the infant church fear for its own welfare? Whatever the reason, Paul is sent eastward, toward the coastline.

The narrative offers another gap as it notifies readers that Silas and Timothy—the latter is finally mentioned explicitly as having been with Paul all this time—are safe to remain in Beroea (v. 14). The narrative's explicit notice that Timothy *remained* in Beroea creates tension with Paul's own testimony in 1 Thessalonians 3:1-2 concerning Timothy's travels. [Timothy's Itinerary] First Thessalonians indicates that Timothy was *with* Paul in Athens and that Paul sent Timothy *back* to Thessalonica. Nonetheless, in Luke's narrative world, Paul travels to Athens

Timothy's Itinerary

Acts indicates that Paul went to Athens alone, leaving both Timothy and Silas behind in Beroea (17:14-15). While Acts 17:16 indicates that Paul is expecting Timothy and Silas to join him in Athens, the three do not reunite until Paul reaches Corinth (18:5). Yet Paul states in his letter to the Thessalonians, likely written from Corinth shortly after Paul left Athens, that he sent Timothy *from* Athens *back* to Thessalonica (1 Thess 3:1-2). Then Timothy rejoined Paul, presumably after Paul had moved on to Corinth (1 Thess 3:6).

The reconstruction of history will invariably necessitate the filling in of some gaps or the reconciliation of sources that, on first glance, are not perfectly consistent. One could simply argue that Acts is mistaken—that is, Timothy accompanied Paul to Athens (Lüdemann, 188). One predisposed to reconciling the conflicting sources could argue that Timothy did remain behind in Beroea (Acts 17:14-15), *subsequently* joined Paul in Athens (1 Thessalonians), was sent back to Thessalonica (1 Thess 3:1-2), then rejoined Paul in Corinth (Acts 18:5; cf. 1 Thess 3:6) (Witherington, 510).

Gerd Lüdemann, *Early Christianity according to the Acts of the Apostles: A Commentary* (Minneapolis: Fortress, 1989); Ben Witherington III, *The Acts of the Apostles: A Socio-Rhetorical Commentary* (Grand Rapids MI: Eerdmans, 1998).

without Timothy, accompanied by other anonymous believers. The narrative is not clear whether Paul went to Athens by land or by sea. That is, did Paul exit Beroea toward the sea in order to board a ship or to travel down the coastline on foot to Athens? Whatever route Paul followed, upon reaching Athens he told those who accompanied him to give word both to Silas and Timothy to meet him in Athens as soon as they could.

"What You Worship as Unknown, I Proclaim to You," 17:16-34

The narrative of Paul divides easily into three sections: Paul's initial impressions of Athens (vv. 16-21), Paul's speech to the Athenians, (vv. 22-31), and a brief conclusion (vv. 32-34). [Athens]

Paul and the Idols, vv. 16-21

Paul follows his usual practice of preaching in the synagogue to Jews and to Gentiles sympathetic with Judaism (v. 17a). However, Paul also visits the market place (the agora) each day and offers his message to the crowds gathered there (v. 17b). Wandering teachers, such as the Cynic philosophers, regularly employed the city square to teach. This represents a deliberate change of Paul's strategy, for previously Paul tended to focus only on Gentiles whom he found in the synagogue.[18]

Verse 16b states that Paul is greatly angered by the abundance of idols. The verb *parōzyneto* (NRSV, "deeply distressed") can also denote anger, outrage, or infuriation.[19] The LXX used the verb to denote *God's* extreme anger and wrath due to people's rebellion or false worship (see in LXX Deut 9:18, 19; Ps 106:29; Isa 65:3; Hos 8:5). [Jewish Views of Idolatry]

It is true that much of Athenian art and architecture centered on Greek religion. Based on knowledge, sketchy as it might be, of the layout of Athens, one can imagine what Paul might have seen in the agora. Paul would have seen symbols of Greek philosophy and religion. According to Jackson and Lake, Paul would

---

Athens

Athens reached its zenith in the late fifth century BC, with great building programs, the construction of the Parthenon, and, over time, the establishment of significant schools of Greek philosophy. This legacy continued into Paul's time. The city had the reputation of being religious, curious, and learned—all stereotypical traits that the narrative of Acts alludes to and employs.

Jewish Views of Idolatry

Wisdom of Solomon articulates clearly Jewish polemical views of Gentile idolatry and its ramifications. Idolatry begins when one fails to recognize the Creator behind the creation and gives homage to the creation itself (Wis 13:1-9). Once one confuses that which the Creator made with things worthy of worship, one moves to the construction of idols, which "give[s] the name 'gods' to the works of human hands, gold and silver fashioned with skill" (Wis 13:10; cf. 13:10–14:7). In the logic of Wisdom such accursed idolatry (cf. 14:8) moves one then to immorality, with sexual immorality serving as the primary example of an immoral way of life: "For the idea of making idols was the beginning of fornication, and the invention of them was the corruption of life" (Wis 14:12).

Romans 1 shows that Paul was familiar with such a pattern of thought. He speaks of the confusion of the creation and the Creator (Rom 1:19-21). This leads to the worship of images (Rom 1:22-23), followed by immorality (Rom 1:24-32), with sexual immorality viewed as especially egregious (Rom 1:26-27).

James D. G. Dunn, *The Theology of Paul the Apostle* (Grand Rapids MI: Eerdmans, 1998), 91–93.

The Agora of Athens

Mars Hill is the hill situated just below the Acropolis (loc. 10). One can see that Paul's encounter with the philosophers took place under the imposing presence of the Acropolis. The Royal Stoa (loc. 2) is the likely spot where readers can imagine Paul's speech before the Areopagus to have taken place.

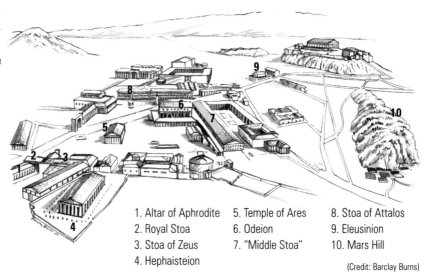

1. Altar of Aphrodite
2. Royal Stoa
3. Stoa of Zeus
4. Hephaisteion
5. Temple of Ares
6. Odeion
7. "Middle Stoa"
8. Stoa of Attalos
9. Eleusinion
10. Mars Hill

(Credit: Barclay Burns)

have seen many religious statues and altars: the statue of Hermes Agoraies, the Temple of Ares, and, nearby, an altar and place of dedication of the city's heroes. Clustered around the southern end of the agora, between the Metroon and Tholos, were the Temples of the Mother Goddess and Apollo Patroos and the Hall of the Twelve Gods.[20]

Among those who happened to be in the agora are followers of two influential philosophical schools: the Epicureans and the Stoics (v. 18). [Epicureans] [Stoics] The NRSV states that these philosophers "debated" with Paul, though the Greek word *symballō* could denote a milder tone, such as "converse" or "confer." Some among these philosophers, perhaps the Epicureans,[21] are quite disparaging, calling Paul a "babbler." The term *spermologos* literally refers to the practice of birds picking up seeds and then dropping them elsewhere along their way. Metaphorically, the term came to denote persons who "picked up" others' ideas then "scattered" them about, depicting themselves as more learned than they really were. [Babbler]

Others among the philosophers infer that Paul is speaking of "foreign divinities." The narrator explains that such an inference came from the fact that Paul was preaching about Jesus and the resurrection. The narrator's interpretive gloss might indicate that these listeners understood Jesus to be one god and "Resurrection" (a femi-

Epicureans

Epicurus (341–270 BC) and his followers held to a materialistic philosophy of life. The eternal universe—there was no "creation"—was made of small building blocks called atoms. These eternally existing solids had shape, size, weight, and motion. They came together to form objects. While particular objects may cease to exist, such as one's body, or even one's soul (Epicureans denied that the soul was immortal), the atoms themselves continued to exist. Epicurus believed that the gods were not concerned with human beings or with matters of this world. This is quite distinct from Stoicism, for if the gods have no interest in human welfare or other matters of this world, it is meaningless to speak of Providence.

Everett Ferguson, *Backgrounds of Early Christianity*, 3rd ed. (Grand Rapids MI: Eerdmans, 2003), 370–79.

nine word in the Greek language) to be another god, perhaps Jesus' female consort.[22]

Paul is then taken to the Areopagus. There is much debate over how to interpret the passage. The NRSV translates the participle *epilabomenoi* rather neutrally as "took" (cf. 9:27; 23:19). The older RSV, however, translates it as "took hold of," implying that Paul was taken by force, a meaning also employed by the narrator (cf. 16:19; 18:17). Is Paul being *led* away for further spirited discussion or *taken* away for some type of hostile interrogation?

Further, what does the narrator refer to when he speaks of the Areopagus? The Areopagus could refer either to a place, Mars Hill, located near the agora and the Acropolis, or to the ruling council, which was called by the same name. In past

---

Stoics

This school was founded by Zeno (335–263 BC). Stoics taught that divine reality, which had many names, such as Reason (Logos), Spirit, or Providence, permeated all of reality. This type of pantheism led Stoics to the logical conclusion that all things are interconnected by a higher intelligence that providentially guides all things to an intended goal. Stoics believed that ethical behavior found its roots in living life in harmony with this Logos that guided all of life. One's social or economic station, which belonged to the "external circumstances" of one's life, was of no real significance. What was important was to understand that one's external circumstances were given by the providential Logos and to live life accordingly. The first-century Stoic philosopher Epictetus (AD 55–135) stated in his *Enchiridion*: "Remember that you are an actor in a drama of such sort the author chooses. . . . If it be his pleasure that you should enact a poor man, see that you act it well. . . . For this is your business—to act well the given part; but to choose it belongs to another."

Everett Ferguson, *Backgrounds of Early Christianity*, 3rd ed. (Grand Rapids MI: Eerdmans, 2003), 354–69. Excerpt from the *Enchiridion* found on p. 367.

Babbler

 Selected uses of the word *spermologos* (or some variation) include:

- Philo, mocking the competence of some of Emperor Gaius's advisors, describes one, a certain Helicon, as a "slave, scrap retailer (*spermologō*), [and] piece of riff-raff" (*On the Embassy to Gaius*, 203).
- Apollonius of Tyana, speaking of the folly of trafficking in the idolatry business, describes idolaters as follows: "It is true that there are babbling (*spermologousin*) buffoons who hang upon their persons images of Demeter or Dionysus . . ." (Philostratus, *Life of Apollonius of Tyana*, 5.20).
- Plutarch speaks of Aristippus, who was captivated by Socrates' teaching when "he had gleaned a few odd seeds (*logōn . . . spermata*) and samples of Socrates' talk" (*Moralia* 516C).

---

times, the council met on Mars Hill—hence, its name. But in Paul's day the ruling council, while keeping its original name, met in the Royal Stoa, located on the northwestern side of the agora. Understanding the Areopagus to refer to the ruling council clearly makes more sense, given particularly that this council was responsible for sanctioning the many speakers who attempted to use the Athenian agora as a public forum.[23] Paul's questioners want to look into this "new teaching" (v. 19b) and these things that sound "rather strange" (v. 20).

Furthermore, the leading of Paul before the ruling council of the city of Athens is consistent with the narrative pattern of this and the previous chapter, as well as the subsequent chapter: in Philippi, Thessalonica, and, later, Corinth, Paul is brought before civil

The Royal Stoa

The ruins of the Royal Stoa are what remains today of the place where Paul was questioned before the Areopagus (Acts 17:22).

See **The Agora of Athens** for its location in relation to the larger Agora.

(Credit: Barclay Burns)

authorities. Hence, while this interrogation lacks the acrimony and violence of other scenes, it continues the motif of Paul's being challenged by civil authorities. Perhaps influenced by stereotypical images of Athens as a city curious about new things (v. 21), the narrator portrays Paul's interrogation in a different light from the interrogations that confronted him in Philippi and Thessalonica. [Athenian Curiosity]

Athenian Curiosity

The Athenian propensity to talk about or listen to new things, about which Luke comments in 17:12, was proverbial in Luke's world. A most colorful description of Athenian curiosity is found in the Chariton's ancient novel, *Chaereas and Callirhoe*:

When they were all alone they debated where to sail to. One of them said: "Athens is nearby. . . ." And they all liked the idea of making for Athens. But Theron did not like the inquisitive ways of the town. "Look, are you the only people who don't know what busybodies they are in Athens? They're a nation of gossips, and they love lawsuits. There'll be hundreds of nosey parkers in the harbor wanting to know who we are and where we got this cargo we're carrying. Nasty suspicions will seize hold of the malicious minds—and it's the Areopagus straightway, in Athens, and magistrates who are more severe than tyrants.

B. P. Reardon, ed. and trans., *Collected Ancient Greek Novels* (Berkeley: University of California Press, 1989), 33.

Paul's Speech before the Council, vv. 22-31
Paul stands (v. 22), as is common among Hellenistic orators. Stating that Paul stood in the midst of the Areopagus would indicate that the narrator means by Areopagus "the council," not the geographical locale. One stands in the middle of a group, not the middle of a hill.

To help establish his credibility, or *ethos*, Paul begins his speech on a seemingly positive note by referring to the Athenians' devotion, something for which they were known in their day. Such "currying of favor," known technically as *captatio benevolentia*, was a common rhetorical strategy. The word Paul uses to denote Athenian devotion (*deisidaimonestepous*) can also mean "superstitious," giving Paul's word a somewhat ironic twist. Though the narrator made clear in v. 16 that Paul was incensed by the idols he saw, Paul is not out to alienate his audience, but to persuade them. Hence, in v. 23 Paul speaks rather neutrally of his observing of the city's "objects of worship." The word Paul employs (*sebasmata*) can have negative connotations in Jewish polemical literature against idolatry (cf. Wis 14:20; 15:17), but the Athenian audience need not hear it that way. Thus, once again, the Lukan Paul chooses his words carefully—words that will not offend his audience but do not imply agreement with his audience's views.

There is much debate over whether there existed in Athens an altar with an inscription "to an unknown God." To be sure, there is no physical evidence discovered among the archaeological ruins, yet there is enough literary evidence to give credence to the reference, even if such literary evidence offers no *exact* parallel to Paul's claim. Nonetheless, in the context of the Lukan narrative, the inscription offers a meaningful point of departure for Paul's speech. The apostle has found some common ground with his audience. [To an Unknown God]

Paul claims that he will make known to the Athenians this "god" to which they pay homage, a god, by their own admission, that they do not know. To be sure, much of what Paul will tell them they *do* already know. His strategy will be to show the Athenians that their manner of worship does not measure up even to the best religious and philosophical thinking of their own heritage and tradition. Yet, at the same time, while Paul's speech will offer many points of contact with Greek thinking, it will remain true to the Jewish theological heritage and to Lukan theology. Paul seeks *common* ground; he does not compromise, however, faithfulness to his own religious heritage.

Verse 24 affirms God as the creator. This is a bedrock claim of Paul's Jewish faith; it forms the foundation of the biblical narrative (Gen 1–3). As such, it became a central feature of early Christian thought, including Lukan theology (cf. Acts 4:24, 28; Rom 1; Col 1; John 1, etc.). However, much of the Greek philosophical tradition also affirmed God as creator, or at least the force behind creation that sustained and maintained it. To be sure, the Epicureans did not, but the Stoics most certainly did, though not in the manner of traditional Christianity.[24] As creator, the ruler of all creation ("Lord of heaven and earth"), this unknown God does not live in humanly constructed shrines. Again, Paul has found common ground between Jewish and early Christian thought (1 Kgs 8:27; cf. Isa 66:1-2; Acts 7:48-50; cf. Heb 8:2; 9:11, 24) and

To an Unknown God

 The literature of antiquity offers rough parallels to the reference "to an unknown god" (Acts 17:23). Talbert (161) lists the following writers of antiquity as making reference to altars to "unknown gods" (note the plural, not the singular, as in Acts) in or around the immediate environs of Athens: Pausanias 1.1.1-3; Diogenes Laertius 1.110; Philostratus, *Apollonius of Tyana* 6.3. For a thorough discussion of the "altar to an unknown god," see Witherington, pp. 521–23.

Charles H. Talbert, *Reading Acts: A Literary and Theological Commentary of the Acts of the Apostles* (New York: Crossroad, 1997); Ben Witherington III, *The Acts of the Apostles: A Socio-Rhetorical Commentary* (Grand Rapids MI: Eerdmans, 1998).

Shrines Made by Human Hands

 Selected voices from antiquity echo the Lukan Paul's claim that the true God does not live in humanly constructed edifices.

Seneca: "Temples are not to be built to Him with stones piled up on high" (Lactantius, *Institutes* 6.25 [Talbert, 162]).

Zeno: "One should not build temples for gods" (Plutarch, *Moralia* 1034B [Talbert, 162]).

Euripides: "What house fashioned by builders can contain the divine form within enclosing walls" (*Fragments*, 968 [Fitzmyer, 608]).

Charles H. Talbert, *Reading Acts: A Literary and Theological Commentary of the Acts of the Apostles* (New York: Crossroad, 1997); Joseph A. Fitzmyer, *The Acts of the Apostles* (AB 31; New York: Doubleday, 1998).

Greek thought, for the Greek philosophical tradition regularly affirmed similar beliefs. [Shrines Made by Human Hands]

Verse 25 offers further connections between the Jewish and Greek heritages. Both affirmed that the creator God did not need what humans had to offer; rather, humans were dependent on the creator. The biblical tradition declares God's independence of human ritual and cult in such texts as Psalm 50:7-15. Postbiblical Jewish materials echoed this thought (see 2 Macc 14:35). Josephus explicitly claimed that "God contains all things, and is a being every way perfect and happy, *self-sufficient*, and *supplying all other beings*; the beginning, the middle, and the end of all things" (*Ag. Ap.* 2.190; emphasis added). Within the Greek literary and philosophical traditions one can find the same idea. "For God, if indeed God he be, is in need of nothing" (Euripides, *Hercules Furens* 1345-46).[25] Said Senecea, "God seeks no servants; He himself serves mankind" (*Epistle* 95.47).[26]

In v. 26 Paul alludes to the character of Adam. Paul's Greek audience, unfamiliar with the specifics of the biblical tradition, would not catch this specific allusion. However, the Stoics in Paul's audience did affirm the common kinship of humanity, a clear implication of Paul's statement that all nations derive from one ancestor.[27] Such an emphasis on the common bonds that unite all humans was not universally held, however, in Greek thought.[28]

The second part of v. 26 refers to God's providential care of the creation. There is debate over what exactly Paul means when referring to allotted periods and boundaries. He could mean by "periods" the natural seasons (cf. Ps 74:17; Acts 14:17) and by "boundaries" God's setting aside specific places on the earth to make them fit for human habitation (e.g., Gen 1:9-13, 24-26; Job 38:8-11). This reading might have been more amenable to Paul's Greek listeners.

Or Paul might mean by allotted "periods" the purposeful movement of history, commonly seen in Jewish apocalyptic thought, which often viewed history has divided into predetermined periods.[29] By "boundaries" Paul could be referring to the different areas where various groups within the human family dwell (e.g., Gen 10; Deut 32:8). Regardless of one's particular reading, the speech asserts that "the historic limitations set upon humanity, the times and places where they dwell, are all the object of divine determination."[30]

In vv. 27-28, Paul directs his speech toward humanity's purpose for existence: human beings are to seek this creator God, "feeling after God" and, possibly, "finding God." The words translated as "feeling after" (*psēlapheseian*) and "finding" (*heuroien*) deserve comment. *Psēlepheseian* can carry the connotation of groping, as someone who is blind might feel her or his way along in a room (cf. Isa 59:10). *Heuroien* is expressed in the optative mood, a mood rarely employed in the New Testament. The mood expresses in the Greek language a high degree of uncertainty that the action will be fulfilled. Hence, while God created humanity with the intention that humans should seek after God, the quest is characterized by a kind of blind groping with little chance of success. This is in spite of the fact that God is not remote; God is not very far from humanity (v. 27b). It is as though Paul were saying that God is within reach, but as humans reach out in the darkness to lay hold of God, the Creator proves elusive to the human grasp.

Paul's Greek audience would likely hear the phrase of v. 28 (NRSV, "in him we live and move and have our being") as an affirmation of divine immanence. Seneca said something quite similar: "God is near you, He is with you, He is within you" (*Epistle* 41.1-2).[31] Psalm 139 offers a biblical expression of the idea. The Greek text could also be translated to say, "*by means of God* we live and move, etc." This would place more of an emphasis on humanity's dependence upon God, rather than God's innate nearness to humanity. Whether God is spatially "near" to humans or humans are dependent on God for life and being, God is portrayed as integral to human life.

Paul's quotation of the Greek poets in v. 28b (likely Eratus, *Phaenomena* 5), stating that humans are God's offspring, can, like so much of Paul's speech, be heard at least two ways. One could hear an affirmation of humanity's natural kinship with God, as though humans were in some sense divine or, at least, possessed some type of divine nature. Paul's Stoic audience could very well have heard Paul to be saying this. It is doubtful that either the Lukan or historical Paul would entertain such a notion. For the Lukan Paul and Christian reader, Eratus's quotation would likely denote that God created humans. In Luke 3:38, Adam is said to be a "son of God." In Luke's genealogy such a statement served to affirm that Adam was created by God, not that Adam possessed some divine nature.

Thus far, Paul is saying that humans have been created to seek for God; they can feel after and sense God's nearness and even have some type of kinship with God as God's creatures. Paul has offered no explicit assessment of the success of humanity's quest for God, though the thrust of the speech makes it apparent that the quest is not successful. The very fact that the speech began with reference to an altar dedicated "to an unknown god" speaks for itself. The Athenians do not *know* this God who has created them to seek after him. In v. 29 Paul draws upon the implications of vv. 27-28 to provide a severe critique of idolatry. As God's children, persons created by God in God's own image and likeness (cf. Gen 1:26-27), humans should realize that God is no more like stones or precious metals than are humans. More importantly, human beings, who are created and sustained by God, should fully realize that what humans fashion with their own hands cannot be confused with the Deity. God is the creator; God cannot be captured by that which humans, in turn, create themselves.

On this the traditions of Judaism and certain streams of Greco-Roman philosophy agreed. Dio Chrysostom, an influential Roman thinker of the first century AD, said that living things can only be represented by the living.[32] The Wisdom of Solomon is most emphatic that idolatry represents the height of human foolishness. After all, if it is wrong to confuse what *God* creates with the Deity (Wis 13:4-9), it is more egregious to confuse what *humans* create with the Deity (Wis 13:10-19). When Paul's audience is willing to heed the guidance of even its own philosophical heritage, it will recognize the error of its ways: "The popular religion in Athens does not live up to the insights of the pagan philosophers and poets."[33]

The Athenians' failure to acknowledge the true God, glimpses of whom even the best of their own tradition should have provided, requires that there be a change of mind—a change of thought. Such a "change of mind" (*metanoein*, commonly translated as "repentance") is precisely what Paul demands in v. 30. The God of which humanity had been ignorant, an ignorance epitomized by the Athenian altar dedicated to an unknown god, is now made known through the proclamation of the gospel. The times of ignorance will be overlooked no longer.

In the narrative of Acts, ignorance is a common theme. The Jewish audience is called to repentance for its act of ignorance—rejecting God's anointed one (Acts 2:38; 3:17, 19; 13:27). Gentiles are called to account for their not knowing the true God (Acts 14:15, 16). The Jews now know, through the apostolic witness, the identity of God's anointed one. Through that same witness the Gentiles now know the identity of the Creator. Both groups are called to turn away from their respective errors.

Behind the call to repentance is a positive invitation to receive the good benefits of God, such as salvation and forgiveness (2:38; 3:19) or knowledge of the true God, as in this text. But there is also the threat of judgment from the one whom God appointed to serve as judge. The assurance of God's appointment of this man to the role of judge is found through God's raising of this man from the dead. The resurrection as the definitive sign of God's affirmation of this Jesus (though unnamed in this particular sermon) is echoed in earlier sermons to audiences of both Jews and God-fearers (2:31-32; 3:15; 5:30-33; 10:41; 13:31). On this crucial point, there can only be straightforward proclamation; there can be no "common ground" in addressing this Hellenized audience. After all, Aeschylus, the Greek composer of tragedies, placed on the mouth of Apollo: "When the dust has soaked up the blood of a man, once he has died, there is no resurrection" (*Eumenides* 647-48).[34]

Paul Went Out from among Them, 17:32-34

Verses 32-34 provide the brief conclusion to the narrative of Paul's mission to Athens. The transition to the conclusion is quick, as the narrator reports the immediate reaction of Paul's audience to the notion of resurrection. As mentioned above, the idea of the resurrection of the body was foreign to Greek thought. But Greeks, represented in the Lukan narrative by these philosophical schools, differed on the broader idea of "afterlife." Epicureans denied any notion of afterlife, while Stoics accepted the idea that one's soul survived, connected as it was to the larger "world soul." However, the Stoics did not have any concept of *personal* immortality.[35] Stoic openness to some notion of the survival of the soul may imply that it was they who were willing to hear Paul further on this matter. Some reject the message immediately, while others are open to further discussion.

Yet openness to further discussion is not the same as belief. Luke concludes his narrative on a positive note by explicitly noting that some came to actual faith (v. 34). One such new believer, Dionysius, is a member of the Areopagus. Though later church tradition asserted that this Dionysius became the first bishop of Athens, there is no solid historical basis for this claim.[36] The narrator is also careful, as he has been in other places in his narrative (see 17:4, 12), to note that a woman was among the believers.

History offers no further information on the identity or destiny of this Damaris.

CONNECTIONS

Years ago I listened to a woman share her strategies for witnessing. The only specific comment that I remember was something to this effect: "I don't know how to witness when I'm talking to someone who doesn't believe the Bible." She raised an interesting point. If we are offering witness to folk who *already* "believe the Bible," then we are witnessing to persons who already have some connection with the very tradition to which we are urging them to commit more fully. But what if "they don't believe the Bible"? What if they do not already share some common assumptions on which we can build our testimony?

Paul's sermon to the Areopagus offers the best example from Acts to address such a situation. The main characters of Acts are Jewish, and, most often, the sermons presented are delivered in Jewish contexts, such as the temple or synagogue, and to audiences who are either Jews or non-Jews immersed in the tradition of Judaism. In this speech, however, the audience is one that appears to have no familiarity at all with the Jewish tradition or its sacred texts. How can an effective mission be offered where there appears to be no explicit connections between the speaker and the audience?

Robert Tannehill's comments on this text are worth reading in their entirety.[37] The following statement offers a taste of Tannehill's insight:

> Effective mission . . . requires reflection on theological foundations in order to discover a message that can address the whole world. More than instruction in the Jewish gospel is needed. The mission must discover latent resources within the tradition (discovered, perhaps, in conversation with the larger world) in order to preach a universal message. Otherwise the world cannot hear, and the preachers themselves lose sight of the worldwide dimension of the message they proclaim. . . . The Areopagus speech may provide a helpful model of the delicate task of speaking outside the religious community through critical engagement with the larger world. A mission that does not engage the presuppositions and dominant concerns of those being approached leaves these presuppositions and concerns untouched, with the result that the message, even if accepted, does not transform its hearers.[38]

Effective "outreach" to those truly "outside" the circle of our tradition requires a careful balance: finding common ground of discourse, while, at the same time, not emptying the Christian gospel of the transformative power of its distinctive message.

Paul begins his sermon by seeking to establish a positive relationship with his audience. The narrator makes clear that Paul was personally incensed at the many idols that confronted him in the agora, but Paul refrains from any kind of tirade that would serve only to alienate his listeners. Rather, Paul begins by speaking of the Athenians' devotion.

One might compare the Lukan Paul's more gentle approach in this sermon with the Paul of Romans. Absent from the Athenian sermon are such heated words as,

> though they knew God, they did not know him as God or give thanks to him, but they became futile in their thinking, and their senseless minds were darkened. Claiming to be wise, they became fools; and they exchanged the glory of the immortal God for images resembling a mortal human being or birds or four-footed animals or reptiles. (Rom 1:21-23) ["Natural Revelation" in Acts and Romans]

Paul's approach in Athens can be contrasted with that of the missionary of Barbara Kingsolver's haunting novel *The Poisonwood Bible*. Nathan Price reached the Congo in 1959, with his family—his wife, Orleanna, and four daughters—full of zealous determination to convert the heathen. He wanted to bring them not only to faith, but, more importantly, to *true* faith. Upon the Prices' arrival at the village of Kilanga, the swarm of well-wishers among the residents greeted the newcomers. A fellowship meal had been arranged as part of the festive greeting.

The Prices, proper folk from the South, could not help but notice that most women moved about the village "all bare-chested and unashamed,"[39] with naked children clinging to their long skirts. Nathan Price was, like Paul in Athens, incensed at what he saw: "He had that narrow-eyed, lockjawed look like he was starting to get steamed up."[40] The leader of the gathering asked Nathan Price, the newly arrived and honored guest, to pray. But rather than pray a sincere word of thanks, he used the opportunity to shame and castigate his hosts for their evil nakedness. [Nathan Price's "Prayer"]

There was no compromising Nathan Price's conviction. When this holy man of God saw that which incensed him, he let it be known, without hesitation and without mincing words. He had come to call the worthy out of the darkness, and would let his hearers know, without qualification or exception, what was right

---

"Natural Revelation" in Acts and Romans

Important issues pertaining to the question of "natural revelation" or "natural theology" face interpreters of the Areopagus speech. Does the speech really appeal to natural revelation, that is, the idea that somehow God is truly revealed in and through nature, even if such revelation is not complete? If the speech does assume a type of natural revelation, does it employ such a notion positively or negatively?

For example, Wisdom of Solomon 13:1-9 asserts that God is revealed through creation, but also emphatically claims that those ignorant of God "were unable from the good things that are seen to know the one who exists" (Wis 13:1). This represents a negative and polemical appeal to "natural revelation." Second-century Christian apologists such as Justin Martyr, on the other hand, could employ the concept of natural revelation more positively, arguing that non-Jewish philosophy and religion, informed by natural revelation, actually served to prepare the Gentiles for Christ.

Does the Lukan Paul of Acts 17 employ "natural revelation" affirmatively, as something that had successfully prepared his Greek audience for the fuller revelation of the gospel? Is Philip Vielhauer on track when he says that in Acts 17 natural theology "is evaluated positively and employed in missionary pedagogy as a forerunner of faith" (36)? Or is Ben Witherington closer to the mark when he argues that natural revelation was, in fact, not terribly successful and offered no useful foundation on which the gospel could build? Witherington contends, "[Luke] does not believe that a Jewish or Christian knowledge can simply be added to what pagans already knew about God, with salvific results. Conversion to a new worldview, not merely additional knowledge, is required" (531).

The Lukan Paul clearly appealed to many ideas that biblical and Jewish religion *shared* with Greek religion and philosophy. Paul could *assume* his audience would understand these thoroughly *biblical* and *Jewish* ideas without having to allude to Moses, the prophets, or any particular Jewish texts or traditions. The very fact that Paul could even assume he would be understood would indicate some success on the part of natural revelation. And yet the fact that natural revelation could and did lead toward idolatry simultaneously indicates that it is not adequate. It is that inadequacy that the gospel can address. The fact, however, that such natural revelation is incomplete does not mean that it is a failure.

Another important issue is whether the "natural revelation" as employed in Acts 17 is consistent with Paul's employment in Romans 1. Romans 1 is quite similar to Wisdom 13–14: any divine self-disclosure through nature served only to demonstrate human culpability, not prepare humanity in any *positive* way for the gospel. This would imply an inconsistent employment of natural revelation, if one concludes (as not all do) that Acts 17 employs natural revelation rather positively.

If Romans 1 does have a more pessimistic view of the effectiveness of natural revelation than does Acts 17, there is no need to pit one against the other. "I am of Paul. I am of the Lukan Paul." Rather, the presence of each testifies to the richness of the *whole* of the scriptural tradition. It further reminds modern interpreters that awareness of and sensitivity to varying rhetorical situations requires the skill to know when it is appropriate to emphasize that which the Christian tradition has in common with other traditions and when it would be more appropriate to highlight the differences.

Philip Vielhauer, "On the 'Paulinism' of Acts," in *Studies in Luke–Acts*, ed. Leander E. Keck and J. Louis Martyn (Philadelphia: Fortress, 1980), 33–50; Ben Witherington III, *The Acts of the Apostles: A Socio-Rhetorical Commentary* (Grand Rapids MI: Eerdmans, 1998); James Barr, *Biblical Faith and Natural Theology* (Oxford: Clarendon, 1993).

---

and what was wrong and just where he stood on the subject. This was a war of cultures, values, and faiths and there was no common ground to be found between the two sides. Nathan Price let go a battle cry with his very first utterance. He was going to conquer the Congo. Yet, in the end, the Congo conquered both Nathan and his family—but one needs to read the rest of Kingsolver's narrative to get the rest of that story.

Christian proclamation has as its goal the transformation of lives into the image of Christ. There will inevitably be confrontation and a clash of cultures. But success is not assured because the proclaimer, anxious to demonstrate pious zeal, initiates the presentation of the gospel with vitriolic speech and tone. One sus-

Nathan Price's "Prayer"

The following is Nathan Prices prayer with original emphases. It is the prayer only, with intermittent narration omitted.

The Lord rideth upon a swift cloud, and shall come into Egypt. *Into* Egypt and *every* corner *of* the earth where *His* light, where His *light* has *yet* to *fall!* The Lord *rideth* in the person of His *angels of mercy*, His *emissaries of holiness* into the *cities* on the plain, where *Lot* dwelled amongst the *sinners!* And Lot *said* unto the *sinners* who *crowded* at his door, I *pray ye, brethren*, do not do so *wickedly!* For the *sinners* of *Sodom* pressed their *evil will* against the entrance to his *household*. The *emissaries* of the Lord *smote* the sinners, who had come *heedless* to the sight of God, *heedless in their nakedness. Nakedness* and *darkness* of the *soul!* For we shall *destroy* this place where the *loud clamor* of the *sinners* is waxen *great* before the *face* of the Lord. And Lot went out and *spake* unto those there *worthy.* And Lot said unto them, '*Up!* Get ye *out* from this place of *darkness! Arise* and come forward into a *brighter land!* O Lord, let us pray. Lord, grant that the worthy among us here shall rise above wickedness and come out of the darkness into the wondrous light of our Holy Father. Amen.

Barbara Kingsolver, *The Poisonwood Bible* (New York: HarperPerennial, 1999), 26–28.

pects that Paul would not have received much more of a hearing had he used the same rhetoric and tone that one finds in Romans 1. Is the proclaimer's goal to make a point or to get a hearing? If the latter, tact and respect are always in good order.

Though the Athenian sermon urges proclaimers today to establish rapport with an audience, it also urges Christian testimony to challenge views that need correction in the light of the gospel. However, such challenge *begins* by finding some common points of departure. Throughout the sermon, Paul finds several points of connection between the biblical/Jewish tradition and the Greek tradition: God as creator, God as one who does not live in humanly constructed temples, God as one who does not need human offerings, God as one who is to be sought after, God as one who is in some way present among humans, God as one with whom humans have some sort of relationship or kinship, and God as a living one who cannot be captured in dead objects of stone or metal.

But Paul is not merely interested in identifying what the two cultures have in common. His motivation for finding common ground is, ultimately, to challenge the Athenian proclivity to idol worship. He wants to turn his audience toward the true and living God—one whom the Athenians do not know. Paul found within Greek religious, philosophical, and literary traditions ideas that give assent to Paul's biblical and Jewish tradition and that question and challenge the practice of idolatry. This allows Paul to offer a critique of Athenian practice based not on values and ideas foreign to the Athenians, but very much at home among the Athenians.

Within American culture, Dr. Martin Luther King Jr. was most adept at such a method of prophetic critique. His sharp challenges to American culture and values consistently emerged from wellsprings that the larger culture would have affirmed: the Bible and

Martin Luther King, Jr.'s Appeal to Common Values

📖 King's appeal to deeply embedded American values in order to challenge current attitudes is well represented in his "I Have a Dream" speech:

When the architects of our republic wrote the magnificent words of the Constitution and the Declaration of Independence, they were signing a promissory note to which every American was to fall heir. This note was a promise that all men—yes, black men as well as white men—would be guaranteed the unalienable rights of life, liberty, and the pursuit of happiness.

It is obvious today that America has defaulted on this promissory note insofar as her citizens of color are concerned. ...

I have a dream that one day this nation will rise up and live out the true meaning of its creed: "We hold these truths to be self-evident, that all men are created equal."

Martin Luther King Jr., "'I Have a Dream' (1963),"
International Information Programs,
http://usinfo.state.gov/usa/infousa/facts/democrac/38.htm
(2 October 2007).

the sacred texts of American history. [Martin Luther King Jr.'s Appeal to Common Values] Had King, an admirer of Mahatma Gandhi, quoted regularly from Hindu texts or from Marxist literature, he would have lost his audience immediately. Rather, he took the very texts and ideals that America revered and held them up before the American conscience. In so doing, he demonstrated that racism and segregation cut against the grain of the very values we professed to hold sacred.

Finding common ground in order to change that very ground binds the Lukan Paul and Martin Luther King Jr. together. Allowing people to recognize how they fail to live up to their own highest standards is likely a more effective instrument of change than imposing foreign standards that will be instantly suspect.

The proclaimer of the gospel should attempt to establish rapport and establish common ground in order to allow for the necessary critique of perspectives in need of transformation. However, the proclaimer cannot avoid, in the end, the scandal of the gospel. Paul's sermon moved toward the inevitable climax of a call to repentance to turn from false worship to the God whom Paul had now made known to his audience. The demand of Christian proclamation requires that however much common ground one can find between the gospel and other attempts at seeking and finding God, the gospel insists that the quest for God can only find its realization when one meets the One whom God raised from the dead.

We need not enter into speculation about who will go to heaven or who will go to hell. God will ask none of us on the day of appointed judgment for our input. But we are speaking of satisfying the desire that compels and moves human beings to know one's creator. The gospel dares to assert that its message points humanity in the only truly reliable direction to satisfy that desire. That hunger to experience that which transcends us appears universal among humans. There exists what Rudolf Otto called the sense of the *numinous*, a sense of the presence of something beyond us, real but indefinable and beyond our grasp. We can sense that it is, as Paul says, "not far from each one of us" (17:27). Otto uses the expression *mysterium tremendum* to denote the sensing, or "feeling"

Mysterium Tremendum

Rudolf Otto offers the following description of the experience of the mysterious and terrible presence of the Other that compels humans to seek and to find this transcendent power:

The feeling of it may at times come sweeping like a gentle tide, pervading the mind with a tranquil mood of deepest worship. It may pass over into a more set and lasting attitude of the soul, continuing, as it were, thrillingly vibrant and resonant, until at last it dies away and the soul resumes its "profane", non-religious mood of everyday experience. It may burst in sudden eruption up from the depths of the soul with spasms and convulsions, or lead to the strangest excitements, to intoxicated frenzy, to transport, and to ecstasy. It has its wild and demonic forms and can sink to an almost grisly horror and shuddering. It has its crude, barbaric antecedents and early manifestations, and again it may be developed into something beautiful and pure and glorious. It may become the hushed, trembling, and speechless humility of the creature in the presence of—whom or what? In the presence of that which is a *mystery* inexpressible and above all creatures.

Rudolf Otto, *Idea of the Holy* (London: Oxford University Press, 1958), 12–13.

(to employ Otto's word) of that which is "hidden and esoteric that . . . is beyond conception or understanding, extraordinary and unfamiliar."[41] The Athenians felt the presence of that which was hidden from and unfamiliar to them—and to that "unknown god," they dedicated an altar. Paul was there to make this mysterious one known. [*Mysterium Tremendum*]

Augustine's words are most apropos: "Thou hast prompted him [humans], that he should delight to praise thee, for thou hast made us for thyself and restless is our heart until it comes to rest in thee."[42] The goal of the proclaimer is to lead persons to the rest that they are seeking. But such rest can only be found when the seeker comes to rest in the living God. Herein lies both the universal and distinctive character of the God of the gospel. This God is universal in that human beings across time and culture sense God's presence and seek to find this God. This God is distinctive in that this God has chosen to be most assuredly known through the man Jesus of Nazareth, whom God raised from the dead.

NOTES

[1] Bertil Gärtner, *The Areopagus Speech and Natural Revelation* (Uppsala: Gleerup, 1955), 71.

[2] Ben Witherington III, *The Acts of the Apostles: A Socio-Rhetorical Commentary* (Grand Rapids MI: Eerdmans, 1998), 503.

[3] Joseph A. Fitzmyer, *The Acts of the Apostles* (AB 31; New York: Doubleday, 1998), 593.

[4] Gerd Lüdemann, *Early Christianity according to the Traditions in Acts: A Commentary* (Minneapolis: Fortress, 1989), 187.

[5] Wayne Meeks, *The First Urban Christians: The Social World of the Apostle Paul* (New Haven: Yale University Press, 1983), 27–28.

[6] Witherington, *Acts*, 504.

[7] Ibid., 505. Cf. F. J. Foakes Jackson and Kirsopp Lake, *The Beginnings of Christianity: The Acts of the Apostles*, 5 vols. (Grand Rapids MI: Baker, 1979): "*paratithemenos* apparently means presenting evidence," 4.203.

[8] See Fitzmyer's discussion, *Acts*, 594.

[9] Mikeal C. Parsons and Martin M. Culy, *Acts: A Handbook on the Greek Text* (Waco TX: Baylor University Press, 2003), 326, understand the Greek syntax to say that the "some" refers exclusively to the devout Greeks and leading women. That is, *only* Gentiles responded in an affirming way.

[10] John B. Polhill, *Acts* (NAC 26; Nashville: Broadman, 1992), 361.

[11] Jackson and Lake, *The Beginnings of Christianity*, 4.205.

[12] Ibid. See also Luke Timothy Johnson, *The Acts of the Apostles* (SacPag 5; Collegeville MN: Liturgical Press, 1992), 307.

[13] Witherington, *Acts*, 504.

[14] Ibid., 508.

[15] See I. Howard Marshall, "Political and Eschatological Language in Luke," in *Reading Luke: Interpretation, Reflection, Formation*, ed. Craig G. Bartholomew, Joel B. Green, Anthony Thiselton (Scripture and Hermeneutics Series 6; Carlisle UK: Paternoster/ Zondervan, 2005), 157–77.

[16] Polhill, *Acts*, 363.

[17] Ibid.

[18] Robert W. Tannehill, *The Narrative Unity of Luke–Acts: A Literary Interpretation*, 2 vols. (Minneapolis: Fortress, 1990), 2.213. The one major exception would be 14:8–18, Paul's preaching in Lystra.

[19] See Johnson, *Acts*, 312; Polhill, *Acts*, 366.

[20] Jackson and Lake, *The Beginnings of Christianity*, 4.210.

[21] Ernst Haenchen, *The Acts of the Apostles: A Commentary* (Philadelphia: Westminster, 1971), 517–18, suggests that comments about Paul being a "babbler" came from the Epicureans and the speculation that Paul was preaching foreign deities came from the Stoics.

[22] Jackson and Lake, *The Beginnings of Christianity*, 4.212, are among the minority of commentators to dispute this widely held interpretation.

[23] See Jackson and Lake, *The Beginnings of Christianity*, 4.212–13; Polhill, Acts, 368.

[24] Everett Ferguson, *Backgrounds of Early Christianity*, 3rd ed. (Grand Rapids MI: Eerdmans, 2003), 358. Stoics did not advocate an "individual" immortality. But some held that "the soul is part of the World Soul and will reappear in the new world" (Ferguson, 358).

[25] Cited from Fitzmyer, *Acts*, 608.

[26] Cited from Charles H. Talbert, *Reading Acts: A Literary and Theological Commentary of the Acts of the Apostles* (New York: Crossroad, 1997), 163.

[27] Witherington, *Acts*, 526.

[28] Ibid.

[29] E.g., Daniel 7 has four periods, 4 Ezra 14 has 12 periods, and 1 Enoch 90–91 has ten periods.

[30] Fitzmyer, *Acts*, 609.

[31] Quoted from Talbert, *Acts*, 163.

[32] Ibid., 164.

[33] Ibid.

[34] Cited from Fitzmyer, *Acts*, 612.

[35] Ferguson, *Backgrounds*, 358.

[36] See Eusebius, *Church History* 3.4.11 and 4.23.3.

[37] Tannehill, *Narrative Unity*, 2.210–20.

[38] Ibid., 211, 215.

[39] Barbara Kingsolver, *The Poisonwood Bible* (New York: HarperPerennial, 1999), 25.

[40] Ibid.

[41] Rudolf Otto, *The Idea of the Holy* (Oxford: Oxford University Press, 1958), 13.

[42] Cited from John R. Tyson, ed., *Invitation to Christian Spirituality: An Ecumenical Anthology* (Oxford: Oxford University Press, 1999), 104.

PAUL WENT TO CORINTH AND REACHED EPHESUS

Acts 18:1-28

COMMENTARY

Readers divide the chapter differently, but it seems to fall easily into two broad sections. Acts 18:1-17 describes Paul's Corinthian ministry and trials. Acts 18:18-28 serves as a transitional passage to Acts 19, which will focus on Paul in Ephesus. Acts 18:18-22 offers a compressed description of Paul's travels, while vv. 24-28 tell of Apollos in Ephesus and his subsequent journey to Corinth.

"Speak and Do Not Be Silent," 18:1-17

This passage divides further into two sections, vv. 1-11 (Paul's ministry) and vv. 12-17 (Paul's hearing before Gallio).

Paul's Ministry in Corinth, vv. 1-11

Corinth was located approximately thirty-seven miles due west of Athens. As a city of economic and political significance, Corinth was the next logical stop. [Corinth] Pauline Christianity was a thoroughly urban phenomenon.[1]

The narrative of vv. 2-4 requires readers to fill in many gaps. Readers learn that Paul finds his way to the home of a Jewish couple who shared in Paul's trade of tent making. Aquila is described as a Jew from Pontus. His geographical/ethnic place of origin is of no direct significance, but Luke regularly informs readers of characters' places of origin (see Acts 2:22; 4:36; 6:5; 9:11), though not always, as readers do not learn from where Priscilla, his wife, hails.

Paul's own testimony confirms his association with the couple (Rom 16:3; 1 Cor 16:19; cf. 2 Tim 4:19). Perhaps Luke's implied readers knew the couple well enough that it could go without saying that they were believers. The narrative clears up any ambiguity later, however (see 18:26).

Corinth

The Corinth of Paul's day served as the capital of the Roman province of Achaea, a status it had held since 27 BC. The city was economically significant, as well. Its strategic location allowed the city to serve as a bridge connecting mainland Greece and the Peloponnesian Peninsula, as well as to two major seas, the Aegean and Adrian. Two ports, Cenchreae and Lechaeum, situated to the east and west, respectively, kept commerce and travelers moving in and out of Corinth.

Religiously, the city was quite diverse. Older Greek religions experienced something of a revival, including the worship of Apollo, Aphrodite, Poseidon, Asclepius, and Demeter. Non-Greek religions, such as those honoring the Egyptian deities of Isis and Serapis and the Phrygian goddess Cybele, and Judaism were also prominent in Corinth. Paul's lengthy discussions regarding the issue of Christian participation in pagan rituals and cultic practices (see 1 Corinthians 8–10) speaks to the deep-seated cultural currents that could affect believers in Corinth.

Wendell Willis, "Corinth," *EDB* 279–81.

(Credit: Jim Pitts)

The narrator states that the couple had recently arrived from Rome. Why they settled in Corinth is not stated, though why they left Rome is: Emperor Claudius had recently expelled the Jews from Rome. This comment creates a major narrative gap, for Luke offers no other information as to why such an expulsion occurred. Almost universally, interpreters believe Luke to be alluding to an incident to which the Roman historian Suetonius refers (*Life of Claudius*, 25.4). He relates that Claudius the Emperor had to expel Jews from Rome because "the Jews constantly made disturbances at the instigation of Chrestus."[2] [Edict of Claudius] The "instigation of Chrestus" may refer to disturbances created in the Jewish community at Rome by Christian Jews proclaiming Jesus to be the Christos. Chrestus was a rather common Latin name and was pronounced like the Greek word Christos. Suetonius may be alluding to the first preaching about Jesus among the synagogues of Rome by Jewish messianists. Aquila and Priscilla apparently got caught up in the disturbances and expulsions.

Guilds and trade organizations, which drew together people who shared a common craft or trade, were common in Mediterranean antiquity. The practicing of a common trade, combined with the fact that the couple shared Paul's faith in Jesus, drew Paul to them. The trade that they shared was tent making. The term *skēnopoioi* can be understood in the broader sense of "leather worker."

Paul occasionally notes that he would work with his own hands in order to support himself (1 Cor 4:12; 9:6; 1 Thess 2:9; 2 Thess 3:6-8), a fact of which Luke is aware (20:33-34). Some rabbinic and philosophical traditions extolled such self-support as virtuous. *Aboth* 2:2 states, "Study of Torah along with worldly occupation is seemly; for labor in the two of them makes sin forgotten."[3] Within the Greek tradition, Diogenes Laertius says of the philosopher Clesthenes, "He was renowned for his industry, being indeed driven by extreme poverty to work for a living. Thus, while by night he used to draw water in gardens, by day he exercised himself in arguments" (*Lives*, 7.168).

Paul may have elected to support himself not only to emulate some of the more noble traditions of his time, but also to avoid scandal. Some itinerant philosophers, particularly of the Cynic school, relied on begging for support in order to demonstrate their "freedom" from material concerns. Like modern itinerant preachers who "trust the Lord" for their support (that is, who "beg" from supporting congregations), such traveling beggars were regularly viewed as charlatans, willing to fleece credulous supporters.[4] Paul avoids such scandal, not burdening or taking advantage of potential followers of Jesus.

Though Paul worked regularly to support himself, he would have been free to frequent the synagogues on the Sabbath in order to preach. Luke offers no details of Paul's preaching, saying only that he persuaded both Jews and Greeks. Readers can fill in the gaps from recent scenes that Luke has painted with more detail (Philippi [16:11-40]; Thessalonica [17:1-9]; Beroea [17:10-15]).

Things change once Silas and Timothy arrive from Macedonia (v. 5). Specifically, Paul devotes full attention (the verb *synechō* carries the metaphorical meaning of being hard pressed by a sense

---

Edict of Claudius

"Since the Jews constantly made disturbances at the instigation of Chrestus, he expelled them from Rome" (Suetonius, *Life of Claudius* 25.4). As noted in the commentary, most interpreters connect this "edict" with Acts 18:2 and generally date the event to AD 49.

That date 49 comes from the fifth-century writer Orosius, who states that this event occurred in the ninth year of Claudius's reign (25 Jan AD 49–24 Jan AD 50). Orosius claims to have derived the date from Josephus. However, Josephus makes no mention of this event at all. Most historians affirm Orosius's dating of the event and simply believe that his citation of Josephus was in error. Hence, most scholars date Paul's arrival to around the year AD 49 or 50 (see [Pauline Chronology in Corinth]).

Dio Cassius (60.6.6) speaks of another incident involving Claudius and the Jews, which dates to the year AD 41: "As for the Jews, who had again increased so greatly that by reason of their multitude it would have been hard without raising a tumult to bar them from the city, he did not drive them out, but ordered them, while continuing their traditional mode of life, not to hold [open?] meetings." Though Dio explicitly states that Claudius did *not* expel the Jews from Rome, a minority of interpreters (e.g., Lüdemann, 164–71) believes Suetonius and Dio to be referring to the same event, though there is obviously confusion between the ancient writers on exactly what transpired. These interpreters follow Dio's dating of the event, thereby linking Acts 18:2 to the year 41—a step that would have implications in reconstructing Pauline chronology.

Gerd Lüdemann, *Paul, Apostle to the Gentiles: Studies in Chronology* (Philadelphia: Fortress, 1984); Ben Witherington III, *The Acts of the Apostles: A Socio-Rhetorical Commentary* (Grand Rapids MI: Eerdmans, 1998), 539–44.

of urgency) to "the word." The thrust of his proclamation was that Jesus is the Messiah. The narrative leaves a gap as to why the arrival of Paul's two coworkers would allow Paul to devote more attention to the word. Readers familiar with 2 Corinthians 11:8 and Philippians 4:15 might infer that Paul's companions brought financial support from Philippi, freeing Paul from having to carry out his trade.

While v. 4 indicated that Paul persuaded both Jews and Greeks, v. 6 implies a change of response. The Jews are portrayed now as opposing Paul. The narrator uses strong language to note their opposition: *blasphēmountōn* (NRSV, "reviled") is a cognate of "blaspheme." Paul's response is just as strong. By announcing the Jews' blood to be on their own heads (cf. Ezek 33:1-7), Paul declares them to be responsible for any punishment or judgment that comes their way. Paul has declared the truth to them; he is innocent, therefore, of any judgment that befalls them. Paul now declares that he will turn to the Gentiles.

This last statement can create some confusion. Paul has made a similar statement before (cf. 13:46). Whatever Paul means by this, he does not mean that he will never speak again to Jews about the gospel, for Paul maintained a consistent pattern of visiting synagogues when he entered a city. Perhaps Paul meant that in each location, once he offered the gospel to Jews, he felt free to move on to Gentiles. But that might imply that had Jews been receptive to the gospel, Paul would never have "moved on" to Gentiles. Perhaps Paul was simply making clear that, despite Jewish rejection, the proclamation would not cease—Paul would offer the gospel to any who would listen, regardless of Jewish response. Within the larger flow of the narrative, such declarations may serve to give expression to Luke's and the readers' awareness that the future of "the Way" lies with Gentiles.

Interpreters debate whether v. 7 means that Paul changed his place of *residence* to the house of Titius Justus or simply changed the primary location for his *preaching*. The fact that Justus is said to be "worshiper of God" indicates that he is a Gentile. Regardless of precisely what Luke means by Paul going to his house, it is consistent with Paul's change of focus toward the Gentiles. Gentiles, perhaps even Gentiles who might not feel comfortable entering the synagogue, would now have easier access to Paul. The location of Justus's house next to the synagogue might indicate that Paul had not closed off all hope of leading some Jews to recognize Jesus to be their Messiah.

If such were Paul's hopes, they are realized in that Crispus, the ruler of the synagogue, becomes a believer, along with his household (v. 8). [Crispus] Clearly, not all Jews in Corinth rejected Paul's proclamation. Verse 8b implies some direct connection between Crispus becoming a believer and "many of the Corinthians" following suit. The NRSV translates the text to say that it was as a result of hearing *Paul* that many Corinthians came to believe. The Greek text, however, literally says, "having heard, many of the Corinthians believed and were baptized." This could mean that what motivated many Corinthians to believe was that they heard about Crispus's faith. If so, one might infer that among these many Corinthians were Jews, influenced by the example of Crispus. One must concede that the narrator is not clear on this point.

Crispus

The synagogue ruler of Acts 18:8 who became a follower of Jesus is likely the same person named by Paul in 1 Cor 1:14 as one of the persons whom Paul baptized in Corinth. As a ruler of the synagogue, a position that assumes relatively high social and perhaps also financial status, the community of Jews and God-fearers would certainly have noticed his acceptance of Jesus as Messiah.

Paul's vision (vv. 9-10) interrupts the flow of the narrative. Given what follows in vv. 12-17, the vision serves as a reassuring foreshadowing (see [Vision]). This particular vision follows broadly a pattern familiar to Old Testament readers (cf. Exod 3:2-12; Josh 1:1-9; Jer 1:5-10). In such visions, God (or God's representative) appears to a human being (v. 9a, where "the Lord" most likely refers to Jesus), gives a task to perform (v. 9b), and offers a word of assurance (v. 10).[5] The assuring word offered to Paul is not that his days would be free of trials, but that no harm would come to him as a result of such trials.

Part of the basis of the Lord's reassuring word is that the Lord has many people in the city of Corinth. The significance of such language lies in the fact that Luke consistently employs "people" (*laos*) to denote Jews, the ethnic descendants of Abraham, as "the people of God." There are only two exceptions, Acts 15:14 and here. In Corinth, from among Gentiles, God is adding to the ranks of God's people. The vision implies that God is calling so many people from among the Corinthians that an extended stay is necessary for Paul.

This section ends with a statement that Paul spent eighteen months teaching the word among the Corinthians. One does not know whether the narrator means that Paul spent a total of eighteen months for the entire period of his ministry prior to leaving (v. 18, which offers its own imprecise statement of time ["many days"]), or whether eighteen months elapsed prior to the next incident that Luke narrates (vv. 12-17). [Pauline Chronology in Corinth] In the narrative world of Acts, the point is clear enough:

Pauline Chronology in Corinth

Traditional reconstructions of Pauline chronology revolve around dating the edict of Claudius to AD 49 (see [Edict of Claudius]) and the initiation of Gallio's proconsulship to AD 51 or 52 (see [Gallio]). Further, such traditional reconstructions assume the historical reliability of Acts.

Acts 18:2 states that Priscilla and Aquila had recently arrived in Corinth and that their arrival was directly related to Claudius's expulsion of the Jews. The couple arrived in Corinth as early as AD 49 and Paul a little later.

Acts 18:11 reports that Paul stayed in Corinth about eighteen months and implies in 18:12 that Paul was taken before Gallio after the eighteen months had transpired. If Gallio began his tenure as proconsul in the early summer of AD 51 *and* if Paul were taken before him early in his proconsulship *and* if Paul had been in Corinth eighteen months prior to his appearance before the tribunal, that would place Paul's arrival in Corinth in early AD 50. However, Gallio could have begun his tenure in the early summer of AD 52, which would place Paul's arrival in Corinth closer to early AD 51. This is all quite speculative, for one does not really know how many months Gallio was in Corinth prior to Paul's appearance before the tribunal. Further, it is possible that Acts 18:11 intends to communicate that the *total* duration of Paul's stay in Corinth was eighteen months, including the months before and after his appearance before the tribunal. However, if Acts 18:11 indicates the duration of Paul's Corinthian stay prior to his appearance before Gallio, then it is difficult to determine when Paul left Corinth, for Luke offers only the imprecise statement that Paul remained in Corinth for "many days longer" after the hearing before Gallio.

The task of historical reconstruction is even more tenuous if one reads the ancient sources, biblical and extra-biblical, with less credulity. For example, Gerd Lüdemann generally reads Acts through a skeptical lens (162–73). He argues that in Acts 18 Luke has actually collapsed two separate Corinthian visits of Paul, visits separated by several years, into a story of a single visit. The fact that readers encounter in Acts 18 two separate synagogue leaders (vv. 8, 17) is one example offered by Lüdemann to indicate that Acts 18 speaks of separate visits.

Further, Lüdemann rejects Orosius's dating of Claudius's expulsion of the Jews from Rome, given that Orosius wrongly attributes the date of AD 49 to Josephus, who, in fact, makes no mention of this incident. This makes Orosius unreliable. Lüdemann argues that Dio and Suetonius offer varying versions of the same incident regarding Claudius's dealings with some Jews of Rome. Further, Dio's dating of the action to the year AD 41 is historically accurate; hence, Acts 18:2 refers to a Pauline visit to Corinth in AD 41. Acts 18:12-17 makes reference to a second visit that Paul made to Corinth, corresponding with the proconsulship of Gallio and dating to AD 51 or 52. Clearly, Lüdemann's methods do not allow one to reconstruct history simply by reading the Lukan narrative at face value. Chronology derived from the Lukan narrative and the chronology derived from critical historical reconstruction can have little in common.

Gerd Lüdemann, *Paul, Apostle to the Gentiles: Studies in Chronology* (Philadelphia: Fortress, 1984).

Paul had an extended ministry, fulfilling in part the promise of vv. 9-10 that God would protect him from harm.

Paul before Gallio, vv. 12-17

Between vv. 9-11 and v. 12 rests a gap. Whether eighteen months has elapsed is not clear (see [Pauline Chronology in Corinth]), but the narrative obviously assumes some duration of time. The narrative introduces Gallio briefly, setting the following event in the context of his proconsulship of Achaia. Most scholars date the initiation of Gallio's administration to the summer of AD 51 or 52. [Gallio]

The narrator states that the Jews made a united attack on Paul (v. 12). He does not mean by this that every single Jew was opposed to Paul (recall v. 8), but does portray the great bulk of the Corinthian Jewish community as opposed to Paul's ministry. Consequently, they bring Paul before the tribunal (*bēma*) of Gallio. The *bēma* was a raised platform in the midst of the agora (town

Gallio

Gallio's actual name was Lucius Annaeus Novatus, son of Annaeus Seneca and older brother of the Roman philosopher Seneca. Lucius Annaeus was later adopted by one who bore the name Gallio and so assumed the name Lucius Junius Gallio.

An inscription discovered at Delphi refers to Gallio and assists historians in dating the time of his proconsulship of Corinth (see image below). It reads, in part (as reconstructed):

> Tiberius Claudius Caesar Augustus Germanicus, invested with tribunician power for the 12th time, acclaimed imperator the 26th time . . . sends greetings to . . . . But now since it [Delphi] is said to be destitute of citizens, as L. Junius Gallio, my friend and proconsul recently reported to me . . . .

The inscription offers two clues as to the date of Gallio's proconsulship. First, it is dated to Claudius's twelfth year as emperor. Second, it is dated to the twenty-sixth acclamation of Claudius as imperator. Most commentators conclude that these two clues date the inscription between 25 Jan AD 52 and 1 Aug AD 52. It is during this time that Gallio is said to be serving as proconsul.

One generally assumed proconsular duties in early summer. Hence, Gallio could have assumed his duties in either the summer of AD 51 or AD 52 and fallen within the date range established by the inscription. Given that one generally served as proconsul for one year, two at most, Gallio's tenure of service could have begun as early as AD 51 and ended as late as AD 54.

The inscription is quite fragmentary, hence the ellipses in the quotation. The fragment pictured above is the portion specifically mentioning Gallio (four lines up from the bottom, in the middle of the line).

Joseph A. Fitzmyer, *The Acts of the Apostles* (AB 31; New York: Doubleday, 1998), 621–23. (Credit: Image courtesy of www.holylandphotos.org)

square) on which governmental leaders sat to render official judgments. The archaeological remains of such a *bēma* have been located among the ruins of Corinth, though one cannot be sure that it is the first-century *bēma* of Gallio.

In the logic of the Lukan narrative, the response of the Jews follows patterns that readers have come to expect, namely that Paul or his associates are brought before government officials (cf. 16:19; 17:5-6; 17:19) and Jews offer opposition to their ministries (cf. 13:45; 14:2, 19; 17:5, 13). The charge that the Corinthian Jews make against Paul is ambiguous (v. 13). Are they offering strictly a religious accusation (*This man is teaching people to worship our God contrary to Jewish law*) or a more politically charged accusation (*This man is teaching people to worship in a manner that violates Roman law*)? Readers have encountered before political accusations against Paul or his colleagues (cf. 16:20-21; 17:6-7, 19-20 [pos-

Bema at Corinth

According to Acts 18:12, Jews who opposed Paul brought him before the *bēma* [NRSV, "tribunal"], the seat of judgment located on the town square (Agora). The *bēma* pictured here may not date back to the first century.

(Credit: Image courtesy of www.holylandphotos.org)

sibly]), and it might make most sense to follow such an understanding here.

Gallio, however, has no interest in hearing the case (vv. 14-15). He is not interested in hearing any elaboration of the charges or Paul's defense. Rather, he makes clear that he views this dispute, regardless of the Jewish community's motives, as an internal debate among Jews. As such, he dismisses the case with the formal, legal declaration that Roman officials employed when they chose not to adjudicate over a case (v. 15b).[6] With regard to Roman law, he finds Paul guilty neither of a "crime" (*adikēma*) nor of "serious villainy" (*rhadiourgēma*). The two Greek terms together cover both malicious and careless wrongdoing. However, in Gallio's view this dispute is about "words" (perhaps the proper interpretation of Jewish Scriptures or traditions), "names" (perhaps the claim that Jesus is Messiah), and Jewish law.

Once again, consistent with the patterns within the Lukan narrative, Roman officials recognize Jesus and his followers *not* to be a legal threat to the Roman Empire (cf. Lk 23:4, 13-16; Acts 16:39). Rather, Gallio places what he knows of Paul's words squarely within the context of the Jewish tradition. This is precisely where Luke also places the message of "the Way." The Jesus movement is not a new-fangled religion, but the fulfillment of the promises of the God of Abraham, Isaac, and Jacob, promises contained in the Scriptures of the Jewish tradition.

Though Gallio helps Luke's agenda to portray Christianity as non-threatening to the Roman Empire, it is not because Gallio is a paragon of justice. His dismissal of all the Jews, including Paul, from the tribunal is abrupt, perhaps even forceful (v. 16). The

Greek verb *apēlasen* (NRSV, "dismissed") can also be translated as "drove" (so RSV).

That Gallio was not greatly concerned with matters of justice, beyond what Roman law demanded of him, is evident from the curious events that conclude this scene. "They" (the antecedent is ambiguous) seize Sosthenes, the ruler of the synagogue, and beat him before the tribunal. Such mob brutality is of no concern to Gallio (v. 17). [Sosthenes]

On the level of the Lukan narrative, the story can yield a number of insights. While historians can rightly be curious whether this Sosthenes is to be identified with the Sosthenes of 1 Corinthians 1:1, indicating that the Jewish leader later became a follower of Jesus, in Luke's narrative he is given no such identity—he is simply a Jewish leader. Sosthenes may have shared leadership responsibilities with Crispus, also identified as "the ruler of the synagogue" (v. 8). Acts 13:15 speaks of multiple leaders of a synagogue. Or perhaps Sosthenes succeeded him after Crispus became a believer. Regardless, there is some irony that a Jewish leader, perhaps even one who might have been responsible for leading the Jews in making charges against Paul, is the one who is beaten. The Jews take Paul to Gallio, hoping to have Paul disciplined, and it is their own leader who receives the blows.

The text does not say who, precisely, is inflicting the blows on Sosthenes. The Western text makes explicit that it was Greeks, an interpretation that several modern interpreters follow, even if they reject the Western text as representing the oldest textual tradition. Luke has portrayed Gentiles as capable of mob reaction against Jews (cf. 16:20) and will do so again (19:34). Gallio's dismissal of the Jews perhaps unleashed latent anti-Jewish feelings of the Gentile bystanders against the leader of this group of Jews who appeared before Gallio (see [Anti-Jewish Sentiment]). One could also understand the "they" to be Jews, angered that their leader failed to bring charges against Paul. Shamed as they were before the tribunal, they take their rage out on their leader who, as head of the group, must atone for the group's shame.

Readers need not solve these riddles to grasp the main point: the one whom God promised would not be harmed (v. 10) was not, despite Jewish attempts. Those who tried to inflict such harm were not only dismissed by Gallio, whom they sought as an ally, but their own leader was the one to whom the harm had come. If such harm came to Sosthenes by the hands of his own people, the irony is even richer.

Sosthenes

Sosthenes was a ruler of the synagogue in Corinth (Acts 18:17). Acts is not clear with regard to his role in the attempted prosecution of Paul before Gallio. Nor does Acts offer any hint that Sosthenes later became a follower of Jesus. Given that Paul mentions a Sosthenes as a co-author of 1 Corinthians (see 1 Cor 1:1), some have concluded that this leader eventually became a follower of Jesus and companion of Paul.

Paul's Travels and Apollos in Ephesus, 18:18-28

Paul Takes His Leave, vv. 18-23

This section begins with the kind of chronological imprecision that readers have encountered before: Paul remained "many days" in Corinth (v. 18; cf. 9:23, 26). The narrative confirms that the promise made to Paul holds true: despite the attempt of Jews to have Paul disciplined before Roman authorities, Paul actually is able to stay longer in Corinth. After "many days" Paul departs for Syria, the home base of Paul's mission (cf. 15:30-41), accompanied by Priscilla and Aquila.

He journeys to Cenchreae, a port city just southwest of Athens. Luke notes that while there he cut his hair, "for he had a vow." Most likely, this refers to the Nazirite vow, the requirements and procedures of which are found in Numbers 6:1-21. This whole scene creates some interpretive problems, particularly for interpreters who feel compelled to vindicate Luke's historical veracity at every point. [Nazirite Vow] Within the context of the narrative, the comment functions in two ways. First, it shows Paul to be a loyal Jew, laying a foundation for the defense speeches of Paul to follow later. Second, it prepares the reader for the scene in 21:23-24, where Paul plans to attend the Jerusalem temple, with some others, to fulfill this vow. The faith that Paul proclaims is the *fulfillment* of Jewish hopes and Scriptures, offered by a loyal and faithful Jew.

Verses 19-21 prepare readers for later scenes in which Ephesus will play an important role (see 19:1-41; 20:17-35). Paul argues with the Jews there (v. 19), as was his custom. Their request that he stay longer (v. 20) implies a more receptive hearing. Paul promises to return, God willing, in the future. Readers would rightly infer that God would grant such a hope.

Paul leaves Ephesus and lands at Caesarea (v. 22). If Paul's ultimate destination was Antioch of Syria, there were many ports closer than Caesarea Maritima. But the narrator wants Paul to visit the Jerusalem church (the standard way to interpret the phrase "go up" ["to Jerusalem" is added to NRSV, though it gives the right interpretation]), so Caesarea is an appropriate port. The brief visit offers further assurance of Paul's loyalty to the "mother church" of Jerusalem. Following the visit of undefined duration, he returns to Antioch, spends some indeterminate time there, and then elects to revisit churches of Galatia and Phrygia in order to strengthen the disciples there. Compressed into these few words are over 1,500 miles of travel and, therefore, several months of time. While Paul

---

Nazirite Vow

Luke's description of the details of Paul's vow does not match up precisely with the steps delineated in Numbers 6:1-24. First, according to Numbers 6:5, the hair is not to be shorn until the *end* of the vow period. That would imply that Paul was *ending* a period of living under a vow. Yet Acts makes no allusion to Paul having begun a vow. In fact, Acts 21:23-24 speaks of Paul planning to go to the temple to perform the *concluding* rituals with some other persons who were under a Nazirite vow. This implies that Luke understood Acts 18:18 as the *beginning* of the vow period, which culminated when Paul arrived in Jerusalem in Acts 21.

Second, according Num 6:18 the hair is to be shorn at the temple and burned along with the sacrifice that the one who had taken the vow offers at the conclusion of period of consecration. So why is Paul cutting his hair at Cenchreae?

One can address these issues in a number of ways, none of which is totally satisfying. Perhaps the narrator is simply confused. He wants to portray Paul as a loyal Jew, so he offers this anecdote about Paul taking a vow. This is not totally satisfying, since Acts 21:24 seems to reveal the narrator's awareness that it is proper to cut the hair in the temple at the end of the vow period.

One might argue that Paul is, in fact, ending a period of Nazirite consecration, the initiation of which the narrator simply did not report. But why is Paul cutting his hair outside the temple boundaries? Polhill (390n126) argues that Josephus, *J. W.* 2.3.13 can be read to say that Aquila cut his hair outside Jerusalem and offered the sacrifice of

the hair later. Yet there is no section 13 to chapter 3 of book 2 of *J. W.*, so Polhill's argument cannot be confirmed (and I could not locate the actual text to which Polhill is referring).

Witherington (557) argues that references in the Mishna (*Nazir* 3.6; 5.4) allude to the cutting of the hair outside Jerusalem. However, a review of these texts reveals that they do not actually address the issue at hand. Hence, it is difficult to find precedent in Jewish tradition for Paul's actions. If one assumes, nonetheless, that Acts is offering an accurate portrayal of events, one would then conclude that when Paul visited Jerusalem in Acts 18:22 he completed his sacrifice there. Yet Luke makes no reference to this at all.

Such reconstructions of *history* may be possible, but one must concede that such reconstructions are not really interpretations of the Lukan *text*. Rather they constitute the filling in of major gaps in the text: Luke fails to report either the initiation of the vow (following Polhill) or the final ceremony to conclude the vow (following Witherington).

Johnson (329–30) rightly recognizes that Acts 18:18 should be connected with Acts 21:23-24, where the period of consecration ends. He suggests that perhaps Paul cut his hair just before the vow period began since he knew that some time would transpire before shaving his head at the conclusion of the consecrated period.

John B. Polhill, *Acts* (NAC 26; Nashville: Broadman, 1992); Ben Witherington III, *The Acts of the Apostles: A Socio-Rhetorical Commentary* (Grand Rapids MI: Eerdmans, 1998); Luke Timothy Johnson, *The Acts of the Apostles* (SacPag 5; Collegeville MN: Liturgical Press, 1992).

---

tours Asia Minor, the narrator takes the readers back to Ephesus, where he left Priscilla and Aquila.

Scholars who speak of Paul's so-called three missionary journeys in Acts regularly identify this section, vv. 18-23, as the conclusion of the second and initiation of the third journey. However, the forthcoming section (18:24–21:16, which begins with Paul's arrival in Ephesus and culminates with Paul's arrival at Jerusalem) is marked not so much by "journeys" as extended stays in various locations.

Apollos at Ephesus, vv. 24-28

This story about Apollos at Ephesus serves as a transition to Acts 19, which speaks of Paul's ministry in that city. The narrator informs readers that Apollos is from Alexandria. Alexander the Great founded Alexandria in 323 BC. Located there was a great library and museum, which made the city known as a great center

Map of Paul's Third Missionary Journey

Paul's so-called third missionary journey is narrated in Acts 18:23–20:38, beginning from Antioch of Syria. At the conclusion of this "journey" Paul set sail for Jerusalem, arriving there in Acts 21:17.

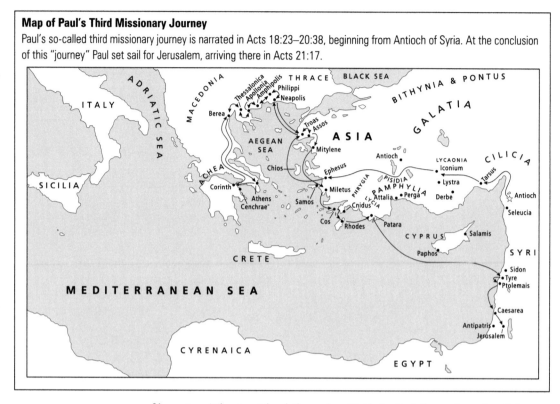

of learning. The Jewish philosopher Philo hailed from that city. It is fitting that one described as an "eloquent man, well versed in the scriptures" (v. 20) would come from the cosmopolitan center that bore Alexander's name. [Apollos]

Apollos

What one learns from the portrayal of Apollos in Acts 18 corresponds well with what Paul says of him in 1 Corinthians. For example, Acts indicates that Apollos went to Corinth after Paul established a community there (18:27). Paul describes himself as one who plants and Apollos as one who watered (1 Cor 3:6), as though Apollos followed the apostle (cf. 1 Cor 3:10).

Acts makes reference to the eloquence of Apollos (18:24). While Paul never explicitly contrasts himself with Apollos on matters of rhetorical eloquence, Paul does imply, with some defensiveness, a certain *lack* of eloquence on his part (cf. 1 Cor 1:18-25; 2:1-5), as though he knew that he was being criticized for such (cf. 2 Cor 10:10). Paul also was aware of some divided loyalties at Corinth, which included some rivalry between followers of Apollos and Paul (1 Cor 1:12). Further, Paul felt compelled to give special attention to his relationship with Apollos as fellow ministers to the Corinthians (1 Cor 3:5-15; 4:6-7). This all *might* imply that the supporters of Apollos were attracted to his skills of eloquence in speech and interpretation, especially as compared to Paul's lack of the same.

Verse 25 states that Apollos is a follower of Jesus, having been instructed in "the Way" of the Lord. The NRSV's description of Apollos as one who "spoke with burning enthusiasm" is more literally rendered as "being fervent in the spirit he spoke." Commentators debate whether one should understand the Greek phrase in a psychological sense, referring to Apollos's fervent spirit (so NRSV), or in a spiritual sense, as referring to the Holy Spirit (see Connections).

The text also describes Apollos as one who taught accurately "the things concerning Jesus." Luke adds the curious comment that Apollos knew only the baptism of John, implying at least two things. First, the narrative assumes the influence of John the Baptist to extend beyond Palestine and the duration of John's life (cf. 19:2-3). Luke does not make much of this, but it offers historians of early Christianity interesting morsels on which to ruminate.[7] Second, Apollos had not been initiated into Christian baptism. Further, the narrator offers no hint that he *ever* was so initiated (see Connections).

Though not fully initiated into the fellowship of "the Way" through baptism, Apollos could speak boldly to Jews in the synagogue (v. 26). Verse 25 made clear that he spoke accurately, as well. Though Apollos spoke boldly and accurately, he still had room for growth. Priscilla and Aquila took him aside and "explained the Way of God to him more accurately." Note that Luke is quite explicit that it was *both* Priscilla and Aquila who taught this very learned man. He offers no hint that it was inappropriate for this woman to serve as a teacher to this man, offering an interesting contrast with 1 Timothy 3:11-12. The narrator leaves readers with another gap to fill concerning what the couple taught Apollos "more accurately." Some speculate that it may have had to do with the issue of baptism.

Apollos decides to go to Achaia (v. 27). Again, the text offers no reason. The Western text fills this gap, adding that some Corinthians who heard Apollos speaking in Ephesus invited him to return with them to their city. Regardless of what initiated Apollos's thinking, the Ephesian congregation supported his decision and sent him to Corinth bearing a letter of recommendation. The New Testament refers to such letters elsewhere (cf. Rom 16:1-2). The narrator describes Apollos as one who was most beneficial to the disciples there, helping the believers. Verse 30 explains just how Apollos helped the believers: by confuting the Jews in public, showing by means of scriptural exposition that Jesus was the Messiah. Why such a "total rout of the opposition"[8] would give encouragement to the Corinthian believers is not said. Perhaps the young believers found reassurance and renewed confidence in their faith that, indeed, this one in whom they believed *was* the Messiah promised in the Jewish Scriptures—a belief that most Jews in the Corinthian community vehemently rejected (recall vv. 5-6).

CONNECTIONS

The mission of Paul and other believers in Corinth and other cities of the empire has much to say about the life of discipleship and the quiet ways that God can play a hand in such lives.

Few modern believers have experiences exactly like that of Paul, as recorded in 18:9-10. Visual and audible encounters with the Lord are not the common fare of most twenty-first-century Christians. Paul's *encounter* with the Lord is, therefore, not so much that with which moderns can "connect." The promise itself offered Paul in that encounter might offer a more realistic connection: The Lord promises Paul that he will not be harmed as he engages in the mission to which he was called.

It's dangerous to take any isolated story, be it from life or from Scripture, and transform it into a paradigm for living. That is, the promise that no injury would come to Paul should not lead one to conclude that so long as one is doing God's will no trials or harm will come one's way. Both Jesus and his followers encountered both trial and harm in the Lukan narrative world. Jesus endured Pilate and the crucifixion. Paul endured a severe beating in Philippi (16:19-40). Peter suffered beatings (5:40) in Jerusalem. James, one of the Twelve, was executed (12:2).

Divine protection does not come in Acts as a fixed formula. In the world of Acts, certainly more so than in the world of most modern Christians, mission comes regularly with trials and pain. Divine protection from harm in the midst of trial is often the exception, not the rule. Something significant is going to happen in Corinth. God's promise, offered through James, the leader of the Jerusalem church, that God would call out from among the Gentiles a people for God's name (15:17) is finding special realization in this city. *Many* people of God are to emerge from Corinth (18:10). And Paul's ministry of nurturing, indeed of "fathering" (cf. 1 Cor 4:14-15), this people requires, in this instance, special protection from the Lord. Paul's presence will be needed for some time in Corinth. And for his ministry to be effective, Paul will need to be kept from harm, though not necessarily from trial.

Paul's protection from harm is directly linked to his hearing before Gallio. Gallio's total lack of interest in Jewish concerns foiled the schemes of Paul's opponents to persecute him. Gallio did not act from incredibly noble motives. It was not his burning desire for justice that compelled him to drive all the Jews, including Paul, from the tribunal. The fact that he ignored the beating of Sosthenes confirms this. Yet, ironically, and even providentially, it was Gallio's casual disregard for the Jewish religion and matters internal to its interests that contributed to Paul's protection.

God's providential care in life and history is often portrayed in the Bible in more dramatic ways: wind and tongues of fire, prison doors opening, chains falling off, earthquakes, resuscitations, and the lame walking. But sometimes the lesson learned by Elijah as he hid in the cleft of the rock repeats itself in other portions of the biblical narrative. God is not always in wind, fire, or shaking rocks (cf. 1 Kgs 19:11-13). Sometimes God's purposes are accomplished in ways imperceptible to most eyes. Paul's protection in Corinth came not through any miracle, but through Gallio's own indifference.

The quiet, virtually invisible workings of God through human action, or inaction, are part of the biblical portrait of providence. It was certainly not the intention of Joseph's brothers, when they sold him into slavery, to set in motion events that would allow Joseph one day to deliver his family from famine. The author of Second Isaiah sees the providential care of God guiding the history that allowed the Jews to return to their homeland. Yet Cyrus is not portrayed as intentionally seeking to be an instrument of God's purposes; in fact, Isaiah 45:4-5 states explicitly that Cyrus does not even know God. It is well known that the Hebrew version of Esther does not even mention God (a silence that the Septuagintal version could not bear, adding, as it did, several sections with explicit references to God). Part of the mystery of more subtle and thoughtful understandings of providence is how life seems to move in a direction that achieves purpose even when God appears to have no involvement. "Coincidences," someone has said, "are God's way of remaining anonymous." [Synchronicity]

Because God, more often than not, works in such a subtle manner, it is not possible to formulate some sure doctrine of providence that one can apply, like a scientific formula, to any situation in life. God works so intricately in the nooks and crannies of human decisions, indecisions, prejudices, and good and bad intentions that we must all live with a sense of openness

Synchronicity

"Synchronicity" is a term coined by Carl Jung. Walter Wink employs the word to talk about providence. Wink quotes Jung, defining synchronicity as "a concurrence or meaningful coincidence of events not causally connected with one another" (Wink, 75). Wink goes on to say,

> Causality is merely a statistical hypothesis of how events evolve one out of another, whereas synchronicity takes the coincidence of events in space and time as meaning something more than mere chance, namely, a peculiar interdependence of objective events among themselves as well as with the subjective (psychic) states of the observer or observers. (75)

The narrative of Acts relates a series of "objective events" that took place in Corinth, including many such events that most would call "bad" or "evil," such as determined, even violent opposition against Paul and Gallio's disregard for justice. But the narrator implicitly sees within these events a meaningful order and tells his story in a way that invites readers as they observe these events to find such meaningful order. It is the "coming together" of "incidents" (co-incidents → coincidence) as subjectively perceived by observers (readers) that allows them to recognize the working out of God's providential care so that Paul could remain in Corinth to carry out his ministry.

Walter Wink, "Providence and the Powers," in *Transforming the Powers: Peace, Justice, and the Domination System*, ed. Ray Gingerich and Ted Grimsrud (Minneapolis: Fortress, 2006), 67–83.

The Working of God

The Lord assures Paul that no harm will come to him (18:10) and then steps off the stage of the narrative immediately following. The Lord's providential care is actualized not by explicit intrusions of God, but through the unfolding of events, all of which seemingly consist of the free actions of human characters on the stage. How are readers to understand God's providential care or ways of working in such events?

John Sanders offers a helpful discussion of views of providence. He speaks first of "meticulous providence," also called "specific sovereignty." He writes, "God has *exhaustive* control over each situation: Only what God purposes to happen in that particular time and place to that specific creature will happen. God does not take risks in governing the world because God micromanages every detail" (211).

Applied to this particular story (and all events that happen in Acts or in life), the particular ways in which God's providential care for Paul is "worked out" are willed or ordained by God. Gallio's quick dismissal of charges against Paul, rooted ultimately in his disregard for justice, which is instrumental in this story to preserve Paul from harm, is "purposed" and "micromanaged" by God. There are ethical problems associated with this view of providence, for though God's micromanagement of affairs, including Gallio's disregard for justice, delivers Paul, it would also be evident in the beating of Sosthenes before the tribunal. This act of violence against Sosthenes is also "purposed" by God.

Sanders also speaks of "general sovereignty" or "general providence."

> God has sovereignly established a type of world in which God sets up general structures or an overall framework for meaning and allows creatures significant input into exactly how things will work out. . . . Since God macromanages the overall project (while remaining free to micromanage some things), God takes risks in governing the world. . . . [T]his model does not claim that God has a specific purpose for each and every event which happens. . . . God's normal way of operating is to allow the creatures significant freedom and, consequently, not to control everything. (213–14)

Applied to this narrative, God has a "project" for Paul, which, broadly, is to be a witness to both Jews and Gentiles (cf. 9:15). In this particular setting, God's purpose is for Paul to remain unharmed in Corinth so that he might do the work of God. The specific means by which God's "project" finds realization include the violent opposition against Paul by some of the Jews in Corinth and Gallio's apathetic disregard for justice. But God does not "will" or "purpose" such evil to happen. God gives God's creatures the genuine freedom to act in ways that violate God's perfect means of achieving God's project. Hence, God takes risks.

Such a view of providence is certainly more complex than meticulous providence. While those who embrace specific sovereignty may not understand much of the evil that God purposes or wills, they can surrender to the comforting thought that, in the larger scheme of God's will, such events have a specific purpose. Those who embrace "general providence" must concede that some events have no specific divine purpose. Mysteriously, however, as the story (be it the story of Acts or the story of one's life) unfolds one can, with a discerning eye, see how the divine project finds realization.

John Sanders, *The God Who Risks: A Theology of Providence* (Downers Grove IL: InterVarsity Press, 1998).

and mystery to how God can possibly accomplish God's purposes. Hence, we reiterate what we said earlier: it is dangerous to take an isolated biblical story and make it a fixed and absolute foundation on which to construct a paradigm for all of life. [The Working of God]

The cautionary word against seeking firm and fixed paradigms is reiterated in Luke's story of Apollos at Ephesus (18:24-26). As discussed in the Commentary, interpreters are not sure whether *to pneuma* refers to Apollos's spirit or to the Holy Spirit. The ambiguity arises because the text states that Apollos knew only the baptism of John, implying that he had not experienced Christian baptism. Christian baptism is the normal means in Acts through which one receives the Holy Spirit (cf. Acts 2:38).

Yet the narrative of Luke–Acts refuses to tie the presence of God's spirit to any fixed or orthodox formula. Luke refuses to offer a "doctrine of the Spirit" that limits the God's freedom. [Freedom of God] Before concluding that Apollos cannot be moved by the Spirit since he knew only the baptism of John, one should recall that the great characters of Luke's birth narrative were moved by the Spirit, even before there was a baptism of John, much less one in the name of Jesus! Elizabeth (1:41), Zechariah (1:67), and Simeon (2:25) are all said to have been moved by the spirit of God. One should not overlook that none of those who received the Spirit on the day of Pentecost were said to have been baptized.

Ritualistic patterns are important to religion. They provide a sense of order, predictability, and stability. Such is not a bad thing. Human beings need order. Yet when the quest for order requires placing restrictions on God, order can become a subtle idol. The text of Acts is ambiguous. Perhaps the narrator wanted only to refer to the fervent spirit of Apollos, rather than the fervent spirit of God. But readers must live with the ambiguity and not sweep it away because Apollos "knew only the baptism of John," as though the rituals with which Apollos was familiar could restrict God's freedom to inspire and use him.

Freedom of God

Eduard Schweizer offers the following thoughtful insight that bears on the issue of Apollos, baptism, and the Spirit:

> Nor is there a definite Pneumatology in Luke. How confusing are the reports in Acts! Once the Spirit is given without baptism (2:4), often immediately after or in baptism (2:38, etc.), once also before (10:44) and twice quite a time after baptism (8:16-17; 19:6). Moreover, the Spirit once given to someone has still to come anew (for instance, 4:31). There is no doctrine of the Spirit which would shield us against ever-new surprises by the living God, of whose love we know, but not how he will act on us.

Eduard Schweizer, *Luke: A Challenge to Present Theology* (Atlanta: John Knox Press, 1982), 91–92.

NOTES

[1] See Wayne Meeks, *The First Urban Christians: The Social World of the Apostle Paul* (New Haven CT: Yale University Press, 1983), 1–50.

[2] Cited from C. K. Barrett, ed., *The New Testament Background: Writings from Ancient Greece and the Roman Empire That Illuminate Christian Origins*, rev. ed. (New York: HarperSanFrancisco, 1989), 14.

[3] Quoted from R. Travers Herford, ed. and trans., *Pirke Aboth: The Ethics of the Talmud: Sayings of the Fathers* (New York: Schocken Books, 1962), 41.

[4] John B. Polhill, *Acts* (NAC 26; Nashville: Broadman, 1992), 384.

[5] See Benjamin J. Hubbard, "The Role of Commissioning Accounts in Acts," in *Perspectives on Luke–Acts*, ed. Charles H. Talbert (Special Studies Series 5; Danville VA: Association of Baptist Professors of Religion, 1978), 187–98.

[6] Ben Witherington III, *The Acts of the Apostles: A Socio-Rhetorical Commentary* (Grand Rapids MI: Eerdmans, 1998), 554.

[7] More will be said about the enduring influence of John the Baptist in the Commentary on Acts 19.

[8] This is how Luke Johnson understands the Greek verb Luke employs (*diakatēlecheto*). See *The Acts of the Apostles* (SacPag 5; Collegeville MN: Liturgical Press, 1992), 333.

TEACHING THE WORD OF
GOD AMONG THE EPHESIANS

Acts 19:1-41

COMMENTARY

Acts 19 connects with the story of Apollos in Ephesus (18:24-28), though the focus on Paul in this chapter gives the chapter its own literary integrity. The chapter divides as follows: Verses 1-10 describe Paul's ministry in Ephesus, with a focus on the disciples of John. Verses 11-22 tell the story of the sons of Sceva and Paul's confrontation with magic at Ephesus. Verses 23-41 offer an interesting story of Paul's confrontation with peddlers of paganism (vv. 23-27), a confrontation that sparks a riot (vv. 28-34), which is quieted only by a speech from the town clerk (vv. 35-41).

The Residents of Asia Heard the Word, 19:1-10

The first verse connects the ensuing narrative with what precedes. Reference to Apollos being in Corinth recalls 18:27-28. Reference to Paul passing through "the interior regions" (lit., "the upper [or "higher"] regions") alludes back to 18:23. Fitzmyer states that these upper regions denote the "more mountainous, inland parts of Asia Minor, the upper regions of Galatia and Phrygia (18:23)."[1] Paul then found his way to Ephesus, alluding back to 18:21, where Paul had announced his intention to return. The narrator states straightforwardly that Paul found some disciples there. [Ephesus]

In vv. 2 and 3 readers learn that these disciples had not received the Holy Spirit. In fact, they had not even heard of the Holy Spirit and had not experienced Christian baptism, but only the baptism of John. On first glance, it would appear that Paul is talking with non-Christians who were disciples of John the Baptist. These are persons, Paul insists, who need to follow up on John's own message, which was one of preparation through repentance for the one to come after John, namely Jesus (v. 4).

Ephesus

In Paul's day, the city of Ephesus was over 900 years old and had experienced, as any city of that age, quite a history. It had been ruled by the Persians, Alexander and his various successors, and rulers of the region of Pergamum, until moving under Roman control in 133 BC. From that time it served as the official residence of the governor of the Roman province of Asia.

Ephesus was among a select group of cities during the Roman imperial period to have the honor to build temples dedicated to patron deities. The patron deity of Ephesus was Artemis.

According to Acts, Paul was instrumental in founding the Christian community at Ephesus (18:19), though his coworkers, particularly Priscilla and Aquila, made significant foundational contributions (18:26). Paul's extended stay of some three years (19:10, 22; 20:31) speaks to the importance of the city in the Pauline mission.

David E. Aune, "Ephesus," *EDB* 413–15.

However, four things suggest that these persons are Christians. First, they are called "disciples," and Luke–Acts only uses "disciples" to denote disciples *of Jesus*, unless the text adds some qualifying descriptor (e.g., Luke 5:33 and 7:18 speak of "disciples of John"). Second, these disciples appear to be somewhat like Apollos, whom readers encountered in the previous chapter (see [Apollos]). Apollos, too, "knew only the baptism of John" (18:25), yet he clearly was a follower of Jesus. One could be a "disciple of Jesus" and not be baptized into the name of Jesus. Third, Paul assumes these persons to be "believers." In v. 2 he asks whether they had received the Holy Spirit when they became *believers* (*pisteusantes*). Would Paul have had any kind of believer in mind other than a believer in Jesus? Fourth, though Paul directs these "disciples" to "believe in the one who was to come after [John]" (v. 4), he mentions only Jesus' name; he does not offer any summary of the kerygma (see [Kerygma]), as though Paul could assume that they had already heard of Jesus.

And yet each of these arguments is not without weaknesses. Though Luke's tendency is to use "disciple" without any qualifying statement to denote only followers of Jesus, one cannot confidently and rigidly require such consistency from the narrator. Luke may have wanted only to communicate that Paul had encountered some persons who had some broad connection with the Way, the precise nature of which required clarification.

Second, though there is some connection with Apollos in that both had experienced the baptism of John, the narrator explicitly says that Apollos knew about Jesus and even taught accurately concerning Jesus (18:25). Further, there is no indication that Apollos was baptized into the name of Jesus, leaving the impression that he was, in some very real sense, a disciple of Jesus. These disciples, on the other hand, were baptized "into the name of the Lord Jesus" (v. 5; see [In the Name of Jesus]), indicating a status different from that of Apollos.

Third, while Paul uses the term "believer" to address these persons, he apparently is not clear concerning their status. Had Paul felt absolutely confident that they were "believers in Jesus," one wonders why he would have asked them if they had received the Holy Spirit. In the Lukan narrative world, belief in Jesus consistently goes hand in hand with receipt of the Spirit. Luke's character, Paul, would certainly have known that. Hence, Paul's very inquiry raises questions concerning the status of these persons.

Fourth, the fact that Luke offers no summary of the kerygma is of little significance. Luke has presented numerous summaries thus far and can assume that readers would fill in the gap of what Paul might have said (cf., e.g., 18:4, 19, 25).

One could also add that the narrative logic of the story must assume that these "disciples" were not a part of any Christian community in Ephesus. Had they been, it is difficult to understand how they would never have heard of the Holy Spirit or that John's message was one (only) of repentance and preparation. It seems odd that Priscilla and Aquila, presented as characters who would go to such lengths to set Apollos straight (18:26), would not take steps to ensure that Ephesian congregations were properly schooled in the essentials of the gospel message.

Though commentators are divided, the evidence would appear to indicate that these disciples are not "Christians." However, whether these Ephesian disciples were Christians of a sort or only followers of the Baptist, it is clear that subsequent to their baptism they receive the Holy Spirit and either become Christians or "Christians in the full sense."[2] The evidence that they receive the Spirit is manifested in their speaking in tongues and prophesying (v. 6; see [Tongues]). The text could mean that they engaged in two separate activities: they *both* spoke in tongues *and* prophesied. However, the word *kai* (NRSV, "and") can also be used in an explicative manner, rendering the translation, "they spoke in tongues; that is, they prophesied." This is reminiscent of the Pentecost experienced by the Twelve and others in 2:1-4 and 17. There it is said that they spoke in tongues (2:4) and prophesied (2:17). It is also similar to the experience of Cornelius and his household (10:44-48).

These followers of John (and, perhaps, in some sense, Jesus) are now (fully?) incorporated into the people of God and receive the sign of such incorporation. Luke Johnson finds it significant that there were about twelve of these persons, as though Luke were intending "to symbolically represent a realization of 'Israel.'"[3]

While interpreters will never solve the riddle of the status of these disciples, the text may address issues more significant than the exact

Followers of John the Baptist

Biblical testimony makes clear that John the Baptist had his own circle of disciples (Matt 9:14; 11:2 || Luke 7:18; Luke 11:1; John 1:35; 4:1). And testimony from texts such as Acts 18:25 and 19:3 indicate that John's message of baptism reached out into the larger Greco-Roman world.

The Gospels seem concerned to make clear that John is subordinate to Jesus (see such texts as Matt 3:14 and John 1:8, 20; 3:30). In fact, many believe that one of the major points of the Lukan birth narrative, as he offers his narrative of Jesus' and John's respective annunciations and births, is to show Jesus to be superior to John. Attention to such a concern on the part of New Testament writers offers indirect evidence that followers of the Baptist continued to offer some competition to the Jesus movement at the time these narratives were composed. The story of Paul and followers of John in Acts 19 is one such story that serves to show that, properly understood, John's purpose is to *prepare* the way for Jesus.

J. Bradley Chance, "John the Baptist," *MDB* 458–59.

status of these disciples prior to their meeting Paul. At least two other issues emerge. First, there is wide consensus among historians of early Christianity that John the Baptist continued to have a following after his death. [Followers of John the Baptist] This story, combined with other references in Acts (see 1:5; 11:16; 13:25; 18:25), makes clear that John's role was to *prepare* for Jesus; John was not of sufficient importance or authority to warrant a long-standing following of his own. The story of the Ephesian disciples presses the message that those who continued in *Luke's own time* to follow the Baptist were missing the point of the Baptist's own message: the Baptist offered a message of repentance and a baptism of water to prepare for the coming of the Messiah, who would offer salvation and a baptism of the Spirit.

A second issue is somewhat related. The narrative has portrayed Jesus' followers as bringing Jews of all sorts into the fold of the faith community centered around Jesus: ordinary people (on whom Jesus focused his work in the Gospel), priests (6:7), Pharisees (15:5), Hellenistic Jews (6:5-6), and even Samaritans (8:4-25), though it is not clear whether Luke perceived them to be "Jews" (see [The Samaritans]). These followers of the Baptist may represent yet one more sort of Jewish group that finds its completion—its fulfillment—in the ranks of the church. Jesus has not come to offer a new religion, but to complete and fulfill a very old and rich religious tradition.

In a series of brief statements, Luke summarizes the essence of Paul's Ephesian ministry, which lasted for an extended period. Verse 8 speaks of Paul's preaching in the synagogue for three months. Verse 10 refers to two additional years, and v. 22 indicates that Paul continued to stay for "some time longer."

Paul's preaching in the synagogue again shows that declarations such as those found in 13:46 and 18:6, namely that Paul would turn to the Gentiles, do not mean that Paul would show no further interest in the Jews. In each location Paul offers all persons, Jews and Gentiles, the opportunity to respond to the message of the kingdom. Reminiscent of the Pauline phrase from Romans 1:16, 2:9, 10, "to the Jew first and also to the Greek," the Lukan Paul gives due attention to the Jews of the cities he visits.

The fact that Paul could preach for three months would indicate some measure of acceptance. While the narrator does not share specifically what Paul said, he states that Paul "argued persuasively" (cf. 17:2, 16; 18:4, 19). Persuasive argument can only be resisted by "stubborn refusal" (v. 9). The Greek text reads more literally, "but some were hardened and not persuaded." The word translated "hardened" or "stubborn" (*esklērynonto*) is found regularly in the Old Testament to denote a turning from the God: "It signifies a stubborn resistance in the face of God's visitation."[4] The intensity of the Jewish resistance to the gospel appears to be growing (see [The Jews]). It will reach a crescendo when Paul reaches Jerusalem. These hardened persons attempt to shame Paul before the Jewish congregation, speaking "evil of the Way" (see [The Way]). Consequently, Paul chooses to withdraw, taking those who had become disciples with him.

Paul moves his mission to the "lecture hall of Tyrannus" (v. 9). The Greek text literally reads "the school of Tyrannus," but the word *scholē* can denote either a gathering of *persons*, such as a philosophical school (see [School]), or a gathering *place*. Most interpreters interpret *scholē* in the latter sense. History offers no further information about Tyrannus, the owner of the hall, presumably to whom Paul would have had to pay rent (though the narrative is silent about this detail, or how Paul would have afforded such rent).

What is apparent is that the lecture hall offered Paul a more open forum, allowing him to preach more widely. Readers can infer that Gentiles who would not have attended the local synagogue might be inclined to attend this type of more public gathering. One can assume Lukan hyperbole when he declares that "*all* the residents of Asia, both Jews and Greeks" had heard the gospel. In Luke's narrative world, this extended stay in Ephesus effectively brings to an end Paul's evangelistic activity in the larger world. With the end of the Ephesian ministry, the narrative will focus on Paul's attention to churches already established, his return to Jerusalem, and his trip to Rome.

The Word of the Lord Grew Mightily, 19:11-22

Verses 11-12 portray Paul as one who is mighty not only in word, but also in deed. The narrator is clear that Paul is an *instrument* of God; that is, it is God who actually works the mighty deeds "by the hands of Paul" (v. 11). Persons who are both physically ill and possessed of demons can find healing through Paul. The power that radiates through Paul is so efficacious that one does not even need to be touched by Paul to receive wholeness. Handkerchiefs (the Greek term *soudaria* could denote a rag tied around the head, like a "sweatband") or aprons that had come into contact with Paul's skin could transfer healing power.

Mana, "the conveying of the healing power through the medium of a piece of clothing . . . from the healer,"[5] could strike readers as quite similar to magic, the very thing that the narrator seems to go to such lengths in this larger story to discredit. Susan Garrett is helpful here, in her argument that "magic" is as much a qualitative as formulaic judgment in ancient literature. Magic is what persons label demonstrations of power that they find offensive or inspired by forces one views as dark or demonic (see [Magic]).[6] From the narrator's perspective, Paul is clearly not an ally of the forces of darkness; hence, he is no magician, no matter how much methods associated with him appear magical.

Clearly the narrative dissociates Paul's abilities to do mighty works from "magic." The darkly humorous story of the sons of the high priest Sceva (vv. 13-17) and the ensuing story of the rejection of magic by the Christians of Ephesus (vv. 18-20) make this apparent. The narrative introduces some unnamed itinerant Jewish exorcists (see [Exorcism]). While specific details about Jews who performed exorcisms are slim, H. D. Betz states that "Jewish magic was famous in antiquity."[7] These exorcists seem to view "the name of Jesus" as something of a magical incantation, using his name in a somewhat formulaic manner to cast out evil spirits. [Magical Incantation] That they identify this Jesus as "the Jesus whom Paul preaches" betrays the fact that they make no claim to know this Jesus personally. That is, they do not appeal to Jesus as one in whom they believe; they simply attempt to invoke his name to secure the desired results.

Magical Incantation

Given the pervasiveness of magic in the ancient world, it is not surprising that archaeologists have recovered a number of magical formulae. Among various magical papyri is one dating to c. AD 300 that offers the following formula for exorcism. Note among the names a variation on the name Jesus:

Standing opposite, adjure him. The adjuration is this: "I adjure thee by the god of the Hebrews Jesu, Jaba, Jae, Abraoth, Aia, Thoth, Ele, Elo, Aeo, Eu, Jiibaech, Abarmas, Jabarau, Abelbel, Lona, Abra, Maroia.

C. K. Barrett, ed., *The New Testament Background: Writings from Ancient Greece and the Roman Empire That Illuminate Christian Origins*, rev. ed. (New York: HarperSanFrancisco, 1989), 34.

The story then zeroes in on some particular Jewish exorcists, the seven sons of the high priest Sceva. Reference to this particular high priest creates some interpretive problems. The Jewish historian Josephus mentions no high priest by this name in his listing of those who held this office (*Ant.* 18.34-20.179). Further, one wonders what this high priestly family is doing in Ephesus! The Western textual tradition addresses the problem by identifying Sceva simply as a priest—not as a *Jewish high priest.*

Interpreters address this problem in numerous ways. Most argue that Luke may have been using the term "high priest" not to denote *the* ruling priest, but someone from the aristocratic priestly families from which the high priest was chosen. According to this understanding it would be more appropriate to translate *archiereōs* as "chief priest," as in Acts 4:23. Fitzmyer argues that the term *archiereōs* was used to denote priestly authorities of the imperial cult. Perhaps Sceva was a Jew who had "defected" to paganism and served now in the Roman cult.[8] Regardless of how one interprets the specific meaning, the narrative serves to contrast the healing power of Paul with the total ineffectiveness of his Jewish counterparts, some of whom can even claim impressive credentials!

While the evil spirit recognizes Jesus and Paul, perhaps acknowledging the authority of these two over it (cf. Jas 2:19), it does not recognize the authority of these sons of Sceva who attempt to exploit Jesus' name. The story illustrates clearly and somewhat comically who has the power in this confrontation between the priest's sons and the demon. The evil spirit comes out of the man and masters and overpowers all the sons of Sceva. Battered and stripped naked, the Jewish would-be exorcists are publicly shamed as they flee the house and expose themselves to the populace of Ephesus.

In some sense, the sons of Sceva do succeed in casting the unclean spirit out of its original victim. The man in need of cleansing is rescued—the narrator does not leave this demon-possessed man, with whom readers are likely to show sympathy, without deliverance. Yet the evil spirit is not conquered—it has found some new hapless victims, persons with whom the reader, however, is presumably not to be sympathetic. The victim is released while villainous characters get what they deserve.

Word travels through Ephesus, both among Jews and Greeks (i.e., non-Jews) so that people are awed by the authentic power they have witnessed (v. 17). This verse offers an intertextual echo with the story of Jesus in Luke 7:16-17. In this text, fear grips the people, God is glorified, and the word is spread. Public reaction and response play a role in validating the claims of the gospel, whether offered by Jesus or one of his followers.

Awed by the demonstration of such power, many who had become Christians, perhaps due to the evidence of spiritual power radiating from Paul, chose to confess their practices (v. 18). The next verse makes clear that the practices of which the story speaks are "the magic arts" (v. 19). Not all who practiced magic brought their books to be burned. This could mean that some held back

Books in Antiquity

In biblical times the word "book" gener-ally denoted what modern persons would think of as a scroll. Sheets, either of papyrus (paper) or leather, would be stitched together and rolled up. One would read the book by unrolling the scroll. The codex, which is more akin to the modern book, became prevalent beginning in the second century AD. It is possible, however, that such codex book forms were avail-able in the first century.

their books or that only some who practiced magic, such as the more affluent, had books to burn. Books in antiquity were very expensive, and magical books, containing formulas and recipes to manipulate the cosmic powers, brought an even greater premium. [Books in Antiquity] Luke's claim that the books were valued at 50,000 silver coins should impress readers of the immense financial sacrifice. The drachma is the coin likely spoken of here. If one assumes the drachma to represent a day's wage, 50,000 days of wages repre-sents an impressive sum!

Luke offers another statement summarizing the success of the gospel. Verse 20 can be translated two ways. The NRSV offers one possible translation. One could also translate the words, "So with the power of the Lord the word grew and prevailed." Each testifies to the gospel's efficacy in the city of Ephesus.

Verses 21-22 serve to foreshadow significant events of the narra-tive. There is debate whether the phrase *en tō pneumati* denotes the Holy Spirit or Paul's spirit. The NRSV assumes the former. If one understands it to mean Paul's spirit, it would render "Paul resolved in his spirit" or simply "Paul decided" (NIV). The Lukan tendency to see behind events the providential hand of God may favor the NRSV translation. However, the hand of God cooperates with human choices (see [The Working of God]). It was *Paul* who *resolved* in the (Holy) Spirit to take certain steps in the future.

What Paul resolved was to revisit churches he had founded in Macedonia and Achaia, then move on to Jerusalem and Rome (v. 21). Luke will give little detailed attention to Paul's revisitation of established churches (see Acts 20:1-5). However, he will give much attention to Paul's trip to Jerusalem, by way of Troas and Miletus (20:7-38), from which Paul would make his way to Jerusalem and eventually on to Rome.

In describing his plans to visit the center of the empire, Paul says, "I must also see Rome," or, more literally, "It is necessary [*dei*] for me to see Rome." Luke regularly uses *dei* to denote divine necessity, most especially with reference to events that happen on the plane of history so that the pur-poses of God can be accomplished. [Divine Necessity] "It is necessary" that Paul see Rome in order to accomplish God's intention that the gospel of the kingdom reach the "ends of the earth" (cf. Acts 1:8). In preparation for Paul's

Divine Necessity

Luke regularly used the Greek verb *dei* to denote necessary action, particularly action that is necessary within the divine scheme of things. He uses the verb in various tenses thirty-six times. Some key texts are Luke 2:49; 4:43; 9:22; 13:33; 17:25; 24:7, 26, 44; Acts 1:16; 3:31; 4:12; 9:16; 14:22; 17:3; 19:21; 23:11.

visits, he sends two of his helpers, Timothy (see [Timothy]) and Erastus, on to Macedonia while Paul remained behind in Asia (Ephesus) "for some time longer" (v. 22). [Erastus] Before Paul can leave he must pass through one more great adventure.

Erastus

It is possible that the Erastus who appears in the Lukan narrative (19:22) is the same as the Erastus mentioned in Rom 16:23, written from Corinth. The Erastus in Rom 16:23 is identified as the city treasurer. Note that Erastus is said to be accompanying Timothy. Apparently, Paul had left Timothy in Corinth (18:5), but at some point Timothy rejoined Paul, for Timothy is now in Ephesus (19:22). Perhaps readers should infer that, historically, Erastus accompanied Timothy to Ephesus from Corinth.

No Little Disturbance Broke Out, 19:23-41

Demetrius's Complaint, vv. 23-27

Around this same time, the narrator reports, "no little disturbance" arose on account of the Way (v. 23). The narrator regularly uses a negative, such as "no little," to denote a positive, such as "large" or "great" (cf. 12:18; 17:4, 12; 19:24). A certain silversmith named Demetrius is the ringleader (v. 24). An inscription from Ephesus identifies one by this name as a temple administrator, but there is no clear reason to identify this as the same person.

Demetrius used his skill to build "silver shrines of Artemis" (v. 24). These were likely small replicas of the temple of Artemis, used as amulets and employed in family worship around the home altar. [Artemis] A mold for such replicas resides in the Metropolitan Museum of Art in New York,[9] and replicas have been discovered in various locations, though no silver ones have survived. Silver

Artemis

Artemis of Ephesus was the local manifestation of a truly cosmopolitan deity in the Greco-Roman world. In fact, she was the most widely followed deity in Paul's day. She was closely associated, particularly among the Ephesians, with fertility and the protection of new life. A statue of Artemis from Ephesus shows numerous eggs or breasts protruding from her torso—symbols of fertility. Ancient inscriptions indicate that devotees looked to her for answered prayer and the offering of salvation, including liberation from fate and demonic forces.

Twice each year the city of Ephesus would sponsor civic celebrations that revolved around the city's devotion to the goddess. Involved in the celebration was the procession of the images of Artemis from the Artemisium, the temple of Artemis, through the city streets. The temple that stood in Paul's day dates back to the fourth century BC and was considered one of the seven wonders of the ancient world. The civic celebrations brought many pilgrims to Ephesus, and the "tourist industry" was the primary means of economic support to the city.

Joseph A. Coray, "Artemis," *EDB* 107.

Statue of Artemis. Ephesus Archaeological Museum, Ephesus, Turkey. (Credit: Vanni / Art Resource, NY)

Professional Guilds

Professional guilds were part of a larger social institution of the Roman world, that of various types of associations: (1) gymnasiums, (2) professional guilds, (3) social clubs, and (4) religious associations. To be sure, the functions of one type of association could spill over into another; e.g., social or professional associations would often have a religious underpinning.

The primary purpose of professional guilds was to offer assistance to those who practiced the trade of the guild, including, perhaps, vocational training. The guilds could also provide a new arrival at the city a place to find lodging and a network to assist in securing work. The narrative in Acts also indicates that such guilds could come together to find ways to protect their economic interests.

Helmut Koester, *Introduction to the New Testament, Volume One: History, Culture, and Religion of the Hellenistic Age* (Philadelphia: Fortress, 1982), 65–67.

---

replicas likely would have been plundered by looters through the ages or melted down for other more practical uses by later generations. Such implements of worship and devotion brought "no little business" to Demetrius and his fellow artisans. This observation sets the stage for the commotion to follow.

Demetrius gathers together his fellow artisans, as well as workers of the same trade (v. 25). Professional guilds, loosely analogous to contemporary unions, were organized for numerous reasons, among which was the protection of their economic interests. [Professional Guilds] Demetrius makes clear that their economic interests are at stake here (v. 25b). But there is even more at stake: silversmiths and other artisans were not of high status within their culture—working with one's hands was not considered a noble calling in antiquity. Their only claim to status would have been the relatively good income produced by their goods. A threat to their business, therefore, threatens not only their livelihood, but also their honor and status within their community.

Demetrius, though he speaks polemically, offers a fair summary of Paul's preaching activity and its effects on the worship of gods. Paul has been active in Ephesus for over two years (see vv. 10, 22), and Demetrius, as well as others, would have had opportunity to hear his message. Readers know from the narrator's account of Paul's preaching in Lystra (14:15-17) and Athens (17:23-31) that Paul did challenge the legitimacy of gods "made with hands" (v. 26).

This challenge has both economic and larger cultural implications (v. 27). Demetrius repeats his warnings of the economic threat and adds a warning that Paul's message could threaten the reputation of both "the great goddess Artemis" (the official cultic title of the goddess) and her temple in Ephesus. Religion is regularly intertwined with the larger fabric of a society, and Demetrius is right to recognize the potential negative impact that Paul's preaching could have on Ephesian society. The worship of Artemis

The Temple of Artemis

The Temple of Artemis was one of the Seven Wonders of the World. The artist's rendition below offers some sense of the grandeur of this temple. All that remains today are remnants of pillars among which, locals say, one often finds grazing animals.

(Credit: Barclay Burns)

(Credit: Wikipedia, "Temple of Artemis, Ephesus, Turkey" [cited 17 September 2007]. Online: http://en.wikipedia.org/wiki/Image:Ac_artemisephesus.jpg.)

did extend far beyond Ephesus, for she was a cosmopolitan deity, perhaps the most widely recognized goddess in the Mediterranean world of antiquity. The greater the success of Paul's gospel, which explicitly called upon people to turn from idols, the more that Artemis and Ephesus, the guardian of her temple, would be diminished. Given the important role that religion played in the larger civic life of the empire's urban centers, the social implications of the demise of the cult would extend far beyond Demetrius and his guild's business ventures.

The Crowd's Response, vv. 28-34

Verses 28-34 form the next subunit of this section, bracketed at the beginning and end by the cry of the populace, "Great is Artemis of the Ephesians" (vv. 28, 34). Artemis was the guardian deity of Ephesus, so the diminishment of one leads to the diminishment of the other. The potential threat to the city itself brings out the crowd who gather at the massive Ephesian theater. The cult of Artemis was an integral part of all aspects of the city's life. What is at stake, therefore, is not merely the welfare of some artisans, but a city's way of life. The kind of chaos that can overcome a people whose way of life is threatened is well represented by this scene.

The narrative employs a stock motif of mob scenes common in both ancient romance and historiography (see [Greek Novels]). [Mob Scenes] The crowd, stirred by the fear that their goddess and city would be demeaned by the gospel, came together in the city's gathering place, the large theater built into the western slope of Mount Pion that could hold up to 25,000 spectators (v. 29). Apparently not being able to find Paul, the mob grabs two of his travel com-

The Ephesian Theater

Pictured here are the remains of the great Ephesian Theater where, according to Acts 19:29, the crowds gathered to defend their "way of life" against the threat the gospel brought. This picture shows people to give viewers a sense of scale. The theater could hold some 25,000 people.

Ephesus Theatre, Turkey
(Credit: Adrian Beesley, istockphoto.com)

Mob Scenes

The appearance of the urban mob was typical of ancient narrative, of both the historical and novelistic genres (though the line between the two was rather thin in antiquity). Mob scenes are certainly common in Acts. Richard Pervo offers an exhaustive list. Below is a selective list:

• 6:12; 7:56-58—Stephen stoned
• 14:19-20—Paul stoned at Lystra
• 16:19-23—Mobs at Philippi
• 18:12-17—Mob at Corinth
• 19:21-40—Riot at Ephesus
• 21:26–22:24—Lynch mob in temple

Pervo states the following as one literary motive for the frequent mob scenes: "As an antithesis to the unruliness of pagan and Jewish crowds there emerges the orderly structure of Christian meetings, in which crowds behave just as the imperial masters believe they ought to act" (35).

Richard I. Pervo, *Profit with Delight: The Literary Genre of the Acts of the Apostles* (Philadelphia: Fortress, 1987).

panions, Gaius and Aristarchus, both said to be from Macedonia. [Gaius] [Aristarchus] Readers may infer that these persons had become followers of the Way and associates of Paul sometime during Paul's missionary activity in Macedonia (see Acts 16:11–17:15).

Paul is aware of the disturbance and its causes (v. 30). Consequently, he wants to enter the theater and the rabble "assembled" there. Whether he thought he could convince the crowd to turn from its course of action that could harm his companions or simply wanted to be with his friends during their time of trial is not said. The narrator wants to portray Paul's courage and to make clear that it is only fellow disciples, as well as some provincial officials known as Asiarchs (v. 31), who dissuade Paul from entering the large theater. [Asiarchs]

Why fellow disciples would hold Paul back is clear enough; they were concerned about the welfare of their important leader. The motive of the Asiarchs is less apparent. The narrator reports only that they were "friendly to him" (v. 31), but does not explain the basis of this friendship. Polhill speculates that they might have been showing deference to Paul's status as a Roman citizen,[10] but one cannot know for sure. Johnson interprets the expression of their concern as consistent with the Lukan literary motif "to show the success of the mission among the better classes (17:4, 12, 34)."[11]

Where Paul goes and what he does afterward is left unspoken. The narrator immediately turns attention back to the crowd, reiterating the general state of confusion and chaos (v. 32). There is some irony in Luke's language, for he uses the term "assembly" (*ekklēsia*, v. 32) to denote this crowd. The assembly was to be an ordered gathering for the conducting of legitimate city business— not a cover for a zealous and raucous mob.

The Jewish would-be and reluctant spokesman, Alexander, comes forward in vv. 33-34. Some within the crowd, presumably Jews caught up in the mob, offer some instructions to and then push out into the midst of the mob the hapless Alexander. He motions, attempting to silence the crowd and to

Gaius

Gaius is identified in 19:29 as a Macedonian. Acts 20:4 mentions a Gaius from Derbe, which is not part of the Macedonian region. Offering two different locations by which to identify "Gaius" implies that readers are not to understand these men to be the same person. The Pauline letters also mention a Gaius from Corinth (1 Cor 1:14, whom Paul baptized, and Rom 16:23, which was written from Corinth; Gaius is there identified as one who provided hospitality to Paul and the whole church). It is possible that the Gaius of Acts 19:29 is to be identified with the man from Corinth. Perhaps Gaius originally hailed from Macedonia and later moved to Corinth, which is located in the region of Achaia, but one cannot know for sure.

Aristarchus

Acts 19:29 identifies Aristarchus as a Macedonian. A character by this name appears in two other places in the Acts narrative—20:4, where he is identified as being from Thessalonica, which is in Macedonia, and 27:2, where he is identified as a Macedonian from Thessalonica. It is most reasonable for the reader to infer that each of these texts refers to the same person.

Aristarchus is mentioned in two letters of the Pauline corpus, Col 4:10, which identifies Aristarchus as Paul's fellow prisoner, and Philem 24, which refers to him as Paul's fellow worker. Nothing in these references would rule out that these texts refer to the same person who appears in Acts.

Asiarchs

AΩ This is the term that NRSV translates as "officials" in 19:31. Their precise duties are not clear, but there is good evidence from antiquity that this is the technically correct term for local leaders in this area. Some ancient sources identify Asiarchs as having a cultic function, serving as priests of the cult of Augustus. Other sources say that such persons were delegates of various towns that formed a league, for which Ephesus served as the place of assembly. It would appear that persons with primarily *political*, as opposed to *cultic* responsibilities would be the ones to urge Paul to stay out of the danger facing him in the theater.

Joseph A. Fitzmyer, *The Acts of the Apostles* (AB 31; New York: Doubleday, 1998), 660.

offer a defense. The narrator does not indicate what kind of defense he was attempting to present. Tannehill argues that he "intended to give a courageous defense of the Jewish rejection of idols."[12] This would certainly explain his reluctance, but it would be surprising for Luke, at this juncture, to portray Jews as indirect allies of Paul. Most commentators understand the defense to mean that Alexander wanted to differentiate non-Christian Jews from Paul and his messianist Jewish message. Though Jews would certainly agree with Paul that idol worship was vain, they are, according to this reading, anxious not to be seen as compatriots of Paul and the Ephesian Christian community.

Readers may discern here a subtle stab at the Jews of Ephesus. Had they been consistently bearing witness to their strong monotheism these many years in the city, Paul's message would likely not have created the stir it did. Is Luke implying that the Jewish community had been too carefully hiding its monotheistic convictions under a basket? Though the Jews want to distinguish themselves from Paul, the Ephesian crowd, like Gallio of Corinth (see 18:12-17), allows for no such differentiation. Once the crowd recognizes Alexander to be Jewish, they shout him down for more than two hours with their thunderous mantra: "Great is Artemis of the Ephesians" (v. 34).

The Town Clerk's Speech, vv. 35-41

At this juncture the town clerk steps forward to bring some order (vv. 35-41). The term *grammateous* literally means "scribe." Commentators disagree on the precise duties of this official, though the title itself is well attested in the ancient sources. Polhill understands this term to denote the "chief administrative office of the city" who presided over the city magistrates and the public assembly, as well as serving as liaison to the provincial Roman authorities.[13] Fitzmyer believes the official to be *either* the clerk of the city council *or* that of the city assembly. Either way, this character represents the voice of the official city government of Ephesus, offering the reader the ordered and civil verdict on the validity of the charges that Demetrius, his fellow guild members, and the city "assembly" make against the gospel.

His speech is deliberative (see [Types of Rhetorical Persuasion]), in that he will attempt to persuade the audience to take a certain course of action, specifically a course of action other than the one it is currently taking.

The clerk begins his appeal by reassuring the crowd concerning Ephesus's well-known status as the world center of the Artemis cult. He reminds the crowd that Ephesus is "the temple keeper of the great Artemis" (v. 35). The term "temple keeper" could denote the rather menial task of fulfilling the standard custodial duties of the temple. However, it could also denote the title of a city that housed important temples, which is how the clerk uses it here. The title was one of Ephesian pride, as it appeared on some Ephesian coins. The clerk also appeals to a legend that a statue of the goddess in Ephesus had fallen from heaven. Euripides refers to a similar legend in reference to the city of Taurus (*Iphigeneia in Taurica* 87–88, 977,

1384–85), but the reference in Acts is the only ancient allusion to such a legend pertaining to Ephesus.

Given the secure status of Ephesus, the clerk appeals to the crowd to silence itself and do nothing untoward (v. 36). He defends Gaius and Aristarchus, claiming that they were guilty of being neither "temple robbers nor blasphemers of our goddess" (v. 37). The term temple robbers could refer either to the literal act of plundering temples or, metaphorically, to being sacrilegious. [Temple Robbers] Candidly, the clerk is being rather generous. To be sure, one may find ways to claim that a particular religion's way of worship is totally without merit and illegitimate without technically blaspheming against that tradition or being sacrilegious. However, the demeaning implications of Paul's gospel as pertains to the veneration of Artemis are difficult to ignore. In many ways, Demetrius is more on target than the city clerk.[14]

Still, the clerk is correct to point out that Demetrius's manner of addressing his complaint violates the government's respect for order. He has avoided going through official channels, the courts and the proconsuls (v. 38). [Proconsuls] The city also provides "the regular assembly" (lit., "the *lawful* [*ennomous*] assembly") to address matters of interest to the municipality (v. 39). The implication is clear: this *unlawful* assembly is not the proper way to conduct municipal business. The clerk makes this point explicit in v. 40 as he warns the crowd that it is *they*, as opposed to Paul and his companions, who are "in danger of being charged with rioting," for the crowd has no just cause for its current course of action. With this, the clerk dismissed the crowd (v. 41).

Luke does not always portray Roman government officials or their duly recognized representatives in a positive light. Yet through this story Luke reinforces once again the message that readers may glean from earlier episodes in places such as Philippi and Corinth: Christianity is no legal threat to the Roman Empire, a claim

Temple Robbers

The reference to temple robbers in 19:37 offers an intertextual echo with Rom 2:22, where Paul, speaking rhetorically to Jews, alludes to the charge against them of robbing temples. The Jewish historian Josephus reports an incident that would have occurred a few years before Paul wrote Romans. Four Jews, purporting to be teachers of the Law, convinced a woman Jewish convert to donate "purple and gold to the temple at Jerusalem." However, once the men secured the valuables "they employed them for their own use." Consequently, Emperor Tiberius (ruled AD 14–37) "ordered all the Jews to be banished out of Rome. . . . Thus were these Jews banished out of the city by the wickedness of four men" (*Ant.* 18.81–84).

Other texts from Josephus indicate the prevalent charge against Jews was that they were sacrilegious and did not respect others' religious traditions, even profaning others' shrines and temples (*Ag. Ap.* 1.248–50). Josephus interprets Exod 22:28 to prohibit stealing from temples of other gods, a matter about which the text from Exodus says nothing (*Ant.* 4.207). In fact, one charge against the Jews was that the etymology of the original name of the Jewish holy city, *Hierosyla*, meant "temple robbers," which the Jews later changed to *Hierosolyma* in order to deflect away from themselves the stigma of being sacrilegious.

Proconsuls

Generally, Roman imperial districts were administered by one of two types of rulers. Legates, procurators, or prefects administered regions that required, for reasons of security, a standing army. Such administrators answered directly to the emperor. More tranquil provinces were under the supervision of the senate and were administered by proconsuls.

corroborated by appropriate government officials. In fact, those who disrupt the stability of the empire are regularly those who oppose Christians.

CONNECTIONS

This story, like stories of Paul's exploits in Lystra (14:8-18) and Athens (17:16-34), invites reflection on the impact and implications of the gospel message among non-Jews in the larger Greco-Roman culture. It will also allow for some connecting reflections on the gospel's impact on our own culture.

Luke's narrative presents two reactions to the implications of the gospel message from Gentile spokesmen, that of Demetrius (and those whom he stirs up, vv. 23-34) and that of the town clerk (vv. 35-41). Demetrius and his allies feel instinctively the threat of Paul's message. To be sure, Demetrius's initial reaction voices concern over the economic implications of Paul's message against idols (vv. 25b, 27a). The fear of losing potential profit from the business of making shrines offers an interesting contrast with the believers who were willing to burn their books of magic, books that the narrator values at 50,000 pieces of silver (v. 19). Readers may infer from this contrast that acceptance of the gospel message can have economic implications: either wittingly or unwittingly, acceptance of the gospel's message can require financial sacrifice.

Luke Johnson has long recognized that in Luke–Acts financial sacrifice serves as a metaphor or symbol for submission to the message and authority of the gospel and its proclaimers. Laying one's goods at the feet of the apostles in such texts as 4:32-37 amply illustrates this.[15] Acceptance of the authority of the gospel requires that one store one's treasure somewhere other than bigger barns (Luke 12:18). One is called upon to lay up one's treasures in heaven (Luke 12:33-34). The implications of Acts 19 are clear: one cannot be devoted either to magic or to idols, and the potential profit to come from each, and be simultaneously devoted to the gospel. One cannot serve two masters (Luke 16:13).

But Demetrius and his allies, whether they are his fellow artisans or the larger populace of Ephesus, are not only concerned about wealth. They are equally concerned about the welfare and reputation of their guardian deity, Artemis, and her temple located in Ephesus (v. 27b). The cry of the larger populace, "Great is Artemis of the Ephesians" (vv. 28, 34), reveals a concern not only for the deity, but the deity of *the Ephesians*—the goddess of the great city of Ephesus. There is assumed a close connection between the goddess and the city.

The town clerk is well aware of this connection. Consequently, he begins his appeal to calm the crowd by reassuring them that the reputation both of Artemis and the city are firmly established (vv. 35-36). The people need not fear, therefore, that the message of Paul and his companions will undermine either. Robert Tannehill offers the insightful observation that the town clerk "is a naïve Ephesian who assumes that the Christian criticism of idol worship has no importance."[16]

Indeed, he is naïve. Jewish and Christian resistance to idolatry was grounded in the profound awareness that the Creator was not in any way to be confused with the creation (see [Jewish Views of Idolatry]). If God is not to be confused with that which *God* has created, then certainly God is not to be confused with that which *humans* create (see Wis 13:1-19). At the heart of the criticism of idolatry lies the insight that the God who is immanent, who is not far from us (17:27), is also transcendent, above all creation, including even the most sacred spaces within creation: "Heaven is my throne, and earth is my footstool, what is the house that you would build for me, and what is my resting place?" (Isa 66:1; cf. Acts 7:49). Such an understanding of God cannot rest easily with views of the Deity that fail to acknowledge such transcendence.

Challenging the way that a people views its deity can affect more than narrowly focused religious beliefs. Religion is intricately woven into the complex fabric of society and culture. It is an integral part of the whole of a people's life, for religion is that which offers to life a larger sense of meaning and purpose. As far as we know, we are the only creatures capable of asking questions of meaning; consequently, we are the only creatures capable of seeking answers to questions of meaning. Historically, religion has been the primary means through which human beings have sought such meaning.

Clifford Geertz, the cultural anthropologist, has written extensively on the powerfully significant role that religion plays in humans' lives: "The drive to make sense out of experience, to give it form and order, is evidently as real and as pressing as the more familiar biological needs."[17] Human beings crave meaning; they yield to the "drive to make sense out of experience." Ernest Becker has given us the title *homo poeta*: humankind the meaning maker.[18] [Homo Poeta] Peter Berger's modern classic *The Sacred Canopy* fully explores how human beings, yearning to satisfy the hunger for meaning and order, construct worlds of meaning under which they

Homo poeta

"Even our nearest relatives in the animal world are endowed with far more set and specific instinctive guidance systems than are we. Matters such as mating, building dens or lairs, searching for food and knowing how to care for their young are far more programmed even in the chimpanzee than they are in us. But as far as we know none of these other creatures bears the glory and burden we carry of asking what life is about. They do not struggle under the self-consciousness of shaping their lives through commitments they make or of searching for images of meaning by which to give sense to things. *Homo poeta* Ernest Becker calls us, man the meaning maker. We do not live by bread alone, sex alone, success alone, and certainly not by instinct alone. We require meaning. We need purpose and priorities; we must have some grasp on the big picture."

James W. Fowler, *Stages of Faith: The Psychology of Human Development and the Quest for Meaning* (New York: HarperSanFrancisco, 1981), 4.

can live, like a protective canopy, "as a shield against terror," the threat of meaninglessness.[19]

Artemis, the guardian deity of Ephesus, was not merely a means to economic gain among artisans who molded miniature temples. She was more than a source of civic pride to Ephesus as the "temple keeper of the great Artemis" (v. 35). She was the goddess around whom civic, political, cultural, and economic life revolved. She was the goddess who gave meaning to being an Ephesian. To threaten the status of Artemis was to threaten a way of life that had come to find its direction and purpose in her. The violent reaction of the mob, shouting repeatedly, "Great is Artemis of the Ephesians," bears witness to the city's instinctive awareness that much is at stake if Paul and his gospel are believed to be true. The sacred canopy that they had constructed to give stability, order, and meaning to their lives could be in danger of being shredded.

But the Judeo-Christian warnings against idolatry, gods made with human hands that so aptly symbolize humans' drive to *construct* and *create* symbols that give them a sense of order and meaning, serve as warnings for us as well, those who worship the true and living God. We are far too sophisticated to take piece of wood, carve it carefully into the shape of a human being or animal, slap some paint on it, and hang it our wall. Yet can we deny that we do not in our own far more sophisticated ways carve out in our thoughts and minds abstract and intellectual *images* of God? And images matter. They greatly influence the way we make sense out of life and give purpose, order, and meaning to our lives. [Images of God]

Christians informed by the biblical tradition have inherited from our spiritual ancestors deeply meaningful and influential images of God. King, Father, and Creator are probably among the most influential. But dare we take seriously enough our own affirmations of God's *transcendence* that we will confess that our images, as embedded in sacred tradition as they are, cannot contain the eternal essence of God? Can we bring ourselves to acknowledge

Images of God

Our images of God matter. Just as how we conceptualize God affects what we think the Christian life is about, so do our images of God. Ideas (which include both concepts and images) are like families: they have relationships. How we image God shapes not only what we think God is like but also what we think the Christian life is about. People who think of God as a warrior may become warriors themselves. . . . People who think God is angry at the world are likely to be angry at the world themselves. (Borg, 57)

Marjorie Suchocki presses her readers to "image" God as truly *relational*, who touches and *is touched* by God's creation. In an interdependent creation touched and touched by a relational God,

[W]e receive from God[;] God receives from us. Who we are, in every newly becoming moment, is received by God, known by God, felt by God. . . . But the image of God I am proposing is of a God pervasively present, like water, to every nook and cranny of the universe, continuously wooing the universe toward continuous transformation toward its greater good. . . . I am proposing an image of a God who

interacts with the universe not partially, but *totally*. Such a God creatively gives to and receives from all forms of existence. Only a God could do that. A king, of course, never could. (Suchocki, 26–27)

Applied to this story in Acts, to *all* the stories of Acts, indeed to all experiences of life, such an *image* of God urges human creatures to *imagine* God totally and fully receiving from all characters in this narrative. God feels, receives, and is touched by the anger of Demetrius, the frenzy of each individual in the mob, the fear of Gaius and Aristarchus, the courage of Paul, the cautiousness of the city officials, the helplessness of Alexander, and the sobriety of the town clerk. But God also offers, gives, and touches. "God's energy meets and mingles with the energy of all other relations" that interact in this—and every!—story (Suchocki, 26). God makes no explicit appearance on the stage of Ephesian theater where the riot is taking place. And yet God is there. Paul and the other disciples are delivered and the gospel of God moves forward.

Marcus Borg, *The God We Never Knew: Beyond Dogmatic Religion to a More Authentic Contemporary Faith* (New York: HarperSanFrancisco, 1997); Marjorie Hewitt Suchocki, *In God's Presence: Theological Reflections on Prayer* (St. Louis: Chalice, 1996).

that when we engage in the important task of theology, which literally means "God talk," that *we* are the ones doing the talking? Can we recognize that even the theology that *we* embrace is *constructed*?

[Constructive Theology]

And like the Ephesians, the theologies we construct serve not only religious ends. They serve larger social and cultural ends, as well. For just as Artemis served to legitimate and sanction the Ephesian way of life, our theologies often serve as well to legitimate and sanction our way of life. God as King has given legitimacy to the divine right of kingship, lending support to tyrannical monarchies and other forms of despotism. God as Father has given legitimacy to patriarchal structures that privilege men and subjugate women. God as Creator, who has given humans dominion over creation, has more often been employed to legitimate the exploitation of nature than to encourage the nurturing and care of nature.

Constructive Theology

"Constructive activity is interpretative activity. To *construct* is to 'construe,' that is, to explain, deduce the meaning of, interpret. The task of constructive theology is to work out a construal of the meaning and truth of faith's language about God in light of a particular cultural situation. . . . Theology, we must acknowledge, is a project of the human imagination, not a direct description of what things are in and of themselves—whether divine things or human things. The question is whether theological constructions are nothing other than illusory fantasies, extensions of the human ego, . . . or whether they respond to something real, transcendent, and overwhelming that presents itself in experience, demanding reverence, and transition from self-centeredness to reality-centeredness. . . . The task of constructive theology is to make the best possible case for the validity and truthfulness of Christian faith, but the risk of faith and the need for courage are never eliminated."

Peter Hodgson, *Christian Faith: A Brief Introduction* (Louisville KY: Westminster/John Knox, 2001), 39–40.

The first part of Acts 19, vv. 1-20, gives considerable attention to Paul and his work in Ephesus. In the latter part of the chapter, Paul virtually disappears, making only a brief appearance outside the theater, wanting to enter the fray but being prevented from doing so by his disciples and friends in the government. But the enduring impact of Paul's message, despite his absence, retained its power to challenge a mighty city and the goddess who guarded that city.

All that remains of Paul in our time, centuries after Paul has departed this life, is the echo of his voice and the gospel he proclaimed. If Paul could have his way, he might wish to venture into the theaters of our own time, roll up his sleeves, and enter the fray. Paul's gospel challenged the Ephesians to look to the true and living God, the God who transcended their humanly constructed images.

We should not belittle ourselves for needing images and symbols that offer glimpses of the Wholly and Holy Other, the One who transcends our highest ideas and escapes the comprehension of our deepest thoughts. But the same gospel that Paul preached to those who practiced *other* religions also continues to preach to us, calling us, even as Paul Tillich reminds us, to "break-through the particularities" of our own traditions, symbols, and images, as sacred and necessary as they are. The gospel of the true and living God regularly calls us to recognize that God lies beyond the reach of even our most profound expressions and experiences of the sacred. [Breaking through the Particularities] When we hear this challenge we can either heed its call or gather with the masses and defend the god, whom we assume to be God, who defends *our* way of life.

Breaking through the Particularities

"Religion cannot come to an end, and a particular religion will be lasting to the degree in which it negates itself as religion. Thus Christianity will be a bearer of the religious answer as long as it breaks through its own particularity. In the depth of every living religion there is a point at which the religion itself loses its importance, and that to which it points breaks through its particularity, elevating it to spiritual freedom and with it to a vision of the spiritual presence in other expressions of the ultimate meaning of man's existence."

Paul Tillich, *Christianity and the Encounter of the World Religions* (New York: Columbia University Press, 1963), 96–97.

NOTES

[1] Joseph A. Fitzmyer, *The Acts of the Apostles* (AB 31; New York: Doubleday, 1998), 642.

[2] Ibid., 644.

[3] Luke Timothy Johnson, *The Acts of the Apostles* (SacPag 5; Collegeville MN: Liturgical Press, 1992), 338.

[4] Ibid., 339. Johnson cites Deut 2:30; 10:16; Ps 94:8; Isa 63:17; Jer 7:26; 17:23; 19:15.

[5] Ben Witherington III, *The Acts of the Apostles: A Socio-Rhetorical Commentary* (Grand Rapids MI: Eerdmans, 1998), 578.

[6] Susan R. Garrett, *The Demise of the Devil: Magic and the Demonic in Luke's Writings* (Minneapolis: Fortress, 1989), esp. the introduction and ch. 1.

[7] As cited by Witherington, *Acts*, 580.

[8] Fitzmyer, *Acts*, 650.

[9] Witherington, *Acts*, 590.

[10] "Paul was well-respected by his fellow Roman citizens in high places" (John B. Polhill, *Acts* [NAC 26; Nashville: Broadman, 1992], 411).

[11] Johnson, *Acts*, 349.

[12] Robert W. Tannehill, *The Narrative Unity of Luke–Acts: A Literary Interpretation*, 2 vols. (Minneapolis: Fortress, 1990), 2.243.

[13] Polhill, *Acts*, 412.

[14] See Tannehill, *Narrative Unity*, 2.244.

[15] See Commentary above on 4:32-37.

[16] Tannehill, *Narrative Unity*, 2.244.

[17] Clifford Geertz, *The Interpretation of Cultures* (New York: Basic Books, 1973), 140.

[18] Ernest Becker, *The Structure of Evil* (New York: Macmillan, 1968), 210.

[19] Peter Berger, *The Sacred Canopy: Elements of a Sociological Theory of Religion* (New York: Anchor Books, 1967), 22.

"YOU WILL NEVER SEE MY FACE AGAIN"

Acts 20:1-38

COMMENTARY

Acts 20 brings to a conclusion Paul's missionary efforts throughout Asia and southeastern Europe. With the conclusion of this chapter Paul will journey to Jerusalem where he will encounter opposition from the Jewish leadership, face hearings and trials, and, finally, head for Rome. The climactic feature of Acts 20 is Paul's farewell address to the Ephesian elders, representing the only major speech of Paul in Acts that is directed toward the faith community.

The chapter divides into three major sections: (1) Paul's revisitation of churches in Macedonia and Greece (vv. 1-6); (2) Paul's stay in and departure from Troas, which contains the tale of the resuscitation of Eutychus (vv. 7-12), followed by the brief report of Paul's journey to Miletus (vv. 13-16); and (3) Paul's farewell address to the Ephesian elders (vv. 17-38).

Paul Gives the Believers Much Encouragement, 20:1-6

Verses 1-6 are filled with gaps that require the reader's imagination to fill in and supplement. The narrative begins abruptly, noting that when the great riot of Ephesus had come to an end, Paul summoned the disciples of Ephesus to offer them encouragement. The participle that NRSV translates "encourage" (*parakalesas*) could also be rendered as "exhorted" (cf. RSV), but *encouragement* is more fitting given the uproar the disciples had just witnessed. The narrator offers no word on what Paul said. Rather, he moves the narrative quickly along, reporting that Paul "left for Macedonia" (v. 1). This notice recalls Paul's stated plans in 19:21 to pass through Macedonia and Achaia and then head on to Jerusalem. The riot in Ephesus slightly delayed, but did not deter, Paul's resolve to go to Jerusalem.

Readers confront another gap as the narrator does not report where specifically Paul went in Macedonia. One may infer that Paul visited churches he had established there, for, once again, readers are told that he offered "them much encouragement" (the NRSV reasonably renders "them" as "the believers" to fill in the gap created by the Greek text). Cities in Macedonia in which Paul had established churches were Philippi (16:11-40), Thessalonica (17:1-9), and Beroea (17:10-15).

Then Paul moves on to Greece, more specifically, the southern part of Greece, known as Achaia (v. 2b), where he stayed for three months (v. 3). The narrative does not indicate where exactly Paul stayed in Greece during this period, but earlier Paul had stayed for more than a year and a half in Corinth (18:11), so likely this is where Paul spent his time while in Greece.

Because the New Testament includes two letters from Paul to the Corinthians, interpreters know much about Paul's relationship with the Corinthian congregation. This leads some to fill in the narrative gap with historical information that one can deduce from the Corinthian correspondence.[1] Relations between Paul and the Corinthians were rocky, but the narrative of Acts shows no awareness of this. [Paul's Relationship with the Corinthian Churches] Rather, Acts focuses on the Jews' scheming against Paul, even as they had done during his first stay (cf. 18:12-17). According to Acts, the Jewish plot against Paul was not hatched until he was about to set sail for Syria. Again, the narrative is silent as to why the Jews waited until Paul was ready to depart before plotting against him. The narrative indicates that, for some reason, this plot motivated Paul not to sail to Syria, but rather "to return [to Syria? Jerusalem?] through Macedonia" (v. 3).

The narrative does not say why Paul wished to go to Syria. Perhaps the ship he had intended to take to Jerusalem (cf. 19:21) was going to take him only as far as Syria. Perhaps he intended to visit Antioch of Syria.[2] Nor does the narrative report exactly what the Jews were planning against Paul that deterred him from taking this voyage. Some have speculated that some Jews intended to attack Paul while en route to Syria.[3]

Verse 4 reports that a number of persons accompanied Paul, though the text is silent as to why these men were accompanying

---

Paul's Relationship with the Corinthian Churches

Acts shows no awareness of the tumultuous relationship between Paul and the Corinthian congregation. Yet, historically, behind Acts' notation in 20:2, which speaks of Paul's staying in Greece (likely Corinth) for three months, is a complex and interesting story.

During Paul's stay in Ephesus, Paul wrote a "painful letter" to the Corinthian congregation (see 2 Cor 2:3-4). There were those in Corinth who questioned Paul's legitimacy. This letter was sent by way of Titus. Some scholars identify this letter with the current text of 2 Corinthians 10–13, though there is hardly consensus on this matter. While according to Acts 20:1, Paul went to Macedonia from Ephesus, 2 Cor 2:12-13 indicates that Paul apparently went to Macedonia by way of the port city of Troas. Paul had hoped he would meet Titus there and get a report on how the Corinthian congregation had responded to his letter. Not finding Titus there, Paul then proceeded to Macedonia. It was there, as 2 Cor 2:14-17 implies, that Paul received a favorable report from Titus and, in reply, wrote 2 Corinthians (or, at least, 2 Corinthians 1–9). Eventually, Paul followed his own letter to Corinth, and stayed with the Corinthians for three months (Acts 20:2-3). New Testament historians suggest either the winter of 55–56 or 57–58 for this stay.

John B. Polhill, *Acts* (NAC 26; Nashville: Broadman, 1992), 414–15.

The Collection

Acts makes only passing reference (24:17) to the fact that Paul's final visit to Jerusalem was to offer financial relief for the Jerusalem saints, which Paul had collected from various Gentile churches. However, the collection was very much on Paul's mind, according to his letters, as he planned his trip to Jerusalem (see 1 Cor 16:1-4; 2 Cor 8 and 9; Rom 15:25-29). Paul expressed some apprehension about whether he would fare well in the face of the perceived attacks by Jewish nonbelievers in Jerusalem (Rom 15:31a). He was also a bit concerned that this gift from the Gentile churches to the Jerusalem saints would not be well received (Rom 15:32b). Possible tensions between Paul and the Jerusalem leadership (minimized in Acts 15 but highlighted in Gal 2) might have been the cause both of Paul's taking the initiative to gather a collection from the Gentiles for the Jerusalem saints and his apprehension that the gift would not serve its intended purpose of reconciling the Jewish and Gentile believers. It is possible that Acts downplayed the importance of the collection, for it did not accomplish Paul's purpose; the saints of Jerusalem did not accept this service from the Gentile churches, as Paul had hoped they would.

---

him or whether they had been with Paul the whole time in Corinth or joined him along the way as he journeyed through Macedonia. Interpreters generally fill this gap by alluding to the collection for the Jerusalem saints, of which there are many references in the Pauline letters. [The Collection] The narrator is certainly aware of this collection, for he makes passing reference to it in 24:17. But for the narrator of Acts, the collection was not Paul's primary motive for returning to Jerusalem. Consequently, readers are left without explicit explanation as to why these men are accompanying Paul.

Luke Johnson finds it significant that these men, collectively, represent the major areas of Paul's missionary endeavors.[4] Sopater of Beroea, along with Aristarchus and Secundus of Thessalonica, represent Macedonia (see [Aristarchus]). Gaius of Derbe and Timothy of Lystra (cf. 16:1) represent the region of Phrygia and Galatia (cf. 16:6). Tychicus and Trophimus represent Asia, more specifically Ephesus (readers later learn in 21:29 that Trophimus is from Ephesus). This broad geographical representation makes sense if these men were accompanying Paul as representatives of Gentile churches offering a gift to the Jerusalem saints. The fact that there are seven representatives is even more fitting, given that in Jewish thought there were "seventy nations" of the Gentiles.[5] But the narrative of Acts offers no such explanation.

Verses 5-6 report that "they went ahead and were waiting for us in Troas; but we sailed from Philippi." First, readers note that the first-person narrator has reentered the narrative. This is reasonable, given that it was in Philippi that readers last encountered the first-person narrator (16:16). The narrator is not clear, however, exactly *who* went ahead to Troas, the port city on the far western border of Asia from where the mission to Macedonia and Achaia originated (16:6-10).

Haenchen offers three possibilities: (1) Paul plus the seven companions went on to Troas, leaving behind in Philippi the narrator and some additional, unnamed believers. (2) The narrator and Paul remained in Philippi, and the seven went ahead to Troas. (3) Only the last two named in the list, specifically Tychicus and Trophimus, who were from Asia, went to Troas.[6] Most commentators prefer the last option. Whoever remained with the narrator, they stayed in Philippi through the feast of Unleavened Bread (see [Passover]). Sometime thereafter they set sail for Troas from Philippi, or, more precisely, Neapolis, Philippi's port city. The trip normally took five days. Readers may recall that the sail from Troas to Neapolis took only two days (16:11); the difference in time would be due to the power and direction of the prevailing winds. The entire group then remained in Troas for seven days.

Paul Conversed until the Dawn, 20:7-16

The narrator offers a brief description of the worship service in Troas, noting that the time of gathering was the first day of the week and that it involved the "breaking of bread" (v. 1; see [The Breaking of Bread]). The gathering also involved Paul's "holding a discussion" (*dielegeto*) with those gathered. Paul was intending to leave the next day, and this would be his last opportunity to talk with the disciples. Thus, the conversation lasted well into the night.

If the narrator is reckoning days in the Jewish manner, that would mean "the first day of the week" began on what most Westerners would call "Saturday evening," with Paul intending to depart the following morning, or "Sunday morning." Thus, Paul's discussion up until midnight would have lasted a few hours. If the narrator is reckoning time according the Roman method, then "the first day of the week" would be Sunday, and Paul would have been intending to leave on "Monday" morning. It is possible that Paul's discussion would not have run any longer than had the church gathered on "Saturday" night, for the evening may have been the regular time for worship in the first century. The ancient world did not have "weekends," and Sunday, like any other day, would have been a "work day" for the believers.

Regardless of the exact day of the week, Paul spoke long enough for Eutychus, whose name appropriately means "good fortune," to suffer the consequences of the windy discussion. Eutychus is described as a young man (*neanias*) in v. 9 and a "boy" or "lad" (*pais*) in v. 12. The two Greek terms together probably denote someone between nine and fourteen years of age.[7] The community was gathered in the upper chamber of the house, with the room being lit by torches. The combination of lack of sleep, the droning on of adult conversation, and possibly the flames' consumption of oxygen contributed to the boy's dozing off and falling out the window to the ground below. Most modern readers will have no problem empathizing with such nodding off; most, hopefully, can only imagine falling out a window.

Sometimes interpreters, seeking to offer a rationalistic reading of the story, have understood Paul's statement "his life is in him" (v. 10) to mean that the boy's fall was not fatal. However, v. 9b states emphatically that the boy was taken up "dead" (*nekros*). Most likely, one is to understand the story as belonging to the category of resuscitation miracles, similar to Luke 7:11-15, 8:49-56, and Acts 9:36-41 (cf. John 11:1-44). Comparing this story to Peter's resuscitation of Tabitha in Acts 9 allows Paul to do the kinds of the things the Jerusalem apostles do, illustrating continuity between the Jerusalem apostles and Paul. This further legitimates Paul's authority in the Lukan narrative. Just as Peter's resuscitation offered echoes of the activities of Elijah, Elisha, and Jesus (see [Scriptural Patterns of Resuscitation Narratives]), so too Paul's action of bending over and embracing the boy resembles that of Elijah stretching himself upon the dead boy whom he resuscitated (cf. 1 Kgs 17:21).

The response to the resuscitation is almost anticlimactic. To be sure, the boy is taken away by those who are said to have been greatly comforted (v. 12). But following the miraculous revival, Paul returns to the upper room and continues to break bread and converse with the disciples until morning. The theme of breaking bread is reminiscent of both the Last Supper (Luke 22:14-23) and Jesus' post-resurrection meals (Luke 24:30-31, 41-43; Acts 1:4). This theme, of course, brackets the story of the resuscitation of Eutychus (cf. vv. 7, 11), allowing the conclusion that Christian worship on "the first day of the week," or resurrection day (cf. Luke 24:1), provides the appropriate context in which to illustrate and demonstrate the renewal of life that the resurrected Lord can bring.

Verses 13-16 describe the sail from Troas to Miletus, setting the stage for Paul's address there to the Ephesian elders. For reasons not given by the narrator, Paul elects to travel by land to Assos, the first port stop on the sail from Troas to Miletus (v. 13). Only there does Paul board the ship. The next stop along the way to Miletus was Mitylene, the port city of the island of Lesbos. They then sailed southeast toward the island of Chios, then south the next day to Samos, arriving the following day at Miletus. The narrator explicitly tells readers that Paul deliberately bypassed Ephesus. Paul did not want to get detained in Asia, as he was anxious to reach Jerusalem by Pentecost. The narrative leaves another gap in that

Miletus

The city where Paul offered his farewell address to the Ephesian elders was a significant seaport city and commercial center, having four harbors and three market areas. One of the agoras is pictured below on the left. Due to silt deposits over the centuries, modern Miletus (Palatia) is now five miles inland. Two symbols of the cosmopolitan character of the city were its theater and public bath, the ruins of the latter pictured below on the right.

The Agora at Miletus. (Credit: Todd Bolen, "Miletus in the Bible," [cited 17 September 2007]. Online: http://www.bibleplaces.com.)

The Bathhouse at Miletus. (Credit: Todd Bolen, "Roman Bathhouse," [cited 17 September 2007]. Online: http://www.bibleplaces.com.)

readers are not explicitly told why Paul thought stopping in Ephesus might delay him. Perhaps Paul believed his presence might fan the embers left by the riot months before, the result of which might have detained him from moving on to Jerusalem.

"Keep Watch over Yourselves and All the Flock," 20:17-38

Paul has offered three major speeches in the narrative, including this one. Acts 13:16-41, offered at the synagogue of Antioch of Pisidia, is presented to an audience of Jews and Gentile God-fearers steeped in Jewish tradition and Scripture (see [God-fearer]). Paul's speech in Athens to Gentiles unfamiliar with Jewish tradition is found in Acts 17:22-31. This speech represents Paul's counsel to Christians, particularly Christian leaders.

Formally, the speech resembles a testament, a popular genre within Jewish and Christian literature. This form of speech offers the parting words of a heroic character to those whom the character leaves behind. [The Testament] Rhetorically, the speech is difficult to pin down. The testamentary genre can function, at least in part, to pay honor to the parting hero. Such payment of honor would match most closely speeches of the epideictic sort (see [Types of Rhetorical Persuasion]). However, much of Paul's speech is hortatory, looking to the future and offering exhortation to the elders to do specific things in the times to come, making the speech more deliberative in function.[8]

Interpreters also note that the themes and vocabulary of this speech most closely resemble the themes of Paul's Epistles. [Paul's Farewell Speech and the Pauline Epistles] Witherington suggests that Luke took notes of the speech.[9] Fitzmyer attributes the Paulinisms to Luke's use of a Pauline source, which Luke reworked into his own distinctive composition.[10] There is no clear consensus as to how to outline the speech, but several commentators pick up the repetitiveness of the phrase "and now" in vv. 22, 25, and 32 as points of division, rendering the following outline:

• Paul's history among the Ephesians (vv. 18b-21)
• The present situation (vv. 22-24)
• The future situation (vv. 25-31)
• Commendation and blessing (vv. 32-35)

The speech is framed by a brief narrative introduction and conclusion (vv. 17-18a and 36-38).

The Testament

The testament, or "farewell address," is well known from biblical and extra-biblical materials. Examples from within the Bible include farewell addresses from the following: Jacob (Gen 49:1-17), Joshua (Josh 23–24), Samuel (1 Sam 12:1-25), and Moses (Deuteronomy). In deuterocanonical and extra-biblical sources one finds many other examples of farewell addresses by Tobit (Tobit 14:3-11), Abraham (*Jub* 19:17–21:26), Isaac (*Jub* 36:1-16), and each of the patriarchs in *Testament of the Twelve Patriarchs*. Typical, formal elements of the farewell speech that are found in Acts 20:18b-35 include:

• Discussion of relevant past events (20:18-19)
• Notice of departure (20:22-25)
• Planning for future leadership (20:29-30)
• Exhortations to faithfulness in the future (20:31)
• Final commendation or blessing (20:31, 35b)

Joseph A. Fitzmyer, *The Acts of the Apostles* (AB 31; New York: Doubleday, 1998), 674.

Paul's Farewell Speech and the Pauline Epistles

Ben Witherington notes that the content and vocabulary of this address, the only one in Acts in which Paul addresses a Christian audience, offer many connections with the Pauline corpus. He lays out the data and offers a helpful discussion of the issues (610–11). Some of the more important similar features are summarized below:

Vocabulary/concept	Reference in Acts	Reference in Pauline letters (indisputably authentic only)
Summarizing work as "serving the Lord"	20:19	Rom 1:1; 12:11; Phil 2:22
Jewish persecution	20:19	2 Cor 11:24, 26; 1 Thess 2:14-16
Teaching from house to house	20:20	Rom 16:5; Philem 21
Preaching to both Jews and Gentiles	20:21	Rom 1:16; 1 Cor 9:20
Faith in the Lord Jesus	20:21	Rom 10:9-13
Uncertainty about Paul's future	20:22	Rom 15:30-32
Willing to surrender his own life for the gospel	20:24	2 Cor 4:7–5:10; 6:4-10; Phil 1:19-26; 2:17; 3:8
Preaching the gospel of the grace of God	20:24	Gal 1:15-16; 2 Cor 6:1

Ben Witherington III, *The Acts of the Apostles: A Socio-Rhetorical Commentary* (Grand Rapids MI: Eerdmans, 1998).

Narrative Introduction, vv. 17-18a

The introduction is brief. It seems curious, if Paul were in such a rush to get to Jerusalem, that he would have created further delay by calling the Ephesian elders all the way down to Miletus, particularly since he intentionally bypassed Ephesus (see v. 16). There would be considerable time delay to get word to the elders, have them pack their bags for the journey, and then make the trip to meet Paul. Further, how could Paul have assumed that these people would have been free simply to vacate work and family and make the trek to Miletus to meet him? The sword can cut either way. The scenario seems so unreasonable that one might be inclined to argue that the narrator has been inept here, constructing a narrative too full of implausibilities to be considered historical. On the other hand, one could argue that sometimes truth is stranger than fiction. Why would the narrator, if he were simply artificially setting the stage, create these apparent problems?

Paul's History among the Ephesians, vv. 18b-21

In outlining the pattern of his ministry, Paul is not so much being defensive as offering himself as an example to emulate. There is no reason to assume that either the narrative's readers or the audience within the speech (the Ephesian elders) would have needed to hear a "defense" of Paul's behavior.

Paul sums up his life among the Ephesians as one of "serving the Lord" (v. 19). "Service" (*douleuōn*), which also carries the connotation of being a slave, was characteristic of Paul's self-description in his epistles, denoting total devotion. By "the Lord" Paul means the living Lord Jesus. "Humility" characterizes such service, not putting himself first, but the needs and concerns of others, particularly within the Christian community (cf. Phil 2:3). Paul also makes reference to the trials he faced due to the plots of the Jews. This reference offers a clue that the speech is likely directed to readers even more than to the Ephesian elders, for the Jewish opposition to Paul at Ephesus was not very effective (19:9, 33). Readers, however, will recall several instances of more intense Jewish opposition in other towns (cf. 13:50; 14:2, 5, 19; 17:5, 13; 18:12; 20:3).

Despite such trials, Paul declared and taught openly and in homes the message of repentance and faith in Jesus Christ (vv. 20-21). Such open declaration recalls specifically Paul's preaching in Ephesus both within the Jewish synagogue (19:8) and the hall of Tyrannus (19:9). Paul's message had an impact on both Jews and Greeks in Ephesus (19:10, 17). Paul's proclamation of repentance was directed primarily at Gentiles, as he urged them to turn to the true and living God. This was demonstrated in Ephesus when masses turned from the magical arts (19:18-19). Jews did not need *that* kind of repentance, but Paul consistently urged Jews to turn to Jesus as the Messiah (cf. 13:38-39; 17:3; 18:5).

The Present Situation, vv. 22-24

Paul's present situation actually deals with his immediate future, his upcoming trip to Jerusalem. Paul had resolved already "in the Spirit" to make this trip (19:21). That same Spirit still grips his resolve and determination. Paul does not know exactly what to expect there. Again, one who chooses to fill in the narrative gaps by alluding to the collection could appeal to texts such as Romans 15:31b, where Paul asks the Roman Christians to pray that his gift to the Jerusalem saints will be acceptable to them.

But the Lukan Paul knows, based on what the Spirit has told him, that he will face hardships there, specifically "imprisonment and persecutions" (v. 23), as he has faced everywhere (cf. Rom 15:31a). In 9:16 the Lord revealed to Ananias, who would subsequently baptize Paul, that Paul would suffer. This prophecy will serve as a clear foreshadowing of events to come in Jerusalem.

Paul, however, values his calling, his ministry "to testify to the good news of God's grace" (v. 24) as of greatest value, even compared to his own life. Such talk is not empty rhetoric. Paul's pattern of life from the time of his call (Acts 9) to the present offers concrete testimony of how much he values his ministry even more than his own life (cf. 9:23-25, 29; 13:50; 14:5; 16:19-40; 17:10, 13; 18:12-17; 20:3). His ministry, it seems, is Paul's life.

The Future Situation, vv. 25-31

Here readers come to the heart of Paul's address. Certainly this is the longest section of the speech and consists primarily of warnings to the elders/overseers to be faithful in Paul's absence to the teaching Paul has commended to them. Verse 25 states specifically that Paul's audience will not see his face again. Typical of the genre of "the testament," the assumption is that the speaker is not long for this world. That does not fit the narrative situation precisely, for even as the narrative of Acts ends, a number of years after Paul offered this speech, Paul is alive and well in Rome preaching the gospel. However, most likely from the *readers'* perspective (and, as a genre, the real audience of the testament is the *reader*), Paul is now gone. His words are offered, therefore, not so much to these particular elders sometime in the mid-50s, but to the leaders of the church of Luke's time.[11]

The Whole Purpose of God

AΩ The Greek word translated "purpose" is *boulē*, often rendered by such other English words as *intention*, *plan*, or *decision*. In the Lukan writings, the term, when used in reference to the *boulē* of God, can best be rendered as "plan" or "purpose," depending on the context. The line between the two renderings, however, is quite thin, for God's plans are in accordance with God's purposes and God's purposes eventuate in God's plans. Luke

Johnson summarizes the Lukan use of the phrase as follows: "The 'will of God' (*boulê tou theou*) is a favorite term of Luke's, denoting God's plan for history (see Acts 2:23; 4:28; 13:36; 20:27). Contrasted to it is the 'will of man' in Acts 5:38" (123).

Luke Timothy Johnson, *The Gospel of Luke* (SacPag 3; Collegeville MN: Liturgical Press, 1991).

Paul offers rhetoric that implies a dire warning, announcing that he is innocent of his audience's blood (v. 26). One finds here an intertextual echo of Ezekiel 33:1-6. Here the prophet is compared to a sentinel whose task is to warn the city of approaching danger. If the sentinel offers such warning, but the citizens refuse to heed it, the blood of those who are lost will be on their own heads and the sentinel is innocent. Paul is offering here the warning of dangers to come. He, therefore, is innocent if any disaster falls upon the church after he departs.

But Paul is not only offering a warning. He reminds his audience (including readers who have followed Paul's story) that he has declared the "whole purpose of God" to the leaders. The precise content of this "whole purpose" is not given, but one may conclude that it alludes back to "the kingdom" that Paul has preached (v. 25) and "the good news of God's grace" (v. 24). [The Whole Purpose of God]

Readers have the advantage not only of having followed Paul's story, but also of having followed the whole Lukan narrative. Luke offers through the resurrected Jesus a good summary of "the whole purpose of God," that is, the message of "the kingdom" and "the gospel of grace."

Then he opened their minds to understand the Scriptures, and he said to them, "Thus it is written, that the Messiah is to suffer and to rise from the dead on the third day, and that repentance and forgiveness of sins is to be proclaimed in his name to all nations, beginning from Jerusalem. You are witnesses of these things" (Luke 24:45-48).

The good news of the death and resurrection of Jesus and the offering of forgiveness of sins to everyone, all in fulfillment of Scripture, are at the heart of the "whole purpose of God."

Verses 28-31 clearly set up something of a siege or fortress mentality. Verse 28 begins with the exhortation to "keep watch," and v. 31 concludes with the call to "be alert." The elders are exhorted to keep watch over both themselves and over "the flock." Flocks, sheep, and shepherds were common metaphors to denote the people of God and their leaders, respectively.[12] In this specific context, however, Paul refers to the leaders as "overseers" (*episkopoi*), rather than "shepherds," although the verb Paul employs to describe their leadership is properly translated by the NRSV as "to shepherd" (*poimainein*). These overseers, or elders, are legitimate in their roles of leadership by the fact that it was the Holy Spirit who set or appointed (*etheto*, from *tithēmi*) them to such roles. How *precisely* the Holy Spirit appointed these leaders is not said. [Elders and Overseers] Yet in Acts the work of the Spirit regularly goes hand in hand with human will and choice (cf. 13:1-3; 15:28; 19:21; see [The Working of God]). Polhill suggests that, humanly speaking, these leaders were chosen by the church, whose selection would have been perceived as being guided by the Spirit.[13] These overseers are "to shepherd" the church of God, that is, to care for the flock who constitute God's people.

Some manuscripts read "church of the Lord," rather than "church of God" in v. 28. The key to understanding the change lies in the phrase "that he obtained with *tou haimatos tou idiou*." The simplest way to translate the Greek phrase is "his own blood," with the antecedent of "his" being "God" (from the earlier phrase "church of God"). The idea that *God* bled on the cross is a peculiar way to talk about the cross—even later church creeds consistently spoke of the suffering and death of the Son, not the Father. It is likely this peculiarity that led subsequent copyists to change "church of God" to "church of the Lord," allowing the blood to refer back to the blood of the Lord (Jesus). If, however, one retains the reading "church of God," how is one then to understand the phrase *tou haimatos tou idiou*? An alternative way to render the Greek is "the blood of his own," with "his own" referring to God's own Son. This is the rendering of the NRSV.

Paul continues to employ shepherding imagery to warn his audience of impending danger. He employs the metaphor of fierce wolves to denote persons from outside the community who will attempt to injure the flock (v. 29). And he also warns that persons from within the community will "distort the truth" (lit., "speaking distorted or crooked things," v. 30). Note that all of this

Elders and Overseers

ΑΩ The Greek terms translated as "elders" (*presbyteros/oi*) and "overseers/bishops" (*episkopos/oi*) occur primarily in the deutero-Pauline letters. Within the Pauline corpus the term elder(s) is found only in the Pastoral Epistles (1 Tim 5:1, 2, 17, 19; Titus 1:5). The term "overseer" or "bishop" is found in Phil 1:1, 1 Tim 3:2, and Titus 1:7. It is difficult to discern from Phil 1:1 the function of the "overseers." One must keep in mind that the Greek term *episkopos*, while it came to denote an office within the church, was originally a secular term used to designate a leader within a group. Acts 20 implies, as do the Pastoral Epistles, that "elders" and "overseers/bishops" were virtually synonymous. Titus 1:5 and 7 seem to use the terms elders and bishops/overseers interchangeably. In addition, the requirements for bishops spelled out in 1 Tim 3:1-7 are quite similar to the requirements for elders in Titus 1:5-9. In time, the "bishop" became a singular official who, apparently, presided over the larger ruling body of elders. The structure of church leadership assumed in Acts 20 and the Pastoral Epistles seems to represent a transitional phase to the later, more formal structures of leadership and authority.

L. Michael White, "Christianity: Early Social Life and Organization," *ABD* 1.926–35.

is prophesied to begin after Paul has gone (v. 29). Clearly what is being denoted here is some type of heresy, particularly in the area of Ephesus (see [School]). Other New Testament texts allude to trouble in Ephesus (cf. 1 Tim 1:3, 19-20; 4:1-3; cf. 2 Tim 2:15-18; Rev 2:2, 6). Recent commentators appear reluctant to identify precisely the nature of false teaching about which Paul warns. A generation ago, interpreters commonly identified such false teachings with some version of Gnosticism.[14]

Even if one cannot identify specifically the heresy in question, it does appear that the narrator assumes a model that one finds often in the later church. This model assumes that following the apostolic period, after the first generation leaders such as Paul departed (cf. v. 29), false teachings became a problem for the church. During the apostolic generation, however, heresy was kept in check.[15] The church, however, should be able to protect herself, for she has had the consistent and persistent witness of Paul, and implicitly the other first-generation leaders, on whom to rely for guidance.

Commendation and Blessing, vv. 32-35

The final section of Paul's testament begins with the declaration that Paul commends the church both to God and the message (lit., "word") of God's grace. The word "commend" (*paratithemai*) is used similarly in 1 Timothy 1:18 and 2 Timothy 2:2, both of which exhort Timothy to stand faithfully for the gospel and urge others to do the same. It can carry the meaning of "commit" or "entrust." Paul is committing and entrusting these leaders to God and the gospel, confident that both can build up the leaders and, implicitly, the church. The word translated "build up" (*oikodomēsai*) and its various cognates are common in the indisputably authentic Pauline epistles (cf. 1 Cor 8:1; 10:23; 14:4, 17; Gal 2:18; 1 Thess 5:11). The deutero-Paulines do not employ the word or its cognates. Such edification results in the receipt of the inheritance. The content of the inheritance is not spelled out, but use of the term in other New Testament texts indicates that it has to do with the rewards of salvation and life (cf. Eph 1:14, 18; 5:5; Col 3:24; Heb 9:15; 11:8; 1 Pet 1:4).

Verses 33-35 cumulatively exhort church leaders to emulate Paul's manner of life. They are not to be greedy or covetous (v. 33). Verse 34a alludes to Paul's practice of supporting himself, as well as those who assisted him (v. 34b). Paul's pattern of self-support is attested in the Pauline letters (cf. 1 Cor 9:8-18; 2 Cor 11:7-9; 1 Thess 2:9) and alluded to in Acts 18:3. Paul's model of self-support was not the norm, but the practice of avoiding greed and helping the weak (v. 35) was always to be followed. Paul legitimates this pattern by appealing to a saying of Jesus not found in the gospel tradition (v. 35b). Rough parallels to the saying do exist, however, in other early Christian materials (1 Clement 2.1; Didache 1.5).

Narrative Conclusion, vv. 36-38

The chapter concludes with a brief description of Paul praying with the elders. The narrator attempts to capture the pathos of the moment, referencing the weeping, embracing, and kissing among the believers (v. 37). The kiss was a common greeting within the early church (cf. Rom 16:16; 1 Cor 16:20; 2 Cor 13:12; 1 Thess 5:26; 1 Pet 5:14). Most of all, the group is sorrowful for they know that they will never see Paul again (v. 38). In the narrative of Acts, Paul's mission to the churches as a free man has come to a close. Henceforth, Paul will minister to churches that he established by means of the word that he leaves behind, be it a farewell address, as in Acts, or, for the church of subsequent generations, his letters.

CONNECTIONS

Paul's resuscitation of Eutychus and farewell address to the Ephesian elders offer excellent material for reflection upon contemporary application and connections.

The commentary noted that the resuscitation of Eutychus was couched in between clear allusions to the worship of the faith community in Troas. The framework offered by the narrator makes reference to "the breaking of bread" (vv. 7, 11). The breaking of bread not only signifies fellowship among the believers, but also offers a reminder of the last meal that Jesus shared with his disciples (Luke 22:14-23) and the resurrected Jesus' continuing fellowship with his disciples (Luke 24:30-31, 41-43). In the breaking of bread the community of faith both remembers the body broken and experiences the presence and power of the "author of Life, whom God raised from the dead" (3:15).

The resuscitation of Eutychus demonstrates, dramatically to be sure, the power of this author of life to give life to those who have tasted death. Philistine readers who can find contemporary application only when they witness a resuscitation from physical death will miss much of the point of the story. Commendable and praiseworthy are the heroic measures taken by paramedics who apply the electrical shock of defibrillators and who "bring back to life" victims of heart attacks or car accidents. And certainly family members experience great joy and relief from such resuscitations. But the power of the gospel to offer life is not something to be replaced by, or compared to, the modern marvels of medical science.

The death that people face, the kind of death that the gospel has power *here and now* to overcome, is not physical death, but spiritual death. As it states in Ephesians, "But God, who is rich in mercy, out of the great love with which he loved us even when we were dead through our trespasses, made us alive together with Christ" (Eph 2:4-5a). A similar note is sounded in Colossians: "And when you were dead in trespasses and the uncircumcision of your flesh, God made you alive together with him, when he forgave us all our trespasses" (Col 2:13). The language of death and resurrection, though clearly metaphorical in its application, is offered to describe the *present* life of believers, persons who share here and now in the power of the life of the resurrected one.

The Gospel of John offers a similar account of the good news. The Johannine Jesus boldly declares that he is "the resurrection and the life" (John 11:25) and, further, "Very truly, I tell you, the hour is coming, *and is now here*, when the dead will hear the voice of the Son of God, and those who hear will live" (John 5:25). Death comes in many forms in human experience beyond the cessation of physical life.

In his modern classic *The Courage to Be*, Paul Tillich employs the word "nonbeing" to denote what we might more popularly call "spiritual death," that is, a notion of death that transcends the cessation of physical life. Tillich argues that the threat of nonbeing creates in all humans, simply as a part of living the human experience, a pervasive anxiety. Humans experience such anxiety in three distinct, but broadly related ways. There is the anxiety of fate and death. Here we are speaking of the sense that so much in our lives is out of our control and that we all face, inevitably, the cessation of this (physical) life. There is, secondly, the spiritual anxiety of emptiness and meaningless, when "everything is tried and nothing satisfies. . . . The anxiety of emptiness drives us to the abyss of meaningless."[16] Finally, there is the anxiety of guilt and condemnation, an anxiety that we may be tempted to resist either by laying upon ourselves more and more moral demands or releasing ourselves from any restrictions whatsoever. But neither path works; either way "the anxiety of guilt lies in the background and breaks again and again into the open, producing the extreme situation of moral despair."[17] Ultimately, human beings long to be set free from nonbeing and the anxiety of fate and death, emptiness and meaningless, and guilt and condemnation. To be set free from such would be, indeed, to have life and to have it more abundantly (John 10:10b).

The gospel message, the message of the death and resurrection of Jesus, symbolized by the breaking of bread as a memorial both to Jesus' death (the Last Supper) and resurrection (Jesus' eating with his disciples on Easter—and beyond!), offers such abundant life. The gospel promises not only life beyond the cessation of physical life (e.g., 23:6), but the Lukan emphasis on the guidance of the Spirit in the life of the church and individual believers (e.g., 8:29, 39; 10:19; 11:12; 13:2, etc.) offers hope that something other than blind and indifferent fate moves our lives along. The gospel addresses the spiritual anxiety of emptiness and meaningless. The Athenians' longing for meaning in their countless gods (17:22-23) and the Ephesians' quest for something substantive in magic (19:18-19) can be satisfied by the word of the gospel, if only one will hear.

Finally, the anxiety of guilt and condemnation is addressed in the gospel. This is certainly Luke's main interest as he zeroes in on the word of "salvation" that the gospel offers, most emphatically in the offering of forgiveness of sins. From Zechariah's declaration in the Benedictus (Luke 1:77) to Paul's speech before Agrippa (Acts 26:18), the proclamation and offering of forgiveness of sins resonate through the Lukan narrative. The resuscitation of Eutychus, therefore, can be about far more than resuscitation. It can be about resurrection.

Paul's farewell address to the Ephesians also deserves comment. The Connections portion of Acts 19 invited readers to consider the fact that our theological language and imagery, no matter how sacred, grows out of our own imaginations. Thus, we need to be cautious that we not confuse our language and imagery with the Transcendent One to whom we are pointing. Humbly acknowledging our own limits is important. Paul's speech to the elders, however, also reminds us that there is something substantive to the Christian "gospel of grace" (vv. 24, 32). It is a message that can be twisted, bringing danger or ruin to the lives of people who succumb to or are enticed by those who distort the truth (v. 30).

Finding the balance between acknowledging the human, imaginative element in our theological talk and the stable tradition of the gospel to which persons such as "elders" and "overseers" are to remain faithful is tedious and complex. Of course, one can avoid the complexity by essentially denying the human element within our "God-talk," or theology. We can assert, as does traditional

The Council of Trent on Scripture and Tradition

"Furthermore, in order to restrain petulant spirits, It decrees, that no one, relying on his own skill, shall,—in matters of faith, and of morals pertaining to the edification of Christian doctrine,—wresting the sacred Scripture to his own senses, presume to interpret the said sacred Scripture contrary to that sense which holy mother Church,—whose it is to judge of the true sense and interpretation of the holy Scriptures,—hath held and doth hold; or even contrary to the unanimous consent of the Fathers; even though such interpretations were never (intended) to be at any time published. Contraveners shall be made known by their Ordinaries, and be punished with the penalties by law established. "

Council of Trent, Decree Concerning the Edition, and the Use, of the Sacred Books, Hanover College Department of History, http://history.hanover.edu/texts/trent/trentall.html (28 June 2006).

Roman Catholicism and, less officially, fundamentalist expressions of Protestantism, that both our scriptural witness and interpretations of such witness are absolutely trustworthy and free from the potential human frailties that emerge when we admit that we carry the treasure of the gospel in earthen vessels (2 Cor 4:7). [The Council of Trent on Scripture and Tradition] By submitting, not simply to the testimony of Scripture, but to a certain view of those Scriptures and others' interpretations of them, we can confidently formulate summaries of the faith to which we can yield all allegiance and insist upon the same from others. Failure to submit, not so much to the gospel, but to certain understandings of the gospel, Scripture, and views on various and sundry topics can result in various forms of discipline, expulsion, and/or termination.

The voice of those such as Karl Barth represents a somewhat less strident position than that of Catholicism or fundamentalism. Barth readily acknowledges that theology and dogmatics represent human voices, witnesses, and words. To be sure, such voice and witness must emanate from within the church, the community of faith; one cannot engage in meaningful Christian God-talk outside the context of the faith community. Nor can one, Barth insists, engage in meaningful God-talk unless one faithfully acknowledges that, while our God-talk is a human response, it is not a human response to some ethereal "religious experience," but the revealed word of God: "Theology itself is a word, a human response; yet what makes it theology is not its own word or response but the Word which it hears and to which it *responds*. Theology stands and falls with the Word of God."[18]

Barth does not simplistically equate this revealed word with the Bible. The Bible, for Barth, is the authoritative, yet human *witness to* the revelation of God. Hence, Barth acknowledges that our theological discourse is *ours*: "dogmatics is not a thing which has fallen from Heaven to earth."[19] [Karl Barth and Church Dogmatics]

Emphasizing as he does the revelation of God through the word of God, with such a word placing appropriate boundaries on our theological expositions, goes a long way toward preserving the church from straying into the kinds of distortions of the truth (20:30) to which Paul refers in his farewell address. But we cannot forget what Paul has said to his Greek audience in Athens, where Paul insisted that we are all near to God and live in and by God. God's revealed word finds its clearest expression in the gospel, though that gospel is always mediated through human witness and word. But God's revelation is not confined to a particular history (that of Israel and the church) or tradition (that of the prophets and the apostles)—on this point Barth appears to have placed too many restrictions on God's revealing power. Ancient church thinkers, such as Justin Martyr allowed the logos the freedom to speak where he will; such is worthy of our consideration. [Justin Martyr's Understanding of the "Word"]

As we take seriously Paul's injunctions to "keep watch" (v. 28) and to "be alert" (v. 31), we also need to take seriously that God deals with human beings as distinct and unique creatures, with each person possessing, or being possessed by, his or her own gifts, talents, stories, and experiences. And it is through these distinctive human stories that the interpretation and understanding of the experience and word of God are filtered. Alertness and vigilance need not silence the disparate voices of persons who, in good faith, respond to their own hearing of God's word in many and various ways. The experience of believers as they encounter, or are encountered by, the word is a legitimate, though not solitary, source of theological truth. [Experience and the Believer]

Karl Barth and Church Dogmatics

"In the science of dogmatics the Church draws up its reckoning in accordance with the state of its knowledge at different times . . . . The Christian Church does not exist in Heaven, but on earth and in time. And although it is a gift of God, He has set it right amid earthly and human circumstances, and to that fact corresponds absolutely everything that happens in the Church. The Christian Church lives on earth and it lives in history, with the lofty good entrusted to it by God. . . . It is because the Church is conscious of its limitations that it owes a reckoning and a responsibility to the good it has to administer and to cherish, and to the good One who has entrusted this good to it. It will never be able to do this perfectly; Christian dogmatics will always be a thinking, and investigation and an exposition which are relative and liable to error. "

Karl Barth, *Dogmatics in Outline* (New York: Harper and Row, 1959), 10–11.

Justin Martyr's Understanding of the "Word"

"We have been taught that Christ is the firstborn of God, and we have proclaimed that he is the Logos, in whom every race of people have shared. And those who live according to the Logos are Christians, even though they may have been counted as atheists—such as Socrates and Heraclitus, and others like them, among the Greeks. . . . For all writers were able to see the truth darkly, on account of the implanted seed of the Logos which was grafted into them."

(*Apology* 1.46; 2.13)

Cited in Alister E. McGrath, ed., *The Christian Theology Reader*, 2d ed. (Oxford: Blackwell Publishers, 2001), 4.

Experience and the Believer

"Experience is also a source for theology to consult. The gospel is also experienced, not only in earlier generations, but in our own space and time as well. Our own encounters with God's Word can be added to the already vast range of experiences and recollections of the historical community. . . . Truth needs to become personally convincing by being confirmed in individual experience, when the faith of the whole church becomes real for me in my own life today. Daily life provides experiential confirmation of the reliability of the truth of the Christian story."

Clark Pinnock, *Tracking the Maze: Finding Our Way through Modern Theology from and Evangelical Perspective* (Eugene OR: Wipf and Stock, 1998), 178.

NOTES

[1] John B. Polhill, *Acts* (NAC 26; Nashville: Broadman, 1992), 415.

[2] Gal 2:11-14 could imply that Paul's relationship with Antioch was strained at best. But Acts shows no awareness of this. The *character* in the narrative might very well want to visit Antioch.

[3] According to Joseph A. Fitzmyer, *The Acts of the Apostles* (AB 31; New York: Doubleday, 1998), 665, this was Ramsey's speculation.

[4] Luke Timothy Johnson, *The Acts of the Apostles* (SacPag 5; Collegeville MN: Liturgical Press, 1992), 355.

[5] The list of nations in Gen 10 names seventy nations. Negatively, the Deuteronomistic tradition lists seven nations that stand in opposition to Israel (see, e.g., Deut 7:1; Josh 3:10; 24:11).

[6] Ernst Haenchen, *The Acts of the Apostles: A Commentary* (Philadelphia: Westminster, 1971), 581–82.

[7] Polhill, *Acts*, 419n63.

[8] Ben Witherington III, *The Acts of the Apostles: A Socio-Rhetorical Commentary* (Grand Rapids MI: Eerdmans, 1998), 612–13.

[9] Ibid., 615.

[10] Fitzmyer, *Acts*, 675.

[11] Witherington, *Acts*, 612–13 and 618–20, offers the strongest exception.

[12] Ps 78:52, 70-71; Mic 5:4; Isa 40:11; Jer 13:17; 23:1-4; Ezek 34.1-6, 11-12, Zech 10:2-3; 11:4-17.

[13] Polhill, *Acts*, 427.

[14] In reference to v. 30, Haenchen, *Acts*, 593, states, "[T]he defection to the Gnostic heresy could not well be more clearly described in this prophecy. The reader moreover had it before his very eyes."

[15] Charles H. Talbert. *Reading Acts: A Literary and Theological Commentary of the Acts of the Apostles* (New York: Crossroad, 1997), 188.

[16] Paul Tillich, *The Courage to Be* (New Haven: Yale University Press, 1952), 48.

[17] Ibid., 53.

[18] Karl Barth, *Evangelical Theology: An Introduction* (New York: Holt, Rinehart and Winston, 1963), 16–17.

[19] Karl Barth, *Dogmatics in Outline* (New York: Harper and Row, 1959), 10.

"WE ARRIVED IN JERUSALEM"

Acts 21:1-40

COMMENTARY

Here begins the final phase of the third major section of Acts. In Acts 21 Paul takes the last steps on his journey to Jerusalem, and by the time the chapter ends, Jerusalem is turned upside down.

This chapter divides into three sections. Verses 1-16 describe Paul's journey from Miletus to Jerusalem, noting various ports and stops along the way. Verses 17-26 speak of Paul's meeting with the leadership of the Jerusalem church, rumors of Paul's encouraging Christian Jews to abandon Jewish ways, and a plan to address such rumors. Verses 17-40 narrate the riotous events that led to Paul's arrest and offer a transition to Paul's defense speech before his Jewish critics.

They Urged Him Not to Go to Jerusalem, 21:1-16

Much of this section reads in a very straightforward manner. This has led some interpreters to conclude that the author is following a source, either his own travel notes or those of another.[1] If so, the narrator's own hand intrudes on these sources, particularly in the references to the prophetic activities of the Spirit (vv. 4b, 9, 10-11).[2] Readers will find it helpful in following this discussion to refer to a map.

Verses 1-3 briefly describe the trip from Miletus to Tyre of Syria, several hundred miles away. Verse 1 tells of "port hopping" from Miletus, to Cos, to Rhodes, to Patara. Hugging the coast during the day, while setting into port in the evenings when the winds tended to die down, was a typical means of sea travel.[3] At Patara, Paul and his companions found a cargo ship going directly to Phoenicia (v. 2). Hitching a ride on cargo vessels was typical in the ancient world; passenger vessels, with private cabins and dining halls, are a modern luxury readers should not assume to have existed in antiquity. [Sea Travel]

Sea Travel

Most ships on the Mediterranean were military or cargo vessels. Persons needing to travel by sea would generally hitch a ride on a cargo vessel that was going their direction. Since proceeds from travelers were a secondary source of revenue for the ship owners, travel was relatively inexpensive (about two days' wage for a family). The fare did not include food and there were no cabins for passengers. If the ship hugged the coastline (as was typical) and went into port at night, passengers could disembark and find lodging in local inns, which offered their own dangers, or they could sleep on deck under the stars (see [Inns]). There was always the danger of storms, shipwreck (cf. Acts 27; 2 Cor 11:25), and pirates, though Roman power had dealt rather effectively with the last of these threats.

Everett Ferguson, *Backgrounds of Early Christianity*, 3rd ed. (Grand Rapids MI: Eerdmans, 2003), 86–87.

A look at the map reveals that it is almost a straight shot southeast from Patara to Tyre, if one were to sail close to the south side of Cyprus. Verse 3 indicates that the ship passed Cyprus on the boat's "left side" (the side of the boat the island would appear on from an eastern bound vessel sailing by the south side of Cyprus). The journey across the Mediterranean would likely have taken about five days, if the winds were cooperative.

Apparently Paul made the voyage in good time, for despite the fact that he was determined to reach Jerusalem for Pentecost (20:16), he decided to stay in Tyre with the disciples who lived there. Acts has offered no explicit description of the establishment of the faith community in Tyre. However, Tyre is in the region of Phonecia, and Acts 11:19 makes passing reference to Hellenistic Christians fleeing from Jerusalem speaking the word exclusively to Jews of Phonecia. Whether the disciples with whom Paul stayed were only Jews, the narrative does not say.

Verse 4b offers the curious statement that it was "through the Spirit" that the community there urged Paul *not* to go to Jerusalem. Readers are not told what the disciples knew through the Spirit that led to this warning. In addition, the characters in the story do not know what readers know. Readers should recall that Paul, "bound in the Spirit" (20:22), was convinced that he was to go to Jerusalem, with the likely result that he would face affliction there (20:23). Readers encounter a similar paradox below in vv. 11-12, and more comment will be offered in that context. The departing scene of vv. 5-6 is reminiscent of the scene when Paul left Melitus (20:36-38).

The narrative offers no details as to what type of ship Paul and his companions took. It states only that the ship sailed down the coast to Ptolemias, where they stayed with disciples for one day. Since Ptolemias is only twenty-five miles south of Tyre, the text probably assumes that they joined the disciples for the balance of the day and night, leaving the following day (v. 8a) for Caesarea (see [Caesarea]).

Upon arrival in Caesarea, Paul and his traveling companions joined Philip (v. 8), with whom they remained for a few days (see v. 10). The narrator explicitly identifies Philip as "the evangelist" and as "one of the seven" (cf. 6:5). These comments should spark readers' memory of Philip's sharing the gospel with the Ethiopian eunuch (8:26-39), after which time Philip journeyed to and settled in Caesarea (8:40). Such explicit identification should prevent readers from confusing this Philip with Philip, one of the Twelve, but both ancient and modern commentators have confused the two anyway (see [Philip]).[4]

The narrative also states that Philip had four unmarried daughters who prophesied (v. 9). The Greek participle used to describe their prophesying is in the present tense, which would likely indicate that such prophetic activity was a regular, ongoing activity, not sporadic or exceptional. The reference alludes back to Peter's first Pentecost sermon, in which context he spoke of "sons and daughters" prophesying (2:17).

Though Philip's daughters had the power to prophesy, attention shifts to another prophet, Agabus from Judea. Acts 11:28 introduced readers to a prophet from Jerusalem named Agabus, and this most likely denotes the same person. Agabus the prophet offers both a prophetic action and prophetic word that interprets the action. Enacted prophecies occur in the Old Testament (see, e.g., Jer 19:1-13; Ezek 4:1-17). Agabus imitates Old Testament prophetic speech, as well, initiating his announcement with the words, "Thus says the Holy Spirit." The introductory words are clearly reminiscent of the prophetic messenger formula, "Thus says the Lord."

As Jeremiah placed a yoke upon himself to represent that Judah and the surrounding nations would fall under the yoke of Babylonia (Jer 27:1-15), so Agabus binds himself with Paul's belt to represent what would happen to Paul in Jerusalem: the Jews of that city will bind Paul and deliver him to the Gentiles (v. 11). As the narrative unfolds, Agabus's prophecy is not fulfilled precisely. For example, the Jews don't actually bind Paul and deliver him to the Gentiles. They attack Paul, the Romans (Gentiles) come to rescue him, and then bind him in order to lead Paul away for interrogation.

Two comments are in order. First, in ancient narrative *precise* fulfillment of prophecy or prognostications within a narrative were not necessary. Prophecies or prognostications that foreshadowed events to come within the narrative offered readers a general sense of the direction that the narrative would take.[5] Second, Luke here may be shaping Agabus's prophetic utterance to resonate with the words that Jesus offered about his own fate in Jerusalem. This would encourage readers to see a comparison between Jesus and his

Jesus and Paul

The narrator offers a portrayal of Paul that high-lights similarities and parallels between the Lord and the disciple. Charles Talbert lays out the parallels most systematically, only a summary of which is presented:

• Both Jesus' and Paul's final and climactic journeys to Jerusalem receive focused attention (Luke 9:51, 53; 13:22, 33; 17:11; 18:31; 19:11; 19:28; Acts 19:21; 20:22; 21:4, 11-12, 13, 15, 17)
• Both are initially well received (Luke 19:37; Acts 21:17-20a)
• Both go to the temple (Luke 19:45-48; Acts 21:26)
• Both discuss the issue of resurrection, dividing Sadducees

and scribes or Pharisees (Luke 20:27-39; Acts 23:6-9)
• Each is the victim of mob action (Luke 22:54; Acts 21:30), which cries "Away with this man [or him]" (Luke 23:18; Acts 21:36)
• Each has four trials or hearings
• Jesus: Sanhedrin (Luke 22:26), Pilate (23:1); Herod (23:8); Pilate (23:13)
• Paul: Sanhedrin (Acts 23); Felix (Acts 24); Festus (Acts 25); Agrippa [a Herodian] (Acts 26)
• Each is declared innocent by government officials (Luke 23:4, 14, 22; Acts 23:9; 25:25; 26:31)

Charles H. Talbert, *Literary Patterns, Theological Themes and the Genre of Luke–Acts* (SBLMS 20; Missoula MT: Scholars Press, 1974), 17–18.

faithful follower Paul who lives as Jesus did. [Jesus and Paul] Compare especially Agabus's prophecy here with Jesus' words found in Luke 18:32. Here Agabus says that the Jews will "deliver [*paradōsousin*] him into the hands of the Gentiles" (v. 11, RSV). Luke 18:32 says of the Son of Man that "he will be delivered [*paradothēsetai*] to the Gentiles" (RSV).[6]

The response of the believers, including the narrator, to this dire prophecy is to beg Paul not to go up to Jerusalem. This protest is similar to what the text said earlier in v. 4b, where believers "through the Spirit" urged Paul not to go to Jerusalem. It may strike readers as odd that believers *inspired even by the Spirit* should urge Paul *not* to do what he was convinced *in the Spirit* (cf. 20:22) he should do: go to Jerusalem. Robert Tannehill offers insightful commentary:

> It is interesting that the narrator has allowed to surface at least a superficial contradiction in the divine guidance that Paul is receiving, an indication that it is seldom easy to separate divine revelation from human interpretation. Appeal to divine guidance is not an easy escape from the ambiguities of human life.[7]

Fittingly, at the end of the day, what matters most is how the one who is being directed by God's spirit responds to such guidance. In v. 13 Paul shows his readiness to go to Jerusalem and face whatever awaits him there. He replies to his fellow believers that their weeping is "breaking his heart" (v. 13). Is Paul broken-hearted because fellow believers have urged him to go against the guidance of the Spirit? In this case, Paul's reply that he is ready both to suffer and die for the Lord may serve as a kind of retort: *Even though you have urged me to disobey the Spirit, be assured that I am ready both to be imprisoned and die on behalf of Jesus.* Or is he broken-hearted that they are sad? If so, his reply would serve more to offer comfort and reassurance: *It breaks my heart to see you so saddened, but you can be confident that I am prepared for whatever awaits me in Jerusalem.*

Whatever the intent of Paul's response, whether it be to shame or to comfort, the community realizes that Paul is going to go to Jerusalem. Thus, they cease to attempt to persuade him to do otherwise and leave Paul's future to the will of the Lord (v. 14). With this closure, Paul and his companions, now joined by some believers from Caesarea, complete the journey to Jerusalem (vv. 15-16). Upon arrival they lodge with a believer named Mnason of Cyprus. The narrator only tells readers that he had been a believer from the early days of the church. Given that he was from Cyprus, he might well have belonged to the circle of Greek-speaking Jews (see [The Hellenists and the Hebrews]).

"So, Do What We Tell You," 21:17-26

Luke's opening sentence to this section leaves the impression that Paul's arrival in Jerusalem got off to a good start. "The brothers" who gladly welcomed Paul and his companions (v. 17) may not refer to the whole Jerusalem congregation, but perhaps only the leadership. One suspects that the myriads of Christian Jews zealous for the law and skeptical of Paul's fidelity to Judaism (see v. 21) would not have been among those who gladly greeted Paul.

Verses 18-22 describe Paul's more focused meeting with James and "the elders," the leadership of the Jerusalem congregation (see [Elders]). The last time Paul met with the leadership of the Jerusalem church "the apostles" were also present (15:4). The apostles no longer lead the Jerusalem congregation.

Luke offers no explanation for this transition of leadership. The narrative may reflect the social reality of its own time of composition. The leadership had passed to "the elders." More specifically, "the bishops and elders" to whom Paul had passed on the responsibility of caring for the church now led the flock (20:26-32).

Paul speaks to these leaders about his work among Gentiles, similar to what he had done in Acts 15. The narrator offers no specific word of what Paul said, beyond summarizing "what God had done." This would certainly refer to Paul's success in turning Gentiles away from idols to the true and living God. The response of the leadership is positive: "they glorified God." Luke regularly uses this phrase to denote a positive recognition of the saving work of God (see Luke 2:20; 5:26; 7:16; 13:13; 18:43; Acts 4:21; 11:18; 13:48). There is no question but that the leadership is affirming of Paul's ministry.

However, other members of the Jerusalem church may create something of a problem. The leadership speaks of thousands of Christian Jews, describing them as "zealous for the law" (v. 20). Zeal for the law often involved more than internal passion. Such texts as 1 Maccabees 2:26-27, 50, 54 and 58 point to the kind of zeal that resists, even violently, attempts to undermine the practice of God's commands. Paul will later admit that he once had a similar zeal—a zeal that led him to persecute the church (22:3-4; cf. Gal 1:14). Such zeal would not accept well rumors that Paul's gospel among the Gentiles was also encouraging Jewish believers to abandon their Jewish ways: forsaking Moses and not practicing circumcision and other Jewish traditions.

Readers know that such charges are unfounded. Paul circumcised Timothy (16:3), assumed the obligations of the Nazirite vow (18:18), and observes Jewish festivals (20:6, 16). There is no hint that the leadership doubts Paul's fidelity to his Jewish heritage. But they are concerned that something be done to appease the zealous Jewish believers (v. 22). What lies behind this concern in the narrative to show Paul to be a loyal Jew who preaches a gospel that does not advocate that Jews abandon their traditions?

Historically, the collection may have had something to do with this concern (see [The Collection]). Statements that Paul makes in his letters seem to indicate that the Jerusalem church needed the funds (Rom 15:25-27). And yet Paul's openness to Gentiles and his advocacy of a "law-free" gospel did create suspicion among more traditional Christian Jews. The issues that gave rise to the letter to the Galatian churches offer evidence of that. To have received this gift from Gentile churches, while not requiring anything of Paul to show his loyalty to his own Jewish tradition, might have greatly alienated those believers who were zealous for the law.

On the literary level, which need not necessarily clash with historical matters, the narrative is apparently quite concerned to portray Paul to be loyal to his Jewish heritage. It is not an exaggeration to say that for the *historical* Paul, the delivery of the gift to Jerusalem was the primary reason for his journey to Jerusalem. For the Paul of Acts, a *character* in Luke's narrative world, the display of loyalty to Jewish ways, evidenced in Paul's behavior and the speeches he will eventually give, is a primary reason for this final journey.[8]

In vv. 23-25, the leadership lays out what Paul can do to demonstrate his fidelity to Jewish tradition. They note that four men are currently under a special vow. The whole of the speech, with its reference to the shaving of heads, makes clear that the men are under a Nazirite vow, the details of which may be found in Numbers 6. Luke Johnson has argued that Paul is also concluding his own Nazirite vow, which began in Acts 18:18,[9] but not all commentators read the text this way (see [Nazirite Vow]).

There is some confusion over how to interpret the phrase of v. 24, which NRSV translates: "Join these men, go through the rite of purification with them." This translation, which is a fair rendering of the Greek text, makes it sound as though Paul *and* those under the vow will undergo purification. But those under the vow would already have been pure or they would not have been able to complete the vow. According to Numbers 6:8, Nazirites are to remain "holy to the LORD" for the entire duration of the period of the vow, avoiding contact even with the corpse of a close family member. Should contact with the dead be unavoidable, Numbers 6:9-12 allows for a special purification rite so that the one having taken the vow can renew and complete the vow. But there is no indication that all four of these men had unavoidably come into contact with the dead.

One might resolve this by arguing that Luke intends to say that only Paul would need to purify himself. Such purification would have been necessary so that Paul, after having spent time among Gentiles, could be clean and enter the Jerusalem temple.[10] Jewish law and tradition assumed that one living outside the land among Gentiles would become ritually defiled, living among people who did not adhere to laws of cleanness. Haenchen argues that *historically* this is how one should understand the event. But Luke misunderstood the procedure and thought that *all* members of the party were to be ritually purified and that Paul actually assumed a Nazirite vow for the balance of the seven days. It was this misunderstanding that led Luke to write that the leadership instructed Paul to purify himself "together with them [the other four men]" (Gk., *syn autois*).[11]

Upon completion of the purification period, Paul was then to pay the expenses for the sacrifices that would conclude the period of the Nazirite vow (v. 24a). The required sacrifices and offerings are spelled out in Numbers 6:13-15. One was to sacrifice a one-year-old male lamb, a one-year-old ewe lamb, and one ram; one was to present as an offering a basket of bread, cake, and grain. Further, Numbers 6:21 stipulates that the Nazirites who take a vow are to provide additional offerings, based on what they can afford. It is these considerable expenses that Paul agrees to incur on behalf of the four who have taken the vow. The text does not say or imply that Paul used funds from the gift he brought from the Gentiles to pay these expenses.

Historical issues aside, in the narrative world the leadership is convinced that Paul's providing the funds for the sacrifices and offerings will convince people that he is loyal to his Jewish heritage, that he lives in observance of the law (v. 24b). In this same narrative world, this will help to reinforce for the reader that Paul is a loyal Jew and that the gospel he and others preach is not opposed to Judaism, but actually fulfills Jewish hopes for life and salvation.

One could interpret the comment of v. 25 to reiterate both to Paul (historically) and to the reader (literarily) that the leadership is not reneging on its commitment of Acts 15. Gentiles would not be required to be circumcised, but would only need to observe minimal laws of purity to distinguish themselves from their former way of life and to allow association with Jewish believers. That is, neither Paul nor the reader should understand that Paul's agreeing to undergo rites of purification and to pay the expenses for the Nazirites compromised the essence of Paul's gospel to the Gentiles.

The comment also reinforces for the reader that the Pauline mission to the Gentiles showed sensitivity to Jewish law, custom, and tradition. The requirement that Gentiles abstain from certain patterns of behavior shows the kind of respect for Jewish tradition and law that believers zealous for the law suspect that Paul does not honor. The picture is quite clear: believers zealous for the law have no reason to believe that Paul undermines their traditions or customs.

Paul's actions reinforce this, for the following day he went to the temple with the men to begin the process of purification (v. 26)— a process that would take seven days (see v. 27). The Greek text can be read to say that Paul went through the process of purification *along with* the four Nazirites (see RSV). The text can also be read to say that Paul alone went through the process of purification, after which time he entered into the temple *along with* the Nazirites (NRSV).

They Seized Paul, 21:27-40

Paul never gets the chance to show his faithfulness to his own Jewish traditions. The narrator reports in v. 27 that before the seven days for purification were completed, Jews from Asia, perhaps in Jerusalem to celebrate Pentecost (cf. 20:16), initiated a near riot in the temple precincts. The specific charge that they made against Paul was that he had been speaking against the Jewish people, law, and sanctuary and that he had brought Greeks into the temple area, thereby defiling the sacred space (v. 28). The Asian Jews are perhaps Jews from Ephesus, who had already shown a proclivity to create trouble for Paul (cf. 19:9), even though they were not terribly successful there—as evidence by Paul's more than two-year stay in the city (cf. 19:10, 22). In addition, these Jews specifically recognized Trophimus, a Gentile believer and native of Ephesus, whom these fellow Ephesians would have known to be an associate of Paul. It was this Gentile, specifically, whom they supposed Paul had taken into the temple.

The outer courts of the temple area were open to Gentiles. However, the inner courts were for Jews only, protected not only by a wall, but by signs warning non-Jews that they were not to violate the sacred space of the temple. [Temple Inscription]

The charge is full of irony. First, it is patently false. There is no evidence within the narrative that Paul had brought Trophimus or any Gentile into the inner courts of the temple. Second, Paul is so concerned about honoring the purity of the temple that he has

---

Temple Inscription

 Josephus and archaeology offer rich background for the scene in Acts 21 depicting the violent reaction of the Jews to the supposed desecration of their temple.

Thus was the first enclosure. In the midst of which, and not far from it, was the second, to be gone up to by a few steps; this was encompassed by a stone wall for a partition, with an inscription, which forbade any foreigner to go in, under pain of death. (*Ant.* 15.417)

When you go through these [first] cloisters, into the second [court of the] temple, there was a partition made of stone all round, whose height was three cubits: its construction was very elegant; upon it stood pillars, at equal distances from one another, declaring the law of purity, some in Greek, and some in Roman letters, that "no foreigner should go within that sanctuary." (*J. W.* 5.193–94)

One of the warning inscriptions was discovered in 1871 (pictured at right.) It reads as follows:

No man of another nation is to enter within the fence and enclosure round the temple. And whoever is caught will have himself to blame that his death ensues.

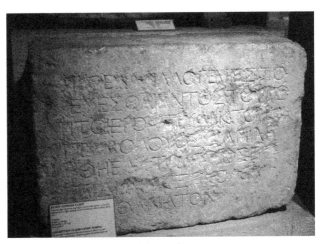

(Credit: Image courtesy of www.holylandphotos.org)

Quoted from C. K. Barrett, ed., *The New Testament Background: Writings from Ancient Greece and the Roman Empire That Illuminate Christian Origins*, rev. ed. (New York: HarperSanFrancisco, 1989), 53.

The Jerusalem Temple

The Jerusalem temple increasingly restricted access the closer one came to the holy of holies. Note in the diagram of the temple that the Court of the Gentiles is in the outermost areas, *outside* the inner courts. The first inner court is that of the Court of Women. Looking at the model of the Jerusalem temple (here one is looking at the temple from the East), the Court of Women is the first "inner court," located in the bottom portion of the picture. The gates entering into the Court of Women may be the "doors" or "gates" that "were shut" (21:30). At the end of the Court of Women, one can see steps leading up to a second gate (this is the Nicanor Gate and, possibly, the Beautiful Gate to which Acts 3:2 refers). Beyond this is the Court of Israel, where men were permitted to view the work of priests in the Court of Priests, just outside and in front of the Sanctuary (*naos*) proper. The Sanctuary proper represents even holier space, with access restricted to priests who, by lot, were assigned roles within the Sanctuary (see Luke 1:8-9). Within the Sanctuary was the holy of holies, into which the high priest would enter on the Day of Atonement.

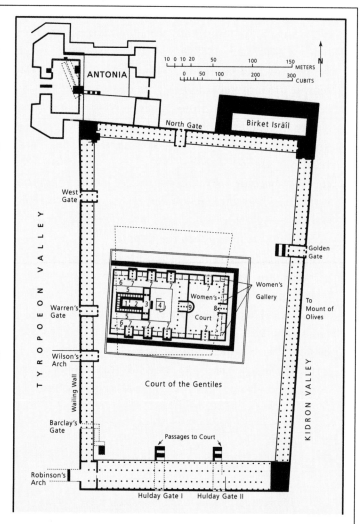

Model of Jerusalem Temple

(Credit: Wikipedia, "The Second Jewish Temple. Model in the Israel Museum." [cited 17 September 2007]. Online: http://en.wikipedia.org/wiki/Image:P8170082.JPG.)

been undergoing the appropriate rites of purity so that *he* could enter the inner courts to provide the sacrifices for the four Nazirites. Third, though more subtly, *readers* would know that even if a Gentile had entered the inner courts, he or she would not have defiled (*kekoinōken*, v. 28) the temple, for God had already explicitly declared through his vision to Peter that what God has cleansed one must not call "common" (see 10:15; 11:9), the root of which, *koin-*, is the same as the word translated "defile" in 21:26. Gentiles are no longer "common" or "defiled." They are, therefore, not capable of rendering God's holy space common or defiled.

It may seem surprising that such a charge could so quickly arouse "all the city," even if one allows for Lukan hyperbole (vv. 30-31). There is some literary license here, no doubt, but readers of Acts have grown accustomed to Paul's actions affecting whole cities, often in less than peaceful ways (cf. 13:44, 50; 14:4; 16:20; 17:5; 19:29; see [Mob Scenes]). But there is also verisimilitude in Luke's narrative, for the historian Josephus does report that Jews took quite seriously, with Roman sanction even, the radical protection of their sacred courts.[12] Some claim that "Jews believed the Temple remained profane until the trespasser had been executed."[13]

The narrator reports that once Paul was dragged out of the temple, "immediately the doors were shut" (v. 30). On the literal level, the shutting of the gates, ironically, would have served to protect the temple from being further defiled by what was about to happen—the summary execution of Paul.[14] On a more symbolic and literary level, the shutting of the gates could represent Jerusalem's final word of rejection to the gospel—Jerusalem has "closed the door" on the messenger of the gospel and, therefore, the gospel itself.[15]

The larger Roman fortress, known as Fortress Antonia, stood at the northwestern corner of the massive temple complex, looming over the courts where Romans could keep an eye on things. During the religious festivals, the Roman cohort, which consisted of 1,000 troops when at full strength, would likely have been on high alert. Hearing of the commotion (v. 31), the tribune took a contingent of "soldiers and centurions" to stop the beating of Paul (v. 32). Given that a centurion led 100 men, this might imply that at sizeable contingent of troops poured out of the fortress and into the outer courts of the temple.

Interestingly, the tribune assumes Paul to be in the wrong and not the mass of people beating him, for he arrests Paul and binds him with two chains (v. 33). Perhaps readers should picture Paul with a chain on each wrist, with a soldier on the other end of each

Fortress Antonia

These pictures of the model of Jerusalem, located at the Holy Land Hotel in Jerusalem, are looking at the temple complex from various angles. Looking from the SW (left photograph), Fortress Antonia is the massive structure in the upper right of the photograph. Looking from the SE (right photograph), one can see how close Fortress Antonia is to the northern Court of the Gentiles. This allows one to get a sense of how Roman troops could quickly enter the courts to quell the ensuing riot (21:31-32). The Fortress had a "bird's eye" view of the temple courts.

(Credit: Jim Pitts)

(Credit: Jim Pitts)

chain. After securing Paul the tribune turns to the crowd in an attempt to discover the cause of the disturbance, but this only adds to the confusion, so he orders Paul taken to the barracks located within Fortress Antonia (v. 34).

Verse 35 confuses some interpreters, for it is not clear to some how carrying Paul, presumably above the heads of the soldiers, would have protected Paul from the volatile crowd; in fact, this could very well have exposed him to further danger. The violent intentions of the crowd are evident in their cry, "Away with him" (v. 36), a clear echo of the cry against Jesus (cf. Luke 23:18). Haenchen attributes the scene of the soldiers carrying Paul to Luke's poetic license. Witherington asserts that "there is nothing improbable about this action by the soldiers."[16] The disagreement between Haenchen and Witherington illustrates how so much in the interpretation of Acts as a historical record is dependent on the disposition of the reader.

Verses 37-40 conclude the chapter and set the stage for the defense speech to follow in Acts 22. Assessing the scene historically is problematic, and, again, such assessment is regularly dependent on the disposition of the interpreter. Haenchen thinks it unlikely that the tribune would leap to the conclusion that Paul was the revolutionary Egyptian, then, upon hearing Paul speak Greek, immediately conclude that he was not the revolutionary (many people spoke Greek!). [The Egyptian] Haenchen also finds it improbable that the tribune would then honor Paul's request to make a speech—a speech that the riotous crowd would stop to listen to.[17] Witherington attempts to address Haenchen's assessment by arguing that tense times could have led the tribune to conclude that Paul was some type of troublemaker, that Paul's refined Greek allowed him further to infer that Paul was no local-yokel (hence, he must not be "the Egyptian"), and that the tribune allowed Paul to speak to show and restore honor to one whom he had dishonored by assuming him to be a revolutionary.[18]

Literally, however, the scene flows well with the narrative. Paul, in v. 37, is portrayed as taking control of the situation; he is no passive instrument of the whims of others. While it may seem problematic historically that the tribune should be shocked that Paul spoke Greek or that Paul could have been the revolutionary Egyptian who led an army of assassins, the scene serves to show that Christians, even Christian leaders, are not a threat to the Roman state. As Haenchen reiterates, "Christianity has nothing to do with political Messianism."[19] [Sicarii] Readers have encountered this theme before (cf. Acts 18:12-17; 19:37-40).

In fact, Paul is a citizen of Tarsus, a respectable city. Readers know, and the tribune will later learn (22:25-29), that Paul is also a Roman citizen. The contrast could not be greater. The tribune assumed Paul to find his roots in the wilderness, which represented alienation from and opposition to the established order of Rome. In fact, Paul is well grounded in the social stability and order of Rome. He identifies himself in proper fashion: his nationality (*natio*) (Jewish), his place of origin, or *origo* (Tarsus), and his civil status (*civitas*) (citizen).[20] In the narrative world of Acts, Paul has thus earned the right to speak, and speak he does. With the wave of the hand, a stereotypical rhetorical gesture, Paul hushes his

---

The Egyptian

The Roman tribune suspected that Paul might be "the Egyptian." The narrator uses the tribune's short address to Paul to inform the reader about this revolutionary. After stirring up a revolt he led 4,000 assassins (see [Sicarii]) into the wilderness (21:38).

The Jewish historian Josephus twice speaks of "the Egyptian" in his historical annals (*Ant.* 20.169–72; *J. W.* 2.261–63). The Egyptian claimed to be a prophet who led 30,000 men (Luke's number of 4,000 seems more realistic) from the desert to the Mount of Olives. From there they were to witness the collapse of the walls, whereupon he and his followers would secure the city. Felix, who served as the procurator from AD 52–60, stopped the effort, killing about 400 of the rebels and capturing around 200. The Egyptian got away.

Josephus's account helps modern readers understand the complex intertwining of religion and politics among first-century Jewish revolutionaries. The trek from the wilderness to the outskirts of the city of Jerusalem, which was to result in the collapse of the walls, was clearly a reenactment of ancient Israel's sojourn through the wilderness and its invasion of the promised land, including the collapse of the walls at Jericho. Many Jews were hoping to experience in their own time a demonstration of God's liberating powers similar to what their ancestors had experienced during the birth of Israel as a nation under Moses and Joshua.

Sicarii

AΩ The word NRSV translates as "assassins" in 21:38 is *sikariōn*, the plural of the Greek word *sikarios*, a transliteration of the Latin *sicarius*. These assassins would employ as their primary weapons small daggers. They were quite active in the revolt against Rome (AD 66–73) and were among the last to fall, having committed suicide at the fortress of Masada rather than surrender to the Romans. Luke, who is ultimately responsible for the tribune's comments, is not correct to identify the followers of the Egyptian with the Sicarii, unless he is using the term in the more generic sense of "revolutionary."

David Rhoads, "Zealots," *ABD* 6.1043–54; see especially the section on "Sicarii," p. 1048.

audience and proceeds to speak to them in Hebrew. This most likely refers to Aramaic, a dialect of the Hebrew language (cf. 22:2; 26:14).[21]

CONNECTIONS

Two issues for contemporary application emerge from the reading of this story. The first issue might be labeled, "the necessity of compromise for the sake of the gospel." The second we might title, "the futility of compromise." The paradox gives expression to the complexity of discipleship.

Paul's willingness to purify himself and pay the expenses for the four men who had taken the Nazirite vow is consistent with his behavior throughout Acts. The Paul of Acts regularly shows deference to the Jerusalem leadership. He delivered the letter to Gentiles telling them to observe minimal laws of purity in order to distinguish themselves from their former way of life and also to allow ongoing fellowship with Christian Jews (15:30; 16:4). He circumcised Timothy "because of the Jews" (16:3). And in this story Paul follows the council of the Jerusalem leadership in an attempt to persuade zealous Jewish believers that he is a loyal Jew.

Among interpreters, the question regularly arises whether the "historical Paul," or the Paul one meets in the Epistles, would have agreed to such a "compromise." The text most commonly cited to offer an affirmative response is 1 Corinthians 9:20: "To the Jews I became as a Jew, in order to win Jews. To those under the law I became as one under the law (though I myself am not under the law) so that I might win those under the law."

Paul's actions in Acts 21 illustrate this statement well. To be sure, the zealous believers who are skeptical of Paul's loyalty are already "won" to the gospel. He need not "become as one under the law" in order to turn these Jews to Christ. However, Paul firmly believed that "there is no longer Jew or Greek . . . for all . . . are one in Christ" (Gal 3:28). The church is the "body of Christ" that is to be marked by unity of purpose and mission, guided by being of one mind (cf. Phil 1:27; 2:2; 3:15). The writer of Ephesians captured well this feature of Paul's view of the church when he wrote:

> For he is our peace; in his flesh he has made both groups [Jews and Gentiles] into one and has broken down the dividing wall, that is, the hostility between us. He has abolished the law with its commandments and ordinances, that he might create in himself one new

humanity in place of the two, thus making peace, and might reconcile both groups to God in one body through the cross, thus putting to death that hostility through it. So he came and proclaimed peace to you who were far off and peace to those who were near; for through him both of us have access in one Spirit to the Father. (Eph 2:14-18)

Compromise for the sake of unity within the body of Christ comes forth in Paul's Letter to the Romans, as well. Paul urges the Jewish and Gentile believers in Rome not to allow differences of opinion over food or drink or holy days (Rom 14:1-6) to cause quarrelling and division within the body: "For the kingdom of God is not food and drink but righteousness and peace and joy in the Holy Spirit. . . . Let us then pursue what makes for peace and for mutual upbuilding" (Rom 14:17, 19).

While the narrative of Acts pays little attention to the collection that Paul, accompanied by several Gentile believers, was bringing to the saints of Jerusalem, Paul's motive for the collection was to demonstrate in a concrete way that, in Christ, there is neither Jew nor Greek (cf. Gal 3:28). [The Unity of Jew and Gentile in Christ] In Paul's words, "If the Gentiles have come to share in their [the Jews'] spiritual blessings, they ought also to be of service to them in material things" (Rom 15:27). And Paul's own testimony makes clear that he was not sure that this gift, or "ministry," as Paul called it, would be accepted (Rom 15:31). If showing his loyalty to his Jewish heritage would have increased the likelihood of the Jewish believers' acceptance of this ministry, it is consistent that he would "compromise" and "live as one under the law," though he did not consider himself to be under the law (cf., again, 1 Cor 9:20).

But does not the Paul of Galatians show a strident, uncompromising attitude? In this letter Paul pronounces damnation upon those who are "preaching a different gospel" (Gal 1:8-9). He even states caustically that those bewitching the Galatian believers with talk of circumcision should mutilate and castrate themselves (Gal 5:12).

We would not be wise to understand the apparent contrast of tone within Paul by appealing to something as subjective as "Paul's mood." It is not as though he was more open on some days than others to the spirit of compromise. What was at stake in Galatia

---

The Unity of Jew and Gentile in Christ

In speaking of the practical and "applied theological" implications of the collection, James D. G. Dunn offers the following:

The shared "participation" in grace/Spirit (it is implied) should come to expression in the "sharing" of relative prosperity in "shared" ministry. . . . Here it is especially noteworthy that the sharing and service are not limited to the local church or even the churches of the region, but reach across the ocean to another church, one regarding which feelings were somewhat mixed. The interdependence of the body of Christ is not limited to relationships within individual congregations.

James D. G. Dunn, *The Theology of Paul the Apostle* (Grand Rapids MI: Eerdmans, 1998), 709.

was the essence of the gospel itself. For the Galatians to have submitted to circumcision would have been to deny that faith in what God had offered in Christ was sufficient. It would have had the effect of declaring that Christ had died for nothing (cf. Gal 2:21). Rather, one can find a consistent thread running through Paul's letters on this matter of compromise: Paul will compromise *for the sake of the advancement* of the gospel or the unity within the body that the gospel is to engender. But Paul will not compromise the gospel itself.

Paradoxically, the narrative of Acts 21 also shows the potential futility of compromise. The charge that the Jews from Asia make against Paul, that he encouraged Jews to abandon their ethnic heritage and religious traditions and that he defiled the temple by bringing a Gentile into the inner courts, are patently false. One may infer from their charge that, within the narrative logic of Acts, it was these Asian Jews who stirred up the zealous Jewish believers of Jerusalem with talk of Paul's infidelity to Judaism.

One could wish that the zealous Jewish believers had listened more to their leaders than to the Asian Jews. Or perhaps one could wish that the leaders of the Jerusalem church had themselves been more zealous to defend Paul to the Jewish believers on fire for the law. Since the narrator never returns again to either these zealous believers or the Jerusalem leadership, we simply cannot know how the saints of Jerusalem came to understand Paul or whether they were open to receiving the gift he had worked years to collect.

For the duration of Paul's stay in Jerusalem, the narrative will focus almost exclusively on Paul's non-believing Jewish opponents. One theme seems persistent: those vehemently opposed to Paul's inclusive and open-armed, law-free gospel will not accept or, as subsequent chapters will show, even listen to Paul. They are totally unimpressed by his Jewish heritage or credentials. While Paul is dutifully and carefully going through the appropriate ceremonies of purification so that he could pay the expenses of four Nazirites, his opponents see only what they want to see. "There's none so blind as they that won't see," quipped Jonathan Swift. Except, perhaps, those who see what isn't even there: a man disparaging their religious traditions.

Religious opposition is often the most blind, or at least has the foggiest vision. And yet it can deceive itself into believing that it sees with absolute clarity. The narrator never accuses Paul's Jewish opponents in this chapter of intentional deceit. He states quite clearly that "they *supposed* that Paul had brought him into the temple" (21:29). The word translated as *supposed* means "to think" and is consistently used in Acts to denote sincerely held conclusions or inferences, even if they are often incorrect (see 7:25; 16:13, 27). The Asian Jews really do believe Paul had profaned their temple. And the fact that they are mistaken bears no weight with them.

Such is the potential curse of "knowledge" that is too self-assured, especially in matters of religion. It seems that anything that some don't fully understand or that challenges what some believe they do understand is open to suspicion, ridicule, or worse: violent opposition. Anything that raises questions of any kind becomes the enemy. Such persons do not know the liberation that can come when one dares to risk or question. [Questions]

People who cannot live with doubt and who live with and in the midst of those who might call into question carefully crafted paradigms for living may be prone to surrender their own freedom—and demand the surrender of the freedom of others. [Surrendering the Freedom to Doubt]

Faced with this kind of self-assured fanaticism, compromise proves futile. Compromise requires openness and a willingness to find common ground. And both of these may require letting go of some of those beliefs that one grasps so tightly. And all Paul can do, as the subsequent chapters will show, is say what he has to say: offer his testimony, his witness, and let his audience decide for itself. But the violence of this scene offers a clear harbinger that his testimony will fall on deaf ears.

Questions

"It was years before I learned that *living* the questions, not *answering* them, was what true faith required." (Stella, 94)

"The main questions of religion—Who am I? Where have I come from? Where am I going?—are not questions with an answer but questions that open us to new questions which lead us deeper into the unspeakable mystery of existence. . . . This quest, precisely because it does not lead to ready answers but to new questions, is extremely painful and at times even excruciating. . . . The pain of the human search is a growing pain. When we prevent that pain from entering into consciousness, we suffocate the forces of human development." (Nouwen [Durback], 99)

"[H]ow do we know that it's God that we know when we think we know God? The very asking of such questions leads to one of the oldest definitions of Christian theology: faith seeking understanding. To probe the questions is to trust God in the very probing, knowing that God can handle all the questions we can devise. Questions can be a way of drawing us into deeper realms of faith, taking us from belief in our beliefs to belief in the God who is more than our beliefs can express." (Suchocki, 2)

Tom Stella, *A Faith Worth Believing: Finding New Life Beyond the Rules of Religion* (New York: HarperSanFrancisco, 2004); Robert Durback, ed., *Seeds of Hope: A Henry Nouwen Reader*, 2d ed. (New York: Doubleday, 1997); Marjorie Hewitt Suchocki, *In God's Presence: Theological Reflections on Prayer* (St Louis: Chalice, 1996).

Surrendering the Freedom to Doubt

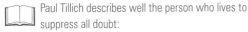

Paul Tillich describes well the person who lives to suppress all doubt:

He flees from his freedom of asking and answering for himself to a situation in which no further questions can be asked and the answers to previous questions are imposed on him authoritatively. In order to avoid the risk of asking and doubting he surrenders the right to ask and to doubt. . . . And since the conquest of doubt was a matter of sacrifice, the sacrifice of the freedom of the self, it leaves a mark on the regained certitude: a fanatical self-assertiveness. Fanaticism is the correlate to spiritual self-surrender: it shows the anxiety which it was supposed to conquer, by attacking with disproportionate violence those who disagree and who demonstrate by their disagreement elements in the spiritual life of the fanatic which he must suppress in himself.

Paul Tillich, *The Courage To Be* (New Haven: Yale University Press, 1952), 49–50.

NOTES

[1] Joseph A. Fitzmyer, *The Acts of the Apostles* (AB 31; New York: Doubleday, 1998), 686.

[2] Gerd Lüdemann, *Early Christianity according to the Traditions in Acts: A Commentary* (Minneapolis: Fortress, 1989), 230–31.

[3] Ben Witherington III, *The Acts of the Apostles: A Socio-Rhetorical Commentary* (Grand Rapids MI: Eerdmans, 1998), 629.

[4] In *Church History* 3.31.3–5 Eusebius speaks of "Philip, one of the twelve apostles, who sleeps in Hierapolis, and his two aged virgin daughters, and another daughter who lived in the Holy Spirit and now rests at Ephesus." He further states in 3.39.9, "That Philip the apostle dwelt at Hierapolis with his daughters has been already stated." It is possible that the apostle Philip also had "virgin daughters," but most historians conclude that Eusebius confused the two men, though some believe he rightly identified the two.

[5] J. Bradley Chance, "Divine Prognostications and the Movement of Story: An Intertextual Exploration of Xenophon's *Ephesian Tale* and the Acts of the Apostles," in *Ancient Fiction and Early Christian Narrative*, ed. Ronald F. Hock, J. Bradley Chance, Judith Perkins, vol. 6 (SBL Symposium Series; Atlanta: Scholars Press, 1998), 219–34.

[6] See Robert W. Tannehill, *The Narrative Unity of Luke–Acts: A Literary Interpretation*, 2 vols. (Minneapolis: Fortress, 1990), 2.265. Witherington, *Acts*, offers an alternate view (634). He minimizes the parallels between Paul and Jesus, noting, among other things, that Paul was not actually killed in Jerusalem and Paul defended himself. Echoes that allow for comparison, however, should perhaps not be limited to tit-for-tat correspondence.

[7] Tannehill, *Narrative Unity*, 2.263.

[8] The abundance of speeches that Paul makes while in Jerusalem and Caesarea allow the conclusion that in the narrative world of Acts, Paul makes his final journey to Jerusalem *in order to speak*. And much of what Paul talks about is his loyalty to his Jewish tradition. See Jacob Jervell, "Paul: The Teacher of Israel: The Apologetic Speeches of Paul in Acts," in Luke and the People of God: A New Look at Luke–Acts (Minneapolis MN: Augsburg, 1972), 153–83.

[9] Luke Timothy Johnson, *The Acts of the Apostles* (SacPag 5; Collegeville MN: Liturgical Press, 1992), 329–30. Also see [Nazirite Vow].

[10] Johnson, *Acts*, 375–76; John B. Polhill, Acts (NAC 26; Nashville: Broadman, 1992), 449.

[11] Ernst Haenchen, *The Acts of the Apostles: A Commentary* (Philadelphia: Westminster, 1971), 612.

[12] Josephus attributes a speech to Titus in which the Roman leader says, "Have we not given you leave to kill such as go beyond it [the temple boundary], though he were a Roman?" (*J. W.* 6.126).

[13] W. J. Larken, *Acts* (Downers Grove: InterVarsity, 1995), 314, cited in Witherington, *Acts*, 656.

[14] Haenchen, *Acts*, 616.

[15] Johnson, *Acts*, 382, and Polhill, *Acts*, 453.

[16] Witherington, *Acts*, 658.

[17] Haenchen, *Acts*, 620–22.

[18] Witherington, *Acts*, 661–64.

[19] Haenchen, *Acts*, 622.

[20] Fitzmyer, *Acts*, 700.

[21] The Gospel of John also uses "Hebrew" to denote the Aramaic language (see John 5:2; 19:13, 17, 20; 20:16).

"LISTEN TO THE DEFENSE THAT I NOW MAKE"

Acts 22:1-30

COMMENTARY

Acts 22 offers the first of several defense speeches to follow. A central theme of this speech and those that follow is Paul's—that is, Christianity's—relationship to Judaism. Ben Witherington comments, "The overwhelming impression left by the speech material in the last quarter of Acts is that 'the Way's' relationship to non-Christian Judaism is still very much a live issue for the author, requiring repeated instruction to his audience on the subject."[1] The close examination of what that relationship is will unfold as the speeches unfold. However, in short, the narrator, through the voice of Paul, will highlight that Christianity is the loyal extension of Judaism and the fulfillment of Judaism's Scriptures and hopes.

The chapter can be divided into four sections: (1) Paul: a Jew zealous for God (vv. 1-5), (2) Paul's call to be a witness to all the world (vv. 6-16), (3) Paul's vision of Jesus notifying him that the Lord would send him far away to the Gentiles (vv. 17-22), and (4) Paul's near interrogation by the Romans (vv. 23-30).

A Jew Zealous for God, 22:1-5

Paul is about to offer a defense, or *apologia*, to his Jewish audience. [Defense Speeches] One possible rhetorical outline is to view v. 1 as the *proem*. Verses 3-5 serve both to complete the *proem*, part of the function of which is to gain the audience's goodwill, and to begin the *narration*. Verses 6-21 continue the *narration*. Paul never formally gets to present the *proposition* or subsequent *proof*, for the crowd interrupts the speech at v. 22. However, the central thesis, that Paul is a loyal Jew and, therefore, is not guilty of defiling the temple or disparaging Jewish traditions, is at least *implicitly* addressed in the narration of facts. "The facts speak for themselves": a man with Paul's history cannot be justly accused of being a disloyal Jew.

Defense Speeches

📖 Defense speeches come under the type of discourse known as "judicial rhetoric" (see [Types of Rhetorical Persuasion]). According to George A. Kennedy defense speeches tended to follow a typical outline:

I. The *proem* or *exordium*, "which seeks to obtain the attention of the audience and goodwill or sympathy toward the speaker."

II. The "*narration* of the facts, or background information."

III. The "*proposition* which the speaker wishes to prove."

IV. The *proof* is the section where "the speaker then presents his arguments."

V. The *refutation* provides the speaker an opportunity to challenge opposing views.

VI. The *epilogue* or *peroration* "summarizes the argument and seeks to arouse the emotions of the audience to take action or make judgment."

Not every defense speech will have all sections and commentators will often disagree over how the various elements of the defense speeches of Acts fit into these formal categories of rhetorical analysis.

George A. Kennedy, *New Testament Interpretation through Rhetorical Criticism* (Chapel Hill: University of North Carolina Press, 1984), 23–24.

Paul immediately moves to establish rapport and credibility, or what Aristotle called *ethos*, with this hostile audience by claiming kinship—Jewish kinship—with them, referring to them as "brothers and fathers" (v. 1). Paul moves to create rapport in other ways in the opening of his speech (v. 3): he speaks of being brought up "in this city" (see below), claiming civic kinship with his Jerusalem audience; he makes reference to "the law of our fathers" (NRSV, "our ancestral law"); he acknowledges that his audience consists of Jews who are zealous for God's law. What is more, he communicates his ideas through the medium of the Hebrew, or Aramaic language (v. 2)—the native, nationalistic tongue of Palestinian Jews (see comment on Acts 21:40).

Having attempted to establish a good *ethos*, the thrust of v. 3 is to portray Paul as a good Jew, zealous for God. His autobiographical summary follows the standard conventions of his time, noting his place of birth and where he was reared and educated.[2] Commentators agree that the phrase "brought up in this city" connects grammatically with what follows, "at the feet of Gamaliel" (so NRSV), making clear that, though Paul was born in Tarsus, he was both reared and educated in Jerusalem. Paul's connection with Gamaliel, the leading rabbi of his time (see [Gamaliel]), would certainly enhance Paul's Jewish credentials. [Paul and Gamaliel]

Gamaliel was a Pharisee (5:34; see [Pharisees]), and though Paul does not explicitly identify himself as such here in v. 3, his self-description as one "educated strictly according to our ancestral law, being zealous for God" would comport with one educated under a Pharisee's tutelage. The noun *akribeian*, translated by the adverb "strictly" in the NRSV, is found only here in the New Testament. However, in his autobiography, Josephus used the term to describe Simon the Pharisee, and son of Gamaliel, (Josephus, *Life* 191).[3] And in his letters Paul used similar language to describe his Jewish

Paul and Gamaliel

Paul claims in Acts 22:3 to have studied with Gamaliel I. The Paul of the Epistles makes no such claim, implicitly or explicitly. As with so many of the historical and biographical claims of Acts that cannot be confirmed from other sources, scholars are divided as to the veracity of this claim of the Book of Acts.

Lüdemann thinks it "may be . . . historical" that Paul was educated in Jerusalem, but renders no judgment on his having studied with Gamaliel (Lüdemann, 240). Haenchen, following Rudolf Bultmann, argues that the claim is "scarcely correct" since Gal 1:22 implies that Paul was not well known among Judean Christians; therefore, he could not have spent much time in Jerusalem as either a student of Judaism or persecutor of Christians (Haenchen, 625).

N. T. Wright argues that Paul's great zeal, which manifested itself in the violent persecution of Christian Jews whom he perceived to be living in violation of the law,

would be consistent with a Pharisee of the more stringent school of Shammai. Gamaliel was of the school of Hillel (in fact, Hillel was his grandfather) and "the Hillelites, broadly speaking, pursued a policy of 'live and let live.' . . . The Shammaites believed that . . . Torah itself . . . demanded that Israel be free from the Gentile yoke, free to serve God in peace, calling no-one master except YHWH, the one true God, himself" (Wright, 27). If Wright's conclusion is correct, one would at least have to deduce that if Paul did once study under Gamaliel, he chose not to follow his "way" of being Jewish. In which case Paul's claim to have studied under the great rabbi, thereby attempting to ride Gamaliel's coattails into the hearts of his audience, is accurate but not wholly truthful.

Gerd Lüdemann, *Early Christianity according to the Traditions in Acts: A Commentary* (Minneapolis: Fortress, 1989); Ernst Haenchen, *The Acts of the Apostles: A Commentary* (Philadelphia: Westminster, 1971); N. T. Wright, *What St. Paul Really Said: Was Paul of Tarsus the Real Founder of Christianity?* (Grand Rapids MI: Eerdmans, 1997).

credentials as Luke depicts him employing here. Paul writes in Galatians 1:14 both of "zeal" and "the traditions of the elders [lit., *fathers*]" (cf. Phil 3:6). This compares closely with the language Luke places in Paul's mouth in this scene: "trained in the law of our fathers and . . . zealous for God" (RSV).

Zeal commonly translated into action in the Jewish tradition, including violent action against those perceived as threatening the law and will of God (see Num 25:6-13 [cf. Sir 45:23]; 1 Macc 2:26-27, 50, 54, 58; Phil 3:6a; Gal 1:13-14). Thus, Paul's reference to his zeal for God flows logically into his narration of his persecution of the Way (see [The Way]). Paul here is about to offer his rendition of what the reader already encountered in Acts: the story of Paul's call by the risen Lord to be his witness to the nations. Paul will offer another recounting of this event in Acts 26.

The triple narration of this event is an indication of its key importance for understanding Paul's mission. The place of the three accounts supports this observation. The first appears at the beginning of Paul's mission as its foundation, the second and third in the two major defense speeches at the beginning and end of the defense sequence in Acts 22–26, all prominent positions.[4]

The accounts are not identical, though they are complementary. [The Accounts of Paul's Conversion] The following will note significant differences and offer explanations for such, taking into account the narrative setting of the various accounts.

Verses 4-5 speak of Paul's persecution of "the Way to death" and the official sanctioning of such by the Jewish leadership. Paul's

The Accounts of Paul's Conversion

Luke presents three accounts of Paul's conversion, or call: Acts 9, 22, and 26. As one can see from synopsis, each account, while complementing the others, is its own composition. The first is the narrator's account. The latter two accounts are in the form of a speech by Paul. Paul is presented as sensitive to his rhetorical situation, with his speech shaped accordingly. See the commentary.

Acts 9

Meanwhile Saul, still breathing threats and murder against the disciples of the Lord, went to the high priest 2 and asked him for letters to the synagogues at Damascus, so that if he found any who belonged to the Way, men or women, he might bring them bound to Jerusalem.

3 Now as he was going along and approaching Damascus, suddenly a light from heaven flashed around him. 4 He fell to the ground and heard a voice saying to him, "Saul, Saul, why do you persecute me?" 5 He asked, "Who are you, Lord?" The reply came, "I am Jesus, whom you are persecuting. 6 But get up and enter the city, and you will be told what you are to do." 7 The men who were traveling with him stood speechless because they heard the voice but saw no one.

Acts 22

4 I persecuted this Way up to the point of death by binding both men and women and putting them in prison, 5 as the high priest and the whole council of elders can testify about me. From them I also received letters to the brothers in Damascus, and I went there in order to bind those who were there and to bring them back to Jerusalem for punishment.

6 "While I was on my way and approaching Damascus, about noon a great light from heaven suddenly shone about me. 7 I fell to the ground and heard a voice saying to me, 'Saul, Saul, why are you persecuting me?' 8 I answered, 'Who are you, Lord?' Then he said to me, 'I am Jesus of Nazareth whom you are persecuting.' 9 Now those who were with me saw the light but did not hear the voice of the one who was speaking to me. 10 I asked, 'What am I to do, Lord?' The Lord said to me, 'Get up and go to Damascus; there you will be told everything that has been assigned to you to do.'

Acts 26

4 "All the Jews know my way of life from my youth, a life spent from the beginning among my own people and in Jerusalem. 5 They have known for a long time, if they are willing to testify, that I have belonged to the strictest sect of our religion and lived as a Pharisee. 6 And now I stand here on trial on account of my hope in the promise made by God to our ancestors, 7 a promise that our twelve tribes hope to attain, as they earnestly worship day and night. It is for this hope, your Excellency, that I am accused by Jews! 8 Why is it thought incredible by any of you that God raises the dead? 9 "Indeed, I myself was convinced that I ought to do many things against the name of Jesus of Nazareth. 10 And that is what I did in Jerusalem; with authority received from the chief priests, I not only locked up many of the saints in prison, but I also cast my vote against them when they were being condemned to death. 11 By punishing them often in all the synagogues I tried to force them to blaspheme; and since I was so furiously enraged at them, I pursued them even to foreign cities.

13 when at midday along the road, your Excellency, I saw a light from heaven, brighter than the sun, shining around me and my companions. 14 When we had all fallen to the ground, I heard a voice saying to me in the Hebrew language, 'Saul, Saul, why are you persecuting me? It hurts you to kick against the goads.' 15 I asked, 'Who are you, Lord?' The Lord answered, 'I am Jesus whom you are persecuting. 16 But get up and stand on your feet; for I have appeared to you for this purpose, to appoint you to serve and testify to the things in which you have seen me and to those in which I will appear to you.'

8 Saul got up from the ground, and though his eyes were open, he could see nothing; so they led him by the hand and brought him into Damascus. 9 For three days he was without sight, and neither ate nor drank.

10 Now there was a disciple in Damascus named Ananias. The Lord said to him in a vision, "Ananias." He answered, "Here I am, Lord." 11 The Lord said to him, "Get up and go to the street called Straight, and at the house of Judas look for a man of Tarsus named Saul. At this moment he is praying, 12 and he has seen in a vision a man named Ananias come in and lay his hands on him so that he might regain his sight." 13 But Ananias answered, "Lord, I have heard from many about this man, how much evil he has done to your saints in Jerusalem; 14 and here he has authority from the chief priests to bind all who invoke your name."

15 But the Lord said to him, "Go, for he is an instrument whom I have chosen to bring my name before Gentiles and kings and before the people of Israel; 16 I myself will show him how much he must suffer for the sake of my name." 17 So Ananias went and entered the house. He laid his hands on Saul and said, "Brother Saul, the Lord Jesus, who appeared to you on your way here, has sent me so that you may regain your sight and be filled with the Holy Spirit." 18 And immediately something like scales fell from his eyes, and his sight was restored. Then he got up and was baptized, 19 and after taking some food, he regained his strength.

11 Since I could not see because of the brightness of that light, those who were with me took my hand and led me to Damascus.

12 "A certain Ananias, who was a devout man according to the law and well spoken of by all the Jews living there,

13 came to me; and standing beside me, he said, 'Brother Saul, regain your sight!' In that very hour I regained my sight and saw him. 14 Then he said, 'The God of our ancestors has chosen you to know his will, to see the Righteous One and to hear his own voice; 15 for you will be his witness to all the world of what you have seen and heard. 16 And now why do you delay? Get up, be baptized, and have your sins washed away, calling on his name.'

17 "After I had returned to Jerusalem and while I was praying in the temple, I fell into a trance 18 and saw Jesus saying to me, 'Hurry and get out of Jerusalem quickly, because they will not accept your testimony about me.' 19 And I said, 'Lord, they themselves know that in every synagogue I imprisoned and beat those who believed in you. 20 And while the blood of your witness Stephen was shed, I myself was standing by, approving and keeping the coats of those who killed him.' 21 Then he said to me, 'Go, for I will send you far away to the Gentiles.'"

17 I will rescue you from your people and from the Gentiles—to whom I am sending you 18 to open their eyes so that they may turn from darkness to light and from the power of Satan to God, so that they may receive forgiveness of sins and a place among those who are sanctified by faith in me.'

summary of v. 4 accords well with what the narrator reported in 8:1-3. In 8:3, the narrator states that "Paul was ravaging the church; . . . dragging off both men and women, he committed them to prison." Paul's reference in v. 4 to persecuting "the Way to death" recalls Paul's indirect participation in the execution of Stephen.

Verse 5 speaks of the formal commissioning by the Jewish leadership and Paul's journey to Damascus for the purpose of rounding up followers of the way (cf. 9:1-2). Acts 9:1-2 speaks of Paul taking the initiative to procure letters from the high priest alone that would authorize his seizing of Damascus Christians. Acts 22:5 leaves out that Paul took the initiative and indicates that Paul received his letters of authorization from the high priest and the elders. Furthermore, Paul appeals to the high priest and elders as witnesses, as though they could attest to the truth of this statement.

Commentators note that the high priest at the time of Paul's persecution of the church (Caiaphas) was not the same as the high priest at the time Paul made the speech (Ananias; cf. 23:2). Such observations invariably will turn conversation to whether or not Paul could have really said what is credited to him in this and the other speeches of Acts. Would the "real Paul" not have known that the high priest had changed and, therefore, could not have been one to whom he could have appealed as a witness? One could speculate endlessly, offering explanations and arguments as to why the "historical Paul" might have said what he did or could not possibly have said what was credited to him. Luke Johnson offers a sane approach: "The main point is that these leaders stand as 'witnesses' (*martyreō*) for Paul's deeds and motivations; the citation of such witnesses was a key component in ancient defense speeches."[5]

One must remember that speeches in Acts are aimed *ultimately* at the reader, not the audience in the story, though a good narrator will present a speech that is *appropriate* to the context within the story. It would be appropriate for Paul, in this narrative setting, to refer to various Jewish leaders as witnesses to his persecution of the church, for within the larger Lukan narrative Paul's violence against the church was not something that *readers* would have concluded Paul did in a dark corner, known only to him and the high priest. The larger body of Jewish authorities would surely have known about the activities of Paul as such are portrayed in Acts 8–9. The audience of Paul's speech *in the narrative setting* is not being asked simply to trust Paul's testimony that he was "zealous for God."

A Witness to All the World, 22:6-16

Verses 6-16 correspond roughly to Acts 9:3-19. Comparing accounts yields no clear conclusions on the matter of the historicity of Paul's speech. Inconsistencies do exist, but these can be explained as due to the *historical* Paul's memory lapses or misinterpretations or subjective impressions, which the author dutifully recorded. Or they may be explained as the narrator's attempts to make the character giving the speech *appear* to be offering a believable retelling of the event from his own perspective, complete with memory lapses or subjective impressions. Working on the assumption that the speeches are, finally, the responsibility of the author of Acts, the narrator does offer a credible presentation of Paul's recounting of his experience.

As Paul speaks of what happened to him on the way to Damascus, he emphasizes details that would highlight for his audience within the narrative the stupendous character of the event. He notes, unlike the narrator's account in Acts 9, the time of day (around noon) and that the light was "great." Paul's rendition of the experience tries to make clear to his audience the "objective" character of what happened. Encountering a "great light" in the middle of the day is no subjective vision. Paul's traveling companions further attest to the objective character of the light, for, according to Paul's account, they "saw the light" (v. 9). This can stand in tension with 9:7, which says that these men "saw no one." Of course, Paul saw in this great light the risen Jesus—that is, he saw more than a bright light. Paul had a personal revelation, a revelatory experience of the living Lord that his companions did not have. They may have seen a light, but not "the Light," "the living one."

Paul's emphasis on the revelatory character of the event on the Damascus road can offer some explanation of a further tension. Paul says that his companions "did not hear the voice of the one who was speaking to me" (v. 9), while the narrator of 9:7 says that "the men . . . heard the voice." If one hears Paul's speech as emphasizing his own, personal revelatory experience the inconsistency does not disappear (it is there), but it makes sense. The men heard a voice (Acts 9). They did not hear the voice of the living Lord who revealed himself to Paul (Acts 22). This was *Paul's* encounter with the living Lord. There were, to be sure, "objective" events to attest to the authenticity of the encounter (they saw a bright light [Acts 22] and heard a voice [Acts 9]). But the real meaning of the encounter is the interpretation that Paul, who met the Lord, gives to these events.

Paul's remembers that the Lord's command for him to continue on to Damascus was prompted by him asking, "What am I to do, Lord?" (v. 10). The question provides a transition to the Lord's command and makes for a more balanced rhetorical presentation by Paul.

A. Who are you, Lord?
   B. I am Jesus of Nazareth whom you are persecuting.
A. What am I to do, Lord?
   B. Get up and go.

The narrator of Acts 9 is not offering a speech; the narrator (Paul) in Acts 22 is, calling for more rhetorical polish.

Because the narrator in Acts 22 is Paul the speechmaker, his telling of Ananias's role is offered, appropriately, from the subjective point of view of Paul, not the omniscient narrator. Consequently, Acts 22 makes no mention of the details of Acts 9:10-14, which speaks of Ananias's own visionary encounter with the risen Jesus. Paul would not have been privy to what was narrated in 9:10-14. Thus, Paul's recollection picks up when Ananias came to Paul (vv. 12-13), commanded him to regain his sight (v. 13), and offered to Paul the Lord's commissioning to be his "witness to all the world of what you have seen and heard" (vv. 14-15).

The Paul who speaks in 22:12-15 is sensitive to his rhetorical situation within the narrative—a situation of offering a defense speech to a hostile, nationalistic Jewish audience. For example, Paul's summation of his call, to be a "witness to all the world" is consistent with Ananias's words in Acts 9, but not as provocative, given Paul's rhetorical situation. Ananias was instructed to tell Paul that the Lord had chosen him "to bring my name before Gentiles and kings and before the people of Israel" (9:15). Paul's summation in 22:15 avoids, at least at this juncture, explicit reference to the Gentiles. Paul is "building up" to that declaration.

Further, the narrator of Acts 9 describes Ananias as a "disciple in Damascus" (9:10). Paul in Acts 22 describes Ananias to his audience "a devout man according to the law and well spoken of by all the Jews living there" (v. 12). Additionally, as Paul offers his own reminiscence of Ananias's commission to Paul, Ananias employs vocabulary appropriate to a devout Jew. He refers to God as "the God of our ancestors" and employs the term "Righteous One" to refer to Jesus. "God of our ancestors" emphasizes the deep scriptural and Jewish roots of these folk who encounter the Lord (cf.

Exod 3:15-16; Deut 1:11, 21; Josh 18:13), and "Righteous One" is reminiscent of the messianic title "Righteous Branch," which also had scriptural precedent (cf. Jer 23:5-6; 33:15).

Acts 9 offers a straightforward statement that Paul was baptized (9:18). In Acts 22 Paul alludes to his baptism through the voice of Ananias exhorting Paul to be baptized, have his sins washed away, and call upon the Lord's name. The association of baptism with the name of the Lord is rather common in Acts (2:38; 8:16; 10:48; 19:5). The association of baptism with the washing away or cleansing of sins is found in Acts only here, though the motif is found elsewhere in the New Testament (1 Cor 6:11). Baptism, understood as a kind of cleansing, would have made sense to Paul's Jewish audience for whom ritual bathing for purposes of cleansing was quite common. [Baptism]

Far Away to the Gentiles, 22:17-22

There is no parallel to this account in Acts 9. Acts 9 reports that, upon his return to Jerusalem after his call, Paul preached in Jerusalem and encountered stiff, life-threatening resistance resulting in his departure from that city (9:28-30). It is left to readers to merge the two accounts, but Paul's report supplements from the point of view of personal experience what readers already know from Acts 9.

Paul speaks of his "return to Jerusalem" (v. 17), which alludes back to 9:26-27. There is no need for Paul to dwell on the fact that the disciples of Jerusalem did not initially trust him or his introduction by Barnabas to the apostles. He moves in his own account to an experience that took place in the temple sometime during this stay in Jerusalem. Paul's reference to "praying in the temple" speaks of his piety, implicitly challenging those who had called into question Paul's loyalty to his Jewish heritage and customs. Recall that it was a questioning of Paul's piety by Jews from Asia (21:27-28) that created this riotous scene in the first place.

Baptism

AΩ The Greek word *baptein* literally means to dip. The rite of baptism was widespread in the ancient world, commonly understood as a ritual associated with purity. The rite could be practiced either as a rite of initiation into a community or to offer ongoing purification to persons. Some mystery religions practiced the rite, as did the Jews of Qumran. John was known for calling Jews to be baptized as a sign of repentance to prepare for the coming eschatological judgment of God (cf. Luke 3:7-17).

Scholarly consensus argues that the earliest Christians practiced baptism as a rite of initiation (Acts certainly assumes this to be the case [cf. Acts 2:38-41; 8:12, 35-39, etc.]), perhaps as a direct outgrowth of John's practice, which included baptizing Jesus (Mk 1:9). In Rom 6:1-14, Paul interprets baptism as a participation in the death and resurrection of Jesus, which he applies to the moral behavior of Christians: they have died to sin and are to walk in a newness of life.

First Peter offers a similar understanding of the rite, assuming, as many scholars do, that much of the letter is a reflection on an early Christian baptismal liturgy. First Peter stresses rebirth with the resulting transformation of life (1:3, 23) that is to issue in a life of holiness and obedience (1:11-17, 22; 2:1-10). Receiving the Holy Spirit was also associated with baptism (Acts 1:5; 11:16), with the Spirit serving as the initiated Christian's guarantee of ultimate salvation at the close of the age (2 Cor 5:5).

L. Hartman, "Baptism," *ABD* 1.583–94; G. R. Beasley-Murray, "Baptism," MDB, 86–86; G. R. Beasley-Murray, *Baptism in the New Testament* (London: Macmillan, 1963).

Paul speaks of falling into a trance. Johnson suggests that Paul may be offering an intertextual echo to the scene of Isaiah's call (cf. Isa 6).[6] The Paul of the Epistles has shown his willingness to compare himself to prophets, as a comparison of Galatians 1:15-16 with Jeremiah 1:5 clearly shows. Further, the Paul of Acts has compared himself to the "servant" of Isaiah (cf. Acts 13:47; Isa 49:6). Employing scriptural intertexts and allusions in his rhetoric offers subtle reassurance that Paul is one who grounds his own experience in the story of Scripture and the piety of Judaism.

Whereas it was God who appeared to Isaiah in his temple vision, it is Jesus, at least implicitly, who appears to Paul (NRSV reads "Jesus"; the Greek text reads "he"). He warns Paul to get out of Jerusalem "because they will not accept your testimony about me" (v. 18). Acts 9:29-30 would have left the impression that Paul left Jerusalem to escape threats against his life. Paul's account here supplements Acts 9: It was at the urging of the Lord, who also recognized the trouble Paul was in, that Paul left Jerusalem.

But not without a fight! Even in the face of a divine command, Paul protested. Such protests of divine commands are, themselves, part of the biblical tradition.[7] Paul wanted to stay and preach, thinking that his well-known history as a persecutor of the followers of Jesus and a willing bystander to the execution of Stephen would offer some credibility to his Jewish audience. The implication is that one who had such a radical turnabout—from violently opposing believers to becoming a believer—must have experienced some kind of valid and life-changing encounter with a power greater than he.

But Jesus' goal is not simply to get Paul out of Jerusalem. Paul's larger mission to be a witness to all the world, alluded to in v. 15, is what the Lord has ultimately in view. Paul pulls no punches here: The Lord is sending Paul "far away to the Gentiles" (v. 21). Previous speeches in Acts had hinted to Jewish audiences that the gospel was to extend its reach beyond Jews. Peter concluded his Pentecost speech with a quotation from Joel, that "all who call upon the name of the Lord will be saved" (2:21). In that same sermon to the Jews of Jerusalem, Peter spoke of how the promises of God are "for you, your children, and for *all who are far away*, everyone whom the Lord our God calls to him" (v. 39). The reference to those "far away" could be an allusion to Gentiles. Peter later spoke to Jews of the promise made to Abraham that "in your descendants *all the families of the earth shall be blessed*" (3:25, alluding to Gen 22:18). While each of these hints at Gentile inclusion can be found in speeches to Jewish audiences, none is as explicit as this word from the Lord.

On the other hand, as Paul traveled throughout the Roman Empire, it became clearer and clearer to Jewish audiences that inclusion of the Gentiles was, indeed, part of God's plan of salvation to *everyone* who called upon the name of the Lord. With such clarity came increased resistance (see, e.g., 13:44-50; 14:2; 17:4-5, 12-13). Hence, Jewish reaction to Paul's unambiguous declaration that the Lord had commissioned him to go far away to the Gentiles should come as no surprise to the reader.

And what a reaction it is! In words reminiscent of exclamations made at Jesus' appearance before a Jewish audience under the watchful eye of a Roman official, the crowd makes clear its view of Paul's commissioning by the Lord: "Away with this fellow from the earth. For he should not be allowed to live" (v. 22; cf. 21:36; Luke 23:18). The verb translated "away" (*airō*) is the same in all three verses. The cry that Paul should not be allowed to live echoes in content, if not in diction, the demand that Jesus be crucified (cf. Luke 23:21).

Ernst Haenchen makes the observation, following Martin Dibelius, that it is common for Paul's speeches to be "interrupted" at "just that point which is important to the author."[8] So, here, the interruption at the point of clear allusion to a Gentile mission allows readers to know "what's important." The pattern that readers have detected in the narrative is replicated in Paul's speech. Just as Jewish audiences did not react negatively to hints of Gentile inclusion in Peter's speeches early in Acts, they did not so react at Paul's hints of such inclusion in the earlier part of his speech (see v. 15 and Paul's reference to being a "witness to all the world"). And just as Jewish audiences did react, violently no less, to clear markers of Gentile inclusion later in the narrative, so this Jewish audience responds violently to Paul's declaration that the Gentiles were to be included in God's work of salvation.

Following Haenchen, this is an important juncture in the speech and in the narrative. For here it is made clear to readers that God's offering of salvation is for *all*, both Jew and Gentile. And it is made equally clear that many Jews cannot accept this feature of the salvation story. From the first unambiguous announcement placed on the lips of Simeon in Luke 2:32, stating that Jesus was "a light for revelation to the Gentiles and for glory to your people Israel," to this point in the narrative, salvation for both Jews and Gentiles drives the plot of the Lukan story.

The rejection of Jesus at Nazareth, a story commonly viewed as "programmatic" by Lukan scholars,[9] offered a harbinger of things to come in the Lukan drama. For there, Jesus' Jewish audience initially responded positively to Jesus' announcement that these promises of Scripture were fulfilled in their hearing this day (Luke 4:21-22). But once Jesus made clear that this good news was also for those beyond the borders of Israel, the reaction turned violent (Luke 4:25-29). And so the pattern is set. And here the pattern finds expression once again, for this violent reaction sets in motion a series of determined efforts to silence this man who unabashedly offers God's word of salvation to all, both Jews and Greeks.

They Were about to Examine Him, 22:23-30

The threatening verbal declaration of the crowd is highlighted and intensified by their actions, for "while they were shouting, [they were] throwing off their cloaks and tossing dust into the air" (v. 23). The precise meaning of such gestures is debated among the commentators. For example, was the crowd throwing off their garments to prepare themselves to stone Paul?[10] Recall that Paul stood over the garments of those who stoned Stephen to death (7:58). Johnson offers a helpful literary comment: "The crowd goes through the whole repertoire of apotropaic gestures exhibited elsewhere in the narrative: shouting (Acts 7:57; 14:14), tearing the garments (14:14; 18:6), throwing dust (13:50)."[11] Ben Witherington's comment is also on target: the total impact of the crowd's response shows that "they consider Paul's words wicked, blasphemous, and thus totally repugnant."[12]

The tribune, who presumably has understood neither what Paul had said nor the words of the crowd, can see that the mob's reaction, once again, verges on a riot. Thus, he decides to take Paul back into the barracks, Fortress Antonia, no doubt, and interrogate him as to the cause of this latest disruption (v. 24). There is apparently something wrong with what this man is doing and saying, given that Paul has now twice, in the eyes of the Roman official, created a violent outburst from a large crowd.

The chosen method of interrogation was a scourging, using the dreaded instrument of the *flagellum*. This was no ordinary whip; rather, it was leather tongs, on the end of which were inserted pieces of bone or metal, designed to tear into human flesh. This form of "discipline" or "questioning" was far more severe than that which Paul had experienced in Philippi, where he was subjected to a beating with rods (16:22). Readers of the Lukan narrative note another loose parallel with the story of Jesus, who also was subjected to the threat of Roman flogging (Luke 23:16, 22). Luke does not actually record in his Passion Narrative that Jesus was flogged. This may offer another comparison between Jesus and Paul, as Paul, in the end, is not flogged either (see [Jesus and Paul]).

Paul is prepared for the interrogation. He is tied up with thongs, likely binding at least his hands around a pole or, perhaps, outstretched, exposing the back and making a wide, stationary target for the one administering the blows. It is at this juncture that Paul raises a protest (v. 25). This is good storytelling. Readers already know that Paul is a Roman citizen and that Roman officials quake at the thought of abusing one of Rome's citizens (cf. 16:37-38). Waiting until the last possible moment to bring a halt to the scourging creates dramatic tension. On the level of historical verisimilitude, Paul's dramatic delay is also appropriate: waiting until he was bound allows the Roman officials no wiggle room—clearly they were intending to scourge this man.

Paul's question whether it is legal to whip a citizen is rhetorical. All present knew that it was not (see [Roman Citizens]). Paul was not only "uncondemned" (v. 25), but he had not even been properly interrogated—interrogation by flogging was not to be an option of first resort: "According to Roman law (cf. *Digest* 48.18 prol. 1) this procedure [flogging] was recommended only when all noncoercive means had failed to resolve the matter, or perhaps when the situation was so extreme it was deemed necessary."[13] At the very least,

Roman Scourging

The diagram needs little commentary. The whip (*flagellum*) was designed to inflict maximum pain. Note how the victim is tied to the pole, fully exposing the back. The soldier stands to side, allowing his full momentum and strength to inflict the blows.

(Credit: Barclay Burns)

there has been here a severe breach of protocol. The centurion overseeing the interrogation knows this and immediately reports to his superior, the tribune (v. 26; see [Centurion]).

The tribune now becomes personally involved, approaching Paul to inquire of his citizenship status, which Paul confirms (v. 28). How one, in fact, confirmed such status is unknown. Did one carry papers? Possibly. But to claim such a status falsely was itself a severe crime, and it is possible that this alone might deter non-citizens from making such a false claim. [Falsely Claiming Roman Citizenship]

Why does the tribune share with Paul that he had obtained his citizenship at a high price (v. 28a)? After all, to obtain citizenship for money likely would have involved the bribing of a corrupt, mid-level bureaucrat who was responsible for preparing for the emperor's review a list of candidates for citizenship.[14] Such an action was neither honorable nor legal. On the level of historical verisimilitude, the tribune might have been so shocked to hear that this Jew, whom he had not many minutes before suspected of being an anti-Roman revolutionary (21:38), claimed to be a citizen that his remark betrays his own incredulity: "I, a Roman tribune, had to pay a large sum to acquire citizenship. Do you really expect me to believe that a nobody like you is a citizen?" On the level of literary irony, however, the tribune's remark sets Paul up, even though bound, to show himself to be superior to his inquisitor, for Paul "was born a citizen" (v. 28b), giving him one leg up in this match of wits. [Contest of Honor]

As to how Paul acquired such citizenship from birth is, frankly, unknown, if such a status were even true for the historical Paul (see [Roman Citizens]). But readers tend to trust narrators as reliable, so on the literary level such questions are moot: Paul is a free-born citizen of Rome. Consequently, Paul's interrogators withdraw in fear, knowing that they had committed a grave error binding this Roman citizen. According to Roman law it was a violation even to *bind* a Roman citizen: "To bind a Roman citizen is a crime, to flog him an abomination, to slay him almost an act of parricide" (Cicero, *Against Verres* 2.5.66).

Verse 30 offers a transition to chapter 23. The tribune now takes a more sober approach: wishing to discover more thoroughly and sanely the nature of the accusations of the Jews against Paul, the tribune released him and convened a meeting of the Jewish ruling council (see [Sanhedrin]). Some interpreters question whether a

Falsely Claiming Roman Citizenship

Two ancient sources address this issue:

Those who falsely claim Roman citizenship are severely punished (Epictetus, *Discourses* 3.24, 41).

Those who usurped the privileges of Roman citizenship he [Claudius] executed in the Esquiline field (Suetonius, *Life of Claudius* 25.3).

Contest of Honor

According to Bruce Malina, among the "pivotal values of the first-century Mediterranean world" were those of "honor and shame." "Honor . . . is basically a claim to worth that is socially acknowledged," Malina explains (29). It involves one's self-perception ("a *claim* to worth"), but self-perception alone is not enough to give one honor; such a claim must be "socially acknowledged" by one's social group. In a world where honor is supremely valued, "contests of honor" were quite common. In the legendary past of North American culture, the closest analogy to such "contests of honor" would be the duel, in the context of which one "defended to the death one's honor." Ongoing contests of honor were not always so deadly in the Mediterranean world.

Some sort of challenge initiated contests of honor. The motive for initiating the challenge was to enhance the Challenger's own honor or to diminish the honor of the other person, the Receiver of the challenge (these often went hand-in-hand). In the case of Paul and the tribune, Paul (the Challenger) initiated the challenge when he made a claim to Roman citizenship. Such a claim is a claim to honor—and a claim to be treated honorably. The tribune, the representative of the Roman Empire, represents the Receiver of the challenge. The tribune (now the Challenger) offers a counter-challenge by implicitly questioning Paul's (now the Receiver) claim to citizenship. In the honor tug-of-war, the Receiver (who is now Paul) can maintain honor by issuing yet another counter-challenge. Paul assumes this role when he not only reaffirms his Roman citizenship, but also ups the ante by claiming that he was born a citizen. Note in v. 29 the reaction of the tribune and the whole group to Paul's final counter-challenge: "Immediately those who were about to examine him drew back from him; and the tribune also was afraid, for he realized that Paul was a Roman citizen and that he had bound him." The silence and fear of the group offers the appropriate "social acknowledgment" of Paul's "claim to worth." Paul has come forth the victor in this "contest of honor."

Bruce J. Malina, *The New Testament World: Insights from Cultural Anthropology*, 3rd ed. (Louisville KY: Westminster/John Knox Press, 2001), see esp. ch. 1.

tribune had the authority to convene the Jewish council. However, Fitzmyer claims that there is precedent for the assembling of local ruling councils "in an advisory role," as opposed to an official "judicial trial." Consequently, he argues, the gathering of the council for such an informal, yet significant hearing is not impossible.[15]

The verb that the NRSV translates as "released" is rendered as "unbound" in the RSV. The Greek word *luein* can be translated either way. The King James translation has "loosed him from his bands." King James is following Greek manuscripts that actually contain the words "from his bands," but most textual scholars believe that these words do not best represent the original text of Acts.

The RSV translation implies that it was only the next day that Paul was "unbound," which is clearly the way that copyists behind the textual tradition followed by King James translators understood the term. Within the logic of the narrative, however, it makes little sense that the Romans who were so fearful because they had tied Paul up (v. 29, employing a different Greek verb, *dedeka*) would only "untie" him the following day. Surely readers are not to assume that Paul remained bound to the flogging pole for the night. Paul was likely held in custody over the night, perhaps with some type of bonds or chains (cf. 26:29), and "released" from such custody the following day, with or without some bonds, so that he could attend the hearing before the Jewish council.

CONNECTIONS

Paul's initial defense speech offers the first truly autobiographical speech in the book of Acts. Earlier speeches talked much in a direct manner about Jesus and God and even, in the case of Paul's speech in Athens, religion in general. But here Paul talks about himself: his upbringing, his education, his zeal for God, his call by the risen Lord, and his commission by this same Lord to go far away to the Gentiles. Paul offers, in short, what many in the pietistic, evangelical tradition call "his testimony."

The autobiographical testimony has other names. Sallie McFague uses the terms "religious autobiography" and "confession." [Religious Autobiography] In Christian literature, the classical expression of religious autobiography or confession is St. Augustine's *Confessions*. The purpose of the religious autobiography is not to bring attention to oneself, but to say something about God, as any reader of Augustine knows. The confession expresses theology; it is, ultimately, to "talk about God." [Augustine's *Confessions*] However, it is to talk of God not in abstract propositions, but in the context of how God is revealed in the nooks and crannies of a real life. In the case of Paul's speech in Acts 22, the real life in question is that of Paul, as that life was given expression by the narrator of the book of Acts.

When one reflects on the significance of the "personal testimony" or one's "religious autobiography" as a medium for theological discourse, one cannot sidestep the central role that *experience* plays in such theology (see [Experience and the Believer]). Experience is a slippery thing. One can make one's experience an absolute, as if one's "experience of God" is all that matters, boldly and arrogantly declaring to the world that the only experience of God that is valid is *my* experience. While one's experience of God is unavoidable if God is to be personal, experience alone is too subjective to form an independent source for our God-talk, apart from other sources, such as Scripture, tradition, and reason.[16]

Religious Autobiography

"An autobiography is a story, the story of a life, and the best autobiographies are written precisely as a story, that is, as an ordering of events around a central focus. Like a good story, a good autobiography deals with something unfamiliar, the mystery of the self, in and through the familiar, a multitude of events and circumstances. If the autobiography is true, it points to the self elliptically through these events and circumstances; in other words, a successful autobiography resembles a parable. A religious autobiography is similar, except here the unfamiliar is not the "interesting" self but the self in relation to God. What shines through indirectly in a confession is God's hand in the intricacies of an actual, historical life."

Sallie McFague, *Speaking in Parables: A Study in Metaphor and Theology* (Philadelphia: Fortress Press, 1975), 145

The focus of theology is *God*, not one's experience of God. Experience is the channel of theological reflection, but not the focus.[17] Further, our God-talk needs a central, organizing theme, lest it become random musings, as thoughtful as they might be, about this God of whom we speak. McFague explains, "The purpose of theology is to glorify God by reflecting on how we might live better on the earth. Theology is about thinking, but it is not primarily an intellectual activity. It is a practical one—so that we might live better, more appropriately, in the world."[18]

How does Paul's testimony offer a good example of a confession that gives meaningful expression to Paul's experience of God and how it shaped the way that Paul came to view his life—that he "might live better, more appropriately, in the world"?

Though one's experience of God is a crucial part of the religious biography, "there is no such thing as raw experience; there is no innocent eye; nothing is seen nakedly."[19] The *context* in which we live shapes the *way* we experience things. Authentic religious autobiography honestly acknowledges that one's experiences of God emerge from one's particular context. Paul begins his own confession or testimony by acknowledging his context. He is Jewish, having been reared in Jerusalem and educated in the Pharisaic tradition under the tutelage of Gamaliel I. He had a great zeal for God that was firmly grounded in his study of the law as such law came to him through his spiritual ancestors. Such zeal found its expression in persecuting persons whom he believed deviated from the required faithfulness.

Recognizing our context allows us to acknowledge that our experiences of God come to us filtered, that "nothing is seen nakedly." Had Paul not been a particular type of zealous Jew, he would not have been a persecutor of the church. It was within the context of being such a persecutor that Paul encountered the risen Lord: "Saul, Saul, why are you persecuting me?" (v. 7). For the Paul of Acts, his role as a persecutor of the church was a significant filter through which he remembered his experience of having met the Lord.

Augustine's Confessions

Augustine's journey of faith is a fascinating one. His *Confessions*, written AD 397–398, shortly after he assumed the office of the bishop of Hippo, tells of his pilgrimage from "sinner to saint" in the form of a confessional prayer to God—though he occasionally addresses his own "soul," as well. The following excerpt illustrates how "religious autobiography," while talking about oneself, engages, ultimately, in theology—talking about God.

How shall I call upon my God for aid, when the call I make is for my Lord and my God to come into myself? What place is there in me to which my God can come, what place that can receive the God who made heaven and earth? . . . Or since nothing that exists could exist without you, does this mean that whatever exists does, in this sense, contain you? If this is so, since I too exist, why do I ask you to come into me? . . . Or is it rather that I should not exist, unless I existed in you? . . . But if I exist in you, how can I call upon you to come to me? (1.2)

Saint Augustine: Confessions, trans. R. S. Pine-Coffin (London: Penguin Books, 1961), 22.

Such is also the case for the Paul of the Epistles. Paul's own summary autobiographical statement says, "as to zeal, a persecutor of the church" (Phil 3:6). And had Paul not been such a persecutor he would not have *experienced* the grace of God in exactly the manner that he did. In another autobiographical reflection Paul commented on his apostleship, stating, "For I am the least of the apostles, unfit to be called an apostle, because I persecuted the church of God" (1 Cor 15:9). This is not false modesty. The specific and particular context in which and out of which Paul met the living Lord, that of being one who was persecuting him and his church, shaped the way that Paul came to *experience* in a very specific way the saving grace of God. There was no way that Paul could, given his own particular history, understand the grace of God as anything but wholly unmerited.

Paul's particular experience of God's grace shaped his own understanding of his call. In Acts, Paul's commission was to be a witness to all the earth (v. 15), going "far away to the Gentiles" (v. 21). To be sure, in Acts that mission was not to avoid Jews, for Paul was to be a witness to *all* the earth. Paul, even as he offers this speech, is offering witness to Jews. But readers of Acts know that as Paul has moved through his journeys, he has found more fruitful ground among non-Jews.

Theological reflection is to result not in abstract ideas about God but in life-changing patterns of behavior. To quote again Sallie McFague: we engage in theology "so that we might live better, more appropriately, in the world." Paul's encounter with the grace of the living God made him live better. His realization that his call and his status before God rested in no way on his own merit guided him to recognize God's openness even to those whom certain expressions of zealous Judaism excluded: the Gentiles. And *that* realization shaped the way Paul lived his life, moving about the Roman Empire for the purpose of bearing witness to the living Lord who had revealed himself to Paul as Paul was neck-deep in persecuting the Lord and his followers.

Paul had hoped that his audience could share his particular experience of the grace of God. After all, Paul was not merely offering rhetorical fluff when he said that he and they had in common a certain kind of zeal for God (v. 3). In both Paul's history and the crowd's present this kind of "zeal for God" manifested itself in the persecution of the Lord's followers: those in Damascus in Paul's case and Paul himself in the case of his audience. Paul's reputation as one who imprisoned and beat followers of Jesus and consented to the death of Stephen (vv. 19-20) established his credentials as one who was possessed by a certain kind of zeal. If Paul could experience the grace of God given his particular context, his particular type of zeal, surely his audience could.

But such was not to be the case. The grace of God is a mysterious thing. It is quite literally a mystery why some respond to the offering of such grace while others do not. One could speculate endlessly on the tension that stands between human will and divine sovereignty (see [Providence and Fatalism]). In Acts, however, it is clear that openness to the grace of God for me and my kind requires the extension of such grace to others, even those who are not of "my kind." [A Radical Grace]

In the Lukan narrative, "the Jews" are those characters who embody the kind of exclusive spirit that resists the universal gospel (see [The Jews]). We miss the point today if we read this particular narrative, coming as it is out of its own particular context, as a universal denunciation of Jews. Today, such texts are not about Jews who lived as characters in a narrative composed some 2,000 years ago. Today, the question for us is, "Whom do *we* exclude from experiencing the grace of God?"

Modern Christian readers, most of whom are non-Jewish, might recoil at the thought that "the people of God," due to their zeal for God, thought it imperative that *we* be excluded from experiencing the grace of the living God. Non-Jewish believers, of all people, should *know* what it feels like to be excluded: "remember that you [Gentiles] were at that time without Christ, being aliens from the commonwealth of Israel, and strangers to the covenants of promise, having no hope and without God in the world" (Eph 2:12).

But the fact is that we non-Jewish believers, especially those of us who come from white, middle-class North America, no longer know the feeling of exclusion. It is now we who guard the temple gates, making sure that no unacceptable folk pass through our doors. And it is too often we, the new insiders, who shout down those whose experience of God's grace compels them to include those who also "are not fit" or "worthy" to be the recipients of God's call of grace. Being a Christian "by the grace of God" does not always translate into being channels of such grace for others.

A Radical Grace

"God as the lawgiver and judge is the God of 'works' that Paul and Luther and the Protestant Reformation in general rejected. Instead, they affirmed radical grace: God's acceptance of us is unconditional, not dependent upon something we believe or do. But radical grace has most often been too radical for most Christians. We must often put conditions on God's grace: God accepts if . . . . And whenever an 'if' clause is added, grace becomes conditional and ceases to be grace." (Borg, 76–77)

"But if . . . we are lost and blind, it is not because we lack grace, but because we are not attuned to God's grace-presence. Our own life, and indeed life itself, is the stage upon which the performance of grace never ceases to be enacted. We do not earn grace; it is a gift given from the start. Quickly . . . we lose a sense of the pervasive presence of grace. But the reality of it is undefeated, and our periodic awakenings to this truth are indeed "graced moments." (Stella, 179)

Marcus Borg, *The Heart of Christianity: Rediscovering a Live of Faith* (New York: HaperSanFrancisco, 2003); Tom Stella, *A Faith Worth Believing: Finding New Life Beyond the Rules of Religion* (New York: HarperSanFranciso, 2004).

Lasse Hallström's film *Chocolat* illustrates well this sad feature of Christian faith.[20] The Comte de Reynaud, mayor of the small French village of Lansquenet, a village that "believed in tranquility," embodied a firm and resolute spirit of self-denial and discipline. "If you lived in this village," says the voice of the narrator, "you understood what was expected of you. You knew your place in the scheme of things. . . . So through good times and bad, famine and feast, the villagers held fast to their traditions. Until one winter day, a sly wind blew in from the north."

The film opens on the first Sunday of Lent in the year 1959. The villagers plod into the church, its door guarded by the overbearing Comte de Reynaud. It is on that day that Vianne and her illegitimate daughter Anouk blow into town—with the "sly north wind" that whirled around the village finding its way to the church and blowing open its large double doors. In this village, people who did not conform, people who forgot their "place in the scheme of things," were quickly put back in place. Those few folk who, for whatever reason, could not find their way back into the scheme of things felt the chill of being outsiders, excluded from the good "graces" of the Comte—and the church, which he so thoroughly mastered by controlling the parish priest, Pere Henri.

Vianne's chocolate shop, which she opened over the stern protests of the Comte, becomes a symbol of defiance. But hers was not a defiance that was mean-spirited, intentionally political, or explicitly religious. Vianne's expression of defiance came primarily through her willingness to extend generous hospitality to those who were hurting and whom the town, at the Comte's urging, ostracized.

It was Holy Saturday. The Comte had had enough of Vianne and her chocolate shop, which in a rage he vandalizes. Some of the shards of chocolate that flew about as he unleashed his zealous anger against this place of inclusion found their way into the Comte's mouth—and he succumbed to the temptation to taste these decadent treats, gorging himself until he collapsed in fatigue in the open window of Vianne's shop—for all to see the following Easter morning as they went to Mass.

There was neither praise for nor condemnation of the Comte. But there was forgiveness. And he was changed, as was the town. The homily offered that Easter morning by Pere Henri was not the one that the Comte had approved, but his own homily, inspired by what he had seen. It focused, appropriately, on the theme of inclusion and acceptance. [Easter Homily of Pere Henri]

The film's narrator comments on the priest's sermon: "It was certainly not the most fiery sermon Pere Henri would ever preach, nor the most eloquent. But the parishioners felt a new sensation that day, a lightening of the spirit. Even the old Comte de Reynaud felt strangely released."

The village of Lansquenet and its mayor had lived with a kind of zeal for God that Paul once knew by bitter experience. What released both Paul and the Comte were the taste of grace and the experience of forgiveness. Both became new creatures. Both were "strangely released" from the dark and angry bondage of the exclusion of "the other," those who were different. Both discovered that to be embraced by the love given supreme expression in the gospel liberated them finally to include others, even as they had been included.

The audience of Paul's speech in the narrative of Acts did not learn that. But the relevant question *now* is whether the audience of Paul's speech today—Christians who read the speech in the book of Acts—will experience with enough power the kind of inclusive release that the gospel offers to extend that same grace to others who, today, stand outside the large, closed double doors of the church. The Spirit blows where it wills. Will the sly north wind of the Spirit today be able to blow open the gates of our temples, which many choose to guard so zealously?

> **Easter Homily of Pere Henri**
>
> "I don't want to talk about Jesus' divinity. I would rather talk about his humanity. . . . How he lived his life here on earth, his kindness, his tolerance. . . . We can't go around measuring our goodness by what we don't do, by what we deny ourselves, what we resist and who we exclude. I think we've got to measure our goodness by what we embrace, what we create, and who we include."
>
> From the film *Chocolat*, DVD, directed by Lasse Hallstrom (2000; Brisbane CA: David Brown Productions).

NOTES

[1] Ben Witherington III, *The Acts of the Apostles: A Socio-Rhetorical Commentary* (Grand Rapids MI: Eerdmans, 1998), 659–60.

[2] Luke Timothy Johnson, *The Acts of the Apostles* (SacPag 5; Collegeville MN: Liturgical Press, 1992), 387.

[3] Ibid., 388.

[4] Robert W. Tannehill, *The Narrative Unity of Luke–Acts: A Literary Interpretation*, 2 vols. (Minneapolis: Fortress, 1990), 2.275.

[5] Johnson, *Acts*, 388.

[6] Ibid., 390.

[7] John B. Polhill, *Acts* (NAC 26; Nashville: Broadman, 1992), 462.

[8] Ernst Haenchen, *The Acts of the Apostles: A Commentary* (Philadelphia: Westminster, 1971), 628, quoting Martin Dibelius, "The Speeches in Acts and Ancient Historiography," *Studies in the Acts of the Apostles*, ed. Heinrich Greeven (Mifflintown PA: Sigler Press, 1999), 160.

[9] See, e.g., I. Howard Marshall, *Commentary on Luke* (NIGTC; Grand Rapids MI: Eerdmans, 1978), 177–78; Robert C. Tannehill, "The Mission of Jesus at Nazareth (Luke 14:16-30)," in *Jesus in Nazareth*, ed. Erich Grässer (Berlin and New York: Walter de Gruyter, 1972), 51–75.

[10] "In spite of prolonged study by scholars, and the inferences which may be drawn from the texts and contexts of the several passages, and the citation of parallels elsewhere, the interpretation of these gestures remains without settled conclusion." (Henry J. Cadbury, "Dust and Garments," in F. J. Foakes Jackson and Kirsopp Lake, *The Beginnings of Christianity: The Acts of the Apostles*, 5 vols. [Grand Rapids MI: Baker, 1979], 5.269.)

[11] Johnson, *Acts*, 391.

[12] Witherington, *Acts*, 675.

[13] Ibid., 677.

[14] Joseph A. Fitzmyer, *The Acts of the Apostles* (AB 31; New York: Doubleday, 1998), 712.

[15] Ibid., 716.

[16] Stanley J. Grenz, *Theology for the Community of God* (Nashville: Broadman and Holman), 20–21.

[17] Sallie McFague, *Life Abundant: Rethinking Theology and Economy for a Planet in Peril* (Minneapolis MN: Fortress Press, 2001), 52.

[18] Ibid., 25.

[19] Ibid., 40.

[20] From the film *Chocolat*, DVD, directed by Lasse Hallstrom (2000; Brisbane CA: David Brown Productions).

FROM JERUSALEM TO CAESAREA

Acts 23:1-35

COMMENTARY

This chapter continues Paul's "trials" in Jerusalem. Having been taken before the Sanhedrin, Paul participates in a hearing before this ruling body (vv. 1-11). The balance of the chapter (vv. 12-35) tells of the plot to assassinate Paul and the Roman response to foil the plot, culminating in the transfer of Paul to Caesarea.

Paul Looked Intently, 23:1-11

The concluding verse of Acts 22 offered the transition scene as the Roman authorities escorted Paul from Fortress Antonia to the Sanhedrin (see [Sanhedrin]). Ancient sources differ as to the location of the council hall, whether it was within the temple courts (so rabbinic sources) or outside the temple complex (so Josephus).[1] If Jewish zealots intended to kill Paul en route from the fortress to the building where the Sanhedrin met (see below), that might imply that Luke assumed the location of the Sanhedrin to be outside the temple complex. It would be difficult, perhaps, for forty or so assassins to lie in wait in a large, open courtyard.

Though the tribune has supposedly gathered the council to learn more about the charges of the Jews against Paul (22:30), the narrator has Paul take control of the meeting and begin to make a speech. Readers should assume a narrative gap to stand between 22:30 and 23:1; surely, some type of preliminary discussion, presentation of charges, or the like must have taken place. But that is not the narrator's concern. The final section of Acts is about the relationship between Judaism and Paul, that is, Judaism and Christianity. Thus, the storyline stays on task.

Paul is not intimidated by the council, which he looks keenly in the eye (v. 1). He refers to the members of the council as "brothers," as equals, certainly not as superiors or judges. And Paul declares

Conscience

AΩ The word "conscience" (*syneidēsis*) is found one other place in Acts (24:16) and quite frequently in the Pauline corpus, specifically in Romans, 1 and 2 Corinthians, and the Pastorals. The conscience is that *within* humans that either convicts or exonerates that person (Rom 2:15; 1 Cor 10:25, 27, 28; 2 Cor 1:12; 1 Tim 3:9). The human conscience is not infallible, however. It can be weak, leading to a "false conviction," a conviction that, no less, still affects the person in a negative way (1 Cor 8:7, 10, 12). Paul is declaring before the council that his conscience is clear, despite his having participated in the persecution of believers. Paul's conscience did not at that time convict him, for the conscience is not infallible. Paul, convinced of his zeal for God, undoubtedly did persecute followers of Jesus "with a clear conscience." This is broadly related to the affirmation that Paul makes in Phil 3:6, where he states in one breath that he was a persecutor of the church and in the next that he was blameless with respect to righteousness under the law.

unequivocally that his manner of life, his citizenship (*pepoliteumai*)—note the root of the English word for "politics"—before God has been conducted in "good conscience" [Conscience]. His point is that, despite his being in Roman custody and standing before the Jewish supreme council, nothing within Paul convicts him of any wrongdoing; in fact, his conscience exonerates him.

Commentators are stumped as to motive, but for some reason the high priest Ananias orders that Paul be slapped for making such a statement (v. 2; see [Jewish Rulers of Acts]). The lack of motive may reveal the narrator's motive: the high priest does not come off looking judicious or fair for ordering the corporal punishment of a man who is guilty of nothing more than declaring his innocence.

Paul's boldness continues (v. 3). Though lackeys of the high priest have struck (*typein*) Paul, he declares that it is *God* who will strike (*typein*) Ananias. Luke's readers who knew their history would know that, in fact, Jewish zealots struck down Ananias at the outbreak of the revolt against Rome (AD 66). In calling the high priest a "whitewashed wall," Paul was employing a vivid metaphor for hypocrisy. Perhaps alluding to Ezekiel 13:10-15, which employs the image of the whitewashed wall to refer to false prophets, Paul portrays the high priest as one whose inner character is corrupt and false and who wears only a veneer of holiness.

Paul makes the hypocrisy explicit as he declares that this one who sits to render judgment in accordance with the Jewish law himself violates the very law it is his place to uphold. The word in v. 3 that the NRSV translates as "in violation of the law" is *paranomeō*, which carries the connotation of "flouting the law."[2] As to what specific law the priest was violating, neither Paul nor the narrator says. Perhaps Paul is alluding to Leviticus 19:15, which states that one shall not render unjust judgment and shall judge the neighbor with justice. The allusion is subtle, but that might be part of the rhetorical strategy: Paul is showing himself to be something of an "insider" on matters of Jewish law who can spar even with the high priest.

Ananias's lackeys come to the priest's defense, asking Paul rhetorically whether he would revile God's high priest (v. 4). Paul's response may betray actual ignorance; he really did not know who the high priest was. Historically, that might be so (there is no way contemporary readers can know), but the Lukan Paul likely would not be so out of the loop. Perhaps Paul is employing biting irony: "How could I have known that one who flagrantly flouted God's law would be the high priest?" Paul, ever portrayed by Luke as the loyal Jew, shows proper deference, if not to the man Ananias, at least to the office. He, again as the loyal Jew, legitimates such deference by quoting the Torah (Exod 22:27)—the very Torah that Ananias so casually violates.

Paul, totally in control of the session, notices that the assembly is divided between Pharisees and Sadducees (v. 6; see [Pharisees] and [Sadducees]). Luke has already asserted Pharisaic influence on the Sanhedrin (cf. 5:34), though historically it is likely that the Sadducees, more economically and ideologically aligned with the priestly aristocracy, would have held the sway of power on the ruling council. Paul explicitly identifies himself with Pharisees, even claiming a Pharisaic pedigree. He then claims that he is on trial "concerning the hope of the resurrection of the dead." Such statements are clearly intended to provoke the council *and* say something to the reader of "the Way's" relationship with Judaism.

Paul's claim to be "a son of Pharisees" could mean that Paul's ancestors were Pharisees. Since most evidence indicates that Pharisaic schools existed only in Palestine that would imply either that Paul's ancestors became Pharisees *before* they migrated to Tarsus, where Paul, according to Acts 22:3, was born. Paul, then, was later sent to Jerusalem to receive his education or the family moved backed there (22:3). Or Paul's whole family moved to Jerusalem after he was born, and Paul, as well as other members of his family, including perhaps his father, became Pharisees. Such historical speculations are interesting, but there can be no resolution. Rhetorically, Paul's audience, both characters in the text and readers in front of the text, would not need to resolve such historical issues in order to get Paul's point: Paul identifies with the Pharisees!

Paul's affirmation that he stands on trial with respect to the hope of the resurrection serves in the narrative to set Paul and the other Pharisees apart from the Sadducees. The narrator specifically states that Pharisees, unlike Sadducees, believed in the resurrection (vv. 7-8). [Resurrection of the Dead] The narrator clearly wants to make this distinction as he explicitly observes that "the Sadducees say there is no resurrection, or angel, or spirit; but the Pharisees acknowledge all three" (v. 8).

Resurrection of the Dead

Little is said in the Old Testament of this belief. Some statements are actually metaphorical expressions relating to the restoration of the nation of Israel (cf. Isa 26:19; Ezek 37:13-14; Hos 6:1-2). Dan 12:2 (mid-2d century BC) offers the first clear expression of the hope. As evidenced in the conflict of the Sanhedrin in Acts 23:8, there was no uniform belief among Jews regarding afterlife or resurrection. Views seemed to exist within a wide range:

- Sheol was the place of death where one was cut off from God (Sir 17:27–28). There is, effectively, no afterlife in any meaningful sense.
- Belief in immortality of the soul, though such immortality is not understood as an intrinsic property of the soul, but a gift of God, preserved for the righteous (Wis 1–6).
- A resurrection of the righteous, understood quite literally (2 Macc 7): it is implied that mutilated bodies would be restored (2 Macc 14:46). *1 Enoch* seems to envision a resurrection of the righteous, with the evil people being destroyed (*1 En.* 91:10-11).
- A resurrection of both the just and unjust to receive their due rewards (*2 Bar* 50-51; 2 Esd 7:32-44).

George W. E. Nickelsburg, "Resurrection: Early Judaism and Christianity," *ABD* 5.684–91; David Rolph Seely, "Resurrection," *EDB* 1120–22.

Josephus on the Sadducees

"The Sadducees . . . do away with Fate. . . . They maintain that man has the free choice of good or evil. . . . As for the persistence of the soul after death, penalties in the underworld, and rewards, they will have none of them." (*J. W.* 2.164–65)

Interpreters generally explain the Sadducees' rejection of belief in resurrection by alluding to the fact that these Jews recognized only the Pentateuch as authoritative and normative.[3] The Pentateuch offers no explicit teaching about resurrection, yet the Pentateuch has more than a score of references to angels (see, e.g., Gen 16:7-11), as well as several references to a divine spirit (e.g., Gen 6:3; 41:38; Exod 31:3; 35:31; Num 11:25-29; 24:2; 27:18). The narrator's assertion that the Sadducees rejected "angels and spirits" is therefore more difficult to understand. In addition, while Josephus confirms Acts' claim that the Sadducees reject resurrection, he makes no comment regarding their rejection of "angel and spirit." [Josephus on the Sadducees]

Some suggest that by "angel and spirit" Luke is simply elaborating on the Sadducean rejection of resurrection.[4] Joseph Fitzmyer's translation of v. 8 illustrates this interpretive approach: "For the Sadducees maintain that there is no resurrection, neither as an angel nor as a spirit, whereas Pharisees acknowledge them both."[5] This approach avoids the problem of having the narrator claim that the Sadducees did not believe in something—angels and spirits—that the Pentateuch clearly affirmed. The Greek phrase of v. 8 (*ta amphotera*) that the NRSV renders as "all three" and that Fitzmyer translates as "both" does literally mean "both." Hence, there is good reason to follow Fitzmyer's translation and interpretation.

Recognizing that Paul was in some very real sense one of their own, some of the scribes of the Pharisees actually rise to Paul's defense: "We find nothing wrong with this man" (v. 9b). [Scribes] The suggestion that it might even be possible that an angel or spirit had spoken to Paul (v. 9c) is particularly significant, especially in light of the translation and interpretation of v. 8 offered above. If "angel or spirit" refers to a way of talking about "afterlife," these scribes appear to be open to considering Paul's claim to have heard and spoken to the resurrected Jesus—that is, his "angel or spirit."[6]

Scribes

At its most basic level, a scribe was one who could read and write. Hence, scribes were essential for keeping records, both in matters of business and politics. In the post-exilic period, the term was expanded to include those competent in matters of Jewish law (cf. Ezra 7:6, 10). Sirach presents the scribe as the thoughtful interpreter of Scripture, parables, proverbs, and the inherited wisdom of the ancients (Sir 38:34–39:2). He is well respected, a man of piety and wisdom (Sir 39:3-11).

The New Testament is often viewed skeptically as a valid historical source, but broadly it affirms what is known from other sources: scribes are often presented as experts in matters of biblical and legal interpretation, as well as application (cf. Mark 1:22; 2:6; 7:1-5). When associated with another group, scribes are regularly associated with Pharisees (eighteen references in the Synoptic Gospels). This occurs especially in Matthew, which regularly uses the phrase "scribes and Pharisees" as though they represent one tightly knit group (ten references). On one occasion, the synoptic tradition speaks of "scribes of the Pharisees" (Mark 2:16; cf. the Lukan parallel [Luke 5:30], which speaks of "the Pharisees and their scribes"), implying that scribes were not exclusively associated with Pharisees. Very often, scribes are associated with the priests or chief priest(s) as part of the official leadership of the Sanhedrin (twenty-two references). Even in this capacity, they might very well have given expression to their primary loyalty to the Pharisaic party.

Kim Paffenroth, "Scribes," *EDB* 1173; Anthony J. Saldarini, "Scribes," *ABD* 5.1012–16.

The association of Paul with the Pharisees, especially with reference to the common belief in resurrection, would have been most relevant to Luke's audience of *readers*. During the time of the narrative's composition the Pharisaic element of Jewish leadership was emerging as the rulers of the Sanhedrin. How Christianity, represented by Paul, related to *Pharisaic* Judaism would have been a relevant issue to Luke's original reading audience. Ernst Haenchen offers this comment:

> For [Luke] the charge against Paul is not a matter of the past, but the burning issue of contemporary Christianity. . . . It is Luke's honest conviction that fellowship between Pharisaism and Christianity is in the end possible; the Pharisees also hope for the Messiah [and] await the resurrection of the dead. . . . The wild tumult between Pharisees and Sadducees shows that Christianity is a matter within Judaism, even if it gives rise to such strong passions.[7]

If representatives of Pharisaic Judaism, the leading voice within the Judaism of Luke's time, also affirm the hope of the resurrection *and* are at least open to the possibility that the angel or spirit of Jesus did speak to Paul, Luke's readers receive yet one more affirmation that their belief in Jesus is not out of step with the religion from which their faith emerged. The Lukan narrative presses the conclusion that Jesus and his followers actually represent the *fulfillment*, not the displacement, of Jewish hopes as rooted in Scripture (cf. Luke 4:21; 22:37; 24:44; Acts 3:18; 13:33). Indirectly, the Pharisees on the council affirm such a claim to be possible.

The council is divided enough over the issue of "the hope of the resurrection" that the tribune must, once again, come to Paul's rescue (v. 10). This scene does not present the council in a good light. The last time the tribune had to rescue Paul responsibility lay with a mob in the outer courts of the temple. The Jewish Sanhedrin acts no better.

Paul, back in custody, receives a vision, not from an "angel or spirit," but from the living Lord. This confirms that the hope of the resurrection is a *realized* hope (v. 11). The appearance of Jesus not only shows the hope of the resurrection to be a reality in him, but also offers Paul (and readers) assurance that the gospel will "reach the ends of the earth," as prophesied in Acts 1:8. "It is necessary" (*dei*; NRSV, "you must") that Paul testify in Rome, even as he has testified in Jerusalem (see [Divine Necessity]).

The Jews Joined a Conspiracy and the Romans Took Paul, 23:12-35

Verses 12-25 tell of the murderous conspiracy against Paul (vv. 12-15), the discovery of the plot (vv. 16-22), the tribune's plan to foil Paul's assassination by removing Paul to Caesarea (vv. 23-30), and the journey to and arrival at Caesarea (vv. 31-35).

"We have bound ourselves with an oath," vv. 12-15
The following day "the Jews," more accurately, "some Jews" who numbered more than forty, conspired to assassinate Paul (vv. 12-14). They are so determined and zealous that they bound themselves with an oath, swearing not to eat or drink, until they had accomplished their mission. The phrase used to denote their oath is *anathemati anethematisamen* ("with an oath we have oathed," v. 14). One can see the English word *anathema* in both the noun and the verb. "May we damned with damnation if we do not accomplish this!" There is precedent in Jewish tradition for attaching to such oaths the promise not to eat and drink. The narrator leaves it to the reader to infer the fate of these zealous conspirators, but Jewish law allowed one the means to be released from such oaths should it prove impossible to fulfill them. [Oaths and Release from Oaths]

The conspirators feel that elements within the Sanhedrin, the chief priests and elders, will conspire with them (v. 14). Perhaps it is significant that the Pharisees are not explicitly listed among those whom the conspirators had approached to assist them in their plot. The previous day this group had shown itself to be broadly sympa-

Oaths and Release from Oaths

In the Mishnah, the collection of Jewish law as interpreted by the Rabbis, one finds discussion of oaths in the tractate *Shebuoth*, or "Oaths." One also finds herein some discussion of oaths attached to food (*Shebuoth* 3.1-5): ["If a man said.] 'I swear that I will not eat', and he ate aught soever, he is culpable. . . . [If a man said,] 'I swear that I will not eat', and he ate and drank, he is liable only for one count; but if he said, 'I swear that I will not eat and that I will not drink', and he ate and drank, he is liable on two counts" (3.1; Danby, 411).

There is also precedent in rabbinic materials for release from an oath should mitigating circumstances prevent fulfillment of the oath: "[Which are accounted] 'vows [that cannot be fulfilled by reason] or constraint'? If, to wit, his fellow made him vow to come and eat with him and he fell sick, or his son fell sick, or a river-flood hindered him, such would be a vow [that cannot be fulfilled by reason] of constraint" (*m.Nedarim* 3.3, Danby, 266–67).

Herbert Danby, *The Mishnah: Translated from the Hebrew with Introduction and Brief Explanatory Notes* (Oxford: Oxford University Press, 1933).

thetic with their fellow Pharisee (v. 9). The zealots urge these leaders of the Sanhedrin, along with the whole of the council, to ask the tribune to bring Paul back to the council for further examination (v. 15). Reference to the rest of "the council" implies not that the co-conspirators within the Sanhedrin would bring the balance of the council in on their treachery; rather, they would dupe the larger council into becoming unwitting co-conspirators. This group of chief priests and elders could not alone, without consent of the larger council, persuade the tribune to bring Paul back to them. En route to the meeting, the exact time of which the conspirators on the Sanhedrin would pass along to the zealots, the assassins would carry out their plan.

"Do not be persuaded by them," vv. 16-22

Paul's nephew, the son of his sister, got wind of the plot. The narrator offers no help in assisting readers in filling in the gap as to how he found out. Was he one of the zealots? After all, he was part of Paul's family and he too, like Paul in his earlier days, might have been one who expressed his zeal for God through violence. Did family loyalty outweigh his "zeal for God"? Did word of the conspiracy leak out and become part of the buzz on the narrow streets of Jerusalem? Regardless of how one fills the gap, Paul's nephew visits Paul at the fortress to make him aware of the plot (v. 16). How he gained access to Paul is not said, though there are statements in other portions of the New Testament that assume that Paul had access to visitors while in custody (cf. Phil 2:25; 2 Tim 1:16-17). The narrator clearly did not believe his readers would find such a visit incredulous or he likely would have felt compelled to offer some explanation as to how he gained access to his uncle.

Paul commands one of the centurions to take his nephew to the tribune, informing him only that the young man had something to tell the Roman officer (v. 17). One can ask why the centurion would have done what a man in custody told him to do. Again, the narrator leaves readers another gap to fill. Perhaps readers are simply to be impressed by the protagonist's control of the situation. Or perhaps word had spread that this was a Roman citizen who had been illegally bound and almost flogged and the centurion thought it best to err on the side of caution, giving Paul the benefit of the doubt.

The centurion escorts Paul's nephew to the tribune, informing his superior that the young man had something to tell him (v. 18). If the tribune were willing to hear the nephew's report, it is not surprising that he would desire privacy, so he takes the nephew aside, leading him by the hand (v. 19). Physical contact between males, with which most modern Western men would not feel comfortable, is not peculiar for this culture. A kiss on the cheek between men is still a common greeting in many cultures.

In vv. 20-21 Paul's nephew repeats the gist of the plot. The narrator is inferring the exact conversation, most likely, though one cannot rule out that the narrator had heard the story from Paul—assuming that one even grants any historical truth to the story at all. Included in the nephew's summation is also his advice to the tribune not to agree to take Paul to the council, for if he does Paul will be assassinated along the way. Knowing now of Paul's Roman citizenship it is most believable that the tribune would not take offense at the advice; in fact, he would certainly not want to be responsible for the murder of a Roman citizen by Jewish brigands. Appropriately, the tribune urges Paul's nephew to keep the matter between the two of them (v. 22).

"Take him safely to the governor," vv. 23-30

The tribune makes immediate plans to send Paul to Caesarea. Readers may wonder why the tribune would go to such lengths. Would it not make more sense simply to refuse the Sanhedrin's request and keep Paul in protective custody? Because Paul was a Roman citizen, it was likely (perhaps inevitable) that his case would have been transferred to the jurisdiction of the Roman governor. The tribune simply saw the present threatening situation as an opportunity to effect the change of venue.[8]

In addition, it is not an exaggeration to say that Paul had been nothing but trouble for the tribune. Paul, at least indirectly, had incited two near-riots (21:27-36; 22:22-23); the tribune had almost found himself in hot water by binding and ordering the flogging of this Roman citizen (22:24-29); Paul's hearing before the Sanhedrin resulted in disorder (23:7-10); now, Jewish zealots were plotting his assassination (23:20-21). The tribune, responsible for maintaining order in Jerusalem, as well as wanting to watch out for his own career, had nothing to lose by removing this source of irritation. The tribune moves decisively to do precisely that.

He orders a large contingency of Roman troops to move Paul to Caesarea that night (v. 23). Moving out under the cover of darkness would make sense if there were reason to suspect that Jewish assassins were preparing Paul's murder. The size of the Roman force seems to defy credibility. Two hundred soldiers, seventy cavalry, and an additional 200 spearmen would have constituted one-half the entire Jerusalem force! Again, Luke may simply want to impress the reader with how important his hero is.

Interpreters who seek to provide credulity to these numbers suggest that the tribune might have wanted to outnumber the brigand band, which numbered "more than forty" (v. 21), with overwhelming force, either to deter them or utterly route them should they catch wind of the transfer and attempt to follow through on their vow.[9] Readers, like the two centurions to whom the tribune conveys his orders, are not told why Paul was to be provided with multiple mounts (v. 24). Was one for Paul's baggage? Was Paul to be provided with a donkey, rather than a horse, and a spare mount would be necessary for Paul to transfer to en route so that his donkey could keep up with the cavalry, which (readers learn only later, v. 32) was the only part of the escort that would complete the trip?[10] Was the other mount for one of Paul's companions, perhaps even Luke?[11] Such speculations are interesting, but no resolution is really possible.

The tribune, whose name readers now finally learn is Claudius Lysias (v. 26), composes a letter to accompany Paul to the Judean governor Felix (see [Felix]). The narrator introduces the letter with the comment that it was "to this effect" (v. 25). Is the narrator claiming that what follows is actually the gist of the letter? Or is he acknowledging that he is simply inferring that the letter, which is actually his composition, must have said something like what follows?[12] Witherington argues that Paul would have likely heard the letter read before Felix, given that it was the practice of ancients to read aloud, even if reading to themselves (vv. 33-34). Hence, Luke could actually have learned the gist of the letter from Paul.[13] Regardless, the letter, as the narrator presents it, passes the test of verisimilitude: it does not say anything that a reader would find surprising or inappropriate.

The letter comes close to what was known as *litterae dimissoriae*: "the letter that had to be sent according to Roman law from one official to a superior in the case of appeal."[14] To be sure, no formal appeal has yet been made, but readers could rightly assume that Lysias would certainly have written some type of letter explaining to the governor why Paul was being transferred to his custody.

The letter follows the standard form of ancient missives and certainly conveys "the facts of the case" to a superior in a manner appropriate to the setting (see [Letter]). In v. 27, Lysias states succinctly enough the relevant facts: the Jews had seized Paul and threatened his life. Lysias and his soldiers had rescued him. Lysias is not lying to say that he learned that Paul was a Roman citizen, but he is spinning the fact to his advantage to imply that it was his having learned of this fact that motivated him to rescue Paul. And, of course, Lysias makes no mention of the near flogging.

Lysias summarizes accurately in v. 28 the essence of the hearing before the Sanhedrin. Lysias also shares with Felix, and with readers, his assessment of the situation from the standpoint of Roman law (v. 29). Lysias is convinced, as other Roman officials who preceded him (cf. 18:15), that disputes between Paul and his Jewish accusers have to do exclusively with matters of Jewish law and are not deserving of Roman punishment, be it death or incarceration (v. 29). This is a persistent theme in Acts: Christians, as irritating as they might be, are not criminals; they do not violate the laws of the Roman Empire (16:20-21, 38-39; 18:14; 25:8, 24-27; 26:32). Lysias concludes the letter by informing Felix of the plot against Paul's life and letting the governor know that Paul's accusers would be appearing before him to present their charges against Paul (v. 30). The concluding statement also informs readers of what will develop and prepares them for the next chapter when Ananias and other representatives of the Sanhedrin appear before Felix (24:1).

They Came to Caesarea, vv. 31-35

According to the narrative, Paul and his military escort made the trip overnight to Antipatris (v. 31). From there, the foot soldiers returned to Jerusalem, and the balance of the trip was made only by the cavalry (v. 32). Antipatris, which Herod the Great built in honor of his father, Antipater, was located about thirty-five to forty-five miles (commentaries differ on the distance) northwest of Jerusalem, about halfway between Jerusalem and Caesarea. Apparently, Paul was now far enough away from the immediate threat that an escort of seventy cavalry would provide sufficient security; this allows the foot soldiers to return to Jerusalem and bring the military presence in that city back to almost full strength.

Even assuming the shorter distance of thirty-five miles, this is an incredible distance for 400 soldiers on foot to cover overnight. Moving at the relatively rapid clip of four to five miles per hour, it would have taken the soldiers seven to nine hours to reach Antipatris. Verse 32 then states they returned the following day to their barracks in Jerusalem. That is a grueling seventy-mile march in less than a full day!

Commentators deal with this in varying ways. Interpreters such as Haenchen and Lüdemann are simply incredulous. They conclude that Luke must not have known Palestinian geography very well to have pressed the march into such a narrow timeframe.[15] Polhill suggests that the soldiers did not actually make the trip all the way to Antipatris, but escorted Paul and the cavalry far enough beyond Jerusalem to be assured that the rest of the trip could be made safely.[16] Witherington, who is regularly inclined to give Luke the benefit of the doubt, takes him at his word: "It does not pay to underestimate what Roman troops were capable of when a crisis situation was involved."[17] As with so many issues pertaining to Luke's historical accuracy, there is no clear resolution, and the interpreters' ideological and theological perspectives always color their conclusions.

The narrator does not tell readers exactly when Paul and his escort arrived in Caesarea. He simply notes only that, upon their

---

Location of Paul's Imprisonment at Herod's Palace, Caesarea Maritima

Excavation of Caesarea Harbor and Palace. (Credit: Todd Bolen, "Caesarea harbor aerial from west," [cited 20 September 2007]. Online: http://www.bibleplaces.com.)

arrival, they delivered Paul and Lysias's letter to the governor (v. 33). Upon reading the letter Felix inquired as to Paul's provincial home. When he learned that Paul was from Cilicia (v. 34), he determined that he could hear the case. Cilicia and Judea were both under the single provincial administration of the imperial legate of Syria. Hence, Felix, as an official within that region, would be competent to hear the case. Felix's concern to make sure that it is appropriate for him to hear the case might raise the expectation in readers that Paul will get a fairer hearing than he received in Jerusalem. While Felix was no paragon of judicial virtue, as Acts will later make clear, he is clearly a breath of fresh air compared to the Jerusalem Sanhedrin, whose own presiding officer is a "whitewashed wall" (cf. v. 3) and is complicit in an assassination attempt.

The story will pause until Paul's accusers arrive. In the meantime, Paul is kept in custody in Herod's praetorium until his hearing begins. Herod built the palace, and it would have been taken over by the Romans when Judea was transferred to direct Roman rule in AD 6, overseen by governors. According to Barrett, its location is not known, as no archaeological remains have been discovered.[18]

CONNECTIONS

The two most explicitly theological statements in this chapter are found in vv. 6 and 11. In v. 6 Paul declares that he is on trial for the hope of the resurrection. In v. 11 Paul receives confirmation that he will bear witness for Christ in Rome. These two statements work together in a synergistic way to invite theological reflection.

One can only offer informed speculation as to what exactly "the hope of the resurrection" would have implied for Paul's audience in the narrative—at least those among his audience who even affirmed it. The resurrection of the dead was inextricably linked with other eschatological hopes. Jewish expressions of eschatological hope allow for the conclusion that many Jews looked forward to a very literal fulfillment of such hopes. [Restoration Eschatology] For example, the exile would come to an end and Jews would be restored to their land, Jerusalem would be rebuilt in splendor, and a new temple would stand within it. The messianic throne would be restored and a descendant of David would, once again, rule over God's people. The unrighteous, including Gentiles, would be purged from Jerusalem, and many Gentiles would actually come to worship the true and living God.

Luke seems to be broadly aware of such hopes. He speaks of liberation from enemies (Luke 1:71, 74) and the exaltation of the righteous and oppressed poor and the judgment of the oppressive rich (Luke 1:51-53; 6:20-25). The redemption of Israel (Luke 24:21), including the restoration of the kingdom to Israel (Acts 1:6), was one such hope. There is obviously much in Luke–Acts that revolves around messianic hope and the fulfillment of such hope in Jesus (Luke 1:32-33; Acts 2:30-36; 13:30-39). There are even hints at some type of restoration for Jerusalem (Luke 21:24). And Luke most certainly holds to the hope of the salvation of the Gentiles, the leading of the Gentiles to worship the true and living God (Luke 2:32; Acts 11:18; 14:15; 26:17-19). And all of this—from the story of Jesus to the mission of the church—represents the "fulfillment of Scripture" (Luke 24:46-47).

Claiming to hold to the hope of the resurrection of the dead, Paul and Christianity are claiming association with a whole network of beliefs that were connected with such hope. Messiah had come. In him the resurrection finds its fulfillment. Salvation and liberation are here. Scripture is being fulfilled. And yet traditional Jewish hopes are fulfilled in surprising ways. Liberation comes primarily through release from forces of possession and sickness and, most especially, through forgiveness of sin (Luke 1:77; 5:20-24; 7:47-49; 23:34; 24:47; Acts 5:31; 10:43; 13:38; 26:18). The one who fulfills messianic hopes fails to fulfill traditional messianic expectations. Oppressive kingdoms, with their riders and chariots (cf. Hag 2:22), do not fall. It is, rather, Satan who falls, and only Jesus claims to have seen it happen (Luke 10:18). And the one who fulfills such messianic hope follows a path of crucifixion and resurrection, something of which traditional Jewish hopes never conceived. Even those sympathetic with Jesus had to be taught to read their Scriptures in a new way to see that death and resurrection was the path to messianic glory (Luke 24:45). [Political Hopes, Spiritual Fulfillment]

Restoration Eschatology

Restoration eschatology is a term some scholars use to summarize essential features of Jewish eschatological hopes: hopes centered on the "restoration" of Jewish religious and national life. Sanders points out that, "In general terms it may be said that 'Jewish eschatology' and 'the restoration of Israel' are almost synonymous" (97). Texts such as Acts 1:6 and 3:21 show that Luke or his traditions had some awareness of restoration eschatology. Two texts from Jewish religious literature are as follow:

After this they all will return from their exile and will rebuild Jerusalem in splendor; and in it the temple of God will be rebuilt, just as the prophets of Israel have said concerning it. Then the nations in the whole world will all be converted and worship God in truth. They will all abandon their idols, which deceitfully have led them into their error; and in righteousness they will praise the eternal God. All the Israelites who are saved in those days and are truly mindful of God will be gathered together; they will go to Jerusalem and live in safety forever in the land of Abraham, and it will be given over to them. Those who sincerely love God will rejoice, but those who commit sin and injustice will vanish from all the earth. (Tobit 14:5b-7)

See, Lord, and raise up for them their king, the son of David, to rule over your servant Israel in the time known to you, O God. Undergird him with the strength to destroy the unrighteous rulers, to purge Jerusalem from Gentiles who trample her to destruction; in wisdom and in righteousness to drive out the sinners from the inheritance; to smash the arrogance of sinners like a potter's jar. (*Pss Sol* 17:21-23)

E. P. Sanders, *Jesus and Judaism* (Philadelphia: Fortress Press, 1985), see esp. part 1, "The Restoration of Israel."

Embracing Jesus as the fulfillment of the hope of the resurrection required transformed ways of thinking; it required the adjustment of expectations and new ways of seeing that allowed one to recognize such fulfillment in Jesus. Over the years, Christianity has come to adopt its own set of very specific expectations. Some contemporary Christian expressions of eschatological hope share the pattern of some ancient Jewish expressions of hope. They envision the fulfillment of such hopes primarily in stupendous events that are destined to take place in an (unknown?) future and the unfolding of which will signal in an unambiguous way the dawn of the times of fulfillment.

Within the creeds, such as the Apostles' Creed, eschatological expectations are rather laconically stated:

He ascended into heaven
and sits at the right hand of God the Father Almighty,
whence He shall come to judge the living and the dead.
I believe in . . .
the resurrection of the body,
and life everlasting.

Hopes and expectations stated so broadly leave much room for interpretation, as well as speculation. For many, the fulfillment of eschatological hopes in Jesus have come to be associated with very specific scenarios: a "rapture" of the elect, whereupon millions will mysteriously disappear from homes, hospital beds, and cradles, followed by a seven-year period of tribulation, culminating in a great battle to be led by Jesus himself. After this Jesus will bind Satan and set up a literal earthly kingdom for a period of 1,000 years, at the end of which period will take place the great judgment and the establishment of a new heaven and new earth.

Various smaller expectations can accompany this larger outline, such as the establishment of a Jewish state, the rebuilding of a literal temple in Jerusalem, and the reinstitution of literal sacrifice during the millennial reign of Christ. And speculations can abound as to what exactly will constitute the number or mark of the beast

---

Political Hopes, Spiritual Fulfillment

I. Howard Marshall explores the political, militaristic language of the Lukan birth narrative, found especially in Mary's Magnificat and Zechariah's Benedictus. He offers the following insights:

[T]he mission of Jesus is of such a kind that the metaphor of politics can be used to interpret it. Its deeper meaning and overall significance is brought out. It is 'political' but, to appropriate a well-known catch phrase, 'not as we know it'. Politics is concerned with the security of the realm, the maintenance of law and order within it, and the development of its communal life and its material prosperity. Here we have the establishment of a kingdom that is significantly different and, for want of a better term, is spiritual in that it is concerned with the inward allegiance of people to God as a result of which they live in a new way.

In large measure, Luke absorbs the language of political militancy offered in his birth narrative and subverts it by redefining the manner in which it is fulfilled as the narrative of Jesus and the church unfolds. Hence, while Luke is aware of many of the traditional elements of "restoration eschatology" that shaped the Judaism of his time, they do not capture his imagination or control the way he presents the good news of the reign of God.

I. Howard Marshall, "Political and Eschatological Language in Luke," in *Reading Luke: Interpretation, Reflection, Formation*, ed. Craig G. Bartholomew, Joel B. Green, Anthony Thiselton (Scripture and Hermeneutics Series 6; Carlisle, UK: Paternoster/Zondervan, 2005), 161.

(cf. Rev 13:18; 19:20). For many, such an array of hoped-for events has come to constitute the "signs" that the hope of the resurrection is coming to realization.

But like the Pharisees, who were busy looking for signs and who could not see the realization of kingdom hopes right under their noses (Luke 17:20-21), how many contemporary Christians, like the apostles looking into the sky (Acts 1:11), miss the clear, even if more subtle signs of the fulfillment of the hope of the resurrection? The God of Acts has clear aims and goals, and chief among them are the offering of liberation, as we have outlined just above: the "hope of the resurrection"—God's aims and goals to offer redemption, salvation, liberation, and forgiveness—comes to expression in the Lukan story about Jesus and the church.

Yet in the gospel narratives the fulfillment of Scripture "today in your hearing" (cf. Luke 4:21) and the fulfillment of the hope of the resurrection (Acts 23:6) carry all the significance but very little of the extravagance of popular notions of fulfillment, be they those of some ancient Jews or contemporary Christians. As the "fulfillment of Scripture today" plays itself out in the narratives of Luke and Acts, there are eruptions of the miraculous, to be sure. But the fulfillment of eschatological and scriptural hopes unfolds just as significantly in the seemingly ordinary events of history.

In Acts the realization and fulfillment of end-time, resurrection hopes become manifest in the tumble of events and the nooks and crannies of life. Among these are the Jerusalem church's struggle with the temple authorities, both at the beginning (5:17-42) and end of the narrative (ch. 23), internal disputes over the welcoming of Gentiles (chs. 11 and 15), the many fracases with religious zealots opposed to the inclusion of non-Jews in God's salvific work (13:44-50; 14:2; 17:4-5, 12-13), interpersonal quarrels over who will constitute a workable mission team (15:36-41), run-ins with economic opportunists and the political authorities vested with the responsibility of guarding entrepreneurial interests (16:19-40; 19:23-41), and various hearings before representatives of Roman power (18:12-17 and much of the concluding chapters of Acts). How does the tumble of such events give expression to the realization of the hope of the resurrection of the dead, the realization of God's redemptive aims for all flesh?

It is simply this: as history moves forward through seemingly unrelated events the story moves steadily toward its dénouement: the witness of Paul—the witness of the church—to Rome and, with that, the extension of the liberating message of God's salvation "to the ends of the earth." Right in the midst of Paul's trials of Acts

Living Water

"Think of water as a . . . metaphor for God. Water rushes to fill all the nooks and crannies available to it; water swirls around every stone, sweeps into every crevice, touches all things in its path—and changes all things in its path. The changes are subtle, often slow, and happen through a continuous interaction with the water that affects both the water and that which the water touches. . . . The water doesn't exert its power by being 'single minded' over and above these things, but simply by being pervasively present to and with all things. It does not evoke the 'command' of power over its creation: it is more like a 'persuasive' power with and around its creation. Its power is a power of presence."

Marjorie Heweitt Suchocki, *In God's Presence: Theological Reflections on Prayer* (St. Louis: Chalice, 1996), 4–5.

23 both he and readers hear the reassuring word that Paul will bear witness in Rome (v. 11). The Lord makes a quick appearance and then, just as quickly, disappears into the background. In the rest of the chapter the Lord is absent, as well as silent. And yet a calm sense of God's presence pervades all that follows. [Living Water]

On the stage we see a Roman tribune attempting to find a way to deal with this curious preacher who seems to stir up trouble wherever he appears in Jerusalem. We find a hypocritical high priest who ignores the law that it is his duty to enforce. We see zealots bent on murder who find helpful allies among the leaders of Jerusalem society. We find an anonymous relative of Paul who—in ways unknown to readers—makes his way to Paul to inform him of the devious plot against Paul's life. We find another anonymous character, a centurion who, again for reasons unexplained, decides to heed Paul's counsel and take this young man to see the Roman tribune. This military officer chooses not to dismiss this no-account Jewish lad, but takes him into his confidence. We find the stage now populated by almost 500 Roman soldiers, none of whom is said to have any interest at all in being instruments of God's redemptive purposes. And, finally, we meet a Roman governor, whose precise role is left undefined as the chapter comes to a close.

Save for one brief appearance and a few words, the Lord is absent and silent. And yet, when the reader comes to the end of the chapter, Paul is out of Jerusalem, out of immediate harm's way, and several miles closer to Rome than he was when the chapter began. The history that unfolds in this narrative and that tells the story of the realization of the hope of the resurrection moves silently and unnoticed by all the players on the stage, save for Paul, one step closer to fulfilling its purpose: the offering of God's liberating salvation to all flesh, even to the ends of the earth.

Reflecting on the mysterious ways that history unfolds toward what appear to be goals or aims raises questions. Does history move toward seemingly positive aims because God has so scripted it? That is to say, does God stand *over* history, like Christof in the movie *The Truman Show*, sitting up in the sky, looking down and directing the action and players? Or is it simply coincidence, and it is left to our interpretive abilities to find the meaning? That is to say, is God not involved at all? Or does God work within the

Process and Providence

Process theology is a term used to denote a view of God wherein "God as becoming" is a more apt way of thinking of God than "God as being." God is not a static being who pushes reality to conform to God's will, but One who becomes along with creation, "luring" creation and reality to embrace the aims of God for God's creation.

Process thinking, as well as "open theism," the more evangelical theological expression of a somewhat similar sentiment, takes seriously human freedom and the contingent nature of history that must accompany any serious notions of human freedom. God and the world *together* move history along toward or away from God's aims or goals for life.

What is the connection between God's reign *in* history and God's reign *beyond* history? Process theology addresses these questions through the dynamics describing the interaction between God and the world. God works with the world as it is to guide it toward what it might be. This means that God's own nature influences the world in every developing moment. Insofar as the world responds positively to this influence, the world will be living according to the reign of God in history. . . .

But the process dynamics do not stop with the influence of God on the world; the world also has an effect upon God. This return dynamic relates history to God's own everlastingness, intimating that in God, beyond all histories, there is a fully actualized reign of God in which the world participates. But once again, the dynamics call for the return motion toward history. The world does indeed have an effect upon God, meeting its own judgment and transformation in God—this is precisely the event in God that God turns into a redemptive influence in ongoing history.

Marjorie Hewitt Suchocki, *God, Christ, Church: A Practical Guide to Process Theology* (New York: Crossroad, 1989), 188.

---

context of (and fully respect) our choices as freely created human beings? Does God work within the context of the contingencies of history, quietly and unobtrusively guiding the world toward God's aims for creation? Perhaps Marjorie Suchocki is on to something: "God works with the world as it is in order to bring it to where it can be" (see [The Working of God]).[19]

This last option is far more complex to grasp. But the way that the narrative of Acts moves along toward the realization of God's aim, that the word of salvation reach to the ends of the earth so that all flesh may experience the salvation of God, and moves along only occasionally disrupted by manifestations of God's coercive power invites us to consider this last way of thinking about "providence." [Process and Providence]

NOTES

[1] Kirsopp Lake, "Localities in and near Jerusalem Mentioned in Acts," in F. J. Foakes Jackson and Kirsopp Lake, *The Beginnings of Christianity: The Acts of the Apostles*, 5 vols. (Grand Rapids MI: Baker, 1979), 5.477–78.

[2] Luke Timothy Johnson, *The Acts of the Apostles* (SacPag 5; Collegeville MN: Liturgical Press, 1992), 397.

[3] According to Josephus the Sadducees do not "regard the observation of anything besides what the law enjoins them" (*Antiquities* 18.16).

[4] Joseph A. Fitzmyer, *The Acts of the Apostles* (AB 31; New York: Doubleday, 1998), 719; Ben Witherington III, *The Acts of the Apostles: A Socio-Rhetorical Commentary* (Grand Rapids MI: Eerdmans, 1998), 692; C. K. Barrett, *Acts*, 2 vols. (ICC; Edinburgh: T&T Clark, 1994/1998), 2.1063–64 offers a thorough discussion and survey of the literature offering this interpretation.

[5] Fitzmyer, *Acts*, 714.

[6] Luke, of course, does not view the resurrection of Jesus as that of a "spirit" (cf. Luke 24:37). But on the level either of history or of verisimilitude the text is saying that there exists between Christians and Jews the common ground of resurrection. See the discussion that ensues.

[7] Ernst Haenchen, T*he Acts of the Apostles: A Commentary* (Philadelphia: Westminster, 1971), 641, 643.

[8] John B. Polhill, *Acts* (NAC 26; Nashville: Broadman, 1992), 472–73.

[9] Johnson, *Acts*, 405.

[10] Haenchen, *Acts*, 647.

[11] Witherington, *Acts*, 697–98.

[12] Fitzmyer, *Acts*, 726.

[13] Witherington, *Acts*, 698. Given that Witherington thinks that Luke might have accompanied Paul (the other mount of v. 24 was for him), the author of the narrative might actually have heard the letter himself.

[14] Fitzmyer, *Acts*, 726.

[15] "The narrator makes great demands upon the poor infantry. . . . Evidently he has only an inaccurate conception of the geography of Palestine" (Haenchen, *Acts*, 648). Gerd Lüdemann, *Early Christianity according to the Traditions in Acts: A Commentary* (Minneapolis: Fortress, 1989), 245, challenges interpreters, such as Martin Hengel, who vouch for the essential historicity of Acts 23 by arguing, in part, that Luke's description of the trip to Antipatris is not historically plausible: "Luke gets the distance between Jerusalem and Antipatris wrong (he presupposes a distance of forty-five miles can be covered in a night)."

[16] Polhill, *Acts*, 475.

[17] Witherington, *Acts*, 697.

[18] Barrett, *Acts*, ICC 2.1088.

[19] Marjorie Suchocki, *In God's Presence: Theological Reflections on Prayer* (St. Louis: Chalice, 1996), 188.

PAUL BEFORE FELIX AND THE COUNCIL

Acts 24:1-27

COMMENTARY

Paul's trial before Governor Felix is the first formal trial that Paul undergoes in this section of Acts. There are two primary speeches in this chapter, both employing judicial rhetorical aims (see [Types of Rhetorical Persuasion]).[1] Tertullus lays forth the formal accusations against Paul, and Paul replies in defense. Paul's defense speech will, like all of Paul's defense speeches in this section, steer ultimately toward "testimony" of "the Way."

Passing judgment on the historical veracity of events is very much guided by—often unexpressed—theological and ideological predispositions that one brings to the text. One so inclined can find only a bare kernel of historical tradition: Paul was imprisoned in Caesarea, Jewish authorities brought charges, assisted by a lawyer named Tertullus, and there was eventually a trial, but only before Festus, Felix's successor. There was never an actual trial before Felix.[2] On the other hand, one can make a case that readers find before them a good accounting of the actual trial before Felix, where careful and official notes would have been recorded. Paul would have taken these records with him to Rome, which Luke could have examined on the ship and committed to memory (presumably such records would have become lost in the shipwreck). Not to mention that Luke would have had as a direct source Paul himself to offer details on his numerous encounters with Felix.[3] While not ignoring historical issues, the following comments will focus on the narrative *as narrative*, viewing events and characters as literary constructs of the narrator.

The chapter divides into three sections: the charges against Paul (vv. 1-9), Paul's defense (vv. 10-21), and Felix's response (vv. 22-27).

They Began to Accuse Him, 24:1-9

Chapter 23 concluded with Paul in prison, awaiting his day in court. Five days later his accusers arrive. Among them are the high priest himself, Ananias, certain elders, who are likely select members of the Sanhedrin, and an attorney (*rhētōr*), Tertullus (v. 1a). The presence of the high priest and the retaining of an attorney combine to make clear the importance of this matter to the Judean powers-that-be.

Readers (both ancient and modern) who are broadly familiar with Roman jurisprudence would be impressed by at least the verisimilitude of the narrative, and perhaps even its factual veracity. First, the narrative employs appropriate legal terminology. Tertullus is designated as a *rhētōr*, which can mean "attorney." The verb that the NRSV renders as "they reported their case" (*enephanisan*, v.1) was a legal technical term, as was the term translated as "began to accuse" (*katēgorien*, v. 2).[4] Paul's response is denoted by the phrase "make my defense" (*apologeomai*, v. 10b).

Further, the progression of the events conforms to Roman legal procedure. Such trials would develop in five steps: (1) the presentation of basic charges *before* Paul appeared before the governor (v. 1), (2) summoning the accused (v. 2a),[5] (3) the formal presentation of the charges (vv. 2b-9), (4) the defense of the accused (vv. 10-21), and (5) the disposition of the case (vv. 22-23), with the governor being under no obligation to settle things in a timely matter (vv. 24-27).[6]

Tertullus begins his appeal to Felix with the customary *captatio benevolentia*, a rhetorical device to curry the favor of one's audience. Such was offered "to establish the proper rapport so that the political charges would be considered viable."[7] As a professional, legal rhetorician Tertullus offers a polished speech, something expected by judges of antiquity. [Rhetoric and Judges] Tertullus's flattering words constitute the bulk of his speech, as presented by the narrative.

He portrays Felix as the quintessential Roman ruler. First, he has done well in promoting *Pax Romana*, the peace of Rome (v. 2b). Second, Felix is credited with "foresight" or "forethought" (*pronoia*, v. 2c). Having prudent foresight was deemed necessary to allow for effective planning and ruling. Tertullus makes clear that his Jewish subjects are enriched and gratified by his important contributions to their

Rhetoric and Judges

Quintilian offers a relevant comment on the Sanhedrin's employment of a professional orator:

The judges themselves demand the most finished and elaborate speeches, thinking themselves insulted, unless the orator shows signs of having exercised the utmost diligence in the preparation of his speech, and desire not merely to be instructed but to be charmed.

Charles H. Talbert, *Reading Acts: A Literary and Theological Commentary of the Acts of the Apostles* (New York: Crossroad, 1997), 205.

social life. Tertullus speaks as though he assumes flattery will get him far.

Two comments are in order. First, readers aware of the ineptitude of Felix would know that Tertullus's words ring hollow. [Felix] Felix was most competent at oppressively squashing public dissent and of crucifying brigands, but this was not the ideal implementation of *Pax Romana*. Second, while Tertullus is, at best, stretching and spinning the truth by emphasizing to Felix his contributions to maintaining peace, the charges against Paul take on more weight. In essence, Tertullus is saying to Felix, "You, who have done so much to bring peace to our region, are faced today with one who threatens that peace."

Tertullus, sensitive to Roman demands for succinctness and brevity (v. 4),[8] gets on with the formal charges. The narrative proposes two broad charges against Paul: (1) being a political agitator (v. 5) and (2) profaning the Jerusalem temple (v. 6).[9] Both actions would threaten public peace and social stability.

Tertullus describes Paul the agitator as "a pestilent fellow" (v. 5). The word *loimos* literally denoted a disease of epidemic proportions, such as plague or pestilence. Metaphorically, it could be used to denote one who brought harm and sickness to society. Tertullus is describing Paul as a cancer, capable of corrupting, injuring, and debilitating the social structures of Rome.

Tertullus attempts to substantiate his charge with two specific examples. First, throughout the whole of the empire, Paul has been "an agitator among all the Jews." The Greek phrase *kinounta staseis* can be rendered as "stirring up insurrections" or "causing uproars." The latter would be truer to the facts, for even readers sympathetic with Paul would have to concede that he did have a way of unsettling Jews throughout the world, though it was hardly Paul's intent to "stir up insurrections." Unfortunately for Tertullus and his clients, Felix's jurisdiction doesn't reach beyond Judea, and no witnesses are present to substantiate his claims that Paul stirred up trouble virtually everywhere he went.

The second example that Tertullus offers is to describe Paul as "a ringleader of the sect of the Nazarenes." The term rendered as *ring-*

Felix

Felix governed from c. AD 52–60. He was a former slave and not an able administrator. Even the Roman historian Tacitus characterized him as "practicing every kind of cruelty and lust; he exercised royal power with the instincts of a slave" (*Histories* 5.9). During his administration he had a number of encounters with Jewish revolutionaries. The Jewish terrorist group known as the Sicarii, which specialized in political assassination, was especially active. While Felix made it a point to rid Judea of these and other brigands (Josephus, *J. W.* 2.252), he was willing to conspire with these enemies of the Roman Empire to assassinate the high priest Jonathan, with whom Felix was having serious political disagreements (Josephus, *Ant.* 20.173–78). It was also during this administration that a major disturbance erupted under the leadership of the Egyptian with whom Paul was confused in Acts 22. According to Josephus, it was Felix's forces that killed so many of his followers (*Ant.* 20.169–72). Further, though Felix was assured by Claudius Lysias that Paul was guilty of no political crimes, one can understand why Felix, so accustomed to having to deal with Jewish agitators, would want to look into this case. Acts 24:26 indicates that Felix was hoping that Paul would offer him a bribe in order to secure his release from prison. This is not out of character for Felix.

Nazarenes

Acts 24:5 is the only place in the New Testament where followers of Jesus are referred to as Nazarenes (Gk. *Nazoreans*). Despite there being only one reference in the New Testament, there is evidence from subsequent testimony that the term was used to denote followers of Jesus. Tertullian (c. AD 200) writes that Jews still referred to Christians as "Nazarenes." About 100 years later the church historian Eusebias states that Christians used to be called Nazarenes. Jewish Christians apparently continued to call themselves "Nazarenes," or some close derivation, according to church fathers (who considered Jewish Christianity to be a heresy). Finally, there is evidence that the synagogue used the term *Nosrim* to denote Christians (or, perhaps only Jewish Christians).

Stephen Goranson, "Nazarenes," *ABD* 4.1049–50.

leader can also denote a legitimate leader among the ranks of the Roman army. Used pejoratively, it carries the implied ominous tone captured by the English word "ringleader." Paul is the leader of a splinter group of Jews, which Tertullus refers to as a sect (*hairesis*). The Greek word can be used in a more neutral manner to denote differing parties or schools within a larger religious or philosophical tradition (cf. Acts 5:17; 15:5; 26:5). The term also can have pejorative definition (cf. the English word "heresy"), and that is how Tertullus is using it here (see [School]). The movement of which Paul is a ringleader, the Nazarenes, is a subversive, seemingly illegitimate sect within the Jewish tradition. [Nazarenes] In the speech, at least as the narrator presents it, Tertullus offers no evidence for his claim.

The second charge accuses Paul of profaning the temple, followed by the claim that "we [Jewish authorities] seized him" (v. 6). Roman authorities did respect Jewish protection of their sacred precincts, including the sanctioning of the use of force to protect their sacred space from profanation by Gentiles (see [Temple Inscription]). Tertullus, again, offers no evidence for this charge, not even describing exactly what Paul supposedly did. Presuming that "at the real trial" he would have done so offers no meaningful insight into the narrative as Luke chooses to present it. The failure of Tertullus to provide evidence sets the stage for Paul's defense, the gist of which will be that his accusers have no case, due to lack of evidence.

The claim of Tertullus that "we seized him" stretches the truth to the point of perjury. Readers *and* Felix, who have read Lysias's letter (Acts 23:26-30), know this. The Greek verb *krateō* can carry the connotation of "arrest," as well as simply "laying hold of." Tertullus, clearly, wants to imply that it was Jewish authorities who *arrested* Paul, while both readers and Felix know that it was a Jewish mob that "seized" Paul and *Roman* authorities who rescued him.

Tertullus ends his case by encouraging Felix to "examine" Paul for himself, presumably employing whatever methods of interrogation he deemed appropriate, confident that such an interrogation would confirm the Jewish authorities' accusations (v. 8). [The Western Addition of vv. 6b-8a] This section concludes with "the Jews" corroborating Tertullus's case, "asserting that all was true" (v. 9). The verb that the NRSV translates "asserting" (*phaskō*) connotes speaking

---

The Western Addition of vv. 6b-8a

AΩ The so-called Western text of Acts adds the following after "and we seized him" (v. 6): "and we would have judged him according to our law. But the chief captain Lysias came and with great violence took him out of our hands, commanding his accusers to come before you." It is not readily explainable why later copyists would have struck these words had they been a part of the original text of Acts. The words summarize events from the previous chapter from a Jewish point of view, but "spin" events to the point of making Tertullus almost guilty of perjury, for the words imply that Jewish authorities were conducting everything in good order and the only one guilty

of any violence, aside from Paul, was the Roman tribune. Tertullus does not come off looking good in the reader's eye, again prompting the question why Christian copyists, who, not having been sympathetic with Tertullus, would have omitted the lines. In addition, the Western text tends to show anti-Jewish tendencies; this may be one more example. If one does include these lines, it changes the meaning of v. 8, where Tertullus says to Felix, "By examining him yourself you will be able . . . ." The insertion of the verses in question makes the antecedent of "him" to be Lysias, not Paul.

---

with certainty. The fact that the narrator refers to the Jewish authorities as "the Jews" implies that Tertullus was not a Jew himself. Rather, he was a Gentile lawyer, retained by the authorities to make the strongest case possible.

Readers know the case of Tertullus to be weak; further, readers know that Felix, having read Lysias's letter, should know it to be weak. This could raise expectations that justice will prevail in Paul's case. Paul's adroit defense should raise such expectations even more.

"I Cheerfully Make My Defense," 24:10-21

So wrapped in his own power that he merely nods in Paul's direction, Felix grants Paul permission to speak (v. 10a). Paul's *captatio benevolentia* is much more succinct than that of Tertullus. Paul speaks as a man convinced that the facts are on his side; he need not rely on flattery. Confident of the facts of the case, Paul is more than happy to offer his own defense (v. 10c).

The essence of Paul's *captatio* is to acknowledge that Felix has been ruling over the Judean territory now "for many years" (v. 10b). Given that the narrator rarely offers any hints of absolute dates (he does not say when Felix came to power or when Paul arrived in Jerusalem), readers can only understand Paul's words to mean that he is confident that Felix has been in power for a sufficient period of time to know the national situation well enough to make a reasonable judgment. Haenchen states that this was a rhetorically conventional expression from which one should not attempt to derive precise historical information.[10]

Tertullus had encouraged Felix "to learn" (*epiginōskō*) the facts of the case by examining Paul (v. 8). Paul, who is now being examined, asserts confidently that Felix can "find out" (*epiginōskō*) the facts that Paul was not long in Jerusalem (v. 11). The phrase "it is

Paul's Twelve Days in Jerusalem

A strict reading of 24:11b, where Paul says "it is not more than twelve days since I went up to worship in Jerusalem" does not match exactly with the rest of the narrative. Clearly the initial impression left by the text is that "no more than twelve days" had elapsed since Paul's arrival in Jerusalem and the present day, when Paul stands before Felix. A careful reading of the narrative, however, reveals that at least seventeen days have elapsed:

Day One: Paul arrives in Jerusalem (21:17)
Day Two: Paul meets with the leadership (21:18)
Day Three: Paul begins the period of purification (21:26)
Days Three through Nine: The period of purification (21:27)
Day Ten: Paul appears before the council (22:30)
Day Eleven: Some Jews plot to assassinate Paul (23:11-12).

Day Twelve: Paul departs (23:23) for Caesarea. Keeping in mind that Jewish days begin at sundown, Paul would have left Jerusalem in the early hours of Day Twelve. According to Acts, he arrived "the next day" (23:32-33) *at the earliest.* The narrator appears to be using "next day" to mean after the sun came up from the previous night, not the next "date."
Five days later Paul appears before Felix (24:1).

Note that according to the above reconstruction, Paul was in Jerusalem for twelve days. Some interpreters understand the words of 24:11b to refer only to the time Paul spent in Jerusalem (e.g., Haenchen, 654; Witherington, 711).

Ernst Haenchen, *The Acts of the Apostles: A Commentary* (Philadelphia: Westminster, 1971); Ben Witherington III, *The Acts of the Apostles: A Socio-Rhetorical Commentary* (Grand Rapids MI: Eerdmans, 1998).

---

not more than twelve days since I went up to worship in Jerusalem" does not match up exactly with the earlier Lukan narrative. [Paul's Twelve Days in Jerusalem] But it makes the point: as Felix himself would have to know, Paul was not in Jerusalem long enough to do what he has been accused of doing.

Paul flatly denies the charge that he was stirring up trouble in Jerusalem, declaring emphatically that his accusers did not find him engaging in any type of agitating behavior, whether it be in the synagogues, the temple, or anywhere else in Jerusalem (v. 12). Readers of the narrative know Paul to be speaking the truth. Consequently, Paul is quite confident that his accusers cannot prove their charges against him.

Paul is willing, however, to "confess" to something. In the offering of his confession, Paul shares his "testimony," his "witness," before the governor. He will confess that he is a faithful Jew, worshiping the ancestral God of the Jewish faith (v. 14). To be sure, Paul worships in accordance with what he calls "the Way" (see [The Way]), which, to his mind, is not a mere "sect," or even one party or school among others. The Way "is more than just a form of Judaism such as Pharisaism or Sadduceeism. He regards it as a God-inspired 'way' to salvation, not something that someone prefers or chooses."[11]

While Paul firmly believes the Way to be *the* Way, he is confident that it is a faithful way. He believes *everything* in the law and prophets, that is, the Jewish Scriptures. He embraces the widespread hope of his Jewish faith that there will be a resurrection of both the just and unjust. To be sure, not all Jews literally believe this—certainly not every Jew standing before Felix accusing Paul, for many, perhaps all of these representatives of the Sanhedrin denied the resurrection (see [Josephus on the Sadducees]). Still, belief in the resurrection of judgment was a widespread belief among many Jewish people. Paul is not being "sectarian" to embrace such a hope.

Paul's hope in a resurrection of judgment motivates how he lives his life. He "does his best" or "exerts effort" to have a clear conscience, both before God and other people. The Greek word *aproskopos*, translated as "clear," carries the idea of not being a cause of stumbling or offense in one's interpersonal relationships (cf. 1 Cor 10:32; see [Conscience]). C. K. Barrett comments, "His conscience shall not accuse him of offending against God or man."[12]

Paul moves back into a more explicit defense in v. 17, noting that after some years he decided to come to Jerusalem to bring alms to his nation and to "offer sacrifices" (NRSV) or, more generally, to bring "offerings." One cannot be sure, for the Greek word *prosphoras* could denote more general kinds of offerings, distinct from animal sacrifices (cf. Sir 34:23 [NRSV]; Eph 5:2; Heb 10:5, 8), though the term could also denote animal sacrifices (Sir 46:16). His point to Felix is clear enough—the only reason Paul returned to Jerusalem was to practice his Jewish faith in customary ways. Readers will recall Paul's desire to reach Jerusalem in time to celebrate Pentecost (20:16). This corroborates for readers Paul's claim that his desire to participate in his Jewish faith motivated him, at least in part, to return to Jerusalem. He certainly did not come to Jerusalem to stir up trouble.

Readers of the Lukan narrative might assume that Paul's desire to give alms to his nation would have been a simple act of piety, typical of a Jewish pilgrim.[13] Readers familiar with the Pauline corpus know that the historical Paul visited Jerusalem for the specific purpose of offering financial relief to the saints of Jerusalem (see [The Collection]). If one brings this knowledge to the speech,[14] one will hear Paul claiming before Felix that what he intended as a gift for Jerusalem Christians should be interpreted as gift of alms for his *nation*. If this is the case, readers will be required to be generous with Paul's testimony, for "the collection for the saints" would not have been part of Paul's intention to worship at the temple and could only loosely be construed as alms "for his nation." Yet this would not have been a problem for Luke's reader, who is *not* aware of this "collection" as Paul describes it in his letters.

Paul has claimed that his intent in returning to Jerusalem was to practice his faith. In the midst of his attempts to be a faithful Jew, completing rites of purification in deference to his tradition and people (recall 21:24, 26), Jews from Asia found Paul in the sacred precincts (v. 18). Paul was not creating any disturbance. Paul was not profaning the temple; he has made a point to inform Felix that he was completing rites of purification.

Paul's terse introduction of "some Jews from Asia" would sound a bit laconic to Felix; he has not heard of them and Paul does not report what they did. Felix knows from Lysias's letter only that "Jews" had "seized" Paul (cf. 23:27). But it is enough perhaps to spark the readers' memory and to vindicate to readers Paul's defense: it was these Asian Jews, not Paul, who created the disturbance in the temple. With this knowledge readers can make perfect sense of Paul's broken syntax, that the Jews from Asia should be there offering testimony against him. But they are not. The prosecution has no witnesses who can testify firsthand as to what happened in the temple precincts (v. 19). Failure to bring witnesses who could reliably corroborate the charges was a gross violation of Roman jurisprudence. The failure of the Asian Jews to appear at the trial should lead to the dismissal of their charge of Paul's profaning the temple.[15]

The only witnesses for the prosecution who are present are members of the Sanhedrin. Paul challenges them to put forth whatever evidence they have of Paul's criminal activity when he stood before them (v. 20). These witnesses had emphatically affirmed that Paul was guilty both of being an agitator and of profaning the temple (v. 9). But the fact is that these so-called witnesses could testify only to what Paul said and did while being interrogated by them. The *only* thing Paul said or did before the council that could in any way be construed as rabble-rousing was declaring his hope in the resurrection of the dead (v. 21; cf. 23:6). To be sure, Paul did declare his faith in the resurrection, but it was the council members themselves who created the "dissension," the noun the NRSV uses to translate the Greek word *stasis*, the very crime of which Tertullus has accused Paul (v. 5).

With Paul's defense complete, readers should expect immediate dismissal of the charges. Tertullus has offered no evidence and no witnesses, save members of the Sanhedrin who can only testify that Paul believes in the resurrection. Paul has denied the charges and claimed that he is a good, loyal Jew. Felix has heard no evidence or testimony to the contrary.

Keeping Paul in Custody, 24:22-27

Felix offers both a public and private response to the case. His public response is found in vv. 22-23: he refuses to pass judgment on the case. The initial reason given seems baffling, for the narrative states that Felix had rather accurate knowledge of the Way (v. 22), with the construction of the Greek sentence actually implying that such knowledge served partially as his reason for adjourning the proceedings.[16] Where he had acquired such knowledge is not said, for that is not the issue. The issue is that "being rather well informed about the Way" (NRSV) should have led Felix to recognize that this Jewish movement presented no political threat.

Felix presents as his rationale for delaying judgment another motive: he will wait for Lysias to appear before deciding Paul's case. But this too would be baffling to the reader, for Felix already has Lysias's statement in the letter he wrote, the contents of which are known to the reader (see 23:26-30). And this letter explicitly stated that accusations against Paul were solely about matters of Jewish law and involved "nothing deserving death or imprisonment" (23:29).

Felix orders Paul to remain in custody, but with some liberty, a practice known technically as *custodia libera* (v. 23). As the narrative states, Paul was not to be deprived visitors or the receiving of care from such visitors. Some modern commentators employ the phrase "protective custody." It is also important for contemporary readers to keep in mind that "for Romans prison was not a punishment but a means of keeping people available for trial and future punishment."[17] The fact that Paul is in prison means that the outcome of the trial is still very much up in the air.

Felix's private response would perhaps strike readers as even more curious, for Felix and his Jewish wife appear to be fascinated with Paul. The narrative states that "some days later" Felix and Drusilla "came" and "sent for Paul" (v. 24). Given that the prison was located in same place as the residence (see Commentary, Acts 23:35), it is not exactly clear where Felix "came" to or from in order to speak to Paul. Did he visit the actual prison? Had he been away from Caesarea and now come back? Readers will have to fill the gaps from their own imaginations. The crucial issue is that both the governor and his wife heard Paul speak "concerning faith in Christ Jesus" (v. 24).

According to v. 25a, the message that Paul preached focused on "justice, self-control, and the coming judgment." The word translated as "justice" is *dikaiosynē*, which is also regularly rendered as "righteousness," particularly in the Pauline corpus. Further, the term *righteousness* carried not only the usual Pauline meaning of being "justified [by faith]," but also the idea of justice or ethical virtue, in the sense of doing what is right. So readers can understand Paul to have spoken about justification (by faith), justice, or doing what is right. Given that the narrative states that Paul also spoke of self-control, justice and right behavior might be the more appropriate understandings here. The narrator certainly employs *dikaiosynē* in this sense in other places (cf. 10:35; 13:10). Such right behavior would both grow out of and into self-control, or discipline. Paul also reminds them that there is a judgment coming and they will be held accountable (cf. Acts 17:31).

Paul's message strikes a chord with Felix: he actually becomes frightened and sends Paul away (v. 25b). The narrative does not state exactly what it was about Paul's message that frightened Felix. Readers aware of the improper marriage that existed between Felix and Drusilla might conclude that Paul is condemning their relationship. [Drusilla] If such is the case, then the scene offers a faint echo of the relationship between John the Baptist and Herod, who was improperly married to Herodias (cf. Luke 3:19-20). The difference is that the narrative of the Gospel of Luke makes the reader privy, though only subtly so, to the relationship between Herod and Herodias. Acts is totally silent with regard to the scandalous nature of the relationship between Felix and Drusilla. Or perhaps readers, armed with the knowledge of just how inept and unjust a ruler Felix was, might read into the governor's fears his awareness that his corruption and oppression would one day catch up with him.

Readers compelled to rely only on what the narrative tells them cannot yet be clear why Felix was so frightened by Paul's message of justice/right behavior, self-control, and the threat of coming judgment. Yet the narrator fills this gap in the following verses. Verse 26a explicitly states that Felix hoped that Paul would offer him a bribe. [Bribery] One does not need to be an expert in Roman law to know that holding people in prison in order to exact a bribe is neither just nor right behavior. Verse 26b indicates that it was the hope for money that induced Felix to speak often with Paul, the implication being that during one of these many preaching sessions the offering of a bribe would come forward. Greed, hardly a demonstration of self-control, is what drives this ruler to imprison Paul unjustly.

Drusilla

Her full name was Julia Drusilla. She was the daughter of Agrippa I (the Herod of Acts 12), born around the year AD 38. Around AD 53, she married Azizus, king of the Syrian region Emesa. Felix, captivated by her beauty, persuaded her to leave her husband, promising her great happiness. Drusilla was not well treated by her sister Bernice and, though he is not clear as to exactly how this bad relationship affected Drusilla's judgment, Josephus indicates that the stormy relationship between the sisters prompted Drusilla to "transgress the laws of her forefathers, and to marry Felix" (*Ant.* 20.142).

David C. Braund, "Drusilla," *ABD* 2.238–39.

Verse 27 further indicts Felix for his lack of justice and right behavior. The narrative states that he held Paul for another two years in prison. The sole reason given was in order "to grant the Jews a favor." To be sure, Felix had to work with the Jews, and appeasing his subjects was part of the hard political realities of life. But holding a man in prison for two years, a man whom Felix knew to be innocent, is by no measure just or right behavior, no matter what politically expedient rationalization one might offer. Even when succeeded by the next governor, Porcius Festus, Felix refused to release Paul. When a new administration took charge, it was not unheard of for the outgoing ruler to release prisoners held in undecided cases.[18] And what is more, Felix, about to be liberated from his troublesome Judean post, no longer has even the motive of political appeasement to excuse his behavior.

Bribery

The taking of bribes was both officially condemned and widely practiced in the Roman Empire. Recall that Lysias likely secured his Roman citizenship through bribery (see Commentary on 22:28). Charles Talbert offers a number of excellent examples from ancient sources that attest to pandemic bribery. Following are a few of his quotations:

Cicero, speaking of the Roman governor Piso: "What need for me to adduce . . . your bargains with defendants, your selling of justice, your savage condemnations and your capricious acquittals? (In *Pisonem*, 87)

Josephus, speaking of Florus, governor of Judea: "He thought it but a petty offense to get money out of single persons, so he spoiled whole cities (*J. W.* 2.278).

Suetonius, speaking of Emperor Vespasian: "[He] thought nothing of . . . selling pardons to the innocent and guilty alike" (*Vespasian* 16).

Charles H. Talbert, *Reading Acts: A Literary and Theological Commentary of the Acts of the Apostles* (Macon: Smyth & Helwys, 2005), 203.

CONNECTIONS

Paul stands before the two most powerful ruling institutions of his world: a representative of the Roman Empire and representatives of the Sanhedrin, including the high priest. Secular (Roman) and sacred (temple) authorities confront Paul. It is before "the Powers" that Paul offers his defense.

Walter Wink's trilogy on "the Powers" offers to contemporary Christians a lens through which to "connect" this text with our worlds.[19] A volume of essays published in 2006 complements well Wink's trilogy.[20] Wink's thesis is three-fold: (1) the Powers are good, (2) the Powers are fallen, and (3) the Powers are redeemable.[21] We need also to understand that the Powers are *real*.

The Powers Are Real

The reality of the Powers, both visible and invisible, was taken for granted in the ancient world. The reality of the *visible* Powers is obvious. Paul stands before the visible Powers: persons, backed by institutions, who had the power to seize, interrogate, incarcerate, bind, and almost lacerate Paul.

But there were also the invisible Powers, the gods, spirits, demons, angels, and sprites that hovered over, above, and around the "visible" world, energizing and empowering that world (cf. Eph 6:12). We take seriously the "invisible Powers" not by making ourselves think that we live in the kind of world that we enter when we open the pages of a Harry Potter or Frank Peretti novel, worlds of magic forces or invisible, personified spirits hovering in the rafters. The "traditional worldview" that ancients took for granted was that "everything earthly has its heavenly counterpart and everything heavenly has its earthly counterpart. . . . Everything has a visible and an invisible counterpart."[22] This is still true, but our worldview understands this reality differently.

Peter Berger's modern classic *The Sacred Canopy* offers us a way to understand the reality of the invisible Powers and their interconnectedness with the visible Powers.[23] We long for order. To assist us in the establishment of order we construct customs, traditions, principles, laws, morality, and even theologies—in a word, we construct culture. That which we construct soon takes on a life of its own, what Berger refers to as objectivation and reification. "Ideas," "values," "philosophies," "customs," "traditions," and "theologies" (the list could go on) are "unseen." They are *invisible.* One cannot touch an idea the way one can touch a tree. Yet ideas and other similar "invisible" things have real *power.*

We also construct "visible" things that embody the invisible. Schools, churches, councils, court systems, armies, etc., embody the invisible "Powers" and give them concrete substance. And we populate these institutions with people: principals and teachers, priests and deacons, mayors and city managers, judges and clerks, generals and privates. The systems we construct allot power to different people within the systems, depending on what makes the systems work most effectively.

We all live under these Powers in some way. When we go to work, we live under the power of the corporate culture; when we go to school, we have to complete assignments; when we join the police force, we join that "thin blue line" and feel the pressure to take care of our own; when we go to church, we know without having to think about it what's expected of us. Review the description of life in the village of Lansquenet, France, in the Connections of chapter 20 (Acts 22). It offers a good picture of the interconnectedness of the visible and invisible dimensions of the Powers.

Intertwined in the fabric of the Powers is religion: the sacred canopy. Historically, according to Berger, a key social function of religion has been to give to the socially constructed Powers divine legitimacy; religion "sanctions" the Powers (our word "sanction" comes from the Latin *sanctus*, meaning "holy"). [Religious Legitimation] Religion is among the "Powers."

Starting from the day we are born, we internalize the values, customs, traditions, ideas, and God-thoughts of our world. The "Powers" become a part of us. The Powers are *real* subjectively, as we feel their influence on us, shaping us into what we are, and they are real objectively. We can "prove" the objective reality of the Powers through a simple experiment: challenge them and we will experience the power of the Powers, whether it be a fine, an in-school suspension, the loss of a letter grade on a paper, getting demoted or fired, or a trip up the river for a few years. The Powers are real.

Religious Legitimation

"Religion legitimates social institutions by bestowing upon them an ultimately valid ontological status, that is, by *locating* them within a sacred and cosmic frame of reference. . . . All legitimation serves to maintain reality—reality, that is, as defined in a particular human collectivity. Religious legitimation purports to relate the humanly defined reality to ultimate, universal and sacred reality."

Peter Berger. *The Sacred Canopy: Elements of a Sociological Theory of Religion* (New York: Anchor Books/Doubleday, 1967), 33, 35–36.

The Powers Are Good

The Powers are good because they, like all creation, come from God. The fact that we *construct* these Powers, following Berger's theory, only attests to the reality that, in God's way of "creating" things, we are God's created co-creators.

The story of Acts portrays Paul as loyal to and respectful of Jewish institutions and traditions. Paul's opponents charge that he has flouted and disrespected his Jewish religion; it is a charge that Paul emphatically—and honestly—denies. Acts has consistently insisted that Paul and other Christians are *not* disloyal to the empire. It is those who oppose Paul who violate the empire's systems of order (recall the mobs who have opposed Paul in virtually every city he visited). The deference that the narrative of Acts shows both to the empire and to Jewish religion speaks to the goodness of the Powers.

Implicitly, at least, we in our own context acknowledge these Powers as good. We may be annoyed when we get pulled over for going a few miles over the speed limit, write a check to the IRS, or have to work on a weekend. But, ultimately, we value the stability and order that the Powers offer. The Powers, both visible and invisible, allow us to move through the day, not having to "reinvent the wheel" each morning to discover what we are to do and how we are to behave. The alternative to living under the Powers is to live in chaos and anarchy, and humans do not like living that way. That is why we construct cultures and societies.

The Paul of the Epistles affirms most clearly the goodness of the Powers in Romans 13:1-7. Paul affirms that the God has instituted the specific embodiment of the Powers, the empire (Rom 13:1). Consequently, to resist the Powers is to resist God (Rom 13:2). Many interpret the passage as Paul's offering carte blanche to "the Powers": *whatever* the Powers do is ordained by God. That is a naïve reading of the text, at best. God has instituted the Powers not to be ends in themselves, but to be "a servant for your good" (Rom 13:4). Paul does *not* say that whatever the Powers do is good. He affirms that God ordained the Powers for the good, punishing the one who does wrong and approving the one who does good. Often the Powers fail to live up to their calling, however. Why?

The Powers Are Fallen

One cannot understand the complex dynamic of the Powers if one fails to see that they are fallen. The fact is that the Powers regularly do not reward and uphold the good and dissuade and punish the evil. The Powers can, themselves, become instruments of injustice and evil. Paul would have no doubt of that. Neither should we as read the story.

The Powers before which Paul stands are clearly fallen. The religious authorities have condoned and contrived false charges against Paul. They have collaborated with zealous assassins in the attempted murder of Paul. Felix is in dire need to hear a word about "justice, self-control, and coming judgment" (v. 25). There is no question but that the leadership of both Roman political and Jewish religious power is corrupt. Both Felix and the Sanhedrin pervert justice (cf. Exod 23:2; Mic 7:3). A quick review of Paul's story from the day the mob went after him in the temple courts displays the fallen nature of the Powers that occupy the stage.

It is not simply a question of "bad" people. To be sure, people are fallen, as well. But it is *also* the Powers that are fallen. The "spirit" that pervades our institutions of Power is often dark. The corporate culture (invisible Power) can condone sexual harassment and the belittling of employees. The judicial system is quicker to incarcerate people of color than white people.

Our economic system (an invisible Power) works itself out in such a way that equally qualified women make a fraction of the pay as their male counterparts and racial minorities continue to make up the majority of those who live in poverty and without health-care. And the economic materialistic philosophy and ideology (one of the invisible Powers) tempts us with a constant stream of "goods" that we "need," as well "easy credit" to subsidize our "needs."

Religion, too, is among the fallen powers. The interconnectedness of religious and civil life is made clear in the story of Paul's troubles at Ephesus (Acts 19). The Powers at Ephesus were in a frenzy. The Jewish religion of Jerusalem is also fallen. It, too, is in a frenzy. Perceived threats against both the "invisible" and "visible" Powers" of that religion ("Help! This is the man who is teaching everyone everywhere against our people, our law, and this place!" [21:28; cf. 21:21]) inspire physical and legal violence against Paul.

To confine our critique to the fallenness of "other" religions is to ignore the logs in our own eyes. In his farewell speech to the Ephesian elders (20:29-31) Paul attests to the reality that the church itself is susceptible to the fallen nature of the Powers. The Christian *sanctioning* (sacred legitimation) of the Crusades, the Inquisition, the drowning of Anabaptists, the slaughter of the peasants (endorsed by Martin Luther), the public stocks, and the burning of witches in the Massachusetts Bay Colony, and slavery, racism, segregation, sexism, militarism, eugenics, and unbridled capitalism and consumerism in our own national history all testify that even "our" religion is fallen. Fallen religion too often offers comfort and legitimacy to the rest of the fallen Powers.

The Powers Are Redeemable

This is the good news! It was the Powers that crucified the Lord (1 Cor 2:8), and it is these Powers over whom the crucified Lord has triumphed (Col 2:15). Acts begins with the ascension of Jesus (1:9-11), assuring us that as we take the redemptive witness into the world, we do so under the one who has put *power* "to work in Christ when he raised him from the dead and seated him at his right hand in the heavenly places, far above all rule and authority and power and dominion" (Eph 1:20-21). The good news not only tells individuals "how to get saved," but it confronts the Powers, even religious powers, with the fact of their fallen nature and the good news that God reigns and offers salvation even to them!

The church stands as one of the Powers. The church is to stand as a beacon for and model to the world, showing and demonstrating what "Power redeemed" looks like. "Through the church the wisdom of God in its rich variety [is] now . . . made known to the rulers and authorities in the heavenly places" (Eph 3:10). But the church not only serves as an example of Power redeemed, it is also an instrument to redeem the Powers. Both individuals and the Powers are fallen and redeemable. They both are the objects of God's redemptive concern.

> For in [Christ] all things in heaven and on earth were created, things visible and invisible, whether thrones or dominions or rulers or powers—all things have been created through him and for him. . . . For in him all the fullness of God was pleased to dwell, and through him God was pleased to reconcile to himself all things, whether on earth or in heaven, by making peace through the blood of his cross. (Col 1:16, 19-20)

"All things" are the object of God's redemptive love (cf. Rom 8:19-23; 2 Cor 5:17-19). "All things" are the objects of the church's redemptive witness.

Paul offers this good news to the Powers, whether it be the mob filled with the Power of religious zeal (Acts 22) or the Sanhedrin, which embodied the Power of Paul's ancestral religion (Acts 23). In his speech before the crowd, Paul used his own story to illustrate both that religion is fallen (he was persecuting people under by the sanction of the religious Powers [22:4-5]) and that it is redeemable (God transformed Paul to be God's redemptive instrument to all the world) [22:14-15]). As Paul stands before the Sanhedrin, the fallen nature of his own religion is manifested as Paul is struck (23:2). But Paul offers a word of redemption as he speaks not only of judgment (23:3), but also of the hope of resurrection (23:6). Before Felix and representatives of the Sanhedrin Paul attests to the goodness of his religious traditions (v. 14), including his loyalty to his people (v. 17), the fallen nature of his own religious institutions (vv. 19-20), and the redemptive word of resurrection (v. 20). Before Felix and Drusilla, Paul continues to offer a word of redemption (v. 25).

A paradox of "life in Christ," whether we are speaking of "the body of Christ" or of "members" of that body, is that, though we are reconciled to God and redeemed, we have not yet attained "the full stature of Christ" (Eph 4:13). We, like Paul, have not yet "reached the goal" (Phil 3:12a). Hence, too often the church fails in its mission to be both a beacon of redemptive light and example of what redeemed life looks like. The church's affinity with the unredeemed Powers, as noted in the previous section of these Connections, too regularly shows itself.

But, like Paul, we are called "to press on to make it [our] own, because Christ Jesus has made [us] his own" (Phil 3:12b). As we press on, it is imperative that we remember that we live in a world very different from Paul's. Paul lived in a world where the transformation or redemption of the *institutional Powers* was not much of an option. "The right of the people peaceably to assemble, and to petition the Government for a redress of grievances," assured in the First Amendment, was *not* a right that our spiritual ancestors enjoyed. The idea that

> Governments are instituted among Men, *deriving their just powers from the consent of the governed*—That whenever any Form of Government becomes destructive of these ends, it is the Right of the People to alter or to abolish it, and to institute new Government, laying its foundation on such principles and *organizing its powers* in such form, *as to them shall seem most likely to effect their Safety and Happiness*

was not a view of the Powers that our spiritual ancestors likely even imagined, much less could apply (from the Declaration of Independence [emphases added]). The slow plodding of history has brought us to a point where "we the people," including "the people of God," have real power to transform the Powers.

We make a mockery of the cosmic lordship of Christ to ignore this calling and the power we now have to be instruments of redemption and ministers of reconciliation (cf. 2 Cor 5:18). People are not to be *the exclusive* focus of our good news of redemption. Walter Rauschenbusch in the nineteenth century and Martin Luther King Jr. in the twentieth recognized the power and responsibility of the Christian faith to confront and transform the Powers. [Social Gospel] See also [Martin Luther King Jr.'s Appeal to Common Values]. The church now has "power to make a difference" that Paul could never have envisioned. The church should not ignore the Scriptures' cry for justice, while keeping in mind that such justice is often illustrated with explicit calls to protect those least able to protect themselves.

As the church enters the fray to take on the Powers of injustice and oppression, she should bear in mind two things. First, we do not enter

Social Gospel

The name most often associated with "the Social Gospel" is that of Walter Rauschenbusch. The selection below comes from his reflections on the Lord's Prayer. Rauschenbusch's observations show his awareness of the "power of the Powers," even if he does not use such precise language.

In the prayer, "Lead us not into temptation," we feel the human trembling of fear. Experience has taught us our frailty. Every man [*sic*] can see certain contingencies just a step ahead of him and knows that his moral capacity for resistance would collapse hopelessly if he were placed in these situations. . . .

But such situations are created largely by the social life about us. If the society in which we move is rank with sexual looseness, or full of the suggestiveness and solicitations of alcoholism; if our business life is such that we have to lie and cheat and be cruel in order to live and prosper; if our political organization offers an ambitious man the alternative of betraying the public good or of being thwarted and crippled in all his efforts, then the temptations are created in which we go under, and society frustrates the prayer we utter to God. No church can interpret this petition intelligently which closes its mind to the debasing or invigorating influence of the spiritual environment furnished by society.

Walter Rauschenbusch, *For God and the People: Prayers of the Social Awakening* (Norwood MA: Plimpton Press, 1910); quoted from John R. Tyson, *Invitation to Spirituality: An Ecumenical Anthology* (New York: Oxford University Press, 1999), 374–75.

God with Us

📖 While the "traditional worldview" no longer is taken for granted and simply accepted by modern Westerners, Walter Wink argues that moderns need not simply succumb to the "materialist" worldview, which asserts that only the "material" is real. Wink proposes what he calls an "integral worldview."

In the Integral Worldview, soul permeates the universe. God is not just within us but within everything. The universe is suffused with the divine. This is not pantheism, where everything is God, but panentheism (*pan*, everything; *en*, in; *theos*, God), where everything is in God and God in everything. . . .

This Integral Worldview is no more essentially "religious" than the Traditional Worldview, but I believe it makes the biblical data more intelligible for people today than any other available worldview, the Traditional Worldview included.

Walter Wink, "The New Worldview: Spirit at the Core of Everything," in *Transforming the Powers: Peace, Justice, and the Domination System*, ed. Ray Gingerich and Ted Grimsrud (Minneapolis: Fortress, 2006), 22, also 17–28. For a very readable discussion of panentheism see Marcus Borg, *The God We Never Knew: Beyond Dogmatic Religion to a More Authentic Contemporary Faith* (New York: HarperSanFrancisco, 1997), 32–54. For a thorough discussion see Philip Clayton and Arthur Peacocke, eds., *In Whom We Live and Move and Have Our Being: Panentheistic Reflections on God's Presence in a Scientific World* (Grand Rapids MI: Eerdmans, 2004).

---

the fray alone. God is with us, not as one hovering above us "up there," passively watching and occasionally working a miracle to set our course back on the right track again. Rather, "God is with us" immanently and pervasively. [God with Us]; see also [Living Water] God patiently works within us, enabling us to will and work for God's good pleasure (cf. Phil 2:13). By means of those who love God, God works all things together toward the good (cf. Rom 8:28; see [The Working of God]).

Second, Peter Hodgson keeps before us the implications of the painful reality of the cross. Our redemptive projects are doomed to failure if we define "success" as the unambiguous and total victory over the forces of darkness and human oppression. [The Cross and the Christian Commission] Our calling is to establish what J. Christiaan Beker called "beachheads of the kingdom," not to delude ourselves into thinking that we can "build the kingdom of God" in all its fullness here on earth.[24] [Beachheads of the Kingdom]

The Powers are real; we carry out the call of witness at our own peril if we do not take seriously what we are up against. The Powers

The Cross and the Christian Commission

📖 "The significance of the cross for humanity is its indication that all our historical projects of liberation ultimately fail. . . . The shape of the cross . . . remind[s] us that [the kingdom's] vision of inclusive wholeness, of a liberated communion of free persons, forever remains marginal in this world. . . . It reminds us that God does not rescue us from history or provide miraculous victories. God suffers alongside us, and it helps to know that God is there as a faithful friend, providing companionship, sharing our struggle and fate."

Peter Hodgson, *Christian Faith: A Brief Introduction* (Louisville KY: John Knox Press, 2001), 118.

Beachheads of the Kingdom

📖 "Although Christians must do battle against the power of death and against the unjust power structures of this world, they should not overrate their own capabilities. . . . Unless Christians know that their ethical activity is essentially an anticipation of that greater reality of God's coming kingdom, they cannot but wonder about the futility of their own efforts in view of the overwhelming structures of evil and suffering in our world. And unless

Christians know that it is their task to establish nothing but beachheads of the kingdom of God in this world, then not only the sheer magnitude of the ethical task will suffocate them, but also their frequent inability to measure ethical progress will stifle them."

J. Christiaan Beker, *Paul's Apocalyptic Gospel: The Coming Triumph of God* (Philadelphia: Fortress, 1982), 86–87.

are good. We are not anarchists. Ours is not a God of chaos, but of peace (cf. 1 Cor 14:33). The Powers are fallen. We need to view all the Powers, even, perhaps especially, the Power of *our own religion*, with caution (see [Hermeneutics of Suspicion]). But—glory to God—the Powers are redeemable.

NOTES

[1] Marion L. Soards, *The Speeches in Acts: Their Content, Context, and Concerns* (Louisville KY: Westminster/John Knox, 1994), 117–18.

[2] Gerd Lüdemann, *Early Christianity according to the Traditions in Acts: A Commentary* (Minneapolis: Fortress, 1989), 251.

[3] Ben Witherington III, *The Acts of the Apostles: A Socio-Rhetorical Commentary* (Grand Rapids MI: Eerdmans, 1998), 702–703.

[4] Luke Timothy Johnson, *The Acts of the Apostles* (SacPag 5; Collegeville MN: Liturgical Press, 1992), 410.

[5] NRSV translates v. 2 as "When Paul had been summoned," stating in a footnote that the Greek literally reads "when he had been summoned." The narrator's Greek is not precise, as the antecedent of "he" is not clear. One could make the case, based on the "rules of Greek grammar," that Tertullus, who is actually named later in the verse, would be the one who was summoned. But literally that makes little sense, given that he was already before the governor.

[6] Witherington, *Acts*, 703.

[7] Ibid., 705.

[8] Johnson, *Acts*, 410 says that Roman courts actually used a water timer to limit the duration of presentations.

[9] Joseph A. Fitzmyer, *The Acts of the Apostles* (AB 31; New York: Doubleday, 1998), 732, argues that there were four charges against Paul: he was a pestilent presence, an agitator, a ringleader, and a profaner of the temple. Most commentators collapse Fitzmyer's first three charges into one.

[10] Ernst Haenchen, *The Acts of the Apostles: A Commentary* (Philadelphia: Westminster, 1971), 654. Cf. Fitzmyer, *Acts*, 734.

[11] Ibid., 735.

[12] C. K. Barrett, *Acts: A Shorter Commentary* (London: T&T Clark, 2002), 369.

[13] Robert W. Tannehill, *The Narrative Unity of Luke–Acts: A Literary Interpretation*, 2 vols. (Minneapolis: Fortress, 1990), 2.300. See also Beverly Roberts Gaventa, *Acts* (ANTC; Nashville: Abingdon, 2003), 328.

[14] Many commentators do just this; e.g., Haenchen, *Acts*, 655; C. K. Barrett, *Acts*, 2 vols. (ICC; Edinburgh: T&T Clark, 1994/1998), 2.1107–108; Lüdemann, *Early Christianity*, 249; Witherington, *Acts*, 712; Johnson, *Acts*, 413.

[15] So Barrett, *Acts*, 2.1109, following A. N. Sherwin-White, *Roman Society and Roman Law in the New Testament* (Oxford: Clarendon, 1963), 52–53.

[16] See Barrett, *Acts*, 2.1090. He translates the verse: "Felix adjourned [the hearing] since he had accurate knowledge of the Way. . . ."

[17] Barrett, *Acts: Shorter Commentary*, 371.

[18] So Fitzmyer, *Acts*, 741. Josephus recounts that when Albinus was to be succeeded by Gessius Florus, he released prisoners who were being held "on some trifling occasion" (*Antiquities* 20.215).

[19] *Naming the Powers: The Language of Power in the New Testament* (Minneapolis: Fortress, 1984); *Unmasking the Powers: The Invisible Forces That Determine Human Existence* (Minneapolis: Fortress, 1986); *Engaging the Powers: Discernment and Resistance in a World of Domination* (Minneapolis: Fortress, 1992).

[20] Ray Gingerich and Ted Grimsrud, eds., *Transforming the Powers: Peace, Justice, and the Domination System* (Minneapolis: Fortress, 2006).

[21] E.g., Wink, *Engaging the Powers*, 5.

[22] Walter Wink, "The New Worldview: Spirit at the Core of Everything," in *Transforming the Powers*, 18.

[23] Peter Berger, *The Sacred Canopy: Elements of a Sociological Theory of Religion* (New York: Anchor Books, 1967), esp. ch. 1.

[24] J. Christiaan Beker, *Paul's Apocalyptic Gospel: The Coming Triumph of God* (Philadelphia: Fortress, 1982), 86.

FESTUS, KING AGRIPPA, AND BERNICE ARRIVE IN CAESAREA

Acts 25:1-27

COMMENTARY

Acts 25 serves a transitional role. It continues Paul's legal dealings, though now with the new governor, Festus (24:27). Paul's appeal to Caesar prepares the narrative and the reader for the trip to Rome, to be narrated in Acts 27–28. The introduction of Agrippa and Bernice sets the stage for Paul's final and most comprehensive defense speech in Acts 26. Acts 25 itself falls into two major sections: Paul's hearing before Festus, culminating in his appeal to Caesar (vv. 1-12) and the introduction of Agrippa and Bernice, in the context of which Festus takes the opportunity to summarize his understanding of the case relating to Paul (vv. 13-27).

"I Appeal to Caesar," 25:1-12

Festus wastes no time in visiting Jerusalem, the center of religious and political life in the territory of his newly acquired office (v. 1). [Festus] The narrator offers no motive for the visit. Historically, it makes sense that Festus would seek to establish a relationship with the ruling elite of the Jews. Literarily, the visit allows the narrative to move forward, as the subject of Paul will again come up.

While in Jerusalem, the "chief priests and the leaders of the Jews," likely a reference to the Sanhedrin, give Festus "a report against Paul" (v. 2) (see [Sanhedrin]). Two years have passed (cf. 24:27); indeed, a new

---

Festus

Porcius Festus assumed the office of governor (or procurator) c. AD 60 and ruled until c. AD 62. According to Josephus, he made conscientious attempts to deal with anti-Roman insurgents, particularly the assassination squads, known as the *sicarii* (see [Sicarii]). "Now it was that Festus succeeded Felix as procurator, and made it his business to correct those that made disturbances in the country. So he caught the greatest part of the robbers, and destroyed a great many of them" (Josephus, *J. W.* 2.271; cf. *Ant.* 20.188).

chief priest has now come to power: Ishmael, who had been recently appointed by Agrippa II. Though two years have passed and a "new administration" has come to power, Paul is still a primary concern to the leadership. They offer the new governor an attempt to curry the favor (*charis*, v. 3) of the local, ruling elite, requesting that Festus transfer Paul to Jerusalem, presumably to allow them to handle this matter. In fact, they were actually planning to assassinate Paul en route (v. 3). Luke *the historian* can only infer this, with or without justification. Narrators of literature, however, can always discern the inner motives of their stories' characters.

Earlier, Jewish radicals with the support of some members of the Sanhedrin had plotted to assassinate Paul (cf. 23:12-15). The injustice of the Judean ruling body is again evident, for now it is the leaders themselves spearheading the plot. Paul will not find justice before the Sanhedrin.

Festus refuses to grant the Sanhedrin's request, stating that Paul would continue to be held in Caesarea, to which Festus would be returning soon (v. 4; see [Caesarea]). He does state that these authorities were free to travel and to bring accusations against Paul there (v. 5). Luke has used the term translated as "accuse" several times in Acts, all in contexts implying formal, legal charges (22:30; 24:2, 8, 13, 19). Festus implies that he is open to further charges being brought against Paul, though one wonders what new charges the authorities could offer, since Paul has been in prison for the past two years.

Festus remains in Jerusalem for several more days (v. 6), though the narrator offers no report of what transpired. Luke here speaks of Judean politics only as it affects Paul. The authorities do take Festus up on his offer, for the day after Festus returned, the governor holds a formal, legal hearing, taking his seat "on the tribunal" (Gk., *bēma*) and ordering Paul to appear before him. The *bēma* denoted the platform from which Roman authorities "would hear cases and dispense judgment"[1] (see 18:12, 16, 17). This is very much a formal hearing.

Luke describes Paul's accusers, whom he refers to as "the Jews . . . from Jerusalem," as "surrounding" Paul. The picture painted is that of Paul standing in the midst of an ominous circle of powerful people. These powerful people were "bringing [*katapherō*] many serious charges [*aitiōma*] against him" (v. 7). Again, Luke employs technical, legal terminology. However, Paul's accusers fail to prove their charges. Luke offers no details as to what the Judean authorities said, leaving readers to surmise that it was something of a rehashing of what they have already read.

Paul's reply in defense reinforces such an impression, as he emphatically claims that he has "in no way committed an offense against the law of the Jews, or against the temple, or against the emperor" (v. 8). Readers are familiar with such charges. The Jews of Asia had accused Paul of speaking against the law (21:28), charges with which Claudius Lysias was familiar (23:29). The charge of profaning the temple was also first made by Jews from Asia (21:28) and offered as a formal charge against Paul by Tertullus in Paul's trial before Felix (24:6). Paul was never specifically charged with crimes "against the emperor." Yet Tertullus's accusation that Paul was an "agitator among all the Jews" and a "ringleader of the sect of the Nazarenes" (24:5) clearly had political overtones. Thus, readers can conclude that the Jewish authorities offered a mere reiteration of well-worn accusations.

Festus's reaction is curious. While he refused to grant the Jews a favor by sending Paul to Jerusalem (vv. 3-4), he now asks Paul if he wants to go to Jerusalem to be tried before him on these charges (v. 9). All this was motivated by his desire "to do the Jews a favor" (*charis*). The text is ambiguous as to whether Paul would be tried in Jerusalem "before" Festus, in the sense that Festus would *preside* over the hearing, or whether Festus would simply be an *observer* to a trial that the Sanhedrin would conduct.

Commentators tend to lean toward the former, but one wonders what Festus could accomplish legally by moving the trial to Jerusalem. Perhaps, some suggest,[2] given that the charges were of such a religious and theological nature, Jerusalem would be a more appropriate setting. But if the charges were of a religious and theological nature, why would Festus be concerned to preside over or even observe such a trial? There appears to be no legally strategic reason to suggest a change of venue. Hence, the narrator's claim that Festus made the suggestion in order to do the Jews a favor may be the most reasonable explanation.

Festus refused to grant the favor of the Sanhedrin's initial request—that the case simply be transferred to their jurisdiction (vv. 3-4). But he was willing at least to allow the trial to be conducted on their turf. This would, perhaps, placate the aristocratic leadership with whom Festus would have to maintain good relations, while, at the same time, ensuring that Paul's fate would remain firmly in Roman hands. Candidly, the narrative leaves many gaps here for the reader to fill.

Regardless of how one interprets Festus's motives, within the flow of the narrative the governor's suggestion prompts Paul to make his appeal to Caesar. Making such an appeal propels the plot toward its inevitable goal: Paul would see and bear witness in Rome (19:21; 23:11).

Though Festus seemingly leaves the decision to Paul, one suspects that offers from a Roman governor are not really suggestions or offers, but indirect statements of what is to be. In effect, Festus has said to Paul, "I think it best that we transfer the venue of this trial to Jerusalem. You do agree, don't you, Paul?" Paul does not agree.

Paul has no desire to have his destiny determined in Jerusalem where the Sanhedrin could likely wield more influence. In addition, even if Paul is not aware of the latest plot against his life, he surely has not forgotten (and readers should not either!) the earlier attempt to take his life. Going to Jerusalem is out of the question for Paul.

Beyond this, Paul might think that it would not be in his best interest to press the governor to continue the case in Caesarea, which could possibly result in his acquittal, given that Paul realized that the charges against him were unfounded. As C. K. Barrett states, "Paul had as much to fear from acquittal as condemnation. Released from custody in Caesarea with no Roman soldiery at hand to protect him he would have been an easy victim to the assassin's knife."[3] Finally, Paul is aware, as are readers, that he is to see and witness in Rome. Appeal to Caesar could ensure safe passage to his divinely appointed destination. Thus, for any number of reasons, Paul declines Festus's "offer" and appeals to the emperor.

The Lukan Paul makes his appeal with tactful bravado, making clear his own assessment of the matter, but in such a manner that he does not overstep appropriate boundaries. Paul begins by stating the fact that he is now standing before "the emperor's tribunal" (lit., "the *bēma* of Caesar"; v. 10a). What he means is that Festus, as the duly appointed representative of Rome, represents the power and authority of Rome. To stand before the *bēma* of Festus is to stand before the *bēma* of Caesar himself.

Paul declares that this is the appropriate venue for his trial (v. 10b), implying that no other venue, that is, the Sanhedrin, is appropriate. Paul has been charged with crimes against Rome—it is to Rome that he should answer. There is no good reason for him to be tried before any Jewish authority, for Paul has committed no crime against the Jews—a fact of which, Paul claims, Festus is well

Nero

Though Nero is not explicitly mentioned in Acts, this is the emperor to whom Paul would have been making his appeal. Nero came to power in AD 54. He was the last emperor from the actual family of Caesar (see [Caesar]). He committed suicide in AD 68. Nero is most remembered in the history of Christianity for persecuting Christians in the mid-60s, in part to deflect rumors that it was Nero who was responsible for the great fire of Rome in AD 64. At the time Paul made his appeal, Nero's assault on Christians had not yet begun. The New Testament does not offer details of Paul's death. He may have been executed after he had spent two years preaching in Rome, in which case Paul died prior to the outbreak of the Neronian persecution. Or Paul may have been released and subsequently rearrested in Rome, getting caught up in the persecutions of the mid-60s.

John F. Hall, "Nero," *EDB* 960; Marion L. Soards, "Paul," *MDB* 657–62.

(Credit: Wikipedia, "Head of Nero" [cited 17 September 2007]. Online: http://commons.wikimedia.org/wiki/Image:Nero_Glyptothek_Munich_321.jpg.)

aware (v. 10c). Paul concedes that if he is "in the wrong," that is, committed some act of injustice (*adikō*) for which he is worthy of the death penalty, he does not seek to evade such just punishment. Paul, in his boldness, stands in company with heroes of antiquity such as Socrates who refused to fear death, or those capable of imposing such a sentence upon him. [Socrates and the Fear of Death] Still, Paul appears confident that he is guilty of no capital crime and that Festus is aware of this, as well.

Paul reasserts that if there is no basis for the charges of the Jews against him, "no one [including Festus!] can turn me over to them." The word that the NRSV translates as "turn me over" is *charisasthai*. It shares the same stem as the word used twice in the passage, both times referring to the "favor" requested by (v. 3) and granted to (v. 9) the Jewish authorities. Luke Johnson captures the sense in his translation: "no one is able to deliver me to them as a favor."[4] It's a play on words discernable only to the reader, for only the reader is privy to the narrator's voice, and it is the narrator who has twice spoken of this "favor" to the authorities. Having stated his reasons, Paul appeals to the emperor. Paul does not claim his right to do so as a Roman citizen; readers are well aware of Paul's legal status.

Socrates and the Fear of Death

"For to fear death, men, is nothing other than to seem to be wise, but not to be so. For it is to seem to know what one does not know: no one knows whether death does not happen to be the greatest of all goods for the human being; but they fear it as though they know well that it is the greatest of evils" (Plato *Apol.* 29a; West, 35).

Paul's confident faith in resurrection would offer him even more reason than Socrates not to fear death, for, though Paul considered death a great evil, he considered the power of resurrection to be even greater (cf. Phil 1:23; Rom 8:38-39).

Thomas G. West, *Plato's Apology of Socrates: An Interpretation, with a New Translation* (Ithaca and London: Cornell University Press, 1979).

Appealing to Caesar

Historically, evidence indicates that the right of Roman citizens to appeal to the Emperor was absolute. Witherington's quotation of Paulus, *Sent.* 5.26.1, is self-explanatory:

> Anyone invested with authority who puts to death or orders to be put to death, tortures, scourges, condemns, or directs a Roman citizen who first appealed to the people, and now has appealed to the Emperor, to be placed in chains, shall be condemned under the Lex Julia relating to public violence. The punishment of his crime is death, where the parties are of inferior station; deportation to an island where they are of superior station.

Given this, it would seem that, historically, Festus had no option but to grant Paul's appeal. Readers should assume that a Roman-appointed procurator would have known this, leaving Festus's consultation with his council (25:12)

something of a mystery. Of course, one could argue that Festus was not really sure what the legal ramifications were, explaining why he sought counsel.

Modern readers should not anachronistically assume the contemporary situation of American jurisprudence, where the often-exorbitant costs of appeals are regularly assumed by the state, particularly for defendants who "cannot afford an attorney." In Roman jurisprudence, the defendant had to assume all costs of the appeal, including her or his own transportation to Rome. Talbert notes, "The appellant would personally have to undertake the costs of travel to Rome, the living expenses while there, and perhaps the costs of actually litigating the case, including securing witnesses" (210).

Ben Witherington III, *The Acts of the Apostles: A Socio-Rhetorical Commentary* (Grand Rapids MI: Eerdmans, 1998), 725; Charles H. Talbert, *Reading Acts: A Literary and Theological Commentary of the Acts of the Apostles* (New York: Crossroad, 1997).

Festus then confers with his council. These are Roman citizens who lived in the area: "military personnel and officials who attended the governor, among whom would likely be at least an expert in Roman . . . law."[5] Their role was advisory, and Luke does not report what their recommendation was. He reports only that Festus grants the appeal. On the literary level, the plot is prepared to move forward. The expectation raised by such texts as Acts 19:21 and 23:11, that Paul would see and bear witness in Rome, moves one step closer to fulfillment. On the historical level, commentators debate whether the governor was obliged to grant the appeal once made or whether, as the conferring with the council might imply, he was free to reject the appeal. More recent commentators lean in the direction that, once made by a Roman citizen, the request must be granted.[6] [Appealing to Caesar]

Meeting Agrippa and Bernice, 25:13-27

Readers now meet "Agrippa the king and Bernice," who have come to Caesarea to greet the new Roman ruler (v. 13). [Agrippa] The visit was prolonged, and one can assume the two rulers had much to talk about. Luke is only

Agrippa

Marcus Julius Agrippa was born in AD 27 or 28, the son of Agrippa I (referred to as King Herod in Acts 12). Upon the death of his father in AD 44, Rome thought it best, owing to Agrippa's adolescence, not to allow him to succeed his father, whose kingdom had expanded to the approximate size of that of Herod I (Herod the Great). At the age of 22 (c. AD 50), he was given the kingdom of Chalcis. Around the year 53, however, this was exchanged for the former territory of his great uncle Philip, the son of Herod (the territory to the northeast of Galilee). Later, perhaps around the mid-50s, he was given rule over limited areas of Galilee and Peraea. Agrippa also had appointive powers for the office of high priest. Though, as a Jew, Agrippa was sensitive to Jewish concerns, he was unswervingly loyal to Rome and attempted to intervene to stop the revolt against Rome that would erupt by the end of decade of the 60s, several years after the encounter with Paul about which Acts 25–26 speaks.

David C. Braund, "Agrippa," *ABD* 1.98–100.

interested in what was said about Paul. Verses 14b-21 offer what one must concede is totally a Lukan composition, since even the most credulous of Lukan interpreters can offer no plausible explanation for how Luke could have been privy to the private conversation of these two men.[7] Readers can understand the speech as Festus's interpretation of the situation Paul is facing.

In vv. 14b-15 Festus reports straightforwardly that Paul had been imprisoned under Felix and that, upon his initial visit to Jerusalem, the Judean leadership had made charges against Paul and asked for a judgment against him. Festus's summary could leave the impression that the Judean leaders had requested Festus to pass sentence right then and there—not that they actually requested that Paul be sent to them.

Festus's continued summary in v. 16 indicates, however, that the Sanhedrin did request that Paul be "handed over" to them. The Greek word is, again, *charizomai*, the same root as the word "favor" found in vv. 3 and 9. Though the irony is lost on Agrippa, readers are reminded that Festus was willing to "grant the Jews a favor"—a fact that Festus never mentions to Agrippa. In fact, Festus portrays himself as behaving according to the best standards of Roman justice, flatly denying the Sanhedrin's request, all in the interest of proper jurisprudence.

Festus tells Agrippa that he told the Judean authorities that it would violate customary standards of Roman justice to hand Paul over, without the accused being able to face his accusers and answer their charges. Festus is quite right about Roman law here; the principle of *aequitas romana* (Roman fairness) was to be followed. [Ulpian on Roman Justice] Readers might note that the narrator did not report in vv. 4-5 that Festus made any explicit appeal to this Roman custom. However, as the narrator reported in v. 5, Festus did insist that the Jewish leaders must come to Caesarea to face the accused—an insistence that is, at least, consistent with the principle of Roman fairness.

Verse 17 offers a straightforward summary of what the narrator reported earlier in v. 6. Verses 18-19 leave the impression that the charges against Paul were exclusively of a *religious* nature—not the kinds "of crimes that I was expecting" (v. 18). The narrator had not explicitly reported what charges the Sanhedrin members made against Paul; the narrator states only that they could not prove their charges (v. 7). Hence, one cannot ade-

Ulpian on Roman Justice

Ulpian offers statements on matters of Roman jurisprudence that provide insight into some of the legal proceedings described in Acts 25. On the matter of Roman fairness (*aequitas romana*), to which Festus alludes in 25:16: "This is the law by which we abide: No one may be condemned in his absence, nor can equity tolerate that anyone be condemned without his case being heard" (Ulpian, *Digest* 48.17.1; cited from Fitzmyer, 750.) On the matter of the letter that Festus had to write in view of Paul's appeal (25:26): "After an appeal has been made, records must be provided by the one with whom the appeal has been filed to the person who will adjudicate the appeal" (Ulpian, *Digest* 49.6.1; cited from Fitzmyer, 748).

Joseph A. Fitzmyer, *The Acts of the Apostles* (AB 31; New York: Doubleday, 1998).

quately compare Festus's summary with what "actually happened," even in the world of the story. Paul's response of v. 8, stating that he did not commit any crimes against Caesar, does imply, however, that some type of political charges were brought. Festus's summary, therefore, is curious, unless readers keep in mind that the narrator, who could have no idea what Festus really said anyway, is using Festus's words to further the narrative's apologetic interests.

This is made apparent by the continued summary of v. 19. Here Festus reports that the charges had to do only with "certain points of disagreement . . . about their own religion." The word the NRSV translates as "religion" is *deisidaimonias*, which denotes literally reverence for divine beings (note the root of the word "demon"; originally, in the history of Greek thought, "demons" were "divine beings" and not necessarily malevolent spirits). The term could also carry the more pejorative connotation of "superstition" (cf. RSV; AV) when used in contexts implying a "reverence for divine beings" that bordered on irrational or excessive. Paul used precisely this ambiguous term in his opening address to the Athenians (17:23).

The narrator has chosen the word carefully for his character. Festus, as a Roman governor, might very well consider these matters "superstition." But he knows that he is speaking to a *Jewish* leader who would consider these matters to be of a legitimately *religious* nature. Festus can offer his own implicitly negative judgment on the whole matter without directly offending his guest.

But Festus adds another detail that should take the reader totally by surprise. He states that the charges concerned not only matters of "their own religion," but also matters about Jesus, a man who had died, but whom Paul claimed to be alive. There is no hint in the narrative above that the issue of the resurrection of Jesus had come up in the hearing before Festus—though readers might recall that in an earlier hearing before the Sanhedrin (more than two years previous!) the matter of resurrection *in general* did arise (23:6; cf. 24:21).

Perhaps readers can conclude that Festus is simply filling in a narrative gap. Even so, the fact that Festus raises the issue of Jesus' being alive allows this Roman official, even if unwittingly, to state what is at the heart of the matter: the disagreements between Paul (and others who believe in Jesus) and Jewish religious authorities do not have to do with Roman law or crimes against Rome. They have to do with matters of "their own religion" (Judaism) and, most especially, the issue of Jesus, whom Paul and other Christians claim is alive. The resurrection of Jesus will be a major issue in Paul's final defense speech of Acts 26, and the narrator has Festus set the stage for it.

In v. 20 Festus concedes that the charges against Paul are totally beyond the purview of his competence as a Roman governor. He admits that he is "at a loss" when it comes to making judgments about such matters. Such an acknowledgment reinforces the narrative's apologetic interest: "Paul and the Christians were guilty of no crime against the state."[8] It is this lack of expertise in matters of Jewish religion that Festus claims prompted his suggestion that the trial be continued in Jerusalem. Readers know that Festus was actually attempting to placate the Judean authorities—to do them a favor (v. 9). Festus puts the best spin on it that he can before Agrippa: it would make him appear vacillating and, perhaps, weak to admit that what prompted him was the desire to grant a favor to the Sanhedrin body.

Festus implies that Paul is at least partially responsible for the current situation, for it was Paul who appealed to the emperor (v. 21). The word actually used is *Sebastos*, the Greek rendering of Augustus. This was the name given to Octavian, the successor of Julius Caesar and, like "Caesar," had evolved into one of the many titles for the Roman emperor (see [Caesar]). Festus states that Paul actually "appealed to be kept in custody." These were not Paul's words, of course—Paul actually stated that he was appealing to the emperor since "no one can turn me over to them [the Judean authorities]" (v. 11)—a fairly bold slap at Festus. Again, it would diminish Festus in the eyes of his guest to admit that Paul's implied low assessment of Festus's dedication to justice was what motivated his prisoner to appeal to Caesar.

Perhaps Agrippa's request to hear Paul for himself (v. 22) is what Festus was hoping for. As readers will later learn, Festus is going to seek Agrippa's help in assessing the charges against Paul as he prepares his prisoner for his appeal to Rome. With a little empathy, readers can imagine the bind that Festus finds himself in. He is about to send to Rome a Roman citizen who, Festus must admit, is guilty of no crime against the empire. How will the governor justify this? Perhaps Agrippa can help.

Verse 23 sets an elaborate stage, describing the grand entrance of Agrippa and Bernice into the "audience hall." [Bernice] Attending the session, as well, are all the leading persons of the city. Note that this hearing is not before the *bēma*, but in the "audience hall" or "auditorium." The setting is almost surreal—why do all the leading military officers and residents of Caesarea need to be there? There is a sense that Paul's hearing is as much a form of entertainment for the idle aristocracy as a legal proceeding.

Bernice

Bernice was born about one year after her brother Agrippa (c. AD 28). Her younger sister, Drusilla, was married to Felix (24:24). Bernice had a short marriage to Marcus Julius Alexander. When he died she married her uncle Herod, king of Chalcis. He too did not live long, dying in AD 48, whereupon she took up residence with her brother Agrippa II. Rumors abounded as to the incestuous nature of their relationship. According to Josephus, Bernice married Polemo, king of Cilicia, primarily to silence the rumors. But this marriage did not last long either (*Ant.*

20.145–146). She then resumed her relationship with Agrippa, with whom she was living at the time that Paul appeared before the both of them in Acts 25–26. Bernice was not always loyal to the ethical demands of her Jewish religion, particularly in her sexual liaisons (she later had an affair with Titus, who eventually became emperor). But she did remain loyal to her people, intervening personally and at risk to her own life to procurator Gessius Florus on behalf of the Jews whom he was persecuting.

Douglas S. Huffman, "Bernice," *EDB* 167.

Yet it serves the narrative well, for it will allow Paul a large audience before which to offer his final defense speech. As Ernst Haenchen notes, this scene offers one more example of how the important message of Christianity is not presented "in a corner," as Paul will state in the speech to follow (cf. 26:26). The presence of such a grand audience allows Luke in this literary setting to raise Paul and the Christian message "above the hole-in-corner existence in which great things cannot come about."[9]

Festus prepares the scene for Paul by summarizing for his audience, and again for the reader, what this hearing is all about. In v. 24 he says that "the whole Jewish community" (*plēthos*) had made petition against Paul. The Greek word *plēthos* most often means multitude, often (though not always) followed by some qualifying noun to make clear what or who the multitude consists of: people (Luke 1:10; 23:27; Acts 5:14; 21:36), angels (Luke 2:13), fish (Luke 5:6), disciples (Luke 6:17; 19:37; Acts 6:2), residents of a region or city (Luke 8:37; Acts 5:16; 14:4), authorities (Luke 23:1), believers (Acts 4:32), worshipers (Acts 14:1), and even sticks (Acts 28:3).

Careful study of the narrator's use of *plēthos* is important, for here Festus identifies Paul's accusers as "the whole *plēthos* of the Jews." Some commentators argue that Festus here means the Judean authorities,[10] but it appears that Festus (and the narrator!) is casting the net of Paul's accusers much more widely. While Luke regularly distinguished the Jewish people from their leaders in the gospel narrative and the earlier chapters of Acts, the line has become increasingly blurred as the story progresses in Acts and "the Jews," as a group, take on a more consistent role as opposing the followers of Jesus (see [The Jews]).

Festus summarizes the accusations of "the multitude of the Jews" against Paul by saying that they claimed he did not deserve to live. The statement echoes the cry of the "multitude of the people" in Acts 21:36, which said "Away with him" and later explicitly said that Paul should not live (22:22). How Festus knows this is not the point. The narrator brings to his apologetic agenda the voice of the Roman governor: the whole of the Jewish community does not want this man to live and, as such, has brought charges against him.

The governor furthers the narrator's cause, explicitly declaring that he had found that Paul had done nothing deserving death (v. 25). The charges of "the multitude of the Jews" against Paul are totally unfounded. Nonetheless, Paul has appealed to the emperor, and Festus has decided to grant the appeal.

But Festus has a problem, as stated above. He has "nothing definite to write to our sovereign about" Paul (v. 26a). [Sovereign] Festus now makes explicit his reasons for granting Agrippa's request to hear Paul. He needs his assistance in knowing what to write to the emperor. It is a gross understatement when Festus says that it would be "unreasonable to send a prisoner without indicating the charges against him" (v. 27).

Readers may feel some sympathy for Festus, but just as likely they will find in Festus's dilemma a clear affirmation of Paul's innocence. Festus has a problem precisely because he is about to send to the emperor a man against whom he can find no legitimate charge. Luke never even reports that Festus wrote a letter, showing that Festus's bind is neither the narrator's nor the reader's problem. The governor's tenuous situation serves only one purpose in the narrative: to affirm the innocence of Paul and, implicitly, the Christians reading Luke's narrative.

Sovereign

AΩ The word NRSV translates in 25:26 as "sovereign" is actually "lord" (cf. RSV). Lord clearly is being used here as a title of the Roman emperor. Between the time of Augustus and until the rise of Claudius (AD 41–54), the title "lord" fell out of general usage (Johnson, 427). However, by the time of Nero (54–68), at which time the story of Acts 25 is set, the title was widely used, especially in the eastern provinces (Fitzmyer, 752)—Judea being one of these "eastern provinces."

Luke Timothy Johnson, *The Acts of the Apostles* (SacPag 5; Collegeville MN: Liturgical Press, 1992); Joseph A. Fitzmyer, *The Acts of the Apostles* (AB 31; New York: Doubleday, 1998).

CONNECTIONS

One of the underlying themes of the narrative of Acts is the way in which human choices integrate with the quiet movement of God's providence. To be sure, the narrator can portray God as intervening very obtrusively and directly to "move the story along." Most evident, of course, are Paul's call (Acts 9) and Peter's vision at Joppa (Acts 10). But God also works seemingly unobtrusively to move the world toward God's aims and intentions in human choices. [Human Freedom and Human Choice] This chapter offers a clear example of this. In fact, "God" is not even mentioned in Acts 25. Yet the reader can sense God's presence (see [Images of God]).

Human Freedom and Human Choice

The dynamic relationship between human freedom and human choice, particularly in the context of discussing God's providence, is complex. Just how much freedom do human beings have (see [**The Working of God**])? Can human beings make choices that could thwart the will and intention of God, or is it necessary that human beings must choose that which accords with God's purposes, aims, goals, and providential will?

Those who maintain that human freedom must conform to the will of God hold to what is often called "compatibilist freedom." According to John Sanders, compatibilists argue that "a person is free as long as she desires to do" such and such (p. 221). However, God can *determine* such *desires*, ensuring that one will freely choose what God desires her or him to choose, resulting in the fulfillment of God's providential will. In the case of Acts 25, Festus freely chose to offer Paul the option of having his trial continued in Jerusalem—an option he was willing to offer because he desired to do the Jews a favor (25:9). God, however, is behind the "desire." And Paul freely chose to appeal to the emperor because he desired not to have his case continued in Jerusalem and the appeal was his only option. But, here again, God's will determines Paul's desire.

"Libertarian freedom" asserts that human beings have freedom to choose what they desire, but that humans have power over their own desire *and* can also choose what they do not desire. Within the context of such freedom, God's providential will can still be perfectly "worked out," for God could have the power to "foresee" perfectly what choices people will make and, with such perfect foresight, shape and announce God's will for the future. In the case of Acts, God would perfectly foreknow what would transpire at Paul's trial and, based on such foreknowledge, know that Paul would appeal to Rome and that the appeal would be granted. On that basis, as well God's foreknowledge of all other events, God could inspire the prophecies that Paul would see and bear witness in Rome (19:21; 23:11), simply because *God knew what would happen*.

Certain "libertarians," however, offer more provocative views as they pertain to God's providence. These libertarians, known as "open theists," argue that God's omniscience does not include exhaustive knowledge of the future. According to open theists, God knows all that "is," but the future "is not yet." Hence, God knows only what will likely happen in the future, based on his exhaustive knowledge of "what is." Applied to Acts 25, and indeed the whole of biblical, as well as cosmic history, for that matter, the future is truly "open." Festus *could* have chosen to dismiss Paul's case or Paul *could* have chosen to allow the case to be transferred to Jerusalem. And God might not have expected these choices! Further, God would have to "respond" to these choices and adjust God's providential plans accordingly. According to this view of God, God's will is continually being worked out in the complex give and take of divine action and human response, as well as human action and divine response. God, according to this view, is truly relational with, responsive to, and risk-taking toward the creation.

John Sanders, *The God Who Risks: A Theology of Providence* (Downers Grove IL: InterVarsity Press, 1998), esp. 220–24.

In the context of this chapter, Paul makes the fateful decision to appeal his case to the Roman emperor. Commentators can speculate as to Paul's motives, and some even speculate that Paul was motivated because he saw such an appeal as a means to accomplish God's aim of getting Paul to Rome.[11] But Paul doesn't say this. And we can't forget that our narrator is not the least bit reticent to inform readers of characters' inner thoughts and motives. We know, for example, that Festus wanted to grant the Jews a favor (v. 9), not because of anything he said publicly, but only because the narrator told us. Hence, had the narrator wanted to make clear that Paul's motives were to move along in some deliberate way "God's plan" to get him to Rome, he could have told us that. He didn't.

Paul's stated motives are quite immediate and pragmatic. He does not feel that he will get a fair shake before Festus. Paul realizes that in offering him the "option" of being tried in Jerusalem, Festus was shirking his responsibility as Caesar's representative, passing the buck, so to speak (v. 11). Paul simply does not want to hand his destiny over to the Judean Sanhedrin. Justice will not be found there. So he pursues his best option among limited options. He chooses to appeal to Caesar, knowing that in doing so he had the best chance to avoid having his case determined by the Sanhedrin or by a Roman governor who, for whatever reason, doesn't want to make the hard choices that justice demands.

But it is not only "men of God" who make choices that move the story toward God's aims and goals. Characters who have no interest at all in "God's will" also make choices that move the story in the direction God would have it to go. Festus clearly illustrates this. Festus chose not to grant the Judean leadership the "favor" it initially requested in v. 3: to transfer Paul to Jerusalem. Festus later explains to Agrippa that he was motivated by his duty not to "give up" an accused to his accusers *before* the accused had the opportunity to face those accusers and offer a defense (v. 16). Perhaps that was his real motive.

Regardless, he did choose not to deliver Paul to the Jerusalem Sanhedrin and thereby foiled yet another assassination attempt—an attempt that, had it proven successful, would have brought to an abrupt end God's desired aim that Paul bear witness in Rome. Clearly, Festus was not moved by any desire to be an instrument of accomplishing God's purposes. Yet he became just such an instrument.

The narrative leaves readers facing a gap as we try to discern why Festus, after Paul's hearing before him and the Judean authorities in Caesarea, decided now to grant the aristocracy "a favor" by suggesting a change of venue for Paul's trial (v. 9). Whatever his deeper motives, it was precisely this suggestion that prompted Paul to appeal to Caesar. Apparently the "change of venue" was now no longer a viable option for Festus.

The narrative leaves the impression that Festus had still one more choice to make. Verse 12 indicates that Festus consulted with his council, after which he chose to grant the appeal. As stated in the Commentary section, interpreters debate whether, historically, Festus really would have had any option but to grant the appeal. But, history aside, in the *narrative* world of Acts, Festus did have such a choice—why else consult with his council if it were out of his hands?

Perhaps Festus could have chosen to have dealt with the case then and there and dismissed the charges against Paul. The narrative makes clear that even Festus realized that the charges against Paul did not warrant Roman prosecution. The narrator, Paul, and Festus himself make this point a number of times (vv. 7, 11, 18, 25). In fact, Festus has actually put himself in a bind, for he doesn't even know what reason he will write in his report to the emperor as to why Paul is being transferred to Rome for the settlement of his case (vv. 26-27). But Festus, even knowing that the charges against Paul were unfounded, opted not to dismiss the case. Had he done so, Paul's most direct route to Rome to accomplish God's intended aim might not have been thwarted, but it certainly could have been frustrated. Paul would now have had to avoid his opponents, bent on his violent destruction, without the protection of Roman custody. And, assuming he would have survived this, he would, in order to reach Rome, have had to make his own arrangements.

But as the chapter comes to an end, none of this will be necessary. Choices that Paul made in his own best interests of seeking justice combine with choices that Festus makes, for any number of convoluted reasons, to press the story forward to God's intended aim: Paul *will* be sent on to Rome where he will have the opportunity to bear witness to the gospel.

NOTES

[1] Luke Timothy Johnson, *The Acts of the Apostles* (SacPag 5; Collegeville MN: Liturgical Press, 1992), 420.

[2] E.g., Joseph A. Fitzmyer, *The Acts of the Apostles* (AB 31; New York: Doubleday, 1998), 744; C. K. Barrett, *Acts: A Shorter Commentary* (London: T&T Clark, 2002), 376–77.

[3] Barrett, *Acts: Shorter Commentary*, 375.

[4] Johnson, *Acts*, 418. See also his comment on p. 421.

[5] Ben Witherington III, *The Acts of the Apostles: A Socio-Rhetorical Commentary* (Grand Rapids MI: Eerdmans, 1998), 723.

[6] C. K. Barrett, *Acts*, 2 vols. (ICC; Edinburgh: T&T Clark, 1994/1998), 2.1131; Witherington, *Acts*, 723.

[7] Even Witherington, *Acts*, 728 concedes that here "Luke followed the historical convention of making the persons say what they were likely to have said on the occasion."

[8] John B. Polhill, *Acts* (NAC 26; Nashville: Broadman, 1992), 494.

[9] Ernst Haenchen, *The Acts of the Apostles: A Commentary* (Philadelphia: Westminster, 1971), 679.

[10] Johnson, *Acts*, 427.

[11] See Beverly Roberts Gaventa, *Acts* (ANTC; Nashville: Abingdon, 2003), 335; Witherington, *Acts*, 725–26.

PAUL'S FINAL DEFENSE

Acts 26:1-32

COMMENTARY

The entire chapter is devoted to Paul's final "defense" speech and reaction to it. Given the setting, a hearing before government officials, one might initially expect Paul to offer a *judicial* speech (see [Types of Rhetorical Persuasion]). But the speech moves quickly to a different type of defense. Paul's speech is not really a defense against legal charges made against him. Such charges, for all practical purposes, have been dealt with in previous speeches and declarations by governing officials. This is a testimony of the gospel—a defense of the gospel message itself before an august audience that represents "the sophisticated Greek world."[1] It also involves Paul's defensive insistence, and implicitly Christianity's defense, that what he stood for did not transgress the hopes of Judaism.[2]

Commentators differ in their attempts to outline the chapter/speech. The following outline makes no claim to follow patterns of strict standards of Hellenistic rhetoric.[3] It is more functional in scope. Verses 1-11 offer an introduction to the speech and lay forth Paul's credentials. Paul's conversion and call are the focus of vv. 12-18. This is followed directly by Paul's testimony of his faithfulness to his call (vv. 19-23). The speech and chapter conclude with Paul's appeal to his audience and their response (vv. 24-32).

"The Jews Know My Way of Life," 26:1-11

Agrippa is clearly in charge, as it is he who gives Paul permission to speak (v. 1). Employing the typical rhetorical gesture of the outstretched hand (cf. 13:16; 19:33; 21:40), Paul proceeds. He introduces his speech with the customary *captatio benevolentiae*, a show of deference required by the standards of Greek rhetoric (v. 2). Paul speaks of how "fortunate" he is to be able to speak to Agrippa and to defend himself against the accusations the Jews have made against him. Actually, Paul will not devote much attention to specific charges; rather, he will present a more sweeping defense, demonstrating, initially, that he is a loyal Jew and, eventually, a faithful follower of Jesus.[4]

Part of the reason Paul considers himself fortunate is that Agrippa is familiar—even "expert," compared to Festus—with Jewish customs and controversies (v. 3). The narrator has never explicitly said that Agrippa was Jewish (cf. Josephus, *Ant.* 14.403, on the Herodian family as Jewish). Paul's assertion, however, that the king understands Jewish customs would imply that Agrippa's status as a Jew is assumed by author and reader alike. Paul concludes his rhetorical flattery by appealing to the king to listen to him "patiently." Tolerant patience was the ideal attribute of a good ruler (cf. Luke 18:7, which employs a cognate of the adverb used here).

Paul wastes no time defending his loyalty to his Jewish heritage. His zealous loyalty is well known to "all Jews" (v. 4). He has spent his entire life as a member of the Jewish community, which he identifies as "my own people." He also emphasizes his long-standing connection with Jerusalem (cf. Acts 22:3, where Paul speaks of being born in Tarsus, but brought up in Jerusalem). Paul speaks of his association with Pharisees, which he describes as "the strictest [*akribestatēn*] sect of our religion" (v. 5). Josephus employs a cognate of Greek word translated as "strictest" in his description of the Pharisees (*J. W.* 2.162). It is perhaps significant that Paul employs an aorist (past) tense verb, saying that he "*lived* as a Pharisee." Paul does, like the Pharisees of his time, hold to a belief in resurrection (cf. 23:6). But he no longer *lives* as a Pharisee (cf. Phil 3:5-8).

In vv. 6-8 Paul comes closest to actually addressing the "charges" for which he stands on trial. He claims that he stands where he does because he embraces the hope of his fellow Jews—a hope for the realization of the promises that God made "to our ancestors" (v. 6). It is a hope for which his people long and "worship night and day" (v. 7). [Eighteen Benedictions] "For this *Jewish* hope I am being accused *by Jews*," is how C. K. Barrett paraphrases the last line of v. 7.[5] Paul has not mentioned Jesus, and he will not mention "resurrection" until the next verse, but readers know that the hope of which Paul speaks is the resurrection. And readers know that, for Paul, that hope is finding present fulfillment in that God has raised Jesus from the dead.

The hope of resurrection for Jews meant far more than the hope of an individual afterlife (though it included that). Resurrection had become an inclusive symbol of the hope of liberation from all

Eighteen Benedictions

The so-called *Eighteen Benedictions*, known in Hebrew as *Shemoneh Esre*, refer to the formal prayer or blessings offered by Jews in worship. The modern version is not identical to ancient versions. However, scholars believe that some version of the prayers reaches back to the Second Temple period. To be sure, "one should not . . . speak of an original early version of the eighteen benedictions at the start. There was a variety of versions, which were elaborated in various circles and gradually took on a fixed structure . . ." (Safrai, 925).

Though one cannot know the precise wording of the ancient benedictions, a tentative reconstruction of these prayers is possible. The following selections from the Eighteen Benedictions offer a feel for the longing for liberation for which, Paul says in Acts 26:7, the Jewish people "earnestly worship day and night."

Benediction 7: Look upon our affliction and plead our cause, and redeem us speedily for thy name's sake; for thou art a mighty redeemer. Blessed art thou, O Lord, the Redeemer of Israel.

Benediction 10: Sound the great horn for our freedom; lift up the ensign to gather our exiles, and gather us from the four corners of the earth. . . .

S. Safrai, "The Synagogue," in *The Jewish People in the First Century: Historical Geography, Political History, Social, Cultural and Religious Life and Institutions*, 2 vols., ed. S. Safrai and M. Stern (Philadelphia: Fortress, 1974/1975), 2.908–44; quotations from C. K. Barrett, ed., *The New Testament Background: Writings from Ancient Greece and the Roman Empire That Illuminate Christian Origins*, rev. ed. (New York: HarperSanFrancisco, 1989).

---

that oppressed God's people (see [Restoration Eschatology] and [Resurrection of the Dead]). With such liberation, "we [Jews], being rescued from the hands of our enemies, might serve [God] without fear" (Luke 1:74). Paul asks incredulously why "any of you" (plural) think it incredible (lit., "unbelievable") that God raises the dead (v. 8).

The question seems out of place, given Paul's audience in the story—a Roman governor and the leading citizens of Caesarea, most, if not all, of whom would be Gentiles. It seems odd that he would think it incredible that such folk would not hold to the *Jewish* hope of resurrection—and *liberation*. Johnson, who takes the audience to be Gentiles, interprets it as a rhetorical question.[6] Polhill posits that there would have been, in addition to Agrippa and Bernice, some Jews among the audience and Paul addresses the question to these.[7] Fitzmyer regularly keeps in mind that Paul's speeches are *Lukan* compositions and suggests that the statement is addressed rhetorically to the Jews of Luke's time.[8] Luke's *Christian readers* need reminding that their faith in the resurrection of Jesus represents the fulfillment of the hopes of Israel, whether the Jews in the surrounding culture find it incredible or not.

Witherington sees Paul's discussion of Jewish resurrection hope as something of a digression that foreshadows the more explicit talk of Jesus' resurrection presented in vv. 22-23.[9] But it need not be viewed that way. Paul is establishing his credentials as a faithful and even zealous Jew in these opening sentences. His affirmation that he shares the same hope of his fellow Jews for the fulfillment of the promises that God made to their ancestors contributes significantly to his particular defense.

In vv. 9-11 Paul will continue to present his "credentials" as he speaks of his zeal—a zeal that led him "to do many things against the name of Jesus of Nazareth" (v. 9). The many things Paul did against the name were actually directed at the followers of Jesus, allowing the conclusion that "the name" stands here as a synonym for the disciples of Jesus, the church. Paul rehearses activities with which the reader is already familiar. However, readers learn some details that are either new or greatly amplify earlier accounts (see [The Accounts of Paul's Conversion]).

By the authority of the chief priests Paul shut many Jerusalem saints up in prison (v. 10a). This information is not new. Acts 8:3 and 22:4 state that Paul rounded up Jerusalem saints and put them in prison.

Paul indicates that a number of these saints were put to death and that he cast his vote against them (v. 10b). Acts 8:1 introduces Paul (Saul) by saying only that Paul consented to the death of Stephen—not that he had any direct role in it or cast a vote to authorize it. In Acts 22:4 Paul speaks of persecuting followers of the Way to the point of death, but explicitly defines such persecution as binding and imprisoning. Clearly if readers take Paul at face value here, he has more blood on his hands than one would have assumed. Some commentators suggest that Paul's reference to "casting his pebble," a literal rendering of the Greek, implies that he was an ordained rabbi who participated in formal, legal proceedings against the saints[10] or, at least, had some official duties associated with the Sanhedrin.[11] It could be a vivid metaphor, indicating that Paul was "on board" and approved of the deaths of disciples.[12]

Paul speaks of punishing disciples in "all the synagogues," trying "to make them blaspheme" (v. 11). The punishment might very well refer to the imposition of the thirty-nine lashes[13] and the blasphemy would, of course, not be an attempt to make them blaspheme the God of Israel, but to renounce Jesus the Messiah. [Pliny and Blasphemy] This is new information; however, it is not inconsistent with the zealous temperament of Paul before he became a follower of Jesus.

In v. 11b Paul speaks of pursuing disciples "even to foreign cities." To this point readers have known only of Paul's authorization to journey to the foreign city of

Pliny and Blasphemy

"Real" Christians do not, indeed cannot, "blaspheme" against or curse Christ. Paul asserts as much in 1 Cor 12:3. The Roman governor Pliny, writing to Emperor Trajan in the early second century, said the same thing. In attempting to discern whether one accused of being a Christian really was or not, Trajan would subject the accused to certain "litmus tests." If one offered "an invocation to the Gods, and offered adoration . . . to your image, . . . and who finally cursed Christ—none of which acts, it is said, those who are really Christians can be found performing," Pliny concluded that such a person was not a Christian and let her or him go (Pliny, *Epistles*, 10.96).

Damascus to round up Christians—a mission that was unsuccessful, due to the abrupt interruption of the Lord.

The expanded details are not inconsistent with the kind of person Paul was before he met the Lord. It is curious, however, that Luke, whether we view him as a good historian or primarily as a creative author striving for historical verisimilitude, would have passed over the fact that Paul had more actively participated in the *deaths* of disciples and had pursued them to foreign cities other than Damascus. One can only conclude that the addition of new details did not bother the author—whatever reason one may put forth for his lack of concern. In this context, the details of Paul's speech have an important rhetorical effect. They make vividly clear Paul's zeal for and loyalty to (as misdirected as it often was) his Jewish heritage.

Appointed to "Open Their Eyes," 26:12-18

Verses 12-18 offer yet a third account of Paul's conversion and call. The narrator offered his rendition of Paul's experience on the Damascus road in Acts 9:1-9. Paul recounted his version of events in Acts 22:6-11. Both Acts 9 and 22 speak of the important role of Ananias (9:10-19; 22:12-16). In both earlier accounts it was actually Ananias who conveyed to Paul the specifics of his call. But Ananias disappears from Paul's telling of his experience in this speech.

The removal of Ananias will require Paul to attribute *directly* to Jesus the call to which he has been appointed. Further, as with Paul's narration of his persecution of the church in the immediately preceding verses, the details of this call will be expanded. Readers will not learn, however, anything that is inconsistent with what they have witnessed Paul's call to be as they have already read about Paul.

Readers should allow Paul's words to have their full rhetorical effect. Paul is recounting in this speech his *memory* of this most decisive experience. And memory is always a blend of "fact" and "interpretation." Perhaps Jesus did not, in so many words, "say" to Paul everything recounted here. But through the voice of Ananias and the word that came from experience, Jesus did "call" Paul to the mission of which he speaks in these verses.

Verses 12-14 are very consistent with details of the previous narratives of Paul's call. Verse 12 speaks of his journey to Damascus under authorization of the high priests. Acts 9:1 and 22:5 speak of a singular high priest, though 22:5 speaks also of "the whole council of elders." "High" or "chief priests" could be employed to denote the priestly representatives of these Sanhedrin officials (see [High Priest]). Verse 13 speaks of the midday vision, brighter than the sun (cf. 9:3; 22:6), and v. 14 recounts Paul's falling to the ground and his hearing a voice, calling him by name and asking why Saul is persecuting him (cf. 9:4; 22:7). Verse 14b adds a detail, as the voice declares to Saul that it hurts to kick against the goads.

The goad, like a cattle prod, served to goad, prod, or spur one in a certain direction. The implication is that God had other plans for Paul and Paul was only hurting himself to be resisting these by persecuting the very ones whose ranks God fully intended Paul to join. Commentators regularly point out that the expression was proverbial and it "always has the meaning of resisting one's destiny or fighting the will of the gods. . . . [Paul] was fighting the will of God. . . . It was a futile, senseless task."[14]

In vv. 15-18 Paul speaks in detail of his call. It is here, as stated above, that the specific details vary most from earlier accounts. Whether one views this as a paraphrase of an actual speech, the words of a character who exists only as a narrator's creation, or something in between, readers should keep in mind that the Paul who stands before both the Caesarean assembly *and the readers* has had years to reflect on the significance of this Damascus road experience. What Paul's audiences hear is what this experience has come to mean to him and his life.

Verse 15 adds nothing new (cf. 9:5; 22:8). The call for Paul to stand on his feet (v. 16a), though echoed in the other accounts (cf. 9:6a; 22:10b), takes on added meaning in the context of this telling of the call experience, for Paul's call is replete with allusions to and echoes of language from the prophets. [The Prophetic Character of Paul's Call] Paul's call is to offer a prophetic word. Verse 16b indicates that Jesus has appeared to Paul for a specific purpose, namely to appoint him to a number of very specific tasks, tasks that are fleshed out in one long Greek sentence, extending to the end of v. 18. (The NRSV breaks Jesus' words into two sentences. One can consult the RSV for an English rendering as one sentence.)

Paul is appointed, first, "as a servant and witness" (NIV, which offers a more literal rendering here of the Greek) of what he has and would see: the things in which the Lord has appeared and would appear again to Paul. Paul, in hindsight, can "remember" the call of Jesus this way for, indeed, the Lord would again appear to Saul (cf. 16:9; 18:9; 22:17-21; 23:11). As a servant and witness of things seen, the words "serve" and "witness" loosely hark back to the Lukan prologue, where Luke speaks of those who are

---

The Prophetic Character of Paul's Call

This account of Paul's call contains many allusions to God's encounters with prophets, couching the language of Paul's call in a prophetic mantle.

Paul's Call	Prophetic Echoes
Get up and stand on your feet (26:16a)	O mortal, stand up on your feet. … A spirit entered into me and set me on my feet (Ezek 2:1-2)
I will rescue from your people and from the Gentiles—to whom I am sending you (26:17a)	Do not say, "I am only a boy;" for you shall go to all to whom I send you, and you shall speak whatever I command you. Do not be afraid of them, for I am with you to deliver you (Jer 1:7-8)
To open their eyes (26:18a)	To open the eyes that are blind (Isa 42:7a)
So that they may turn from darkness to light (26:18b)	I have given you as a covenant to the people, a light to the nations (Isa 42:6b)

Echoes of prophetic language not only associate Paul with the prophets, but specifically associate Paul with the servant of Isa 42. Earlier in Acts Paul identifies himself with this servant (Acts 13:47, cf. Isa 49:6). The fact that twice Paul is associated with the servant of Isaiah does not mean that Luke (or Paul) saw Paul as the one who fulfilled exclusively this prophetic text. Later in Acts 26 Paul says that it is the Lord who proclaims light to the people and Gentiles (v. 23). But the text does illustrate how the narrative can portray Paul as the distinctive human servant to fulfill the role of the ultimate Servant who brings the light of salvation to people.

"eyewitnesses" (though a different Greek root is employed) and "servants of the word" (Luke 1:2). Implicitly, Paul is included among these "witnesses" who serve as the source of "the events that have been fulfilled among us" (Luke 1:1).

The call of the Lord also includes a promise of future deliverance from both Jews (the people) and the Gentiles (v. 17a). Again, Paul can legitimately remember the call experience this way for the protective presence of the Lord regularly accompanied him in his work (cf. 16:35-40; 18:2-16; 19:23-41; 20:3). Verse 17b states what initially Ananias had told Paul, namely that his mission would be to both Jews and Gentiles (cf. 9:15; 22:15).

The call of Jesus includes the opening of blind eyes so that his hearers "may turn from darkness to light and from the power of Satan to God" (v. 18a). The language employed is that of dualism, quite reminiscent of the language of Qumran. [Dualism] The clear implication is that apart from the liberating word of the gospel, people are blind, trapped in darkness and the grip of Satan (cf. Luke 13:16 for a powerful visual image of the binding power of Satan). To experience light, one however must "turn" or repent (*epistrepsai*), a word that gets much play in the Lukan narrative.[15] Paul will be an instrument or vessel of the Lord (cf. 9:15) to bring the healing light to people. The theme of bringing light to blind

Dualism

Statements from the Qumran scrolls offer contemporary readers a good sense of the "dualistic" perspective that shaped much of first-century Jewish thought. The covenanters of Qumran are exhorted to

love all the sons of light, each according to his lot in God's design, and hate all the sons of darkness, each according to his guilt in God's vengeance" (1 QS 1:9-10).

For the M[aster. The Rule of] War on the unleashing of the attack of the sons of light against the company of the sons of darkness, the army of Belial (1 QM 1:1).

Note that the last quotation associates those of darkness with the personified force, Belial. Other texts from Qumran associate the power of darkness with a personification. For example, 1 QS 1:18, 23 and 2:19 make reference to "the dominion of Belial." This is not unlike what one sees in Acts, where the power of darkness is associated with the personified Satan.

eyes echoes Jesus' own interpretation of his call in Luke 4:18, which itself contains an intertext with Isaiah 61:1 (LXX only).

The good result of repentance from darkness to light is the liberating gift of "forgiveness of sins" (v. 18b). The word generally translated as "forgiveness" (*aphesis*) has as its root meaning "release." Release from sins is the most concrete form of liberation that the gospel message offers, and the Lukan narrative never tires of saying it.[16] But it is not only forgiveness that the Lord offers through Paul, but also "a place among those who are sanctified by faith in me" (v. 18b). The word translated as "place" is *klēron*, regularly translated as "share" (Acts 1:17; 8:21; cf. Col 1:12). Acts 20:32 employs a cognate of the word to mean "inheritance," where Paul says to the Ephesian elders that God would give them "an inheritance among all who are sanctified." It is, however, not just the church leaders, as in Ephesus, who have a place, share, or inheritance among the saints, but *all* who believe in the Lord, as Paul's final words of v. 18 make clear.

The echoes of prophetic language, the association of Paul with the witnesses and servants, and the mission of offering light and "release" (forgiveness) associates Paul with the prophets, the apostolic witness, and Jesus, respectively. Such important associations are clear to Paul in hindsight and, at this important juncture in the narrative—Paul's final speech—are made clear to readers, as well.

"I Was Not Disobedient to the Vision," 26:19-23

Paul declares that he was faithful to the vision that he had received (v. 19). He proclaimed the message of repentance and forgiveness in Damascus (cf. 9:19b-22). He also preached in Jerusalem, which Acts implies Paul visited shortly after he left Damascus (cf. 9:28-29; see [Acts and Galatians]). Paul's claim to have preached throughout Judea (v. 20) has no explicit record in the narrative of Acts, though Acts 15:3-4 could imply such preaching.[17] Paul's preaching among the Gentiles is well documented throughout Acts. Paul's message to the Gentiles was that "they should repent and turn to God" (cf. esp. 14:15). It was required that they have a "change of mind" (*metanoein*) with respect to their adoration of idols and false gods and turn toward (*epistrephein*) the true and living God. Following such a change of mind and direction they were to "do deeds consistent with repentance." In point of fact, Paul did not explicitly press the doing of deeds in his preaching. But the phrase offers, at least for readers, an echo of the message of John the Baptist (Luke 3:8), as well as the exhortation offered to Gentile believers in James's letter (15:29). And "Luke does describe actions that illustrate repentance just following incidents of conversion (e.g., Acts 2:41-47; 4:4, 32-27)."[18]

Paul then declares that it was "for this reason that Jews seized [him] in the temple" (v. 21). Clearly, interpretation is in play here. A review of Acts 21 reveals that Jews did not seize Paul in the temple because they thought he was encouraging Gentiles to turn to God. However, the Lukan narrative pattern had made clear that Jewish "zeal" or "jealousy" often prompted Jews to oppose Paul when it became apparent that Gentiles were responding favorably to the gospel (cf. 13:44-45, 48-50; 14:1-2, 19; 17:4-5, 13; 18:1-17).

Paul's inclusive gospel resulted in a caricature of Paul's mission reaching the Jerusalem church, claiming that he was actually attempting to persuade Jews to turn from the law and the temple (21:21). It was this misunderstanding of Paul's mission that contributed to the frenzy that led to Paul's being attacked in the Jerusalem temple, supposedly for bringing a Gentile into the inner courts. Yet Paul, standing here before Agrippa, does not offer such a nuanced interpretation of the incident that has led to his incarceration. In Paul's view, a view perhaps intended to persuade the reader more than Agrippa, the ultimate cause of his arrest, imprisonment, and seemingly countless hearings was his faithful preaching of the gospel of inclusion.

Even as Paul stands before Agrippa he presents another offering of his inclusive gospel, "testifying to both small and great" (v. 22). Paul's gospel crosses ethnic, as well as economic and cultural divides. Paul summarizes the essence of this gospel in vv. 22b-23. First, he insists that the message he preaches finds its grounding in "what the prophets and Moses said would take place" (v. 22b). This claim continues a persistent Lukan theme, namely that the gospel of Jesus is not a "new religion," but the "fulfillment" of the faith of Abraham, Moses, David, the prophets, and the whole of Jewish

Scripture. This was what the resurrected Jesus emphasized in Luke's narrative (cf. Luke 24:25, 32, 44-45).

Central to the fulfillment of the prophets was the suffering and resurrection of Christ (v. 23a). Some commentators note that the *ei* (lit., "if") that introduces v. 23 implies that what follows is, in fact, a "matter of debate." Culy and Parsons render the verse as follows: "If the Christ was destined to suffer, [and] if he was the first to rise from the dead, [then], he would be eager to proclaim light to both the (Jewish) people and the Gentiles!"[19] As sure as Paul is that Christ's suffering and resurrection do, in fact, represent the fulfillment of Jewish scriptural hopes, the initial *ei* "may hint at the fact that what is being is said may possibly be denied."[20]

The suffering and resurrection of Jesus, however, are not ends in themselves. It is as the crucified and resurrected one that Jesus "would proclaim light" to both Jews and Gentiles (v. 23b). The proclamation of light echoes what Paul had said of his own commissioning by the Lord in v. 18, namely that Paul was to open blind eyes and turn people to light that they might receive forgiveness of sins. Here in v. 23 it is *Jesus*, the crucified and resurrected one, who proclaims light; in v. 18 it is Paul.

But that may well be the point: the means through which the resurrected one proclaims the liberating light to all is through those whom he has called to preach the gospel. Jesus' commission to the apostles in Luke 24 is that "repentance and forgiveness of sins is to be proclaimed in his [Jesus'] name to all nations" (Luke 24:47). The commission of Acts 1:8 to these same men makes explicit that it is *they* who will do the preaching. Human beings, such as Paul and the apostles who preceded him, are the ones through whom the risen Lord offers light and liberation to the nations. Even as Paul stands before Agrippa and Festus he is offering such liberating light.

"Do You Believe?" 26:24-32

Paul's speech is interrupted at this point by Festus (v. 24; cf. 2:37; 17:32; 22:22). The abrupt intrusion allows readers to conclude that Paul has made a crucial point—and indeed he has: he has just spoken of the crucifixion and resurrection of Jesus and the liberating light that the Resurrected One offers. The interruption betrays Festus's total incredulity, rooted in his being convinced that Paul is "out of his mind" (*mainē*; cf. "maniac"). It seems curious that Festus would attribute Paul's "madness" to his great learning. The Greek phrase is literally rendered as "many letters." While letters (*grammata*) can denote basic learning (such as one's ABCs), the phrase was also often used to denote advanced education. [Higher Learning] Perhaps Festus is being hyperbolic, claiming that Paul simply "is given to outlandish ideas because of his 'much learning.'"[21] Apparently, pejorative and prejudiced attitudes toward those who think about things too much and too deeply have been around for some time.

Paul's retort is quick and to the point (v. 25). He is not "out of his mind" at all; in fact, he speaks words of "truth" and "reasonableness" (NRSV, "sober truth"). Truthful sobriety was the ideal of Greek philosophy,[22] and Paul claims to stand in that same, respected tradition.

The attention of Paul and the reader is immediately turned back toward Agrippa in v. 26, as Paul refers to "the king." Paul again appeals to Agrippa's awareness of these issues of Jewish religion (cf. v. 3 above). His astute knowledge of such matters allows Paul to claim that he can speak freely to him. Surely none of these important matters of which Paul speaks has escaped the king's awareness. These things have happened quite publicly. [In a Corner] The gospel that Paul has proclaimed and proclaims even now has taken place "in time, in human history, and in world history."[23] Haenchen's comment is insightful, even if one does not share his total skepticism regarding the historicity of this scene. In this climactic speech of Acts, Paul is giving voice to the stance that Christians will assume vis-à-vis the world: they "are preparing themselves—Paul is the model!—to step out of their corner into the world of history and culture."[24]

Paul's direct appeal to Agrippa appears to offer a good rhetorical strategy, as he assumes—at least on the rhetorical level—the king's acumen in matters of Jewish faith. But now Paul cuts to the marrow, asking the king directly whether he believes the prophets—those whose message, Paul has just claimed, has found fulfillment in Jesus. Surely one so knowledgeable would believe the

Higher Learning

AΩ Reference to one's letters can refer to basic education. Plutarch speaks of the Persian practice of educating its young men in matters of justice "just as in our country they say that they [boys] are to learn to read and write [*grammata*]" (*Cyropaedeia* 1.2.6). Plato employs the word *grammata* in his *Apology* to denote one who is well read and informed (*Apology* 26D).

Paul's claim not to be mad but, rather, quite "sober" (*sōphrosynēs*), places him in company with good thinkers. Plato says that "soberness [*sōphrosynē*] is a kind of beautiful order" that allows one to be master of oneself: "The soul of a man within him has a better part and a worse part, and the expression self-mastery means the control of the worse by the rationally better part" (*Republic* 430E and 431A). Diogenes Laertius, in his life of Plato, lists among the Platonic virtues "temperance" (*sōphrosynē*): "Temperance causes mastery over desires, so that we are never enslaved by any pleasure, but lead an orderly life" (*Lives*, III.90–91).

In a Corner

AΩ One cannot say that the phrase "in a corner" was proverbial, but the phrase did convey the generally pejorative image of something done in seclusion and, hence, being of little value. Plutarch speaks of the "person who in private station . . . wished to run away from the midst of cities and quietly in some corner solve or quibble over syllogisms of philosophers" (*Moralia* 777B). In another essay he uses the phrase to denote trivial talk, such as "what A's and B's private conversation in a corner was about" (*Moralia* 516B).

Gorgias disparages the philosopher who, in old age "is bound to become unmanly through shunning the centres of marts of the city; . . . [H]e must cower down and spend the rest of his days whispering in a corner with three or four lads, and never utter anything free or high spirited" (*Gorgias* 485D). The Roman comic Terance finds "the corner" a good place to "sleep off a drunk" (*The Brothers*, Act 5, Scene 2 [section 780 in LCL]). What Paul has done has not "happened in a corner."

prophets. In fact, Paul answers the question he puts to Agrippa for him: "I know that you believe."

Readers can only infer Agrippa's motives for putting an end to this brief debate. Agrippa's response makes clear that he recognizes that Paul is pressing him to make a decision. The narrator does not allow readers to be privy to his facial expression or tone of voice. Perhaps Agrippa is conceding with some regret that "almost thou persuadest me to be a Christian" (KJV)—a rendering echoed in the old evangelistic hymn "Almost Persuaded." The King James translation renders the Greek phrase *en oligō* as "almost." Most commentators and modern translations render the phrase temporally as "so soon" or "so quickly."[25] Further, modern translations appear to render his response not as a concession that he has been "almost persuaded," but rather that Paul is premature to think that he can, in such short order, persuade him to be a Christian (cf. NIV and NRSV; see [Christians]).

Paul's reply in v. 29 seems to assume that Agrippa is not persuaded. But it is Paul's desire that he be! The Greek phrase that the NRSV renders as "I pray to God" contains a rare example of the optative mood (*euxaimēn*), which often expressed remote desires. In fact, the verb *euchomai* can mean "wish" or "want" (cf. KJV and RSV: "I would to God"). Paul could only hope, but apparently not very realistically, that all his listeners, whether the time taken is long or short, become as he is, absent his chains, of course. Readers may detect some irony in Paul's allusions to his chains. He has offered a summary of liberating gospel of Christ. It is a liberation that he claims he now experiences, in spite of his chains. The implication appears clear: those before whom Paul stands are bound in a manner far more perilous than he.

The hearing comes to an end, signaled by the standing of Agrippa. Festus, Bernice, and those sitting with them follow suit. They move offstage, but the omniscient narrator moves with them, allowing readers to hear their brief deliberations. Readers will not learn anything new, but prior conclusions will be reinforced. The whole group—a Jewish king and his wife, a Roman governor, and those from among the leading citizens of Caesarea (recall 25:23) who have exited with them—reaches the same, redundant conclusion: "This man is doing nothing to deserve death or imprisonment" (v. 31).

This is now the fifth time that readers have heard sanctioned, governing officials, both Jewish and Gentile, declare Paul's innocence (cf. 23:9, 29; 25:18-19, 25). However, like Jesus, also seen as guilty of no crime before both a Roman governor and a Herodian,

Jewish leader (cf. Luke 23:4, 14-15, 22), technical innocence is no guarantee of real justice. Paul will remain in Roman custody. Agrippa's concluding comment that, had Paul not appealed to Caesar, he could have been released (v. 32), ensures that Paul will continue to wear his chains.

One cannot know what meaning Luke intended his original readers to glean from this final speech and the reaction to it. But perhaps it offered a word of realistic encouragement. Christians of Luke's day can go forth with a clear conscience. What they preach is the fulfillment of an old and honorable faith as given expression in the Jewish Scriptures. And what they promote is in no way criminally subversive. Yet the message of the gospel threatens the established order. And like Jesus and Paul, as well as other heroes of Acts who suffered, they too need to be prepared to wear the chains. Protection will come from God (cf. v. 22), not the state.

CONNECTIONS

Acts 26 represents Paul's final, and perhaps most significant, speech. Joseph Fitzmyer calls it "a finely crafted discourse" and "the christological climax of Acts."[26] As such, Paul's final speech presents an excellent précis of the gospel to which Lukan readers are to bear witness.

The core of the gospel that Paul is appointed to proclaim is given expression in the culmination of the Lord's disclosure to Paul. The Lord is going to send Paul to both Jews and Gentiles "to open their eyes so that they may turn from darkness to light and from the power of Satan to God, so that they may receive forgiveness of sins and a place among those who are sanctified by faith in me" (v. 18). C. K. Barrett interprets the meaning of these words to imply "that men [sic] are held captive by Satan and are released by the Gospel to return to God their Creator."[27] Beverly Gaventa offers a similar understanding: "Transfer from the realm of Satan to that of God is central to Luke's understanding of salvation."[28] As a review of v. 18 makes clear, the metaphors of darkness and light represent these respective spheres of life, under Satan or under God.

The darkness from which people need the light of liberation comes in many forms. For Gentiles, it may be the darkness that pervades the life of one who does not acknowledge and worship the true and living God. The citizens of Lystra, who mistook Paul and Barnabas for Greek gods (14:11-17), and the philosophers of Athens, who represent the groping of humanity to find the unknown god for whom they are seeking (17:22-31), represent in the narrative of Acts some who live in darkness. Ironically, it is a darkness that is not illuminated by their interest in things religious.

The countless governing officials whom readers meet whose only concern, while looking to curry Roman favor, seems to be to maintain order, even at the expense of justice, also are gripped by a certain kind of darkness (16:20-24; 17:6-9; 18:12-17). Roman authorities with whom Paul has to deal in the final chapters of Acts, such as Lysias the tribune or the governors Felix and Festus, also fall into this category. The leaders, unlike the citizens of Lystra or the philosophers of Acts, do not strike us as being terribly concerned with religion, except insofar as religion disrupts the social order. Darkness grips all sorts of Gentiles, religious and irreligious alike.

But many Jews, too, are gripped by darkness. It is perhaps these blind guides whom Paul would understand best. He was once blinded by a kind of zeal that inspired him to pursue followers of Jesus, rounding them up, taking them to prison, and inflicting punishing blows to urge them to renounce what he considered to be a false and damaging faith. Paul knew the God of Abraham, Isaac, and Jacob. Paul knew the Scriptures. Paul knew the law, having sat at the feet of the great teacher Gamaliel (22:3). The Paul of the Epistles effectively sums up his credentials in texts such as Galatians 1:13-14 and Philippians 3:5-6.

Both of these texts speak of Paul's zeal—a zeal that led him to persecute the church. The opening lines of Paul's speech in Acts 26 vividly portray that zeal. Paul speaks in another of his letters of the zeal of his fellow Jews: "I can testify that they have a zeal for God, but it is not enlightened. For, being ignorant of the righteousness that comes from God, and seeking to establish their own, they have not submitted to God's righteousness" (Rom 10:2-3).

E. P. Sanders offers a provocative interpretation of this text. He argues that Paul is not saying that the Jews were attempting "to establish their own righteousness" in the sense of striving to earn a meritorious salvation. Rather, they sought a righteousness, a saving relationship with God, that was *exclusively* "their own," to the exclusion of others, that is, "the gentiles."[29] [Their Own Righteousness]

A zeal for God that excludes others is a zeal that blinds one to the reality that God is the God of all, who longs to have a relationship with all

Their Own Righteousness

"If God's righteousness is the righteousness which is by faith in Christ and which is available to Gentile as well as Jew, then the Jewish righteousness which was zealously sought is the righteousness available to the Jew *alone* on the basis of observing the law. 'Their own righteousness,' in other words, means 'that righteousness which the Jews alone are privileged to obtain' rather than 'self-righteousness which consists in individuals' presenting their merits as a claim upon God.'"

E. P. Sanders, *Paul, the Law, and the Jewish People* (Philadelphia: Fortress, 1983), 38, emphasis original.

people, not just some people. The light that stopped Paul in his tracks on the way to Damascus made that clear to him. The Lord who confronted Paul that day was the Resurrected One who "would proclaim light both to our people and the Gentiles" (26:23). And Paul was to be a primary instrument of that proclamation.

The offering of salvation to all people—Jews and Gentiles—lies at the heart of the Lukan gospel. Simeon's declaration in the temple, that the Christ child would be "a light for revelation to the Gentiles and for glory to your people Israel" (Luke 2:32), and the resurrected Jesus' commission to the apostles "that repentance and forgiveness of sins is to be proclaimed in his name to all nations" (Luke 24:47) bracket the narrative of Luke's Gospel.

It is *this* gospel—this universal gospel—that created for Paul so much resistance from his fellow Jews. The hope for which they worshiped night and day (26:6-7) was not a hope for just one people. It was a hope for all people. We can too easily miss this important point if we are deaf to its implications for us. To focus our attention on how the Jews "back then" did not understand the universal implications of their own hopes, while remaining blind to our own narrow exclusiveness, is to risk putting ourselves in the tenuous position of guarding "our own righteousness" to the exclusion of others. The gospel offers a message of salvation that pushes through barriers and boundaries, providing a liberating testimony "to both small and great" (26:22; see [Breaking through the Particularities]).

Some potentially provocative universal implications of the gospel message are explored in the next chapter. But the universal inclusiveness of the gospel of salvation does not mean for Luke that all will embrace such salvation. To be sure, Paul is sent to all—to Jews and Gentiles "to open their eyes" (v. 18a). But it is imperative that we not overlook the rest of the verse. Paul is sent to open eyes "so that they may turn from darkness to light and from the power of Satan to God, so that they may receive forgiveness of sins and a place among those who are sanctified by faith in me."

The universal, inclusive message of the gospel is a universal and inclusive *invitation* to accept the good news of salvation. But eventually all hearers of the gospel find themselves where Agrippa found himself, having to make a decision whether to believe (vv. 27-28). But belief is not mere acceptance of some dogmatic formula. Belief is to turn to and follow the God *as revealed in Jesus.*

As outlined in the Magnificat (Luke 1:46-55), and worked out through the Lukan narrative, salvation is concerned with a fundamental redefinition of human social interaction which has its basis

Responding to the Gospel

"What is the appropriate response to the good news of salvation? Luke addresses this question with an arsenal of possibilities—e.g., believe, be baptized, turn to God, listen, see, repent, and so on—but singles out no particular pattern of response as paradigmatic. God has acted graciously in Christ to bring salvation to all humanity. All humanity are called to welcome the good news, to respond with receptivity, and thus to share in that salvation not only as recipients but also as those who serve God's redemptive aim."

Joel Green. "'Salvation to the End of the Earth' (Acts 13:47): God as Saviour in the Acts of the Apostles," in *Witness to the Gospel: The Theology of Acts*, ed. I. Howard Marshall and David Peterson (Grand Rapids MI: Eerdmans, 1998), 83–106, esp. 105.

in the wide embrace of the graciousness of God. Salvation entails status inversion and the reversal of conventional values as God accepts those who have otherwise been rejected.[30]

To be sure, faith in the God who is revealed in Jesus offers one "a place among those sanctified by faith in [Jesus]" (v. 18c). But it doesn't end there. It includes not only being embraced by the saving mercy of God, but also acknowledging such mercy is extended to all. Our calling is to urge all to be embraced by it. It requires saying, with Paul, "I pray to God that not only you but also all who are listening to me today might become such as I am" (v. 29). [Responding to the Gospel]

NOTES

[1] Luke Timothy Johnson, *The Acts of the Apostles* (SacPag 5; Collegeville MN: Liturgical Press, 1992), 440.

[2] Ernst Haenchen, *The Acts of the Apostles: A Commentary* (Philadelphia: Westminster, 1971), 682; Joseph A. Fitzmyer, *The Acts of the Apostles* (AB 31; New York: Doubleday, 1998), 755.

[3] For such an outline see Ben Witherington III, *The Acts of the Apostles: A Socio-Rhetorical Commentary* (Grand Rapids MI: Eerdmans, 1998), 737.

[4] "Paul is establishing that he is and has been a sincere Jew who became and remains a witness for Christ" (Ibid., 738).

[5] C. K. Barrett, *Acts: A Shorter Commentary* (London: T&T Clark, 2002), 386.

[6] Johnson, *Acts*, 433.

[7] John B. Polhill, *Acts* (NAC 26; Nashville TN: Broadman, 1992), 499.

[8] Fitzmyer, *Acts*, 757.

[9] Witherington, *Acts*, 741.

[10] Barrett, *Acts: Short Commentary*, 387.

[11] Witherington, *Acts*, 742.

[12] Polhill, *Acts*, 501.

[13] Fitzmyer, *Acts*, 758.

[14] Polhill, Acts, 503. Cf. Johnson, *Acts*, 435; Fitzmyer, Acts, 758–59; Witherington, *Acts*, 743.

[15] Luke 1:16, 17; 2:39; 8:55; 17:4, 31; 22:32; Acts 3:19; 9:35, 40; 11:21; 14:15; 15:19, 36; 16:18; 26:18, 20; 28:27.

[16] Luke 1:77; 3:3; 5:20, 21, 23, 24; 7:47, 48, 49; 11:4; 17:3, 4; 24:47; Acts 2:38; 5:31; 10:43; 13:38; 26:18.

[17] Fitzmyer attributes the claim to "Lucan hyperbole" (*Acts*, 760).

[18] Beverly Roberts Gaventa, *Acts* (ANTC; Nashville: Abingdon, 2003), 345–46.

[19] Mikeal C. Parsons and Martin M. Culy, *Acts: A Handbook on the Greek Text* (Waco TX: Baylor University Press, 2003), 501.

[20] Barrett, *Acts: Shorter Commentary*, 390. Cf. Witherington: "The major function of *ei* is to signal what the essential proposition of propositions under dispute are" (*Acts*, 748).

[21] Witherington, *Acts*, 749.

[22] Ibid.

[23] Fitzmyer, *Acts*, 764.

[24] Haenchen, *Acts*, 692.

[25] Witherington acknowledges this but renders the phrase as "with so few arguments" (*Acts*, 751). Some commentators take the phrase to mean "so easily" (cf. Parsons and Culy, *Acts: Handbook*, 504).

[26] *Acts*, 754–55. Witherington offers similar assessments (*Acts*, 735).

[27] *Acts: Shorter Commentary*, 389.

[28] *Acts*, 345.

[29] *Paul, the Law, and the Jewish People* (Philadelphia: Fortress, 1983), 38.

[30] Joel B. Green, "'Salvation to the End of the Earth' (Acts 13:47): God as the Saviour in the Acts of the Apostles," in *Witness to the Gospel: The Theology of Acts*, ed. I. Howard Marshall and David Peterson (Grand Rapids MI: Eerdmans, 1998), 89.

"IT WAS DECIDED THAT WE SHOULD SAIL FOR ITALY"

Acts 27:1-44

COMMENTARY

After more than two years in captivity (24:27) and several chapters of narrative, Paul is finally setting out for Rome. Readers have expected such a journey in order to fulfill prophetic foreshadowings (19:21; 23:11). As is commonly the case in Acts, commentators cover the gamut of opinion concerning the historicity of the narrative. [History and Paul's Voyage] While not avoiding historical issues, the commentary will concentrate on the narrative *as story*.

The chapter does not divide easily or neatly into distinct sections, as the action flows smoothly over the course of the many days that Paul's ship was at sea, hopping from port to port until finally, after

---

History and Paul's Voyage

Unless one assumes either that Paul never actually went to Rome or, if he did, he went by land, then even the greatest skeptic must conclude that, at its core, the story of the sea voyage is historical. That is, Paul sailed to Rome.

As is regularly the case in the critical reading of Acts, views regarding the historicity of the narrative of Acts 27 vary almost as widely as the Mediterranean Sea itself. Lüdemann argues that the narrative "is a literary entity, the result of his reading to which Luke has added the person of Paul" (259). Verses 6-44 "probably have no point of reference in history. . . . In all probability Paul did not suffer any shipwreck before Malta on his last journey to Rome . . ." (260). Similar to the position of Lüdemann, at least with regard to historicity, is that of Dibelius, who argues that Luke took over a separate account of a sea voyage and ship-wreck and inserted Paul in various places (107).

Other interpreters argue that the account is essentially historical, rooted in the report and

memory of an eyewitness (Luke), though one may adopt this position and still concede that Luke employed stylized and popular literary devices to make the story as vivid as possible (Witherington, 755–56). Luke Johnson, in some measure, straddles the sea of opinion, granting Luke a very free and creative hand, while reminding readers that the employment of "fictional" literary techniques does not mean "that the events were created entirely out of the author's imagination" (457). Apparently, Johnson is affirming a voyage, a storm, and a ship-wreck—a historical event that Luke narrates with considerable literary artistry and freedom.

Gerd Lüdemann, *Early Christianity according to the Traditions in Acts: A Commentary* (Minneapolis: Fortress, 1989); Martin Dibelius, *Studies in the Acts of the Apostles* (Mifflintown PA: Sigler Press, 1999); Ben Witherington III, *The Acts of the Apostles: A Socio-Rhetorical Commentary* (Grand Rapids MI: Eerdmans, 1998); Luke Timothy Johnson, *The Acts of the Apostles* (SacPag 5; Collegeville MN: Liturgical Press, 1992).

having endured a terrible storm, the ship is beached. Paul is the primary character, and the narrator brings him to the fore on a number of occasions. It is around the scenes featuring Paul that one can outline the narrative.

In vv. 1-12 Paul foresees the danger lying ahead. Verses 13-26 feature Paul as offering encouragement to the people on the boat in the midst of the storm. Paul thwarts an attempted escape by some sailors in vv. 27-32, while in vv. 33-38 Paul urges people to take in nourishment in preparation for their escape from the soon-to-be-doomed ship. Finally, the centurion's desire to save Paul's life is an important feature of the last verses of the chapter (vv. 39-44). Readers will find that the narrative will be much easier to follow if they refer frequently to the map.

"I Can See Much Danger," 27:1-12

The first-person narrator, last encountered in 21:18, has returned to the story (v. 1), resuming once again the so-called "we sections" (see [We Passages]). Paul and some other prisoners are put under the command of a centurion named Julius, who belonged to the Augustan Cohort. The *Cohors la Augusta* was made up primarily of Syrian mercenaries and was stationed during the first century AD in Syria.[1] Though a centurion, it is not likely that a full contingent of 100 soldiers would have been required, even though there were

Paul's Voyage to Rome

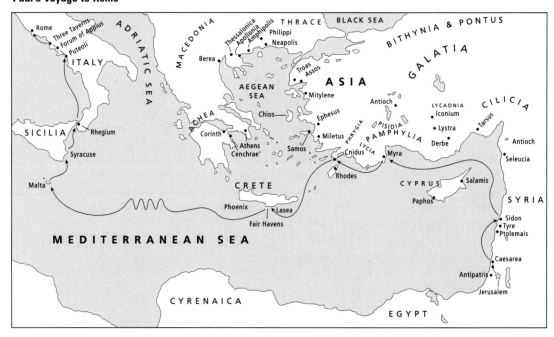

more prisoners than Paul on board (cf. v. 37). Though the *narrator* is not interested in this feature of the story, *readers* may presume that Julius would have been carrying *Festus's* letter explaining the reasons that Paul was appearing before the emperor. The ship should not be thought of as a special vessel whose sole purpose was the transport of prisoners. Rome did not have such ships.[2] Rather, the centurion would have secured passage on a private vessel, heading west, likely a cargo ship (see [Sea Travel]).

The destination of this particular ship was Adramyttium (v. 2), situated on the western coast of Asia Minor, between Pergamum and Troas. Another vessel would have to be secured to reach Rome, but this ship could get Paul and the other prisoners a considerable distance toward their ultimate destination. Joining Paul and the narrator is Aristarchus, a fellow believer introduced to readers in 19:29 and 20:4 (see [Aristarchus]). He is not mentioned again in the narrative of Acts.

The ship makes a one-day voyage to Sidon, approximately seventy nautical miles (eighty land miles) from Caesarea (v. 3). Given that the ship was likely a cargo vessel, it could have stopped to load and/or unload goods. The centurion Julius is described as *philanthrōpōs* (cf. philanthropist), a term used in ancient Greek literature to denote one who was humane, kind, and civilized.[3] As such, he allows Paul, surely under guard, to visit "friends" in Sidon. This likely denotes believers, even though Acts has not explicitly spoken of the establishment of a Christian community in the city (but cf. 11:19 and 15:3, which speak of Christian communities in the region of Phoenicia). Paul's friends are said to have cared for him, which may also have included offering provisions for him for his journey (ancient sea travelers, even prisoners seeking appeal, had to provide for themselves while en route; see [Appealing to Caesar]).

The narrator does not say how long the ship remained in port before putting out to sea again (v. 4). Had the winds been more favorable, the ship would have taken a more direct western course to the south of Cyprus. However, there was a strong wind coming from the west, so the ship sailed "under the lee of Cyprus," meaning that it sailed in a northern direction close to the island, allowing the land mass to buffer the strong westerly winds. Having rounded the island, the ship then took a more direct course toward the west, sailing between Cyprus and the regions of Cilicia and Pamphylia, eventually reaching the city of "Myra in Lycia." Actually, the port of Myra, Andriace, was located about three miles away from Myra.

It is here that Paul, the other prisoners, and the Roman contingent change ships (v. 6), boarding an Alexandrian vessel. Readers later learn that the primary cargo of this vessel was wheat (v. 38). This makes sense given that Egypt was the primary source of grain for Rome. Grain ships would sail directly north out of Alexandria to Andriace (Myra) and from there move west toward Rome. Julius would have known that he could likely have found a vessel to Rome at this port.

According to John Polhill, the normal route from Myra would have been to sail southwest, to the south of Rhodes then west to the north of Crete toward Sicily.[4] However, the winds did not cooperate, so the ship hugged the coast off Asia Minor, eventually reaching Cnidus (v. 7), some 130 nautical (150 land) miles from Myra. From Cnidus, the goal likely would have been to sail southwest, intending to sail to the north of Crete toward Sicily. Yet "the wind was against us," so the ship is forced to sail southward toward Crete and eventually "under the lee of Crete off Salome," which was located on the eastern side of the island. The ship will now have to sail around the island to the south and attempt to get back on course. The ship passes "a place called Fair Havens" (v. 8), located near the city of Lasea on the southern side of the island.

The narrator has not offered any precise indication of the time that has elapsed. He volunteers only that "much time had been lost" (v. 9). Furthermore, "the Fast had already gone by." The fast is a reference to the Day of Atonement, which occurred in the Jewish calendar on the tenth of Tishri, which would correspond to late September or early October in the Roman calendar. Such information is relevant to the story, for it informs readers that the ship was sailing in the autumn when sea travel was becoming more hazardous. In fact, within a few weeks, beginning around November 11 and extending through March 10, sea lanes would be officially closed.[5]

This prompts Paul to offer his first words in this chapter (v. 10), stating that "the voyage will be with danger." He predicts the loss both of cargo and life. Commentators differ whether Paul is offering a prophetic word or a prudent warning, based on his experiences at sea (Paul himself reports that he had been shipwrecked three times in his life [2 Cor 11:25]). If the former—a prophetic word—his prophecy is not accurate, for there will be no loss of life. If the latter, he would not be telling experienced sea hands anything they did not already know.

Readers would think it wise to listen to Paul, the hero of the narrative. The centurion, not surprisingly, gives more heed to the owner and captain of the ship than to a prisoner (v. 11). Besides, the owner and captain were not contemplating heading out to open sea in order to make Rome. "The majority" (the narrator is not clear just who was in on this decision: the centurion and ship's officers? Other sailors? Passengers?) knew that they would have to harbor for the coming winter, and they concluded that Fair Havens was not suitable for this (v. 12a). Phoenix, located nearly forty miles from Fair Havens (assuming Phoenix to be the modern Phineka Bay), should have been reachable. Since it faced southwest and northwest it would provide "safe harbor" against the winter winds. They would not make it.

"Keep Your Courage," 27:13-26

A favorable south wind began to blow (v. 13), so they weighed anchor and began the journey toward Phoenix, hugging the coast of Crete. Steep mountains, reaching as high as 8,000 feet, guarded the Cretan coast, and a violent wind rushed down on the ship from the island.[6] Acts employs the word *typhōnikos* (cf. typhoon) to describe this wind. The Greek word, like its English cognate, indicates "a whirling, cyclonic wind."[7] Luke describes it as a "northeaster," indicating that it is coming from the direction of the island. The wind is so strong and sudden that the seamen could not turn the ship into it (v. 15); hence, the ship is driven in a southwestern direction, away from the island, toward the small island of Cauda, some twenty-five miles away from Crete (v. 16). They find

The Mountains of Crete
Commentators often identify the specific mountain from which the "northeaster" blew as Mount Ida (Acts 27:14). The mountains of southern Crete pictured here are not specifically identified as Mount Ida. Still, the image offers readers a sense of what Paul and his fellow travelers would have seen as they sailed along the southern coastline. It was from this kind of terrain that the northeaster blew down on the ship carrying Paul, leading to his harrowing adventure.

Boat in Lagoon, Crete Island
(Credit: Vladimir Melnik, istockphoto.com)

Undergirding Ships

Henry J. Cadbury offers a full discussion of what exactly the Lukan narrative might mean when it speaks of the ship's crew taking "measures to undergird the ship" (27:17). John Polhill offers a helpful and concise discussion of the options (521n23). There are four possible ways to "undergird" or "reinforce" the ship:

(1) Supporting cables/ropes would run under the hull, securing more tightly the planks of the ship against its ribs, "as the hoops hold the staves of a barrel" (Cadbury, 348). The NIV's translation assumes this understanding: "they passed ropes under the ship itself to hold it together." Imagine wrapping a string around a toy boat, over the top and under the bottom of the boat.

(2) Supporting cables/ropes would run around the outside of the hull longitudinally. Imagine wrapping a string around the outside of a toy boat from the front of the boat to the back of the boat. Roman warships apparently reinforced their hulls in this manner, but the procedure was done while the ship was in port. It is difficult to imagine this being done at sea, while in the midst of a storm.

(3) Supporting cables/ropes would be attached under the deck to the interior ribs of the ship, and then tightened to brace the ribs internally. Imagine taking the deck off the toy boat and attaching strings from one side of the hull to the other.

(4) A supporting cable/rope would run from stem to stern above the deck. Imagine running a string from the front end to the back end of the toy boat, above the deck. Some ancient pictures of Egyptian ships show a thick cable/rope in such a manner.

Among commentators, numbers 1 and 4 seem to be preferred.

Henry J. Cadbury. "*Hypozōmata*," in F. J. Foakes Jackson and Kirsopp Lake, *The Beginnings of Christianity: The Acts of the Apostles*, 5 vols. (Grand Rapids MI: Baker, 1979), 5.345–54; John B. Polhill, *Acts* (NAC 26; Nashville: Broadman, 1992).

---

temporary respite from the "northeaster" as they sail around to the south side "under the lee" of the island. The dinghy, which was in tow behind the ship, could barely be kept under control. Perhaps it was filling with water or colliding dangerously against the hull of the main vessel.

The sailors take advantage of the protection of the lee and hoist the dinghy on board the ship (v. 17). They then take "measures to undergird the ship." [Undergirding Ships] There is a fear that if they stay on this course they will "run on the Syrtis." The Syrtis was 400 miles from the ship's present location. Yet it struck fear in ancient sailors. It was a zone of shallow waters and quicksand off the coast of Cyrenaica, infamous for destroying sailing vessels.[8] The Jewish historian Josephus describes it as "a place terrible to such as barely hear it described" (*J. W.* 2.381). Fear of destruction prompts the sailors to lower "the sea anchor," which would have the effect of dragging the floor and slowing the ship's advance.

The word that NRSV translates as "sea anchor" is *skeuos*, a very imprecise term, whose meaning can only be discerned by its context. Some understand it to refer to rigging of the sails (the feminine form of the word is apparently so used in v. 19).[9] This would indicate that they lowered the rigging of the topsails, leaving up only the smaller storm sail. Regardless of the precise meaning, the narrator is clear as to the result: the ship was being driven by the wind, with little to no control.

Things are getting more desperate as the ship is thrown about out of control (v. 18). Hence, to lighten the load the crew begins to jettison some of the ship's cargo. The next day, the third day of the storm, they then "threw the ship's tackle overboard." Perhaps the precise rigging being referred to was the mainyard, "the long spar used to support the mainsail."[10] If so, it denotes the virtual surrender of the ship to the power of the sea. Without the main rigging, the crew was forfeiting any future hope of being able to control the ship once the storm subsided.

All aboard, including the narrator, lose hope (v. 20). Many days have now passed and the winds have not subsided. What is more, the thick cloud cover by day and night does not allow the seamen to see either the sun or stars: they have no idea where they are, the lights of heaven being the only means whereby ancient sailors could discern their location. Perhaps, historically speaking, at some point during the passing days of darkness Paul too had feared for his life. After all, he had earlier predicted (v. 10) that there would be a loss of life if the voyage continued. Further, the Paul of the Epistles was not immune from experiencing despair for his life (2 Cor 1:8-10). The Paul of the narrative of Acts, however, knows no such concern.

In fact, in the midst of the storm Paul experienced a vision that would offer him and all aboard a word of real hope. The people on board the ship had not eaten for some time (v. 21). Not eating is consistent with the loss of hope. In the midst of such hopelessness, Paul offers words of encouragement, based on his visionary experience (vv. 21b-26).

It may be difficult for readers to imagine Paul making an inspirational speech in such a setting. Perhaps it would not have seemed so strange to ancient readers, for speeches, even in the midst of a storm, could be found in the literature of the time. The fact that it was something of a literary convention might render the historicity of such a speech suspect. Ben Witherington suggests, however, that the commonness of the motif may, in fact, render it unlikely that "this widespread convention was based on pure human imagination. . . . There must surely have been historical incidents in antiquity in which people attempted to exhort and rally crew and

Roman Wine Ship

Transporting wine barrels by ship. Stone relief, 2d C. Rheinisches Landesmuseum, Trier, Germany. (Credit: Erich Lessing / Art Resource, NY)

Stormy Speeches

Readers of ancient literature would not find it odd for characters to make brief speeches in the midst of turbulent storms. However, a review of some specific examples does not shed much light on either the content of Paul's speech of encouragement or the historicity of the speech.

In Homer's *Odyssey*, the god stirs up a storm that threatens Odysseus (5.285–97), in response to which Odysseus makes a woeful speech *to himself* (5.299–312). In Seneca's *Agememnon* (510–27) and Virgil's *Æneid* (1.92–101), prayers of lament and woe are offered to the heavens in reaction to the storm. Such texts actually offer the closest parallel to what 27:29 speaks of, the sailors praying for daylight to come. Hence, "informed" ancient readers might not be shocked that Paul says something in the midst of the storm, but they would likely not expect a pep talk. Reflecting on one's woes, either to oneself or to the gods, was more "the convention." Perhaps readers would be impressed at Paul's courage and faith, as opposed to the conventional practice of focusing on one's plight.

Exploration of the "parallels," if they can be called that, sheds no light on the historicity of the speech. Ben Witherington suggests that the literary convention itself emerged out of actual practice—people made speeches during storms, hence the literary convention emerged to offer verisimilitude to accounts of sea storms (767–68). This would allow the implicit inference that Paul could make such a speech (see Commentary). Readers should not press the logic, however. The concrete examples of speeches explored above are either prayers or inward reflections. Can one deny that during a sea storm people might cry out to the gods? Of course not. But can one move from that to making any kind of historical judgment on the specific prayers that one reads in the ancient literature? No. Similarly, is it impossible to suppose that one might offer words of encouragement during a storm? Of course not. But that, in itself, does not allow any inference with regard to the historicity of any particular speech.

Ben Witherington III, *The Acts of the Apostles: A Socio-Rhetorical Commentary* (Grand Rapids MI: Eerdmans, 1998).

---

passengers in such situations."[11] [Stormy Speeches] Perhaps so, but, even if historical, it would seem probable that only a few actually heard the speech. That is of little concern to readers, however, for readers are permitted to hear the speech and admire Paul's courage and faith.

Paul begins by enhancing his credibility with a quick reminder that he was right—they should not have sailed from Crete (cf. v. 10). Only a few were privy to Paul's advice, unless one surmises that conversations between the centurion, captain, and the ship's owner were conducted before the entire contingent of those on board. Perhaps one can infer that word of the conversation had circulated around the ship over the past several days. Or, perhaps, Paul is actually speaking only to the reader anyway.

Paul moves quickly to the heart of his speech, offering an immediate word of hope: the ship will be lost, but there will be no loss of life (v. 22). This is not what Paul said earlier, when he did predict the loss of life (cf. v. 10). That pronouncement was likely based on Paul's own opinion, given his past experiences at sea. The amendment to his message is based on the angelic message, which readers and characters on the ship learn about together.

Paul reports that the previous night an angel of the God whom he worshiped stood beside him (v. 23; cf. for other angelic appearances 5:19; 7:26; 10:3; 12:7, 23; see [Vision]). Paul, aware that he is speaking to an audience who would be unfamiliar with the specifics of his religious faith, is content to identify the God of the angelic visitor simply as the God to whom he belongs and whom he worships. Readers know exactly the God of whom he speaks.

The message of the angel was simple, but greatly encouraging, as the messenger made clear that (1) Paul would stand before the emperor and (2) all on board the ship would be saved (v. 24). The crew, soldiers, and fellow passengers who heard Paul's words would likely not care about his personal hearing before the emperor, but readers have heard before that Paul would make it to Rome (23:11), and the angelic vision offers a reminder that God's aims for Paul will not be thwarted, even by such a life-threatening storm. Of more interest to Paul's audience in the story is his declaration that none of them would die.

The implication is clear: the salvation of Paul would result in the salvation of all. Here the divine protection offered to one provides safety to all. This offers a twist to the literary motif of sea storms, where the *guilt* of a passenger who had earned divine wrath put all at risk (cf. the story of Jonah). Given that gods tended to use storms to afflict the guilty, the divine protection offered to Paul in the midst of the threatening storm offers another, at least implicit, attestation to Paul's innocence.[12] It further says something about God's concern for all life on board the ship. If God were concerned *only* that Paul reach Rome, it would hardly be necessary to save the lives of *all* others on board the doomed vessel. In short, there is no *necessary* connection between saving Paul's life and the life of everyone else. The deliverance of *all* is grounded not in necessity, but in mercy.

Paul's "faith in God that it will be exactly as I have been told" (v. 25) is strong enough that Paul urges all to take heart. He concludes with a brief announcement that the ship will have to run aground on some island (v. 26). The narrator is silent as to whether Paul's hearers, in fact, did take any hope from his words—at least at this point.

That there would be a shipwreck may very well be an inference that Paul is making. Looking at the precise content of the vision (v. 24), Paul was told only that there would be no loss of life. He was not explicitly told that the ship would be lost or grounded on an island. Perhaps the ferocity of the storm led Paul to conclude it unlikely that the ship could survive this storm. And if there would be no loss of life, the safety of an island to provide haven for passengers and crew until they could be rescued would be necessary.

Whether this aspect of Paul's prediction is an inference or due to inspiration (or both!), he will be proven correct.

"Unless These Men Stay" 27:27-32

Readers learn that the fierce storm has lasted fourteen nights (v. 27). The boat had been drifting out of control across the Sea of Adria, not to be confused with the modern Adriatic. The Sea of Adria is the open sea between Crete and Malta, to the south of Greece and Italy. Around midnight, the sailors sensed that the boat was nearing land, due perhaps to the sound of the surf.

The sound of the surf prompts the sailors to take soundings (v. 28). At first the sea floor is found to be twenty fathoms (120 feet) deep, then, a little later, only fifteen fathoms (90 feet). The ship is definitely approaching land. It is still night, and not wanting to collide with the rocks (rocks against which the sailors can likely hear the crashing waves), the crew drops four stern anchors to hold the ship in place, or at least slow its progress toward the land. Then they prayed for day to come.

Some sailors apparently contemplated an escape, employing the dinghy that had been hoisted aboard a couple of weeks earlier (v. 30). As the narrator tells it, they lowered the boat under the pretext that they were going to put out anchors from the bow. A boat would be needed since the bow anchors would not simply be dropped straight down into the water, but would need to be placed farther out in front of the ship. Anchors to the front and rear of the ship would offer the ship more stability.

Clearly the narrator, as well as Paul, thinks they are planning to abandon ship. Paul warns both the centurion and soldiers that they cannot be saved if these men leave the ship (v. 31). Is Paul predicting that some type of "punishment" will befall the ship if these men succeed in leaving? Is he simply being practical and noting that the crew would be needed to keep the ship intact as it approached the land ahead? Or is he acting on his conviction that God had determined to save all on board and this simply required all to remain together and none "set out on their own," abandoning the others while seeking only their own safety? Whatever Paul's meaning, the centurion and soldiers take him seriously and make sure that no one will have the opportunity to escape by cutting loose the lifeboat (v. 32).

The whole scene is actually a bit confusing when read at the *historical* level. First, it would make sense that anchors would need to be placed out from the bow of the ship to stabilize it. Second, in order to do this, the dinghy would have to be deployed. Third, it is unlikely that sailors would presume that they could, on their own authority, lower the boat, supposedly to put out the anchors, unless they had been ordered to do so by the captain or owner of the ship. Fourth, why would experienced sailors think they had a better chance of survival sailing off into the darkness in a small dinghy than to remain on the larger ship?

Perhaps, at the historical level, the sailors were simply carrying out their orders, and frightened and confused soldiers and passengers, including Paul, thought that they were trying to abandon ship. But if that were the case, why would the soldiers cut loose the boat? Could they not secure the sailors until they were reassured by the ship's officials that these men were following orders and doing what was necessary to make the ship more stable?[13]

The narrative is simply full of gaps when read historically. Regardless of how readers fill such gaps, should they even be interested in doing so, the story—as story—allows Paul to step forth again to center stage and show his command of the situation. Even at the narrative level, the reaction of the soldiers, cutting loose the dinghy, could be interpreted as an *over-reaction*—the kind of action that soldiers might take to ensure that no further escape attempts would occur. Of course, if passengers and crew would eventually have to abandon ship, the dinghy would have proven useful. C. K. Barrett offers a blunt assessment, describing the cutting loose of the dinghy as "[a] foolish act, some think; with the dinghy it would have been possible to sit out the gale and row ashore, without losing the ship."[14] Apparently, the soldiers weren't thinking that far ahead. One can only imagine, even at the narrative level, the tongue-lashing they might have received from the ship's captain.

"I Urge You to Take Some Food," 27:33-38

In v. 29, the sailors had prayed to the gods of their choosing for day to come. Of course, day was going to come, with or without their prayers. What they really had been praying for was that they would live to see the dawn. Dawn is now breaking, and Paul again steps to center stage, this time to encourage all on board to take in nourishment (v. 33). "It's been two harrowing and suspenseful weeks," Paul in effect says, "and you haven't eaten." It's not likely that everyone on board ate absolutely nothing for two weeks, but the hyperbole drives home the point that the people on the ship had passed through a most trying time; they were discouraged, hungry, and exhausted.

Paul urges the people to take food, once again assuring them that they will survive. "For this will be for your salvation," the text literally says. He employs a biblical phrase, one used even by Jesus, to speak of their eventual deliverance: "you will not lose a hair from your heads" (Luke 21:18, cf. 1 Sam 14:45; 2 Sam 14:11; 1 Kgs 1:52; see also Luke 12:7).

As a good Jew, Paul precedes the meal with a blessing. Many commentators note the eucharistic tone of the language.[15] The narrative says that Paul "took bread," "gave thanks," and "broke" the bread. C. K. Barrett observes, "As far as language goes, the present passage is more 'eucharistic' than any other in Acts."[16] The Western text also picked up on eucharistic tones, adding, "distributing [it] also to us." Yet commentators consistently conclude that this is not a eucharistic meal.[17] That is certainly correct in a strict sense. If the narrator had wanted to portray this as a eucharistic meal it is unlikely that he would (1) have emphasized the meal as necessary *only* for physical sustenance and (2) have presented it as a meal shared by *all* on board.

Still, one wonders if the consistent detection by ancient copyists and commentators alike of eucharistic language does not imply that Luke's Christian readers could have discerned at least some sacramental quality to the meal and that the narrator would have known that. Narrators choose what words they will employ to present a narrative, and this narrator chose to employ language that would offer echoes of the eucharistic language of early Christian tradition. [The Breaking of Bread in Acts 27]

Is it insignificant that the narrator employs the word "salvation" or its cognates so many times throughout this narrative (vv. 20, 31, 34, 43, and 44; cf. 28:1, 4), a word that Acts consistently uses to

---

Breaking Bread in Acts 27

The following table demonstrates the presence of language in Acts 27:35 and the meals in the Gospel of Luke where Jesus was present.

Acts 27:35	Luke 9:16	Luke 22:19	Luke 24:30
After he had said this, he took bread; and giving thanks to God in the presence of all, he broke it and began to eat.	And taking the five loaves and the two fish, he looked up to heaven, and blessed and broke them, and gave them to the disciples to set before the crowd.	Then he took a loaf of bread, and when he had given thanks, he broke it and gave it to them, saying, "This is my body, which is given for you. Do this in remembrance of me."	When he was at the table with them, he took bread, blessed and broke it, and gave it to them.

Building on the language of the gospel narrative, the "breaking of bread" serves in Acts as a shorthand way of referring to fellowship, implicitly at least, in the presence of Jesus (Acts 2:42, 46; 20:7, 11). In this final reference to the breaking of bread, perhaps significantly, the fellowship that is shared is not exclusive to Christians, but is inclusive of all.

denote *God's* deliverance (4:12; 7:25; 13:26; 13:47; 16:17)? Or that he presents Paul as employing a phrase of divine protection that Jesus used specifically to assure the faithful that they would experience deliverance in the midst of trial (v. 34; cf. Luke 21:18)? And all set within the context of words that commentators cannot help but notice have eucharistic overtones? To be sure, this is not *literally* a celebration of the Eucharist, but it does invite reflection on the efficacy of the "breaking of bread" *for the whole world* (see Connections).

At this point, the narrator reports that 276 persons were on board (v. 37). The Western text speaks of only "about 76," but most accept the larger number as representing the most reliable textual tradition. Josephus speaks of a voyage he took on which there were about 600 persons on the ship (*Life* 15); Luke's number is credible. Verse 36 reports that all on board were both encouraged and ate. Finally, having satisfied their hunger, they threw the primary cargo, wheat bound for Rome, overboard (v. 38). It would be necessary to lighten the ship's load as much as possible so that the ship could make it in as close to shore as possible, especially since they no longer had a dinghy to use to get to shore!

The Centurion, Wishing to Save Paul, 27:39-44

Day has fully dawned, and those on board can see land ahead (v. 39). Fortuitously, there is within sight a bay with a welcoming beach conducive for running the ship aground. This may well be what today is called St. Paul's Bay, though the contemporary name is clearly the reflection of subsequent tradition

St. Paul's Bay
This bay is traditionally the site of the shipwreck that left Paul and 275 other persons stranded on Malta. Today it is a bustling resort, offering accommodations that Paul and his shipwrecked companions could not even have imagined.

View over St. Paul's Bay in Lindos (Island of Rhodos), Greece
(Credit: Angelika Stern, istockphoto.com)

Verse 40 succinctly lists the steps taken to prepare for the beaching of the ship. The four stern anchors that had been dropped the night before (v. 29) are cut loose and left on the sea floor. Second, the steering oars are set in place. The "rudder" of ancient ships actually consisted of large oars that extended from the back of the ship. During a storm, these would be hoisted on board and tied down.[18] Third, they raise the small foresail to allow the wind to blow the boat in toward the beach.

Regrettably, the ship gets snagged on a shoal, reef, or sandbar (v. 41). The Greek text reads literally "a place of two seas" (cf. KJV; NAS [1995 ed.]). This implies to many commentators and translators (cf. NRSV, RSV, NAB, NIV) something like a sandbar—a geographical structure that "separated" the sea on either side of itself. One would assume that it was well below water or the narrative would have offered some word about attempts to avoid it.[19] The bow is now stuck and the stern takes a beating and begins to break up. There is no hope of getting the ship any closer to the shore. Crew, soldiers, prisoners, and other passengers will have to swim for shore.

The soldiers' plan is to kill the prisoners (v. 42). These soldiers have already proven how rash they can be, cutting loose the dinghy the night before. Their fear was that the prisoners would escape. Though the narrator does not say this, one may conclude that the soldiers feared that they would face severe discipline from their superiors should this happen. Though later, the code of Justinian stipulated that guards who allowed prisoners to escape would encounter the same punishment to which the escaped prisoner had been sentenced.[20] Readers familiar only with the narrative world of Acts would have encountered before guards who paid with their lives for letting prisoners escape (12:19; cf. 16:27).

One still can view the action as rash. First, to where did the soldiers think the prisoners would escape? That they would swim out to sea? Perhaps the soldiers feared that some prisoners would escape once all had reached the island. Second, even if some should escape, it would seem that it would not prove difficult to make a case that they had been lost at sea during the storm. Regardless, the soldiers' callousness is transparent and a threat to Paul's welfare.

The centurion relieves whatever tension the reader might feel that Paul's life was once again threatened (v. 43). Wishing to save Paul, he countermands whatever orders an underling might have issued to execute the prisoners. Once again, others are saved along with Paul. And, once again, it was not *necessary* for all to be saved in order for Paul to be saved. The centurion could have taken Paul under his wing and left the other prisoners to their own doomed fate. The kindly providence that underlies this narrative is *not* concerned only about Paul—or only about the other Christians on the boat, for that matter. It is concerned for *all.*

Those who can swim are ordered off the boat first. Those who could not swim are ordered to make use of planks or "other things" [NRSV, "pieces"] or even "other persons from the ship" and head for shore (v. 44). The Greek word that the NRSV renders as "pieces" could denote "other persons," hence the alternative translation offered in the preceding sentence. Conceivably, some made it safely to land riding the backs of more able swimmers. After a harrowing experience, the chapter ends, finally, on a good note: "all were brought safely to land." Paul's words of assurance and hope prove true.

CONNECTIONS

Finding meaningful connections with the story about a storm at sea may prove challenging. This may explain why commentators such as Luke Johnson warn against allegorizing the story.[21] One such allegorical approach might be to view the ship as the church, making its way through the danger and chaos of the stormy sea. To be sure, stories about storms at sea with Jesus and his disciples in the boat can tempt one in this direction (cf. Luke 8:22-25; par. Matt 8:23-27; Mark 6:45-52; John 6:16-21). However, in these stories those in the boat are limited exclusively to the disciples and Jesus, making a symbolic interpretation of these scenes more palatable.

Even interpreted on a more literal level, however, the story still yields thoughtful insights. The positive witness that faith can offer in the midst of trial is certainly evidenced in this story. To be sure, when Paul first offered words of encouragement, sharing his vision (vv. 21-26), there is no record of any immediate positive reaction by those on board the periled ship. Perhaps it's easy to dismiss those who seem to be coming fresh off manic moments of ecstasy. But Paul's testimony continued, as he encouraged the people on board to take food, leading the way by taking the bread, giving thanks to God, breaking the bread, and eating (v. 35). Then, we are told, "all of them were encouraged and took food for themselves" (v. 36).

John Wesley, while en route to the American colonies to convert Native Americans under the auspices of the Society for the Propagation of the Gospel in Foreign Parts, found himself caught

John Wesley and the Moravians

Wesley offered this observation about the faith of the Moravians, with whom he shared the experience of a storm at sea en route to the Colonies.

At noon our third storm began. At four it was more violent than before. At seven I went to the Germans. I had long before observed the great seriousness of their behavior. Of their humility they had given a continual proof by performing those servile offices for the other passengers, which none of the English would undertake; for which they desired and would receive no pay, saying, "it was good for their proud hearts," and "their loving Saviour had done more for them." And every day had given them an occasion of showing a meekness which no injury could move. If they were pushed, struck, or thrown down, they rose again and went away; but no complaint was found in their mouth. There was now an

opportunity of trying whether they were delivered from the spirit of fear, as well as from that of pride, anger and revenge. In the midst of the psalm wherewith their service began, the sea broke over, split the mainsail in pieces, covered the ship, and poured in between the decks, as if the great deep had already swallowed us up. A terrible screaming began among the English. The Germans calmly sang on. I asked one of them afterward, "Were you not afraid?" He answered, "I thank God, no." I asked, "But were not your women and children afraid?" He replied, mildly, "No; our women and children are not afraid to die."

Christian Classics Ethereal Library, "Journal of John Wesley," http://www.ccel.org/ccel/wesley/journal.vi.i.v.html (4 July 2006). Cited in Sally Smith Holt, "Frailty and Faith," chapel sermon at William Jewell College, 28 October 2004.

in a frightening storm at sea. The courage that he saw evidenced in the many Moravians who were sharing the voyage left an indelible impression on him. [John Wesley and the Moravians] The Moravians were quite influential in shaping Wesley's early theology that minimized the importance of works and emphasized a doctrine of justification that was experienced through sudden conversion and new birth. (The later Wesley, of course, placed great emphasis on the importance of sanctification in the Christian walk.)[22] One never knows the impact that one's courageous faith will make on another.

It is not stretching the narrative into allegory or symbolism to note that the story represents well what the disciples of Acts earlier came to realize: "through many tribulations we must enter the kingdom of God" (14:22, RSV). We are accustomed to seeing the God of Acts help the disciples through trying times with miraculous works, such as the times that Peter and Paul were delivered from prison (12:6-12; 16:25-34). Yet it would be a short-sighted reading of Acts to conclude that miraculous rescue from the trials of discipleship and life are the norm. Peter, recall, was delivered from prison, but just before his imprisonment, James had been executed (12:1-5). And Paul experienced the earthquake that shook open his prison doors only after he had been beaten with rods (16:22-23). Despite God's occasional interruptions, more often than not the trials of life's journey simply come and have to be endured. [We, O God, Unite Our Voices]

We, O God, Unite Our Voices

We, O God, unite our voices,
Raised in faithful praise to thee.
Thou, unchanging, safe hath brought us
Through the ever-changing sea.
Days of calm and days of conflict,
Nights of darkness prove thy grace.
Hands beneath us, arms around us
And above—your shining face.

Not our choice, the wind's direction;
Unforeseen, the calm or gale.
Thy great ocean swells before us
And our ship seems small and frail.
Fierce and gleaming is thy mystery,
Calling us to shores unknown.
Plunge us on with hope and courage
Till thy harbor is our home.

Paul Duke and Grady Nutt, "We, O God, Unite Our Voices," 1981.

The deliverance of the ship from the horrendous storm was no literal miracle; deliverance did not come from any "divine intervention" that silenced the winds and waves. Paul experienced nothing like the disciples of the Gospels for whom Jesus calmed the winds with his word. The story can offer encouragement to the faithful that God's purposes can find their realization and fulfillment. But the human beings whom God has chosen to accomplish God's ends have to pass through all the struggles of life, buoyed by hope and faith, but rarely rescued apart from their own efforts to hang on and to act prudently. [Living through Life Realistically] Our story offers no hints that those on board would have been delivered anyway, regardless of the efforts made by able deckhands. In fact, Paul is quite emphatic that should the sailors, whose skills would be needed to help beach the ship, succeed in escaping the earlier promise that there would be no loss of life (v. 22) would not come to pass: "Unless these men stay in ship, you cannot be saved" (v. 31).

One feature of the story is God's concern for *all* on board the ship, only a handful of which are believers. Had even a respectable number of those on board come out alive, many would still be there to give God the credit for a miracle of sorts, much like the credit God gets when a handful of people walk away from plane crash. Josephus relates how a ship on which he was sailing to Rome with 600 on board was sunk. Only eighty survived—"by God's providence" (*Life* 15). Survivors have a way of preserving God's honor, regardless of how small that number may be. But, at least in this instance, *all* are delivered. "The 'all' who are promised rescue consist primarily of pagans who do not worship the one God. Nevertheless, God has decided to rescue them."[23]

Robert Tannehill finds here universal implications of the gospel. He points out that the narrator regularly employs the word "saved/salvation" or its cognates in this story (27:20, 31, 43, 44; cf. 28:1, 4). And while the word can certainly be understood in the more mundane sense of "rescue," one wonders whether Luke's Christian readers could not help but hear deeper echoes.

Living through Life Realistically

"Like Paul, Luke's readers are caught in depths beyond their control; they too are always close to death in the risky adventure of living, they too are caught as prisoners of complex social entanglements. Their faith in God must not be focused so much on the elimination of these circumstances (that would be fatuous) or even on the amelioration (that might be foolhardy), but on God's power that enables them to 'endure' and so 'gain possession of their lives' " (Johnson, 459).

"Hope is not wishing things were different; it is choosing to make the most of our lives given the given—that is, accepting the reality of our circumstances and the reality that the strength of a 'motherly' presence accompanies us. . . . It seems paradoxical to say that pessimism is akin to hope, but in the same way it can also be true that hope is related to, and requires hopelessness. It is only when the bottom drops out of our hopelessness, only when we have reached the end of the rope of hope and have been enveloped by the realization that all is lost, that we are positioned to experience the hope that is of God. . . . Hope for the 'wrong thing' is hoping life will change, or hoping our attempts to muscle change will work. Hope for the right thing is relying on Mystery's muscle, whose strength is manifest through our efforts." (Stella, 108–10)

Luke Timothy Johnson, *The Acts of the Apostles* (SacPag 5; Collegeville MN: Liturgical Press, 1992); Tom Stella, *A Faith Worth Believing: Finding New Life Beyond the Rules of Religion* (New York: HarperSanFranciso, 2004).

"[Salvation] is not only the hope of those in a storm at sea but the purpose of God for all humanity, announced at the beginning of Luke (2:30-32; 3:6)."[24] Further, Tannehill is willing to recognize the echoes of eucharistic language in Paul's breaking of bread, arguing that for Paul the meal was, indeed, a Eucharist: "By eating before them [the pagans], Paul finally achieves his goal of encouraging them."[25] At this point "we" no longer refers exclusively, as it had in past episodes, to those explicitly associated with Paul, that is, believers. Now, "the entire ship's company becomes a single 'we' as the narrator numbers the company so that readers will know what 'all' means. . . . The meal on the ship is an act that benefits all, Christian and non-Christian, and an act in which community is created across religious lines."[26] Consequently, "the fulfillment of God's promises to Paul that all those in the ship will survive the storm becomes a sign in miniature of God's promises of salvation for all flesh, which has not yet been fulfilled."[27]

Commentators have been reticent to follow Tannehill's reading. And while it might be too hopeful to find in the Lukan narrative a universalism, particularly "a universalism that involves every creature in God's ultimate salvation,"[28] two things, at least, are worth considering. First, we should probably move away from debates over the "eucharistic" language of Paul's breaking of bread. What, however, we should not shy away from is the fact that the language of v. 35 echoes scenes in the Gospel of Luke where Jesus broke bread with others (see [The Breaking of Bread in Acts 27]). If the "words of institution" (cf. Luke 22:17-20), as we now call them, were read or recited at "eucharistic" settings in the Lukan community, then Lukan readers, like modern readers, would catch eucharistic undertones. What cannot be debated is that the words echo those meals where *Jesus was present*, be it with the masses (Luke 9:16), the disciples before his crucifixion (Luke 22:17-20), or the travelers to Emmaus after the resurrection (Luke 24:30). As Paul engages in the act of eating, the narrator employs language that calls to mind the meals of Jesus. At the very least, the breaking of bread before all and the invitation to all to share in the bread, calls to mind meals where the Lord is present. On this ship, in this storm, the Lord is present not only with the handful of the faithful, but also with all.

The second consideration need not lead us to quibble over how far the word *universalism* reaches when applied to the Lukan narrative. But there can be no dispute that God is quite concerned in this story with the lives of more than just Paul or the handful of believers. God is not content for Paul to reach Rome and stand before Caesar. Why, after all, is it so important for Paul to get there? Simply so that a "prediction" can come true? Paul's reaching Rome becomes the narrative expression of the fulfillment of the concern of God and the Lord that the word of salvation reach to the ends of the earth (1:8)—a phrase that does not denote merely geographical expansion, but reaching out to the nations, the non-Jews (cf. 13:37; cf. Isa 49:6). At the heart of the commission of Jesus to his followers is the concern that all humanity, Jewish and non-Jewish, experiences the saving power of God. God's determination to rescue—save!—all on board the ship gives narrative expression to God's determination to extend God's protective deliverance to all, "not wanting any to perish, but all to come to repentance" (2 Pet 3:9).

NOTES

[1] Joseph A. Fitzmyer, *The Acts of the Apostles* (AB 31; New York: Doubleday, 1998), 769.

[2] Ben Witherington III, *The Acts of the Apostles: A Socio-Rhetorical Commentary* (Grand Rapids MI: Eerdmans, 1998), 760.

[3] Luke Timothy Johnson, *The Acts of the Apostles* (SacPag 5; Collegeville MN: Liturgical Press, 1992), 445.

[4] John B. Polhill, *Acts* (NAC 26; Nashville: Broadman, 1992), 517.

[5] Fitzmyer, *Acts*, 775.

[6] Commentators regularly identify Mt. Ida as the specific mountain from which the wind descended (Ernst Haenchen, *The Acts of the Apostles: A Commentary* [Philadelphia: Westminster, 1971], 701; Witherington, *Acts*, 765).

[7] Polhill, *Acts*, 520.

[8] Johnson, *Acts*, 448.

[9] Ibid. Polhill, *Acts*, suggests this as one possible reading (521).

[10] Polhill, *Acts*, 522.

[11] Witherington, *Acts*, 767.

[12] Ibid., 769.

[13] Ibid., 706 and 709–711 for such historical issues.

[14] C. K. Barrett, *Acts: A Shorter Commentary* (London: T&T Clark, 2002), 407.

[15] Johnson, *Acts*, 455; Fitzmyer, *Acts*, 779; Polhill, *Acts*, 527.

[16] Barrett, *Acts: Shorter Commentary*, 408.

[17] Tannehill is a major exception, arguing that it was a eucharistic meal for Paul and the few Christians, though for the others it was an ordinary meal (Robert W. Tannehill, *The Narrative Unity of Luke–Acts: A Literary Interpretation*, 2 vols. [Minneapolis: Fortress, 1990], 2.335–36).

[18] Polhill, *Acts*, 529. Barrett understands the phrase to mean that the steering oars were cut loose and let out to sea. The crew would count entirely on the wind to guide them to shore (*Acts: Shorter Commentary*, 410).

[19] Haenchen, *Acts*, 708, notes that in the modern St. Paul's Bay there is a shoal some thirty-nine feet under the surface of the water. In Paul's time, he claims, it was "probably only about 13 feet" underwater.

[20] Fitzmyer, *Acts*, 780.

[21] Johnson, *Acts*, 457.

[22] Henry D. Rack, "Wesley, John," in *The Dictionary of Historical Theology*, ed. Trevor A. Hart (Grand Rapids MI: Eerdmans, 2000), 568–70.

[23] Tannehill, *Narrative Unity*, 2.333.

[24] Ibid., 2.336.

[25] Ibid., 2.335.

[26] Ibid.

[27] Ibid., 2.337.

[28] Ibid., 2.338.

ADVENTURES ON MALTA AND ARRIVAL IN ROME

Acts 28:1-31

COMMENTARY

As readers come to the final chapter of Acts, some may feel that they are left with many unanswered questions. The chapter begins with a short narrative describing the hospitality of the island's natives and leading citizen, hospitality reciprocated by Paul through the healing of the sick (vv. 1-10). There follows a relatively terse narrative that describes how Paul reached Rome, a destination that readers have been anticipating for several chapters (vv. 11-16). Upon arrival in Rome, the narrative focuses attention not on any hearing before Caesar but on Paul's encounter with the Jewish leadership of the city to whom he proclaimed the kingdom of God (vv. 17-30).

The Island Was Called Malta, 28:1-10

The shipwrecked survivors soon learn that they had found refuge on the island of Malta. [Malta] The Greek text of v. 1 could read that "we *recognized*" the island to be Malta; perhaps some of the veteran sailors, having been here before, recognized the location. The latter reading could indicate that the narrator still includes in the "we" the entire band of 276 persons and not only Paul and the other Christians.

Where the natives came from is not said (v. 2). The narrative employs the Greek *barbaroi* to denote them, a general term used by

---

Malta

The large island is located sixty miles south of Sicily. The name *Malta* is from the Semitic word melit, which means refuge. It provided "safe harbor" for more than Paul and his fellow travelers down through history. Before coming under Roman rule in 218 BC, Malta had been a Phoenician trading colony for centuries. Punic/Phoenician language and culture remained deeply embedded on the island, even centuries after coming under Roman rule.

W. Ward Gasque, "Malta," *ABD* 4.489–90.

persons of Greek culture and language to designate those who did
not share Greek language or cultural heritage. The "unusual kindness" and hospitality (v. 2) make clear that Paul and his fellow
travelers have nothing to fear from these local residents. Hospitality
has regularly been a positive characteristic of persons in Acts who
are at least receptive to the good news that Christian missionaries
proclaim. The Greek word translated in v. 2 as "welcome" (*prose-
labonto*) is not the word that Luke generally uses. Luke regularly
employs *dechomai* or compound verbs built off the root (cf. 2:41;
15:4; 17:11; 18:27; 21:17). Given the context, the meaning
appears the same.

It has started to rain and though all the survivors are already wet,
a fire would be well received (v. 3). At this juncture some commentators, such as Haenchen,[1] conclude that Luke has narrowed the
"we" down to Paul and his Christian companions. Readers likely
are not to envision a fire large enough to warm 276 persons. At the
very least, readers know that Paul and his fellow Christians are
being cared for; God's care continues to manifest itself. The narrative will no longer focus attention on the rest of the survivors.
However, the natives or local leaders would likely not simply ignore
the balance of the prisoners and soldiers, leaving them to fend for
themselves for the next three months.

Paul assists with the work of bringing fuel for the fire, something
readers would expect a man of his proven character to do (v. 3).
The pile of wood harbored a snake (*echidna*), which fled the heat
once the pile of wood was thrown onto the flames. It attached itself
to Paul. The modern island of Malta has no poisonous snakes, and
snakes tend to "strike" not "cling." Based on such insights incredulous readers question the veracity of the story. Readers inclined to
give the narrator the benefit of the doubt point out that modern
interpreters have no way of knowing what types of snakes were
native to this island 2,000 years ago. Further, it is not wise to pass
historical judgment based on the use of the verb "fasten," as
opposed to "strike." The narrator's fondness for verisimilitude is
well demonstrated. Even if spinning a tale out of thin air, he would
likely not employ details that would only raise the eyebrows of his
ancient readers.

A viper clinging tenaciously to Paul's hand (v. 4) creates a powerfully dramatic scene. One can imagine the natives stopping in their
tracks and starring at the viper as it clings to Paul. Ancient supersti-
tions of justice provide them the hermeneutical key to make sense
of this. This man who has just survived a shipwreck must, in fact,
be a murderer, and "justice" has meted out her sentence. Many

commentators personify "justice." Note that natives speak as though this "justice" has acted with an independent will ("justice [*dikē*] has not allowed [*eaō*] him to live"; compare the use of the Greek verb *eaō* in such texts as Luke 4:41; Acts 14:16; 16:7; 19:30). Behind the natives' logic is the assumption that *Dikē*, the Greek goddess of *justice*, has exacted her revenge. The mother tongue of these natives was Punic, a Semitic dialect. The deep cultural roots of this island were Phoenician, but this religion had its equivalent of the god of justice, *Sydyk*, which the narrator has rendered into the Greek idiom of his readers.[2]

But justice does not exact revenge on Paul; rather, he shakes off the viper (v. 5). The natives continue to watch, convinced that, eventually, the poison will have its effect. But nothing happens. Their hermeneutical key remains intact—something supernatural is going on here. They simply change their minds about the significance of the event: Paul must be a god (v. 6).

The conclusion echoes a scene earlier in the narrative when the citizens of Lystra, after witnessing a miracle, conclude Paul and Barnabas to be gods (14:8-11). There, Paul and Barnabas were quick to correct such false conclusions. Here, neither Paul nor the narrator expends any energy for that purpose. This story simply comes to an end. Readers should likely not conclude that Paul was happy to be considered a god—nothing one has read in Acts would justify such a conclusion of this character. Once again, Paul has been spared by the kindly providence that has moved the story along to this point. Whether Paul took the opportunity to share the gospel is not said. The narrator is ready to move to the next scene.

Verse 7 introduces the "leading man of the island, named Publius." Publius is a Roman name, the equivalent of the Greek name Poplios. Whether this man was the official Roman governor of the island or simply the most notable citizen of the island is not said and cannot be determined. The Roman name might indicate that he is a Roman citizen. Paul regularly attracts the attention and sometimes even the sympathy of local leaders (13:7; 16:22; 17:19; 18:12; 19:31). Publius proves to be most hospitable. He welcomed "and entertained us hospitably for three days." Again, does the "us" mean only Paul and his Christian companions or the entire body of 276 survivors? The text is silent. The narrator seems content to assure the readers that Paul is being cared for.

The warm hospitality of Publius proved quite fortuitous, given that his father was ill "with fever and dysentery" (v. 8). The father appears to be ill with "Malta fever," a "gastric fever caused by a microbe in goat's milk."[3] Paul prayed over him and laid his hands on him, curing him. While it may not be significant, this is the only time in Acts that *both* prayer and the laying on of hands accompany healing. There is no mention of preaching the gospel, much less any word that the faith of Publius or his father contributed to the healing. Readers would know, of course, that God is behind the cure and can only conclude that thoroughly unmerited grace provided the power for the cure.

Jesus cured Peter's mother-in-law of a fever (Luke 4:38-39), after which Jesus drew a crowd (Luke 4:40-41). Paul's healing activity also draws "the rest" of the people on the island who were ill (v. 9). They, too, were cured. Again, the narrative is silent with respect to any preaching on Paul's part. Readers do not violate the text to fill the silence with the assumption of preaching,[4] but neither do readers violate the text to conclude that acts of mercy need not be contingent first on Christian proclamation and audience acceptance of such proclamation. An act of mercy is always a good thing to offer those in need, even apart from explicit proclamation.

In response to Paul's mercy, the natives "honored us with many honors" (literal translation of v. 10). The Greek word "honors" (*timai*) consistently denotes funds of some sort in Acts (cf. 4:34; 5:2-3; 7:16; 19:19). The text says nothing to imply that such gifts were refused. In fact, when the group prepared to leave the island, further provisions for the balance of the trip were provided and received

The gospel tradition occasionally mandates that one who offers healing is not to receive pay (cf. Matt 10:8). Perhaps what the gospel tradition has in view is payment for personal gain or financial enrichment. Paul is headed for Rome to face legal charges, and, under Roman jurisprudence, persons on trial were responsible for meeting their own expenses, legal and personal (see [Appealing to Caesar]). Historically, Paul would receive gifts to sustain him while in custody (cf. Phil 4:10, 15-20).

And So We Came to Rome, 28:11-16

Three months pass between vv. 10 and 11, presumably with nothing of significance happening. It is time to set sail (v. 11). The narrative focuses now on Paul and company; it has no interest in the balance of prisoners. "We" boarded a ship with Alexandrian registry that had been wintering in Malta. This may have been another grain vessel.

If readers understand the "three months" as a precise designation of time, it would now be February.[5] This is a bit early, in that the sailing season officially resumed in mid-March. But it is possible, if the weather was fair, that the captain of the Alexandrian vessel was anxious to reach his destination and unload his cargo. Luke indicates that the "Twin Brothers" were the ship's figurehead. This would be a reference to Castor and Pollux, twin sons of Zeus. Some translations insert their names (cf. KJV, NIV). The cult of the Twins was popular in Egypt, and they were traditionally "venerated as protectors of seamen."[6]

The itinerary is succint. The story is moving quickly toward its dramatic conclusion—Paul's arrival in Rome. Syracuse (v. 12) is ninety miles from Malta. Readers are not told how long the trip took, but one full day should have proved sufficient. The ship anchored in this harbor of Sicily for three days.

The next stop was Rhegium, a Greek colony located on the "toe" of Italy (v. 13). The NRSV begins the verse with the phrase "then we weighed anchor." If one follows this translation, then Luke can still employ "we" to denote the whole of the ship's company (he is certainly not saying that Paul and his companions "weighed anchor"). A variant reading says "we sailed around" (cf. RSV), which might imply that the voyage to Rhegium encountered some minor difficulties. The ship anchored in Rhegium for one day, then caught a favorable wind and sailed on to Puteoli, a two-day voyage of 210 miles.

Puteoli was the most prominent port of Italy and was the usual port of arrival for passengers. Under the reign of Claudius, a new port had been built at Ostra, where cargo was regularly unloaded. So, perhaps, the Alexandrian vessel sailed on, but readers are not told. Luke has no interest in the story of grain.

"Brothers" offered hospitality to Paul and company for seven days (v. 14). Whether such hospitality would have included Paul's guards is not said, but readers should imagine them to be nearby.

The NRSV translates brothers as "believers," following the consensus of commentators that "brothers" does not mean Jews, but Christians who could also have been Jewish. Twice, Acts uses "brothers" to denote non-believing Jews (2:29; 13:26), but in both these instances it is Jewish speakers—Peter and Paul, respectively— using the term to address fellow Jews. When the narrator employs his own voice, "brother" consistently means "believers." There exists no corroborating evidence of a Christian community in Puteoli, though Josephus does speak of Jews who lived in the city

(*J. W.* 2.104; *Ant.* 17.328). Perhaps it was out of this Jewish community that the Christian community was born.

Verse 14 concludes with the important, but somewhat anticlimactic statement, "And so we came to Rome." Curiously, Paul has not yet reached the city of Rome, which lies 130 miles away. Perhaps the narrative assumes "Rome" to be the whole of Italy. It is also possible to understand the phrase translated as "and so" (*kai houtōs*) as pointing forward, anticipating the narrative to come. "And so, by way of Puteoli and the few-days journey to follow, we came to Rome."

The narrative is quite brief. Abruptly, readers are introduced to believers from Rome, though only as a group. As Paul made his way from Puteoli to Rome, first up *Via Compania* until it intersected with *Via Appia*, he would have had to pass through a couple of cities, the Forum of Appius (forty-three miles south of Rome) and Three Taverns (thirty-three miles south of Rome). Luke reports that believers from Rome came and greeted Paul and company in these cities. Paul is encouraged and grateful to see them. It is all a bit low-key. Any expectations raised in readers that the Roman Christian community would play some important role in the story to follow will be disappointed. This is all readers encounter of the Roman Christian community—faceless and voiceless extras on a stage where the spotlight consistently focuses only on Paul.

How these believers came to hear of Paul's arrival is not said. Paul's Letter to the Romans offers testimony not only of a Christian community in the city, but also bears witness to the fact that Paul knew people there (e.g., Priscilla [Prisca] and Aquila, cf.

Via Appia

Also known in translation as the Appian Way, this was the most important road through Italy in the days of the empire. It ran from the "heel" of the boot of Italy, across the peninsula in a northwest direction, turning north toward Rome just north of Puteoli. It was here that Paul would have picked up the road to lead him to the city of Rome. It fell out of use with the fall of the empire. A new road was built in the late eighteenth century that roughly parallels the "old Appian Way" (*Via Appia Antica*). Some sections of the old road are still in use.

Appian Way Mist
(Credit: istockphoto.com)

Rom 16:3). Original readers of Acts may not be privy to this information. Still, readers can imagine that while Paul remained in Puteoli for seven days, some of the people accompanying Paul moved on to Rome and reported that Paul was on his way. The journey to Rome on foot is five days, so, presumably, had believers from Rome set out immediately, then they could have met Paul en route. If accompanied by those who had been Paul's traveling companions, the Roman Christians, of course, would have had no problem recognizing Paul. But, admittedly, this is sheer speculation, prompted by readers' instincts to fill narrative gaps. Given the narrative's proclivity to visions, a reader could just as easily surmise that the believers from Rome were told in a dream that Paul was on his way.

With v. 16 Paul reaches the city of Rome. Paul does not meet with the Christian community. Rather, he lives alone under Roman guard, under what contemporary readers would think of as "house arrest." The Western text, followed by the KJV,[7] explicitly notes that the centurion transferred Paul and the other prisoners over to the jurisdiction of the garrison commander. While likely not part of the "original text" of Acts, the copyist has made a reasonable inference, even if only for the sake of verisimilitude. Certainly the centurion who had been accompanying Paul would have delivered him to the appropriate officials in Rome.[8]

The City of Rome

This is a view of the city of Rome from the SW. The circular building is the famous Coliseum (the Flavian Amphitheater). The elliptically shaped building is the Circus Maximus, famous for chariot races. Paul would have approached from the south on the Appian Way. On the southern edge of the city, the Appian Way merged with *Via Latina* and became *Via Nova*. *Via Nova* headed directly toward Circus Maximus. There is no way to know where in Rome Paul stayed or if he even entered the heart of the city.

Model of Ancient Rome. (Credit: Todd Bolen, "Rome Model view north," [cited 20 September 2007]. Online: http://www.bibleplaces.com.)

Proclaiming the Kingdom of God, 28:17-31

At this juncture, the narrative takes something of a surprising turn. Paul does not meet with representatives of the Christian community, nor is there any word on the disposition of Paul's legal case. Rather, Paul calls together the leaders of the *Jewish* community (v. 17). This gathering is the first of two encounters with representatives of the Jews of Rome (vv. 17-22 and vv. 23-31).

The population of the Jewish community of Rome was considerably large (some estimate as many as 50,000 plus). There had been a Jewish presence in Rome for perhaps as many as 200 years prior to Paul's arrival.[9] Archaeological evidence indicates at least five synagogues, and one suspects that other synagogues may have existed for which no material evidence remains.[10]

It is curious that leaders of this large community would have come to hear Paul. But, as the story in Malta reminds readers, Paul has regularly attracted the attention of local leaders, whether such attention boded well or ill for Paul. Additionally, toward the end of the first meeting the narrative offers a partial explanation for why these leaders would have come to hear Paul: they had heard of the Jewish "sect" of which Paul was a member and wanted to know more about it (v. 22).

Paul launches into a speech that explains, from his point of view, why he is in Rome. The brief speech offers the protagonist's interpretation of events that had transpired over the past couple of years since Paul had arrived in Jerusalem. Comparative analysis of Paul's interpretation of events and the narrative's presentation of events yields interesting insights, among which is to highlight—at least for readers—the similarities between Paul's trials and that of Jesus. [Paul's Interpretation of His Trials in Jerusalem] Paul has no way of knowing what his audience knows about his case, so he has nothing to lose by putting his best foot forward. Whatever they might know of his case (readers learn later [v. 21] that they knew nothing about it), his audience certainly does not know what readers know.

Paul insists on his innocence, not with reference to Roman law at this juncture, but with reference to the shared Jewish heritage and tradition of Paul and his audience. He insisted that he had done nothing against either the people or the traditions of "our ancestors" (v. 17). Paul's use of *laos*, which Acts usually employs to denote the Israel, the people of God (cf., e.g., Acts 2:47; 3:23; 4:10), and "our ancestors" points clearly to Paul's identification with his Jewish heritage. Paul declares that, nonetheless, he was delivered as a prisoner from Jerusalem to the Romans. Paul is laying the responsibility for his incarceration squarely on

Paul's Interpretation of His Trials in Jerusalem

Paul's first speech to the Jewish leaders of Rome (28:17-20) offers a summary of his trials in Jerusalem. In some instances, Paul employs language that calls to mind the trial of Jesus. Significantly, these Pauline interpretations do not match up with what the *narrative* of Paul's trials reports. Further, these echoes of Jesus' passion would have been totally lost on Paul's audience *in the story* (the Roman Jewish leadership). This fact serves to remind readers that these echoes are present in the narrative for the benefit of the *readers*, reinforcing critical awareness that the speeches of Acts are composed by the *narrator* to inform and edify the reading audience; they are not "composed" by the speaker in the story primarily to inform the audience in the story.

Paul's interpretation	The account of Acts	Jesus' passion
V. 17b: "Yet I was arrested in Jerusalem and handed over (*paredōthēn*) to the Romans." More literally, "I was handed over as a prisoner from Jerusalem to the Romans."	Paul is not arrested and then handed over to the Romans (or delivered as a prisoner from Jerusalem to the Romans). Paul is being attacked by a Jewish mob. The Romans move in to stop the violence, whereupon the Romans arrest Paul, presuming him to have been the cause of ruckus (21:31-33).	One of Jesus' prophecies of his passion speaks of being "handed over (*paradothēsetai*) to the Gentiles" (Luke 18:32). Further, Luke's Passion Narrative speaks of Jesus' being brought to the Romans by the Jewish authorities (Luke 23:1, 14). Paul's interpretation of events highlights this echo of Jesus' experience.
V. 18b-19a: "The Romans wanted to release (*apolusai*) me, because there was no reason for the death penalty in my case. But when the Jews objected, I was compelled to appeal to the emperor . . . ."	The narrative does report that various Roman officials had declared that Paul had done nothing worthy of death (23:29; 25:25; 26:30). Yet there are no declarations that the Romans wanted to *release* Paul. The closest one gets to such a statement is Agrippa's comment, made in private to Festus, that had Paul not appealed to the emperor he might have been "released" (26:32). But this statement comes only at the *end* of Paul's trials and after Paul had appealed to Caesar. Hence, in the narrative of Acts, Jewish opposition to Paul (while intense) does not consist of any "objections" to Roman desires to release Paul. Paul's summary statement that it was such Jewish objections that compelled him to appeal to Caesar stands in tension with the narrative of Acts. The narrative states that Paul appealed to the emperor because Festus suggested moving the venue of the trial to Jerusalem (25:9-12).	In Jesus' passion, Pilate on three occasions specifically expresses the desire to release Jesus (Luke 23:16, 20 and 22), each time employing a cognate of the verb *apoluō*, the verb Paul employs in his summary. Further, after each of the three times, Pilate's declaration is met with intense protests and objections from the Jews (23:18, 21, 23). Paul's way of recounting the story highlights the similarity with Jesus' trial.

"Jerusalem," by which he would mean, of course, not the city, but the leadership (much like people today can refer to "Washington" or "Wall Street" as a means of referring to the leadership of the institutions these places symbolize).

The Roman authorities, however, after examining Paul actually wanted to release him (v. 18). The Jewish leadership of Rome might prefer not to align themselves against "the Romans" who, at least, according to Paul, found that he had done nothing deserving of death. But readers could just as easily imagine that Paul's audience might be a bit incredulous—if Paul were so innocent, why is he in Rome living under guard? Paul continues his defense: it was only objections from "the Jews" that compelled Paul to appeal to Caesar, and, thus, he now finds himself in Rome.

Paul adds an interesting footnote, insisting that he has no charge to bring against his own nation. Witherington takes seriously the possibility that, historically, Paul might have had good grounds for a counter suit for "malicious prosecution"[11] and that Paul might actually be browbeating his audience a bit. The threat of a lawsuit to cower one's potential opponent is, apparently, not just a modern convention.

Rhetorically, the line assures Paul's listening audience that he holds no grudges at all against "his nation." Literarily, the speech affirms that Paul is a loyal Jew and is in command of the situation. Though under house arrest, he is capable of calmly presenting his case to the leadership of the Jewish community of Rome. Ethically, Paul is a noble man who, even though he might have legitimate cause for counter legal action, will not pursue his rights.

It is "for this reason" (v. 20) that Paul wanted to speak to the Jewish leadership. "This reason" points back to the whole of the preceding speech. Paul declares that he is in Rome because of his steadfast loyalty and conviction to "the hope of Israel"—a hope that Paul holds with enough tenacity that even chains will not weaken his resolve. Readers know the content of this hope—it is the hope of resurrection, a hope that Paul and Luke's readers believe finds its initial realization in the resurrection of Jesus (see [Resurrection of the Dead]). Paul's audience would have a more generic vision of this hope, but it would certainly include the hopes of Israel's vindication and restoration (see [Restoration Eschatology]).

The Jewish leadership shows no hostility toward Paul. Readers and Paul learn together that the leaders are totally unfamiliar with Paul's case. Further, they have not heard any negative reports about Paul at all (v. 21). A prejudicial spirit against Paul, that he is some renegade speaking against the Jewish people and heritage, does not appear to blind their eyes. The Roman Jewish leadership, unlike the leadership of Jerusalem, might be more open to hearing what Paul has to say. This initial perception of Paul is very different from that of the Jerusalem Jews, even the Christian Jews of Jerusalem (recall 21:20-21).

Though ignorant of Paul, the Jewish leadership has heard some things about the movement of which he speaks—and what they have heard is not favorable (v. 22). Candidly, based exclusively on what Paul has said in vv. 17-20, the Jewish leadership would have no reason even to know that Paul represented this "sect" of the Messiah. This is not a very serious problem, however, for one can conclude that these Jewish leaders would have known at least that Paul had something to do with this messianic movement or they would not even bothered to come to see him in the first place. The effect of the comment, particularly when combined with their statement that they did not harbor negative feelings toward Paul, raises expectations that the group is at least open to hearing more of what Paul has to say. They explicitly state that the reason they indulged Paul's invitation was that, though they had heard less than favorable things about the messianist movement, they were open to hearing Paul's views on the matter. The historical veracity of their comments is another matter, however. [The Jewish Leadership: What Did They Know?]

Paul's second meeting with the Jewish leadership of Rome takes place sometime later; the narrator does not report the duration of time between the meetings (v. 23). This time the crowd is larger. Polhill makes the observation that this, the final scene of Paul's ministry, is structurally reminiscent of the first major scene of Paul's ministry, his preaching in Antioch of Pisidia (13:13-41). The similarities provide a kind of inclusio to introduce and conclude Paul's missionary work.[12] [Paul at Antioch and Rome]

Paul spends the entire day preaching to his audience. The narrator graciously offers readers the briefest of a précis. Readers, however, should easily be able to fill in the gaps.

Paul testified concerning the kingdom of God. The good news of God's reign has been a central feature of the message of both Jesus and his followers. The Gospel of Luke and the book of Acts together offer thirty-seven verses that refer to "the kingdom of God." Most, to be sure, are in the Gospel. But, perhaps fittingly, when Luke wishes to summarize the teachings of the resurrected Jesus at the beginning of Acts, he states that Jesus appeared to his disciples for forty days and spoke to them of the kingdom of God (1:3). Further, as Acts brings the narrative to a close it speaks of Paul's "preaching the kingdom of God" (28:31). Paul's preaching of the kingdom complements well his affirmation earlier in the chapter that he was on trial for "the hope of Israel." The coming of God's reign, which included the restoration and liberation of Israel (cf. the Benedictus, esp. Luke 1:69-75), was certainly part of Israel's hope.

The Jewish Leadership: What Did They Know?

Why would the Roman Jewish leadership have heard nothing about Paul, either from Jerusalem or other Jews passing through Rome (28:21)? With respect to having heard nothing from Jerusalem, interpreters wanting to reconstruct the history behind the narrative offer a number of explanations: Paul arrived before any official (or even unofficial) word had reached Rome (Haenchen, 727; Polhill, 540); communication between the leadership of the respective communities was sparse and infrequent (Polhill, 540); the Jerusalem leadership had, in fact, abandoned the case and, hence, no word had arrived or was even forthcoming (Witherington, 799).

Haenchen is not bothered that the Roman leadership has not heard the specifics of the *case* against Paul—it is quite understandable that Paul could have reached Rome before news of his Jerusalem trials did. "But the Roman Jews have apparently still heard nothing unfavourable about Paul at all, and that is unbelievable" (Haenchen, 727). It is curious that, historically, the Roman Jewish leadership would have heard no negative reports whatsoever about Paul. Paul's letters tend to leave the impression that he had opponents everywhere, and it seems odd that none ever passed through Rome or, when they did, they either had nothing at all to say about Paul or chose not to say anything bad about him.

Further, it stands in tension with the testimony of Acts itself. Acts portrays zealous Jews as following Paul about stirring up trouble against him almost wherever he went. And when Paul reached Jerusalem, his reputation as one speaking against Judaism had preceded him. It was, in fact, this negative reputation that stirred up Jews of the Diaspora against Paul. And yet readers are to conclude that the Jewish leadership of Rome has heard absolutely nothing negative about Paul? More credulous interpreters can always reconstruct history or offer hypotheses that allow their credulity to remain intact. But Haenchen seems on target here. His assessment may be blunt, but it's not unfair.

While the Jewish leaders of Rome know nothing negative of Paul, they have heard bad things about the sect that he represents. They offer no summary of the sort of negative things they have heard. Still, the narrative leaves the impression that the Jewish leadership of Rome has only the most remote knowledge of the Christian movement: "Everyone, everywhere says bad things about these people (v. 22)." Their wanting to hear Paul's views on the sect would imply that they simply do not know enough about Christianity to render a judgment.

Paul's letter to the Romans proves the existence of Christian community in Rome. The long list of people whom Paul can greet by name at the end of the letter implies a numerically significant community. Furthermore, many of the specific conflicts that Paul talks about in Romans indicate that there were enough Jewish Christians in the community to create substantial tensions within the Roman Christian community. None of this proves that the Jewish leadership of Rome could not have been poorly informed about the Christian movement, but it does require some explanation.

John Polhill finds the leaders' statement "puzzling," but he surmises that Claudius's expulsion of Jews from Rome, due perhaps to conflicts between Christian and non-Christian Jews, created an intentional distancing between the Jewish leadership and Christian communities (see [Edict of Claudius]). Even with such official distancing, however, it would still seem odd that the Jewish leadership did not know more than they indicate (Polhill, 540).

C. K. Barrett sums up the implications of the whole of 28:21 and attempts a literary solution: "The verse suggests an almost complete cleavage between Jews and Christians in Rome, and between Jews in Rome and Jews in Jerusalem. Neither of these seems probable. The effect is to represent Paul as not only a pioneer missionary but as the spokesman of Christianity to the Jews. This at least seems to be Luke's intention" (Barrett, 2.1242).

Ernst Haenchen, *The Acts of the Apostles: A Commentary* (Philadelphia: Westminster, 1971); John B. Polhill, *Acts* (NAC 26; Nashville: Broadman, 1992); Ben Witherington III, *The Acts of the Apostles: A Socio-Rhetorical Commentary* (Grand Rapids: Eerdmans, 1998); C. K. Barrett, *Acts*, 2 vols. (ICC; Edinburgh: T&T Clark, 1994/1998).

Paul also attempted to persuade his audience "about Jesus both from the law of Moses and the prophets." Paul cannot speak of the kingdom without speaking of Jesus. It is in this man, Jesus, that the hope of the kingdom finds its realization. Again, as early as the Benedictus, one finds allusion to Jesus (referred to as "a mighty savior" from "the house of God's servant David" [Luke 1:69]) as

Paul at Antioch and Rome

The narrative of Paul's preaching of the gospel to the Jewish community at Antioch (Paul's first major "preaching scene") offers many structural parallels with Paul's encounter with Jews of Rome (Paul's last major "preaching scene"). The following table, which builds on but does not reduplicate Polhill's observations, presents the structural similarities.

Event	Antioch (Acts 13:16-47)	Rome (Acts 28:17-31)
First encounter concludes with attitude of openness on the part of the Jews to Paul's message.	"As Paul and Barnabas were going out, the people urged them to speak about these things again the next sabbath. When the meeting of the synagogue broke up, many Jews and devout converts to Judaism followed Paul and Barnabas, who spoke to them and urged them to continue in the grace of God" (vv. 42-43).	"They replied, 'We have received no letters from Judea about you, and none of the brothers coming here has reported or spoken anything evil about you. But we would like to hear from you what you think, for with regard to this sect we know that everywhere it is spoken against'" (vv. 21-22).
Second encounter draws a larger audience.	"The next sabbath almost the whole city gathered to hear the word of the Lord" (v. 44).	"After they had set a day to meet with him, they came to him at his lodgings in great numbers" (v. 23a).
Jews are not as open after the second encounter. Some explicitly reject Paul's message.	"But when the Jews saw the crowds, they were filled with jealousy; and blaspheming, they contradicted what was spoken by Paul" (v. 45).	"Some were convinced by what he had said, while others refused to believe. So they disagreed with each other" (vv. 24-25a).
Paul responds, quoting Isaiah.	"For so the Lord has commanded us, saying, 'I have set you to be a light for the Gentiles, so that you may bring salvation to the ends of the earth'" (v. 47; quoting Isa 49:6).	Quotes Isa 6:9-10 in vv. 26-27.
Paul declares that his Jewish audience is responsible for its decision.	"Since you reject it and judge yourselves to be unworthy of eternal life, . . ." (v. 46b).	"For this people's heart has grown dull, and their ears are hard of hearing, and they have shut their eyes; so that they might not look with their eyes, and listen with their ears, and understand with their heart and turn—and I would heal them" (vv. 27, quoting Isa 6:9).
Paul announces that he will preach to Gentiles.	"Behold, we turn to the Gentiles" (v. 46c).	"Let it be known to you then that this salvation of God has been sent to the Gentiles; they will listen" (v. 28).

The structurally similar narratives that begin and end the focus on the Pauline mission provide a kind of "interpretive frame" for making sense of the preaching mission of Paul. Paul *begins* and *ends* his mission by inviting Jews to accept the gospel that Paul believes is the fulfillment of the hopes of Israel. Paul *begins* and *ends* his ministry encountering a mixed reaction. Paul *begins* and *ends* his ministry announcing that he will go to the Gentiles. The Pauline mission is framed by the consistent pattern of preaching the gospel to all. The same framework also reveals a pattern of mixed reception from the Jewish community and the expectation of a more open reception from non-Jews. But the pattern remains consistent: "turning to the gentiles" does not mean "turning away from the Jews."

John B. Polhill, *Acts* (NAC 26; Nashville: Broadman, 1992), 541–42.

the one in whom Israel's hopes find their fulfillment. The depository of Israel's hope was Israel's Scriptures—the law and the prophets. Thus, Paul appeals to the scriptural heritage of his audience in his attempt to persuade them about Jesus.

Fittingly, this summary of Paul's preaching to his audience in Rome again echoes the Benedictus, for it too speaks of the word that God spoke to the holy prophets of old (Luke 1:70). Further, the resurrected Jesus also spoke of how the law and prophets found their fulfillment in him and the subsequent mission of his followers (see Luke 24:27, 44-47). As to precisely what Paul said concerning the law and prophets, readers have several examples from the other speeches in Acts to fill the narrative gap (see esp. 2:16-36; 3:12-26; 7:1-53; 8:30-37; 13:16-47; 15:13-21).

The reaction of Paul's audience is mixed (v. 24). Though readers might have initially been more hopeful that Paul would have proven more persuasive, this reaction should not surprise readers. A "mixed" reaction is the pattern in Acts.[13] The gospel has consistently divided ethnic Israel, a division that perhaps was foreseen as early as Simeon's postscript to the Nunc Dimittis (Luke 2:29-32), wherein he spoke of Jesus being "destined for the falling and rising of many in Israel, and to be a sign that will be opposed" (Luke 2:34). The day is over and Paul's best attempts to persuade the leaders of the large Jewish community have met with mixed reviews. Paul's audience now departs, disagreeing among themselves. Paul's final word is an (almost) direct quotation of the Greek text of Isaiah 6:9-10, preceded by a brief introduction and application (vv. 25b-28). [Analysis of Isaiah 6:9-10]

Paul introduces the quotation from Isaiah by stating the Holy Spirit was right to speak the oracle of Isaiah to "your ancestors." Paul, like the other characters in Acts, can view the Scripture as speaking with the voice of the spirit of God (cf. Acts 1:16; 4:25). The Holy Spirit offered guidance to those who spoke God's word of old, even as that same Spirit consistently offered guidance to those who spoke God's word and offered God's leadership throughout the narrative of Acts (cf. 1:2; 2:4; 4:8, 31; 6:10; 8:29, 39; 10:19; 11:12, 28; 13:2, 4; 15:28; 16:6-7; 19:6, 21; 20:23, 28; 21:4, 11).

Paul distances himself from his audience as he says that it was to *their* ancestors that the prophecy of Isaiah applies. Paul is not denying his Jewish heritage. But in Luke–Acts "ancestors" can refer not only to the ancestors of ethnic Israel, which would include all Jews, but also to the *specific* ancestors of that part of Israel that is resistant to the gospel of the kingdom.[14] While Paul shares the ancestry of his audience in the former sense, he does not share their ancestry in this latter sense.

The original oracle of Isaiah 6 is found in the context of Isaiah's prophetic call to preach to an obstinate nation. In its originating

Analysis of Isaiah 6:9-10

The following table lays out in English translation the various texts of Isa 6:9-10. With the exception of the introductory formula that introduces what Isaiah is to say to the people, the Greek text of Acts 28:26-27 and the Greek text of Isa 6:9-10 are identical and the English translations reflect that identity.

Hebrew Bible (NRSV)	Septuagint	Acts (NRSV)
9 "Go and say to this people: 'Keep listening, but do not comprehend; keep looking, but do not understand.' 10 Make the mind of this people dull, and stop their ears, and shut their eyes, so that they may not look with their eyes, and listen with their ears, and comprehend with their minds, and turn and be healed."	9 "Go and say to this people, You will indeed listen, but never understand, and you will indeed look, but never perceive. 10 For this people's heart has grown dull, and their ears are hard of hearing, and they have shut their eyes; so that they might not look with their eyes, and listen with their ears, and understand with their heart and turn—and I would heal them."	26 "Go to this people and say, You will indeed listen, but never understand, and you will indeed look, but never perceive. 27 For this people's heart has grown dull, and their ears are hard of hearing, and they have shut their eyes; so that they might not look with their eyes, and listen with their ears, and understand with their heart and turn—and I would heal them."

The most significant difference between the Hebrew and Greek texts is the moods of the verbs. Note that in the Hebrew text Isaiah *commands* the people of Israel to "keep listening, but not comprehend, keep looking, but do not understand." In the Greek version, Isaiah does not *command* the people not to comprehend or understand; rather he simply announces that they will not comprehend or understand.

And *why* will the people not comprehend or understand? Again, the two versions offer differing explanations. In the Hebrew the people will not comprehend or understand for the prophet himself will *make* their minds dull, *stop* up their ears, and *shut* their eyes. The Hebrew text presses how the people of Israel are to be *acted upon*, thereby rendering them virtually powerless to comprehend and, thereby, repent and be healed.

The Greek text transforms the verbs to declare, first, that the heart of the people *has grown dull*. Already the hearts to which the prophet will appeal are dull. So with the ears. The prophet is not to be the one who stops up their ears—their ears are *already* hard of hearing. But why? The next line clearly implicates Israel herself: "they have shut their eyes." Israel's hardness in the Greek text is not a passive reception of the action of God or the prophet. It is Israel's active decision not to see or hear. Consequently, Israel's failure to repent, to turn and be healed, is the consequence of Israel's own decision.

By quoting the text of Isaiah from the Septuagint, Acts does conclude that Israel's rejection of the gospel is a rejection of her own choosing. Hence, no reader of Acts could conclude that "God has rejected Israel" by blinding their eyes, deafening their ears, and hardening their hearts. A reader would conclude, however, that Israel has rejected Paul's message of her own will.

But further analysis of the use of Isaiah reveals that the quotation still ends on a more hopeful note than it had to. Isaiah 6:11-12 goes on to say (quoting the translation of the Septuagint, since this would have been the version Luke employed):

11And I said, How long, O Lord? And he said, Until cities be deserted by reason of their not being inhabited, and the houses by reason of there being no men, and the land shall be left desolate. 12 And after this God shall remove the men far off, and they that are left upon the land shall be multiplied.

Luke's Bible provided him a text that could have allowed Paul's last words to allude to the decimation of the land. Luke (and Luke's readers) could easily have associated such a text with the destruction of Jerusalem and temple by the Romans in AD 70—surely an event of history from the perspective of the narrator and his readers. The quotation could have ended on a note of divine wrath and punishment. Rather, given Luke's quotation, it ends with a reminder that God is able to heal. This requires repentance. Repentance requires a change of heart. But it is within Israel's power to effect such a change.

context "this people" (v. 26) would have referred to Isaiah's audience. Paul finds the words apropos to his own time. He can now say to his divided audience that they shall hear but never understand, see but never perceive. In the case of Paul's particular audience, they have heard his testimony and they have heard his appeals to Scripture. They have witnessed with their own eyes Paul's conviction, bound as he is in chains, for the hope of Israel. But hearing does not always translate into understanding, and sight does not always translate into perception. It takes more than an openness to give Paul another "hearing" to respond positively to what he is saying.

Verse 27, continuing the quotation from Isaiah, offers something of a reason for the kind of response Paul's message engenders. Their heart, the seat of volition and thought, is dull. Their ears are heavy, an idiomatic expression that means that one cannot hear or grasp what is being said. And they have, as Paul quotes the text, closed their eyes. In ancient anthropology, the eye was not so much that which admitted light as that which emitted light.[15] One cannot shine one's inner light of discernment on something if one's eyes are shut.

One needs a heart that is willing to understand, ears that are willing to hear, and eyes that are open and willing to explore or there can be no perception of sight, discernment of sound, and understanding of the heart. With such receptivity, and only with such receptivity, can one then turn (repent) and experience the healing power of God. That is what Paul had hoped for this audience. That has been the consistent plea of Paul throughout the narrative of Acts. Consistently, however, a mixed reaction was the best Paul encountered.

Paul's blunt commentary of v. 28 is that "this salvation of God has been sent to the Gentiles; they will listen." The text employs the middle form of the verb *akouō*, implying not only that Gentiles will *hear*, but also that they will *listen*; that is, they will hear with understanding. This final declaration of Paul has created much conversation among interpreters. Is Paul stating that the Jews have now received their "final offer," that, henceforth, the word of God's salvation is exclusively for the Gentiles? Has the door now been shut on Israel?

Luke Johnson leans in this direction. He notes that Paul has previously made the announcement that he would turn to the Gentiles (cf. Acts 13:46-47; 18:6). But this declaration is different: it is Paul's "third and final 'turn to the Gentiles.'"[16] God has been faithful to God's promises and has given Israel many chances to repent. The narrative of Acts bears witness to this as Peter, Stephen, and Paul have offered the word of salvation to Israel. But Israel, as a whole, has consistently rejected the good news of the kingdom, a rejection manifested in the rejection of those who offered this word of salvation: Jesus, Peter, Stephen, and, now, Paul. Johnson explains, "The final word spoken to the Jewish leaders is therefore one of rejection, but it is a rejection that they have taken upon themselves. . . . For the final time, therefore, Paul announces a turn to the Gentiles with a ringing affirmation: the salvation from God *has* been sent to them and *they* will listen."[17]

The ending of Acts, however, may be more nuanced. Clearly, the narrative does not end on a positive note as it concerns Israel's receptivity to the message of Paul. But Robert Tannehill makes the thoughtful observation that "if the scene's purpose is to show that there is no longer any hope of convincing Jews, and the church must now concentrate exclusively on the Gentile mission, the point is undermined by portraying part of the Jewish community on the verge of acceptance. The reference to some being persuaded indicates that there is still hope of convincing some Jews in spite of what Paul is about to say about the Jewish community of Rome."[18]

To be sure, the words of Isaiah are harsh—they speak to a reality that cannot be denied: the message of the gospel did not find reception among Israel as a whole. Yet these same words are equally harsh in their setting of Isaiah. Still, some of the most comforting words God offers to Israel are found in that same book of Isaiah (note, e.g., Isa 40:1-5). In Isaiah the harsh oracle "did not signal a total rejection of the Jews of Isaiah's day, nor does it do so in this context for Paul's day."[19]

There is no extended narrative of Paul's continued preaching to Jews. It is time for this narrative to draw to a close. But as the narrative closes, it closes with a clear reference that Paul continued to preach the message of the kingdom for two whole years, welcoming "all who came to him" (v. 31). Israel as a whole has not been receptive to the gospel. Such was the historical reality of Luke's time. But readers are not compelled to conclude that Israel will never be receptive to gospel. And certainly readers are not to infer that the gospel is to be one that welcomes all—except Jews.

The narrative closes with a picture of Paul continuing to proclaim the message of the kingdom. Further, such proclamation is unhindered. Paul is under house arrest, awaiting his hearing before Caesar. Yet the gospel is not deterred. The ending of the narrative may impress some readers as lacking meaningful closure. The text speaks of Paul preaching for two years. Tannehill finds a possible intertextual echo with Paul's Ephesian ministry. According to Acts 19:9-10, Paul continued to preach in Ephesus for two years, following his expulsion from the synagogue, during which time "all the residents of Asia, both Jews and Greeks, heard the word of the Lord" (v. 10). The parallel is not exact—it is an echo. But it is a potentially provocative echo. The failure of the Jewish communities of either Ephesus or Rome to embrace the gospel opened up a significant period of continued preaching to *all* the residents of the respective communities.[20]

But what happened after the two years had elapsed? Does the reference to two years imply that the legal waiting period had lapsed and, with no charges forthcoming from the Jews of Jerusalem, Paul had now been released?[21] Not necessarily. Acts is filled with prophetic announcements, most of which find their realization *within* the narrative. It is appropriate at this juncture to focus on some illustrative pronouncements as they pertain to Paul. It was prophesied that Paul would be Christ's instrument to preach to Jews, Gentiles, and kings (9:15), a prophecy fulfilled in the subsequent narrative of Acts. Readers encountered prophecies speaking of how Paul would face hardships in Jerusalem (20:22-23; 21:11), fulfilled when Paul arrived in Jerusalem. The narrative prophesied that Paul would see Rome (23:11). Even the most harrowing storm at sea could not deter this prophecy's fulfillment. In the midst of this storm, Paul received assurances that he and all on board the ship would be delivered, for Paul would stand before the emperor (27:24). This prophecy finds no fulfillment *within* the narrative, but there is no reason to suppose that the prophecy would not find fulfillment. Readers can be confident that Paul would stand before Caesar.

But what of the outcome of this hearing? On this question commentators find less agreement. Readers have encountered no explicit prophecies of the outcome of the trial. The tone of Paul's farewell address to the Ephesian elders (20:18-35), especially hints of Paul's death in vv. 24-25, may imply that Paul would die in Rome. This *may* be another prophecy that does not find fulfillment in the narrative but which readers can be confident was fulfilled beyond the confines of the narrative. To be sure, Acts 20:25 may only mean that Paul would never pass by way of Ephesus again. So it is possible that, historically, Paul was released from Roman custody and was able to fulfill his goal of traveling on to Spain (cf. Rom 15:24, 28). One cannot say for sure, for the author of Acts reported neither the trial before Caesar and, consequently, could not report its outcome.

Narrators end narratives when they have accomplished their purposes. The purpose of Acts is not *primarily* to tell the story of Paul. Paul is an instrument in the story of the gospel's reach "to the ends of the earth." To be sure, Rome may not be the literal end, but it is certainly the hub. With the open proclamation of the gospel of the kingdom of God in Caesar's city, the story of Paul's life may not come to satisfying closure, but the story of Acts does.

CONNECTIONS

Narrative endings, like narrative beginnings, offer important clues and cues to readers as we attempt to construct the meanings of texts. Luke's Gospel, for example, begins and ends in Jerusalem and, more specifically, the temple precincts (cf. Luke 1:5-23, 2:21-38, 41-51; 19:45–21:38; 24:50-53). The center of action as the book of Acts begins is also Jerusalem (Acts 1–7), with the temple often being the setting of the action (e.g., 3:1–4:4; 5:17-26). Jerusalem was center stage for the final, climactic scenes of Paul (21:17–23:30). Again, the temple provided the setting for much of this action (21:27–22:22).

But though Jerusalem and the temple play important roles, the message of the gospel presses beyond the boundaries of this significant city and holy place. Indeed, the pronouncement of Jesus in Acts 1:8 speaks of the message of the gospel progressing from Jerusalem to Judea and Samaria and, finally, to the ends of the earth. The book of Acts, unlike the gospel, does not end in Jerusalem; it ends in Rome, a fitting symbol for (if not the literal location of) "the ends of the earth." The gospel is for *all* people, including, but not limited to, the people of Israel; including, but not limited to, non-Jewish people. And a message for all people must be willing to reach into all places.

Yet, while the gospel presses beyond the borders and boundaries of Jerusalem, readers are regularly "brought back" to Jerusalem. Paul visits Jerusalem after his call (9:26-29). Later, he and Barnabas bring famine relief to Jerusalem (11:27-30). Readers learn of James's execution in Jerusalem (12:1-3) and Peter's imprisonment and deliverance from a Jerusalem jail (12:4-17). Paul visits Jerusalem yet a third time to deal with the issue of Gentile circumcision (15:1-35). Then, yet again, Paul makes visit to Jerusalem in 18:22. No detail is offered. It is sufficient that the readers who accompany Paul drop in on Jerusalem, if only for the duration of a few words. Finally, as already noted, Paul makes a final trip to Jerusalem, where he is arrested.

In the course of Paul's trials following his arrest, Paul appeals to the emperor (25:11). Festus immediately grants Paul's appeal (25:12), and from that point on, the focus of the narrative shifts to Paul's trip to Rome. We would naturally expect that the settlement of Paul's case before Caesar would serve as a fitting climax to the narrative. But this is not the way that the narrative ends. It is almost surprising that the narrative ends not before Caesar, but before the *Jewish* leadership of Rome.

The fact that this is how Luke concludes the narrative allows us to infer that lying close to the heart of Luke's concern is still the issue of Christianity's relationship with Judaism, represented by the relationship of Paul with the Jewish leaders. The narrative's focus on two powerful symbols of Judaism, Jerusalem and the temple, summarized above, reinforces this inference. The appeals to Jewish Scripture, found not only in the concluding scenes of Acts (28:23, 25-27), but also throughout Luke and Acts, further reinforce this conclusion. The relationship seems clear: in the story of Jesus and his followers the hopes of Israel and of Israel's Scriptures find realization (cf. Luke 24:44-48).

And yet so much of Israel fails to realize this. At best, in this final story (v. 24), as in so many stories throughout Acts, the announcement of the fulfillment of Israel's hopes produces mixed results. Paul's appeal to Isaiah 6 attempts to make sense of this seemingly mystifying fact. One way, however, that this text does *not* make sense of this fact is to portray the prophetic words as *foreordaining* that so many within Israel would not believe.

Paul does not say, as he quotes Isaiah, that God had ordained this response and then prophesied such ordination through the Holy Spirit. As a review of the analysis of Isaiah 6 reveals, the Greek text quoted by Luke removes any hint that Israel's obstinacy was due to anything other than *Israel's* own will (see [Analysis of Isaiah 6:9-10]). Further, Luke is certainly capable of employing prophecies to lay out what God had *ordained* to happen (cf. 1:16-21 and 4:24-28). In this concluding scene Paul specifically states that the Holy Spirit was speaking not to Paul's audience, but to the *ancestors* of Paul's audience (v. 27). This observation allows the text to offer more helpful insight into the mystery of Israel's rejection of her own hope.

Given that Paul specifically states that the words of the prophecy are actually directed to the ancestors of his audience, it reminds us of a fact of which the Jewish Scriptures are well aware. *Israel has* rarely responded with one accord to the call of God. Jack Miles's intriguing "biography" of God makes the following interesting observation: One of the striking features of Israel's Scripture is the candor with which it consistently portrays Israel's resistance to God and God's exasperation with Israel. God is regularly portrayed much like parents with "that child" that they "just don't know what to do with." [Israel's Peculiar Relationship with God]

Jesus' parable of the prodigal son (Luke 15:11-32), more properly titled the parable of the father and his two sons, reflects the same interesting relational dynamics. The father is always worrying about or dealing with at least one of his sons. If the father represents God (a relatively easy association) and the sons represent Israel, either in her rebellion and repentance or surly righteousness, then the parable makes clear that God is always busy having to tend to some sort of trouble stirred up by God's children.

And yet, despite Israel's consistent obduracy, Israel remains. God is faithful. One could read Isaiah 6 to warn that the "story of Israel" is not to last much longer. And yet there are sixty more chapters to read. And in these chapters, the struggle continues. Perhaps most intriguing are such texts as Isaiah 42:18–43:7. Here it is Israel, *God's servant* (cf. Isa 42:1), the servant who is to open the eyes of others who are blind (Isa 42:6-7), who is said to be blind and deaf (Isa 42:18-19). This blind and deaf servant "sees many things, but does not observe them; his ears are open, but he does not hear" (Isa 42:20). The echo of Isaiah 6 is obvious. Israel still does not fully see or clearly hear. The servant is described as a people robbed, plundered, trapped, and "hidden in prisons" (Isa 42:22). Such a state is due to God's judgment upon this people (Isa 42:24-25). And yet the servant lives on. Why? Because of God's unrelenting faithfulness: "Do not fear, for I have redeemed you; I have called you by name, you are mine. . . . For I am the LORD your God, the Holy One of Israel, your Savior" (Isa 43:1b, 3a).

Paul would not quote the text from Isaiah 6 to his departing and divided audience if he did not find the words apropos. The words may have been addressed to ancient ancestors, but they are fitting even in Paul's time. But Paul is not saying anything about Israel

Israel's Peculiar Relationship with God

"[God] complains endlessly about [Israel's] complaining. And yet, from the outside, a certain symmetry may be seen, never more clearly than in the Book of Numbers, as Israel complains about Moses, Moses complains about Israel, God complains about Israel, Israel complains about God, God complains about Moses, and Moses complains about God. That such a narrative should have been preserved and elevated to the status of sacred Scripture and national classic was an act of the most profound literary and moral originality."

"Leaving aside the difference, if any, between straining to keep a covenant and fearing to break one, has Israel done either? Obviously not: The attitude in evidence from the crossing of the Red Sea to the imminent crossing of the Jordan has been all obstinate complaint, skepticism, 'stiff-necked' resentment of God's appointed leaders, and on two occasions desertion to another god."

Jack Miles, *God: A Biography* (New York: Alfred A. Knopf, 1995), 133, 143.

that *Israel hasn't already heard or even said about herself.* This is the tragic pattern of Israel's story. Hers is a story of rebellion, repentance, and restoration, only to be followed by a repetition of the seemingly endless cycle. But God is faithful. Israel remains. Israel remains in Paul's day, as well as our own. Israel stands as the enduring testimony of God's faithfulness.

But what of Paul's statement that this salvation will be sent to the Gentiles (v. 28)? One can read this as a kind of final statement, as though after all these centuries God has finally had enough of Israel. God is going to find a new people. God has waited on the porch for the prodigal to return long enough. "To hell with him." Literally. "I'm going to find a new son to replace my old one." But it is not necessary and certainly not gracious to read the text this way.

Paul has been frustrated before, blustering out the words that he would "turn to the Gentiles" (cf. Acts 13:46; 18:5-6). And yet as the story continues Paul finds himself regularly preaching to Jews. Acts 28:30 explicitly states that for the next two years Paul "welcomed all who came to him." It does not say "all but the Jews" or "all Gentiles." The gospel offers a word of God's redemptive love to all. It always did and always will.

Simeon prophesied that Jesus would create division within Israel (Luke 2:34). When has the word of God *not* created division within Israel? But Simeon also said, "for my eyes have seen your salvation, which you have prepared in the presence of all peoples, a light for revelation to the Gentiles and for glory to your people Israel" (Luke 2:30-32). Gentiles should be eternally grateful that the light of the salvation of God has shown on them. Gentiles, who make up the vast, vast majority of Christians, should also not forget that this same salvation is "for glory to [God's] people Israel."

NOTES

[1] Ernst Haenchen, *The Acts of the Apostles: A Commentary* (Philadelphia: Westminster, 1971), 713.

[2] Ben Witherington III, *The Acts of the Apostles: A Socio-Rhetorical Commentary* (Grand Rapids MI: Eerdmans, 1998), 779.

[3] John B. Polhill, *Acts* (NAC 26; Nashville: Broadman, 1992), 533.

[4] E.g., Polhill, *Acts*, 533–34.

[5] Witherington, *Acts*, 781.

[6] Polhill, *Acts*, 535.

7 "The centurion delivered the prisoners to the captain of the guard."

8 Witherington, *Acts*, 789–93 offers a thorough discussion of the legal and military background to Paul's house arrest in Rome.

9 Joseph A. Fitzmyer, *The Acts of the Apostles* (AB 31; New York: Doubleday, 1998), 792.

10 Witherington, *Acts*, 795.

11 Ibid.

12 Polhill, *Acts*, 541–42.

13 Cf. Acts 2:12-13; 4:1-4; 5:12-17; 6:8-14; 9:21-25; 13:42-25; 14:1-2; 17:1-5; 18:4, 12-17; 19:8-10. See also Jacob Jervell, "The Divided People of God: The Restoration of Israel and Salvation for the Gentiles," in *Luke and the People of God: A New Look at Luke–Acts* (Minneapolis: Augsburg Publishing House, 1972), 41–74.

14 See J. Bradley Chance, "The Seed of Abraham and the People of God: A Study of Two Pauls," *SBLSP* (1993): 384–411.

15 Cf. the saying of Jesus, "The eye is the lamp of the body. So, if your eye is healthy, your whole body will be full of light" (Matt 6:22 || Luke 11:34). Lamps emit light; they do not admit light. Hence, it is not that a "healthy eye" *lets in* light, resulting in a body full of light. Rather, it is that a healthy eye emits light, showing the body to be full of light. See Dale C. Allison Jr., *The Sermon on the Mount: Inspiring Moral Imagination* (New York: Crossroad, 1999), 142–45.

16 Luke Timothy Johnson, *The Acts of the Apostles* (SacPag 5; Collegeville MN: Liturgical Press, 1992), 472.

17 Ibid., 476.

18 Robert W. Tannehill, *The Narrative Unity of Luke–Acts: A Literary Interpretation*, 2 vols. (Minneapolis: Fortress, 1990), 2.347.

19 Witherington, *Acts*, 802–803.

20 Tannehill, *Narrative Unity*, 2.350–51.

21 Fitzmyer, *Acts*, 796–97 leaves this open as a possibility.

BIBLIOGRAPHY

Select Commentaries on the Acts of the Apostles

Barrett, C. K. *Acts: A Shorter Commentary*. London: T&T Clark, 2002.

———. *Acts* ICC; 2 vols. Edinburgh: T&T Clark, 1994/1998.

Conzelmann, Hans. *Acts of the Apostles*. Hermeneia; Philadelphia: Fortress, 1987.

Fitzmyer, Joseph A. *The Acts of the Apostles*. AB 31. New York: Doubleday, 1998.

Gaventa, Beverly Roberts. *Acts*. ANTC. Nashville: Abingdon, 2003.

Haenchen, Ernst. *The Acts of the Apostles: A Commentary*. Philadelphia: Westminster, 1971.

Johnson, Luke Timothy. *The Acts of the Apostles*. SacPag 5. Collegeville MN: Liturgical Press, 1992.

Marshall, I. Howard. *The Acts of the Apostles: An Introduction and Commentary*. NIGTC. Leicester: Inter-Varsity Press, 1984.

Neil, William. *Acts: Based on the Revised Standard Version*. Grand Rapids MI: Eerdmans, 1987.

Polhill, John B. *Acts*. NAC 26. Nashville: Broadman, 1992.

Talbert, Charles. *Reading Luke: A Literary and Theological Commentary on the Third Gospel*. Revised ed. Macon, Ga: Smyth & Helwys 2002.

Tannehill, Robert W. *The Narrative Unity of Luke–Acts: A Literary Interpretation*. 2 vols. Minneapolis: Fortress, 1990.

Witherington, Ben, III. *The Acts of the Apostles: A Socio-Rhetorical Commentary*. Grand Rapids MI: Eerdmans, 1998.

Critical Studies on the New Testament and Early Christian History and Culture

Allen, Jr., O. Wesley, Jr. *The Death of Herod: The Narrative and Theological Function of Retribution in Luke–Acts*. SBLDS 158. Atlanta: Scholars Press, 1997.

Allison, Dale C., Jr. *The Ends of the Ages Has Come: An Early Interpretation of the Passion and Resurrection of Jesus*. Philadelphia: Fortress, 1985.

———. *The Sermon on the Mount: Inspiring Moral Imagination*. New York: Crossroad, 1999.

Anderson, J. C. and S. D. Moore, eds. *Mark and Method: New Approaches in Biblical Studies*. Minneapolis: Fortress, 1992.

Aune, David E. *The New Testament in Its Literary Environment*. Philadelphia: Westminster, 1987

Barrera, Julio Trebolle. *The Jewish Bible and the Christian Bible: An Introduction to the History of the Bible*. Grand Rapids MI: Eerdmans, 1998.

Barrett, C. K., ed. *The New Testament Background: Writings from Ancient Greece and the Roman Empire That Illuminate Christian Origins*. Revised ed. New York: HarperSanFrancisco, 1989

Bartholomew, Craig G., Joel B. Green, and Anthony Thiselton, eds. *Reading Luke: Interpretation, Reflection, Formation.* Scripture and Hermeneutics Series 6. Carlisle UK: Paternoster/Zondervan, 2005.

Beker, J. Christiaan. *Paul's Apocalyptic Gospel: The Coming Triumph of God.* Philadelphia: Fortress, 1982.

Borg, Marcus. *Meeting Jesus Again for the First Time.* New York: HarperSanFrancisco, 1994.

Brawley, Robert L. *Luke–Acts and the Jews: Conflict, Apology, and Conciliation.* Atlanta: Scholars Press, 1987.

Chance, J. Bradley. *Jerusalem, the Temple, and the New Age in Luke–Acts.* Macon GA: Mercer University Press, 1988.

———. "The Seed of Abraham and the People of God: A Study of Two Pauls." *1993 SBLSP*: 384–411.

Conzelmann, Hans. *History of Primitive Christianity.* Nashville: Abingdon, 1973.

Crossan, John Dominic. *Jesus: A Revolutionary Biography.* New York: HarperSanFrancisco, 1994.

Dibelius, Martin. *Studies in the Acts of the Apostles.* Mifflintown PA: Sigler Press, 1999.

Dodd, C. H. *The Apostolic Preaching and Its Developments.* Grand Rapids MI: Baker, 1980.

Doty, William G. *Letters in Primitive Christianity.* Philadelphia: Fortress, 1973.

Dunn, James D. G. *The Theology of Paul the Apostle.* Grand Rapids MI: Eerdmans, 1998.

Dupont, Jacques. *The Sources of Acts.* New York: Herder and Herder, 1964.

Ferguson, Everett. *Backgrounds of Early Christianity.* 3rd ed. Grand Rapids MI: Eerdmans, 2003.

Froehlich, K. *Biblical Interpretation in the Early Church.* Philadelphia: Fortress, 1984.

G. R. Beasley-Murray. *Baptism in the New Testament.* London: Macmillan, 1963

Garrett, Susan R. *The Demise of the Devil: Magic and the Demonic in Luke's Writings.* Minneapolis: Fortress, 1989.

Gärtner, Bertil. *The Areopagus Speech and Natural Revelation.* Uppsala: Gleerup, 1955.

Gingerich, Ray and Ted Grimsrud, eds. *Transforming the Powers: Peace, Justice, and the Domination System.* Minneapolis: Fortress, 2006.

Goldingay, John. *Models of Scripture.* Grand Rapids MI: Eerdmans, 1994.

Grant, R. M. and D. Tracy. *A Short History of the Interpretation of the Bible.* 2nd ed. Philadelphia: Fortress, 1984.

Grässer, Erich, ed. *Jesus in Nazareth.* New York: Walter de Gruyter, 1972.

Hengel, Martin. *Acts and the History of Earliest Christianity.* Philadelphia: Fortress, 1979.

Hock, Ronald F., J. Bradley Chance, and Judith Perkins, eds. *Ancient Fiction and Early Christian Narrative.* SBL Symposium Series, vol. 6. Atlanta: Scholars Press, 1998.

Jackson, F. J. Foakes and Kirsopp Lake. *The Beginnings of Christianity: The Acts of the Apostles.* 5 vols. Grand Rapids MI: Baker, 1979.

Jeremias, Joachim. *Jerusalem in the Time of Jesus*. Philadelphia: Fortress, 1969.

Jervell, Jacob. *Luke and the People of God: A New Look at Luke–Acts*. Minneapolis: Augsburg Publishing House, 1972.

Jewett, Robert. *A Chronology of Paul's Life*. Philadelphia: Fortress, 1979.

Johnson, Luke Timothy. *Religious Experience in Earliest Christianity: A Missing Dimension in New Testament Studies*. Minneapolis: Fortress, 1998.

Keck, Leander and J. Louis Martyn, eds. *Studies in Luke–Acts*. Philadelphia: Fortress, 1966.

Kee, Howard Clark. *Medicine, Miracle, and Magic in New Testament Times*. New York: Cambridge University Press, 1986.

Kennedy, George A. *New Testament Interpretation through Rhetorical Criticism*. Chapel Hill: University of North Carolina Press, 1984.

Koester, Helmut. *Introduction to the New Testament. Volume One: History, Culture, and Religion of the Hellenistic Age*. Philadelphia: Fortress, 1982.

Lüdemann, Gerd. *Early Christianity according to the Traditions in Acts: A Commentary*. Minneapolis: Fortress, 1989.

Malina, Bruce J. *The New Testament World: Insights from Cultural Anthropology*. 3rd ed. Louisville: Westminster/John Knox, 2001.

Marshall, I. Howard and David Peterson, eds. *Witness to the Gospel: The Theology of Acts*. Grand Rapids MI: Eerdmans, 1998.

Meeks, Wayne A. *The First Urban Christians: The Social World of the Apostle Paul*. New Haven: Yale University Press, 1983.

Metzger, Bruce M. *A Textual Commentary on the Greek New Testament*. London: United Bible Societies, 1971.

Moore, G. F. *Judaism in the First Centuries of the Christian Era*, 2 vols. Reprint. New York: Schocken Books, 1971.

Nock, A. D. *Conversion*. London: Oxford University Press, 1933.

Parsons, Mikeal C. and Martin M. Culy. *Acts: A Handbook on the Greek Text*. Waco: Baylor University Press, 2003.

Parsons, Mikeal C. and Richard Pervo. *Rethinking the Unity of Luke and Acts*. Minneapolis: Fortress, 1993.

Parsons, Mikeal C. and Joseph Tyson, eds. *Cadbury, Knox, and Talbert: American Contributions to the Study of Acts*. Atlanta: Scholars Press, 1992.

Pervo, Richard I. *Profit with Delight: The Literary Genre of the Acts of the Apostles*. Philadelphia: Fortress, 1987.

Powell, Mark Allan. *What Is Narrative Criticism?* Minneapolis: Fortress, 1990.

Reardon, B. P., ed. and trans. *Collected Ancient Greek Novels*. Berkeley: University of California Press, 1989.

Safrai, S. and M. Stern, eds. *Jewish People in the First Century: Historical Geography, Political History, Social, Cultural and Religious Life and Institutions*. 2 vols. Philadelphia: Fortress, 1976.

Sanders, Jack T. *The Jews in Luke–Acts*. Philadelphia: Fortress, 1987.

Sanders, E. P. *Paul, the Law, and the Jewish People*. Philadelphia: Fortress, 1983.

————. *Paul*. Oxford: Oxford University Press, 1991.

—————. *Jesus and Judaism*. Philadelphia: Fortress Press, 1985.

Schweizer, Eduard. *Luke: A Challenge to Present Theology*. Atlanta: John Knox, 1982.

Soards, Marion L. *The Speeches in Acts: Their Content, Context, and Concerns*. Louisville: Westminster/John Knox, 1994.

Stendahl, Krister. *Paul Among Jews and Gentiles*. Philadelphia: Fortress, 1976.

Talbert, Charles H. *Literary Patterns, Theological Themes and the Genre of Luke–Acts*. SBLMS 20. Missoula MT: Scholars Press, 1974.

Talbert, Charles H., ed. *Perspectives on Luke–Acts*. Association of Baptist Professors of Religion, Special Studies Series, no. 5. Danville VA: Association of Baptist Professors of Religion, 1978.

—————. *What Is a Gospel? The Genre of the Canonical Gospels*. Philadelphia: Fortress, 1977.

Tyson, Joseph B., ed. *Luke–Acts and the Jewish People: Eight Critical Perspectives*. Minneapolis: Augsburg, 1988.

—————. *Images of Judaism in Luke–Acts*. Columbia: University of South Carolina Press, 1992.

Wink, Walter. *Engaging the Powers: Discernment and Resistance in a World of Domination*. Minneapolis: Fortress, 1992.

Winter, B. W., ed. *The Book of Acts in Its First Century Setting*. 6 vols. Grand Rapids MI: Eerdmans, 1993–97.

Witherington, Ben, III, ed. *History, Literature, and Society in the Book of Acts*. Cambridge: Cambridge University Press, 1996.

Wright, N. T. *The New Testament and the People of God*. Minneapolis: Fortress, 1992.

—————. *What St. Paul Really Said: Was Paul of Tarsus the Real Founder of Christianity?* Grand Rapids MI: Eerdmans, 1997.

Other Studies: Theology, Ethics, Religion, and Spirituality

Barr, James. *Biblical Faith and Natural Theology*. Oxford: Clarendon Press, 1993.

Barth, Karl. *Dogmatics in Outline*. New York: Harper and Row, 1959.

—————. *Evangelical Theology: An Introduction*. New York: Holt, Rinehart and Winston, 1963.

Berger, Peter L. *Questions of Faith: A Skeptical Affirmation of Christianity*. Malden MA: Blackwell, 2004.

Berger, Peter L. *The Sacred Canopy: Elements of a Sociological Theory of Religion*. New York: Anchor Books, 1967.

Bonhoeffer, Dietrich. *Life Together*. San Francisco: Harper and Row, 1954.

Borg, Marcus. *The God We Never Knew: Beyond Dogmatic Religion to a More Authentic Contemporary Faith*. New York: HarperSanFrancisco, 1997.

—————. *The Heart of Christianity: Rediscovering a Live of Faith*. New York: HarperSanFrancisco, 2003.

Callahan, J. "The Bible Says: Evangelical and Postliberal Biblicism." *Theology Today* 53.4 (1997): 449–63.

Carter, Stephen L. *Integrity*. New York: Basic Books, 1996.

———. *The Culture of Disbelief: How American Law and Politics Trivialize Religious Devotion.* New York: Doubleday/Anchor Books, 1993.

Clayton, Philip and Arthur Peacocke, eds. *In Whom We Live and Move and Have Our Being: Panentheistic Reflections on God's Presence in a Scientific World.* Grand Rapids MI: Eerdmans, 2004.

Dalferth, Ingolf. "'I Determine What God Is!': Theology in the Age of 'Cafeteria Religion.'" *Theology Today* 51.1 (April 2000): 5–23.

Durback, Robert, ed. *Seeds of Hope: A Henry Nouwen Reader.* 2nd ed. New York: Doubleday, 1997.

Fowl, Stephen E. and L. Gregory Jones. *Reading in Communion: Scripture and Ethics in Christian Life.* Grand Rapids MI: Eerdmans, 1991.

Fowler, James W. *Stages of Faith: The Psychology of Human Development and the Quest for Meaning.* New York: HarperSanFrancisco, 1981.

Geertz, Clifford. *The Interpretation of Cultures.* New York: Basic Books, 1973.

Goodwin, Everett C., ed. *Baptists in the Balance: The Tension between Freedom and Responsibility.* Valley Forge: Judson Press, 1997.

Grenz, Stanley J. *A Primer on Postmodernism.* Grand Rapids MI: Eerdmans, 1995.

———. *Theology for the Community of God.* Nashville: Broadman and Holman, 1992.

Hodgson, Peter. *Christian Faith: A Brief Introduction.* Louisville: Westminster/John Knox, 2001.

Kimball, Charles. *When Religion Becomes Evil.* New York: HarperSanFrancisco, 2002.

King, Martin Luther, Jr. "Letter from a Birmingham Jail." In *I Have a Dream: Writings and Speeches that Changed the World.* James M. Washington, ed. New York: HarperSanFrancisco, 1986.

Macquarrie, J. *Principles of Christian Theology.* 2nd ed. New York: Charles Scribner's Sons, 1966/1977.

McFague, Sallie. *Speaking in Parables: A Study in Metaphor and Theology.* Philadelphia: Fortress Press, 1975.

———. *Life Abundant: Rethinking Theology and Economy for a Planet in Peril.* Minneapolis: Fortress Press, 2001.

Miles, Jack. *God: A Biography.* New York: Alfred A. Knopf, 1995.

O'Connel, Timothy E. *Making Disciples: A Handbook of Christian Moral Formation.* New York: Crossroad, 1998.

Otto, Rudolf. *The Idea of the Holy: An Inquiry in the Non-Rational Factor in the Idea of the Divine and Its Relation to the Rational.* Oxford: Oxford University Press, 1923.

Pinnock, Clark H. "God's Sovereignty in Today's World. *Theology Today.* 53/1 (1996): 15–21.

———. *Tracking the Maze: Finding Our Way through Modern Theology from and Evangelical Perspective.* Eugene OR: Wipf and Stock, 1998.

Rigby, Cynthia. "Free to Be Human: Limits, Possibilities, and the Sovereignty of God." *Theology Today,* 53/1 (1996): 47–62.

Russell, Robert John. "Does the 'God Who Acts' Really Act: New Approaches to Divine Action in Light of Science. *Theology Today* 54/1 (1997): 43–65.

Sanders. John. *The God Who Risks: A Theology of Providence.* Downers Grove IL: InterVarsity Press, 1998.

Segundo, John Luis. *The Liberation of Theology.* New York: Maryknoll, 1976.

Shurden, Walter B. *The Baptist Identity: Four Fragile Freedoms.* Macon GA: Smyth and Helwys, 1993.

Smith, B. K. "Christianity as a Second Language: Rethinking Mission in the West." *Theology Today* 53/4 (1997): 439–48.

Stella, Tom. *A Faith Worth Believing: Finding New Life beyond the Rules of Religion.* New York: HarperSanFranciso, 2004.

Suchocki, Marjorie Heweitt. *In God's Presence: Theological Reflections on Prayer.* St Louis: Chalice, 1996.

Tillich, Paul. *Christianity and the Encounter of the World Religions.* New York: Columbia University Press, 1963.

———. *The Courage to Be.* New Haven: Yale University Press, 1952.

Tyson, John R., ed. *Invitation to Christian Spirituality: An Ecumenical Anthology.* Oxford: Oxford University Press, 1999.

INDEX OF MODERN AUTHORS

INDEX OF SCRIPTURES

INDEX OF SIDEBARS AND ILLUSTRATIONS

INDEX OF TOPICS